RESPONSES TO CRIME

Volume 3

Responses to Crime

VOLUME 3

Legislating with the Tide

Lord Windlesham

CLARENDON PRESS · OXFORD
1996

Oxford University Press, Walton Street, Oxford OX2 6DP

Oxford New York
Athens Auckland Bangkok Bogata Bombay
Buenos Aires Calcutta Cape Town Dar es Salaam
Delhi Florence Hong Kong Istanbul Karachi
Kuala Lumpur Madras Madrid Melbourne
Mexico City Nairobi Paris Singapore
Taipei Tokyo Toronto
and associated companies in
Berlin Ibadan

Oxford is a trade mark of Oxford University Press

Published in the United States
by Oxford University Press Inc., New York

British Library Cataloguing in Publication Data
Data available

Library of Congress Cataloging in Publication Data
Data available
ISBN 0–19–826240–X

1 3 5 7 9 10 8 6 4 2

Typeset by Hope Services (Abingdon) Ltd.
Printed in Great Britain
on acid-free paper by
Bookcraft (Bath) Ltd
Midsomer Norton, Somerset

Once more Pilate spoke to them, offering to set Jesus at liberty; but they continued to answer with shouts of, Crucify him, crucify him. Then for the third time he said to them, Why, what wrong has he done? I can find no fault in him that deserves death; I will scourge him, and then he shall go free. But they, with loud cries, insisted on their demand that he should be crucified; and their voices carried the day.

New Testament, trans. R. A. Knox,
Luke, 23:20–4.

Preface

THE theme of this third volume of *Responses to Crime* is the impact of public opinion on criminal justice policy and legislation. Although the time-span is shorter than the developments described in Volume 2, the scope is wider since the book contains a comparative study of the most recent attempt by the United States Congress to enact a statute designed to control violent crime and strengthen law enforcement (Public Law 103–322).

A timely visit in the Summer of 1994 to the University of California, Berkeley, at the very moment when the 'three strikes and you're out' sentencing initiative was sweeping everything before it throughout the State of California, aroused my interest in the powerful tides of opinion which had already engulfed the more conventional approaches to policy-making. Once politicized, crime control in America had no defences against the populist agitation resulting in the mass incarceration which now looms as such a dark shadow over a land that is still, if deeply troubled, one of the greatest civilizations of the Western world.

Violent crime at unprecedently high levels is, alas, not confined to America, although few other developed societies have experienced comparable rates. A peculiarly American phenomenon can be seen in the frequency of gun-related homicides and other serious offences, as well as self-inflicted injuries, which cannot be dissociated from easy access to a vast and feebly regulated reservoir of firearms. In Britain too over recent decades criminal offending reported to the police has risen to levels previously unknown in the twentieth century, leading to a widespread and debilitating fear of crime, and a creeping normalization. Today, living with high crime rates is regarded as normal, a fact of modern life, like pollution or the perils of heavy road traffic, that has to be accommodated. But normalization does not mean acceptance or passive resignation. On the contrary, anger and frustration are propelled to the forefront of both media attention and electoral politics.

How politicians, and the officials who advise them and have the unenviable task of managing the consequences of their policies, translate the forces of opinion into legislation is a fascinating subject for study. Both categories are, or ought to be, aware of the limited capacity of governments to control, still less reduce, the incidence of crime. Yet democratic electoral politics do not allow for such admissions. Hence the emergence of punitiveness as a reaction which can be exhibited to the general public even if, in anything beyond the short term, it is likely to exacerbate the social blight caused by such extensive criminality rather than ameliorate it. The superficial attraction to the general public of proclaimed toughness is self-evident. It is infectious and quickly spreads across the political spectrum. However, it can serve as a rhetorical smoke-screen, presaging the introduction of questionable policies which then come to be regarded as politically irreversible.

These reflections may sound too sombre a note at the outset of a book. Maybe the growing emphasis on crime prevention, or self-protection, will provide a substitute for the protection of the citizen which the authority of the state can no longer provide. Maybe the bulwark of the judges, fortified by the instrument of judicial review, will prevent too drastic a degradation of standards of justice. Maybe politicians will begin to lead opinion as well as reacting to it. But it is hard to be at the same time confident and realistic about the prospect. The extract from the New Testament chosen for the frontispiece has a contemporary resonance: '. . . they, with loud cries, insisted on their demand that he should be crucified; and their voices carried the day.' It is reproduced with the permission of A. P. Watt Ltd on behalf of The Westminster RC Diocese Trustees.

WINDLESHAM

Brasenose College, Oxford
February 1996

Acknowledgements

This volume calls for two sets of acknowledgements. The first is for the assistance received from many quarters in writing Parts I, II, and IV. These chapters take forward the narrative of Volume 2 and discuss the main legislative developments in criminal justice in England and Wales between 1991 and 1995. The second is to recognize with warm thanks the help of all those who guided the author's footsteps over the less familiar terrain of law-making in America which is the subject of Part III.

The principal sources of information on the domestic changes in the penal system that came thick and fast in the early 1990s have been ministerial decisions, the proceedings in Parliament, government publications, and personal knowledge. The many extracts from Crown and Parliamentary copyright material, including letters from ministers expounding government policy, are reproduced with the permission of the Controller of Her Majesty's Stationery Office. Once again, the Home Office has been a rich mine of source material, and I am grateful to its Research and Statistics Department for checking several of the Tables for accuracy and providing up to date statistical data. With the Editor's permission, Chapter 9 incorporates parts of an earlier article published in the *Criminal Law Review* [1993] Crim. L. R. 644.

The Librarians and staff at the Bodleian Law Library in Oxford and the House of Lords have been unfailingly assiduous in following up countless queries and requests. A special debt of gratitude is recorded to Parthenope Ward, Assistant Librarian at the House of Lords, on whom the burden has been heavier than any other. Another member of the Library staff, G. R. Dymond, was instrumental in obtaining unpublished transcripts of judgments in the courts. As with the previous volume, my Secretary, Patricia Spight, typed the entire book, with many revised versions of each of the chapters, and has been an invaluable support throughout. My association with the Centre for Criminological Research at Oxford is a continuing source of stimulus and has encouraged me to widen the range of my interests. To Dr Roger Hood, its Director and a

Fellow of All Souls College, and David Faulkner, Senior Research Associate and a Fellow of St John's College, I acknowledge debts of gratitude accumulated over many years.

Others who have helped in different ways include: K. Akester, Lord Birkett, W. J. Bohan, Lord Carlisle of Bucklow, Paul Cavadino, Michaela Coulthard, J. M. Davies, Bryan Gibson, Antony Griffiths, Richard Hart, C. Lewis, C. Nuttall, Sir Derek Oulton, Helen Reeves, Viscount Runciman of Doxford, T. Russell, Michael Ryle, L. Scudder, David Shapiro, Stephen Shaw, Paul Silk, P. Spurgeon, Dr David Thomas, and Dr Martin Wright. To all of them, I express my thanks. Other acknowledgements are made in the footnotes to the text.

Two periods spent in the United States, as a Visiting Fellow at the Earl Warren Legal Institute, the University of California, Berkeley, in the Summer of 1994, and at the Library of Congress in Washington D.C. during the following Spring, enabled me to further my investigations for the study which now forms Part III of this book. At both, I was greeted hospitably and granted generous facilities to carry out my research. At Berkeley, I should like to thank in particular Herma Hill Kay, Dean of the School of Law (Boalt Hall); Professor Franklin Zimring, Director, and Gordon Hawkins, Senior Fellow, at the Earl Warren Legal Institute; and Professors Richard Buxbaum, John Fleming, S. H. Kadish, R. A. Kagan, and J. Skolnick, as well as Johan Van Buren for his research assistance. Elsewhere in California, Peter Greenwood, Director of the Criminal Justice Program at RAND, David P. Gardner, John Van de Kamp, and the Office of the Legislative Analyst at Sacramento, each supplied information.

The Librarian of Congress, James Billington, made available the incomparable resources of the Library of Congress and the Law Librarian, Dr Rubens Medina, allocated work space throughout my stay. My research was greatly assisted by Kersi Shroff, a Senior Legal Specialist in the Legal Research Directorate. Prosser Gifford, in charge of Scholarly Programs, and Josephus Nelson, in the Librarian's Office (Oxonians both), as well as Charles Doyle, an experienced criminal law specialist, were unstinting with their time and knowledge. Others who were personally helpful in Washington, often far beyond the bounds of the usual courtesies, included Richard Aborn, Lloyd Cutler, Ronald Gainer, Marc Mauer, and Jerome Miller.

In addition to amassing a large quantity of written material at the Library of Congress and from other sources, I was able to meet members of both Houses of Congress who had played a leading part in the anti-crime legislation passed in 1993-4 and signed into law by President Clinton in September 1994. The list included the ex-Speaker of the House, the then chairmen of the relevant Committees or Subcommittees in the Senate and House of Representatives, a member of the Congressional Black Caucus, and several staff assistants to Senators and Representatives. Contacts at the Department of Justice were a former Attorney General, an Assistant Attorney General, and a Deputy Assistant Attorney General responsible for policy in the Criminal Division. I had the opportunity to attend a hearing of the Senate Judiciary Committee, and of the House Subcommittee on Crime and Criminal Justice. Through the good offices of Robert Litt, Deputy Assistant Attorney General, the Department of Justice subsequently provided factual information on several occasions in reply to my inquiries. John Rabiej at the Administrative Office of the United States Courts, and Ankur Goel, at the time Counsel to the Senate Committee on the Judiciary, did the same. The Washington part of my research was funded largely by a grant from the Andrew W. Mellon Fund at the University of Oxford which promotes studies in American government.

Essential as it was, only a small amount of the time I was engaged on my study was spent in the United States. At Oxford, the Library of Rhodes House contains an extensive collection of contemporary works of reference on American government, while in London the Reference Center of the United States Information Service is a facility of unique value. The staff at the Reference Center are remarkably well-informed about a wide range of subjects, and what is not available in London is rapidly obtained from Washington or elsewhere in America. To Anna Girvan, who was so patient in following up my requests over such a lengthy period, and so expert in tracking down sources which sometimes I did not know existed, I am especially indebted. Also in London, the Bureau Chief of the *New York Times*, John Darnton, supplied numerous items from his newspaper's full and authoritative coverage of the 1994 crime legislation.

The inclusion in Volume 3 of a detailed comparative study has been a new departure for me in writing about criminal justice policy. I have had much to learn and remain apprehensive that there will be errors and misunderstandings. In expressing my thanks to those whose names are recorded above, I can only say that whatever shortcomings the American chapters may have, they would have been even less adequate without the co-operation I have enjoyed.

Nearly a century and a half ago, an earlier observer from Europe, Alexis de Tocqueville, wrote in the preface to the first volume of *Democracy in America*: 'Let us look to America, not in order to make a servile copy of the institutions that she has established, but to gain a clearer view of the polity that will be the best for us; let us look there less to find examples than instruction; let us borrow from her the principles, rather than the details, of her laws'. At a time when changes in sentencing policy imported from the United States are pending, there are salutary lessons to be drawn from the American experience. Mandatory sentencing raises fundamental issues of principle, and often causes unintended and unwelcome repercussions in other parts of the penal system. It is to the principles of justice, rather than their distortions, that we should look when seeking guidance from America in the closing years of the twentieth century.

Contents

List of Tables

PART I

Volte Face

1

The Criminal Justice Act 1993

I

On 13 May 1993, immediately after Prime Minister's Questions in
the House of Commons, the Home Secretary, Kenneth Clarke,[1]
made a statement about the criminal justice system. An 'unexpected
and welcome' opportunity had arisen, he said, to amend a Bill currently before the House so as to 'improve the working of the
Criminal Justice Act 1991' and 'strengthen the powers of the courts
in other important respects'.[2] Useful and necessary, albeit in a
minor key, the Criminal Justice Bill (HL) had attracted little notice
since it was brought from the Lords (where it had originated) on
10 December 1992. It had been given an unopposed Second
Reading on 14 April and was due to go to a Standing Committee
for detailed consideration in late May and early June. The policy
objectives were to extend the jurisdiction of the courts to try various offences of dishonesty when they involve a significant foreign
element; to counter more effectively offences of money laundering;
to amend the confiscation provisions of the Drug Trafficking
Offences Act 1986 and the powers in the Criminal Justice Act 1988
relating to confiscation of the proceeds of other serious crimes; and
to implement a European Community Directive on insider dealing
in securities.[3]

The Bill was narrower than most criminal justice legislation,
being confined to jurisdictional extension and crimes committed for
financial gain. Before its introduction the Lords' Public Bill Office
had advised the Home Office that a proposed Government amendment to make parents responsible for the payment of fines imposed

[1] Kenneth Clarke became Home Secretary after the General Election in April
1992. He had previously been Secretary of State for Health (1988–90) and for
Education and Science (1990–2).
[2] *Parl. Debates*, HC, 224 (6th ser.), col. 939, 13 May 1993.
[3] 89/592/EEC.

on their children would be inadmissible as falling outside the scope of the Bill. The Commons authorities, also consulted in October 1992, had taken a more relaxed attitude towards the doctrine of relevance, indicating that they would probably have allowed such an amendment because of the homogenous nature of the Long Title of the Bill and its Short Title.[4] It was these soundings that paved the way for one of the most sudden about-turns in the history of penal legislation.

The bulk of the Criminal Justice Act 1991, including the sentencing provisions, had come into effect seven months earlier, on 1 October 1992. At that time the Minister of State with responsibility for criminal justice policy at the Home Office affirmed that the Act's implementation was an 'important landmark in the way we deal with offenders in England and Wales'.[5] A personal letter, sent by the Minister to MPs and peers who had taken part in the debates, asserted:

The Act introduces, for the first time, a statutory framework for consistent sentencing based on the severity of the sentence matching the seriousness of the offence. All penalties under the Act, whether custody, community sentences or unit fines are designed to restrict liberty.

A custodial sentence will now only be passed where the offence is so serious that no other form of penalty would be appropriate. A court will, in certain cases, be able to look at the circumstances of past offences in determining whether the offence is more serious than it would be taken on its own. Furthermore, in the case of a violent or sex offender, in deciding whether to impose a custodial sentence the court will be able to take into account not just the seriousness of the offence but also the need to protect the public from harm; and it will be able to pass a longer sentence than would be justified by seriousness alone . . .

Although fines do not restrict the offender's liberty in the same way as a custodial or community sentence they do deprive the offender of money and the ability to enjoy it. The Act introduces a system of unit fines, which

---

[4] House of Commons rules on the admissibility of amendments are determined by the powers of a committee as well as the objects of a bill: 'The objects of a bill are stated in its long title, which should cover everything contained in the bill, as introduced. Amendments, however, are not necessarily limited by the title of the bill, since a committee is empowered by Standing Order No. 63 to make amendments "relevant to the subject-matter of the bill", provided that, where such amendments are outside the title, the committee extends the title so as to cover them.' Ed. C. J. Boulton, *Erskine May's Treatise on The Law, Privileges, Proceedings and Usage of Parliament*, 21st edn., Butterworths, London, 1989, p. 486.

[5] Letter from Michael Jack MP to the author, 1 Oct. 1992.

reflects the seriousness of the offence and the weekly disposable income of the offender. Fines will now be fairer and more effective by restricting offenders' enjoyment of personal disposable income according to their means. Under the Act the maximum fine available in the magistrates' courts is raised from £2,000 to £5,000. In cases of default it is possible to make an attachment of income support for the first time.[6]

The fourteen-month interval between Royal Assent in July 1991 and implementation in October 1992 was needed for the judiciary, the magistracy, their clerks, and the Probation Service to familiarize themselves with a sentencing regime containing many novel features. As sentencers got to grips with the complexity of the statutory restrictions on their discretion, disillusion began to spread. Despite written guidance and the training given at circuit seminars and other events organized by the Judicial Studies Board, once the Act came into force judges in the Crown Court found its requirements frustrating and difficult to explain. Before long the mood of scepticism and disillusion hardened into overt criticism. Although concentrated upon two provisions in particular, much of the criticism was more deep-seated. It was articulated in public when Lord Taylor, who had succeeded Lord Lane as Lord Chief Justice in April 1992, added his voice and authority to the rumbling discontent. In a speech to the Annual Conference of the Law Society of Scotland at Gleneagles on 21 March 1993 Taylor elaborated on the shortcomings of sentencing policy. Those concerned with policy making, he declared, fell into distinct schools of thought:

that which believes in the need for, and efficacy of, punishment and that which does not. The punishment school has gradually lost ground over the years, certainly since the war. Capital punishment for murder, corporal punishment, hard labour, borstal training, short sharp shock sentences have all gone. Speaking for myself I would not wish to see any of them return. But the result is that contention between the two schools of thought has recently been confined to custody versus community sentences and, even here, the punishment school has increasingly lost out in English legislation, culminating in the Criminal Justice Act 1991.[7]

Remarking on the good fortune of Scotland in having comparatively little legislation in its criminal law, the majority of crimes being common law offences, Taylor said that as a result Scotland

---

[6] Ibid.

[7] 'Judges and Sentencing', *Journal of the Law Society of Scotland*, Apr. 1993, p. 129.

had been spared most of the statutory limits and sentencing restrictions which applied south of the border. But the greatest advantage was to have been spared the Criminal Justice Act 1991, or any equivalent of it. Quite apart from the merits of its policies, the drafting had caused English lawyers to tear their hair. He then identified two provisions as running counter to 'all the principles of good sentencing policy' and defying common sense.[8] Coming from such an august source this was strong language. His targets were the rule in Section 1(2)(a) whereby the power of a court to pass a custodial sentence must be related to the seriousness of the offence, or the combination of the offence and one other offence associated with it, and the convoluted wording of Section 29 on the effect of previous convictions or failure to respond to previous sentences. Each had been the subject of unsuccessful judicial representations before the Act had gone onto the statute book.

In the late Autumn of 1990, shortly before the introduction of the Bill in the House of Commons, a delegation from the Judicial Studies Board, led by its Chairman Lord Justice Glidewell and including a representative of the Council of HM Circuit Judges, called on the then Home Secretary, David Waddington, to express their reservations about the limitation in the original draft to the seriousness of a single offence before the court when deciding whether a custodial sentence was justified.[9] The Home Secretary's unforthcoming demeanour conveyed no encouragement, but he did agree to make a concession: that one associated offence could be added to the instant offence in determining whether the threshold of gravity necessary for a prison sentence had been reached. This struck at least one member of the delegation as having been pre-arranged, and did not meet their argument that in the case of a persistent offender who had committed a series of similar offences the

[8] 'Judges and Sentencing', *Journal of the Law Society of Scotland*, Apr. 1993, p. 130.

[9] The draftsman had followed the 'one offence' rule contained in Section 1 (4A) of the Criminal Justice Act 1982, as amended by Section 123 of the Criminal Justice Act 1988, which restricted the use of custody in sentencing young offenders below the age of twenty-one. Whenever two or more offences had been committed, at least one of them needed to satisfy the standard of seriousness required before a custodial sentence could be imposed. It was not permissible, the Court of Appeal had held in *Davison* (1989) 11 Cr. App. R. (S) 570, to aggregate several less serious offences to reach the necessary standard of seriousness. See A. Ashworth and B. Gibson, 'The Criminal Justice Act 1993: (2) Altering the sentencing framework' [1994] Crim. L.R. 101.

cumulative effect and damage caused by the totality of the offences should be regarded as relevant in assessing whether the seriousness of his offending justified a custodial sentence. Nor did the concession impress the judges taking part in sentencing seminars when the legislation was explained by the Minister of State at the Home Office, John Patten, or senior officials. At these sessions, and at meetings of the Judicial Studies Board which, with its Criminal Committee, constituted a convenient forum for consultation,[10] the judges merely took note of the proposals. As they were later to protest, they never approved them.

If multiple offences did not fit easily into the new sentencing order, still harder to reconcile with the canons of proportionality or 'just deserts' which underpinned the legislation[11] was the previous conduct of the convicted but unsentenced offender. According to the Government's stated intention, punishment should be commensurate with the gravity of the offence and the harm done to the victim. The sentence should be related to the actual offence, not to what an offender might have done and been punished for in the past, nor to what he might do in the future. As a statement of principle the policy reflected case-law at the time the legislation was in draft. In criminal cases the courts were expected to decide on the proper sentence for the offence of which the accused had been convicted. Apart from the most serious cases of homicide and violence, a discount would be allowed to a first offender. The amount of the discount would be progressively eroded by previous convictions or failures to respond to previous sentences until exhausted on reaching the ceiling set by the gravity of the offence. Even the worst prior record should not take the sentence above that level.[12] To this extent, therefore, previous convictions were taken into account in deciding upon the sentence for the instant offence. The judgment in

[10] The sentencing seminars, and the expanding role of the Judicial Studies Board, are discussed in Vol. 1, p. 15, and Vol. 2, pp. 174–81 of *Responses to Crime*, Clarendon Press, Oxford, 1987 and 1993.

[11] The White Paper which preceded its introduction, *Crime, Justice and Protecting the Public* (Cm. 965), HMSO, London, 1990, p. 2, stated the aim of Government proposals as 'better justice through a more consistent approach to sentencing, so that convicted criminals get their "just deserts". The severity of the sentence of the court should be directly related to the seriousness of the offence'.

[12] For an analysis of progressive loss of mitigation, see Andrew Ashworth, *Sentencing and Criminal Justice*, Weidenfeld and Nicolson, London, 1992, pp. 147–50. The leading cases before the 1991 Act were *R. v. Queen* (1981) 3 Cr. App. R. (S) 245 and *R. v. Bailey* (1988) 10 Cr. App. R. (S) 231.

Queen was cited approvingly in the White Paper which remarked that a good record may enable the court to reduce the sentence.[13]

In the Bill as first presented to the House of Commons the draftsman chose to incorporate the effect of a convicted offender's previous record as part of Clause 3, which set out the procedural requirements for imposing a custodial sentence. Subsection (2) stated clearly enough that an offence should not be regarded as more serious by reason of any previous convictions or failure to respond to previous sentences. But this statement was promptly qualified by subsection (3): 'In so far as the circumstances of any offences of which an offender has been previously convicted are relevant for the purpose of forming an opinion as to the seriousness of the offence, nothing in subsection (2) above shall prevent the court from taking those circumstances into account for that purpose'. Ministers denied there was any contradiction between the two sub-sections, struggling to explain what was meant by the circumstances of previous offences and the concept of progressive loss of mitigation, but it was uphill work, the reasoning being questioned in both Houses. During the debate on Second Reading in the House of Lords a prominent QC speaking from the Labour benches, Lord Irvine of Lairg, accurately predicted what was to become one of the principal bones of contention following enactment:

If the circumstances of previous offences means the circumstances surrounding the offences, then in practice a sentencer will know nothing, or very little, that is reliable about the surrounding circumstances of previous offences. Of course the sentencer will know the nature of the previous offences and from the sentences imposed how seriously they were regarded by past sentencers. However, that is altogether different. That would simply bring in what Clause 3(2) took out; namely, previous convictions.[14]

At the Committee stage the Government rearranged the sequence of the Bill by removing the references to an offender's previous record from Clause 3, which related only to custodial sentences, and joining it to an identical provision relating to community sentences in a new clause placed later in the Bill. The wording was unchanged, but it attracted adverse comment from Lord Ackner, a Lord of Appeal in Ordinary, who called into question the wisdom

---

[13] *Crime, Justice and Protecting the Public*, p. 9.
[14] *Parl. Debates*, HL, 527 (5th ser.), col. 98, 12 Mar. 1991.

of denying the court the ability to take account of the response of an offender to previous sentences in deciding on the sentence. He pointed out that the provision was at variance with Section 123 of the Criminal Justice Act 1988, under which a young offender qualified for a custodial sentence if he had a history of failure to respond to non-custodial penalties and was unwilling to respond to them.[15] Whatever the age of the offender, Ackner argued, it did not make sense when considering the seriousness of the offence to ignore the response to previous sentences. For the judge it was of 'enormous relevance' to know whether the response had been one of enthusiastic compliance or resolute failure to comply with the conditions of a probation order or community sentence.[16]

At Third Reading the wording of what became Section 29 of the Criminal Justice Act was revised and slightly widened by Government amendment; however, its confusing format of prohibition followed by qualification was maintained. Having consulted in advance Lord Lane, the Lord Chief Justice, Ackner mounted a strong challenge putting down a series of amendments on each of the main issues troubling the higher judiciary. Their objections were not so much to the principle of proportionality between the offence and the punishment it attracted as to its mode of expression. In a powerful speech he illustrated the unreality which would result from legislation that prevented a trial judge in sentencing an habitual offender from having any regard to the response to previous sentences, as well as the number of offences taken into consideration and previous convictions.[17] The first of his amendments would enable a custodial sentence to be passed when a person was found guilty of 'one of a series of similar offences committed by him which together were so serious that a non-custodial sentence cannot be justified'.[18] Lord Roskill, a retired Law Lord, spoke in support saying that the position would be absurd unless the amendment, or something like it, were to be accepted.[19] In the event it was negatived, immediately after an

---

[15] The provision, together with S.1(4A) of the Criminal Justice Act 1982, was repealed by Schedule 13 of the Criminal Justice Act 1991. Thereafter, the criteria restricting the powers of the Crown Court or the Magistrates' courts to impose a custodial sentence did not differentiate between adult and young offenders.

[16] *Parl. Debates*, HL, 527, col. 1617, 18 Apr. 1991.

[17] *Parl, Debates*, HL, 529 (5th ser.), cols. 548–50, 4 June 1991.

[18] Ibid., col. 561.   [19] Ibid., col. 552.

unrelated amendment of my own, which for procedural reasons
had been debated with Ackner's.

A subsequent amendment on the response of an offender to previous sentences was no more successful. Speaking to a later
Government amendment, the Minister of State, Earl Ferrers, re-
affirmed that the mere fact that an offender had previous convictions should not necessarily lead to a heavier sentence. While in
general the Government wished to avoid sentencing on record, the
circumstances of previous offences might point to aggravating factors which under his amendment could be taken into account by
the court for the purpose of forming an opinion as to the seriousness of the offence.[20] It was a devious way round, and although it
was presented as a concession Ackner was to be proved correct in
his forecast that it would not have the effect which the Minister
claimed for it.[21] Therefore, while the judicial reaction had been dis-
creet and in a relatively low-key during the pre-legislative stage, and
Ackner's objections had not attracted wide support when the Bill
was debated in Parliament, a flare had been fired that was soon to
illuminate the political landscape.

In his Gleneagles speech Taylor conceded that there was a sensible idea behind Section 29, but claimed it had been taken too far.
After giving examples of anomalies, he said that he hoped the Act
would be soon reviewed and sanity restored. The fundamental error
underlying the legislation was a misconceived notion that sentencing should be programmed in detail so as to restrict the discretion
of the sentencing judge. The laudable desire to reduce and confine
custodial sentencing to cases where it was really necessary had led
to restrictive provisions 'forcing the judge into an ill-fitting strait-
jacket'.[22] Putting aside the thought that judges may strive for
'sound bites' like politicians eager to attract media attention,
Taylor had coined a phrase that went into instant circulation.
Caricature though it might have been, it struck a responsive chord,
not only with sentencers whose chief spokesman he was, but with
a growing number of MPs, now extending to some new Ministers
at the Home Office who had played no part in the design of the
'strait-jacket'. Unlike the senior officials, who had striven so long
and hard to get the 1991 Act onto the statute book, and the
Ministers (notably Hurd and Patten) who had moved on to other

[20] *Parl, Debates*, HL, 529 (5th ser.), col. 582.   [21] Ibid., col. 585
[22] 'Judges and Sentencing', p. 130.

departments, their successors lacked any sense of ownership of the legislation.

II

Kenneth Clarke's reaction to the criticism was characteristic of his political style. The initial, and predictable, stance of the Home Office was defensive, a spokesman saying rather petulantly that when people had particular grievances they should be directed to where it mattered, to ministers. It was too soon for a full-scale review of the Act, or to amend it, although it was being monitored.[23] The next morning, however, the Home Secretary was to be heard on BBC Radio 4 assuring listeners: 'Plainly if the Act is not working as it is intended, we must revisit it and change it.'[24] On the same day the Chairman of the Magistrates' Association, Mrs Joyce Rose, accompanied by the Deputy Chairman and two other representatives,[25] met the Lord Chief Justice to express their disquiet over the working of the new legislation which they believed had resulted in resignations from the Bench.

Under Section 29 magistrates, in the same way as the Crown Court, were entitled to refer to previous convictions in assessing the seriousness of an offence if the circumstances were similar. Experience had shown, however, that they were normally unable to find out whether or not the circumstances were similar because the records did not show sufficient detail. The Crown Prosecution Service was initially reluctant to produce the detailed information needed, and plans to resolve the difficulties then got bogged down in arguments over resources and computer technology. In the upshot, at the very moment when the judicial critics were concentrating their fire on the practical shortcomings and their objections of principle to the policy, it was estimated that it would take as long as three or four years before a working system was operational. In the meantime, magistrates would have to sentence without taking adequate account of the circumstances of previous convictions as allowed for in the Act. The prospect was causing great unhappiness.

---

[23] *The Times*, 23 Mar. 1993.   [24] *The Times*, 24 Mar. 1993
[25] A representative of the stipendiary magistrates, who also attended the meeting with Lord Taylor, was reported as saying that the concerns of the stipendiaries were the same as the lay bench (*The Times*, 24 Mar. 1993).

Although it was put about that disgruntled magistrates were resigning in droves, leading to a depleted and demoralized lay magistracy, the assertion was not borne out when the official statistics became available. On 1 January 1994 the number of active justices was 30,054, comprising 16,151 men and 13,903 women. New appointments in 1993 amounted to 2,062 and losses from resignations, removals, compulsory retirements on age grounds, and deaths totalled 1,448, making a net gain of 614.[26] Informed estimates of the numbers of resignations by JPs on account of the provisions of the 1991 Act varied from thirteen[27] to about thirty,[28] some of whom were believed to have had additional reasons for their disenchantment.

The magistracy was also the source of a new and highly combustible element which heightened the flames of the existing controversy surrounding the 1991 Act. Magistrates were not only worried about multiple offences and previous convictions, but they were also vociferous in their criticism of the working of the newly introduced system of means-related fines which was confined to the Magistrates' courts. Originally, the policy that the seriousness of the offence should be calculated in units applicable to all offenders alike, but that the amount of the financial penalty payable should be related to their disposable weekly income, had been generally welcomed as a step in the direction of equality of impact. With the co-operation of the Magistrates' Association and the Justices' Clerks' Society, experimental schemes had been piloted successfully and the results evaluated and published by the Home Office.[29] The idea was not novel, similar systems having been adopted in several jurisdictions overseas, including Austria, France, Germany, Greece,

[26] Text of an address by the Lord Chancellor, Lord Mackay of Clashfern, to the Annual General Meeting of the Gloucestershire Magistrates' Association, 4 Feb. 1994, p. 2.

[27] Cf. Professor David Smith, Department of Applied Social Science at Lancaster University, in *Regional Criminal Justice Conferences, 1990–93*, Home Office, 1994.

[28] Letter from Bryan Gibson, 8 Jan. 1994. An experienced Magistrates' clerk, Gibson had been among the most active and persuasive advocates for the introduction of unit fines. His book, *Unit Fines*, Waterside Press, Winchester, 1990, developed the original arguments and was published ahead of the Home Office research, containing much background information and reaching similar conclusions. Gibson was the co-ordinating editor of *Materials on the Criminal Justice Act 1991*, Waterside Press, 1992.

[29] D. Moxon, M. Sutton, and C. Hedderman, *Unit Fines: Experiments in Four Courts*, Home Office Research and Planning Unit Paper 59, 1990. The four Magistrates' courts were at Basingstoke, Bradford, Swansea, and Teesside.

Portugal, Scandinavia, and parts of the United States.[30] No doubts had been expressed during the passage of the legislation through Parliament. Yet within a few months the magistracy was up in arms and the Home Secretary in retreat. What had gone wrong in so short a time?

The explanation lay in the detailed and technical drafting of Sections 17–24 of the Criminal Justice Act 1991 and the rules for assessing disposable weekly income made by the Lord Chancellor under the Magistrates' Courts (Unit Fines) Rules 1992. Under Section 18(2) of the Act the amount of the fine was to be the product of the number of units determined by the court to be commensurate with the seriousness of the offence, or the combination of the offence and other offences associated with it,[31] and the value put on the units. Section 18(4) linked the number of units that could be imposed to offence levels set out in a prescribed scale, achieving proportionality between the level of penalties and the range of offence seriousness.[32] When fining an offender the court would have at its disposal between one and fifty units, limited by the statutory level of the offence under the Magistrates' Courts Act 1980. There were five such levels. Section 17 of the 1991 Act increased the maximum amounts of fines in a graduated range from £200 at level 1 to £5,000 at level 5.

In what turned out to be a fatal miscalculation the maximum value of a unit had been set at £100, whereas in the pilot schemes the maxima within the norms had originally been between £10 and £25. Later the pilot courts (and others operating unit fines voluntarily) had generally moved to a range of between £20–£30 per unit. Although there were dark suspicions that a grasping Treasury had been responsible, the finger pointed additionally to the habitual zeal

---

[30] See a report in the Issues and Practices in Criminal Justice series published by the National Institute of Justice, Douglas C. McDonald (ed.), J. Greene and C. Worzella, *Day Fines in American Courts: The Staten Island and Milwaukee Experiments*, US Department of Justice, Office of Justice Programs, Washington DC, 1992.

[31] It was anomalous that in assessing the seriousness of the offence for the purposes of deciding upon the quantum of this non-custodial penalty (i.e. the number of units) magistrates were empowered to consider 'other offences' rather than being limited to one other associated offence, as with custodial and community penalties.

[32] See M. Wasik and R. D. Taylor, *Blackstone's Guide to the Criminal Justice Act 1991*, Blackstone Press, London, 1991, p. 70. The authors provide a useful commentary on the system of unit fines at pp. 69–73. A second edition, including the amendments made by the Criminal Justice Act 1993, was published in 1994.

for bureaucratic neatness at the stage when instructions to drafts-men were being prepared by Home Office officials. A decision to increase maximum fines was overdue, although the top level was raised well above the rate of inflation from £2,000 to £5,000. When the level 5 maximum permissible fine of £5,000 was divided by the maximum number of units (fifty), the maximum value of each unit worked out at £100. Moreover, there was to be a standard maxi-mum of £100 per unit, irrespective of the level of offence involved. By the time the rules on the assessment of means in terms of dis-posable weekly income were made the Lord Chancellor's Department had taken over responsibility for the finance, organ-ization, and administration of the Magistrates' courts from the Home Office. But the all-important responsibility for determining criminal justice policy, including sentencing policy, remained with the Home Office. Therefore, although the Statutory Instrument was in the Lord Chancellor's name, it was the Home Office, with the approval of the Treasury, which had devised and implemented the scheme.

Whatever the allocation of blame, it was clear that the impact of substantially higher levels of fines, and the inflexibility of the mech-anism for calculating them, had not been anticipated. Magistrates resented their inability to adjust the final amount of the fine once the number of units had been determined by the seriousness of the offence and the offender's means. It was the method of assessing the disposable income of the offender which proved to be the Achilles' heel. All assessments were made by the courts on the basis of information supplied by the offender, usually without any veri-fication. Difficulties arose when an offender failed or refused to complete a means inquiry form, and the court did not adjourn the case or make a post-conviction order that the offender complete the form. The latter course of action put an offender at risk of an extra penalty for non-compliance. Despite representations at the forma-tive stage, the Government had refused to bring the liability to this sanction forward in time so that an offence would be committed if an offender failed to complete and return a means form sent with a summons in advance of the hearing. Partly driven by performance criteria, since too many cases adjourned meant a cash loss to the courts, magistrates tended to set the top rate of £100 per unit in such cases. The effect was to protract the sequence of events, bring-ing the offender back before the court in enforcement proceedings when the value of the units could be varied downwards if appropriate.

The procedure was cumbersome and vulnerable to legitimate public criticism. Most of the rash of well publicized cases of very high fines being imposed on offenders of modest means for trivial offences were attributable to defendants not complying with the requirement to complete a means form. A few voluble magistrates and the plain silliness, not to say unfairness, of the outcome in some of the least defensible cases was a mixture irresistible to the tabloid press, which milked the stories relentlessly. The denouement came when an unemployed man, Vaughan Watkins, was reported to have been fined £1,200 at Cwmbran, Gwent, for dropping litter from a car. Because he failed to attend court, and refused to supply details of his means, the twelve units of his fine were valued at the rate of £100 per unit. A reduction was made when the magistrates were told two weeks later that he had a disposable weekly income of £4. Once in possession of this information, the fine was reduced to £48, being the product of twelve units at the lowest permitted value of £4 per unit. By then, however, the case of the discarded crisp packet had caught the eye of the Home Secretary; indeed he could hardly have missed it given the tabloid exposure.

Then and there, rejecting all pleas from officials for a more carefully considered examination of the alternatives, Clarke decided that outright abolition of the statutory unit fine system was the only answer. In reaching his decision he had been influenced also by the heavy fines imposed on middle-income earners, often for road traffic offences where the fixed penalty was disproportionately lower.[33] Here again there had been a failure on the part of Government to think through the proper relationship between unit fines and fixed penalties.[34] Impetuous as his action may have seemed, and precipitated by sensational press reports as it undoubtedly was, no one could censure Clarke for indecisiveness or not knowing his own mind. It was one of the rare instances of a minister going further, and faster, than his critics were urging him to go.

---

[33] Before the unit fine system had come into effect there had been 5.6 million fixed penalty notices of £40 issued in 1991 for offences under the Road Traffic Offenders Act 1988. Fines for equivalent offences in the Magistrates' courts averaged £60. Following the implementation of the Criminal Justice Act 1991 the Automobile Association reported that the average fine in the Magistrates' courts for speeding had increased to £400. Wasik and Taylor, *Blackstone's Guide to the Criminal Justice Act 1991*, 2nd edn., 1994, p. 84.　　[34] Ibid., p. 85.

Neither the Magistrates' Association nor the Justices' Clerks were pressing for repeal, and urgent work was in hand on a rescue package. Only days before the Home Office had issued a press release in which the Home Secretary was quoted as saying that the scheme was to be made to work. At a meeting on 4 May with representatives of the Magistrates' Association he had suggested that a compromise solution might be found by retaining unit fines but allowing the Bench to take a second look at the cash figures when the units and disposable income had been multiplied. The meeting was followed by the issue of a bulletin circulated to all fifty-eight of the Association's branches encouraging the maximum use of their existing discretion. Clarke's own attitude was unequivocally revealed after the meeting when he commented that while he endorsed the principle of linking fines to an offender's means, plainly the scheme needed to be amended 'to avoid some of the more absurd recent decisions'.[35]

At this critical moment another actor entered an already crowded stage. The Justices' Clerks, responsible for advising lay magistrates on points of law and procedure, were holding their annual meeting at Eastbourne. When the contents of the Association's bulletin was put to the hall on 5 May there was unanimous rejection of the advice it contained. The clerks regarded it as a fudge, and worse, an improper attempt by the executive to interfere with the judicial process. The extension of the controversy to a three-way clash between the Home Secretary, the Magistrates' Association, and the Justices' Clerks' Society fortified Clarke's instinctive judgment that the best way to respond to the mounting ridicule to which unit fines were being exposed was to abandon the whole idea, rather than to persist in seeking some accommodation acceptable to the conflicting interests. Unkind critics, inside and outside Parliament, alleged that his decisive action was intended to improve his chances of becoming Chancellor of the Exchequer, an office he obtained shortly afterwards.[36] However, the explanation is unlikely to have been as simplistic. The Home Secretary saw the danger of being caught in a pincer between influential and disaffected professional groups, reinforced by the higher judiciary, and a surge of populist sentiment fanned, although not initiated, by the

[35] *The Times*, 5 May 1993.
[36] Norman Lamont resigned as Chancellor on 28 May and Kenneth Clarke was appointed to succeed him on the same day.

tabloid press. Political dexterity was required to recognize the perils of this situation and to extricate himself before it engulfed him as had happened to so many of his predecessors. If this demonstration of political skill earned him kudos in Parliament, so much the better. It is in the handling of such awkward incidents that political reputations are made—or lost.

III

If unit fines were beyond saving, could the sentencing provisions of the 1991 Act have been salvaged intact? There is, after all, nothing unusual about new legislation experiencing teething problems and encountering initial resistance. To recap: the primary causes of the abrupt change of course announced on 3 May were the malfunctioning of certain sections of the Criminal Justice Act 1991, leading to complaints from judges and magistrates. Perhaps these consequences could have been avoided if the drafting had concentrated less on the conferment of specific powers, adhering more closely to the general principles which had commanded such widespread support when first enunciated in Green and White Papers. Perhaps an earlier and more determined attempt to involve the judiciary and the magistracy when the Bill was in draft might have helped to exorcise some of the weaknesses. Nevertheless, the main structure of the Act remained sound and the Court of Appeal lost no time in giving guidance on its correct interpretation and application.

In the Crown Court, the legal issues predictably revolved around the two offences rule in Section 1(2)(a), and Section 29(2) on the effect of previous convictions. On the practicalities, frustration was caused by the absence of information about the circumstances of previous convictions and the inability to treat an offence as more serious by reason of an offender's failure to respond to previous sentences. Another objection arose from the need to adjourn and obtain a pre-sentence report from the Probation Service in cases where a custodial sentence of substantial length was inevitable. This was causing problems, especially for part-time recorders who sat in the Crown Court only for a limited number of weeks. Extra expenditure was incurred because Counsel had to appear twice and be paid for doing so, whereas before the Act one appearance would have been sufficient.

Inconvenient as they were, these practical difficulties were not insuperable; solutions could and would have been found. After a slow start, the Crown Prosecution Service was working on a system to supply Crown Court sentencers with the necessary information about previous convictions. The Home Office and the Lord Chancellor's Department had, with the Crown Prosecution Service, issued a joint circular[37] urging that adjournments be minimized by the preparation before trial of as many pre-sentence reports as possible in cases where guilty pleas were known. There were also proposals to keep adjournments as short as possible. Given time, Court administrators would have ironed out inefficiencies in the deployment of professional resources. In a series of cases heard between 23 and 30 November 1992, only weeks after the sentencing provisions of the Act had come into effect, Lord Taylor CJ gave judgment in the Criminal Division of the Court of Appeal on the true construction of the Sections dealing with the use of imprisonment and the length of custodial sentences.[38] There were no surprises and few adverse comments.

The Court made it clear that a custodial sentence could be justified only if the offence was so serious that no other penalty would suffice; that the length of the sentence must be commensurate with the seriousness of the offence, although it could be mitigated or aggravated by the presence of factors relevant to the offender; that a proper pre-sentence report must be obtained and considered before sentence was passed; and that a sentencing judge cannot treat the mere existence of previous convictions as relevant in assessing the seriousness of the instant offence or its combination

---

[37] The circular, issued on 11 May 1992, summarized the main findings of pilot trials carried out at five Crown Court centres (Birmingham, Bristol, Lincoln, Newcastle, and Southwark) in the second half of 1991 to investigate the most effective means of implementing the pre-sentence report provisions of the Criminal Justice Act 1991. An estimated 20,000 additional reports would be required annually, reflecting an increase of more than 10 per cent in the total number of reports prepared for the courts.

[38] In the order reported in the All England Law Reports the cases are: *R.* v. *Okinikan* [1993] 2 All ER 5 (pre-sentence reports and suspended sentences); *R.* v. *Oliver* and *R.* v. *Little* [1993] 2 All ER 9 (seriousness of offence); *R.* v. *Cunningham* [1993] 2 All ER 15 (sentence to be commensurate with seriousness of offence); *R.* v. *Cox* [1993] 2 All ER 19 (seriousness of offence and mitigating factors); *R* v. *Bexley*, *R* v. *Summers*, *R.* v. *Harrison* [1993] 2 All ER 23 (previous convictions); *R.* v. *Baverstock* [1993] 2 All ER 32 (reasons for imposing custodial sentence, previous convictions, and aggravating factors). These cases are also reported in (1993) 14 Cr. App. R. (S), Part 3.

with another offence. In *Bexley*, the leading case, Taylor CJ said that such familiar remarks as 'You have a long history of committing offences of this kind' or 'You have been given every chance, fines, probation, community service, and here you are again' would no longer be appropriate in passing sentence. Previous convictions would be statutorily irrelevant as indicators of seriousness in the instant offence.[39] The application of the reference to 'circumstances of other offences' in Section 29(2) had to be confined to those which disclosed some aggravating factor in the instant offence (A) and one other offence associated with it (B). The Chief Justice continued:

In other words the sentencer must concentrate his attention on A or A and B. Keeping that offence or combination in the forefront of his mind, he may properly ask himself whether there are any circumstances of other offences committed by the offender which shed light on offence A or offence B, so as to disclose some aggravating factor in either of them. If an aggravating factor is revealed by such circumstances, the sentencer is entitled to weigh it in deciding the seriousness of either A or A and B in combination. Relevant circumstances will usually be those which bear upon the offender's guilty mind. For example, they may show an aggravating element of planning, deliberation or selection; or they may disclose some added gravity of criminal purpose in the instant offence.[40]

The only hint of deviance from the notion of proportionality embedded in the Act, and the statements of intention which preceded it in the 1990 White Paper on *Crime, Justice and Protecting the Public*,[41] can be found in the Court of Appeal's acceptance of deterrence as a legitimate consideration in deciding sentence. In the case of *Cunningham* counsel presented an argument deployed by the editor of the *Criminal Law Review* that the White Paper should be relied upon as the basic document for the interpretation of the Act.[42] Deterrence should be eliminated from the considerations which the court could take into account since it appeared neither in the Act, which referred only to the seriousness of the offence, nor in the White Paper. When challenged from the Bench, however, counsel was unable to point to anything in the White Paper saying

---

[39] [1993] 2 All ER 25.   [40] Ibid. 25–6.   [41] Cm. 965.

[42] [1992] Crim. L.R. 230. The Editor of the *Criminal Law Review* is Andrew Ashworth, Edmund-Davies Professor of Criminal Law and Criminal Justice at King's College, University of London.

that deterrence was no longer a proper consideration.[43] In the judgment of the Court of Appeal the primary purposes of a custodial sentence must be to punish and deter. Accordingly, the phrase 'commensurate with the seriousness of the offence' in Section 2(2) must mean commensurate with the punishment and deterrence which the seriousness of the offence requires.[44] That this construction departed from the original intentions of the framers of the legislation is supported by contemporary Home Office records. For example, the senior official in charge of the Bill had written that: 'at the point of sentencing the individual offender, the use of custody cannot be given validity by the presumed deterrent effects and the Act reflects this, in requiring that custody be used only where justified by the seriousness of the offence.'[45]

Whether consciously or otherwise, the reinstatement of deterrence may have been an instance of the judiciary regaining some of the ground which they had lost in the unpopular restriction on their sentencing discretion.

Another straw in the wind can be detected in the adoption by the Court of Appeal in *Cox* of an earlier dictum about the relevance of public opinion when dealing with young offenders. In *R.* v. *Bradbourn* Lawton LJ had said that a custodial sentence was justified under the Criminal Justice Act 1982[46] if the offence committed

[43] Letter of 17 Sept. 1993 from Dr D. A. Thomas who acted as *amicus curiae* in these cases with D. Calvert-Smith, Senior Treasury Counsel at the Central Criminal Court. The role of *amicus* is a neutral one, assisting the court with submissions on the interpretation of legislation or other questions of law which arise, without reference to the outcome of the case. The *amicus* is not concerned to persuade the court to decide the case in favour of one party or another, but to present arguments in a detached way to help the court in coming to its decision. Dr Thomas, a leading authority on sentencing, is University Reader in Criminology and a Fellow of Trinity Hall, Cambridge. He edits the Criminal Appeal Reports (Sentencing) and is a Member of the Judicial Studies Board.

[44] *R.* v. *Cunningham* [1993] 2 All ER at 17.

[45] John Halliday, 'Aims and Objectives of the Act' in *Materials on the Criminal Justice Act 1991*, p. 17. Halliday succeeded David Faulkner as Deputy Under-Secretary of State in charge of the Criminal Department of the Home Office in 1990. He had been Principal Private Secretary to the Home Secretary (William Whitelaw) 1980–3; Assistant Under-Secretary of State at the Home Office, 1983–7; and Under-Secretary at the Department of Health, 1987–90.

[46] Section 1(4) provided that where a person under twenty-one years of age is convicted or found guilty of an offence the court may not impose a custodial sentence on him unless it is of the opinion that no other method of dealing with him is appropriate because it appears to the court that he is unable or unwilling to respond to non-custodial penalties or because a custodial sentence is necessary for the protection of the public or because the offence was so serious that a non-custodial

by a young person was such as 'would make right-thinking members of the public, knowing all the facts, feel that justice had not been done by the passing of any sentence other than a custodial one'.[47] In *Cox* Taylor CJ agreed, saying that although the form of words in the 1982 Act differed from the provision in the 1991 Act, which applied not just to young offenders but generally, the earlier formulation was nevertheless appropriate to any consideration of the expression 'so serious that only such a sentence can be justified for the offence'.[48]

Greater reliance on punishment and heightened sensitivity towards public opinion were soon to emerge as the central planks of a radically reconstructed policy towards criminal offending when Michael Howard succeeded Kenneth Clarke at the Home Office the following summer. Before this came Taylor's climatic speech in Scotland. It was understandable that ministers should wish to rectify an Act that was not working as intended because it was misconceived, or too hurried in preparation, or not properly thought out. But what if it was working as intended (with the exception of unit fines) and had been shown to be workable by the Court of Appeal? Did the alarming prospect occur to officials that too abrupt a change of course, with no opportunity for a thorough review of the operating defects, would upset the still evolving relationships between the component parts of the system of criminal justice?

Retrospectively, some contemporary empirical evidence concerning these questions became available. Early in 1993, about five months after the implementation of the Criminal Justice Act 1991, a large scale survey of the various agencies involved in the Act was launched by the Home Office. The aim of the survey, which had been planned by an interdepartmental working group set up to oversee the implementation of the legislation before it had come under attack, was to elicit the views of those who were operating the Act in practice. Between February and April 1993 over 2,000 respondents were interviewed. The sample was drawn from the

sentence cannot be justified. For the legislative origins of this provision see *Responses to Crime* (vol. 2), pp. 168–70.

[47] (1985) 7 Cr. App. R. (S) 180 at 183, CA.

[48] [1993] 2 All ER 21. The test of the 'right-thinking man' is open to objection on the grounds that it is too vague and imprecise, and that it is susceptible to the pressure of public opinion, in some instances inspired by the popular press.

police, magistrates and their clerks, barristers, defence solicitors, the Crown Prosecution Service, the Probation Service, and the Prison Service. The views of judges were not included in the study.

Although the results were not published until 1995,[49] the survey is an interesting historical document showing how closely the views of many practitioners in the field coincided with the political perceptions which were shortly to bring about the policy reversal. While most respondents had an understanding of the Act, and in this respect the training which had preceded its implementation was considered to have been helpful, many found parts of it to be unclear or ambiguous. Opinion was polarized between magistrates, clerks, barristers, and defence solicitors, who thought that there were major problems which needed amending, and prison staff, probation officers, and social services staff, who thought that although there were short-term problems the Act was generally to be welcomed. Unit fines, Section 29, and the assessment of offence seriousness were seen as the main difficulties by all groups, with the exception of social services staff. Most respondents were positive about community penalties, and magistrates in particular were very satisfied with the work of the Probation Service.[50]

IV

The foreshortened Parliamentary timetable was evident when Standing Committee B resumed its consideration of the Criminal Justice Bill (Lords) on 8 June 1993.[51] Following the Government changes which had translated Kenneth Clarke to the Treasury, the Committee's membership was reconstituted. Michael Jack, the Home Office Minister of State who had been in charge of the Bill in Standing Committee, was moved to the Ministry of Agriculture, Fisheries and Food, making way for David Maclean.[52] In the opinion of the Government's business managers, Maclean was expected

---

[49] G. Mair and C. May, *Practitioners' views of the 1991 Criminal Justice Act: a survey of criminal justice agencies*, Research and Planning Unit Paper 91, Home Office, London, 1995.

[50] Ibid., p. iv.

[51] The first sitting of the Committee had been on 25 May 1993.

[52] David Maclean had succeeded William Whitelaw as MP for Penrith and The Border in 1983. He was Parliamentary Secretary, Ministry of Agriculture, Fisheries and Food, 1989–92, and Minister of State, Department of the Environment, 1992–3.

to bring more bite and political conviction to the ministerial team. Nicholas Baker was replaced by James Arbuthnot as the Government Whip, and Emma Nicholson and Phillip Oppenheim, Parliamentary Private Secretaries to Home Office Ministers, by Jacques Arnold and Bernard Jenkin. Alun Michael and Paul Boateng led for the Opposition on the bulk of the Bill, with Alastair Darling, an Opposition Treasury spokesman, taking the clauses relating to insider dealing. The Economic Secretary to the Treasury, Anthony Nelson, led for the Government on these clauses.

About 150 amendments or new clauses were tabled by the Opposition at Committee stage. However, it was at the initiative of the Government, amending its own Bill which had already completed all stages in the Lords after detailed scrutiny, that the legislation was transformed. In the final total, 207 amendments were incorporated during the Bill's passage through the Commons. Of these 206 were Government amendments with only one Opposition amendment.[53] The main changes fell under four heads: a new Part on the financing of terrorism;[54] an amended definition of the offence of insider dealing, together with a Schedule setting out a series of special defences; the abolition of the unit fines system under the 1991 Act; and the restoration to the courts of the power to take previous convictions into account when sentencing. The last two had been forecast by Kenneth Clarke in his Parliamentary statement of 13 May.

At the start of the Committee's third sitting, Opposition spokesmen pointed out that the wording of the new clauses which had been announced on the floor of the House by the Home Secretary had not yet been tabled. In reply, Maclean said that officials were 'working night and day' on the drafting.[55] He hoped that the Government would soon be able to table the amendments on unit fines, Section 29 (previous convictions), and increasing the penalties for causing death through drunken or dangerous driving. Proposals would be presented and laid as soon as possible so that members had adequate time to consider them before they were debated.

[53] The author is indebted to the Committee's Clerk, Frank Cranmer of the Public Bill Office at the House of Commons, for these statistics. Letter dated 6 Sept. 1993.

[54] Part IV of the Criminal Justice Act 1993 (Sections 36–51) read across into the Northern Ireland (Emergency Provisions) Act 1991 and the Prevention of Terrorism (Temporary Provisions) Act 1989 certain provisions contained in the Drug Trafficking Offences Act 1986 applicable to the proceeds of drug trafficking.

[55] *Parl. Debates*, HC, Standing Committee B, col. 71, 8 June 1993.

In the meantime the Committee occupied itself with insider trading, which since leaving the Lords had been the subject of intensive consultation between the Treasury and representative organizations, including the Stock Exchange, the Confederation of British Industry, the Law Society, the British Merchant Banking Securities Houses Association, and others. The proceeds of trafficking in controlled drugs, and an extension of the powers of confiscation contained in the Drug Trafficking Offences Act 1986 to terrorist-related activities, also took up time in the early sittings. The latter was a sizeable addition, virtually a Bill in itself, made possible at this stage in the legislation only by the generous ruling of the Commons authorities on the scope of the original Bill. Twenty-one pages of amendments were required to spell out the new provisions, but they attracted scant attention apart from a speech by the single Ulster MP on the Committee. They were accepted without dissent at each of the remaining stages of the Bill's passage through Parliament. In this instance, therefore, although an important measure affecting Northern Ireland was brought forward by primary rather than secondary legislation,[56] it was enacted with a minimum of Parliamentary scrutiny and debate.

By its seventh sitting the Committee was ready to turn to the more familiar ground of unit fines. Government amendments had been tabled the previous week, but the Opposition spokesman Alun Michael complained that there had been only three working days to consider them. In a matter of hours, he said, the Opposition had tried to improve on something which the Minister and his advisers had had weeks to tackle.[57] Maclean explained that rather than attempting to modify the scheme the Government had decided to abolish unit fines because of widespread dissatisfaction with its operation among sentencers and the general public. He went on: 'We are concerned about the anomalous results that have been produced in several cases. On reflection, and with the benefit of experience of the scheme's operation, we believe it to have been over-mechanistic and over-complicated. It interfered unnecessarily

---

[56] Since the prorogation of the Northern Ireland Parliament at Stormont in 1972 the bulk of legislation relating to the Province was passed at Westminster in the form of affirmative Orders in Council, not subject to amendment or to scrutiny by the Joint Committee on Statutory Instruments, and generally disposed of perfunctorily in both Houses.

[57] Standing Committee B, col. 245, 17 June 1993.

with magistrates' discretion to impose appropriate fines in individual cases.'[58]

The alternative of amending the scheme, as suggested in the Opposition's amendments, in particular by the introduction of banded allowances, had been carefully considered. The conclusion, however, was that it would complicate matters still further, creating more scope for misunderstanding with disproportionate and anomalous results. Instead, the Government had decided that the best way forward was to restore the courts' discretion and to rely on magistrates to use their common sense to relate fines to the seriousness of the offence, taking into account the means of offenders.

In reply, Michael protested that the Opposition had called for an end to the unit fines system well before ministers had been willing to contemplate the need to make a change, but that the replacement now proposed would not prevent a recurrence of the inconsistencies and unfairness which had existed before the 1991 Act. The pilot schemes had worked well, receiving warm approval as a way of improving justice, fairness, and effectiveness in the courts. Despite the universal support which had been expressed for the principle of unit fines at the time of the earlier legislation, the implementation of the process had not enjoyed the same unqualified support: 'Either the Home Office became greedy, or—more likely—the dead hand of the Treasury bore down on the arrangements.'[59] As a result, over the months since the scheme had been in operation criticism had grown. There had been pleas for amendment from magistrates, from the media, and from representatives of other organizations. They wanted limits on the discretion of the courts to be lifted, and for the systems which had operated successfully in the pilot projects to be allowed to continue instead of the inflexible statutory scheme in Section 18 of the Criminal Justice Act 1991.

After a lengthy and at times heated debate the Opposition amendments were not pressed to a division, Michael urging the Government to use the period before the Report Stage to find a way to introduce a better and fairer system. The new clause, which subsequently became Section 65 of the Criminal Justice Act 1993,[60] was then read a second time, and added to the Bill. A novel

---

[58] Ibid., col. 240.   [59] Ibid., col. 247.

[60] Section 65 (1) of the Criminal Justice Act 1993 substituted a new Section 18 in the Criminal Justice Act 1991. Section 19 of that Act was repealed by Section 65 (2) of the Criminal Justice Act 1993.

feature, which distinguished it from the pre-1991 practice, was the inclusion of a duty to inquire into the financial circumstances of the offender before fixing the amount of any fine. The requirement left it to the courts to determine how, and in what depth, the inquiry should be made in each case. The duty extended to both the Crown Court and the Magistrates' courts, in neither of which there had been any explicit requirement to make such inquiries previously. Unlike the unit fines scheme, it was not intended that there should be a prescribed statutory form for inquiring into financial means. Courts would be encouraged to develop locally those arrangements which they found most useful and which best suited their circumstances. Having burnt its fingers once, the Government now declared that it did not intend to fetter the discretion of the courts.[61]

Although ministers could not be moved from their resolute commitment to outright abolition, either in Standing Committee or when the Bill was reported to the House of Commons, the debates on unit fines were the best informed and the proposals the most thoroughly tested. Several MPs were themselves magistrates, and all were in touch with local opinion on the issue in their constituencies. By contrast, the changes in the powers of the courts to deal with offenders were less immediate, being of more direct relevance to the judiciary than to parliamentarians. In his statement of 13 May Kenneth Clarke had said that sentencers should have reasonable discretion to decide on the right sentence in a particular case, bearing in mind the seriousness of the offences being dealt with, all the circumstances of the offender, and his offending behaviour. The aim of the changes which he would be bringing forward was to ensure that the law allowed the courts to exercise judgment and common sense within a sensible legal framework, enabling justice to be done in the interests of the public, the victim, and the offender. The Government intended:

to amend Section 1 of the 1991 Act so as to allow the courts to take into account all the offences for which the offender is being dealt with, instead of only one offence, or that offence and one other offence, which is the case now. Secondly, we propose to restore to the courts their power to have full regard to the criminal record of an offender and his response to previous sentences when deciding on the sentence for his current offences. We will

---

[61] Standing Committee B, col. 244, 17 June 1993.

do this by repealing Section 29 of the 1991 Act, which prevents a court from regarding an offence as more serious by reason of any previous convictions of the offender, or his failure to respond to previous sentences.[62]

This concise statement met all the main points of criticism advanced by judges when the 1991 Act was before Parliament and subsequently. The immediate response of Opposition Front Bench spokesmen in the Commons had been to chide Clarke on his reversal of policy, reiterating an attachment to sentencing guidelines,[63] but without saying whether they supported the detailed proposals. When a new clause enabling the courts to take account of previous convictions or failure to respond to previous sentences was reached in Standing Committee, Opposition amendments were tabled and debated at some length, but were not pressed. The new clause, which became Section 66 of the 1993 Act, was then accepted without a division. It replaced the original Section 29 in the 1991 Act, for which it was substituted, and came into force on 16 August 1993.[64]

Political sensitivity towards public opinion was reflected in two other late additions to the Bill. Once the cork was out of the bottle, so to speak, it seemed there was little check on the desire of Home Office ministers to top up the Bill with extra infusions. Offending on bail had caught the public eye, largely because of extensive press coverage of some bad cases of breach, backed up by pressure from the police. As a result the opportunity was taken to add a new sub-section to the wording which was to replace Section 29, the unsatisfactory legislative compromise in the 1991 Act on the limited extent to which the circumstances of previous offences amounted to aggravating factors which could be taken into account in sentencing. In future, the straightforward provision in the substituted Section 29(1) that 'In considering the seriousness of any offence, the court may take into account any previous convictions of the offender or any failure of his to respond to previous

---

[62] *Parl. Debates*, HC, 224 (6th ser.), col. 939, 13 May 1993.

[63] Ibid., cols. 941–3.

[64] The treatment of previous convictions and failure to respond to previous sentences in the legislation of 1991 and 1993 has been the subject of several commentaries. See Wasik and Taylor, *Blackstone's Guide to the Criminal Justice Act 1991*, 2nd edn., 1994, pp. 33–8; Ashworth and Gibson, [1994] Crim. L.R. 101; and M. Wasik and A. von Hirsch, 'Section 29 Revised: Previous Convictions in Sentencing', [1994] Crim. L.R. 409.

sentences'[65] would be supplemented by Section 29(2): 'In considering the seriousness of any offence committed while the offender was on bail, the court shall treat the fact that it was committed in those circumstances as an aggravating factor.' According to the Minister of State, it was expected that the new power would in many cases 'rightly result in a heavier sentence than would otherwise have been given'.[66]

The second addition stemmed from a shift in the public mood, accelerated by one of the most vehement of all lobbies, the Campaign Against Drinking and Driving (CADD). CADD argued that the widespread suffering and harm inflicted on innocent victims of road crimes was being trivialized by lenient sentences and inconsistencies in sentencing practice. Growing public sympathy towards this sentiment had led to the inclusion in the Conservative Manifesto for the 1992 General Election of a commitment to increase the penalty for causing death through dangerous or drink driving so that 'the maximum sentence for such a crime should reflect its gravity'.[67] In the Standing Committee a new clause was added to the Bill, honouring the undertaking by doubling the maximum penalty for both causing death by dangerous driving and causing death by careless driving while under the influence of drink or drugs from five to ten years.[68] The resulting difference between the maxima for dangerous driving, which remained at two years, and for causing death by dangerous driving was very large, reflecting the emphasis placed on the consequences of driving dangerously rather than the act of driving dangerously.[69]

That the courts had not been restricted by an inadequate upper limit in passing sentence for the most serious offences was indicated

[65] Wasik and von Hirsch do not agree with Ashworth and Gibson's sombre prediction that even if the law on previous convictions continues to be interpreted in line with common law principles, the reintroduction of the phrase 'failure to respond to previous sentences' may become a clear invitation to sentence offenders on their record: [1994] Crim. L.R. at 106 and 414.

[66] Standing Committee B, col. 271, 17 June 1993.

[67] *The Best Future for Britain*, Conservative Central Office, London, 1992, p. 23.

[68] Criminal Justice Act 1993, Section 67 (1).

[69] Andrew Ashworth has pointed out that a minor lapse of care while driving may occasionally have tragic consequences, whereas a gross lapse may give rise to no harm at all. The result, and consequently the penalty imposed by the courts, will depend on outcome-luck. Moral blame and criminal responsibility, he argues, should be assessed on the degree of fault and the forseeable risk of harm. 'Taking the Consequences' in S. Shute, J. Gardner, and J. Horder (eds.), *Action and Value in Criminal Law*, Clarendon Press, Oxford, 1993, p. 122.

by the rarity of cases in which recourse was had to the maximum penalty. Information reported to the Home Office in the five years preceding the change showed that only four persons (an average of less than one per year) convicted in England and Wales of causing death by dangerous driving (or reckless driving prior to the coming into force of the Criminal Justice Act 1991) or careless driving while under the influence of drink and drugs had received the maximum penalty of five years' imprisonment.[70] Nevertheless, once the ten-year maximum had come into effect it was not long before the Court of Appeal interpreted the will of Parliament by laying down a more stringent sentencing regime in a guideline judgment.[71]

V

Apart from two further Government amendments, one on the forfeiture of cash resulting from the proceeds of drug trafficking and the other on money laundering, the Report stage of the Bill on the floor of the Commons was taken up with debates on a number of general issues raised by the Opposition parties. Amendments ranged from the importance of crime prevention and the interests of victims of crime to a code of practice for the courts in deciding bail applications, pre-sentence reports, and the powers of authorized investigators in Northern Ireland.[72] The House was thinly

[70] The annual statistics were: 1988: 2; 1989: nil; 1990: 1; 1991: nil; 1992: 1. *Parl. Debates*, HL, 550 (5th ser.), col. WA 135, 16 Dec. 1993.

[71] The Attorney General, with leave, referred two cases to the Court of Appeal on the grounds that the sentences passed by the Crown Court appeared to him to be unduly lenient. In quashing the original sentence and substituting an increased penalty in each case, Lord Taylor CJ made use of the opportunity to lay down revised guidelines to be followed by the courts in cases of drink driving resulting in the death of the victim. *Attorney-General's References Nos. 14 and 24 of 1993 (R. v. Shepherd and R. v. Wernet)*, (1994) 15 Cr. App. R. (S) 640. The levels of penalty were revised upwards in the most serious cases of causing death by dangerous driving, especially where there was more than one fatality. In cases of convictions of the new offence of causing death by careless driving, having consumed alcohol above the prescribed limit, a prison sentence would ordinarily be appropriate, other than in exceptional cases where the alcohol level was just over the borderline, the carelessness momentary, and there was strong mitigation. For the legislative history of the power to increase lenient sentences under the provisions of Sections 35 and 36 of the Criminal Justice Act 1988, see *Responses to Crime*, Vol. 1, pp. 17–19, and Vol. 2, pp. 178–80.

[72] *Parl. Debates*, HC, 227 (6th ser.), cols. 839–929, 29 June 1993.

attended, and none of the Opposition amendments were accepted. The Bill was then read a third time and passed.

Since the Bill had started in the House of Lords, all the amendments made in the Commons, either as a result of Clarke's volte-face or the later additions on terrorist finances and insider dealing, had to be referred to the Lords for consideration. Time was pressing, and one of the shortcomings of a heavy legislative programme is that the demands of practical convenience invariably predominate. Government Departments insist in unison that compelling urgency requires their bills to be completed and added to the statute book before the Summer Recess, even though many of their provisions are not due to come into effect immediately. Few bills fail to cross the finishing line, leaving only a handful of stragglers waiting until Parliament returns in the Autumn for a short period before the end of the session. The result is that the amount of time available for each House to perform its constitutional functions of scrutiny and revision is squeezed to the minimum regarded as acceptable.

So it was with the Criminal Justice Bill in 1993. On 26 July, a date confirmed at the last moment and only three days before the start of the Summer Recess, the Lords were asked to consider and agree to no less than sixty-nine pages of printed amendments sent from the Commons. For two and a half hours from 7.13 p.m. until 9.47 p.m. peers debated the main changes, dutifully accepting every one of the 207 amendments without a vote. The House welcomed the rewording of the provisions on insider dealing, which had formed part of the original Bill, and had been criticized when previously before the Lords. Now, following more detailed consultation with the interested parties, the key provisions had been redrafted including the definition of the offence of insider dealing by acquiring or disposing of price-affected securities, or encouraging another person to do so, on the basis of information obtained as an insider.[73] A new clause particularized the defences to the offence of insider trading,[74] again following consultation, and aiming to achieve a greater degree of certainty.

Reactions towards unit fines were more mixed, moving the Minister of State Earl Ferrers to give a frank and dispassionate account of the difficulties which had been encountered in the oper-

---

[73] Criminal Justice Act 1993, Section 52.   [74] Ibid., Section 53.

ation of the scheme introduced by the 1991 Act. Before taking the decision to abolish it, he assured the House, all the options for amending it had been looked at. The Government did not believe that a system of banded expenditure allowances, or indeed any other refinement, would solve the problems which sentencers had experienced.[75] Under the new arrangements the aim was that each fine should reflect the court's view of the seriousness of the offence. Before setting a fine the court would have a duty to inquire into the financial circumstances of an offender and to relate the seriousness of the offence to the offender's means and ability to pay. A court might consider that different levels of fine would be appropriate to reflect the seriousness of the same offence for offenders of differing means.

The closing moments of this most unorthodox Bill's passage through Parliament witnessed some of the most forthright invective. No longer a Lord of Appeal, but still a forceful and eloquent voice of the higher judiciary, Lord Ackner roundly denounced the restrictions placed on the sentencing powers of the courts by the 1991 Act:

Sections 1, 2 and 29 constituted aberrations on the part of the Government of quite monumental proportions. They so startled and astonished the former Home Secretary, the Rt. Hon. Kenneth Clarke, that he thought and so alleged in the radio programme *Today* on 5 May that his predecessor had fully consulted the judiciary who had agreed with the sections which are now to be amended. He withdrew that statement when its inaccuracy was drawn to his attention. But the fact that he thought that consultation must have taken place shows . . . his astonishment that the provisions existed.[76]

Ackner went on to remind the House that in the debates on the earlier legislation he had warned that, while Parliament was entitled to establish a framework within which the judges should operate, if the framework became distorted then so would the decision of the court. In his opinion the Government had ignored the doctrine of separation of powers. They had decided to control the administration of criminal justice by obliging judges to sit in blinkers insulated from reality, unable to focus on vital and relevant facts, and unable to apply the Government's own doctrine of just deserts emphasized

[75] *Parl. Debates*, HL, 548 (5th ser.), col. 1082, 26 July 1993.
[76] Ibid., col. 1088.

in the White Paper which had preceded the 1991 Act. As a result, the judges had been unable to protect the public from the persistent offender.[77]

It was strong meat. Ackner's language may have been more extreme than would have been used by some of the judges sitting regularly in the Crown Court or Court of Appeal, but it was not discordant with the general tenor of judicial opinion. Once enough judges had convinced themselves that the introduction of a statutory framework in which sentencing discretion would have to be exercised in a consistent and visible way, and along known lines, equated to 'sitting in blinkers insulated from reality', the provisions to which they objected most strongly were doomed. In vain the civil servants protested that they had tried to involve the judiciary in consultation during the crucial stages when the general principles contained in the White Paper were being converted into legislative form, but had obtained little in the way of positive response.

VI

The episode exemplified the ambiguity of the judicial role. An innate acceptance of the fundamental importance of the doctrine of separation of powers (brought in by Ackner to buttress his argument) in maintaining a judiciary free from political control makes most judges wary of intervening in policy making. Legislation, although it may be grumbled about in private, is regarded as the province of the politicians. Then there is an awareness that the English judiciary is strictly hierarchical and to speak out of turn is to risk rebuke from higher authority. At the apex of the criminal judiciary stands the Lord Chief Justice, to whom great deference is paid. He expects to be informed directly or indirectly by the Home Secretary, or by senior officials at the Home Office, of any significant proposals for changes in criminal justice policy, whether or not legislation is required. His role is particularly difficult: he is a spokesman for judges collectively whenever he believes such representation necessary, while simultaneously discharging his judicial responsibility in court to interpret and apply the laws enacted by Parliament.

[77] *Parl. Debates*, HL, 548 (5th ser.), col. 1090.

Personalities, and the manner of reacting to proposals from Government, count for much. Although engaged in dialogue with ministers, generally at arm's length although occasionally in person, on policy developments throughout the 1980s,[78] Lord Lane was deliberately more reticent in his public statements than his successor. The contrast between the two was apparent from the start. At his first interview with a national daily newspaper five weeks after his appointment, Taylor told the Legal Correspondent of *The Times* that judges should be more ready to speak out and involve themselves in the machinery of justice. They should not 'hide behind judicial independence' and a 'fear of what might emerge if they do talk to anybody'.[79] In a later interview, after the 1991 Act had been amended, he said that judges had a part to play in sentencing policy: 'It is desirable that the judiciary should have an input, or you get the sort of muddle we had over the 1991 Act.'[80]

Sentencing policy is always sensitive ground for politicians, the more so because of a mutual realization that proposals for a change of direction may be taken as criticism of the judges who have created, through the use of their discretion, a situation calling for reform. While it is seldom if ever made explicit, the Home Office at times sees the judges as part, even a large part, of the problem. Vested interests are then brought into play which if heeded can thwart the introduction of a desired change, or if spurned can lead to a judiciary alienated from the implementation of reforms enacted.[81]

Lords of Appeal in Ordinary, for historical reasons, stand astride the dividing line separating judges and politicians. The most senior appellate judges in the country, they are simultaneously members of one of the Houses of Parliament. Appeals are heard in

---

[78] See *Responses to Crime*, (vol. 2), pp. 173–84, 464.

[79] *The Times*, 2 June 1992. The report disclosed that Lord Taylor was making use of the Lord Chancellor's press office on a daily basis, whereas Lord Lane had never granted a media interview. On 28 May 1993 Taylor gave a press conference to mark his first year in office. *The Times*, 29 May 1993. By judicial standards his practice continued to be unprecedently media-friendly.

[80] *The Times*, 27 June 1994.

[81] For a discussion of the dilemma posed to judges by proposals for major changes in sentencing laws or procedures in the more dispersed jurisdictions of the United States, see M. Tonry, 'Judges and Sentencing Policy—the American Experience' in C. Munro and M. Wasik (eds.), *Sentencing, Judicial Discretion and Training*, Sweet and Maxwell, London, 1992, pp. 137–63. Michael Tonry is Sonosky Professor of Law and Public Policy in the University of Minnesota and an authority on sentencing policy and research.

Committee Rooms in a court-like setting, although less formal. In the Chamber itself the Law Lords sit on the cross-benches. Party politics are eschewed, and the topics on which Law Lords will speak are chosen with care. On the more important criminal justice policies, as Ackner acknowledged, they might consult amongst themselves, and in particular with the Lord Chief Justice. However, each speaks as an individual, and on occasion conflicting views are expressed.[82] Unlikely as it may be that any written constitution would permit judges to influence legislation in this way, it is nevertheless a device which has helped to blunt the sharp edges of the boundaries that have bedevilled the recent history of sentencing reform in the United States.

The fact that the changes made to the sentencing provisions of the Criminal Justice Act 1991 were a victory for the judges does not mean that the Government was faced with the outright rejection of the main purpose of an Act of Parliament. We have seen that for the most part the underlying principles of the legislation were upheld and enforced by the courts without critical comment. Under the new regime custodial sentences and community sentences were distinguished, and the use of custody limited to those cases where the offence was so serious that no other penalty would suffice. The length of the sentence had to be commensurate with the seriousness of the offence. The parole system was reformed and the law on early release rationalized. However, by attempting to stick too closely to the ideal of proportionality between the gravity of the offence and the penalty it should attract, inflexibility had been created in the treatment of multiple offences and inability to take proper account of previous convictions and the offender's response to earlier sentences. Greater reliance on political instinct in the preparatory stages, and less reluctance to risk undermining the precision and structural coherence demanded by the draftsman, might have avoided this trap. More generally, it was typical of Home Office internal procedures to become progressively more remote from the original principles as legislation made its way towards the statute book.

[82] See the speeches of Lords Goff of Chieveley, Lane, and Ackner in the debate on the Report of the House of Lords Select Committee on Murder and Life Imprisonment. *Parl. Debates*, HL, 512 (5th ser.), cols. 467–71, 478–80, and 489–93, 6 Nov. 1989. Also Lord Lane's evidence to the Select Committee, *Report of the Select Committee on Murder and Life Imprisonment* (HL Paper 78–II), HMSO, London, 1989, p. 254.

As it was, these were the features which acted as a lightning conductor for hostile judicial reaction. While implementing the statutory policies in the courts, judges almost universally felt that some of the restrictions placed on their discretion hampered rather than assisted the process of arriving at a just and fair sentence. The magistrates' criticism of the system of unit fines was essentially the same. The amendments made by the 1993 Act corrected these weaknesses, strengthening the structure within which the sentencing of offenders was to be contained in the future. The legislation of 1991[83] did not escape unscathed from the storm which built up so unexpectedly, but in its amended form it endured as a milestone in English penal policy. In November 1993 Taylor went out of his way to demonstrate publicly how far his views had changed from his speech at Gleneagles eight months before. In addressing the Annual General Meeting of the National Association for the Care and Resettlement of Offenders (NACRO) he said:

I believe that the philosophy of the Criminal Justice Act 1991 as it was originally envisaged still holds good. I believe, though, that the amendments have improved it and have made it more realistic. The philosophy of the Act is very simple as far as custody is concerned. It is just this—that the courts should not send anybody to a period of custody unless the seriousness of the offending behaviour makes a custodial penalty the only viable option or where, in the case of serious violent or sexual offences, the public needs to be protected from a dangerous offender.[84]

VII

Would the outcome have been the same without Kenneth Clarke's political intervention? It is possible, but unlikely. The bureaucracy in Whitehall is tenacious and does not change course readily. The team of civil servants, including the draftsman, working on the legislation when it was being taken through Parliament had become convinced that the heart would be torn out of the Bill if amendments on the lines proposed by Ackner were accepted. It was a classic case of defence of the detail overwhelming the underlying principles. Of the ministers, neither of Clarke's immediate

---

[83] *Responses to Crime*, Vol. 2, pp. 404–67, contains a detailed account of the origins and passage through Parliament of the criminal justice legislation in 1990–1.

[84] Extract from Lord Taylor's speech as made available to the press.

predecessors as Home Secretary, David Waddington or Kenneth Baker, had displayed a comparable political touch in their tenure at one of the most difficult of all Departments to manage, and by the time Michael Howard arrived on the scene the die was cast.

The history is one of political pragmatism applied to the administration of the criminal law. It is as much of an over-simplification to say that the judges did not like part of a law made by Parliament and got it changed as it is to claim that Kenneth Clarke acted impulsively and was motivated by political ambition. Diverse factors were present and synthesized. The resulting force would have been unstoppable even if there were any determined effort to stop it, which there was not.

Two casualties were left unnoticed at the roadside as the procession swept by. The first, one of many such instances, was the cavalier treatment of the parliamentary process. Almost every precept of sound law-making was breached in the course of the passage of the Criminal Justice Act 1993. Only the previous year a Hansard Society Commission on the legislative process had analysed the deep dissatisfaction expressed by of many of those most directly involved with the way public bills were handled. It noted that, although some measures will inevitably be required in a hurry, 'getting a bill right should always have priority over passing it quickly'. The Government was urged to make 'every effort to get bills in a form fit for enactment, without major alteration, before they are presented to Parliament'. This should be an overriding objective.[85] The 1993 Act was not the first and will certainly not be the last measure to depart from these aims. Nevertheless, the scale of the additions to the original modest measure, the lack of consultation and lateness of their appearance, and the inadequacy of the parliamentary scrutiny to which they were subjected make it a spectacular departure.

The second is an allegory. Watching the procession was an onlooker, a reasonable man, standing hesitant and apart. He was no casualty in the sense that he was unhurt. However, he appeared worried and ill at ease. He was listening intently and, as he did so, the clamour of a distant multitude could be heard. It was far away and indistinct, and he could not be sure of its meaning. But others had heard it too, and were hurrying towards it.

[85] *Making The Law*, Report of the Hansard Society Commission on the Legislative Process, Nov. 1992, Hansard Society for Parliamentary Government, London, 1993, p. 139.

PART II

Legislating with the Tide

2

Devising the Strategy

Well before the Criminal Justice Act 1993 reached the statute book fresh legislation under the rubric of law and order was taking shape. Early in the decade both ministers and officials had antici-pated that the successor to the 1991 Act would be legislation aris-ing out of the recommendations of the Royal Commission on Criminal Justice set up immediately after the acknowledgement of the wrongful convictions of the Birmingham Six and the Guildford Four. During the Commission's lifetime the likelihood of this hap-pening was first diluted and then submerged by a sea change in the climate of public opinion. Reforms in the criminal process aimed at reducing the possibilities for miscarriages of justice in the future were no longer seen as the most urgent priority. While Lord Runciman and the members of his Commission were investigating with great diligence the faults in the structure and operation of the legal system which had permitted such manifestly unlawful out-comes,[1] the public perception that crime was getting worse and criminals were getting away with their misdeeds interacted with other factors in determining the political weather.

Events played a large part, ranging from some notorious crimes, including serious offences committed by children or young teenagers, to flagrantly anti-social behaviour such as joy-riding in stolen cars, squatting in residential premises or shops, sabotaging fox-hunting, and disruptive assemblies on private or public land without the owner's consent. Anger, resentment, and widespread fear of crime mounted and were exploited by the media. Conservative ministers listened, and listened closely, to their own constituents and other

[1] The Royal Commission held its first meeting on 14 June 1991. Unusually, it was asked by the Home Secretary to complete its work within two years, and met this target. Its report, with 352 recommendations, supplemented by twenty-two separate research studies, was published on 6 July 1993. Royal Commission on Criminal Justice, *Report* (Cm. 2263), HMSO, London, 1993.

MPs. They also listened to a constantly hectoring and strident press. They sensed a compulsion to act, and to act toughly.

At and after the General Election of 1992 the same political imperatives spread to the Labour Party, unwilling to leave the law and order card solely in the hands of their opponents. Under new leadership, John Smith replacing Neil Kinnock as Leader of the Opposition[2] and Tony Blair succeeding the veteran Roy Hattersley as Shadow Home Secretary,[3] Labour adjusted its traditional libertarian stance and style of political discourse on crime and punishment to suit the hardening popular mood. Blair coined a slogan, 'tough on crime, and tough on the causes of crime', which helped his party to regain lost ground in what had previously been one of the safest Conservative-held territories. The wording was adroit: it enabled Labour to compete in the rhetorical display of toughness, while recognizing the context in which criminal offending takes place. Moreover, in terms of party politics the addendum left ample scope for attacking the Government's record on unemployment, homelessness, and other social conditions which could be presented as contributory causes of crime.

When faced with intractable and deeply rooted problems of deviant behaviour over which they have little direct control, legislators, and the governments they uphold, tend to fall back on the one thing they can do, which is to legislate. This may explain the parallel development of the steady growth over four decades in the incidence and severity of offending, and the greater frequency of Criminal Justice Acts. Whereas there were five such Acts in the thirty-five years between 1947 and 1982 (and a Criminal Law Act in 1977 which contained provisions on the powers of the courts and penalties), the seven years from 1987 to 1994 yielded the same number of substantive Criminal Justice Acts for England and Wales.[4]

[2] Parliamentary Under-Secretary of State 1974–5, Minister of State 1975–6, Department of Energy; Minister of State, Privy Council Office 1976–8; Secretary of State for Trade 1978–9. Principal Opposition spokesman on trade, prices, and consumer protection 1979–82; on energy, 1982–3; on employment, 1983–4; on trade and industry, 1984–7; on Treasury and economic affairs, 1987–92. Leader of the Labour Party 1992–4. Died of a heart attack, May 1994.

[3] Labour MP for Sedgefield since 1983. One of a new generation of Labour leaders who had never held ministerial office, Tony Blair was elected Leader of the Opposition in succession to John Smith in July 1994.

[4] Tables 1 and 2 of *Responses to Crime*, Vol. 2, pp. 2–3, summarize details of the substantive legislation for England and Wales, 1947–91, and Scottish legislation, administration, international co-operation, and minor Acts, 1949–90.

In the aftermath of Kenneth Clarke's deft transformation of the 1993 Act, policy responses by Government towards crime and criminal justice became noticeably more reactive. Whereas Clarke had been correcting faults in the operation of an Act which he accepted as otherwise sound policy, the strategy of his successor as Home Secretary, Michael Howard, could not have been more different. He was generally dismissive of professional expertise, including at times advice from his own officials, sensing that the general public was looking for a greater emphasis on punishment than on the rehabilitation of offenders. All elected politicians need to keep an ear to the ground, but Howard's was more closely attuned than most. Before long a consistent pattern could be detected of conforming to perceived public opinion, taking particular notice of the coverage of crime and editorial comment in the broadsheet and tabloid press. As an inevitable result, decisions began to be taken piecemeal, often dictated by what was thought most likely to appeal to an insecure and resentful general public.

Instant decision making, however, was not always followed by speedy action since some of the policies took a long time to bring into effect. For example, difficulties were experienced in extending the criminal law to prevent squatting, an objective announced in 1991 by Kenneth Baker when he was Home Secretary. At that time he said he was receiving almost daily letters showing real grievances on the part of owners and lawful occupiers about squatting, as well as representations from many Members of Parliament.[5] Simultaneously pressure was building to give the police more effective powers to control large and disruptive assemblies and raves on open land,[6] as well as the nuisance caused by gypsies and other unauthorized campers.

The application of the law to squatting was complicated due to the overlap between public and private wrongs, and criminal

---

[5] *Parl. Debates*, HC, 196 (6th ser.), col. 151, 15 Oct. 1991. A review by P. Vincent-Jones of the civil/criminal distinction in the law relating to the unlawful occupation of land or buildings for residential purposes, 'Squatting and the Recriminalization of Trespass', is included in I. Loveland, ed., *Frontiers of Criminality*, Sweet and Maxwell, London, 1995, pp. 219–47.

[6] For a discussion of the concept of public order and its historical development since 1880 see C. Townshend, *Making the Peace: public order and public security in modern Britain*, Oxford University Press, 1993. Aspects of policing and public order are explored in P. A. J. Waddington, *Liberty and Order: public order policing in a capital city*, UCL Press, 1995.

prosecutions or civil remedies for trespass.[7] Enforcement could raise problems; it being argued that homelessness and poverty justified the squatting of empty domestic or commercial premises. The lengthiness and expense of the available civil remedies strengthened demands for criminal sanctions. Nor was the problem limited to a small number of private landlords or occupiers. In the late 1980s it was estimated that the heaviest concentration of squatting was in local authority dwellings, especially in London.[8] While there were fewer than 100 prosecutions under the Criminal Law Act 1977 in each of the years 1988 and 1989,[9] more than 10,000 applications were made in 1989 for relief against squatters or trespassers by way of civil proceedings in the High Court or the County Court in England and Wales.[10] A Home Office consultation paper published in October 1991 commented that there were difficult issues of principle and practice, and that there was 'no unassailable consensus' on many aspects. The Government wished legislative changes to follow broad public discussion.[11]

It was the last time that such an invitation was issued before the publication of a Bill more than two years later. Over the same period a review of the general law on trespass was put in hand, leading to proposals for statutory controls including a new crim-

[7] 'Trespass spans a range of behaviour, from an inadvertent and temporary deviation onto private land to the forcible entry and continued occupation of premises. The traditional view is that the criminal law should concern itself not so much with the impingement on property rights as such—which may be the subject of misunderstanding or dispute—but rather with its manner. If violence is used against another or criminal damage is done to secure entry, it, rather than the resulting occupation, is dealt with under the criminal law. Curbing violent or forcible encroachments is an aspect of preventing disorder and maintaining the Queen's Peace.' *Squatting: a Home Office Consultation Paper*, London, 1991, p. 11.

[8] On 1 April 1990 approximately 5,200 local authority dwellings in England and Wales were reported as being unlawfully occupied, some 90 per cent of them in London. Three boroughs, Southwark, Lambeth, and Hackney, between them accounted for 65 per cent of the national total. (Ibid., p. 3.)

[9] Section 6 of the Criminal Law Act 1977 made it unlawful to use or threaten violence to secure entry if there was someone on the premises who was opposed to entry and if the person using or threatening the violence knew this to be the case. Section 7 introduced into the criminal law the novel feature of causing homelessness, since an occupier was afforded a remedy only where he was rendered homeless by the occupation, or was 'a protected intended occupier' who had purchased a freehold or leasehold interest (with not less than twenty-one years to run) intending to occupy the premises as a residence. The provisions of the 1977 Act did not extend to squatting in non-residential premises.

[10] *Squatting: a Home Office Consultation Paper*, p. 5.

[11] Ibid., p. 1.

inal offence of aggravated trespass, giving the police powers to prevent or deal with trespassers on land in the open air who seek to
intimidate, obstruct, or disrupt a lawful activity. With the addition
of elaborate measures to counter squatting in premises,[12] the resultant part of the Bill extended to sixteen clauses. By then the picture
had changed, with the number of local authority residential properties occupied by squatters going into decline. Between 1990 and
1993 the number of local authority dwellings in England and Wales
which were unlawfully occupied fell from 5,200 to approximately
3,000. In the London Borough of Lambeth as few as 58 local
authority properties were squatted in October 1993, compared with
an all-time high of 1,250 in 1987.[13]

Another contemporary phenomenon, taken up with relish by the
tabloid press, was offending on bail. Baker's immediate response to
so-called bail-bandits, mainly young people, particularly car
thieves, who had been granted bail against police objections and
soon afterwards committed further similar offences, was to create
a new offence of committing a crime while on bail. Faced with legal
reservations, he had to be content with 'a less draconian measure'
(his own words).[14] The the 1993 Act included a provision requiring
the court, when considering the seriousness of any offence committed while the offender was on bail, to treat the fact that it was
committed in those circumstances as an aggravating factor.[15]
Further restrictions on the right to bail had to await the Criminal
Justice and Public Order Act of the following year.

[12] In the light of the responses to the 1991 consultation paper, the Government
decided against the creation of a new criminal offence of squatting, concluding that
the determination of rights of occupation should continue in the civil courts. The
procedures for obtaining possession were to be expedited, enabling a person entitled
to immediate possession of a building or part of a building to apply to a County
court for an interim possession order, provided notice to commence proceedings had
been given to the alleged squatter. The applicant, in the absence of the person in
occupation at the time of service of the order, would be required to attend before a
judge who would decide whether to make an order. If an interim possession order
was made the person subject to the order must leave the premises within twenty-four
hours of the service of the order and not return. Failure to comply became a criminal offence under Section 76 of the Criminal Justice and Public Order Act 1994. See
*New procedures to combat squatting in houses, shops and other buildings: A consulta-
tion paper on proposals for rule changes*, Lord Chancellor's Department, Mar. 1994.
[13] Letter from R. Brooke, Secretary of the Association of Metropolitan
Authorities, 2 Feb. 1994.
[14] Kenneth Baker, *The Turbulent Years*, Faber, London, 1993, p. 438.
[15] Section 66 of the Criminal Justice Act 1993 substituted a new subsection dealing with offending while on bail in Section 29 (2) of the Criminal Justice Act 1991.

The departure from the conventional evolutionary approach to policy making showed itself in various ways. First, the process of preparing legislation and the competition between Government Departments to bring bills before Parliament means that once settled the legislative strategy can seldom be implemented quickly. As the example of squatting showed, the instant solution may not seem as appropriate or as compelling as when the issue was closer to the forefront of public notice. Then there was the question of consultation. Although openness and accountability were themes of the managerial ideology imported into public administration in the 1980s,[16] a marked falling off occurred in the dialogue with professional bodies and outside interests. The flow of Green and White papers which had preceded the 1991 Act, nine in all,[17] was reduced to a trickle. Two White Papers imbued with managerial values were published containing plans to reform police authorities[18] and the administration of the Magistrates' courts,[19] both measures destined to be incorporated in another major bill in the 1993–4 Parliamentary session.

No comparable statement embracing the large number of disparate items to be included in the Criminal Justice and Public Order Bill ever appeared. Instead, Howard chose to give the Conservative Party Conference an unexpectedly detailed, and heavily politicized, preview of its contents in October, the month before the Queen's Speech in 1993. His speech was rapturously received by the party activists to whom it was directed, but set alarm-bells ringing in the ears of the wider, and less politically committed, audience beyond the hall.

Whether intended or not, a by-product of the managerial concepts borrowed from the private sector as a discipline and incentive for improving the quality and efficiency of the public service was to militate against the practice of consultation and dispassionate

[16] The implications of the new managerialist strand in governmental culture for criminal justice and sentencing policy are thoroughly examined by N. Lacey in 'Government as Manager, Citizen as Consumer: The Case of the Criminal Justice Act 1991' (1994) 57 MLR 534. Nicola Lacey is Professor of Law at Birkbeck College, London.

[17] Table 8 of *Responses to Crime*, Vol. 2, lists the Home Office publications linked to the Criminal Justice Act 1991 at p. 249.

[18] Home Office, *Police Reform: the Government's proposals for the police service in England and Wales* (Cm. 2281), HMSO, London, 1993.

[19] Lord Chancellor's Department, *A New Framework for Local Justice* (Cm. 1829), HMSO, London, 1992.

inquiry. Research findings and the experience of practitioners working with offenders were at a discount. Since the values of the market-place were not universally shared by the professional services or penal reform groups, let alone the Opposition parties in Parliament, ministers usually found it more rewarding and less confrontational to restrict their soundings to their governmental, party, or parliamentary associates before reaching, or at any rate announcing, decisions. Management consultants and accountants could then be brought in to develop plans on how policies could be made to work, and their cost-effectiveness. Until the early 1990s the Civil Service culture in the Home Office remained resistant to the ethos of the new managerialism, although gradually, and with little enthusiasm, its precepts became institutionalized.

The fundamental question was, and remained, how to reconcile the demands of managerialism with the interests of justice.[20] The clash was made harder to resolve by the widely differing beliefs as to the immutable principles of justice and the proper objectives of the penal system. The public order part of the Bill added a further perspective, since an inevitable consequence of the new powers and offences would be a diminution of the freedoms of peaceful assembly and association.[21] Although hardly likely to appeal to ministers, a certain symmetry between legislative content and public response was to be seen in the numerous public demonstrations directed against this part of the Bill.

II

The claim that attitudes towards crime and measures to control it are heavily influenced by press reporting and comment is

[20] A working party on criminal justice administration, set up by the Howard League for Penal Reform under the chairmanship of Dr Lucia Zedner, regarded this as 'the greatest challenge facing the criminal justice system today'. *The Dynamics of Justice*, Howard League for Penal Reform, London, 1993, p. 16. Lucia Zedner is a Fellow of Corpus Christi College, Oxford.

[21] Besides squatting, the main public order provisions related to trespass on land, raves, aggravated trespass, trespassory assemblies, and unauthorized camping. Professor Richard Card offers as a rough and ready definition of public order law those statutory and common law rules designed (or having an established application) either to prevent or control conduct which actually or potentially disturbs public order, or to deal after the event with those involved in such disorder. See 'Disorder in public order law' in P. Smith (ed.), *Criminal Law: Essays in Honour of J. C. Smith*, Butterworths, London, 1987, p. 204.

commonly advanced and is well supported by observation and experience. Surprisingly, however, given its significance, there was a paucity of empirical evidence.[22] In August 1993, therefore, a quiet month during the Parliamentary Recess falling between the completion of the Criminal Justice Act 1993 and the introduction of fresh legislation later that year, I carried out a small survey of my own. Selecting three national dailies, with readerships covering distinct categories of the newspaper reading public, the Editors of *The Times*, *The Sun*, and *The Daily Mail* were approached. The two tabloids, *The Sun* and *The Daily Mail*, normally supported Tory interests and were therefore regarded as particularly important by ministers in communicating with the faithful.

The first aspect on which I sought information was the extent of the coverage of crime-related matters. As expected, it was substantial. In the month of August the total number of crime-related stories published in *The Times* (circulation 354,280)[23] amounted to 269. This was an average of just over ten crime-related stories each weekday. They included home news items, editorial features, letters to the Editor, and five leading articles. The total word-count of these items, laboriously calculated by the staff of *The Times* Library, was 72,680. In the same period *The Sun* (circulation 3,832,397) printed 11 short, punchy editorial comments headed 'The Sun Says,' and 59 crime-related stories. Of these, 26 were general home news stories and 33 selectively presented news items grouped under emotive headings: 'The Sun Campaign for Justice'

[22] A report on a three-stage study of the relationship between newspaper reporting of crime and the fear of crime was published by P. Williams and J. Dickinson, 'Fear of Crime: Read All About It?' in *British Journal of Criminology*, 33 (1993), 33–56. An earlier work was S. Chibnall, *Law-and-Order News: An analysis of crime reporting in the British Press*, Tavistock Publications, London, 1977. Ten years later, Professor P. Schlesinger and H. Tumber carried out empirical research in 1987–8 on the news coverage of crime across a range of newspapers and television. Qualitative analyses based on the findings, supplemented by interviews with journalists, editors, and producers and the sources of their information are contained in Schlesinger and Tumber, *Reporting Crime: The Media Politics of Criminal Justice*, Clarendon Press, Oxford, 1994. See also by the same authors 'Crime and Criminal Justice in the Media' in D. Downes (ed.), *Unravelling Criminal Justice*, Macmillan, Basingstoke and London, 1992, pp. 184–203.

[23] Circulation figures are drawn from a table headed 'National Newspaper Sales: average daily sale in August 1993', published in *The Times*, 15 Sept. 1993. *The Daily Telegraph* (1,027,656) led the quality market; *The Daily Mail* the middle market; and *The Sun*, the largest selling national daily, the popular market. As a result of a price reduction in Sept. 1993 *The Times* increased its circulation by 85,000 to reach an average daily sale of 439,327 in Dec. Source: Audit Bureau of Circulation.

(4, 5, and 13 August), 'Call This Justice?' (10, 23 August), 'Special Investigation' (14 August), 'Violent Britain' (25 August), 'Crisis in Our Jails' (28 August), and 'Crisis in the Courts' (30 August). In these features news items and trenchantly expressed opinions were virtually indistinguishable. Including identified editorials, a total of 70 crime-related stories were published by *The Sun* in August, an average of less than three per day.

The Daily Mail (circulation 1,709,420) was unable to supply statistics of its coverage, but the Editor provided the fullest and most illuminating reply to the questions on editorial policy.[24] He agreed that there had been a detectable shift in attitudes, both political and public, towards crime and punishment. Doubtless *The Daily Mail* had played a part in raising awareness of the issue, both reactive and pro-active. His letter continued:

There is nothing new about rising crime. What I think is new is a more acute perception in recent months by the public, the police, the magistrates and the press of the growing gap between crime and punishment. Clear-up rates continue to fall. Persistent offenders under 15 years old are hardly ever taken into custody. Cautions abound, prosecutions dwindle. Criminals become busier and the courts less so.

The Criminal Justice Act, passed by Parliament in a mood of unquestioning liberalism only a couple of years ago, has already had to be substantially repealed. This, I believe, does mark something of a turning point.

The crux of the changing mood is the realisation that legislation and changes in prosecuting practice designed to ease prison overcrowding have only succeeded in deepening the exasperation of those who suffer the effects of crime.

The unhealthy, yet understandable temptation for people to take the law into their own hands is more evident. 'Vigilante' is not a dirty word down most streets where the victims of crime live.

We, in company with other papers and many magistrates, did call for the contentious sections of the Criminal Justice Act to be repealed. We do want custodial sentences for persistent young offenders. We do want those who offend on bail to be suitably punished.

In areas such as these, it is the aim of *The Daily Mail* to influence Government policy. Surely it is salutary for ministers in office to be made aware of the growing anger and anxiety of those who entrusted them with power.

So, yes, this newspaper does seek to articulate the concern of its readers and, thereby, harden the response from this Tory administration.

---

[24] Letter from Paul Dacre, Editor of *The Daily Mail*, 14 Sept. 1993. Quoted with permission.

The Times, too, confirmed that it tried to influence policy rather than just to reflect readers' opinions.[25] An example of its activities beyond the columns of the newspaper was a conference organized jointly with the London School of Economics[26] shortly after the publication of the Report of the Royal Commission on Criminal Justice. One of the principal speakers was the Lord Chief Justice, Lord Taylor, who gave his reactions for the first time. With some of his views *The Times* agreed, notably his forthright opposition to any limitation of the right of a defendant to elect trial by jury. On others it had reservations, such as the Commission's proposal that judicial performance should be more closely monitored, and plea-bargaining.[27] Although the tone of *The Times* coverage was on the whole factual, discerning, and pragmatic, it nonetheless nodded occasionally towards the peremptory intolerance, at times lapsing into bigotry, of *The Daily Mail* and the unremitting populism of *The Sun*. In two leading articles *The Times* dismissed the Criminal Justice Act 1991 as a 'farce' (9 August)[28] and a 'debacle' (26 August). Other attitudes shared with the tabloids were criticism of the practice of police cautioning rather than prosecuting young people for minor offences; the policy of granting home leave for prisoners; and a wholly unfounded belief that the prisons were becoming too comfortable.

Each of the Editors accepted without hesitation that the coverage of crime and criminal justice was a major editorial topic and one on which they aimed to influence government policy, *The Sun*'s

[25] Letter from Peter Stothard, Editor of *The Times*, 17 Sept. 1993.

[26] Hosting conferences on key topics in criminology and criminal justice was one of the stated aims of the Mannheim Centre at the London School of Economics and Political Science. Founded in Nov. 1990, its other aims were to provide opportunities for the advanced study of criminology and criminal justice in courses at the graduate level; to conduct and facilitate research; and to organize short courses and seminars. The LSE is rich in academic resources in the criminological field, including renowned scholars Professors David Downes (Social Administration), Leonard Leigh (Law), Terence Morris (Social Institutions), Robert Reiner (Criminology), Paul Rock (Sociology), and Michael Zander (Law).

[27] *The Times*, 28 July 1993.

[28] This comment elicited a riposte from the General Secretary of the Association of Chief Officers of Probation. In a letter to the Editor, Bill Weston pointed out that most of the Act was still in force, that no previous criminal justice legislation this century had a more coherent rationale, a more sustained policy thrust from Government (over five years from 1987), a fuller process of publicity and consultation, or a more thorough programme of training prior to its introduction. In his view, more material for farce could be found in the efforts to unsettle the legislation since it had come into effect. *The Times*, 11 Aug. 1993.

Editor adding characteristically 'on behalf of our readers'. Having been sent copies of all the *Sun* news stories and editorials carried in August, the Managing Editor's expectation that once I had read them I would be 'fully cognisant of the paper's editorial policy on crime and punishment'[29] was entirely justified. Although the style differed, the editorial values of *The Sun* were in most respects similar to those of *The Daily Mail*, and some of the other tabloids as well. In the month of the sample, and over a longer period, common themes were: an exaggerated emphasis on the extent of crime, with a particular focus on violent crime; the rate at which it had increased and was increasing; the risks of victimization; sensational reporting of details of the most horrifying crimes; repeated calls for the greater use of imprisonment and the iniquity of lenient sentences; and a generally hostile attitude ('soft on crime') towards community penalties and those who administer them.

The impression was deliberately created that the 1991 legislation had been the work of a liberal elite, out of touch with the impact of crime on ordinary people. Criminals, it was claimed, were manipulating to their own advantage the safeguards for suspects; the balance in the criminal justice system had been tilted towards the protection of the innocent at the expense of failing to convict the guilty; and too often the interests of the offender (the description 'the criminal' being invariably preferred) were put above those of the victim. Much of this was based on conjecture rather than evidence, but it was what millions of people read day in and day out. Tabloid editors regard themselves as being in empathy with the opinions of a mass audience. Their skill is to identify and activate the latent opinions of their readers, evoking the response 'that's just how I feel about it'.

However selective, however exaggerated the coverage of crime by the tabloid press may be, the unavoidable conclusion is that newspaper publicity must have an effect, and possibly a profound effect, on the state of popular opinion. Even this crude and empirically rudimentary survey supports the charge that media coverage of crime, extending from newspapers to broadcasting with a proliferation of television programmes re-enacting actual crimes in graphic detail, has been so intensive and often so emotive that it has contributed to, and at times exploited, public anxiety and fearfulness.

---

[29] Letter from William Newman, Managing Editor of *The Sun*, 19 Oct. 1993.

The heightened fear of crime estimated to have occurred between 1987 and 1994[30] was a most harmful consequence, which impoverished the quality of life of a large number of people.

III

Against this sombre background, let us turn to the contents of the 1993–4 legislation. The Criminal Justice and Public Order Bill, when published in December 1993, comprised 117 clauses and ten schedules. The Explanatory and Financial Memorandum summarized the main provisions: the sentencing of juvenile offenders; bail; reform of the right of silence; police powers to take samples; measures against trespassers, squatters, and illegal camping; anti-terrorist provisions; obscenity; and the contracting out of prisons and prisoner escorts. Although the Bill was later greatly expanded, the next six months becoming an open season for the addition of numerous unrelated legislative proposals, the extra-parliamentary antecedents of the original Bill were clearly influenced by some of the emotive, press-led issues enumerated above. An analysis suggests that provisions dealing with each of the following items were shaped by, if not born of, popular opinion:

- secure training orders for the detention of children and young persons aged 12–14;
- restrictions on the grant of bail;
- persons on bail not qualified to serve as jurors;
- curtailment of the right of silence;
- new offences aimed at hunt saboteurs, gypsies, and New Age travellers;
- enhanced remedies against squatters;

[30] A MORI opinion poll taken in Jan. 1994 found that 77 per cent of those interviewed were afraid of having their homes burgled, an increase of 17 percentage points since the same question had been asked in 1987. In the North-East the figure was as high as 89 per cent. 56 per cent of the national sample feared having their homes or other possessions vandalized, a seven-point increase, and 52 per cent feared mugging (i.e. attempted or actual theft of possessions on the person of the victim), representing an increase of 14 points since 1987. 42 per cent feared going out at night alone, compared with the previous finding of 37 per cent. The statistical sample comprised 2,081 people aged fifteen or more in 148 constituencies throughout Britain. MORI/*Reader's Digest* 'Living in Britain' survey, Mar. 1994. Although the Home Office had some reservations about the methodology of the poll, the overall picture is clear enough.

- power to stop and search vehicles for weapons and explosives;
- child pornography including video graphics;
- prisoner escorts to and from court;
- ticket touts at football matches.

Comparing the contents of a Bill, precisely drafted according to established rules and precedents to meet the full range of possible criminal acts that may be affected by its provisions, with press coverage of issues which attracted public attention and excited opinion during the period of its gestation cannot convey more than a partial and impressionistic picture. Almost always there will be many other influences to be taken into account: political, legal, and administrative. Cost is frequently an important factor; it can inhibit action, or sometimes encourage it if savings can be forecast. However, in the context of criminal justice ministers are reluctant to expose arguments for restraining public expenditure. It is feared that the contrast of such arguments with the more acceptable theme of protecting the public may provoke unfavourable comment. Yet the financial implications of every Bill have to be considered in detail by departmental officials and ministers collectively, with the Treasury seldom silent, before the Ministerial Committee on Legislation will authorize its inclusion in the legislative programme. The golden rule throughout the process is that a Cabinet Committee chairman must ensure that if the Treasury maintains its position it should never be allowed to lose the argument.

A telling example of the potency of events in the formulation of policy was the public outrage following the abduction and murder of James Bulger, a two year-old boy who was battered to death with bricks and stones and left on a railway line in February 1993,[31] which caused the Treasury to abandon its opposition to a Home Office proposal for secure training orders. These were intended by their architect, Kenneth Clarke, to provide a means of taking a hard core of persistent young offenders, between the ages of twelve and fifteen, off the streets by combining a period of education and

---

[31] In November 1993 his assailants, two boys playing truant from school and aged ten at the time of the crime, were found guilty after a seventeen-day jury trial at Preston Crown Court of abducting James Bulger from a shopping precinct and battering him to death. Each blamed the other, but both boys were convicted of murder and ordered to be detained at Her Majesty's Pleasure under Section 53(1) of the Children and Young Persons Act 1933, as substituted by Section 1(5) of the Murder (Abolition of Death Penalty) Act 1965.

training in a secure residential setting with effective supervision in the community.

Once agreement has been reached, the financial implications of countless policies are shrouded in the most impenetrable Whitehall jargon. A classic instance involving substantial additional expenditure was a decision announced by the Home Secretary in 1993. Six new prisons were to be designed, built, financed, and managed by the private sector. In this way, dogma and short-term political advantage were brought together to postpone the evil day when the money would have to be found to pay the cost of accommodating the enlarged prison population which would inevitably result from the punitive thrust of Government policies, and the more severe sentencing regime they engendered. New prisons take a long time to build and bring into service, although optimistically it was hoped that the time-scale would be shortened by the desire of the private sector to start earning income as soon as possible. In the meantime 2,000 additional places, taking between fifteen and eighteen months to complete, would be created at the existing prisons by building houseblocks.[32] Including the extension of support facilities such as kitchens, work areas, and facilities for visitors, the total cost was estimated at £117 million.[33] Struck by the Chancellor of the Exchequer's confident assertion in his Budget Speech that 'A re-ordering of priorities will also allow for extra provision to be made for more prison places and for victim support',[34] I put down a Parliamentary Question asking which priorities in Home Office spending plans would be reordered to meet the cost of extra provision of prison places without making additional funds available. A reply of delphic obscurity was tabled by the Minister of State:

The cost of the extra prison places will be met from within the Prison Service's existing capital budget. The relative priority of other building work has been examined, and a revised refurbishment programme has been drawn up. The final decision on which schemes will have to be deferred has yet to be taken, but it is expected that the 1994–95 programme will contain, not only those required to produce additional prison places, but also

[32] HM Prison Service, *News Release*, 24 Nov. 1993.
[33] Letter from the Director General of the Prison Service, Derek Lewis, to Lord Harris of Greenwich dated 10 Jan. 1994, *Parl. Debates*, HL, 551 (5th ser.), col. WA 15, 10 Jan. 1994.
[34] *Parl. Debates*, HC, 233 (6th ser.), col. 931, 30 Nov. 1993.

a number of other schemes to improve security and control and improve conditions.[35]

Few of the original proposals included in the Bill stemmed from the Report of the Royal Commission on Criminal Justice, although more were added during its passage through Parliament.[36] A conspicuous absentee was the most widely forecast and least controversial of the Commission's recommendations: the establishment of a body independent of government to investigate allegations of miscarriages of justice. Acceptance in principle was announced in the autumn of 1993, but ministers showed little disposition to absorb so large a morsel in the pending Bill, saying that more time was needed to work out the relationship between the proposed review authority and the Court of Appeal, and to design an administrative framework.[37] An unspoken reservation was that putting right injustices caused by failures of criminal law or procedure carried libertarian overtones out of harmony with the more blatantly punitive objectives of the legislation. Moreover, any new departure was likely to be costly, and the scale of funding had not yet been agreed with the Treasury.

The issues chosen for early legislative action, as Howard's Blackpool speech made abundantly clear, were those which promoted his strategy to facilitate the conviction and punishment of the guilty: the abolition of the judge's obligation to warn a jury in cases of rape or other sexual assaults of the danger of convicting on the victim's evidence alone;[38] enhanced powers to assist other

[35] *Parl. Debates*, HL, 551 (5th ser.), col. WA 14–15, 10 Jan. 1994.

[36] As published, the legislation would have implemented in whole or in part recommendations 13–20, 35, 94, 195, and 219 of the *Report* of the Royal Commission on Criminal Justice (Cm. 2263). Government amendments while the Bill was before Parliament added three more recommendations: nos. 116–18 (abolition of committal hearings in their present form); 156 (credit to be given for early pleas of guilty in the form of discounts on sentence); and 329 (circuit judges to sit in the Court of Appeal, Criminal Division).

[37] The Home Office published a discussion paper in Mar. 1994 entitled *Criminal Appeals and the Establishment of a Criminal Cases Review Authority*.

[38] The Law Commission was satisfied that the wording of this obligatory warning had 'caused great offence to women in recent years'. *Twenty-Eighth Annual Report 1993*, Law Com. No. 223 (HC 341), HMSO, London, 1994, p. 9. Its report *Corroboration of Evidence in Criminal Trials* (1991), Law Com. No. 202, Cm. 1620, HMSO, London, 1991, recommended the abolition of the inflexible rules of corroboration in sexual cases. Where advice to the jury by the judge was required it should be tailored to the circumstances of the individual case. The Royal Commission on Criminal Justice endorsed this change in its own Recommendation

countries' agencies in the investigation of fraud offences committed overseas; the disqualification from jury service of persons on bail; and police powers to take body samples for DNA analysis.[39] All these stemmed from recommendations by the Royal Commission[40] which were consistent with the public mood; but others, of equal or greater importance, diverged from it.

The contentious issue of the right *of*, or *to*,[41] silence was complicated by an awareness that confused and vulnerable suspects might be at risk if adverse inferences were drawn from their failure to answer questions. Improbable as it may seem, some suspects do confess to crimes which they have not committed, or otherwise incriminate themselves, in the course of questioning at the police station. A former Commissioner of the Metropolitan Police has gone on record as saying that 'one common difficulty with which police have to contend is the number of people wishing falsely to confess to crimes they have not committed'.[42] The most frequent reasons for false confessions are: to obtain notoriety, to protect a third party, to terminate prolonged police questioning, or because a suspect has become temporarily convinced by his interrogators that he really did commit the offence.

The attitude of the general public towards pre-trial questioning

No. 195. (Cm. 2263, p. 206). Section 32(1)(b) of the Criminal Justice and Public Order Act 1994 abolished the need for the judge at a trial on indictment to warn the jury about the danger of convicting the accused on the uncorroborated evidence of the victim where the offence charged was a sexual offence. The Section became effective on 3 Feb. 1995.

[39] The proposals in the Bill allowed the police to take non-intimate DNA samples (including saliva) in the case of all recordable offences without consent, so bringing the law on DNA into line with the rules on fingerprinting. Consent would continue to be required for taking intimate samples (including blood or semen).

[40] The Bill went further than the Royal Commission which recommended that the power to take non-intimate samples without consent should be extended by the reclassification, for this purpose only, of certain offences (Cm. 2263, p. 15). The Bill, and subsequently Section 55 of the Act, substituted 'recordable offences' for 'serious arrestable offences'. Recordable offences are those serious enough to be recorded in national police records. Under Section 61 of the Police and Criminal Evidence Act 1984 a person's fingerprints may be taken without consent if he has been charged with a recordable offence or informed that he will be reported for such an offence, or has been convicted of a recordable offence.

[41] The Reports of the Royal Commission on Criminal Procedure (Cmnd. 8092) in 1981 and the Royal Commission on Criminal Justice (Cmnd. 2263) in 1993 both referred to the right *of* silence. A lack of consistency appeared in the titles of two of the research studies published by the latter Royal Commission (see n. 43 below) which referred to the right *to* silence.

[42] Sir Peter Imbert, *The Times*, 17 May 1994.

was less concerned with safeguarding the vulnerable and innocent than with a belief, strenuously promoted by the police, that refusal to answer questions helped professional criminals to escape prosecution and conviction. Despite these sentiments, but only after making detailed enquiries, the Royal Commission reported there was no conclusive evidence to establish that silence is used disproportionately by professional criminals, nor that silence in the police station improved the chances of acquittal in contested trials.[43] The possibility of an increase in the convictions of the guilty, in the estimate of the Commission, was outweighed by the risk that the extra pressure on suspects to talk in the police station, and the adverse inferences invited if they did not, might result in convictions of the innocent. The second limb of the right of silence, that no person charged with a criminal offence can be required to give evidence in court at any stage of criminal proceedings,[44] was to lead to protracted and acrimonious debate when the Bill came before Parliament. Equally important, but less publicized in the press, was the procedural context which determined the form that adverse inferences might take, the evidence necessary to support such inferences, and the implications for the presumption of innocence and the requirement for charges against the accused to be proved beyond reasonable doubt.[45] These matters are considered below.

That the issue was not simple was shown by the fact that it divided the Commission which, by a majority of nine to two, recommended that the right of silence be retained.[46] Although the

---

[43] Cm. 2263, p. 54. Two research studies published by the Royal Commission on Criminal Justice provided valuable background data: *The Right to Silence in Police Interrogation: A Study of some of the Issues Underlying the Debate* (Research Study No. 10 by R. Leng) and *Custodial Legal Advice and the Right to Silence* (Research Study No. 16 by M. McConville and J. Hodgson), HMSO, London, 1993.

[44] The right to refuse to answer questions applies in many other situations apart from police stations and criminal trials. As Lord Mustill pointed out in *R. v. Director of Serious Fraud Office, ex parte Smith* [1993] 1 AC 1 at 30 the expression 'the right of silence' does not denote any single right. Rather it refers to a disparate group of immunities, which differ in nature, origin, incidence, and importance, and in the extent to which they have been encroached by statute. Amongst them were six general or specific immunities which he identified in his speech.

[45] For further discussion see J. Jackson, 'The Right of Silence: Judicial Responses to Parliamentary Encroachment' (1994) 57 MLR 270.

[46] A similar conclusion had been reached by the Royal Commission on Criminal Procedure in 1981, again by a majority (*Report*, Cmnd. 8092, HMSO, London, p. 87). Nine years earlier the Criminal Law Revision Committee had recommended that the law be amended to allow a court or jury to draw adverse inferences against an accused person if in the course of interrogation he had failed to mention any fact

majority view was endorsed by the Bar Council, the Criminal Bar
Association, and the Law Society it was dismissed contemptuously
by the Home Secretary:

> As I talk to people up and down the country, there is one part of our law
> in particular that makes their blood boil. . . . It's the so-called right to
> silence. That is, of course, a complete misnomer. What is at stake is not
> the right to refuse to answer questions. But if a suspect does remain silent
> should the prosecution and the judge or magistrate be allowed to comment
> on it? Should they have the right to take it into account in deciding guilt
> or innocence? The so-called right to silence is ruthlessly exploited by ter-
> rorists. What fools they must think we are. It's time to call a halt to this
> charade. The so-called right to silence will be abolished. The innocent have
> nothing to hide. And that is exactly the point the prosecution will be able
> to make in the future.[47]

The reference to terrorists was an example of citing the most
extreme case to justify a change in practice that would affect the
vastly larger number of suspects questioned in connection with
non-terrorist offences. Moreover, the majority of cases involving
terrorist offences were tried in Northern Ireland by special courts
where the judge sits without a jury[48] rather than by jury trial as in
the Crown Court in England and Wales. In 1988, following an
upsurge of violent incidents in the Province, the law on the right of
silence had been substantially modified.[49] Because of the special
procedures for the handling of Northern Ireland legislation neces-
sitated by the prorogation of the Stormont Parliament, the change

upon which he later relied by way of defence at committal proceedings or trial.
Criminal Law Revision Committee, *Eleventh Report* (Cmnd. 4991), HMSO,
London, 1972, p. 19.

[47] *Conservative Party News*, 400/93, extract from a speech by Rt. Hon. Michael
Howard QC MP, the Home Secretary, speaking to the 110th Conservative Party
Conference at the Winter Gardens, Blackpool, 6 Oct. 1993.

[48] Offences scheduled under the Northern Ireland (Emergency Provisions) Act
1973 are tried on indictment by a judge alone, sometimes known as Diplock courts
after Lord Diplock, the Chairman of the Commission which recommended the
necessity for non-jury trial. See *Report of the Commission to consider legal procedures
to deal with terrorist activities in Northern Ireland* (Cmnd. 5185), HMSO, London,
1972. In the absence of a jury, the judge alone has to decide what inferences to draw
from the silence of the accused and to state the inferences and his conclusion in his
grounds of decision. See J. Jackson, 'Curtailing the Right of Silence: lessons from
Northern Ireland' [1991] Crim. L.R. 404. For a detailed study of non-jury trials, see
John Jackson and Sean Doran, *Judge Without Jury : Diplock Trials in the Adversary
System*, Clarendon Press, Oxford, 1995.

[49] Royal Commission on Criminal Justice, *Research Study No. 10*, p. 4.

was effected by statutory instrument, which cannot be amended, rather than by primary legislation at Westminster.

The resulting Order in Council, the Criminal Evidence (Northern Ireland) Order 1988, applied generally to criminal proceedings in Northern Ireland, and was not confined to alleged terrorist offences. It permitted a tribunal of fact to draw inferences from the failure of the accused to mention facts when interviewed upon which he later relied in his defence (Article 3). Inferences could also be drawn where an accused was found in specific incriminating circumstances, or in the vicinity of the scene of a crime, and failed to explain himself to the police (Articles 5 and 6).[50] The Order allowed inferences to be drawn from silence both at and before trial (Article 4). The clauses included in the Criminal Justice and Public Order Bill in 1993 were modelled on the Order already in force in Northern Ireland which, it was claimed, had 'worked well'.[51] The moral is clear: exceptional powers, granted to meet exceptional situations, can become normalized, sometimes buttressed by the spurious argument that the criminal law should be the same throughout Great Britain and Northern Ireland,[52] and finally adopted for general application.

IV

When moving the Second Reading of the Criminal Justice and Public Order Bill in the House of Commons in the New Year, the Home Secretary said that of the twenty-seven points announced in his Blackpool speech, which he described as 'pledges', twenty-two required legislation. Of those, eighteen would be dealt with in the

[50] Articles 5 and 6 of the Criminal Evidence (Northern Ireland) Order 1988 adopt, with minimal amendment, the wording of similar legislation in the Republic of Ireland: see Sections 18 and 19 of the Irish Criminal Justice Act of 1984.

[51] Earl Ferrers, Home Office Minister of State, *Parl. Debates*, HL, 554 (5th ser.), col. 383, 25 Apr. 1994.

[52] At the time when the Northern Ireland Order was introduced Douglas Hurd was considering the possibility of modifying the right of silence in England and Wales. However, he moved cautiously, setting up a working group under the chairmanship of a senior Home Office official, W. J. Bohan. Before the Committee reported (*Report of the Working Group on the Right of Silence*, C4 Division, Home Office, 1989) the cases of the Guildford Four and Birmingham Six made it inopportune to try and strengthen the hands of the prosecution, and no further initiative was taken until 1993.

Bill and four taken forward later. The remaining five announcements did not require legislation but were being pursued vigorously.[53] The debate demonstrated the lack of unanimity over what the objectives of criminal justice legislation should be. Echoing the theme of 'Back to Basics',[54] Howard declared that the measure rested on basic, common-sense principles: that protecting the public was the first job of Government; that criminals should be held responsible for their actions; and that the police should be given the powers needed to catch criminals. The aim was to provide the country with the most effective system of criminal justice which it was possible for a government to provide.[55] Effectiveness was the catchword: 'this Bill and the other measures that we are putting in place will achieve the most comprehensive and effective framework that it is possible to devise to prevent crime, to enable the police more effectively to catch criminals and to enable the courts more effectively to convict them and to deal with them when they have been convicted.[56]

From the Opposition Front Bench, Tony Blair hammered away at a single line of argument in reply. If the Bill was the most comprehensive measure ever to fight crime, a judgment would need to be made before long about whether it had succeeded or failed. Would it cut crime or not?[57] If modifying the right of silence was so crucial an objective for a more effective criminal justice system, how was it that since the changes introduced in Northern Ireland in 1988, although crime had been rising, both the number of prosecutions and the number of convictions as a percentage of prosecutions had dropped? Although not proof absolute, that situation was hard to reconcile with the claim that similar reform of the right of silence in England and Wales was required to get more criminals prosecuted or convicted.[58]

The six and a half-hour debate was noisy and argumentative. The

---

[53] *Parl. Debates*, HC, 235 (6th ser.), col. 22, 11 Jan. 1994.

[54] 'Back to Basics' was adopted as a theme by John Major and other ministers at the Conservative Party Conference at Blackpool in Oct. 1993. The following month, in the Debate on the Address, the Prime Minister told the House of Commons that basic values meant 'basic economic values such as low inflation, free markets and a climate that encourages free enterprise, basic social values such as self-discipline, respect for the law, concern for others, individual responsibility and an emphasis on getting the basics of education right first.' *Parl. Debates*, HC, 233 (6th ser.), col. 31, 18 Nov. 1993.

[55] *Parl. Debates*, HC, 235, cols. 20–1.

[56] Ibid., col. 22.   [57] Ibid., col. 21.   [58] Ibid., col. 43.

contrast with the relative disinterestness in the proceedings during the criminal justice legislation three years earlier, when the main action during the Second Reading had been taking place outside the chamber,[59] was striking. The opening speeches were constantly interrupted, with both Howard and Blair at their most combative and eloquent. The front-bench speakers were conscious of their role as rival champions in a trial of strength, even though the composition of the House and the efficacy of the whipping ensured that the outcome was predetermined. Throughout the debate any attempts at thoughtful deliberation were drowned by vociferous partisanship and displays of party loyalty. The climax was bound to be the ritual of a division, but Labour tacticians shrewdly tabled a reasoned amendment which was defeated by 319 votes to 275. The Bill was then given an unopposed Second Reading, thereby avoiding the charge that the Opposition had voted against the Government's unilateral declaration of war on crime. The Labour banner of 'tough on crime, and tough on the causes of crime' was still flying at the end of the proceedings, having survived all Tory efforts to tear it down.

In the customary way the Committee stage was taken off the floor in a Standing Committee, but on 21 February the Bill was returned to a Committee of the whole House to consider new clauses on capital punishment and the age of consent for sexual acts between men. Both were treated as issues of conscience to be decided by free votes. In debates of this sort the Commons is often seen at its best. Whereas the outcome on capital punishment was never in doubt, it being the fourteenth consecutive occasion since 1969 on which the House had declined by substantial majorities to reintroduce the death penalty for any offences,[60] the strength of opinion was undiminished. The speeches were fervent; while some were personal testaments, most speakers combined their convictions with an evident intent to persuade those whose minds were not already made up, inside or outside the Chamber. Once in each Parliament newly elected members, especially on the Conservative side, have to steel themselves for a public avowal of their beliefs, which for a fair number will conflict with the views of many of their

[59] See *Responses to Crime*, Vol. 2, pp. 407, 416.

[60] For details of all votes on capital punishment in the House of Commons between 1955 and 1987, see *Responses to Crime*, Vol. 1, pp. 158–9; updated 1987–91 in Vol. 2, p. 90.

constituency activists. Moreover, on this issue MPs' votes reflect decisions for which they have to accept personal responsibility, without the protective shield of Government or party policy.

Very few of those who had taken part in the previous debates changed their minds, but in 1994 there was a rare and most notable exception. On earlier occasions Michael Howard, together with Margaret Thatcher and Norman Tebbit, had been in the small minority of Cabinet ministers who had consistently supported the restoration of capital punishment for the murder of police or prison officers, or for murders committed with firearms or explosives. He had done so, he told the Commons, because he thought the deterrent effect would be greatest in those categories. Howard justified his position on the basis that a wide-ranging appeal process in capital cases would effectively eliminate the risk of miscarriage of justice. Such a procedure had been adopted in the case of the Birmingham Six, yet had failed to identify any irregularities. That, and other cases since, had led him to re-examine his previous position. He continued in a powerful passage:

Miscarriages of justice are a blot on a civilised society. For someone to spend years in prison for a crime he or she did not commit is both a terrible thing and one for which release from prison and financial recompense cannot make amends. But even that injustice cannot be compared with the icy comfort of a posthumous pardon. When we consider the plight of those who have been wrongly convicted, we cannot but be relieved that the death penalty was not available. We should not fail to consider the irreparable damage that would have been inflicted on the criminal justice system had innocent people been executed.[61]

Following the Home Secretary, Tony Blair, speaking from the Opposition Despatch Box, said that on moral as well as on practical and utilitarian grounds he was opposed to both the new clauses before the Committee.[62] The first, moved by John Greenway, a Conservative MP and former police officer, prescribed the death penalty for any person aged eighteen or above convicted of the murder of a police officer acting in the execution of his duty. The second, moved by a Conservative MP from Yorkshire with experience as a magistrate, Elizabeth Peacock, provided that following the conviction of a person aged eighteen or above for murder the court would be bound to pass a death sentence. The case would

---

[61] *Parl. Debates*, HC, 238 (6th ser.), col. 45, 21 Feb. 1994.   [62] Ibid., col. 46.

then be remitted as soon as practicable to a special sitting of the Court of Appeal to decide whether there were sufficient mitigating circumstances to commute the sentence to life imprisonment. After a three-hour debate, in which the possibilities of innocent or wrongly convicted people being hanged carried far more weight than in the past, each of the new clauses was defeated on a free vote. The divisions were: 186 for and 383 against the first proposal; 159 for and 403 against the second.[63] The Home Office Ministerial team in the Commons was split. The Minister of State with responsibility for prisons, Peter Lloyd, joined the Home Secretary in twice voting against the death penalty, while David Maclean (with responsibility for criminal justice) twice supported its restoration. The Parliamentary Secretary, Charles Wardle, voted for Mrs Peacock's proposal but abstained in the first division.

An attempt to raise the subject of corporal punishment, which Antony Marlow claimed was of far greater interest in the country than the age of consent for homosexuals, having been rejected earlier in the afternoon,[64] the House moved on to consider new clauses moved by Edwina Currie and Sir Anthony Durant. Mrs Currie's proposal was straightforward: that the age of consent for homosexual acts in private should be reduced from twenty-one to sixteen, the same age as for heterosexuals. It was, she said in a speech punctuated by hostile interventions from her own side of the House, an historic debate. For the first time in over a quarter of a century the age of consent was to be discussed by the Commons.[65] The taboo of silence which had denied the sexuality of young gay men had been decisively broken.[66] For once the newsworthiness of capital punishment was eclipsed. Mrs Currie was amongst the most skilled publicists in the House and had recruited a significant body of

[63] Ibid., cols. 66–74. Both majorities against the death penalty were larger than on the previous occasion when similar proposals had been defeated by 215 to 350 votes (murder of a police officer), and 182 to 367 votes (death penalty for murder if upheld by the Court of Appeal). *Parl. Debates*, HC, 183 (6th ser.), cols. 113–20, 17 Dec. 1990.

[64] HC 238, cols. 23–4. The abolition of corporal punishment is described in *Responses to Crime*, Vol. 2, pp. 47–8, 64, 67–8. A previous unsuccessful attempt to reintroduce it is noted at pp. 73–4.

[65] The age of consent for legal homosexual acts had been set at twenty-one in 1967. Under Section 1 of the Sexual Offences Act 1967, a concise and lapidary provision, a homosexual act in private is not an offence provided that the parties consent and have attained the age of twenty-one.

[66] *Parl. Debates*, HC, 238, cols. 74–5.

all-party support, including the former Opposition Leader Neil Kinnock and Tony Blair. Gay rights groups campaigned energetically and conspicuously. MPs were subjected to intense lobbying; Cardinal Hume urged them to be cautious and use 'prudential judgment';[67] and media coverage remained high for several weeks.

Parliamentary opinion remained apprehensive and the uncertainty only began to dissipate when a compromise hove into view. This was the proposal, welcomed with relief by the Government Whips, that the age of consent should be reduced to eighteen, rather than sixteen. The compromise offered a safe haven to MPs caught between the egalitarian argument that the age of consent should be the same for everyone, whether homosexual or heterosexual, and an acknowledgement that many young men between sixteen and eighteen were still uncertain about their sexual orientation and lacked the maturity to make a choice likely to have such a profound effect on their adult way of life. Although the Church of England did not have a common view, an article by the Archbishop of York, reflecting the opinion of a majority of the Bishops, was quoted with approval in one of the calmer moments of a heated debate. He hoped that Parliament would reduce the age of consent to eighteen, 'thus signalling that homosexuality in young men is neither to be treated as uncontroversial nor to be penalised beyond the age of maturity'.[68] The Home Secretary, after confirming that the Government would respect the wishes of the House,[69] also spoke in favour of reduction to eighteen. The purpose of retaining a minimum age for homosexual acts in private, enforced by the criminal law, he declared, was to protect the young and the vulnerable before their sexual orientation was determined.

When the vote was taken Mrs Currie's proposal was defeated by the small margin of twenty-seven votes: 280 in favour and 307 against. The compromise of a reduction to eighteen was then put and carried by a large majority of 427 in favour, with 162 votes

---

[67] *The Times*, 4 Feb. 1994. George Basil Hume, formerly Abbot of Ampleforth 1963–76, had been Archbishop of Westminster since 1976. He became a Cardinal in the same year.

[68] *Independent*, 18 Feb. 1994. The Archbishop of York was able to amplify his views when he spoke in the Lords during the Committee stage of the Bill. *Parl. Debates*, HL, 556 (5th ser.), cols. 16–18, 20 June 1994. John Habgood, previously Bishop of Durham 1973–83, had been Archbishop of York since 1983. He retired in 1995.

[69] *Parl. Debates*, HC, 238, col. 92.

against any change.[70] Furious scenes took place outside the House when a noisy demonstration by a dismayed and angry crowd of gay rights activists, estimated to be about 4,000 strong, erupted into violence causing the police to close the St Stephen's entrance and lock the main gates to New Palace Yard. After the departing MPs had run a gauntlet of abuse, the protesters moved on to Downing Street at midnight, marching hand-in-hand and chanting 'Downing Street, here we come' and 'sixteen now'.[71]

V

The high drama of the two debates on 21 February interrupted the prolonged consideration of the remainder of the Bill by Standing Committee B. When the Bill was first referred to the Committee it was already bulky, with 117 clauses and ten schedules. After thirty-one sittings over seventeen days, from 18 January and 15 March, sometimes meeting in morning, afternoon, and evening, and on one occasion continuing until 5 a.m. the next morning, the Bill was reported to the House. By then it had expanded to 142 clauses and eleven schedules, the vast majority of the new clauses and amendments (145 out of a total of 150) resulting from second thoughts, refinements, and straightforward additions promoted by the Government. Of the recommendations of the Royal Commission, three more were accepted and added to those already included in the original bill.[72] At Report stage another 10 new clauses and 212 further amendments were added.[73]

The statistics in Tables 1 and 2 show that more than 100 hours were spent in the Standing Committee's consideration of the Bill. In all 196 new clauses and 563 amendments were tabled in Standing Committee, with six new clauses and twelve amendments tabled in Committee of the whole House, and a further 127 new clauses and 388 amendments at Report stage. The legislative effort lying behind this bare statistical summary was prodigious. Not only Ministers and MPs, but a team of supporting Home Office officials, Treasury

[70] Ibid., cols. 115–23.   [71] *The Times*, 22 Feb. 1994.
[72] See n. 36, above.
[73] The author is indebted to Paul Silk, Deputy Principal Clerk in the Public Bill Office, for this information and for the statistics contained in Tables 1 and 2. For a comparison with the Criminal Justice Bill 1991 see *Responses to Crime*, Vol. 2, pp. 416–7.

Devising the Strategy

TABLE 1. *Criminal Justice and Public Order Bill 1993–4: House of Commons Standing Committee, hours of sitting*

	Morning hrs/mins	Evening hrs/mins
18 January	2.30	—
20 January	2.30	7.14
25 January	2.30	11.58
27 January	2.30	1.48
1 February	2.30	8.20
3 February	2.30	5.14
8 February	2.30	7.38
10 February	2.30	5.28
15 February	2.30	3.10
17 February	2.30	3.04
22 February	2.30	3.07
24 February	2.30	2.30
1 March	2.30	2.42
3 March	2.30	1.55
8 March	2.30	2.19
10 March	2.30	—
15 March	2.13	—
Total Time:	106 hours 40 minutes	

Source: Public Bill Office, House of Commons.

Counsel for the drafting, and many pressure groups and other interested parties were kept nose to grindstone for several months. What distinguished the proceedings in Standing Committee in 1994 from similar committees scrutinizing the criminal justice legislation in 1991 and throughout the 1980s was not so much their length but the consistently confrontational tone. Previous committees had always had their moments of lively party-political controversy, but typically they had been limited to a relatively small number of clauses which were particularly controversial between the parties.

On the floor of the House Howard could be acerbic, and often was, and his unyielding stance was carried into the Committee stage upstairs. A forthright and articulate right-winger, David Maclean, was the Minister of State in charge of the Bill in Standing

TABLE 2. *Criminal Justice and Public Order Bill 1993–4: new clauses and amendments tabled in the House of Commons*

	(a) Number tabled		(b) Number made		of (b) Government		of (b) Opposition		of (b) Other Members	
	New Clauses	Amendments[a]	New Clauses	Amendments[a]	New Clauses	Amendments[a]	New Clauses	Amendments[a]	New Clauses	Amendments[a]
Committee of whole House	6	12	1	0	0	—	0	—	1	—
Standing Committee	196	563[b]	24	126	24	121	0	1	0	4
Report stage	127	388	10	212	7	211	0	0	3	1

[a] Including amendments to new clauses.
[b] 57 Amendments were withdrawn; in the case of 9 of these withdrawals, a clear undertaking was given.
Source: Public Bill Office, House of Commons.

Committee, and he lost few opportunities to lay into the Opposition with relish. In this task he was enthusaistically supported by Government back-benchers who were allowed, indeed encouraged to speak at length in debate after debate. This was unusual since Government whips, when sure of a majority, tend to discourage their back-benchers from speaking frequently or at length in Committee, being concerned not to delay the passage of the Bill unduly. The departure from this practice, and the Party Conference provenance of many of the proposals, made it certain that the debates in Committee would be characterized by a high level of party-political rhetoric and point-scoring. The Opposition was hampered by the Government's constant refusals to accept, or even to look with an open mind at the most minor and uncontentious amendments. It seemed as though a blanket policy of resistance to all amendments had been decreed, to avoid any suspicion of deviation from the Government's projected image of uncompromising toughness.

The transformation in Labour policy left Opposition MPs in the Committee with a difficult hand to play. They were reluctant to criticize clauses in the Bill, for example on the secure training orders for very young offenders, on the grounds that they were unduly harsh. Even when Labour put forward amendments which would have tempered the severity of proposals in the Bill, they often seemed anxious to couch their arguments in a 'tougher than thou' style, alleging by way of counter-attack that the Government had been too slow to take tough measures in the past. This tactic put their spokesmen at a disadvantage when Government back-benchers forcefully pointed out that Labour amendments would liberalize key aspects of the Bill and attacked the Opposition for seeking to do so covertly. A more robust defence of Opposition amendments on the grounds that some of the Government's proposals were inappropriate in concept or degree to deal with the problem towards which they were ostensibly directed, and would be ineffective in reducing crime, would have been more telling than attempting to demonstrate that Labour was every bit as tough as the Government in its policies and attitude.

It was therefore hardly surprising that the official Opposition left so slight an impression on the face of the Bill, no more than a single amendment being accepted.[74] An experienced and knowledge-

---

[74] To raise the maximum penalty for possession of child pornography from three to six months' imprisonment.

able Liberal Democrat MP, Robert Maclennan, often appeared to be alone in raising traditional libertarian arguments. Measured against the grand total of thirty-one new clauses and 332 amendments inserted into the Bill at the initiative of the Government during its passage through the Commons, the impact of Opposition MPs on the actual content of the legislation seems puny. The overall picture is one of a long drawn-out confrontation between elected representatives, rather than that close examination of the merits of legislative proposals brought forward by ministers which constitutional purists insist is the prerequisite of sound law-making.

The Hansard Society report cited in the previous chapter affirmed that the essential parliamentary function of subjecting governmental proposals to detailed scrutiny should be to consider the workability as well as the political policies embodied in the legislation. Too dominant and sustained a display of partisanship in attacking or defending the underlying policies will only impede a full and effective scrutiny of the practicalities. In November 1992, after taking extensive evidence, a Commission set up by the Society under the chairmanship of a former Conservative Cabinet Minister, Lord Rippon, stressed that the main purpose of a Committee stage was to improve the quality of legislation:

Broad assaults on policy are also counter-productive; it is much easier for a Minister to use political arguments to fend off an amendment which has been given a political flavour, rather than to deal with a carefully argued amendment on its merits. Overmuch concern with broad political points leads to poor scrutiny of legislation, and Ministers and their officials are not properly tested . . . for all the reasons we have given, we believe it is important that debates on bills in committee should not concentrate too much on policy but deal also with practical questions of the bill's operation.[75]

The politicization continued when the Bill was reported to the House. During the first day on Report scant consideration was given to the content of the Bill or the amendments which had been made in Standing Committee. Instead, several new clauses proposed by the Government were added after only cursory debate before the House turned its attention to three highly topical subjects, none of them bearing on the Bill's contents. The first was the

[75] *Making the Law*, Report of the Hansard Society Commission on the Legislative Process, Hansard Society for Parliamentary Government, London, 1993, p. 82.

Government's intention to substitute a new and less generous scheme of compensation for criminal injuries in place of the non-statutory arrangements which had been in force since 1964. The change had been sharply criticized by the Criminal Injuries Compensation Board and had become intensely controversial after a campaign co-ordinated by Victim Support, working with other interest groups, had convinced the Opposition that the proposed introduction of the new scheme by executive order on 1 April 1994 should be delayed. The issue was awkward for the Government, leaving it riding two horses pulling in different directions. One, central to the realization of its economic objectives, was the need to restrict a large and fast-growing item of public expenditure. The other was the potentially embarrassing conflict with the proclaimed policy of putting victims first. The significance of the changing role of victims in the evolution of criminal policy is the subject of a later chapter. All that needs to be said here is that while there were valid arguments on both sides, there was no doubt that the issue of compensation had been handled in a maladroit way by ministers. The challenge was beaten off in the Commons on a strongly whipped vote,[76] but succeeded when linked to dissent on constitutional grounds in the Lords.

Measures to prevent drug abuse by young people and new clauses on drugs and drug-related crime were the second topic of debate on 28 March. Although alternative strategies had been pressed in Standing Committee by Opposition members, the Government had limited its response to increasing the upper limit of fines for a range of offences arising from the misuse of the less harmful controlled drugs, including cannabis.[77] The third issue was raised by a Labour MP who for many years had conducted a personal crusade against miscarriages of justice, especially the convictions of the Birmingham Six. Chris Mullin had done as much, or more, than any other individual in public life to expose the trail of

[76] *Parl. Debates*, HC, 240 (6th ser.), cols. 688–92, 28 Mar. 1994.

[77] Penalties for certain offences under the Misuse of Drugs Act 1971, listed in Schedule 8 of the Criminal Justice and Public Order Act 1994, had not been uprated since 1977 when the maximum fines were set at amounts equivalent to levels 4 and 3 on the standard scale. The Act increased the maximum fine from £500 to £2,500 on summary conviction for offences in relation to Class B or Class C drugs. The offences included the production, supply (or offering to supply), and possession of cannabis, as well as other controlled drugs, mainly in Class C. It is also an offence to be the occupier or concerned in the management of premises and permitting or suffering certain activities to take place there.

wrongful convictions which came to light in the late 1980s and early 1990s and led to the setting up of a Royal Commission on Criminal Justice in 1991.

The legislation in 1994 offered Mullin a fresh opportunity to table a clause to establish an independent review tribunal to examine alleged miscarriages of justice. Two earlier attempts in 1988 and 1990 had been unsuccessful. He reminded the House that during debates on the Criminal Justice Bill in 1988 his claim that innocent people had been convicted of the M62 coach bombing, the Guildford and Woolwich bombings, and the Birmingham bombings, had been greeted with derision by Home Office ministers.[78] As he spoke, he was aware there were Conservative MPs on the benches opposite who did not accept that the setting aside of the defendants' convictions on the grounds that they were unsafe and unsatisfactory meant that all of those who had been released were necessarily innocent. However, it was not the moment for such suspicions to be aired. Mullin was entitled to assert as he did that the convictions of all eighteen of those to whom he had referred in June 1988 had been quashed and that they were 'walking the streets with compensation in their pockets'.[79]

It was a speech of unusual power and authority delivered by a back-bencher who had earned the respect of the House. From all sides, Blair and Howard speaking from their opposing despatch boxes, tributes were paid to Mullin for his tenacity in seeing through to its conclusion what had for most of its duration been a lonely and unpopular cause. Yet again, however, his plea for early action to implement the Royal Commission's recommendation that an independent body should be established to investigate alleged miscarriages of justice was defeated in a division on party lines.

By now the differences were limited to timing rather than substance. The Government had already accepted the Royal Commission's recommendation in principle, and at the start of his speech the Home Secretary agreed that one innocent person convicted was one too many.[80] He wanted to put in place a system which contained the necessary safeguards to minimize the possibility of a wrongful conviction and the most effective appeals procedures that could be devised, so that if any wrongful convictions did occur they could be corrected at the earliest possible stage. If the

[78] *Parl. Debates*, HC, 240, col. 726.   [79] Ibid.   [80] Ibid., col. 742.

Royal Commission had produced a detailed blueprint for the new authority and its relationship with the Court of Appeal and the Government, no one would have been more pleased than himself to include provisions in the Bill.[81] However, important questions remained to be settled before effecting the biggest constitutional change of its kind since the Criminal Appeal Act 1907.[82]

The Home Office, Howard said, had been devoting a great deal of thought to identifying the issues and examining possible solutions. The results were set out in a discussion paper, the publication of which had been brought forward so that it was available to MPs in time for the debate. Careful consideration was required of all the issues when the results of consultation were available.[83] He agreed with the Lord Chief Justice that the creation of a properly constituted body for the investigation of alleged miscarriages of justice should not be rushed.[84] The timetable did not rule out further progress being made before the Bill completed its passage through the Lords, probably late in July, but no hopes were raised of including it in the current legislation. Despite its lack of urgency, the change of tone was noticeable and Howard's speech reflected a greater sense of commitment than before. The subsequent legislative history of the Criminal Appeal Act 1995 is the subject of Chapter 10.

VI

The Report stage was then adjourned until after the Easter recess. This short break, preceding the busiest months of the Parliamentary session building up to a climax in late July or early August, is a time when MPs cultivate their constituency roots. They return to Westminster finely attuned to the concerns and sensitiv-

---

[81] *Parl. Debates*, HC, 240, col. 743.

[82] The Court of Criminal Appeal, replaced by the Criminal Division of the Court of Appeal in 1966, was created by statute in 1907. According to Radzinowicz and Hood, the objective of the reformers was to secure a better guarantee against wrongful conviction of the innocent. A subsidiary aim, which emerged much later, was to provide a way of altering inappropriate sentences and of establishing greater uniformity in sentencing standards. *A History of English Criminal Law and its Administration from 1750*, vol. 5, Stevens, London, 1986, p. 759.

[83] Comments on the Home Office paper *Criminal Appeals and the Establishment of a Criminal Cases Review Authority* were requested by 31 May 1994.

[84] *Parl. Debates*, HC, 240, col. 743.

ities of their constituents. In the spring of 1994 one concern detected by many MPs as troubling their constituents was violent videos. The widespread objections at the political grass roots to the gratuitous and sometimes sadistic violence portrayed in videos available for rental or sale, and the lack of any effective means of preventing them getting into the hands of children and young and suggestible people, had animated many MPs irrespective of party. The fact that the popular press, inspired by the Bulger case and other sensational crimes involving young people who were believed to have watched violent videos in their homes, was running a campaign to ban access by children to such potentially harmful and degrading material served to fuel the MPs' interest.

The Home Secretary had been alerted to the Parliamentary pressure for regulation when David Alton, a Liberal Democrat MP and formidable moral campaigner, accompanied by a Conservative MP, Michael Alison, at one time Parliamentary Private Secretary to Margaret Thatcher and currently the Second Church Estates Commissioner, had been to see him three months earlier to show him the wording of a new clause intended to be put down at the Report stage of the Bill. The drafting provided that either because a video presented an inappropriate model for children, or because it was likely to cause psychological harm to a child, it should not be supplied for private use, or viewed in any place to which children under the age of eighteen were admitted. By the time the Commons resumed after the Easter Recess the favourable breeze had freshened, filling the sails of their proposal. A collective determination to legislate was evident to business managers on both sides.

Once tabled, the Alton amendment, as it was known, rapidly attracted support across the political spectrum. At first Howard had been sceptical. He needed no lessons in how to respond to public feeling, but feared the formulation was too sweeping, and that whatever its sponsors intended by the word 'admitted' it would include private homes. The effect would be to ban the supply to adults for home viewing of all videos unsuitable for children. Quite apart from the legal advice he was receiving from the Home Office officials, such a move would in his judgment go too far and be deeply unpopular with many constituents once they understood its scope.

As the promoters of the new clause continued to gain ground,

securing the signatures of 220 MPs including about 80
Conservatives, some of them like Alison former ministers, and as
press interest became more and more vocal, so Howard's misgivings began to falter. He was right in pointing to the potential
unworkability of the new clause as it stood, but the public disquiet
was unmistakable. His first response, that the British Board of Film
Classification (BBFC) should be encouraged to label more films
and videos as suitable only for those over the age of eighteen, was
roundly denounced in a *Times* leading article as 'a peculiarly feeble
proposal'.[85] Howard was also quoted as saying that a blanket prohibition on home viewing of violent videos would outlaw the innocent boisterousness of films such as *Toad of Toad Hall* and other
classics. *The Times* first leader concluded:

This is an absurd statement, unworthy of a Home Secretary who professes
serious concern about social problems. This amendment does not advocate
a mindless ban on even the most benign horseplay. It seeks to extend the
powers of the British Board of Film Classification to judge, in an intelligent and conscientious way, each individual film on its own merits and to
decide which of them should be put definitively beyond the reach of children. Mr Howard should think carefully before rejecting the substance of
such a sensible idea.

Let us pause here to note the entry into the story of one of the rarer
specimens of British hybrid: a privately established and financed
body exercising public functions. Set up in 1912 as the British
Board of Film Censors, the BBFC had been intended by the bur-
geoning film industry to bring a degree of uniformity into county
council licensing of cinemas under the powers conferred on them
by the Cinematograph Act 1909. Public houses and music halls
were already licensed by local councils or magistrates. The extension of licensing to public cinematograph exhibitions arose from
concern about the risks to physical safety posed by highly inflam-
mable film. Despite the fact that the title of the 1909 Act contained
a specific reference to securing safety at cinematographic exhibitions, the courts construed Section 2 of that Act as conferring upon
county councils an unlimited discretion as to the conditions
imposed in a licence, so long as they were reasonable.[86] In 1952 the

[85] 11 Apr. 1994.
[86] *London County Council* v. *Bermondsey Bioscope Company Limited* [1911] 1 KB
445, per Lord Alverstone CJ at 451. The case was unconnected with the content of
a film, turning on whether a condition in a licence was *ultra vires* if it precluded

power to subject cinema films to prior scrutiny as a reasonable condition of a licence became a duty in relation to the admission of children when for the first time another Cinematograph Act required local authorities to prohibit the admission of children to films classified as unsuitable for them.

Since a growing number of local authorities had neither the expertise nor the desire to scrutinize every film shown in their area, it was not long before the Board set up by the film industry became an accepted body, developing and upholding standards of censorship that were generally respected and applied. The statutory powers remained, however, with the local councils which could, and on occasion did, overrule the Board's decisions, substituting their own judgment. When technology moved on, the Video Recordings Act 1984 introduced a further statutory requirement that, subject to certain exemptions, video recordings offered for sale or hire commercially throughout the United Kingdom must be classified by an authority designated by the Home Secretary. Rather than set up a new body for the purpose, the Government decided to extend the responsibilities of the existing BBFC. On 26 July 1985 the President and Vice-Presidents of the BBFC were designated the classification authority for the purposes of the Act, and charged with applying a new and additional test of suitability for viewing in the home.[87] This was reflected by the categories into which videos were placed, and the types of audience (including children classified by age) deemed suitable to view them.

A Criminal Justice and Public Order Bill seemed hardly the most appropriate vehicle for further regulation of the content of films and videos, but it happened to be to hand when legislators determined to legislate. It was only at the eleventh hour, with the arguments over practicality and the effects of screen violence on the behaviour of child viewers still raging, that Howard gave way. Temperamentally opposed to compromise, he did so reluctantly and because an all-party coalition was on the verge of getting the support of the Labour Front Bench, which would almost assure the

exhibitions on Sundays, Good Friday, or Christmas Day. It is ironic that the early statute and case-law which provided the basis for film, and later video, censorship should have rested upon such unlikely foundations as the requirements of physical safety and Sunday opening.

[87] For a historical note on the origins, powers, and working practices of the BBFC see the *Annual Report and Accounts for 1985*, British Board of Film Classification, London, 1986 Appendix 1, pp. i–iv.

Government's defeat. On the morning of the debate on 12 April he met Tony Blair, the principal Opposition spokesman. Blair warned him that the Government had underestimated the degree of public feeling at the diet of violence being fed to children. He said that unless an acceptable resolution was reached without delay, Labour MPs would be likely to support the Alton amendment and to do so in large numbers. As a way out of the impasse, Blair favoured a Government amendment to the Video Recordings Act 1984. Howard then agreed to the inclusion of statutory criteria for video classification covering the main objectives of Alton's proposal. The actual wording, he maintained, would call for further consultation with the BBFC and careful drafting to ensure that a workable and enforceable provision resulted.

Urgent discussions followed at 10 Downing Street, chaired by the Prime Minister, with anxious Government business managers in attendance, including the Leaders of both Houses[88] and the Government Chief Whip in the Commons. It was decided that as there was insufficient time to prepare a Government amendment to the Video Recordings Act requiring the BBFC to take into account specified factors when considering whether or not to classify a video, and if so in what category to put it, an undertaking should be given that a suitable amendment would be tabled in the Lords.

After checking again with the Director of the BBFC, who had been consulted the previous day and had been party to intensive four-way discussions over the previous twenty-four hours,[89] Howard was ready to see Alton in his room at the Commons at 2.30 p.m. The Home Secretary explained that he would be elaborating on his earlier statement and requiring more rigorous enforcement of controls under the Video Recordings Act. He had discussed with the BBFC a stiffening of the standards it applied in classifying works to respond to public concerns and in recognition of changing public attitudes towards the depiction of violence. In future, some works placed in the fifteen year-old category would be placed in the eighteen year-old category, while others would be refused a certificate altogether. In order to underpin this strategy

---

[88] The Leader of the House of Lords, Lord Wakeham, had circulated a Cabinet paper on violent videos in his capacity as chairman of the Home and Social Affairs Committee.

[89] James Ferman was Director of the BBFC. The other parties were David Alton, Home Office officials, and the Labour Opposition in the Commons.

and help deliver tougher standards, he conceded the principle of a statutory obligation on which Alton set such store, requiring the BBFC to consider the harm which a video might cause. This would be incorporated in a Government amendment to the Bill at a later stage. He believed that the outcome would satisfy the Opposition Front Bench and be acceptable to the BBFC. Alton agreed without hesitation. He had achieved his objective by negotiation rather than by confrontation across the floor of the Chamber.

Throughout the afternoon and early evening Howard lobbied personally as many as possible of the eighty or so Conservative MPs who were known to be sympathetic towards the Alton amendment, some of whom, such as Sir Ivan Lawrence QC, the Chairman of the Select Committee on Home Affairs and a sponsor of the amendment, were especially influential with back-bench MPs. He also gave broadcast interviews to damp down the anticipation of a Government defeat. Alton's new clause was not reached until after 10 p.m., by which time a sense of anti-climax had settled in.

When the moment finally came, in an abbreviated yet magnanimous speech, Alton said that instead of the protracted debate which had been expected, the Home Secretary had been obliging towards MPs who had approached him about the issue, and receptive towards their arguments. He coupled his remarks with thanks to Blair whose intervention had enabled progress to be made. Alton had not been surprised by the scare-mongering activated by his proposal as huge vested interests were involved. In 1993 alone some £650 million had been generated by eighteen- and fifteen-rated videos.[90] He believed that the new clause would catch about 3 to 4 per cent of ultra-violent videos. While welcoming the greater rigour in enforcement of the existing regulations promised by Howard on television during the afternoon, that response would have been insufficient unless he had been ready to go to the extra mile of introducing legislative safeguards, which he had agreed to do. If the Home Secretary was able to repeat the assurances to the Commons which he had given publicly earlier in the day, there would be no need to divide the House.[91]

Howard duly obliged. Blair followed, confirming that the Home Secretary had undertaken to consult the Opposition Front Bench on the amendment to be tabled in the Lords, and Alton then

[90] *Parl. Debates*, HC, 241 (6th ser.), cols. 130–2, 12 Apr. 1994.
[91] Ibid., col. 135.

withdrew his new clause. The weight of opinion was so forcefully expressed, and so uniform, and the hour so late, that no MP pursued the underlying questions of censorship or restrictions on the freedom of speech. Not until a fortnight later when nine well known film directors, the Chairman and members of the Directors' Guild of Great Britain, signed a letter published in *The Times* was a dissenting voice heard. While understanding 'the urge to respond to the increasing violence in society' and sharing 'the desire to protect our children', the directors questioned whether further censorship would be effective in achieving these ends and might be dangerous for society as a whole.[92] However, they were regarded as persons with a vested interest whose timidly expressed protest was to be expected.

Although it was by then 11 p.m., the Commons moved on to consider further new clauses on a series of newsworthy matters not covered by the Bill: anti-terrorism legislation; touting for passengers by drivers of cars not licensed as taxis; and prohibiting the use of cells from human embryos or foetuses in fertility clinics. The first two were withdrawn after debate. On the third the Secretary of State for Health, Virginia Bottomley, made a sympathetic speech about the revulsion felt by many people, which she shared, at a human life being created from an aborted foetus.[93] The question was one of conscience, and she said that the Government believed it should be resolved by a free vote. In the event it was not necessary to test the opinion of the House, since a motion by Dame Jill Knight was agreed without a division to amend the Human Fertilisation and Embryology Act 1990 prohibiting the use of female germ cells taken from an embryo or a foetus for the purpose of providing fertility services. The change in the law was an important one. The crucial decision had been made late at night, in a thin House, after virtually no informed discussion. It was an issue that cried out for more thorough consideration by the second Chamber, which it received when it was opposed by Baroness Warnock, who had been chairman of a Committee of Inquiry into Human Fertilisation in the 1980s,[94] and by Lord Walton of Detchant, a

[92] *The Times* 28 Apr. 1994.   [93] *Parl. Debates*, HC, 241, col. 159.
[94] *Report of the Committee of Inquiry into Human Fertilisation and Embryology* (Cmnd. 9314), HMSO, London, 1984. The Committee was set up in 1982 to examine the social, ethical, and legal implications of developments, actual and potential, in the field of human reproduction. The thorny question of the use of human embryos in scientific research divided the Committee.

leading authority in the fields of medical treatment and scientific research.

The next day the Commons turned its attention to some of the controversies which had dominated the Committee stage: the cautioning of young offenders; secure training orders; the right of silence; a new offence of aggravated trespass; the activities of ticket touts at football matches; and the discretion to be given to the courts to dispense with pre-sentence reports for young offenders. The debate was long drawn out: starting at 3.47 p.m. and ending eleven hours later at 2.43 a.m. Although it was punctuated with divisions, none was lost by the Government. In the early hours of the morning on 14 April the motion 'That the Bill now be read the third time' was put. The MPs, if not the subject, were exhausted and there was no debate. The Government Whips were palpably more successful than the Opposition in keeping their supporters in the precincts, the motion being carried by 220 votes to 44. The Bill was then passed and sent on to the Lords.

3

The Politics of Tactical Withdrawal

I

A second measure, designed to effect structural changes ('reforms' was the word preferred by ministers) in police and Magistrates' courts services, was published on the same day as the Criminal Justice and Public Order Bill, 17 December 1993. For presentational purposes its unveiling was linked to the more politically attractive proposals to strengthen the penal powers of the courts. Yet the 'crack-down on crime' theme was applied to both measures, with Michael Howard claiming that the legislation on the police was intended to help build the close partnership between police and public necessary to fight crime effectively.[1] The police would be given clear published objectives, protecting the public and preventing and detecting crime being the top priority. As their full titles implied, both Bills were composite. The Criminal Justice and Public Order Bill dealt mainly with the prosecution and trial process, sentencing, and the prisons, but also created new public order offences. The Police and Magistrates' Courts Bill had even less integrity in its subject matter, combining in a single statute proposals for the reform of two distinct institutions which public policy had hitherto striven to keep apart: the police service and the Magistrates' courts.

The fusion induced by ideology and the prospect of legislation did not surmount the jealously guarded departmental frontiers of Whitehall. Since 1992, when responsibility for the financing, organization, and management of the Magistrates' courts had been transferred away from the Home Office, it was the Lord Chancellor, and not the Home Secretary, who had the duty to bring forward legislation affecting the magistracy, although not on the content of the criminal law. In a statement Lord Mackay of Clashfern said that the objectives were twofold: to enable Magistrates' courts' committees better to manage the service, and

[1] *Parl. Debates*, HC, 233 (6th ser.), col. 333, 23 Nov. 1993.

to clarify the accountability to Parliament, through him as the responsible minister, for annual public expenditure on the Magistrates' courts in excess of £300 million.[2] When the Bill came before Parliament it was a paradox that a unity unclaimed by ministers was detected by critics across a broad political spectrum who identified in each part of the Bill a predisposition to add to the powers of direction and control in the hands of central government, diminishing still further the role and influence of local government. In both Houses ministers had a hard time convincing sceptics that the Bill was intended as a decentralizing measure, delegating more responsibility to reconstituted police authorities and Magistrates' courts' committees.

In preparing legislation on the police, Howard enjoyed far less freedom of action than he had with the Criminal Justice and Public Order Bill. His predecessor as Home Secretary, Kenneth Clarke, had decided to grasp the nettle of police reform and work was virtually complete on the drafting of a White Paper which was published in June 1993, shortly after Howard had arrived at Queen Anne's Gate.[3] Clarke had also appointed an industrialist, Sir Patrick Sheehy, and four others to conduct an inquiry into the rank structure, pay, and conditions of service of the police, which reported in the same month.[4] Neither document was well received by the police, always amongst the most awkward of vested interests for a Conservative minister to attempt to regulate.

Howard's inheritance was unenviable. Clarke, never one to shirk a scrap, had been persuaded by the statistics showing the extent of the rise in the cost of policing in real terms, and the increase in manpower (see Table 3), that action had to be taken to adjust the relationship between the allocation of resources and the value to society of catching criminals and maintaining public order. As expenditure on the police escalated, so did the statistics on the incidence of recorded crime. After due obeisance in the opening sentence to the Government's commitment to upholding the rule of law, supporting the police, and fighting crime, the White Paper on

---

[2] Lord Chancellor's Department, *News Release*, 17 Dec. 1993.

[3] Home Office, *Police Reform: A Police Service for the Twenty-First Century* (Cm. 2281), HMSO, London, 1993.

[4] Inquiry into Police Responsibilities and Rewards, *Report* (Cm. 2280 I and II), HMSO, London, 1993. Sir Patrick Sheehy had been Chairman of BAT Industries since 1982. The other members were: John Bullock, Professor Eric Caines, Professor Colin Campbell and Sir Paul Fox.

TABLE 3. *Policing: expenditure, wages, and numbers*

	1964/5	1979/80	1992/3
Expenditure on Policing (£ million)			
Total (cash)	160	1,482	5,862
Total (real terms 1992/3)	1,629	3,545	5,862
Wages (per annum)			
Minimum wage for a constable	700	4,086	12,555
Maximum wage for a constable	1,040	6,471	20,952
Police Numbers			
Total police manpower	81,199	113,309	128,259
Male officers	78,548	103,837	112,099
Female officers	2,651	9,472	16,160
Civilians	11,430	35,762	49,494

Source: Home Office, Dec. 1993.

Police Reform stated in the first paragraph that the police had 'received a greater increase in resources than most other public services'.[5] Similarly, the terms of reference for the Sheehy inquiry instructed it to have full regard to affordability and value for money. From the outset the driving force was to obtain a greater degree of control over a major head of public expenditure estimated to reach £6.2 billion for overall spending on the police service in 1993/4, representing an increase of 88 per cent in real terms since Margaret Thatcher's administration took office in 1979.

Curbing the power of local authorities was a subsidiary part of the strategy, albeit a politically significant one. Since the existing police authorities were normally chaired by elected councillors, rather than by magistrates, the decline of Tory fortunes in local government elections meant that an ever-increasing number of councillors belonging to the opposition parties controlling County and Metropolitan areas in England and Wales were moving into the chair. Two areas, Merseyside and Greater Manchester, had been especially sharp thorns in the side of successive Home Secretaries, the chairmen (or, as in both these cases, chairwomen)

---

[5] Cm. 2281, p. 1.

of their police authorities being castigated as fundamentally opposed to the policing objectives of central government.

Lip service was paid to the notion that the tripartite structure of the Home Secretary, police authority, and Chief Constable ensured that each had a say in the allocation of resources. Yet there was no room for doubt that the Home Office was the predominant source of funding. For provincial police forces the Home Secretary paid a specific grant, which was not cash limited, of 51 per cent of expenditure for policing purposes. Whereas local authorities contributed the remaining 49 per cent, in practice most of their contribution came indirectly from central government in the form of the revenue support grant paid to local authorities by the Department of the Environment. For the Metropolitan Police, the Home Secretary paid a grant of 52 per cent of current expenditure, and local authorities contributed 48 per cent, the total being cash limited.[6] His approval was required for any increase in the numerical establishment of a police force, a restraint relaxed in the Bill. He also made regulations governing police officers' pay and conditions of service and approved the appointment by police authorities of senior officers. Historically, there had been no separate police authority for the Metropolitan Police, the Home Secretary acting in that capacity.

In seeking to apply the techniques of corporate strategy and management to these intricate relationships, the informal and unwritten understandings and conventions as well as the statutorily defined functions and powers, and the degree of public accountability which they regarded as necessary for expenditure on such a scale, Clarke and Howard moved towards a set of proposals which left the Government open to the charge that the outcome would be an unacceptable degree of power in the hands of the Home Secretary with a consequent risk of politicizing control over operational policing. From the moment the proposals were published, the warning lights began flashing.

II

With the aim of getting the principal components of a heavy legislative programme completed in the period of a few months

[6] Ibid., p. 5.

between December and July, the decision was taken that the Police and Magistrates' Courts Bill should be introduced in the House of Lords. It was a major Bill, and a politically sensitive one, such as would normally begin in the Commons. However, the Government's business managers were constrained by the shortage of time to get Bills started before Christmas. Because of the unified Budget and Autumn Statement on Expenditure, introduced for the first time in November 1993, and the resulting Finance Bill, four days were lost for Second Reading debates in the Commons in the early part of the session. Moreover, to have three major Bills before the Commons simultaneously (there was also a highly contentious Sunday Trading Bill cutting across party lines) would have put too great a strain on the Home Office ministerial team. A further consideration was that once it had been decided to combine the proposals relating to the police with those on the Magistrates' courts in order to save time, the responsible minister for the latter parts of the Bill was the Lord Chancellor, who sat in the Lords. For these reasons the Police and Magistrates' Courts Bill was first exposed to Parliamentary scrutiny on Second Reading in the Lords on 18 January 1994. Lord Mackay, the Lord Chancellor[7] opened, with the Minister of State at the Home Office, Earl Ferrers, winding up a debate which was to cause the Government acute discomfort before it ended nearly eight hours later.

Mackay's restrained and rational style contrasted with the shriller law and order polemic of his ministerial colleagues, both in the Commons and outside Parliament. Interviewed on BBC Radio 4 on the morning of the debate he said that he intended to approach it with an open mind. As with Howard and the police, he was not the prime author of the proposals designed to improve the performance and the accountability of the Magistrates' courts' service in England and Wales. They had originated from within the Home Office, which had published a detailed scrutiny of the management and funding of Magistrates' courts in 1989. The findings were highly critical. The arrangements for managing Magistrates' courts and their resources dated from 1949, but retained the local, part-time, and almost amateur flavour of an earlier age. No coherent management structure had been identified in a service costing about £200 million a year to run and employing nearly 10,000 staff.

---

[7] Lord Chancellor since 1987.

The service was fragmented, the main organizational unit being the Magistrates' courts' committee (MCC), of which there were 105. Abundant evidence existed to show that the arrangements were incapable of delivering value for money, indeed it would be difficult to think of any less likely to do so. The Home Office was the source of most of the money, but it had no say in how resources were allocated or used, or in controlling the total level of spending. The immediate funding bodies, the local authorities, had too small a stake in the service to provide an effective budgetary discipline, while the MCCs were too dependent on local authorities and their management capacity too underdeveloped to plan or manage resources effectively. Most clerks had little control over resources and inadequate information about costs. Spending was not properly controlled, and the audit arrangements, despite the improvements, were still deficient.[8]

Although the Government had shied away from the most radical recommendation, that the service be reorganized on a national basis and constituted as an executive agency, a shift towards greater centralization was inevitable. One change was especially unpalatable to the Home Office. While retaining the essential structure of a locally based magistracy, the Government's proposals for organizational reforms were preceded by a transfer of ministerial responsibility for the management, operation, and financing of the Magistrates' courts from the Home Secretary to the Lord Chancellor. The declared intention was to improve co-operation between the different tiers of courts within the criminal and civil justice systems, and to build on the role already exercised by the Lord Chancellor's Department in relation to the appointment and training of magistrates.[9]

By the time a White Paper was published in February 1992 the transfer of ministerial responsibility due to take effect in April of that year had been agreed, the resulting paper being presented in the joint names of the Lord Chancellor and the Home Secretary. The co-incidence that both Mackay and Howard[10] were lawyers who had entered national politics from careers as experienced

---

[8] Home Office, *Magistrates' Courts: Report of a scrutiny 1989*, vol. I, HMSO, London, 1989. Summary, paras. 1–5.

[9] *A New Framework for Local Justice* (Cm. 1829), HMSO, London, 1992, p. 1.

[10] Michael Howard had been a QC in practice at the Bar before his election as MP for Folkestone and Hythe in 1983. He had sat briefly as a recorder in the Crown Court.

advocates before the courts may have made it easier for them to defend the reform proposals as being consistent with the general thrust of Government policies, but without any special sense of mission or personal commitment.

The battle-lines were drawn before the Second Reading debate in the Lords began. The police and local authority associations were unanimously opposed to the changes in the composition and chairmanship of the reconstituted police authorities, and the revised relationship between them and the Home Secretary. Equally hostile were the magistracy and the judiciary towards the requirement that the appointment of the chairmen of the MCCs should be approved by the Lord Chancellor, and that justices' clerks should be employed on fixed-term contracts with performance-related pay. Advance publicity in the press had warned ministers to expect strong criticism, especially from the former Home Secretary, Lord Whitelaw, on the police authorities, and from the Lord Chief Justice, Lord Taylor, on the threat to the independence of the magistracy. Both spoke early in the debate, immediately after the Lord Chancellor and the Front Bench spokesmen for the Labour and Liberal Democrat peers, each of whom condemned the proposals with gusto.

As the supreme Tory loyalist, Whitelaw's intervention was the most telling. Four years as Home Secretary, and four years before that as Opposition spokesman on Home Affairs in the Commons,[11] had convinced him that understanding between the political parties on police matters was of great value and that disagreements could damage sensible policing. Agreement between the parties on the principles of policing, he believed, had been a crucial factor in the high standard of the police over the years. The most controversial of the proposed changes in the structure of police authorities was that the Home Secretary should appoint the chairman. As a result he would be regarded as the Home Secretary's man, particularly in moments of stress in policing operations. There was a risk that the Home Secretary would become directly involved in police operations, something that had always been carefully avoided in the past

---

[11] William Whitelaw was Home Secretary from 1979 to 1983 and Lord President of the Council and Leader of the House of Lords from 1983 until his retirement in 1988. His generally benign influence on criminal justice policy in Opposition and Government over a long period (1975–88) is recounted in *Responses to Crime*, Vol. 2.

and should always be carefully avoided in the future. At the very least there would be accusations of interference with the operational independence of chief constables, leading to controversy that would be undesirable and potentially dangerous on politically sensitive occasions. Whitelaw pressed for an answer to the question why the change was being made: 'I should like to know from the Home Secretary, or anyone else in the Government who will tell me, why they really want to make what I consider to be a very dangerous move indeed.'[12]

The proposed alterations in the membership of the new police authorities also needed to be questioned. Was it wise to replace local authority members with the Home Secretary's nominees? It was extremely doubtful that they would know more about local policing and more about their areas than people from the local authorities. Was there not a danger that local councils might lose interest in their police forces? If that were to happen it would certainly be a loss. How would the balance work in those police authorities which had several councils in their areas, such as Greater Manchester and Merseyside? Did it make sense to reduce all police authorities to the same size, irrespective of their areas of responsibility? He found it hard to believe so.

Whitelaw was followed from the Opposition benches by another former Home Secretary, Lord Callaghan, the only holder of the office in the twentieth century, apart from Winston Churchill from 1910 to 1911, to become Prime Minister.[13] His criticism was sharper and more political, the blame being laid on the shoulders of: '. . . a wilful and ambitious group of young Ministers who flit across the political scene from department to department, supping the honey as they go and moving on quickly before their misdeeds catch them out.'[14]

The intention to alter the composition and make up of police authorities and for the Home Secretary to appoint the chairman had met with opposition from more quarters than he could remember. He echoed what had been said by Whitelaw, asking what had gone so wrong that the Government wanted to transfer the power

---

[12] *Parl. Debates*, HL, 551 (5th ser.), col. 480, 18 Jan. 1994.

[13] James Callaghan was Home Secretary from 1967 to 1970, Secretary of State for Foreign and Commonwealth Affairs 1974–6, and Prime Minister 1976–9. Leader of the Labour Party 1976–80. Life peer 1987.

[14] *Parl. Debates*, HL, 551, col. 482.

to appoint the chairman of a police authority from the members of that authority to the Home Secretary. In justifying their proposals, ministers had become past masters in the art of declaiming that their changes were intended to put more power into the hands of local people. However, when examined carefully the result was often to centralize more power in their own hands.[15] He saw an imperative need to prevent the appointment of government sympathizers as chairmen of police authorities, commenting that there had already been complaints about some hospital trust chairmen. To go down this road would be to provoke a mood of revenge, with Labour wanting to turn them out when the time came and replace them with its own nominees.

As the debate went on the condemnation continued from all parts of the House. Out of a total of thirty-eight speeches, all save two, apart from the Ministers' opening and winding up speeches, were critical either of the Bill as a whole or of parts of it. The weight of authority brought to bear was impressive: another ex-Home Secretary (Carr of Hadley), a former Chief Constable and President of the Association of Chief Police Officers (Knights), a Bishop (Norwich), a Law Lord (Ackner), and numerous peers with first-hand experience of the Magistrates' courts or local government. The tenor of the debate was such that one outspoken critic from the Conservative benches said that he had never known the House to be so unanimous in its disapproval of a Government Bill, and that at the conclusion of the debate the Minister should consider withdrawing the motion for a Second Reading.[16] Another Conservative back-bencher sadly confessed that never in twenty-three years' membership of the House had she disagreed with her party as deeply as over the proposals on the Magistrates' courts.[17]

III

The theme of the centralization of power united the opponents of the proposals bearing on the independence of the magistracy with

---

[15] *Parl. Debates*, HL, 551, cols. 483–4.

[16] Ibid., col. 521. Lord Bethell, the longest serving British Member of the European Parliament (1975–94) and an adviser to the Police Federation.

[17] Ibid., col. 504. Baroness Macleod of Borve had been a magistrate for thirty years.

those whose primary concern was the alterations to the composition of the police authorities and the powers of the Home Secretary
to appoint the chairman and five members. The characteristic
features of the new managerialism were evident in both parts of
the Bill, but they stood out more clearly in Part IV since its provisions were confined to the management and organizational structure of the Magistrates' courts service in England and Wales, and
were not intended to affect the judicial decisions taken in individual cases. Taylor supported the Lord Chancellor's aim of securing
greater efficiency by amalgamating some committee areas and giving statutory authority to an inspectorate to report on their organization and administration. He was anxious about whether the
interests of efficiency conflicted with judicial independence, not simply of the lay and professional magistrates but also of their clerks.
Whilst not strictly members of the judiciary, he pointed out that
justices' clerks had important judicial functions. They had a responsibility to provide advice to the Bench on what the law is and how
it should be applied to the facts of a particular case. Clerks also
exercised judicial functions in their own right, in certain cases
granting adjournments, renewing bail, extending the time allowed
to pay fines, and granting or refusing legal aid. The trend was
towards devolving further judicial functions. Soon clerks would be
empowered to commit actions by consent to the Crown Court and
to issue distress and attachment of benefits warrants. To the Lord
Chief Justice it was: '. . . absolutely fundamental that nobody providing legal directions or advice to a tribunal of fact, or who is taking decisions which affect the rights or liabilities of parties to
proceedings, should be or appear to be susceptible to outside influences of any kind.'[18]

Under the powers contained in the Bill the contract of service
between the clerk and his employing committee might contain provisions specified by the Lord Chancellor. The Government's intention, clearly signalled in the White Paper,[19] was that the contracts
should be for fixed terms with performance-related pay. As Taylor
trenchantly observed, a cult seemed to have developed and invaded
the whole of the public sector whereby fixed-term contracts and
performance pay were seen as the panaceas leading to managerial
efficiency. Useful tools as they might be in a purely managerial

[18] Ibid., col. 476.   [19] Cm. 1829, p. 8.

context, in a judicial context, or where there existed a judicial element, they were out of place. He was strongly critical of the proposal that each area committee should appoint a chief justices' clerk, approved by the Lord Chancellor, to be the head of all its paid staff. While he accepted the need for MCCs to be assisted by an able professional, qualified in the management of staff and financial resources, Taylor argued that what was wanted was a manager pure and simple, a chief executive as in the health service, not as provided in the Bill a lawyer who was '. . . capable of exercising any of the functions of a justices' clerk . . .' with a duty to '. . . promote discussions relating to the law, practice and procedure among the justices' clerks for petty sessions areas within the area of the committee'. It was also the intention that the chief justices' clerk would be on a fixed-term contract incorporating performance-related pay.

Later speakers were equally dismissive of applying the value-for-money criterion to judicial procedures. As Lord Lester of Herne Hill[20] contended, it was not for the executive alone to determine whether a particular judicial procedure provided value for money. Although no one deliberately set out to erode the independence of the legal system, he was aware from his own experience, sitting as a Recorder and Deputy High Court Judge, of subtle administrative pressures which amounted to insidious erosion.[21] Several peers commented on the inappropriateness of tacking a measure dealing with the courts which process 95 per cent of all criminal proceedings onto a police Bill for reasons of legislative convenience: 'The whole direction of British justice has been to separate the police from the magistracy in the eyes of the public. Therefore, it seems an odd and retrograde step that this important Bill about the magistracy should be attached to a police Bill.'[22]

Scepticism was expressed about the Government's predictions that the cost of the new arrangements could be accommodated within the existing budget levels, particularly since the available evidence showed that those counties which had already gone some

---

[20] Anthony Lester QC had been an adviser to Roy Jenkins when he was Home Secretary, 1974–6. A specialist in human rights and public law, he was created a life peer in 1993 and spoke from the Liberal Democrat benches.

[21] *Parl. Debates*, HL, 551, col. 488.

[22] Ibid., col. 512. Lord Gisborough, Lord-Lieutenant of Cleveland and a JP, took the Conservative whip in the House of Lords.

way down the road and unified their management structures under a justices' clerk for the whole county were showing higher costs per case than those which had not done so.[23] Some speakers conceded that in the past the administration of the Magistrates' courts had been in need of greater professionalism. However, they claimed that the scrutiny by the Home Office in 1989 had led to many MCCs putting their house in order, reducing costs, setting strategic objectives, streamlining administration, and introducing computer technology. None of the improvements had been enough to 'stop the inexorable and lumbering advance of the government juggernaut'.[24] Irrespective of party, speaker after speaker reiterated, without attributing deeper or sinister motives to the Government, that ministers were mistaken as to the practical implications of their proposals. They were begged to look at them again in the light of the near unanimity of informed opposition.

In his reply Ferrers concentrated mainly on the police, insisting that the Bill provided for the devolution of managerial responsibility to chief constables. The role of police authorities would be enhanced, and they would have a duty to take into account the views of local people about policing in their area. More power would be concentrated in local hands. Smaller sized police authorities would have a sharper cutting edge, and would be strengthened by the addition of independent members. It was never intended that the independent members should be the placemen of the Home Secretary or party hacks.[25]

His protestations were in vain. In the closing moments of the debate Callaghan intervened in the Minister of State's 'defence of the indefensible' to press for an assurance that the Leader of the House would convey to the Cabinet the sentiment of the Lords that on a Bill of major constitutional importance the Government had been almost friendless. Had it been subjected to a vote it would have been very hard to obtain a majority. He hoped that the Lord Chancellor's stated willingness to listen with an open mind would be heeded.[26]

The extent of press and broadcast coverage before and after the debate rendered superfluous the necessity for any late-night

[23] Ibid., col. 513.
[24] Ibid., col. 525. Viscount Tenby, a JP and member of a police authority, was a cross-bencher.
[25] Ibid., col. 563.   [26] Ibid., cols. 568–9.

messages to the Cabinet from the floor of the House. The proceedings in Parliament, at the instance of a second Chamber where party discipline and loyalties had taken second place to experience and personal conviction, made a change of course unavoidable. The policy would have to be trimmed if the strategy was to be saved.

IV

The politics of tactical withdrawal are elusive. Tone and timing can count for as much as the substance of concessions. Party and personal relationships have to be balanced with public presentation. No departmental minister endures a setback in either House of Parliament with indifference, since apart from the merits of the proposals included in a Bill, the adversarial nature of the proceedings means that any withdrawal or change of direction is seen as a defeat. This is where the middlemen come in, senior ministers whose primary task is to ensure that the machinery of government runs smoothly and that the legislative programme is enacted in the time available.

The controversy over the police reforms embraced two of the most experienced managers of Parliamentary business of the era since 1979. Viscount Whitelaw had occupied a unique role in Margaret Thatcher's administrations, first in the Commons until 1983 and thereafter in the Lords until he resigned after suffering a mild stroke in 1988. Following in Whitelaw's footsteps, the current Leader of the House of Lords, Lord Wakeham, had been Conservative Chief Whip and Leader of the House of Commons, besides holding Cabinet Office as a departmental minister.[27] If anyone had inherited the mantle of Whitelaw as the Government's most skilful operator it was Wakeham. Although cutting less of a figure on the floor of the House, and taking no part in the debates on either Bill, Wakeham nevertheless exercised considerable influence on his ministerial colleagues in the Commons through his chairmanship of Cabinet committees.

---

[27] Parliamentary Secretary to HM Treasury and Government Chief Whip 1983–7; Lord Privy Seal 1987–8, Lord President of the Council 1988–9, and Leader of the House of Commons 1987–9; Secretary of State for Energy 1989–92; Lord Privy Seal and Leader of the House of Lords 1992–4.

The Police and Magistrates' Courts Bill was unusual in that two Cabinet ministers, the Home Secretary and the Lord Chancellor, were jointly responsible for its component parts. Mackay had the advantage of sitting in the Lords and being able to defend his own proposals, moving from the Woolsack to the Government front bench at Committee stage to engage in close combat across the floor of the House. More dangerous was the friendly fire from those who sat behind or alongside him on the Conservative benches, and most dangerous of all, the outspoken criticism of the Lord Chief Justice supported by other judges on the cross-benches. The professional hostility was too strong to ignore, and in the ten days following the Second Reading debate Mackay met representatives of the Magistrates' Association, the Central Council of Magistrates' Courts' Committees, the Justices' Clerks' Society, the Association of Magisterial Officers, and the Standing Conference of Clerks to Magistrates' Courts' Committees. Even before the Second Reading debate the Lord Chancellor had not ruled out the possibility of concessions to meet some of the objections put to him. Mindful of the link with the police reforms and the unyielding stance of the Home Secretary, however, he had decided to await events.

Howard's consultations were less extensive, but at the top of the list was the formidable figure of Whitelaw. Disinclined as the Home Secretary was to give way to pressure from the Lords he knew (and Wakeham was on hand to remind him) that unless an accommodation could be reached with Whitelaw there was no prospect of getting the Lords to agree to some crucial parts of the Bill. Nor could the intervention of Callaghan be overlooked. Like Whitelaw, he commanded great public respect, outside Parliament as well as at Westminster.

The fact that the Bill had started in the Lords strengthened the critics' hand. As a former Prime Minister it was rare for Callaghan to take an active part in the scrutiny of a Bill throughout its successive stages. In this instance he brought his full weight to bear, arguing that when a measure of constitutional importance comes before the Lords it normally arrives with the sanction of the Commons after debate and agreement as to its contents. Consequently, there is a natural reluctance on the part of the Lords to make substantial alterations unless either they are absolutely outraged by what is proposed (for example, the War Crimes Act

1991 which reached the statute book without their consent[28]), or they decide it is necessary to give the elected House an opportunity to think again. Whether due to wisdom or accident, Callaghan observed, the Government had introduced this Bill in the Lords. As the first House to look at it there need be no restraint in putting forward amendments.[29]

As a tactician Whitelaw believed in securing his principal objective which was to persuade the Home Secretary to relinquish the right to appoint the chairmen of the police authorities. A secondary objective was to allow for the maximum number of members to be increased beyond sixteen in appropriate cases. His magnanimity led him to offer something in return. If agreement could be reached with Howard on these two changes, Whitelaw undertook to speak in support of the Government's plans for the re-organization of police authorities, both at the next stage of the Bill and in a private meeting at which Howard was due to address Conservative peers before the Committee stage. It was an offer no pragmatic minister could refuse, although neither Whitelaw nor Wakeham were confident that the concessions would be enough to satisfy the House as a whole. Nevertheless, agreement was secured without delay and Government amendments to give police authorities the power to appoint their own chairman and to introduce flexibility in the overall number of members were tabled on 2 February.

The forebodings were borne out on the first Committee day on 15 February. Whitelaw honoured his side of the bargain, affirming his gratitude to the Home Secretary for his 'immediate understanding and recognition' of the very strong feelings expressed in all parts of the House about the chairmen of the police authorities and the method of appointing the members. He concluded a short speech resoundingly: 'I strongly support my right honourable friend the Home Secretary on the plans that he now puts forward for the organisation of police authorities in tackling the serious problems of law and order which we all face in this country today.'[30]

Important as it was to the Government Front Bench, Whitelaw's conversion and the concessions made to achieve it were insufficient to swing the balance of opinion in favour of the Bill. A debate of

---

[28] See *Responses to Crime*, Vol. 2, pp. 206–7, 436–7.
[29] *Parl. Debates*, HL, 551 (5th ser.), , col. 482, 18 Jan. 1994.
[30] *Parl. Debates*, HL, 552 (5th ser.), col. 112, 15 Feb. 1994.

such intensity followed that, most unusually, the sitting had to be adjourned for half an hour to enable discussions off the floor of the House between the Minister of State, Earl Ferrers, and the leading dissentients. The upshot was a compromise that no amendments to clauses 2 to 4 and schedule 2 would be moved, on an undertaking from the Government that these clauses and the schedule would be recommitted for further consideration at the end of the Committee stage proceedings.[31]

A fortnight later, after three additional days in Committee, and much negotiation behind the scenes, the House returned to the vexatious issue of the composition of police authorities and their relationship with the Home Secretary. In his opening speech Ferrers again denied any intention to politicize the appointment of the chairmen or independent members, although he accepted that the House had taken a different view. To meet the undoubted anxiety that had been expressed on 15 February, he had agreed not to move his amendments if other Lords agreed not to move theirs.[32] By this means a head-on collision was avoided. The Government had now reconsidered its position and was willing to make further concessions.

It had not been easy, Ferrers said, to identify common denominators in the earlier debates and to draft amendments to meet them. With the exception of the Government amendment already tabled on the chairmanship of police authorities (the concession to Whitelaw), which could probably be accepted readily, the additional changes would be incorporated in amendments tabled at Report Stage. Although the aim remained to keep the authorities as small as possible, the standard size would be increased from sixteen to seventeen. As proposed earlier, the Home Secretary would have the power to increase the size of the membership where local circumstances made it desirable. There would be no upper limit. The seventeen members would consist of nine councillors, three magistrates, and five independent members. That would leave the local authority members with a majority of one, a hard-fought concession. Where the Secretary of State increased the size of a police authority, the elected councillors would retain a majority of one, the number of magistrates and independent members being increased in proportion to the overall size of the authority.[33]

---

[31] Ibid., col. 144. [32] Ibid., col. 941, 1 Mar. 1994. [33] Ibid., col. 943.

The Minister then embarked upon a description of the procedure proposed for the selection of the independent members who would be co-opted by the other members of the authority. In a standard-size authority of seventeen, five independent members would be selected from a list of ten names forwarded by the Home Secretary. He would choose these names from a short-list of twenty provided by a local selection panel. The previous idea of regional selection panels, possibly chaired by the Lord-Lieutenant of the county, had been abandoned in favour of a local selection panel for each police authority area. In the interval the Lords-Lieutenant, having been consulted by the Home Secretary, had declined to co-operate.[34] The selection panel would consist of three people. One would be chosen by the councillors and magistrates on the police authority, the second would be a local person of independent judgment appointed by the Home Secretary, and the third member appointed by the other two. These details would appear on the face of the Bill, as would some of the selection criteria which the panels were expected to follow.

The complicated and laborious nature of the procedure outlined was greeted with a mixture of relief and ribaldry. Ferrers was personally popular in the House and by far the most experienced of the Home Office ministerial team on police matters for which he had held departmental responsibility under successive Home Secretaries for more than five years. Spokesmen for the Opposition parties and the cross-bench peers who had participated in the negotiations, as well as the leading rebels on the Conservative benches, were aware that he had faced an uphill task in persuading Howard of the need to give more ground. One of those who had been consulted, Lord Allen of Abbeydale, a former Permanent Secretary at the Home Office,[35] saw the result as a compromise hammered out in prolonged and on the whole good-tempered negotiations. While the revised proposals now put forward by the Government fell short of what he regarded as ideal, in that they did not provide a two-thirds majority for the elected representatives, nor an unfet-

[34] The Lord-Lieutenant of Cumbria, Sir Charles Graham, informed *The Times* that the Home Secretary had 'only chucked this idea on us in the week before he put it to the Lords. The way it was done showed desperation'. 24 Feb. 1994.

[35] Formerly Sir Philip Allen, Deputy Under-Secretary of State, Home Office 1960–2; Second Secretary, HM Treasury 1963–6; Permanent Under-Secretary of State, Home Office 1966–72. Chairman: Occupational Pensions Board 1973–8; Gaming Board for Great Britain 1977–85.

tered choice in the co-option of independent members, nevertheless the local authority members would now be in a majority, however slight. In the opinion of this veteran bureaucrat, cumbersome as it sounded the selection procedure should ensure beyond doubt that the independent members were not simply Government nominees.[36]

Other changes affecting the police were made during the subsequent stages in the passage of the Bill; but the St David's Day debate in the Lords on the restructuring of the police authorities stood out as the high-water mark of parliamentary influence. It was a textbook example of the second Chamber bringing to bear informed or expert opinion, typically channelled from organized interest groups, outside the confines of the two-party system which dominates the Commons.[37] In the circumstances the talk of U-turns, humiliating defeats, and climb-downs which characterized the press coverage was out of place. Even so, the Leader of the Liberal Democrats, Lord Jenkins of Hillhead,[38] provided a stylish extension to the vocabulary of partisanship when he remarked that to oppose what was now proposed would be like firing shots into the back of a routed army.[39] The Labour Front Bench spokesman, Lord McIntosh of Haringey, who had been a leading figure in the negotiations off the floor, got closer to the mood of the House in adapting an adage quoted by Theodore Roosevelt: what had been done had been achieved by treading softly, but carrying a big stick.[40] Treading softly had meant a willingness by the Opposition and other interested parties to engage in courteous and civilized consultation with the Minister and his officials. The big stick had been the weight of opinion in the House as a whole.[41]

[36] *Parl. Debates*, HL, 552, col. 954.

[37] See Windlesham, 'The House of Lords: A Study of Influence Replacing Power' in *Politics in Practice*, Jonathan Cape, London, 1975, pp. 115–42.

[38] Home Secretary 1965–7 and 1974–6; Chancellor of the Exchequer 1967–70. President of the Commission of the European Communities 1977–81. Chancellor of the University of Oxford 1987–.

[39] *Parl. Debates*, HL, 552, col. 949.

[40] The actual quotation from Roosevelt's speech at the Minnesota State Fair on 2 Sept. 1901 was: There is a homely adage which runs 'Speak softly and carry a big stick; you will go far'. *The Oxford Dictionary of Quotations*, Third edition, Oxford University Press, 1979, p. 408.

[41] *Parl. Debates*, HL, 552, cols. 948–9.

V

The latter part of the Bill on the administration of the Magistrates' courts was subject to the same forces. Although the setting was identical, and some of the *dramatis personae* the same, the leading actors were different. The Lord Chancellor is simultaneously head of the judiciary and a senior Cabinet minister with a duty to carry out the policies of the Government. The dual role can be uncomfortable at the best of times, and Mackay was already at odds with several members of the higher judiciary including the Lord Chief Justice, Lord Taylor, and his predecessor, Lord Lane. A rationalist and a lawyer of distinction, an accomplished advocate and an experienced judge,[42] Mackay had alienated a clamorous body of judicial opinion, fearful lest the need to save money should take precedence over the quality of justice. Instances cited were the cuts in eligibility and expenditure on legal aid,[43] a perceived inadequacy in the number of High Court judges, and changes in the rules on judicial pensions. Thus, a lack of mutual trust existed well before the Bill was introduced which made it inevitable that the proposals would be subjected to close scrutiny by the Lord Chief Justice and other Law Lords, as well as by peers representing the views of the magistracy and the justices' clerks.

The initial concessions made by the Lord Chancellor were co-ordinated with those by the Home Secretary on the police. In a press statement on 2 February Mackay said that he had considered carefully the points raised during the Second Reading debate and pursued them in his subsequent consultations with delegates from the representative national organizations. Fears had been expressed that the Bill's provisions could give central Government an inappropriate level of control over the management of the Magistrates' courts service and might undermine the independence of the advice received by magistrates when dealing with individual cases. While

---

[42] Lord Mackay had been Dean of the Faculty of Advocates (1976–9) and Lord Advocate of Scotland (1979–84); Senator of the College of Justice in Scotland (1984–5); and Lord of Appeal in Ordinary (1985–7).

[43] The justification for the changes in legal aid is a large subject on which there were sound arguments on both sides. They are fully discussed by one of the best informed and most level-headed journalistic commentators, Joshua Rozenberg, Legal Correspondent of the BBC, in his book, *The Search for Justice: An Anatomy of the Law*, Hodder and Stoughton, London, 1994, pp. 219–74.

he did not believe that the principles were at risk, he would be bringing forward amendments to put the issues beyond doubt.

Their effect would be threefold. First, the chairmen of the MCCs would continue to be appointed by the members without requiring the Lord Chancellor's approval. Second, the terms of the contract of employment between the chief justices' clerk or justices' clerks and their committees should be left to local discretion. In consequence, the Lord Chancellor relinquished the power to insist either that their contracts be for fixed terms or that their remuneration be related to performance. The third concession also affected the employment of clerks in that any renewal of their appointment would not require the approval of the Lord Chancellor, although their initial appointment would need to be approved by him.[44]

The Government amendments were accepted readily enough on the fourth day when the Bill was in Committee on 22 February. Further matters raised included the compulsory amalgamation of MCCs and special provision to meet the needs of disabled people attending the courts. The most contentious remaining issue was the designation of the chief justices' clerk. This led to the debate's climax, another forceful speech by Taylor, in which he insisted that much more was at stake than nomenclature. He welcomed the proposal that in order to strengthen and sharpen the administration of the Magistrates' courts a head of service should be appointed.[45] He or she would be responsible for the line-management of all staff and the best use of resources. The Government's main purpose in instituting the new office of chief justices' clerk was stated to be to 'provide clearer lines of accountability within the service'.[46] But accountability for what? For resources, clearly yes; for the court and its staff, yes; but for judicial decisions and the legal advice of justices' clerks, categorically no.[47] Taylor saw no prospect that the essential distinction between administrative functions on one hand and judicial and legal functions on the other could possibly be maintained if the new office-holder was both legally qualified and denominated as a justices' clerk. On the contrary, the distinction was bound to become blurred with serving justices' clerks feeling themselves to be accountable to their 'chief' for both sets of functions.

---

[44] Lord Chancellor's Department, *News Release*, 2 Feb. 1994.
[45] *Parl. Debates*, HL, 552, cols. 563–4, 22 Feb. 1994.
[46] *Parl. Debates*, HC, 237 (6th ser.), col. WA 248, 9 Feb. 1994.
[47] *Parl. Debates*, HL, 552, col. 564.

Mackay's reply, with over-long quotations from several documents (some of them superseded by later events), failed to convince. Surprisingly sharp ripostes followed, not only from Taylor, who found the Lord Chancellor's speech long on citation but short on answers to the points raised, but also from Lord Donaldson of Lymington. For ten years until 1992 Donaldson had been Master of the Rolls, presiding over the Civil Division of the Court of Appeal.[48] He was unimpressed by Mackay's analogy with the situation in Inner London where the very large Magistrates' courts service had long been headed by a principal justices' clerk. In his opinion, the reason the system worked satisfactorily there was because at the time it had been set up judicial independence was a reality and no one attacked it. For one reason or another, those days had gone. Nowadays, he continued censoriously: '. . . we are forced into the position where, rightly or wrongly, we feel that we must defend judicial independence at every stage. This is one of those crucial stages at which, as the Lord Chief Justice has so clearly demonstrated, a stand must be taken. It is not for me to say whether that should happen at this stage or another stage of the Bill but a stand must be taken.'[49]

Donaldson's brief but telling intervention was a revelation of the undercurrent of antagonism and suspicion which Mackay had to counter throughout. The debate ended uneasily without a division after Whitelaw, speaking as 'a simple non-lawyer who had listened to a great many lawyers for a long time',[50] had appealed for the Lord Chancellor to be allowed sufficient time to consider all the available alternatives. He should be given the opportunity to find a solution.

On 10 March the Justices' Clerks' Society wrote to a number of interested peers saying that the clause dealing with the appointment and functions of the chief justices' clerk struck at the very heart of the organization of Magistrates' courts. It was imperative that the role and duties of the proposed head of service should be clear and under no circumstances be capable of encroaching on the independent exercise by justices' clerks of judicial or quasi-judicial functions. The provisions in the Bill to allow the head of service to be

---

[48] Judge of the High Court of Justice, Queen's Bench Division 1966–79; President, National Industrial Relations Court 1971–4; Lord Justice of Appeal 1979–82.

[49] *Parl. Debates*, HL, 552, col. 576.   [50] Ibid., col. 581.

treated as a justices' clerk and to exercise those functions were unnecessary in order to fulfil his administrative role. It was an issue which must be addressed by Parliament.[51]

Midnight oil was burnt at the Lord Chancellor's Department, and the following day a group of amendments was tabled by the Government for consideration at Report stage. They included a change in the title of the head of service to 'justices' chief clerk', and an amendment to the effect that no head of service would be able to act as a justices' clerk unless so appointed by an MCC. Other concessions were the deletion of the Lord Chancellor's power to lay down a lower, as well as an upper limit to the number of members of an MCC so that each committee would be able to decide its own lower limit, and that default powers should not be invoked without a prior written warning from the Lord Chancellor to the committee concerned.

By Report stage the squall was beginning to blow itself out. The differences had narrowed. In addition to Mackay's amendments the all-party alliance which had pressed for the substitution of the title preferred by the Lord Chief Justice of 'chief executive' had combined it with the Lord Chancellor's determination to retain the prefix 'justices'. When the amendments were reached Mackay was conciliatory, indicating that he was prepared to forego his own amendments to give a clear run to the hybrid title 'justices' chief *executive*' (rather than clerk) which satisfied, in part at least, all of the parties to the dispute. A dying ember of controversy briefly flickered into flame later in the debate when the House accepted Mackay's revised formulation of the circumstances in which a head of service might exercise the functions of a justices' clerk for a petty sessional area, rather than a more circumscribed version in an amendment which was defeated on a division.[52]

VI

At Third Reading the Government sustained a final reverse on the police. Following a recommendation by the Sheehy Inquiry, the Bill proposed a reduction in the number of ranks within the police

[51] Letter from Laurence Cramp, Honorary Secretary, Justices' Clerks' Society, 10 Mar. 1994.
[52] *Parl. Debates*, HL, 553, cols. 438–44, 17 Mar. 1994.

service from nine to six. The justification of streamlining the management hierarchy by simplifying the rank structure had been condemned during the Report stage as being wholly inappropriate to a disciplined service which had to be ready to cope with large-scale emergencies at short notice. A former Commander in the Metropolitan Police, Baroness Hilton of Eggardon, spoke from personal experience of the operational importance of the co-ordination provided by chief inspectors (one of the ranks to be abolished) in a variety of situations.[53]

Her arguments were endorsed by no less a figure than a Field-Marshal joining the sortie from the cross-benches. Lord Bramall pointed out that there were about eighteen ranks in each of the armed forces, three times the number proposed for the police. Having listed the advantages of 'a proper and comprehensive rank structure', he continued brusquely that he was 'amazed and indeed dismayed' that the Government should be engaged in a totally needless exercise of 'petty tinkering with ranks' for a purpose that was not made clear. Service ranks should not be confused with management posts, and ministers should think again before a 'tampering' which would go right to the heart of police morale.[54] Baroness Hilton, with all-party support, returned to the charge on Third Reading, carrying an amendment against the Government which had the effect of limiting the reduction in ranks to seven, rather than six as proposed by the Home Secretary.[55]

Despite the vehement opposition to the Bill as published, the defeat was only the second to be suffered by the Government in the division lobbies during the turbulent passage of the Bill through the Lords. An earlier setback had come on the third day in Committee when Lord Bethell, from the Conservative benches, carried an amendment on police disciplinary procedures against the Government by the narrow majority of 107 to 100 votes.[56] His amendment nullified two provisions which police organizations found objectionable: that a police officer charged with a disciplinary offence should no longer have the right to legal representation,

[53] *Parl. Debates*, HL, 553, col. 171, 15 Mar. 1994.

[54] Ibid., cols. 172–4.

[55] The amendment was agreed by 133 votes for and 107 against. Although the result was unaffected, the tellers for the Contents reported 133 peers as having voted for the amendment, whereas the Clerks recorded 134 names. *Parl. Debates*, HL, 553, cols. 758–9, 24 Mar. 1994.

[56] *Parl. Debates*, HL, 552, cols. 456–8, 21 Feb. 1994.

and that if an officer had been acquitted on a criminal charge in the courts he might still be brought before a disciplinary tribunal on the same charge, and risk dismissal or other penalties if found guilty on the civil, rather than the criminal, standard of proof. Disregarding appeals from Lords Callaghan and Boyd-Carpenter, two heavyweights sitting on opposite sides of the Chamber, to think again before the next stage of the Bill, the Minister of State had shown no hint of compromise in his reply. Apart from the merits, the reality was that even if Ferrers had wished to consider the amendment further, he was unlikely to be able to persuade an increasingly reluctant Home Secretary to make any more concessions to his critics in the Lords.

In the end the Lords' view of the rank structure prevailed. Although avoiding any deference to the Upper House, Howard announced his change of heart when the Bill was debated in the Commons on Second Reading. He had been impressed, he said, by the strength of the Association of Chief Police Officers' argument that the rank of chief inspector provided the greatest management and operational flexibility. Moreover, there was evidence that a thinning out of middle management (the jargon persisted) was already in progress in several forces. Consequently, the rank of chief inspector would be retained, leaving two ranks between inspector and assistant chief constable, chief inspector and superintendent, as provided in the new clause inserted by the Lords.[57]

With his next breath the Home Secretary declared that he would be inviting the Commons to reverse the amendment carried in the Lords which would prevent disciplinary proceedings being brought against a police officer in respect of a matter for which he had already been tried and acquitted in the criminal courts. Howard did not accept that this provision amounted to double jeopardy and believed that the arguments which had been put forward in its favour were 'fundamentally misconceived'. He had been persuaded, however, that police officers should retain the right to be legally represented, both at the original hearing and on appeal, if they were at risk of dismissal, requirement to resign, or reduction in rank.[58] It was a significant concession which helped to secure a favourable outcome when the Commons' amendments were returned to the Lords for further consideration.

[57] *Parl. Debates*, HC, 242 (6th ser.), col. 115, 26 Apr. 1994.
[58] Ibid., cols. 116–17.

By then, the prevention of disciplinary action following acquittal in a criminal court for an offence similar in substance was the only outstanding question on which the two Houses were in disagreement. The tone of the debate was constructive, and after Ferrers had painstakingly explained the distinction between police disciplinary hearings and proceedings in a court of law, the Lords accepted the reasoning that acquittal on a criminal charge did not necessarily mean the defendant had behaved in a way that was fitting for a police officer.[59] Speaking from the Opposition Front Bench McIntosh agreed, saying that on reflection he now believed the Government was right.[60]

The disciplining of policemen and women who step out of line by acting improperly, abusing the authority and status conferred upon them, bears directly on public confidence in the police. Each year some hundreds of errant police officers are punished following formal disciplinary proceedings. The statistics in Tables 4 and 5

TABLE 4. *Police disciplinary proceedings: Metropolitan Police Service, 1989–93*

Punishment[a]	1989		1990		1991		1992		1993	
Dismissed	16	(6)[b]	15	(4)	13	(3)	19	(3)	21	(4)
Required to resign	10	(10)	16	(9)	12	(3)	14	(4)	14	(9)
Reduction in rank	6	(2)	2	(1)	1	(3)	6	(2)	7	(1)
Reduction in pay	3	(3)	3	(1)	9	(2)	6	(6)	10	(1)
Fine	25	(4)	31	(4)	27	(8)	26	(5)	39	(1)
Reprimand	15	(2)	16	(–)	19	(–)	29	(–)	29	(2)
Caution	5	(–)	4	(–)	3	(–)	5	(–)	3	(–)
Total	80	(27)	87	(19)	84	(19)	105	(20)	123	(18)

[a] Main punishment awarded by disciplinary authority, taking account of variation on appeal.
[b] Figures in brackets represent appeals to the Commissioner outstanding at the year end.

Source: Metropolitan Police Service.

[59] *Parl. Debates*, HL, 557 (5th ser.), col. 29, 18 July 1994.
[60] Ibid., col. 30.

TABLE 5. *Police disciplinary proceedings: England and Wales, 1989–93*[a]

Punishment	1989	1990	1991	1992	1993
Dismissed	33	28	42	54	47
Required to resign	48	40	51	55	55
Reduction in rank	20	16	25	12	20
Fine	182	157	165	134	184
Reprimand	83	115	118	126	117
Caution	25	33	27	27	38
Total	406	408	448	433[b]	485

[a] Including the Metropolitan Police Service.
[b] One officer was found guilty but resigned before punishment was decided.
Source: Home Office, *Statistical Bulletin*, 13/94, 6 June 1994.

show a disproportionate rise in the number of Metropolitan Police Service officers punished as a result of disciplinary proceedings over the five years from 1989 to 1993,[61] as compared with similar statistics for England and Wales as a whole. The trend may imply an increased readiness to initiate disciplinary proceedings in the Metropolitan force, rather than an increase in the volume of misconduct. However, where such misconduct occurs in the course of investigating crime, the process of criminal justice and the standards of fairness which should be incorporated within it will suffer accordingly. The extent of disciplinary action is a mattter of importance, upon which Parliament and the public should keep a watchful eye.

Of the many changes introduced by the Lords in the Police and Magistrates' Courts Bill, all save one were eventually accepted by the Government; and when that one was sent back it was agreed on its merits. The way in which this resolution was reached was in some respects as important as the actual result. The sequence of events represented a classic demonstration of the negotiated concession as a tactic superior to defeating the Government in the division lobby. The old hands in the Lords, as well as the elder statesmen who had come up from the Commons, knew that the

---

[61] The assistance of G. L. Angel, Receiver, Metropolitan Police Service is acknowledged for the provision of the statistics in Tables 4 and 5.

path of compromise and concession was not only outwardly more seemly for an unelected assembly, it was also more effective. Although the Bill had started in the Lords, which gave the House greater edge, the reality was that the Government could use its whipped majority in the Commons to reverse any unacceptable amendments. However, once the concessions had been translated into Government amendments, drafted by Treasury Counsel, it was a near certainty that they would survive the Bill's passage through the Commons. The contrast with the Lords' lesser impact on the Criminal Justice and Public Order Bill showed how far procedural tactics, as opposed to the merits or demerits of a proposal, can define the ultimate content of legislation.

VII

As the liners Queen Elizabeth and Queen Mary used to cross in mid-Atlantic, so the Government's flagship bills of the session crossed en route between the two Houses in the Spring of 1994. Attitudes had hardened during the voyages and the revising function left less scope for change than when the Government's legislative proposals had first come under parliamentary scrutiny. In the Commons the Police and Magistrates' Courts Bill attracted less public attention than had the Criminal Justice and Public Order Bill, although providing further opportunities for the Government to reiterate its strategy on law and order, and further opportunities for the Opposition to oppose it. Crime and lawlessness, Howard proclaimed in his speech opening the Second Reading debate on 26 April, posed 'a supreme challenge to all modern democracies'. The Government was determined to meet the challenge 'by taking action across the board to ensure that we have the most efficient and effective criminal justice system possible'. Action had been taken 'to ensure that more crimes are prevented and more criminals are caught, convicted and punished'.[62]

The police were at the centre of the strategy. No Government, on Howard's somewhat partial reckoning, had done more to support them than the Government of which he was a member. Since the Conservatives came to power in 1979 spending on the police had

---

[62] *Parl, Debates*, HC, 242, col. 110.

increased in real terms by 87 per cent, and the total number of
police officers had grown by more than 16,000. What had to be
addressed was how to make sure that such a huge investment, currently amounting to over £6 billion a year, was deployed wisely and
effectively. That called for an examination of the framework within
which the police operated, which had become out of date and was
in need of reform. The financial arrangements for police forces and
police authorities were 'antiquated and arcane'.[63] Too much detail
was referred to the Home Office. The accountability was opaque.
People did not know how to influence the priorities of their local
forces. Personnel and pay procedures were outdated. The rank
structure was top-heavy. Pay depended too much on the length
rather than the quality of service. Technology and scientific
advance offered enormous scope for fighting crime more effectively,
but much local police information technology had been developed
without co-ordination and was incompatible between forces. The
programme of change looked formidable but much of it, according
to the Home Secretary, coincided with changes actively sought by
the police. He went on to itemize the main strands of the reform
programme.

It was an eloquent speech and it was what the troops on the
Government side wanted to hear. Howard was already a talented
performer at the despatch box when he became Home Secretary
and, unlike some of his predecessors in office, his oratorical powers and self-confidence continued to grow during his tenure of one
of the most testing of all the great offices of state. Blair too was
blossoming as a Parliamentarian of the front rank, and later in the
year was to be elected as Leader of the Opposition after John
Smith's untimely death. Whereas Howard had played down the role
of the Lords in forcing changes in the Government's original proposals, Blair was under no such inhibition. The Bill that had come
before the House, he said, was in 'a badly wounded and limping
state—severely mauled in another place, but nonetheless still dangerous'.[64]

In the eyes of the Opposition the Bill remained deeply flawed. It
represented the most determined and least popular attempt ever made
to centralize policing in Britain, to give ministers unprecedented control over the way the police do their work, and to undermine police

---

[63] Ibid.   [64] Ibid., col. 121.

independence. It was driven not just by short-term cost-cutting but by an ideology that resented local freedom and had an aversion, bordering on paranoia, to local government. It had been opposed not only by the Labour Party and Labour councillors, but by Conservative councillors and the police themselves, where the proposals had the extraordinary effect of uniting almost every rank of serving police officers against them. On the latter part of the Bill, magistrates and their clerks sincerely held the view that their independence, and hence that of the judicial system, was being undermined by the Government's proposals.[65]

In a lengthy Commons debate the main lines of argument were again rehearsed. It followed the contours set in the Lords and by independent commentators, with an occasional dissenting voice raised 'in sorrow rather than in anger'[66] heard on the Government back-benches. The most deeply felt criticisms were directed at the provisions dealing with the reorganization of the Magistrates' courts.

One Conservative MP of twenty-four years' standing put on record his opinion that the Bill would be no worse, and probably much better, if the whole part on the Magistrates' courts were to disappear altogether.[67] A particular point of concern was the power of the Lord Chancellor to initiate orders amalgamating Magistrates' courts committees (MCCs), after consultation, but not as previously only when requested to do so by the magistrates themselves. Large-scale amalgamations, it was feared, would be the prelude to an acceleration in the closure of Magistrates' courts in many towns and rural areas, as was happening already in some places where a performance indicator setting a minimum level of court-room use had not been met. Truly local justice would suffer if, as contended by the Justices' Clerks' Society and quoted in the debate, the effect of smaller towns losing their Magistrates' courts, in rural areas especially, was to restrict the availability of justice to defendants who had difficulty in travelling to a more distant court. Witnesses also would be deterred from attending.[68] The supposedly more efficient structures depending on fixed criteria, performance

---

[65] *Parl, Debates*, HC, 242, col. 122.

[66] Roger Sims, a magistrate and MP for Chislehurst since 1974. Parliamentary Private Secretary to the Home Secretary (William Whitelaw), 1979–83., Ibid., col. 139.

[67] Sir Roger Moate, MP for Faversham since 1970. Ibid., col. 186.

[68] Ibid., col. 187.

indicators, and business plans, when combined with the policy of overall cash-limits on the resources allocated to the Magistrates' courts nationally, posed a real threat to the continued existence of smaller court-houses. Since closures occur one at a time, in different counties throughout the country, the process was piecemeal with the result that Parliament was insufficiently aware of a significant change taking place in society. The pressures for amalgamation should be resisted and the dangers of centralization recognized.[69]

In reply, John Taylor, Parliamentary Secretary at the Lord Chancellor's Department,[70] confirmed that it was the Government's policy to reduce the number of MCCs and the areas which they covered so as 'to achieve the right balance between operational needs and maintaining the local nature of the service'.[71] The White Paper in 1992 had anticipated that the total number of committees would be reduced progressively from 105 to somewhere between fifty to sixty.[72] Since then there had been extensive consultation over how the reduction might be effected. Conclusions had been reached on amalgamations in some areas while in others, notably in outer London, negotiations were still in progress. Decisions over closure would remain in the hands of the MCC.[73]

In contrast to the Criminal Justice and Public Order Bill, the Opposition divided the House against the motion that the Bill be read a second time. The Government had a majority of forty-three, 290 MPs voting for the motion and 247 against. In accordance with the usual procedure of the Commons, unlike in the Lords where the Committee stage on Public Bills is normally taken on the floor of the House, the Bill was then sent to a Standing Committee for scrutiny. Standing Committee D, with Charles Wardle, the Parliamentary Under-Secretary at the Home Office as the Minister in charge for the police proposals, and John Taylor for the Magistrates' courts, met for seventeen sessions, reporting the Bill back to the House on 28 June. With MPs hoping to adjourn for

---

[69] Ibid., col. 188.
[70] A solicitor and MP for Solihull, who in 1992 had been appointed as the first Junior Minister to represent the Lord Chancellor's Department in the House of Commons. Previously a Government Whip (1988–92) and a Member of the European Parliament (1979–84).
[71] *Parl. Debates*, HC, 242, col. 197.
[72] *A New Framework for Local Justice* (Cm. 1829), HMSO, London, 1992, p. 5.
[73] *Parl. Debates*, HC, 242, col. 198.

the Summer Recess before the end of July, the timetable began to press.

The Report stage and Third Reading were both taken on a single day on 5 July, when once again the concern of constituency MPs about the policy of amalgamating MCCs was a main theme of the debate. In Committee it had been asked 'time and time again' what was the rationale for the proposed reduction to a total of between fifty and sixty and how had the figure been arrived at.[74] The fact that there had been no voluntary amalgamations over the previous forty-five years did not imply that MCCs were operating inefficiently, nor failing to give value for money. In reply, John Taylor cited the Home Office Scrutiny of 1989, arguing that there was a lack of management responsibility and accountability for expenditure now running at the level of about £350 million per annum, and that the accountability sought was for administrative and not judicial functions. Line-management from the committees was needed, through the justices' chief executive, to the rest of the staff on administrative matters.[75] A mutually acceptable solution to restructuring had been reached in outer London which fell short of amalgamating Committees. The debates on the Bill in the Commons finished as they had begun, with a set-piece political confrontation between Howard and Blair on Third Reading.

VIII

In its consideration of the Criminal Justice and Public Order Bill the House of Lords was the repository of the hopes of penal reformers and representatives of the professional services for reversing or modifying the Government's policies on two proposals in particular: secure training orders for very young offenders and the right of silence. Each raised questions of principle, a clarion call to which the Lords had often responded in the past.

Ever since Howard's Blackpool speech in October 1993 resistance had been mounting to the planned extension of the use of imprisonment for children aged twelve to fourteen. As further information became available a clearer picture emerged of what was intended. Five self-contained units, each accommodating about

[74] *Parl. Debates*, HC, 246 (6th ser.), col. 253, 5 July 1994.
[75] Ibid., cols. 255–6.

forty boys and girls, would be built on sites already at the disposal of the Prison Service, and would be part of the responsibility of the Home Office. The cost was estimated at about £30 million. There was an expectation that the management of the secure training centres would be contracted out to the private sector after competitive tenders had been received and evaluated. Individualized training plans lasting for the duration of the order would be devised for each trainee, concentrating on education and tackling offending behaviour. The period in detention would be followed by an equivalent period of intensive supervision in the community after release.

The model had been a long time in the making, originating as a response by successive Home Secretaries from Baker to Howard to a series of provocative and well publicized incidents of persistent offending by a small but conspicuous group of youngsters, believed to number no more than 200 nationally.[76] The nub of the policy was to target those individuals for whom detention was an unavoidable necessity by means of a filtering process. The filter took the form of statutory criteria which had to be met before a court would be able to make a secure training order.

Clause 1 of the Bill created a new penal sanction. Its opening words specified eligibility for the order in terms of the age of the offender: 'a person of not less than twelve but under fifteen years of age' and the gravity of his offending: who had been 'convicted of an imprisonable offence'.[77] The duration of the order was subject to upper and lower limits: not less than six months nor more than two years, of which half would be spent in detention and half under supervision. The statutory criteria were that the offender must be not less than twelve years of age when the offence for which he is to be dealt with by the court was committed; that he had been convicted of three or more imprisonable offences; and that on either the present or a previous appearance before the court the offender had been in breach of a supervision order or convicted of an imprisonable offence committed whilst he was subject to a

---

[76] The estimate came from police sources in England and Wales. A Home Office survey across thirty-three police forces during three months in 1992 found that 106 young people in this age group had committed ten or more offences. *Parl. Debates*, HL, 554 (5th ser.), col. 459, 25 Apr. 1994.

[77] An imprisonable offence for this purpose was defined as an offence (not being one for which the sentence is fixed by law) which is punishable with imprisonment in the case of a person aged 21 or over. Section 1(8), Criminal Justice and Public Order Act 1994.

supervision order. To remove any doubt as to the classification of the new penalty, and as a safeguard against future challenges, it was stated on the face of the Bill that a secure training order was a custodial sentence for the purposes of Sections 1–4 of the Criminal Justice Act 1991. In truth it was a hybrid, since half of the sentence was to be spent under supervision in the community. However, as a sanction in which punishment and prevention counted for more than treatment, it was important that it should be subject to the restrictions on the use (Section 1) and length (Section 2) of custody, commensurate with the seriousness of the offence, prescribed in the 1991 Act.

By these means the Government hoped to steer clear of the pitfalls revealed by past experience with the detention of children and young people. Borstals, approved schools, and detention centres, with or without the short, sharp shock regimes unsuccessfully tried out it the early 1980s,[78] had all resulted in a very high proportion in the range of 70–80 per cent of juveniles released from custody reoffending within two years of release.[79] The Government itself had admitted candidly in 1988 that even a short period of custody was quite likely to confirm young offenders as criminals by affording them the opportunity to acquire new criminal skills from more sophisticated offenders. They see themselves as criminals and behave accordingly.[80] Intimidation, bullying, poor quality staff, and low standards of education and training had been contributory factors in the decline of these institutions.

Why should it be different this time? Ministers, and the officials who had the task of converting their policy objectives into practical form, put their faith in targeting so that only those persistent offenders who really needed this type of intervention were made subject to the new orders, whereas in the past approved schools and detention centres had admitted a wider range of youngsters, many of whom could equally well have been dealt with in the community.

[78] For the experiment with tougher regimes in detention centres, see *Responses to Crime*, Vol. 2, pp. 158–61.

[79] Out of a total of 3,090 young persons aged fourteen to sixteen discharged from Prison Service establishments in 1987, 2,534 (82 per cent) were reconvicted within two years of discharge. *Parl. Debates*, HL, 553 (5th ser.), cols. WA 21 and WA 87, 22 Mar. and 12 Apr. 1994. The reconviction results for those discharged in subsequent years was not available when the legislation was before Parliament in 1994.

[80] Home Office, *Punishment, Custody and The Community* (Cm. 424), HMSO, London, 1988, p. 6.

It was claimed that the compactness and relatively small size of the secure training centres would help them to set and maintain minimum standards of education and training which would be included in any contract specification.

A clear disadvantage, evident from the start, was that of geographical remoteness. Five units drawing their inmates from the whole of England and Wales inevitably meant that many young people would be held a long way from their home areas. Regular visits would be difficult to maintain during the period of custody, thus reducing the links with families and social workers which are recognized as being so vital during the period of resettlement under supervision. Experience of custodial establishments for older juveniles indicated also that depression, sometimes leading to suicide attempts, is aggravated by lack of contact with families.

The lengthy gestation of the secure training order, and the results of consultation once the main features of the scheme had been announced,[81] enabled the voluntary and professional organizations working with young people and juvenile offenders to consider the proposals in the light of their experience and to put their views on record. Virtual unanimity was reached. The roll-call of national organizations committed to opposing the secure training order was overwhelming. It included the Associations of Directors of Social Services and Chief Officers of Probation, the National Children's Home, Save the Children, the Children's Society, Barnardo's, National Children's Bureau, the Law Society, Children's Legal Centre, Association of County Councils, Association of Metropolitan Authorities, National Association of Probation Officers, NACRO, Rainer Foundation, Royal Philanthropic Society, Community Service Volunteers, British Agencies for Adoption and Fostering, National Council of Voluntary Child Care Organizations, British Association of Social Workers, British Youth Council, Association for Youth Justice, Methodist

---

[81] On 19 March 1993 a consultation letter was circulated by the Home Office C1 Division inviting comments on the implementation of the policy for dealing with persistent juvenile offenders which had been outlined by the Home Secretary in the House of Commons on 2 March. In his statement Kenneth Clarke said that the Government had decided the courts should have a new power to make what had been described provisionally as a secure training order, combining a period of education and training in a secure residential setting with effective supervision on release. He envisaged that the new training centres would be provided through agreements with organizations in the public, voluntary, or private sectors, and that central government would act as the purchaser. *Parl. Debates*, HC, 220 (6th ser.), cols. 139–40, 2 Mar. 1993.

Association of Youth Clubs, National Association of Young People in Care, National Intermediate Treatment Federation, British Association for Community Child Care, Standing Committee on Youth Justice, Penal Affairs Consortium, Prison Governors' Association, and the Justices' Clerks' Society.

Even the few which were in favour, notably the police and the Magistrates' Association, entered the caveat that secure accommodation should be locally based. The strength of feeling amongst the professional services and voluntary organizations was such that five of them[82] resurrected a consortium known as *New Approaches to Juvenile Crime* to campaign against the Government's proposals. Under the chairmanship of Baroness Faithfull, a former Director of Social Services and a greatly respected and independent-minded Conservative peer, the same five organizations had come together in the late 1970s when there was concern over the increasing recourse to custody for juveniles and harsher methods of dealing with young offenders. Between 1978 and 1984 *New Approaches to Juvenile Crime* argued for the development and greater use of community supervision programmes. The methods employed included producing and publishing reports and briefing papers, holding and publicizing conferences, and working to persuade MPs and peers of the case for more constructive ways of dealing with juvenile crime. The consortium was disbanded in 1984, when official policies towards juvenile crime swung towards a more sparing use of custody and the promotion of intensive supervised activity programmes for juvenile offenders.[83]

In the aftermath of the announcement that the Government intended to go ahead with the secure training order, the dormant consortium was revived as a vehicle for joint action to influence public and Parliamentary opinion once again. Baroness Faithfull chaired a committee consisting of representatives of the five member organizations, with Paul Cavadino, Principal Officer of NACRO, acting as Secretary.[84] As before, detailed and well argued

[82] The Association of Chief Officers of Probation, Association of Directors of Social Services, British Association of Social Workers, National Association for the Care and Resettlement of Offenders (NACRO), and the National Association of Probation Officers.

[83] Letter to the author from Paul Cavadino, 17 Aug. 1994.

[84] Paul Cavadino also acted as Clerk to the Parliamentary All-Party Penal Affairs Group. For his role in the Criminal Justice legislation of 1987–8 and 1990–1 see *Responses to Crime*, Vol. 2, pp. 9n., 202, 431–2.

briefing papers were prepared and circulated to the press and sympathetic MPs and peers. Meetings were held at the Houses of Parliament to propagate the views of the member organizations, explaining the practical experience and research from which they were derived. Ministers and officials were lobbied; amendments drafted; and a swift and efficient briefing service supplied when the Bill was before Parliament. On 10 March, in advance of the Second Reading in the Lords, *New Approaches* organized a conference on the Government's proposals for young offenders at Church House, Westminster, which was well supported by practitioners in the various criminal justice services. Yet despite good press coverage and the presence on the platform of a Bishop, an Assistant Chief Constable, and a noted academic authority on the behaviour of young offenders[85] there was an ominous scarcity of legislators in the audience.

When the action moved back to Parliament for the Bill's Second Reading in the Lords the atmosphere was subdued. Although more than forty speakers took part in a long debate on 25 April which continued until shortly after midnight, it remained in a low key throughout. Of the dramatic tension that had characterized the Second Reading of the Police and Magistrates' Courts Bill three months before there was not a trace. As expected, the secure training order, together with the right of silence, was one of the main themes of the debate. Mindful of his unhappy experience at the hands of the Lords on the earlier legislation, the Home Secretary had left no stone unturned in seeking to persuade individual peers, especially potential rebels on the Government benches, to give their support to the main proposals in the Bill. He was on safer ground in that this time the contents of the Bill had been approved by the Commons before arriving at the Lords, but even so he could not afford to chance another reverse. A steady procession of peers was invited to call on Howard in his room at the Home Office for a private talk.

The most prominent opponent of the secure training order, Baroness Faithfull, was exposed to pressure from an even more elevated quarter. On the day of the debate she received a reply from the Prime Minister to a personal appeal she had made to him. In

---

[85] The Bishop of Birmingham; Charles Clark, Assistant Chief Constable, Leicestershire Constabulary; and Professor Spencer Millham, Director of the Dartington Social Research Unit.

her letter she recalled that he had called for loyalty from all members of the Conservative Party, but continued:

> The dilemma for a back bench Conservative member is when, based on long experience, research and the views of many people, our Party is adopting a policy which cannot be right for the country and the Party in the long run even if it appears (which is doubtful) by a few to be wanted in the short term.
>
> I refer to Part I of the Criminal Justice and Public Order Bill, with special reference to the Secure Training Orders. Under this section 5 'Children's Prisons' for 12–14 year olds will, in all probability, be built in the grounds of prisons far from the homes of the children and run by the private sector which has no experience of such work. The cost is £30 million a year for 200 children . . .
>
> . . . For my own part, I have worked with boys and girls of the most delinquent type and know that incarceration will harden such children and they will be worse. I am not soft on crime; I believe that every boy and girl must not be excused their misdemeanours and crimes.
>
> I do not want to be disloyal to the Party, but I cannot stand by and not oppose a policy which I, and many others, know to be wrong. I believe that in the long run I am being loyal to the Party.[86]

In her speech Baroness Faithfull, described by *The Guardian* as the Conservative conscience of the Lords,[87] summarized the main lines of the argument against the new order, making it clear that in common with other objectors she recognized that some child offenders needed to be held in secure conditions. However, she pointed out that local authority Social Services departments, under the auspices of the Department of Health, already maintained secure units, sometimes shared by a number of local authorities, which were located within closer reach of parents, relatives, and other community ties. The problem was that some local authorities had been unable to provide enough places at secure units because of lack of financial resources. There were currently up to 300 secure places, and the Department of Health was providing resources for a further 170. Since an adequate administrative structure already existed to deal with children aged 12–14, why set up a costly parallel structure which was unlikely to succeed? Why should two ministries deal with the same problem?[88] She ended her speech with a request to

---

[86] Letter from Baroness Faithfull to the Prime Minister, 5 Apr. 1994. Quoted with permission.

[87] 16 May 1994. Baroness Faithfull died in 1996.

[88] *Parl. Debates*, HL, 554 (5th ser.), col. 460, 25 Apr. 1994.

bring a deputation to meet the Home Secretary. The inauguration of a separate penal system for the punishment of persistent juvenile offenders was condemned by other peers as a retrograde and expensive step, which would mean locking up more young people in establishments that would increase rather than diminish their chances of reoffending.

Critical as many of the speakers were, the debate focused on no more than about thirty of the Bill's 152 clauses. Moreover, on the cross-benches as well as on the Government side of the House, ministers detected encouraging signs of support for their proposals. On the right of silence, to which we shall turn in the next Chapter, the former Lord Chief Justice of Northern Ireland, Lord Lowry, drew on first-hand experience of the procedure in Northern Ireland in a maiden speech in which he declared a bias in favour of the relevant clauses in the Bill, although 'not a blind acceptance of their entire contents'.[89] The Lord Chief Justice of England was sitting in court in Cardiff and was unable to speak until the Committee stage. Before the Bill had come on to the Lords Howard had made a significant amendment in the Commons to meet Taylor's principal objection, which was to criticize as an 'unnecessary piece of theatre' a requirement in the original proposals that the trial judge should call into the witness box a defendant who refused to answer questions. Any such procedure would in his view tend to introduce an inquisitorial element into the judge's role.[90] With this concession, it was anticipated that Taylor would be willing to back the amended proposals for modifying the right of silence when the moment came.

By the conclusion of the Second Reading debate the indications were that the Government would succeed in getting its Bill through the Lords without losing any of its principal components. Some difficult and important issues which were certain to evoke deeply held beliefs and opinions lay ahead: the age at which homosexual acts should become lawful; the effects of violent videos; racial harassment; the handling of criminal injuries compensation; and some of the new public order offences and police powers. The Bill had been likened to a Christmas tree on which extra parcels had been hung as it progressed through Parliament. Both private members in the Commons and ministers, in responding to public opinion, had been

---

[89] Ibid., col. 396.   [90] *The Times*, 12 Apr. 1994

responsible for furnishing brightly coloured packages. The Lords might, and did, add some contributions of its own. There were likely to be some embarrassing moments for ministers and some concessions by Government. Although an easy ride was not in prospect, the central planks of the Government's strategy on crime and punishment were no longer at risk.

IX

As it turned out the main challenge on the secure training order came not in Committee, when an attempt to omit it altogether was defeated on a division by a comfortable margin of 182 to 144 votes, but on Report. Although some reservations had been expressed on the Conservative benches during the Committee stage debate on 16 May, only three peers taking the Government whip voted against the motion that Clause 1 stand part of the Bill. The large majority accepted the need for such an order, not because of any great faith in what it might be expected to achieve in terms of controlling future offending, but in sympathy with a *cri de coeur* uttered by the Minister of State. Ferrers' exasperation caught the prevailing mood accurately and deserves to be put on record verbatim:

My noble friend Lady Faithfull said (of the secure training order) 'It will not work'. The noble Lord, Lord McIntosh of Haringey, said 'It will not work'. The noble Lord, Lord Merlyn-Rees, said 'It will not work'. And of course the noble Lord, Lord Harris of Greenwich, as one would expect, said 'It will not work'. The noble Lord asked why the Government were going down this road as it would fail. I shall tell the noble Lord . . . and the Committee why we are doing this—because something needs to be done.

It is all very fine to say that approved schools have not worked, community homes have not worked, borstals have not worked and detention centres have not worked. What are we then supposed to do—nothing? Of course not. We are proposing to establish these new secure training centres. But then the right reverend Prelate the Bishop of Southwark said, 'Ah, but there is no hard evidence that these will work'. Of course he is perfectly right. There is no hard evidence because they have not been introduced. They are a new idea and it is quite right that these new ideas should be pursued.[91]

[91] Parl. Debates, HL, 555 (5th ser.), col. 50, 16 May 1994.

On 11 May, in the week before the Commitee stage, Howard received a deputation led by Baroness Faithfull, having been asked by the Prime Minister to see her. She decided not to take with her any representatives of the voluntary organizations, preferring to concentrate on the experience of the public sector statutory services. She was accompanied by a chief probation officer, a representative of the National Association of Probation Officers, an experienced London magistrate, the President of the Association of Directors of Social Services, a representative from the British Association of Social Workers, and the clerk to the North Hampshire Justices. Their arguments were unavailing; at the end of the hour Howard said bluntly 'We are going forward with the secure training units'.[92]

Unyielding as the Home Secretary remained throughout, a perceptible change had occurred in the mood of the House by Report stage. No one questioned that a firm decision had been taken and the Government had won, but some of the objections had left doubts about the way in which the courts might use the orders. To be eligible for a secure training order it seemed that a young offender need not have been before the courts on at least three previous occasions, but to have been convicted of three imprisonable offences. It was argued that the wording of the Bill was not a true reflection of the Government's often repeated aim that the new sentence was aimed at persistent offenders. If the convictions were obtained on one occasion for three separate offences, say of theft, there would need to have been at least one previous court appearance, since to qualify for the order the juvenile must either have offended while subject to a supervision order or have been in breach of it. Lord Allen of Abbeydale put the matter more simply when he remarked that it did not seem consistent with the Government's proclaimed policy that a single afternoon's shoplifting expedition in three stores and the breach of a single supervision order was all that was needed to qualify for consideration.[93]

Another result of the debates on Second Reading and in Committee was that the House became better informed about the existing facilities for the detention and treatment of young offenders in secure accommodation managed by local authorities. Since the vote at Committee stage a small group of peers on the

---

[92] Ibid., col. 56.   [93] *Parl. Debates*, HL, 556 (5th ser.), col. 1181, 5 July 1994.

Conservative benches had conceived the idea of amending the Bill to enable a court, when making a secure training order, to specify that the period of secure detention might be spent either in local authority secure accommodation or at a secure training centre. This time the standard-bearer was a moderate Conservative ex-Minister, Lord Carr of Hadley, Home Secretary during the Heath administration.[94] He was joined by a former Home Office Minister of State, Lord Elton, and by a magistrate and Lord-Lieutenant, Lord Gisborough. In advance of the debate they wrote personal letters to 170 peers explaining the case for the amendments. *New Approaches* assisted with the drafting of the amendments and circulated briefing material on an all-party basis in support.

Carr was an experienced Parliamentarian with an ultra-reasonable style of debating. In moving the first of a series of amendments on Report, he emphasized that they did not alter the proposed new sentencing orders in any way. They neither weakened nor strengthened them. The orders would remain exactly as they had been approved by the House. While he shared the extreme distaste of many people towards putting children into custody, in present circumstances he accepted that a period of detention was necessary for a small number of 'wholly unruly tearaways'.[95] Nor did the amendments alter the nature of the proposed five secure training centres. What they would do would be to give powers to the courts, not to officers of local or central government but to judges or local magistrates, to decide whether the period of detention under a secure training order should be spent in local authority secure accommodation or in one of the new centres. The courts would be given an option which they did not have under the proposals in the Bill as it stood.

Carr claimed several distinct advantages for his amendments. The courts might decide that some children should be kept in secure conditions as close as possible to their homes, and that the maintenance of community ties were all important. Others might benefit from being sent away for a time. Some might be better suited to the regimes of the secure training centres; others to the smaller local authority units, typically with between eight and sixteen places for

---

[94] Secretary of State for Employment 1970–2; Lord President of the Council and Leader of the House of Commons 1972; Home Secretary 1972–4. Chairman, Prudential Corporation 1980–5.

[95] *Parl. Debates*, HL, 556, col. 1141.

offenders and non-offenders. Again the courts would decide. The second advantage was the opportunity for comparison. The concept of a secure training order for children between the ages of twelve to fourteen was an untried innovation. If it depended solely on the experience of just five training centres throughout Britain, separated by long distances, they would have a monopoly of treatment and there would be no basis for comparison. The suggested option would enable future Home Secretaries to make a judgment on the most appropriate way to deal with difficult and dangerous children in secure conditions.

The third and most ingenious advantage postulated by Carr was that the country was 'dying to see something done'[96] and that if the amendments were adopted they would greatly reduce the delay in implementing secure training orders. The secure training centres were not yet built, indeed until the Bill was on the statute book they could not be contracted for. There was bound to be delay, probably measured in years rather than months, before they were built, staffed, and tested. Meanwhile, the demand for urgent action could not be met by secure training orders unless the courts were permitted to make use of the local authority secure accommodation as well as the new centres. The Secretary of State for Health was currently providing resources for local authorities to add another 170 secure places to enlarge the total capacity at their disposal.

It was the epitome of the best sort of House of Lords speech: calm, persuasive, and well informed. Moreover, it was delivered early in the afternoon to a full and attentive House. A spirited debate followed, in which supporters and opponents of the amendment were almost equally balanced. Lord Hailsham, reinforced by Ferrers when he replied for the Government, argued that the powers of the courts to make a secure training order or to send a young offender to local authority secure accommodation were different in kind, and that once a secure training order had been made a child should receive special treatment.[97] Ferrers elaborated, explaining that the Government had considered carefully whether expanding local authority secure accommodation was the best answer, but had decided that it would not be and that a new kind of facility should be created to deal specifically with persistent young offenders. Local authority units were smaller than the

[96] Ibid., col. 1142.   [97] Ibid., cols. 1144 and 1151.

proposed new centres and catered for a more varied range of young people; some as young as ten, some as old as eighteen; some offenders and some not. Of the 1,300 youngsters placed in secure accommodation each year, about one-third were on remand. Half of that number stayed in secure accommodation for less than one month. Valuable as it was as a way of dealing with young offenders, there were inevitable limitations on the kind of regime that could be offered.

The secure training centres, the Government claimed, would be designed specifically to deal with persistent offenders within a relatively restricted age group. They would be able to provide a much more specialized regime in terms of education and programmes aimed at encouraging trainees to confront and reform their offending behaviour. The 170 additional local authority secure places had not yet been built and were not expected to be available until the middle of 1996. They were intended to fulfil a long-standing commitment to end prison remands for fifteen and sixteen year olds; to allow courts to remand twelve to sixteen year-old juveniles who had not yet been convicted directly into secure accommodation; and to cater for children detained for long terms under Section 53 of the Children and Young Persons Act 1933. Under Carr's proposal, it would be into the present stock of local authority secure accommodation, which everyone had complained was inadequate, that the new category of offending juveniles would be propelled. If carried, the amendment would seriously disrupt the Government's plans for bringing secure training centres into being. Plans would literally have to go straight back to the drawing-board. They had been based on assumptions about the numbers of offenders to be catered for which would be thrown into confusion if some were to be diverted into local authority secure accommodation.[98]

Ferrers' reply was well deployed, but it failed to convince a House which had listened to the arguments and had been thoroughly canvassed in advance. Carr pressed the first amendment to a division in which he was successful, it being agreed by 170 to 139 votes. Half an hour later the Government went down to defeat a second time when another group of amendments was agreed on a division by 147 to 128 votes. These had the effect of introducing more flexibility into the period of detention by enabling a local

---

[98] *Parl. Debates*, HL, 556, cols. 1159–61.

authority to apply to the court, where a child had been sent to local authority secure accommodation, to transfer him to a secure training centre or to another specified form of care. Similarly, where a child had been sent to a secure training centre its director could apply to the court to transfer him to local authority secure accommodation or other form of care. In all cases, the decision would be made by the court.

4

From Platform Rhetoric
to Enforceable Law

I

Although there were some strongly expressed objections of principle to the concept of the secure training order, the controversy was dominated by arguments based on practical experience. The second topic which preoccupied Parliament, and the House of Lords in particular, during the spring and summer of 1994 was the Government's intention to modify the right of silence. To some, although not all, of those most familiar with the process of justice the proposal was seen as coming close to encroaching upon one of the most cherished of principles underlying criminal law and procedure: the presumption that in a contested trial the accused is innocent until found guilty by a jury. In Michael Howard's catalogue of pledges unveiled at Blackpool the previous October, none had been applauded more fervently than his emphatic declaration that the 'so called right to silence' would be abolished.[1]

Arguments over the right of silence had been considered more coolly on various occasions over the previous two decades. and opinions had been divided.[2] The conclusion reached by a majority of the Royal Commission on Criminal Justice in its 1993 report, and the Northern Ireland precedents, were discussed in the previ-

---

[1] *Conservative Party News*, 400/93, extract from a speech by the Rt. Hon. Michael Howard QC, MP, the Home Secretary, speaking at the 110th Conservative Party Conference, at the Winter Gardens, Blackpool, 6 Oct. 1993, pp. 13–14.

[2] The right of a suspect not to answer questions before trial and the right of an accused person not to give evidence at the trial both had their origins in the privilege against self-incrimination. In the eighteenth and nineteenth centuries the courts in England were traditionally suspicious of confessions. A brief summary of the historical development of the right of silence in English law precedes an analysis by C. R. Williams of the approach taken by the Australian courts: 'Silence in Australia: probative force and rights in the law of evidence', (1994) 110 LQR 629. Professor Williams is Dean of Law at Monash University.

ous Chapter. The story can be picked up again after the Second Reading debate on the Criminal Justice and Public Order Bill in the Lords on 25 April when Viscount Runciman of Doxford, the Royal Commission's Chairman, stated unequivocally that the proposal to allow juries to draw inferences from a suspect's failure to answer police or prosecution questions significantly increased the risk of wrongful convictions.[3] Lord Alexander of Weedon,[4] Chairman of JUSTICE (the British Section of the International Committee of Jurists) had spoken in similarly critical vein: 'I see this measure as a charter for unlimited police interrogation, which puts the accused at risk if he does not answer immediately, fully and lucidly. This all takes place in an unfamiliar atmosphere and in an interview which, however fairly conducted, inevitably appears to the accused as frightening and intimidating. Indeed, a former President of the Law Society who has great experience in this area recently told me that even duty solicitors often feel intimidated in the police station.'[5]

Against this, some influential speakers on the Conservative benches, including an ex-Attorney General, Lord Rawlinson of Ewell,[6] had robustly supported the Government. The Committee stage was awaited with keen anticipation.

As with the secure training order, where the drafting of many of the amendments and the preparation of briefing material had been prepared by *New Approaches to Juvenile Crime*, so did JUSTICE, Liberty (the National Council for Civil Liberties), and the Law Society co-operate over the right of silence. Shortly before the Committee stage an all-party briefing session was held at the House of Lords in the Moses Room, with its appropriate murals.[7] The panel consisted of the Chairman of the Bar Council, a solicitor in private practice in East London with experience of advising in police stations, legal and academic experts from Northern Ireland, and a psychologist specializing in the reliability of confession evidence. Despite the selective nature of the invited audience, from the

[3] *Parl. Debates*, HL, 554 (5th ser.), col. 419, 25 Apr. 1994.

[4] QC 1973. Chairman, Bar Council 1985–6; Panel on Takeovers and Mergers 1987–9; National Westminster Bank 1989–.

[5] *Parl. Debates*, HL, 554, cols. 452–3.

[6] Solicitor General 1962–4; Attorney General 1970–4. Chairman of the Bar and Senate, Inns of Court 1975–6; President, Senate of the Inns of Court and Bar 1986–7.

[7] Moses bringing down the tablets of the law to the Israelites, by J. R. Herbert, RA.

discussion which followed the opening statements it was evident that not all the peers present were minded to oppose this part of the Bill. Alexander, who chaired the meeting, was a supreme advocate who sat on the Government benches, but it was doubtful that a majority of the other Conservatives who were taking an active part in the debates agreed with him. While Labour and Liberal Democrat lawyers of the calibre of Lord Irvine of Lairg, Baroness Mallalieu, and Lord Wigoder could be relied on to mount a powerful challenge to the proposals, and to carry their parties with them, the numerical strength of their supporters would not be enough to secure the deletion of the clause unless they were joined by a sufficient number of Conservatives and cross-benchers.

The uncertainty was resolved on the third day in Committee when the main debate was on whether clause 32 (the effect of the accused's failure to mention facts when questioned or charged) should stand part of the Bill. Lord Taylor spoke early and emphatically, putting all the weight of his office behind the proposed changes. Although expressing his personal views, he knew that they were shared by very many judges. Despite frequent, loose assertions to the contrary, he said, the Bill did not abolish the right of silence. Under its provisions a suspect or accused person was still entitled to remain silent. Silence constituted neither a criminal offence nor a contempt of court. He did not agree that the proposals would shift or lighten the burden of proof resting on the Crown. The initial burden to establish a *prima facie* case depended on evidence other than the mere silence of the defendant. Unless that was present there would be no case to answer and none of the provisions as to comment on silence would come into play. If the case did go the full distance the question at the end was whether the prosecution had 'established the guilt of the defendant so as to make the court or jury sure of it'.[8]

Anxiety had been expressed about the vulnerable or very young defendants who might be disadvantaged. In such cases it would be for the judge to use his discretion, in fairness to a particular defendant, to direct the jury on whether or not any adverse influence should be drawn from silence, and if so at what strength. If the judge, in a case which called for an indication to the jury that no adverse inference should be drawn, failed to tell the jury so, the

---

[8] *Parl. Debates*, HL, 555, cols. 519–20, 23 May 1994.

Court of Appeal was there to correct any misdirection.[9] The provisions in the Bill, however, were not aimed at vulnerable defendants nor the common run of first offenders. It was the experienced criminals charged with very serious offences who most frequently declined to answer any questions, and it was against them that the proposals were directed, and properly so in the view of the Lord Chief Justice.

Taylor's speech made a deep impression. He was followed immediately by Lord Carlisle of Bucklow, a QC and former Conservative Minister[10] with long experience of prosecuting and defending in the criminal courts. Carlisle's opinion that the balance had been 'tipped too far evidentially in the interests of the accused'[11] ran contrary to the collective views of JUSTICE, of which he was a Vice-President, and the Bar Council, of which he was a member. Coming from such an authoritative source with a known sympathy towards penal reform, his intervention was a counterweight to Alexander and Williams of Mostyn, both former Chairmen of the Bar Council who had opposed the change on Second Reading. By the time Hailsham spoke the likelihood of the Government losing the clause was ebbing fast. He said that he had not been persuaded by the arguments against the proposal. If he thought for a moment that the right of silence, which was a matter of legal procedure and evidence, would be in any way watered down by the clauses in the Bill he would certainly have been in the ranks of those who would have them expunged; but he did not. The argument put forward by the Lord Chief Justice seemed to him to be absolutely conclusive.[12]

Earlier in the debate Alexander had reiterated that interfering with the exercise of the right of silence by changing the emphasis in questioning by the police carried the risk of convicting the innocent. He was less concerned about the hardened criminals who would continue to play the system whatever the law and whatever safeguards were in force. The research which had been carried out for the Royal Commission showed that typical suspects were neither intelligent nor lucid. For many of them a police station was a

---

[9] Ibid., col. 521.

[10] Parliamentary Under-Secretary of State 1970–2; Minister of State 1972–4, Home Office; Secretary of State for Education and Science 1979–81. Chairman: Conservative Home Affairs Committee, House of Commons 1983–7; Parole Review Committee 1987–8; Criminal Injuries Compensation Board, 1989–. Recorder of the Crown Court 1976–9 and 1981–.

[11] *Parl. Debates*, HL, 555, cols. 523–4.   [12] Ibid., cols. 529–30.

strange and intimidating place.[13] In winding up, Runciman asked members of the Committee to consider whether they believed after all they had heard that the risk of wrongful convictions would not be significantly increased if the Bill passed in its present form.[14] He made it abundantly clear, as had Alexander, that he was in favour of defence disclosure, the subject of a separate amendment, so that well before a trial, when the prosecution case was known and the defendant had access to legal advice, he should be required to indicate the nature of his defence. This would deal with the possibility of ambush defences being raised without warning during the trial.[15] If the defendant failed to do so, or at the trial substantially departed from what had been disclosed, then it would be open to the court to draw such inferences as appeared proper.

Replying for the Government, Ferrers accepted that defence disclosure was a relevant factor which he said was under consideration by the Government in preparing its reply to the Royal Commission's recommendations. Important practical questions needed to be resolved before Parliament embarked on a decision. They had not yet been resolved. The amendment was not appropriate for incorporation in the Bill.[16] When the division came the Government's case prevailed, the main clause affecting the exercise of silence at the pre-trial stages being retained in the Bill by a majority of 176 to 114 votes.

That the issue was not entirely disposed of was shown in a coalition which had been forming between some of the speakers who were in favour of modifying the right of silence in the way proposed, and those who wished to uphold the status quo. Peers on both sides of the substantive argument had stressed the importance of adequate safeguards for suspects, especially during the early stages of police investigation. Ackner and Campbell of Alloway, both of whom had voted with the Government in Committee, had put down separate amendments, warning that they intended to return to the matter on Report. Taylor also had stated that he wished to see safeguards for the suspect put in place before attach-

---

[13] *Parl. Debates*, HL, 555, col. 516.   [14] Ibid., col 535.

[15] For a note on so-called 'ambush' defences (p. 19) and a general commentary on the provisions of Part III of the Criminal Justice and Public Order Act 1994 (Sections 31–53) see J. Morton, *A Guide to the Criminal Justice and Public Order Act 1994*, Butterworths, London, Dublin, Edinburgh, 1994, pp. 17–32. James Morton is Editor of the *New Law Journal*.

[16] HL, 555, cols. 533–4.

ing any risk to silence. The question was how far safeguards should go. Ackner's amendment was the most far-reaching. In his view, the obligation upon the courts to see that the accused was treated fairly would not be achieved unless he had been given the opportunity to consult a lawyer, unless he was told in a broad manner why he was being brought to the police station, and unless he was made aware of the sort of questions he was going to be asked.[17] In the original version of his amendment the accused's lawyer would have to be present at the interrogation, unless it had been stated in writing that his services were not wanted. A tape-recording of the interrogation would be obligatory.

Ackner had been invited to meet the Home Secretary to discuss the proposed safeguards, but had found Howard unforthcoming. The presence of a lawyer in particular seemed to be a sticking point, but a further objection was that the tape-recording requirement would mean in practice that the initial questioning would have to take place at the police station rather than at the scene of the crime. Ackner sought to meet the latter objection on Report by altering the wording of his amendment to require a contemporaneous record of the interrogation, authenticated by the lawyer. He also added a requirement that the suspect be informed of the purpose and nature of the questions to be asked, a responsibility on the part of the constable to make clear the possible effect of his failure to mention any fact later relied upon by way of defence. Both requirements were incorporated in Campbell's amendment, which omitted the presence of a lawyer if requested. When replying to the debate in Committee Ferrers had left the door open, saying that the Government did not consider that it had a monopoly of wisdom on the matter, and wanted to listen to what was said about safeguards before reaching a decision.[18]

The House returned to the issue at the start of the second day on Report. Once again Taylor's speech convinced any waverers. Since the Committee stage he had made a number of suggestions to the Home Secretary. As a result, the Government had agreed to move an amendment of its own requiring a new form of caution to be given before a suspect's silence could feature in the evidence against him. The wording of the caution would make it clear to the suspect that the law had changed and that he might no longer be safe in

---

[17] Ibid., col. 498.   [18] Ibid., col. 530.

refusing to give any account of himself.[19] The very fact that a caution had to be administered would ensure that the changes being introduced in the exercise of the right of silence would apply only to someone under active suspicion of being involved in criminal activity. The Government had also given an undertaking that the Codes of Practice under the Police and Criminal Evidence Act 1984 (PACE) would be amended to provide for a post-validation interview on arrival at the police station. A validation requirement, in which the suspect, having been cautioned, would be asked whether he wished to confirm, deny, or modify any earlier statement or silence, was in line with the approach recommended by the Royal Commission on Criminal Justice. In the opinion of the Lord Chief Justice it would: 'enhance the reliability of evidence not only as to silence but as to any significant statement made before arrival at the police station upon which the prosecution seek to rely. In my view it will represent a very significant improvement in our criminal procedure and one which it is both proper and desirable to achieve through amendment to the codes of practice under PACE rather than in primary legislation.'[20]

These additional provisions satisfied Taylor's previously expressed reservations and he urged the House to support the Government's stance. While appreciating the anxieties of Ackner and others, he thought it was going too far to remove the possibility of any inference being drawn from silence until the suspect had reached the police station. A surprise intervention came from Lowry, who lived up to the comment he had made in the Second Reading debate that, while inclined to favour the clauses modifying the right of silence, his attitude was not one of blind acceptance of their entire contents. Now, after the lengthy discussion on safeguards in Committee and the Government's response at Report stage, Lowry reminded the House that matters of principle were still the main focus.

Unfairness, he said, could arise even under a fair system.

---

[19] During the passage of the Bill the Home Office announced the wording of a new caution in the following terms: 'You do not have to say anything. But if you do not mention now something which you later use in your defence, the court may decide that your failure to mention it now strengthens the case against you. A record will be made of anything you say and it may be given in evidence if you are brought to trial.' J. Morton, *A Guide to the Criminal Justice and Public Order Act 1994, op. cit.*, p. 22.

[20] *Parl. Debates*, HL, 556, col. 1401, 7 July 1994.

Parliament had to avoid legislating for a system which is itself unfair or which leads easily to unfairness. In his submission, the clauses on pre-trial questioning, while not in themselves unfair, would lead easily to unfairness unless amended as proposed. Recordings and the presence of legal advisers were of particular importance in verifying evidence. Additionally, he believed that the use of the silence procedure to create a *prima facie* case eroded the standard of proof. He would rather dispense with the clauses altogether than accept them without amendment.[21] For two chief justices to come to such markedly different conclusions showed that the principles underlying the controversy were open to more than one legitimate interpretation by those with the greatest experience of criminal procedure. In the division that followed Taylor and Lowry voted in opposing lobbies. The only current Lord of Appeal in Ordinary to vote was Lord Mustill[22] who supported Ackner's amendment, whereas Hailsham and a former Lord of Appeal, Lord Simon of Glaisdale,[23] went with the Government. The amendment was defeated by 143 votes to 91.

II

Far more than the discussion on other controversial parts of the Bill, the clash on the right of silence was symbolic. In practice the right of silence is an instrument of only limited value for the protection of suspects because of police pressure on them to waive their right. Research carried out for the Royal Commission on Criminal Justice indicated that the right of silence is rarely exercised, and that of those who do exercise it about half are convicted.[24] Some

[21] Ibid., cols. 1412–4.

[22] Judge of the High Court, Queen's Bench Division 1978–85; Lord Justice of Appeal 1985–92; Lord of Appeal in Ordinary 1992–; Chairman of the Judicial Studies Board 1985–9. Lord Mustill had been a member of the Appellate Committee hearing a Northern Ireland appeal to the House of Lords, in which he had made some observations about the meaning of a *prima facie* case and the inferences to be drawn from the silence of the accused. *Murray* v. *Director of Public Prosecutions* (1993) 97 Cr. App. R. 151.

[23] Solicitor General 1959–62. President of the Probate, Divorce and Admiralty Division of the High Court 1962–71; Lord of Appeal in Ordinary 1971–7.

[24] Royal Commission on Criminal Justice, *The Right to Silence in Police Interrogation: A Study of some of the Issues Underlying the Debate*, Research Study No. 10 by R. Leng, HMSO, London, 1993, p. 79.

commentators anticipated that the sections of the Act on the inferences which might be drawn from the silence of the accused when questioned at the pre-trial stages were likely to leave untouched the professional criminal who knows the ropes and is legally represented.[25] Yet to the police the questioning of suspects is a key ingredient in the investigation of crime. It is understandable that they should resist any procedures which they regard as hindering them in bringing those suspected of having committed criminal offences before the courts. At the same time, as the notorious miscarriage of justice cases had shown so vividly, there is always a possibility that police officers in their zeal to bring offenders to justice may use the interrogation of suspects as a means of obtaining confirmation of what they already believe to have happened. So-called 'noble cause' corruption runs deep.[26]

From the moment the Home Secretary first announced his intention of modifying the right of silence it was inevitable that the proposal would be intensely controversial. Neither in Parliament nor outside was there any likelihood of the debate being confined to a comparison of the functional pros and cons. Political considerations intruded, but the arguments went deeper than party politics. In the end, the issue turned on values.[27]

Behind the protracted debates in the House of Lords on the right of silence lay a nagging question. Sometimes it was articulated; more often it remained latent. However, it was lodged in the minds of many of the more thoughtful participators. What effect would curtailing the right of silence have in future on the presumption of innocence and the criminal standard of proof necessary for a criminal conviction? Would the failure or outright refusal of an accused

[25] See J. Morton in *A Guide to the Criminal Justice and Public Order Act 1994*, *op. cit.*, p. 19.

[26] In oral evidence to a Parliamentary Committee the Commissioner of Police of the Metropolis, Paul Condon, rejected an opinion attributed to a national official of the Police Federation that there was nothing wrong with perjury committed by an honest police officer with good intentions: '. . . police officers talk of something which we call "noble cause corruption", the essence of which is that the end justifies the means and, of course, it does not and never can.' House of Commons, Session 1992–93, Home Affairs Committee, *Policing*, Minutes of Evidence, 24 Mar. 1993, (HC 363–ii), HMSO, London, 1993, Q 161, p. 26.

[27] For a discussion of the place of values in the administration of criminal justice, with particular reference to the pre-trial phase, see A. Ashworth, *The Criminal Process: An Evaluative Study*, Clarendon Press, Oxford, 1994.

person to answer questions when first interrogated, without access to legal advice and possibly unaware of what the police had against him or the grounds of their suspicion, be taken as an inference of guilt? That was the conclusion of the most senior prosecuting counsel at the Central Criminal Court whose written Opinion had been sought by JUSTICE:

In my view clauses [Sections 34 and 35 of the Criminal Justice and Public Order Act 1994] affect the presumption of innocence in two ways. First, separately and jointly, they place pressure on an accused in the police station and at trial to provide an explanation in ways unknown hitherto to our system of criminal justice. Secondly, they allow the prosecutor to capitalize on the accused's failure to provide an explanation if he resists the pressure at either stage in ways unknown, hitherto, to our system of criminal justice. No jury would understand that the onus of proof remains at all times on the prosecution if the law expects an innocent explanation from an accused on pain of an inference of guilt if it is not forthcoming.[28]

As already noted Lowry, with his experience of the procedures in Northern Ireland, took a similar view. The Government's rejoinder was that the clauses would leave untouched the principles that the defendant's guilt should be proved beyond reasonable doubt and that the burden of proof should be on the prosecution. A person would not be committed for trial, have a case to answer, or be convicted of an offence solely on an inference drawn from silence. There had to be other evidence against him. If there was sufficient other evidence to constitute a *prima facie* case[29] strong enough to go to a jury, then his silence could be treated by the court or jury as supporting the other evidence for the purpose of deciding whether or not his guilt was established beyond reasonable doubt. Again and again throughout the debates ministerial spokesmen insisted that there was no question of convicting anyone on the basis of silence alone. What the legislation was intended to do, they argued, was to remove the 'special protection'[30] afforded to a

---

[28] R. D. Amlot QC, Junior Prosecuting Counsel to the Crown, Central Criminal Court 1977–81; Senior Prosecuting Counsel 1981–7; First Senior Prosecuting Counsel 1987–.

[29] In *Murray* Lord Mustill defined a *prima facie* case as one 'strong enough to go to a jury, i.e. a case consisting of direct evidence which, if believed and combined with legitimate inferences based upon it, could lead a properly directed jury to be satisfied beyond reasonable doubt (or whatever other formula is preferred) that each of the essential elements of the offence is proved'. (1993) 97 Cr. App. R. at 154.

[30] *Parl. Debates*, HL, 554, col. 383.

defendant by virtue of the trial judge's obligation to warn the jury not to assume that because he had refused to answer questions, or to give evidence, that he was guilty. No one would be compelled to answer questions or to give evidence in court.

The evidential effect of the 1994 legislation on criminal trials in the future will be that the defendant's silence, while not sufficient to obtain a conviction in the absence of other evidence, may be sufficient to convert a provable prosecution case into one which is actually proved.[31] That, however, will be only the tip of the procedural iceberg. A criminal trial contains within it a series of checks and balances which have accumulated piecemeal. The prohibition against adverse comment is a part of a linked series and it is impossible to forecast what repercussions its removal may have. Much will depend how the judges use their discretion. It is conceivable that adverse inferences from silence in the face of police questioning at the pre-trial stage might be allowed at the trial only if the judge is satisfied that the defendant had been fairly treated by being made aware of the case he had to answer. Without knowing the allegations and evidence against him, the initial questioning of a suspect could become a one-sided process contributing to his self-incrimination. The refusal of ministers to accept any amendment providing that a suspect should be informed of the purpose and nature of the questions he is to be asked could yet blunt the intended cutting edge of the new policy.

Conversely, the Government's determination to restrict the use of silence may pave the way for further encroachments on the procedural rights of defendants. While listening to the debates in the Lords, in which the two opposing sides were so deeply entrenched as to leave no middle ground, I wondered more than once whether the scene that was unfolding marked the first steps, unintentional perhaps, but not hesitantly taken either, towards a shift from the criminal standard of proof (beyond reasonable doubt) towards the lesser standard required in civil actions (the balance of probability). There was no doubt which was closer to Howard's proclaimed objective of strengthening the prosecution and convicting more criminals.

In September, before the Commons considered the Lords' amendments the following month, I wrote to the Home Secretary

---

[31] Cf. Lord Mustill in *Murray* at 155.

to say that while the changes announced at Report stage on 7 July fell short of the degree of protection sought in the Ackner amendment, nonetheless they were worthwhile improvements. The only outstanding point was that once cautioned the suspect should be made aware of the purpose and nature of the questions he was to be asked at the initial interrogation. Was it intended that this objective should be achieved by way of amending the PACE Codes of Practice, as with the validation interview, rather than by primary legislation? Or could it be provided for in some other way? The inquiry fell on stony ground.

Home Secretary   Queen Anne's Gate London SW1H 9AT
12 September 1994

Dear David

Thank you for your letter of 6 September.

You suggest, in connection with the provisions of the Criminal Justice and Public Order Bill on inferences from silence, that a means should be found to ensure that the police inform a suspect at the outset of an interview of the purpose and nature of the questions that he is to be asked; and that this matter is in some sense left over from the debates on the Bill.

This aspect of Lord Ackner's amendment was, however, specifically addressed by Robin Ferrers, on behalf of the Government, at Report Stage (7 July, Column 1395, extract attached). I regard the question as having been settled by the House's rejection of the Ackner amendment.

As Robin Ferrers explained, it will be open to a defendant to explain that he did not understand the significance of the questions that were put to him by the police; and it will then be open to the court to find under Clause 34 of the Bill that the matter was *not* one which he could reasonably have been expected to mention at the time. We think that that is the right way of dealing with the question which you have raised, and that it would not be helpful to prescribe a rigid set of requirements for the police to follow in every case, either in the Bill itself or in the revised Codes of Practice under the Police and Criminal Evidence Act for which we have recently published proposals.

Yours ever
Michael

In the Hansard extract attached with the Home Secretary's letter, Ferrers stated explicitly that the Ackner amendment would oblige the police to put a good many of their cards on the table at the beginning of every interview. He doubted whether that would be sensible.

III

The usual channels in the Lords, the leaders and whips of the main parties and a representative of the cross-bench peers, had agreed that adequate time should be allowed for discussion of the main proposals which attracted the keenest interest. The Government's business managers accepted an extended timetable in the belief that it was the best way to secure the Bill's primary goals, but as the weeks went by and the schedule began to slip relationships with ministers in the Commons became increasingly testy as the prospect waned of getting the Bill back to the Commons in time for the amendments made by the Lords to be considered before the House adjourned for the Summer Recess. While it had been apparent from the start that the secure training order and the right of silence were substantial issues which would call for full debate, it was the omnibus nature of the legislation that permitted the attempted or actual addition of so many extra items.

The force of public opinion resulted in three non-party issues touching on social order being brought before Parliament while the Bill was under consideration. The business managers decided that each should be subject either to free votes in both Houses or to agreement between the parties. These issues were: the age of consent for homosexual acts in private; the ban on the use of cells from embryos or foetuses for fertility treatment; and the availability for rental or sale of violent or potentially harmful videos. On other matters not included in the Bill the Government either had no settled policy (the sale of confidential financial information) or was in agreement with the aim but opposed to the method (the reduction of smoking through a statutory ban on the advertising of tobacco products), or had adopted a controversial policy which was being challenged head-on (the altered arrangements for criminal injuries compensation).

A cross-party alliance, with a leading Roman Catholic layman, the Duke of Norfolk,[32] in the vanguard, made a well organized and well publicized attempt to resist lowering the age of consent to homosexual acts below twenty-one. After rehearsing again the arguments previously deployed in the Commons, the Lords

---

[32] Earl Marshal of England since 1975.

accepted the same compromise by voting to reduce to eighteen the age at which males may lawfully perform consenting homosexual acts in private, but not to go as far as sixteen.[33] If either party was under eighteen both would continue to be liable to prosecution regardless of consent.

Deliberation was also given to the ethically difficult question of whether the use of foetal eggs for the treatment of infertility in women should be forbidden by law, and the implications of the signals sent out by the new clause added so perfunctorily in the Commons at a time when active consultation was still in progress with the medical and scientific bodies. Following debates initiated by Lord Walton of Detchant,[34] both in Committee[35] and on Report,[36] the Lords decided to retain the clause promoted by Dame Jill Knight, although not without voting on the issue.[37] Medical peers were seen in action again in an unsuccessful attempt to ban tobacco advertising. Such an improbable subject for inclusion in criminal justice legislation was but the most conspicuous of several examples of the latitude permitted by the drafting of the long title of the Bill. It also reflected a relaxation in the strict interpretation of the doctrine of relevance in the aftermath of the pressure put on the House authorities in the Commons by the Government to facilitate the late additions to the previous Criminal Justice Bill in 1993.

Faced with the evidence that advertising attracts new smokers, particularly among young people, the Government had made a voluntary agreement with the tobacco industry aimed at protecting children aged between eleven and fifteen who were taking up smoking. The need for protection was underlined by scientific research showing that a child who begins to smoke before the age of fifteen is eighteen times more likely to die of lung cancer than someone

---

[33] *Parl. Debates*, HL, 556, cols. 47–9 and 58–60, 20 June 1994. Section 145 of the Criminal Justice and Public Order Act 1994 amended the Sexual Offences Act 1967 by substituting the age of eighteen for twenty-one. Similar amendments were made to the Scottish and Northern Ireland legislation.

[34] President, British Medical Association 1980–2; General Medical Council 1982–9; Royal Society of Medicine 1984–6. Warden, Green College, Oxford 1983–9.

[35] *Parl. Debates*, HL, 555, cols. 1941–56, 16 June 1994.

[36] *Parl. Debates*, HL, 556, cols. 1752–66, 12 July 1994.

[37] Section 156 of the Criminal and Public Order Act 1994 amended the Human Fertilisation and Embryology Act 1990 by prohibiting, for the purpose of providing fertility services for women, the use of female germ cells taken or derived from an embryo or a foetus, or the use of embryos created by using such cells. The maximum penalty for this offence is ten years' imprisonment, an unlimited fine, or both.

who had never smoked.[38] Whereas the Department of Health had set a target of reducing smoking rates among eleven to fifteen year-olds by one-third from 1988 to 1994, there was no prospect of it being achieved. Over the last ten years there had been no significant change in children's smoking rates. Some 24 per cent of fifteen year-olds were smoking in 1982 and the figure for 1992 was virtually unchanged.[39]

The British Medical Association, supported by the Imperial Cancer Research Fund and numerous medical, health, and other organizations, regarded voluntary agreements as ineffective since the industry would always be reluctant to agree to any measure which genuinely restricted the consumption of their products. A Private Member's Bill in the Commons having made no progress, three peers with medical backgrounds, Lords McColl (a surgeon), Walton (a neurologist), and Rea (a retired general practitioner) decided to make a further attempt to ban tobacco advertising by means of cross-bench sponsored amendments to the Criminal Justice and Public Order Bill. The pretext was that although advertising was not the only factor to influence the commencement and continuation of smoking by children, it was the only factor which was solely under the control of Parliament.

The debates provoked by their amendments were some of the most passionate on the Bill. Against the heartfelt desire of many peers, whether medically qualified or laymen, to do anything possible to reduce smoking and the diseases associated with it, was set the argument that if the smoking of tobacco products was not illegal it was wrong in a free society to ban its advertising. Against the freedom of the individual to smoke as a matter of choice was set the inconvenience, sometimes the acute distress, caused to others. Personal reminiscences of peers who had smoked for half a century or more were matched by peers who had given it up. A sub-theme rumbling throughout the exchanges both in Committee and on Report was the inappropriateness of seeking to tack the contents of a previous Private Member's Bill onto an already over-

---

[38] Letter from Sir Walter Bodmer, Director-General, Imperial Cancer Research Fund, 1 June 1994. Those who begin smoking after age twenty-five are (only) five times more likely to die of lung cancer than non-smokers.

[39] Lord McColl, Professor of Surgery, United Medical Schools of Guy's and St Thomas' Hospitals, *Parl. Debates*, HL, 556, col. 109, 20 June 1994.

cluttered measure aimed at dealing with the pressing problems of criminal offending and public order.

In replying for the Government the Junior Health Minister, Baroness Cumberlege, had a difficult path to tread. She did not want there to be any doubt about the importance the Government attached to reducing the level of smoking. Despite the assertions of some speakers to the contrary, the overwhelming body of medical and scientific evidence showed that smoking had a devastating effect on health. It was a serious cause for concern. The Government's strategy to reduce the consumption of tobacco covered the whole range of influences on smoking, by both adults and children. She claimed it was having an effect and that statistics showed the number of people who smoke and the amount of cigarettes sold was falling. New voluntary controls on advertising would shortly be implemented, and the question before the House was whether the evidence justified the further steps set out in the amendments. Their effect would be not just a total ban but the criminalization of tobacco advertising. Those countries in Europe which already had banned tobacco advertising, or which supported a Europe-wide ban, had not found a guarantee of reducing smoking. None of them had a record which compared with that of the United Kingdom, and in some smoking was still increasing. The Government remained convinced that its voluntary approach was correct. She did not believe that the case for the amendments had been made.[40] By a majority of over two to one the House agreed with the Minister's exposition, the amendments being rejected on Report by 51 votes in favour to 117 against.

IV

More closely connected with offending was the Home Secretary's undertaking, given to David Alton in the Commons, to include statutory criteria which the designated authority, the British Board of Film Censors (BBFC), must take into account when considering the classification of videos and the grant of certificates. Hard thought had been given to the drafting and to the desirability of leaving with the BBFC a discretion in classifying videos; provided

[40] *Parl. Debates*, HL, 555, cols. 1732–6, 12 July 1994.

that 'special regard', and not just regard, had been given to a number of prescribed factors. In this it differed from the original Alton amendment which would have had the effect that if a video was psychologically harmful to a child, or presented an inappropriate model for children, then it could not be certified at all for home viewing. The device adopted by a Government amendment introduced in the Lords was to amend the Video Recordings Act 1984 by providing that any harm which might be caused to potential viewers, including children or young persons, or through their behaviour to society should be related to the way a video portrayed a number of factors. These were: criminal behaviour; illegal drugs; violent behaviour or incidents; horrific behaviour or incidents; and human sexual activity. Violent behaviour was defined as including any act inflicting or likely to result in the infliction of injury.[41]

The BBFC had been consulted over the drafting and had pressed for the addition of illegal drug use to the list. One of its Vice-Presidents, Lord Birkett,[42] vigorously supported the Government's proposals in the debates at Report stage and on Third Reading. Once the matter of the regulation of video recordings had been brought before Parliament, the Board wanted to go further in two respects. A loophole existed in the present system, Birkett said, in that a large number of videos were exempt by law from being classified if, taken as a whole, the work was (a) designed to inform, educate, or instruct; (b) concerned with sport, religion, or music; or (c) was a video game.[43] Exemption was forfeit only on grounds specified in the Video Recordings Act 1984.[44]

Sensible as it was that there should be exemptions for these general categories, some unexpected difficulties had arisen. Music and instructional videos, amongst others, were entirely exempt provided they did not offend against the specified factors. Yet they could be highly objectionable. Examples cited were an instructional video

[41] These provisions are incorporated in Section 90 of the Criminal Justice and Public Order Act 1994.

[42] Deputy Director, National Theatre 1975–7; Director for Recreation and Arts, Greater London Council 1976–86; Adviser to South Bank Board 1986–9. A Vice-President of the British Board of Film Classification, 1985–.

[43] Section 2(1) of the Video Recordings Act 1984.

[44] Section 2(2) of the Video Recordings Act 1984 provides that exemption is forfeit if to any significant extent a work depicts: '(a) human sexual activity or acts of force or restraint associated with such activity; (b) mutilation or torture of, or other acts of gross violence towards, humans or animals; and (c) human genital organs or human urinary or excretory functions.'

demonstrating bomb-making techniques and the use of explosives; a martial arts video on how to kill with a single blow; and pop music videos including references to and depictions of the illegal use of drugs and other matters blatantly unsuitable for children. The BBFC had drafted an amendment, moved by Birkett on Report, which retained the principle of exclusions but which broadened the grounds for forfeiture of exempted status. Ferrers agreed that it would be right to strengthen the system of regulation, but had some reservations about the drafting. Nevertheless, both on the need to close the loophole and also on Birkett's second amendment to enable the Board to give additional guidance to parents on videos that were particularly suitable for viewing by young children, he gave a clear indication that the purpose behind the amendments was likely to be acceptable to ministers.[45]

In the same debate an attempt was made to introduce an element of retrospection into the new procedures.[46] Lord Elton pointed out that a large amount of unsuitable material already in circulation would be left untouched. It included some infamous videos which were believed, by the press at least, to have contributed to the actions of those who had committed some of the most notorious of recent crimes.[47] He wanted a way to be found for the classification of these videos to be reviewed by the BBFC against the new statutory criteria. The mechanism suggested for selecting the offending titles from the many thousands of certificated videos already in circulation, in private ownership as well as stock held for sale or hire, got short shrift. Looking to the model of the Ombudsman, Elton proposed that for a fixed period after the legislation had come into effect Members of Parliament should act as the channel for complaints about videos, forwarding them to the BBFC where the certificates could be reconsidered with a view to reclassification or declassification. Neither the Home Office nor the BBFC regarded the scheme as workable, and the amendment was withdrawn.

At Third Reading Birkett's two amendments were accepted, the wording having been redrafted by the Government in the interval. The category of video recordings generally exempt from the

---

[45] *Parl. Debates*, HL, 556, col. 1591, 11 July 1994.

[46] Ibid., cols. 1592–4.

[47] The suggested connection between a video titled *Child's Play 3* and the two boys who abducted and murdered James Bulger was investigated by the police who found no evidence that the video was in any way responsible for the terrible crime, or that either of the boys had ever seen it. *Parl. Debates*, HL, 556, col. 1599.

requirement for classification by the BBFC was revised by extending the list of activities which, if depicted to any significant extent, would remove the video from the exempt category. The changes included techniques likely to be useful in the depiction of the commission of criminal activity, and the depiction of the commission of criminal activity itself when it would be likely to encourage offending.[48] The Bill was also amended to make clear that the BBFC might issue a certificate indicating that a video was especially suitable for viewing by young children.[49]

Elton returned to the issue of retrospection on Third Reading, pointing out that since the previous debate the Home Affairs Committee of the House of Commons had recommended that the Government should think again about its opposition to a transitional scheme whereby a small number of videos which cause great public anxiety could be reclassified under the new criteria.[50] David Alton, with whom Elton had kept in close touch while the issue was before the Lords, made the same point when the Commons considered the Lords amendments to the Bill. The outcome was an agreed amendment to the Video Recordings Act 1984 enabling the Home Secretary to make an order permitting the BBFC to review any classification decision made before the 1994 Act came into force. The selection of videos for re-examination would be at the BBFC's discretion. Following a review, it would be able to cancel any certificate issued before the new criteria came into effect and issue a new and different classification certificate if it thought fit.[51]

Although the new provisions on the regulation of video recordings which finally became law were some way removed from the amendment which Alton had initiated earlier in the year, he and his supporters had succeeded in their overall aim to galvanize the Government into some sort of legislative action. Unusually for a minister so alert to the state of public opinion and so ready to adjust his policies accordingly, Howard's instinctive response, that a tightening up of enforcement was the furthest he was prepared to

[48] Section 89 of the Criminal Justice and Public Order Act 1994 amending Section 2 of the Video Recordings Act 1984.

[49] Section 90 of the Criminal Justice and Public Order Act 1994 amending Section 7(2) of the Video Recordings Act 1984.

[50] House of Commons, Session 1993–94, Home Affairs Committee, Fourth Report, *Video Violence and Young Offenders*, (HC 514), HMSO, London, 1994, p. x.

[51] Criminal Justice and Public Order Act 1994, Section 90(1).

go, later supplemented by a characteristic resort to an increase in maximum penalties,[52] met neither the popular nor the political demand. Much of the public head of steam was in fact based on a misconception. The phrase 'video nasties' had been coined ten years before to describe some particularly unpleasant videos which had always been refused a certificate. To the BBFC, if not to the general public, a video nasty was a video too nasty to receive a certificate at all.[53]

The lukewarm approach of the Home Office towards the further regulation of video recordings was influenced by two factors. The Bill was already so long and diffuse, and taking up so much Parliamentary time, that ministers and officials alike were reluctant to widen its ambit still further by adding new measures not directly related to its central purposes. More important was a recognition of the limitations of legislative enactments in changing established patterns of behaviour. The reality was that the effectiveness of any system of regulation by certifying videos for viewing by children and young people would depend less on the process of classification than on the response of parents. The BBFC conscientiously gave carefully thought-out advice, sometimes debated and thrashed out for weeks before being made official in the form of a certificate. Time and again it was dismayed to find parents not just ignoring its advice, but denying or being unaware of the existence of such advice. Unless and until that situation changed it was unrealistic to expect that altering the Board's certification procedures, and the criteria to which special regard must be given by law, would be likely to have any widespread impact on the type of material viewed by children in their homes.

---

[52] Section 88 of the Criminal Justice and Public Order Act 1994 increased the penalties for supplying videos of unclassified work on conviction on indictment to a term of imprisonment not exceeding two years, a fine, or both, and on summary conviction to a term of imprisonment not exceeding six months, a fine not exceeding £20,000, or both. Similar penalties applied to the offence of possessing videos of unclassified work for supply. The penalties for three other offences: supplying videos in breach of classification, supplying videos in places other than licensed sex shops, and supplying videos with false indication of classification, were increased on summary conviction to a term of imprisonment not exceeding six months or a fine not exceeding level 5 on the standard scale or both. Section 15 of the Video Recordings Act 1984 did not include any penalties of imprisonment.

[53] Letter to the author from Lord Birkett, July 1994.

V

Apart from the time-consuming controversies decided by free votes and the variations in the secure training order and the right of silence, the Lords made three more changes to the Bill which were unwelcome to the Government and resulted from defeats in the division lobbies. The first and most sweeping was a rejection of the high-handed and arguably unconstitutional introduction of a new system of financial compensation for injuries resulting from violent crime while the existing system remained unimplemented on the statute book. The non-statutory origins of the Criminal Injuries Compensation Board (CICB), set up in 1964 to administer a discretionary scheme, and the tardy legislative cover which followed nearly a quarter of a century later in the Criminal Justice Act 1988, are discussed in Chapter 11. Since its inception claims from a sharply rising number of victims of crime had been assessed by practising lawyers experienced in personal injuries work, usually Queen's Counsel, who decided the amount of *ex gratia* compensation on the basis of the common law damages which would have been awarded for the victim's injuries in a civil action against his or her assailant.

The consistently upward trend in the amount of public money committed to an open-ended system of compensation reached £166 million in the year 1992–3.[54] Augmented by the long delays in processing claims,[55] it was the cost factor more than any other which had led to the postponement in implementing the relevant parts of the Criminal Justice Act 1988. Well before then, however, officials at the Home Office had been sceptical of the long-term viability of a system of compensation based on common law damages. The cause of their scepticism, on the mark as later events were to

[54] In that year expenditure on compensation amounted to £152.5 million and expenditure on administration to £14.2 million, making a total of £166.7 million. Home Office, *Annual Report 1994*, including the Government's expenditure plans 1994–95 to 1996–97 for the Home Office and the Charity Commission (Cm. 2508), HMSO, London, 1994, p. 53.

[55] The number of cases outstanding had reached 87,780 in 1989–90. In a critical report the Home Affairs Committee of the House of Commons commented that the 'scandalous backlog' meant that a system designed to help victims was instead frustrating them. House of Commons, Session 1989–90, Home Affairs Committee, Second Report, *Compensating Victims Quickly: The Administration of the Criminal Injuries Compensation Board* (HC 92), HMSO, London, 1990, p. xvi.

demonstrate, was that in the economic and financial climate, with tightening constraints on public expenditure, it was unlikely that the arrangement could be sustained indefinitely. The ministers of the day were aware of these reservations but had felt obliged to legislate in 1987–8 in order to legitimize such a large head of expenditure as a matter of public accounting, while displaying their concern for victims. It would be politically unacceptable, they decided, to do so on any basis other than the existing scheme.

The non-implementation of the statutory provisions on compensation was an instance of how administrative or financial problems experienced by a Government Department or public body can thwart the declared intention of Parliament.[56] What was exceptional was the intention of the Government, announced in November 1992, to introduce a new and less generous scheme by executive action while the existing scheme based on common law damages was still incorporated in a statute that had been neither implemented nor repealed. Chapter 11 gives a full account of the legal challenge which followed, and unravels the confusing sequence of events caused by one of the most inept changes of direction in penal policy for many years.

There was no reference to compensation for criminal injuries in the Bill as published, nor in the amended version passed by the Commons. On Report Tony Blair had severely criticized the Government's policy, calling for the withdrawal of the proposed new scheme until one which better protected the interests of the victim could be devised after proper consultation.[57] Ministers dismissed his plea, turning a deaf ear to the mounting volume of protest from sectors of the legal profession and the main interest groups whose members would be affected by the projected change. The objections were twofold: the constitutional propriety of what was proposed and the operation of the new system in practice. Whereas previously victims of crime had been compensated on the basis of individual assessment, in future a tariff-based scheme would band injuries together according to their relative seriousness, making compensation awards of a fixed sum for a particular injury. There was no consensus on whether a flat-rate tariff might or might

[56] The non-implementation of statutory provisions, with examples of statutes not brought into force, or only partially brought into force, is explored further in Chapter 11, below.

[57] *Parl. Debates*, HC 240, (6th ser.), col. 669, 28 Mar. 1994.

not prove to be quicker and less costly than the system of individual assessment based on common law damages,[58] but of its nature it was incapable of taking account of the differing impact of broadly similar injuries on different people according to their individual circumstances. Nor would it allow for loss of earnings or future earning capacity.

The first ground for objection, the lawfulness of the Home Secretary's decision to introduce a new scheme in the exercise of his ministerial discretion disregarding the provisions of the 1988 Act, led to an application to the courts for judicial review of his decision. Eventually the case was to reach the House of Lords in its judicial capacity,[59] but at the time the Bill was in Committee it had got no further than the first round. This went to Howard, with the Divisional Court finding that the power to activate the 1988 legislation was permissive, leaving the Home Secretary with a discretion, but no obligation, to bring the relevant provisions into force.[60] Leave was granted to appeal to the Court of Appeal, and an undertaking was given by the Home Office that no awards would be made under the new scheme while the appeal was pending, although applications would be processed.

The 'technical legality of the Minister's action', as it was represented,[61] did little to damp the vigour of the claims of unconstitutionality when an amendment on the compensation issue was debated on the seventh day in Committee on the Bill in June. Its effect would be to bring into force those sections of the Criminal Justice Act 1988 which encompassed the scheme then current six months after the Criminal Justice and Public Order Act 1994 had been passed. Only Ackner referred in any detail to the judgment of the Divisional Court which he found 'surprising'. The Lords, he said, had to decide whether to condone a serious affront by the Government to parliamentary democracy. Should a minister be allowed, without first seeking parliamentary approval, to frustrate the will of Parliament by refusing to carry into effect the clearly expressed intention to put the 1988 scheme onto a statutory basis?

---

[58] The text of a letter sent to the Home Secretary, Kenneth Clarke, on 20 Nov. 1992, by the Chairman of the Criminal Injuries Compensation Board, Lord Carlisle, is reproduced in Chapter 11.

[59] *R.* v. *Secretary of State for the Home Department, ex parte Fire Brigades Union and Others* [1995] 2 AC 513.

[60] [1994] PIQR P320.

[61] By Lord Ackner. *Parl. Debates*, HL, 555 (6th ser.), col. 1832, 16 June 1994.

Should he be allowed to compound that refusal by replacing that scheme with a non-statutory *ex gratia* tariff which ignored the fundamental tenet of justice and fairness that compensation must be matched to individual circumstances?[62] The charges of improper, if not actually unlawful, ministerial action continued to be reverberate around the Chamber throughout the debate. They were supplemented by allegations of hypocrisy and humbug directed at the Government for pretending to have produced a better service for victims, whereas in reality the motivation was to reduce the cost of compensation.

Ferrers did his best in reply,[63] but he had a majority of the House against him from the start. He accepted that escalating costs were part of the reasons for making the change, pointing to the steep increase that had taken place in the total cost of compensation from £58 million in 1987–8, when the earlier Criminal Justice Bill was being considered by Parliament, to £166 million in 1992–3. However, there was also the aim of meeting victims' needs in ways that could not be met under the thirty year-old scheme.[64] Under the tariff scheme all victims with similar injuries would be treated in the same way and would have a good idea in advance of how much compensation they were likely to get. That was far from the case under the old scheme. In addition, there would be an appeals system demonstrably independent of those administering the new scheme. As to the charge that in disregarding the provisions of the 1988 Act and bringing in a tariff scheme by executive action the Government had behaved in an unlawful and unconstitutional manner, the High Court had ruled that its action was neither illegal nor improper or irrational. An appeal was pending, and until the Court of Appeal had delivered a judgment the question could not be taken any further.

Nothing that the Minister could have said would have satisfied a predominantly hostile House. In pressing his amendment to a division, Ackner provided a rousing finale. The debate, he declared, was about where power should reside. Should it reside with the legislature or with the executive? Those who believed passionately

---

[62] Ibid.   [63] Ibid., cols. 1842–8.

[64] In the course of the debate the author pointed to some practical shortcomings of the existing arrangements, and drew attention to the alternative proposals for reform contained in the report of an independent working party convened by Victim Support (*Compensating the victim of crime*, Victim Support, London, 1993). Ibid., cols. 1839–42.

in parliamentary democracy would wish to support the amendment. Defying a strong whip, enough Conservatives and cross-benchers joined the Opposition to do so. The amendment was carried against the Government by 131 to 113 votes.[65]

Four months later, when the Commons had disagreed with the Lords' amendment, a last attempt was made by way of an alternative amendment to persuade the House that the mishandling by the Government of criminal injuries compensation was so serious a matter that the Lords should insist on its own views. This time the peers, conscious of their unelected estate, decided to call it a day. As one very experienced Parliamentarian, who had served for thirty-four years in the House of Commons, put it: 'We have the undoubted right, indeed, sometimes the duty, to ask another place to think again. But we should be very careful before exercising a further right which exists to ask them to think again and again.'[66] On a division the amendment in lieu was defeated by 152 to 89 votes.[67]

VI

Earlier in the summer the Government had been defeated twice in the Lords on successive days, 11 and 12 July, when the Bill was being considered on Report. The first topic, which to some had the appearance of an insoluble problem, was what should be done about gypsy encampments on unauthorized sites. It was an uncomfortable and perennial issue with tentacles running deep in rural constituencies, but not one that was delineated by party politics. The second matter, the sale of confidential financial information, was of a wholly practical nature and elicited vocal support from former Law Lords as well as a sizeable contingent of peers on the Government benches.

Gypsies today, as the Bishop of Liverpool[68] had reminded the House in Committee, are analogous to the Jews of yesterday. A civilized country, he remarked, is properly measured by how it treats

---

[65] *Parl. Debates*, HL, 555, cols. 1850–1.

[66] Lord Renton QC served as the MP for Huntingdonshire 1945–79. He was succeeded as MP for the same constituency by John Major. *Parl. Debates*, HL, 558 (6th ser.), col. 508, 25 Oct. 1994.

[67] Ibid., cols. 516–7.

[68] David Sheppard, Bishop of Woolwich 1969–75; Bishop of Liverpool, 1975–.

its minorities, especially minorities who had attracted unpopularity.[69] The Bill created a new criminal offence of unauthorized camping in a vehicle on land after notice of a direction to leave. Although not aimed specifically at gypsies, they would be covered by the clause. The definition of a vehicle included a caravan with or without wheels and irrespective of whether it was in a fit state for use on the roads. The problem arose, for those committed to the nomadic way of life, of where to go when directed to leave if there was no alternative authorized site in the vicinity to go to. It was aggravated by the proposed repeal of the duty imposed upon local authorities by the Caravan Sites Act 1968 to provide authorized sites with the assistance of grants from central Government. Ministers justified the repeal by arguing that the Act had two objectives: the provision of adequate sites for gypsies and the control of unauthorized camping. Yet in spite of the provision of authorized sites, over the years since the Act had been in effect the levels of unauthorized camping had hardly changed.[70]

From discussions with the National Gypsy Council the Government was aware that many gypsies preferred to establish their own sites rather than live on council sites which had to cater for many different family groups in order to achieve reasonable economies of scale. The 100 per cent grant provision had originally been intended as an incentive to stimulate site provision by local authorities for five years. It had now been paid for fifteen years and local authorities had come to depend on the grant entirely. The Government considered it would be wrong to maintain a commitment to provide sites at the public expense for all gypsy families without accommodation, whether or not it was what they actually wanted. Instead of relying on the inadequate provision by local authorities, gypsies should be encouraged to establish their own authorized sites through the planning system.[71]

The origins of this policy of self-help lay not in the Home Office but in the Department of the Environment, for it was their Secretary of State who was ministerially responsible for caravan sites. A degree of deafness would also be called for not to hear an echo of voices at the Treasury cheering on the application of free market principles to one of the more remote tributaries of public policy. Whatever their provenance, the provisions in the Bill were

[69] *Parl. Debates*, HL, 555, col. 1119, 7 June 1994.
[70] *Parl. Debates*, HL, 556, col. 1541, 11 July 1994.   [71] Ibid., cols. 1544–5.

vigorously contested. The official opposition, led by Irving of Lairg, was joined from the Liberal Democrat and Conservative back-benches respectively by Lord Avebury (who as Eric Lubbock MP had been responsible for introducing the Caravan Sites Act in the House of Commons in 1968) and Lord Stanley of Alderley, speaking for farming interests. They were concerned that genuine gypsies, excluding New Age travellers and others who had dropped out of a more conventional way of life, should not simply be moved on from one site to another. It was understandable that the settled population should be offended by the nuisance, dirt, and other unsavoury aspects of unauthorized sites in their immediate neighbourhood, but it was no solution simply to displace the problem elsewhere.

In the same way as its critics, Avebury said, the Government believed that all gypsy families should be ultimately accommodated on authorized sites. However, because of its ideology it had decided that the remainder of the task should be accomplished entirely by private enterprise, and not by local authorities. Ministers had failed to understand that if the efforts of private enterprise, which had made a significant contribution in recent years, and those of local authorities were harnessed together, completion of the task would be reached at an earlier date than would otherwise be the case.[72]

Other arguments were that local authorities would need time to adjust their planning policies and structure plans in the light of the Government's new approach, and to identify satisfactory sites. Time was also needed to sort out where responsibility would lie for the education of the children and the health of the family when a family was moved from one site to another. Organizations as disparate as Save the Children and the National Farmers' Union supported amendments delaying for five years the repeal of the duty of local authorities under the Caravan Sites Act 1968 to provide authorized sites for gypsies. By a majority of 133 to 104 votes the House agreed with amendments to delay repeal, which Stanley of Alderley described as a minor correction to the Bill which was in keeping with the Lords' revising role.[73]

---

[72] *Parl. Debates*, HL, 556, col. 1536.

[73] Ibid., col. 1563. The Lords' amendment was rejected by the Commons, and when it came back to the Lords in October a motion to insist on it was defeated by 208 to 71 votes. *Parl. Debates*, HL, 558, cols. 490–1, 25 Oct. 1994.

VII

Unlike the controversies over criminal injuries compensation and gypsy encampments, with which many outside organizations were involved, the proposal to make it a criminal offence to sell confidential financial information was the initiative of a retired Lord of Appeal in Ordinary, Lord Brightman.[74] He had ascertained that there were agencies which offered to sell, at a price, confidential information about other people's financial affairs. Circulars distributed by such agencies contained a price list for obtaining details of a person's bank balance, most recent bank statements, salary, pension, indebtedness, and other details. A spokesman for an agency claiming to be the acknowledged market leader in the specialist procurement of highly sensitive commercial and personal information was quoted as saying that there was no security system which could not be circumvented. The Director of Public Prosecutions had stated that under present law offers of information dishonestly obtained did not constitute a criminal offence. The aim of the new clause was to make them a criminal offence.[75]

Replying for the Government, Ferrers said that since the matter had first been raised in Committee ministers had reflected on the 'offensive and noxious practice' of the deliberate obtaining of private information by those not entitled to have it. They had concluded that the best way to approach the problem was by way of an amendment to the Data Protection Act 1984 since the information sought was increasingly likely to be held on a computer, and the Act contained clear arrangements determining who was entitled to receive data.[76] Brightman welcomed the resulting Government amendment, which would make the wrongful procurement of computer-held information an offence, regarding it as supplementary to his own. However, it did not go far enough, being confined only to information held on a computer and not to information held outside a computer, nor was it directed at the iniquitous offers to sell information which could only be obtained corruptly.

Alexander of Weedon, a banker as well as a lawyer, agreed; the

---

[74] Judge of the High Court of Justice, Chancery Division 1970–9; Lord Justice of Appeal 1979–82; Lord of Appeal in Ordinary 1982–6. Chairman of several House of Lords Select Committees.

[75] *Parl. Debates*, HL, 556, col. 1668, 12 July 1994.   [76] Ibid., col. 1670.

root of the mischief was that organizations existed which sought to obtain information in order to sell it. That was the vice which the Bill ought to deal with.[77] Since Ferrers was unable to indicate that he would come back with a composite Government amendment at Third Reading, Brightman pressed his amendment which was carried by 163 to 111 votes.[78] A revised Government amendment making it an offence to procure the disclosure and selling of computer-held personal information was subsequently included in the Bill without a vote, and became Section 161 of the Criminal Justice and Public Order Act 1994. Brightman advised the House against insisting on his own amendment when it was sent back by the Commons at a later stage.[79]

Whilst the door is still open it is sometimes possible to slip through a worthwhile reform which, although insufficiently weighty to warrant its own Bill, nevertheless requires legislation. For such a manoeuvre to be successful certain conditions have to be fulfilled. Ministers must be satisfied that the policy behind the change is generally acceptable and unlikely to attract controversy, and consequently that it will take up no more than a minimal amount of parliamentary time. One such reform was the change in the status of the Parole Board to that of a non-departmental public body, to reflect both its independence from Government and the fact that since the Criminal Justice Act 1991 it had exercised a decision-making as well as an advisory role. Home Office officials were amenable, particularly as there was an operational weakness that could be corrected at the same time, but ministerial approval was necessary. The Chairman of the Parole Board, Lord Belstead, a former minister and Leader of the House of Lords,[80] sounded out the Home Secretary who offered no objection. He then asked me, as his predecessor but one, if I would be willing to put down amendments to this effect in the Lords. I agreed, and amendments were drafted covering both the change in status and capacity of the Board, and to rectify a lacuna in the procedures under the 1991

---

[77] *Parl. Debates*, HL, 556, col. 1676.   [78] Ibid., cols. 1681–2.
[79] *Parl. Debates*, HL, 558, col. 519, 25 Oct. 1994.
[80] Parliamentary Under-Secretary of State, Department of Education and Science 1970–3; Northern Ireland Office 1973–4; Home Office 1979–82. Minister of State, Foreign and Commonwealth Office 1982–3; Ministry of Agriculture, Fisheries and Food 1983–7; Department of the Environment 1987–8. Leader of the House of Lords and Lord Privy Seal 1988–90; Paymaster-General 1990–2. Chairman of the Parole Board 1992–.

Act for recalling to custody prisoners who had been released on licence.

The Parole Board amendments were not reached until after midnight on the eighth day in Committee, June 20–21. Throughout the afternoon and evening the Committee of the whole House had been occupied in debating a mixed bag of amendments, including the age at which homosexual acts should be lawful. Homosexuality in the armed forces and other sexual offences between men took up more time before the Committee moved on to consider the arguments for and against tobacco advertising and wheel-clamping by local authorities. When the discussion on my amendments finally began at 12.30 a.m. there were no more than twelve members of the Committee in the chamber, three of them former chairmen,[81] and one the current chairman, of the Parole Board. The lateness of the hour and the sparsity of the attendance led to a protest by Lord Harris of Greenwich from the Liberal Democrat benches,[82] but the purpose of the amendments was welcomed unanimously. For the Government, Ferrers said that as a result of the changes introduced by the 1991 Act the Parole Board had become more of an executive body taking decisions on the release of certain categories of prisoner. The Government agreed that it should now have the status of a non-departmental public body, reflecting fully its independence and accountability in decision making.[83]

A second set of amendments was intended to deal with an unsatisfactory situation whereby parallel procedures existed for taking the initial decision to recall a prisoner released on licence. For some categories the decision was taken by the Parole Board, and for others by the Home Secretary. Emergency recalls, especially at short notice during the night or out of working hours, were a constant source of anxiety. As the Board's secretariat had no delegated powers the police or supervising probation officer had first to contact a Home Office duty officer in order to establish into which category the parolee fell, and thus who should handle the request for his recall. If it was the Parole Board, the Home Office would have to make contact with an on-duty Parole Board member, who in turn had to secure the agreement of two other Board members for the recall to be activated. Once the decision had been made the Board

---

[81] Lord Harris of Greenwich 1979–82; Lord Windlesham 1982–8; and Viscount Colville of Culross QC 1988–92.

[82] *Parl. Debates*, HL, 556, col. 139, 20 June 1994.   [83] Ibid., col. 138.

had no power to sign a warrant for arrest or a revocation order, so the matter had to be handed back again to the Home Office to implement the decision.

The flaws in such an extended procedure, made necessary by the provisions of the 1991 Act, were self-evident. There was also a risk that a parolee whose urgent recall had been requested might commit an offence or disappear before action was taken. Both the Home Office and the Parole Board wanted the immediate decision in all cases of recall to be taken by the Home Office, leaving undisturbed the arrangements for the Board to confirm an emergency recall as soon as practicable, or order re-release if the parolee's representations against recall were successful.

Accepting both sets of amendments in principle, Ferrers undertook to redraft the wording and table suitable Government amendments to achieve their aims at Report Stage.[84] Howard remained silent on the merits of the changes, although he had authorized them. While no one was aware of it at the time, he may have been contemplating the virtual abolition of the parole system which he was to announce with a fanfare of publicity in another speech to the Conservative Party Conference in 1995.

VIII

Throughout the 1980s proposals generated internally within the Home Office were a central element in the policy-making process.[85] By the early 1990s, however, the picture had changed. The fusing of ministerial intentions with departmental expertise had rested on a set of tacit assumptions questioned by Clarke and largely rejected by his successor, Howard, who was openly critical of what had gone before, and of the contribution of civil servants to devising the policies incorporated in the Criminal Justice Act 1991. Consequently the formative stages of the 1993–4 legislation were more overtly political than previously, a significant part taking place outside the Home Office. Political advisers, policy units, parliamentary colleagues, even some ideologically motivated journal-

---

[84] *Parl. Debates*, HL, 556, col. 138. Government amendments were accepted without any dissent on 11 July, and in due course were enacted as Sections 149 and 150 and Schedule 10(70) of the Criminal Justice and Public Order Act 1994.

[85] See *Responses to Crime*, Vol. 2, pp. 12–15.

ists writing for *The Spectator* and *The Daily Telegraph* were the wells from which the Home Secretary drew his inspiration.

Yet, as this and the two previous Chapters show, by no means all the levers of policy making and execution are held in ministerial hands. The transition from platform rhetoric to enforceable law calls for input by those possessing specialist skills: departmental officials, draftsmen of legislation, and practitioners in the operational services. For their practical experience there is no substitute, the last category being of especial relevance. It is the judges, the magistrates and their clerks, the Crown Prosecution Service, the police, probation officers, Prison Service, and all of those engaged in operating the system of criminal justice who have to implement whatever decisions Parliament may make. If their support, or at least acquiescence, is not obtained while legislation is in preparation, or passing through Parliament, there is a risk that the provisions of the new law, once in effect, will fail to command the confidence of those responsible for carrying them out. There is no need to look any further back than the abrupt switch in sentencing policy in 1993 as an example, if an unusual one measured in terms of the speed of ministerial and Parliamentary response, of public criticism by judges and magistrates lighting the short fuse which ignited the decision to abandon some of the restrictions on the powers of the courts contained in the Criminal Justice Act 1991.

Then there is the scrutiny of the Government's legislative proposals by Parliament. Ministers accustomed to rely on the efficiency of party discipline in the Commons like to get their own way. They are inclined to underestimate the Lords where, on matters of criminal justice especially, it is usually far harder to get their original proposals through unamended. Although the Conservative peers make up the largest single group, they do not outnumber the combined strength of the Opposition parties and cross-benchers. The influence of party whips is relatively weak since they have no electoral and few other sanctions at their command. Hence, as we have seen on both of the Bills described in this narrative, Conservative peers, Lord Whitelaw on the Police and Magistrates' Courts Bill and Lord Carr and Baroness Faithfull on the Criminal Justice and Public Order Bill, played crucially important roles in achieving changes in the legislation which conflicted with Government policy. To succeed they had to ensure not only that the main Opposition parties were of the same mind but also that a majority of the independent peers, particularly the Law Lords past and present, were willing to give their support, both in debate and if needed in the division lobbies. Most influential of all was the holder of the august and strictly non-party political office of Lord Chief Justice of England.

That there was less scope for negotiated concessions on the Criminal Justice and Public Order Bill was due to the fact that by the time it arrived in the Lords it had endured a lengthy passage through the Commons, during which positions had been taken up and policies defended in ways from which it would have been difficult for ministers to resile because of pressure from the Lords. Moreover, from the Second Reading onwards it was apparent that there had been an intuitive closing of ranks on the Conservative side of the House. On the earlier Bill it was felt with quiet satisfaction that the Lords had done its duty in promoting worthwhile changes to some ill-judged and potentially harmful reforms to two of the most important of all public services, the police and the Magistrates' courts. Now, faced with the politics of crime and punishment, on which public opinion was in such a febrile state and so much turned, it was time to give the Government the support it was entitled to expect from those who took the Conservative whip and sat on the Government benches.

This was the message persistently underlined by ministers and whips. Dissenting voices were listened to with tolerance and respect, on the secure training order, the right of silence, and numerous other proposals regarded as matters of legitimate concern. However, there were invariably loyalists on hand to defend the Government's proposals and to support the arguments put forward by ministers in reply. The change in the climate of opinion made the prospect of losing divisions less probable, thus reducing the most powerful motive force leading to negotiated concessions. It was not until the closing stages of the Criminal Justice and Public Order Bill in July that the trickle of reverses became a stream.

Ultimately, Howard must have been surprised that the Act he had previewed at Blackpool nearly a year earlier decriminalized homosexual acts between the ages of eighteen and twenty-one; banned the use of foetal germ cells and tissues in fertility treatment; and strengthened the regulations on the supply of videos for home viewing. On none of these controversial matters had the Government any intention to legislate. At the outset Howard had been totally opposed to the inclusion of any provisions on sexual offences, which he recognized as a traditional Home Office minefield. In the event, not only was a reduction made in the age at which homosexual acts between consenting males in private are lawful, but it was accompanied by a redefinition of the offences of rape (including male rape) and buggery, revised penalties for buggery and indecency between men, and new provisions relating to homosexuality on merchant ships and in the armed forces. As enacted, a separate part of the statute amounting to seven sections was devoted to sexual offences.

The proposals on the right of silence survived, although not in their original form, while the secure training order was an addition to the armoury of penal sanctions viewed with foreboding by many of those who would have to administer it.[86] Compensation for criminal injuries remained a raw issue. The Home Secretary had won in Parliament but he had lost in the courts, the House of Lords holding (by a majority of three to two) that the introduction of the new tariff scheme had been unlawful.

Howard's main purpose of reassuring public opinion that a tough line was being taken in punishing criminals was shown by the grand total of thirty-nine new criminal offences which were created by the Criminal Justice and Public Order Act 1994. When the increase in maximum penalties for a further fifty-six offences was added, no one could question that the legislation in its final form was a true reflection of the punitive intentions of ministers. Comprehensive lists under both headings are set out as Appendices A and B at the end of this Chapter.

Apart from the rebuffs over appointments to police authorities and the organization of the Magistrates' courts, a high proportion of the Government's strategic objectives were in the final outcome approved by Parliament. No complaint could be made about the amount of time and dedication expended by both Houses in debating the main proposals and extracting explanations from ministerial spokesmen. In the process, not only MPs and peers, but ministers too, learned more about the institutions of criminal justice: what they did; what they could do; and what they should not

---

[86] Lord Carr of Hadley's amendments were rejected in the House of Commons on the advice of the Home Secretary, and not insisted upon when the House of Lords considered Commons Reasons and Amendments. *Parl. Debates*, HL, 558, cols. 447–65, 25 Oct. 1994.

be expected to do. The special interest groups, which had been so energetic behind the scenes, and the informed press both played an important part in the process of political education.

IX

What of the policies themselves, and the expectations of the general public? The warm glow initially generated by the perception that here at last was a Home Secretary taking a firm grip on the manifold problems of crime, who knew what had to be done and possessed the will to do it, soon dissipated. Initially Howard had shown a sure touch in recognizing as one of the worst aspects of the apparently remorseless rise in criminal offending that people came to accept it as inevitable. He was determined to counter the sense of helplessness which was so corrosive of confidence in the system of criminal justice and those who were responsible for it. Having heightened expectations, Howard was not the first Home Secretary to suffer the consequences of public disillusion.

The slide in his public esteem began when the proposals selected to give substance to the 'crack-down on crime' approach came under the spotlight of Parliamentary scrutiny. Then, not only because of opposition in Parliament but also because the expertise of civil servants had been utilized inadequately in their preparation, many of the policies so forcefully put forward had to be amended. Within a few short months the press was full of reported retreats, U-turns, climb-downs, and miscalculations. The fault-finding was almost all short-term, and some of it was undeserved. But the obloquy stuck. Howard learned the painful lesson that tactical withdrawal, however necessary to secure the passing of legislation, brought with it a price to be paid in the coin of populist politics.

One attack on the Home Secretary and his policies was so outspoken, and the source so august, that it provoked a defence by the Prime Minister. On the Sunday before the opening of the Conservative Party Conference at Bournemouth in October Sir Edward Heath made no attempt to disguise the strength of his feelings:

Perhaps the Home Office, or its minister, has the greatest need for a new approach, particularly on crime and punishment. There has been no full inquiry into these problems for many years. It has been fashionable for the past 15 years to deny that unemployment or social conditions have any-thing to do with them—so obvious a fallacy as to be unbelievable.

At the last party conference Michael Howard, the Home Secretary, pro-duced 27 points which he wished to implement as a matter of urgency. The consequence was that his Criminal Justice Bill was torn to shreds in Parliament. Let us now have a full study which the government can act on. The Conservative party has had distinguished home secretaries, among them Rab Butler and Willie Whitelaw, who have stood up at the party con-ference and spoken for mature and sensible policies against the hysterical screams of the extremists in the party.

Last year Mr Howard took it upon himself to raise the temperature as high as he could. Disastrous results for the government and the party fol-lowed. This year let him completely change his performance, outlaw the hysteria and give us a weighty considered judgment on measures which can later prove to be effective. Is that too much to ask?[87]

In his conference speech Howard's delivery was more moderate than the previous year and John Major spoke up in support of his beleaguered colleague:

I believe we have fostered too easy, too casual a response to crime by too great a tolerance of crime. There have been too many voices excusing crime, explaining crime and justifying crime. We think that's wrong. That's why we have increased penalties for rape, violence against children, firearms offences, drug-related crime and crimes committed on bail. And so that no one can say we've ignored what our opponents call 'our friends in the City', we have also increased sentences for financial crime. For a whole range of crimes we have toughened sentences. And judges are now using them. For the first time in years, a rising proportion of convicted criminals are being sent to prison.

But don't let us fool ourselves. Punishment alone won't do the trick. We have to change attitudes, improve policing and support the innovative methods of chief constables.

The powers in the new Criminal Justice Bill are needed. We will not be deterred by disgraceful riots like the one we saw in London last weekend. It will take a national effort to beat crime. It will take time and must involve everyone but we are determined to succeed and have made a begin-ning.

Many of the changes that I have been talking about have come about in the last year or so. The people who have spent their time criticising my col-league Michael Howard would have been far better off supporting him.[88]

[87] *The Sunday Times*, 9 Oct. 1994.
[88] Abridged text of John Major's speech to the Conservative Party Conference, *The Times*, 15 Oct. 1994.

The absence of any meeting point in the attitudes of the past and present leaders of the Conservative Party showed the depth of the divide over policies towards the control of crime, and perhaps between those who are in office and out of it.

Earlier in the summer, with a ministerial re-shuffle imminent, there had been speculation that the Home Secretary would not remain unscathed and would be moved to another post. The Prime Minister saw no need to make a change at the top of the Home Office, but two of the Ministers of State, Peter Lloyd, the Prisons Minister, and Lord Ferrers, who had laboured so manfully in steering three major Home Office bills[89] through the Lords in a single session, were replaced.[90] From inside the Government, spurred on by its more strident supporters in the Commons, strictures were levelled at the business managers in the Lords, both the Leader, Lord Wakeham, and the relatively inexperienced Government Chief Whip, Lord Ullswater, who had held the appointment for only nine months at the time of vacating it.[91] The complaint was that they had been ineffective in controlling the Upper House, allowed backbenchers too free a rein, and failed to get the Criminal Justice and Public Order Bill back to the Commons in time for it to obtain the Royal Assent before the Summer Recess.[92] Wakeham had already indicated his readiness to retire and could be replaced without causing ill-feeling, while Ullswater was moved to another ministerial appointment. Once again, casualties were left behind as the cavalcade moved on.

---

[89] The Police and Magistrates' Courts' Bill, the Sunday Trading Bill, and the Criminal Justice and Public Order Bill.

[90] Earl Ferrers was appointed as Minister of State for Trade and Industry on 20 July 1994. Peter Lloyd left the Government.

[91] Parliamentary Under-Secretary of State, Department of Employment 1990–3; Government Chief Whip, House of Lords 1993–4; Minister of State, Department of the Environment 1994–5.

[92] The Criminal Justice and Public Order Bill was returned to the Commons on 19 July with 339 amendments made by the Lords. The House of Commons rose for the Summer Recess on 21 July, and did not consider the Lords' amendments until after it resumed in October. The Bill received Royal Assent on 30 Nov. 1994.

Appendix A *Criminal Justice and Public Order Act 1994: New Offences*

Section	Offence
12	(Linked with Schedule 2 para. 5). Making a false statement to obtain certification as Secure Training Centre (STC) custody officer.
13	Assaulting STC custody officer. Resisting or wilfully obstructing STC custody officer.
14	Wrongfully disclosing information about STC trainee.
40	(Linked with Schedule 10 para. 28). Serving on a jury when knowingly not qualified because on bail in criminal proceedings.
44	(Linked with Schedule 4 Part 1, new para. 8A of Magistrates' Courts Act 1980). Making unauthorized report of transfer proceedings.
51	Intimidating a witness, juror, or person assisting in the investigation of an offence. Harming or threatening to harm a witness, juror, etc.
60	Failing to stop when directed to do so by a policeman under S. 60 powers (stop and search in anticipation of violence).
61	Failing to comply with direction under S. 61(1) (trespassing on land); re-entering the land within 3 months of a direction being given.
63	Failing to comply with direction under S. 63(2) (raves); re-entering the land within 7 days of a direction being given.
65	Failing to comply with direction under S. 65(1) (travelling to a rave).
68	Committing aggravated trespass.
69	Failing to comply with direction to leave under S. 69(1) (aggravated trespass); re-entering the land within 3 months of a direction being given.
70	Organizing a prohibited trespassory assembly. Taking part in a prohibited trespassory assembly. Inciting someone else to take part in a prohibited trespassory assembly.

Section	Offence
71	Failing to comply with direction under S. 14 C(1) of the Public Order Act 1986 (travelling to a trespassory assembly).
74	Knowingly or recklessly making a false statement about one's protected intended occupier status.
75	Knowingly or recklessly making a false statement to obtain an interim possession order or to resist the making of an interim possession order.
76	Being a trespasser on premises during currency of interim possession order.
77	Failing to comply with unauthorized campers direction; re-entering the land within 3 months of a direction being given.
78	Obstructing the removal of vehicles of unauthorized campers.
81	Failing to stop when required to do so by a constable or wilfully obstructing a constable from exercising his S. 81 powers (stop and search powers to prevent acts of terrorism).
82	Possessing an article intended for terrorist purposes. Collecting or having information likely to be useful to terrorists.
114	(Link with Schedule 6 para. 5). Giving false information to obtain certification as Scottish prisoner custody officer.
115	Wrongfully disclosing information about prisoner (Scottish Prison Service).
122	(Link with Schedule 7 para. 5). Giving false information to obtain certification as Northern Ireland prisoner custody officer.
123	Assaulting a Northern Ireland prisoner custody officer. Resisting or obstructing a Northern Ireland prisoner custody officer.
124	Wrongfully disclosing information about a prisoner (Northern Ireland Prison Service).
142	Redefining 'rape' to include non-consensual buggery of either a man or a woman.
154	Causing intentional harrassment, alarm, or distress.
156	Using female germ cells taken or derived from embryos or foetuses for fertility purposes.
161	Procuring personal data to which one is not entitled under the Data Protection Act or selling or offering for sale

Section	Offence
	personal data which one has procured or subsequently procures in breach of the relevant Data Protection register entry.
166	Sale of tickets for designated football matches by unauthorized persons (power exists to extend to other large sporting events).
167	Touting for hire car services in a public place.
Schedule 9 para. 43	Giving a false statement to the court about financial circumstances.

Source: The tables of new offences and increased penalties in Appendices A and B were prepared by the Home Office and printed in Hansard in reply to a Question for Written Answer tabled by the author. *Parl. Debates*, HL, 559 (5th ser.), cols. WA 12–18, 23 Nov. 1994.

Appendix B *Criminal Justice and Public Order Act 1994: Increased Penalties*

Section	Offence	New Maximum Penalty
84(6)(e)	Taking/distribution of an indecent photograph, etc. of a child in Scotland.	Summary conviction: 6 months' imprisonment and/or the existing level 5 fine. On indictment: 3 years' imprisonment and/or the existing fine.
84(7)(c)	Possession of an indecent photograph, etc. of a child in Scotland (equivalent to S. 86 for E & W).	6 months' imprisonment and/or the existing level 5 fine.
86	Possession of indecent photograph of a child.	6 months' imprisonment or level 5 fine, or both.
87	Displaying, publishing, selling, or distributing obscene material in Scotland.	Penalty in Scotland brought into line with that in England and Wales. Summary conviction: 6 months' imprisonment and/or the existing level 5 fine. On indictment: 3 years' imprisonment and/or the existing fine.
88	i) Supplying unclassified videos or possessing such videos for supply.	Summary conviction: 6 months' imprisonment or £20,000 fine, or both.
	ii) Supplying videos in breach of classification, supplying certain videos in places other than licensed sex shops, or supplying videos with false classification marks.	On indictment: 2 years' imprisonment or unlimited fine, or both. Summary conviction: 6 months' imprisonment or level 5 fine, or both.
92	Making obscene, offensive, or annoying telephone call.	6 months' imprisonment and/or level 5 fine.
142	Non-consensual buggery (rape) of a man.	Life imprisonment.
144	Attempted buggery with a person under 16 or an animal.	Life imprisonment.

Section	Offence	New Maximum Penalty
157 and Schedule 8	**Sea Fisheries (Shellfish) Act 1967 (c. 83)**	
	Offences under S. 3(3) (dredging etc. for shellfish in contravention of restrictions etc. or without paying toll or royalty).	Level 5 fine.
	Offences under S. 5(7) (obstruction of inspector or other person or refusal or failure to provide information to inspector etc.)	Level 5 fine.
	Offences under S. 7(4) (fishing, dredging etc. in area where right of several fishery conferred or private oyster bed).	Level 5 fine.
	Offences under S. 14(2) (contravention of order prohibiting the deposit or taking of shellfish, or importation of shellfish, or non-compliance with conditions of licences).	Level 5 fine.
	Offences under S. 14(5) (obstruction of inspector).	Level 5 fine.
	Offences under S. 16(1) (selling, etc. of oysters between certain dates).	Level 4 fine.
	Offences under S. 17(1) (taking and selling etc. of certain crabs).	Level 5 fine.
	Offences under S. 17(3) (landing and selling etc. of certain lobsters).	Level 5 fine.
	Misuse of Drugs Act 1971 (c. 38)	New maximum fines on summary conviction
	Offences under S. 4(2) committed in relation to Class C drug (production, or being concerned in the production, of a controlled drug).	£2,500 fine.
	Offences under S. 4(3) committed in relation to Class C Drug (supplying or offering to supply a controlled drug or being concerned in the doing of either activity by another).	£2,500 fine.
	Offences under S. 5(2) committed in relation to Class B drug (having possession of a controlled drug).	£2,500 fine.
	Offences under S. 5(2) committed in relation to Class C drug (having possession of a controlled drug).	£1,000 fine.

Section	Offence	New Maximum Penalty
	Offences under S. 5(3) committed in relation to Class C drug (possession of a controlled drug with intent to supply it to another).	£2,500 fine.
	Offences under S. 8 committed in relation to Class C drug (being the occupier, or concerned in the management, of premises and permitting or suffering certain activities to take place there).	£2,500 fine.
	Offences under S. 12(6) committed in relation to Class C drug contravention of direction prohibiting practitioner, etc. from possessing, supplying etc. controlled drugs).	£2,500 fine.
	Offences under S. 13(3) committed in relation to Class C drug (contravention of direction prohibiting practitioner etc. from prescribing, supplying etc. controlled drugs).	£2,500 fine.
157 and Schedule 8 cont.	**Firearms Act 1968 (c. 27)** Offences under S. 1(1) committed in an aggravated form within the meaning of S. 4(4) (possessing etc. shortened shotgun or converted firearm without firearm certificate).	7 years' imprisonment.
	Offences under S. 1(1) in any other case (possessing etc. firearms or ammunition without firearm certificate).	5 years' imprisonment.
	Offences under S. 2(1) (possessing etc. shotgun without shotgun certificate).	5 years' imprisonment.
	Offences under S. 3(1) (trading in firearms without being registered as a firearms dealer).	5 years' imprisonment.
	Offences under S. 3(2) (selling firearms to person without a certificate).	5 years' imprisonment.
	Offences under S. 3(3) (repairing, testing etc. firearm for person without a certificate).	5 years' imprisonment.
	Offences under S. 3(5) (falsifying certificate, etc. with view to acquisition of firearm).	5 years' imprisonment.

Section	Offence	New Maximum Penalty
	Offences under S. 4(1) (shortening a shotgun).	7 years' imprisonment.
	Offences under S. 4(3) (conversion of firearms).	7 years' imprisonment.
	Offences under S. 5(1) (possessing or distributing prohibited weapons or ammunition).	10 years' imprisonment.
	Offences under S. 5(1A) (possessing or distributing other prohibited weapons).	(a) On summary conviction, 6 months' imprisonment. (b) On conviction on indictment, 10 years' imprisonment.
	Offences under S. 19 (carrying loaded firearm other than air weapon in public place).	7 years' imprisonment.
	Offences under S. 20(1) (trespassing with firearm other than air weapon in a building).	7 years' imprisonment.
	Offences under S. 21(4) (contravention of provisions denying firearms to ex-prisoners and the like).	5 years' imprisonment.
	Offences under S. 21(5) (supplying firearms to person denied them under S. 21).	5 years' imprisonment.
	Offences under S. 42 (failure to comply with instructions in firearm certificate when transferring firearm to person other than registered dealer; failure to report transaction to police).	5 years' imprisonment.
157 and Schedule 8 cont.	**Firearms (Northern Ireland) Order 1981 (SI 1981/155 (NI) 2)** Offences under Art. 3(1) (possessing etc. firearms or ammunition without firearm certificate).	5 years' imprisonment.
	Offences under Art. 4(1) (trading in firearms without being registered as a firearms dealer).	5 years' imprisonment.
	Offences under Art. 4(2) (selling firearms to person without a certificate).	5 years' imprisonment.
	Offences under Art. 4(3) (repairing, testing etc. firearm for person without a certificate).	5 years' imprisonment.

Section	Offence	New Maximum Penalty
	Offences under Art. 4(4) (falsifying certificate, etc. with view to acquisition of firearm).	5 years' imprisonment.
	Offences under Art. 5(1) (shortening a shotgun).	7 years' imprisonment.
	Offences under Art. 5(3) (conversion of firearms).	7 years' imprisonment.
	Offences under Art. 6(1) (possessing or distributing prohibited weapons or ammunition).	10 years' imprisonment.
	Offences under Art. 6(1A) (possessing or distributing other prohibited weapons).	(a) On summary conviction, 6 months' imprisonment. (b) On conviction on indictment, 10 years' imprisonment.
	Offences under Art. 22(5) (contravention of provisions denying firearms to ex-prisoners and the like).	5 years' imprisonment.
	Offences under Art. 22(7) (supplying firearms to person denied them under Art. 22).	5 years' imprisonment.
	Offences under Art. 43 (failure to comply with instructions in firearm certificate when transferring firearm to person other than registered dealer; failure to report transaction to police).	5 years' imprisonment.

Schedule 9

Para. 1	Trespass in search or pursuit of game	
	i) In England and Wales or Scotland	
	Less than five persons	Level 3 fine.
	Five or more persons	Level 4 fine.
	ii) In England and Wales: five or more persons, one or more with a gun and using intimidating behaviour, etc.	Level 5 fine.
	iii) In Scotland, for assaults on persons acting under the Game (Scotland) Act 1832.	Level 3 fine.
Para. 4	Trespass in search or pursuit of game in England and Wales as one of five or more persons.	Forfeiture of vehicle used in committing offence.

The Act also provided in Section 17 for the doubling, from 12 to 24 months, of the maximum length of detention in a young offender institution for offenders aged 15, 16, or 17 years.

PART III

Law-making in America

5

Populist Pressures
and Organized Interests

I

A century before populist pressures on both sides of the Atlantic became such a potent stimulant to legislation aimed at combating crime, 'populism' in America had taken on a more specific meaning. Stemming from the discontent of small farmers at their inability to come to terms with and benefit from the changes sweeping across the agrarian economy in the latter part of the nineteenth century, it developed into an organized political movement. Candidates were nominated for public office, including the Presidency of the United States, but they soon found that converting discontent into votes was another matter. There were some electoral successes, mainly confined to the poor and thinly populated states of the Mid and Far West, and also in the South.[1] The movement did not gain support in the industrialized North, and populism as a coherent force, standing for the interests of the yeoman farmer against exploitation by men with 'more power and fewer scruples—land grabbers, railroad tycoons, credit merchants, bankers, middlemen',[2] was short-lived. Yet the rise and fall of the Populist Party was more than a solitary and passing phenomenon. It was early evidence of a strain in the American political culture which sat uneasily with representative democracy and was to surface many times in many different contexts in the century that followed.

[1] James Baird Weaver of Iowa, who had been a Union General, was the Populist candidate for the Presidency 1892. He received over nine million votes, more than 8 per cent of the national total, and twenty-two electoral votes, all West of the Mississippi. S. E. Morison, H. S. Commager, W. E. Leuchtenburg, *The Growth of the American Republic*, Vol. 2, 6th edn., Oxford University Press, 1969, p. 173.
[2] Richard Hofstadter, in G. Ionescu and E. Gellner (eds.), *Populism and its National Characteristics*, Weidenfeld and Nicolson, London, 1969, p. 15.

The theme of this Chapter and those that follow is the constant play of public opinion, fortified by populist rhetoric and dissipated by the demands of legislative compromise, on the measures incorporated in the long and detailed Violent Crime Control and Law Enforcement Act of 1994 (Public Law 103–322).[3] In retrospect, as in prospect, there can be little doubt that public sentiment was the most dominant influence on policy-making towards crime in the late 1980s and early 1990s. But what were the impulses which stimulated and fed the latent currents of populist feeling? How was the interest of politicians engaged and retained, being converted into legislative proposals finding expression, moderated or in their original crude form, in the corpus of federal criminal law and procedure effecting courts throughout the United States? The preceding Chapters show how populist attitudes bred a punitive virus which quickly infected the body politic in Britain. While the content and the law-making processes differed, there were common features in the concurrent passage of the Westminster legislation and the crime bill, as it was generally known, which after many vicissitudes was enacted by the 103rd Congress and signed into law by the President in September 1994.

The characteristics of populist feeling include broad discontent with the status quo and a sense that government ought to be doing more to improve the situation. There is also a consciousness of remoteness, and resentment at being powerless and detached from the decision-taking process. Frustration and resentment lead to suspicion of those closer to the seats of power, especially anonymous non-elected officials or experts, and an attraction towards simplistic solutions to complex problems. At this stage attitudes may not have hardened into opinions on specific issues. However, the soil is fertile and slender shoots, cultivated by rhetoric, can grow rapidly and branch out into unexpected directions. In the instance of the crime control and law enforcement legislation, the primary trigger was the prevalence of criminal offending, with the emphasis on violent offending, and the often sensational style of its reporting. The heightened publicity accompanying numerous horrific incidents acted as periodic booster injections hardening the popular reaction which, although present earlier, built up so rapidly in the

[3] 108 Stat. 1796.

late 1980s and early 1990s.[4] Although the scale there was larger, the phenomenon was not peculiar to the United States. A pattern of high crime rates, leading to widespread victimization and fear of crime was only too familiar in many other countries of the developed world where the perception of a steady and apparently remorseless increase in the frequency and severity of crime has become a leading issue of public concern.

Fear of crime restricts people's lives. Public anger, fed and exploited by the mass media, anticipates a political response. The clamour for action is orchestrated by elected representatives, and those who are running for election.[5] However, with few exceptions they are responding to a perceived demand, rather than initiating or leading a discourse. In the formation of popular opinion it is perceptions that count. The reality may be different. The popular perceptions in America are that criminal offending is always on the increase, that violence is everywhere, that no one is safe, and that governments are not doing enough to protect the majority of the people from the harmful acts of others. Strongly held as they are, each is a partial misconception, although derived from truisms. Yet these are the assumptions which underlie policies towards crime.

Before considering the reality we should note with curiosity, if not surprise, that public interest in crime can drive up media coverage even when published data show, as was the case in 1993, that there was no appreciable increase either in overall crime or violent crime rates. Taken over a longer period cumulative trends, reinforced by fear-inducing criminal stereotypes,[6] are likely to condition public attitudes and beliefs. In the absence of national newspapers, the electronic news media in the United States have the primary role in disseminating to the population as a whole the message that crime, frequently portrayed as life-threatening, is

---

[4] For a survey of research on public opinion about crime see Julian V. Roberts, 'Public Opinion, Crime, and Criminal Justice' in M. Tonry (ed.), *Crime and Justice: A Review of Research*, Vol. 16, University of Chicago Press, Chicago, 1992.

[5] It is an accurate reflection of the style of campaigning that Americans should run for election, whereas the staider British stand for election.

[6] In a perceptive analysis prepared for the California Policy Seminar entitled 'Is American Violence a Crime Problem?', Franklin E. Zimring and Gordon Hawkins point out that many people have a homogeneous image of 'the criminal'. They suggest that a composite generalized image of criminals incorporating the characteristics of violent crime acts as a factor conditioning public fear. Franklin Zimring is Professor of Law and Director of the Earl Warren Legal Institute at the University of California, Berkeley, where Gordon Hawkins is a Senior Fellow.

omnipresent. Whether or not news values stand for anything more than a volatile indication of audience interest is debatable, but whatever the selection process for news items the fact is that in 1993 a count by a reputable research organization showed that a record number of crime stories were broadcast by the three major television networks to a national audience.[7]

With a total of 1,698 stories in the main evening newscasts, crime occupied the first place in the top ten television news topics of 1993. The economy (1,457 stories) was second, and health issues (1,096 stories) third. Taken together, these three topics accounted for nearly one-third of the 13,474 news stories broadcast on the ABC, CBS, and NBC evening newscasts. An average of nearly five stories per night meant that the coverage of crime was approximately double that for 1992, with murder stories tripling from 104 stories in 1992 to 329 in 1993. On policies, as against news reports, gun control measures such as the Brady bill led the way (138 stories). Other policy options, including more prisons, stiffer sentencing policies, and extra money for law enforcement and crime prevention, received less media attention. Relatively few stories, 66 out of the total of 1,698, focused on illegal drugs, representing a reduction of 83 per cent since 1989 when the concentration on the war on drugs was at its height and 518 stories were broadcast.[8] Declining concern about the economy correlated with indicators showing a recovery in economic activity, thus opening up space for crime or some other social issue to take its place as the leading topic in media coverage, and also in the opinion polls.[9]

II

Crime statistics exist in profusion, but they are a morass through which it is hazardous to try and lay down any certain path. First of all there is a distinction to be made between crimes reported to and recorded by the law enforcement agencies and victimization

---

[7] VIII *Media Monitor*, (1994), published by the Center for Media and Public Affairs, Washington, DC. The Center is an independent, non-profit research organization which conducts scientific studies of how the media treat social and political issues.

[8] Ibid.

[9] See M. Mauer, 'The Fragility of Criminal Justice Reform', 21 *Social Justice*, 17, (1995).

surveys taking account of a much wider range of offences, whether or not they are reported to the police. Both are regularly published, but the results are neither entirely consistent nor entirely comparable.[10] Over the years the findings have indicated that the rate of increase in America, as in England and Wales, is considerably higher in the police figures than the trends shown in victimization surveys. There are several explanations for the discrepancies. Recorded crime figures are subject to such non-criminal factors as the greater availability of telephones and the necessity to report break-ins to domestic or business premises, or loss of property, to support insurance claims. Then there is a great bulk of so-called victimless crimes, notably prostitution and drug-taking, which never come to light. Within the home or domestic setting it is commonplace even for incidents of serious assault or abuse between members of the family or acquaintances to go unreported. Minor thefts, vandalized cars, and other less serious offences also may not be reported because the public hold out little hope that the police will be able to catch the offender. Recording practices vary, and in general the more numerous the strength of the police force, and the more diligent and effective police officers are in investigating crime, so will the number of recorded offences rise.

The Department of Justice administers two statistical programs[11] to measure the magnitude, nature, and impact of crime in the United States. The first is the Uniform Crime Reporting (UCR) program, dating back to 1929, supplemented by the newer National Crime Victimization Survey (NCVS) which began in 1973. The

[10] For a commentary on the methodology of victim reported offences and police recorded offences see D. P. Farrington and P. A. Langan, 'Changes in Crime and Punishment in England and America in the 1980s', 9 *Justice Quarterly*, 5 at 32–8 (1992). This important and controversial article compares offending and imprisonment trends in the United States and England and Wales, and documents changes between 1981 and 1986–7. David Farrington is Professor of Psychological Criminology at Cambridge, and was President of the British Society of Criminology 1990–3. Patrick Langan is at the Bureau of Justice Statistics, US Department of Justice in Washington, DC.

[11] Although American spellings have generally been anglicized, I have retained the American style for 'program'. The term occurs frequently in Pub. L. 103–332, in which context it denotes an organized set of activities directed towards a common purpose or goal, undertaken or proposed by an agency in order to carry out its responsibilities. This definition is taken from *A Glossary of Terms Used in the Federal Budget Process*, 3rd edn., US General Accounting Office, Washington, DC, 1981, p. 71. The Glossary is recommended in the guidance on *Drafting Federal Law*, prepared by the House of Representatives, Office of the Legislative Council.

Uniform Crime Reports collect data each month on a list of offences, known as index crimes, which have come to the attention of law enforcement agencies throughout the country. The index is made up of the violent crimes of murder and non-negligent manslaughter, forcible rape, robbery, and aggravated assault; the property crimes of burglary, larceny-theft, and motor-vehicle theft; and arson, the last being added by Congressional edict in 1979. Unless they fall under existing categories of offence, hate crimes are excluded from the index, although they are separately reported.[12] In addition to the primary collection of data on crime index offences (part I), the UCR program also solicits monthly data on persons arrested for all crimes except traffic violations (part II offences).[13] The resulting reports, published annually, are a method of estimating fluctuations in the overall volume and rate of increase or decrease of reported crime.

The second national measurement, the NCVS, publishes information obtained by way of sample surveys conducted by the Census Bureau[14] on crimes suffered by individuals or households, whether or not they have been reported to law enforcement. Much detailed information is assembled about both victims and offenders, as well as the frequency and nature of the crimes of rape, personal robbery, aggravated and simple assault, household burglary, personal and household theft, and motor vehicle theft.[15] The NCVS excludes homicide, arson, commercial crimes, and crimes against children under the age of twelve, all of which are included in the UCR. While the UCR is a measure based on actual crime counts, the NCVS is an estimate derived from the results of nationwide

---

[12] The Hate Crime Statistics Act, passed by the Congress and signed by the President in Apr. 1990 (Pub. L. 101–275, 104 Stat. 140), mandated the collection of data on crimes motivated by religious, ethnic, racial, or sexual-orientation prejudice. Collection commenced on 1 Jan. 1991. *Crime in the United States, 1993*, Uniform Crime Reports published by the Federal Bureau of Investigation, Department of Justice, US Government Printing Office, Washington, DC, 1994, p. 3.

[13] Ibid., p. 374. The UCR methodology is set out in Appendix I, pp. 374–6.

[14] All household members over the age of twelve are interviewed in a nationally representative sample of approximately 49,000 households, amounting to about 101,000 persons. Households stay in the sample for three years and are interviewed at six-monthly intervals. New households rotate into the sample on an ongoing basis. Ibid., p. 386.

[15] The National Crime Survey Reports are published annually by the Bureau of Justice Statistics of the Department of Justice under the series title *Criminal Victimization in the United States*.

sample surveys. Each set of statistics is hedged about with qualifications, but together they amount to the best available approximation of the extent and nature of criminal offending in America. Until 1993 sampling methods of the NCVS were constant, with the resulting annual reports being tolerably reliable indicators of trends during the 1980s and early 1990s. However, the UCR data is dependent on the extent to which offences are reported to law enforcement and recorded by the police or other agencies. Both the patterns of reporting and recording practices can and do vary. If, for whatever reason, victims, witnesses, and others become less disposed to report criminal incidents then it may be misleading to conclude that the overall volume of crime has decreased. Conversely, if there is an increase in the number of instances of violent behaviour reported to law enforcement, for example domestic assaults, it does not follow that the actual volume of violent crime has gone up in proportion to the number of reported incidents.

With these reservations, it is safe to say that the overall picture portrayed by the statistics between 1983 and 1993 does not match the public perception. According to the UCR, *per capita* rates of recorded property crimes rose slightly by 2.1 per cent in the decade 1983–93, while violent crime increased by 38.8 per cent, mainly in the category of aggravated assault. The total numerical increase in the number of recorded offences over the same period was 16.8 per cent, representing increases of 12.6 per cent for the more numerous property crimes and 52.9 per cent for violent crime. In 1993 the number of offences in the crime index (excluding arson) was 14,140,990, representing a decrease of 2.1 per cent on the previous year. It was the third successive year in which the all-crime total was lower than in the previous year The rate per 100,000 inhabitants declined by 3.1 per cent between 1992 and 1993. Over the decade 1982–92 the NCVS showed generally downward trends for both property and violent crimes.[16] The comparative figures are set out in Table 6.

There is ample evidence that perceptions are influenced more by violent crime than by either property crime or statistics on the overall rate of offending. Even here there are some chinks of light with the rate of increase in the number of violent crimes reported to law

---

[16] In 1993 there was a change in NCVS methodology which meant that the statistics for 1993 and later are not strictly comparable with the series up to 1992.

TABLE 6. *Crime trends in the United States, 1982–92*[a]

Uniform Crime Reports		National Crime Victimization Surveys	
Per capita rates		*Per capita rates*[b]	
Property crime	–3%	Household crime	–27%
Violent crime	+33%	Personal theft	–28%
Total	+1%	Violent Crime	–6%
Number of offences		*Number of offences*	
		Household crime	–17%
Property crime	+7%	Personal theft	–22%
Violent crime	+46%	Violent Crime	+3%
Total	+11%	Total	–15%

[a] For the 1993 survey the NCVS introduced a new questionnaire which makes the statistics for 1993 inconsistent with those for years earlier than 1992. Thus Table 6 shows trends only to 1992, whereas Tables 7 and 8 show trends based on UCR statistics up to and including 1993.
[b] NCVS rates are based on the number of victimizations per 1,000 persons aged 12 or older for personal theft and violent crime. Rates for household crime are per 1,000 households. Because of the different bases, no overall *per capita* rate can be calculated.

enforcement[17] slowing down, and more recently declining. Caution is necessary as there was also a dip in the mid-1980s, followed by increases taking the totals back up to previous levels. In 1993 the total number of violent offences reported by UCR was 1,924,188, a small decrease from the previous year. The rate per 100,000 inhabitants was 746.1, a reduction of 1.5 per cent. (See Table 7.) Of the individual offences composing the crime index only murder and aggravated assault showed increases in the number of arrests from 1992 to 1993. Decreases for the remaining index offences ranged from 1 per cent for robbery and arson to 5 per cent for burglary.[18]

[17] The classification of violent crime in the UCR is composed of four offence categories: murder and non-negligent manslaughter, forcible rape, robbery, and aggravated assault. All violent crimes involve force or the threat of force.
[18] *Crime in the United States, 1993*, p. 6. Downward overall trends of offending continued in 1994. The total number of violent offences reported to law enforcement in 1994 was 1,864,168, a decrease of 3.2 per cent on the previous year. The rate per 100,000 inhabitants was 716.0, a reduction of 4.1 per cent. Reported offences of murder and non-negligent manslaughter showed a decrease of 5.0 per cent, and aggravated assault a decrease of 1.4 per cent. The number of violent crimes reported

TABLE 7. *Violent crime in the United States, 1990–3*

Year	Number of offences	Change from previous year	Rate per 100,000 inhabitants	Change from previous year
1990	1,820,127	n/a	731.8	n/a
1991	1,911,767	+5.0%	758.1	+3.6%
1992	1,932,274	+1.1%	757.5	–0.1%
1993	1,924,188	–0.4%	746.1	–1.5%

Source: Uniform Crime Reports, *Crime in the United States.*

However, it is the sheer scale of violent offending, in excess of 1.9 million criminal incidents reported in 1993, that casts such a long shadow over the penal scene.

The total number of murders reported in the United States during 1993 was 24,526 (see Table 8), falling to 23,305 in 1994. High as they are these figures are unlikely to represent the actual total. Each year a significant number of missing persons are recorded and no one can estimate how many of those who disappear might have been murdered. Taken over a longer period, the murder rate has been relatively constant. In 1980 it was 10.2 per 100,000 inhabitants, falling to 7.9 in 1984 and 1985 before moving up again to 9.4 in 1990, and steadying between 9.4 and 9.8 per 100,000 in the early 1990s. Yet the rate remains far in excess of any comparison elsewhere in the developed world.

In 1993 the chance of becoming a murder victim was more than twice as high in metropolitan areas (eleven victims per 100,000 inhabitants) as in the rural counties and cities outside metropolitan

during 1994 dropped below 1.9 million offences for the first time since 1990. The 1994 total was down 3 per cent from 1993, but was 2 per cent above the 1990 level and 40 per cent above that of 1985. Property crimes were down 0.7 per cent compared with 1993. *Crime in the United States, 1994*, Uniform Crime Reports published in Nov. 1995 by the Federal Bureau of Investigation, US Government Printing Office, Washington, DC, pp. 10–13, 31 and 35. Juvenile arrests (under the age of 18) increased by 7 per cent, with adult arrests showing virtually no change. Over the five-year period 1990–4 juvenile arrests rose by 21 per cent. The general pattern of decreasing levels of offending by adults over the age of 25 being offset by steadily rising rates of offending by juveniles and younger people was maintained. In 1994 the under-25 age group was responsible for 47 per cent of the violent crime arrests and 59 per cent of property crime arrests. (Ibid., pp. 216–17). The trend was alarming since it was estimated that there would be 23 per cent more teenagers in the United States by the year 2005. *New York Times*, 23 May 1995.

TABLE 8. *Murder*[a] *in the United States, 1990–3*

Year	Number of offences	Change from previous year	Rate per 100,000 inhabitants	Change from previous year
1990	23,438	+9.0%	9.4	+8.0%
1991	24,703	+5.4%	9.8	+4.3%
1992	23,760	–3.8%	9.3	–5.1%
1993	24,526	+3.2%	9.5	+2.2%

[a] Including non-negligent manslaughter. The index offence is defined in the UCR as the wilfull killing of one human being by another. The classification is based on police investigation as opposed to the determination of a court, medical examiner, coroner, jury, or other judicial body. It does not include deaths caused by negligence, suicide, or accident; justifiable homicides; attempts to murder or assaults to murder, which are classified as aggravated assaults.

Source: Uniform Crime Reports, *Crime in the United States.*

areas, where the rate was five victims per 100,000.[19] Within the metropolitan areas there are marked discrepancies. Violent crime is disproportionately concentrated in the low-income, predominantly black, districts where the risks of being murdered, assaulted, or robbed are much higher than in the middle and upper-income, predominantly white districts.[20] The most ominous of the UCR statistics are that in 69.6 per cent of the murders, 42.4 per cent of the robberies, and 25.1 per cent of aggravated assaults a firearm was the weapon used. Between 1992 and 1993 assaults with firearms rose by 5.0 per cent.[21] The statistics for each of these categories

[19] *New York Times*, 23 May 1995, p. 14.

[20] See John J. DiIulio, Jr. 'Saving the Children: Crime and Social Policy', in I. Garfinkel, J. Hochschild, and S. McLanahan (eds.), *Social Policies for Children*, Brookings Institution, Washington, DC, 1996. Based on data extracted from a report by the Fire and Police Commission in Milwaukee, the author (a Professor at Princeton) calculated that in 1991 people living in the predominantly black districts of the city had over thirty times as much chance of being murdered, assaulted, or robbed as those residing in the predominantly white areas. After summarizing other research findings, DiIulio concluded: 'never before has violent crime been so concentrated among teenage and young adult male inner-city blacks.' (p. 204). The interaction between race and crime is a highly sensitive topic which readily attracts controversy. It is thoughtfully explored by Michael Tonry in *Malign Neglect—Race, Crime and Punishment in America*, Oxford University Press, New York, 1995.

showed a rise on the previous year. Firearm injuries were far and away the leading cause of death in 1993 for young black males between the ages of fifteen and twenty-four.[22] At 162 deaths per 100,000 of the population, firearm deaths dwarfed the comparable rates for suicide (16.4 per 100,000), deaths resulting from motor vehicle crashes (35.0 per 100,000), HIV infection (6.9 per 100,000), and all other diseases (in aggregate amounting to 15.2 per 100,000).[23] For whites in the same age group, the death rate from firearm injuries was much lower at 32.0 per 100,000.

This summary does not aim to pursue the disagreements which exist over the gathering and interpretation of statistical data. What stands out from any analysis is the salience of violence and the recourse to physical force and firearms which distinguishes crime in America from any other developed nation state. It is the consciousness of life-threatening personal violence which has led so many Americans, and not only in the big cities where the risk is greatest, to live in fear. In an inter-city comparison of crime patterns between Los Angeles and Sydney, and New York City and London, Franklin Zimring and Gordon Hawkins demonstrated the much greater extent to which American criminals kill and wound their victims than elsewhere in the developed world. Whereas the incidence of theft and burglary in Los Angeles and Sydney, two multi-cultural cities of comparable size,[24] was broadly similar, robbery[25] and homicide were notably dissimilar. In 1992 Los Angeles reported 39,508 robberies while Sydney reported 4,942, one-eighth of the Los Angeles rate.[26]

For homicide the difference was even more startling. Eighty homicides were reported by the police in Sydney during 1992, a crime volume equal to 7.3 per cent of the total of 1,094 homicides

---

[21] *Crime in the United States, 1993*, pp. 18, 29, 32.

[22] National Center for Health Statistics, *Health United States, 1993*, Public Health Service, Hyattsville, Maryland, 1994. Tables 42–53, pp. 115–35.

[23] The categories are deaths from heart diseases (7.3), cerebrovascular diseases (0.5), malignant neoplasms (5.4), neoplasms of respiratory system (0.1), and chronic pulmonary diseases (1.9). Ibid.

[24] Los Angeles is the second largest city in the United States with a population in 1992 estimated at 3.6 million for its crime statistics reporting unit. The city of Sydney in Australia also has a population estimated at 3.6 million.

[25] Robbery is defined as the taking of property from the person of another by force or by the threat of force.

[26] 'Is American Violence a Crime Problem?', *op. cit.*

reported by the Los Angeles police in that year. The same pattern emerges from a comparison between London and New York crime rates. Whereas in 1990 London experienced slightly more theft than New York, and a rate of burglary that was 57 per cent higher, the robbery rate was less than one-fifth of the robbery rate in New York. Here again, homicide stood out starkly with homicide rates in London being less than one-tenth of those in New York. This leads to the conclusion that the distinguishing factor between the cities is not the overall amount of crime experienced but the character of the crimes.[27]

The findings of this illuminating survey have direct relevance to national policies towards crime in the United States. A country's crime rate, it is argued, is substantially independent of its violence rate. The death rate from crime in England and Wales, to take one example, was the lowest in a sample of twenty developed countries, although the overall crime rate was just above the average. Failure to differentiate between the grave dangers to personal security posed by violent crime and the generality of non-violent offending, harmful and distressing as it is, can divert attention away from finding the most effective means of achieving greater public safety. Muggings in the streets and armed robberies are more an aspect of a propensity towards violence than part of a broader pattern of crimes against property. It is the violent strain in American social life which leads to the special destruction and disorganization caused by crime.[28] In framing crime control policies it should have priority over all else.

In any society penal policy is misdirected if resources, including prosecutions, criminal trials, and prison places, are not deployed selectively. The contention that violence is the key to grasping the essentials of the overall crime problem in the United States is persuasive. A loss of priority results if, in the well chosen words of Zimring and Hawkins, there is 'a diffusion of focus'.[29] An example of a priority target is that whereas adult homicide rates remained relatively stable between 1985 and 1992, the rate at which young men aged fourteen to seventeen killed increased steeply. According to one estimate the homicide rate for young white males rose about 50 per cent, and for young black males it tripled.[30] In 1992 the pro-

---

[27] 'Is American Violence a Crime Problem?', *op. cit.*   [28] Ibid.   [29] Ibid.
[30] James Q. Wilson in *Commentary*, Sept. 1994, p. 26. The author of many books and articles on crime and criminal behaviour, Professor Wilson is one of America's

portion of all killings by young men in the 14–17 age range reached 15 per cent.[31] Unlike the direct impact on opinion of adult homicides, where many killings (e.g. of spouses, partners, or lovers) take place behind closed doors, the high profile of inner-city violent behaviour by youths heightened the fear of the public at large of random killings, robberies, and assaults in the street or public places.

By the early 1990s crime, depicted by President Clinton as 'the great crisis of the spirit that is gripping America today',[32] was firmly established at or close to the top of the list of issues of greatest public concern. It was also the most politicized, dominating the electoral landscape. Politicians running for elective office, be it local, state, or federal, had no need to consult opinion polls to be reminded of the strength of feeling aroused by criminal offending, above all the violent crimes which coloured attitudes towards all other forms of offending. The anger, fear, and resentment were only too evident. A wave of populism, already aroused and gathering strength, reached all parts of the nation, including those where the risks of victimization were least. Unlike other upsurges of populist sentiment, the tide did not stop at the doors of professional, business, or academic homes. The elites were frightened too. Their homes might be better protected, and located in safer neighbourhoods, but in the streets of the cities they were as vulnerable as anyone else. The pervading climate of violence and the extent of actual and reputed victimization, reflected and magnified by media exposure and supplemented by the velocity of news about crime within personal networks, came together in the creation of a public mood characterized by retribution and punitive values.

Criminologists might warn against over-simplification and exaggeration, but elected representatives almost without exception recognized an imperative need to respond to such an ubiquitous mood, and in many cases attempted to exact political advantage

leading scholars and commentators on criminal policy and its administration. For an assessment of his distinctive contribution and influence, see A. Rutherford, *Transforming Criminal Policy*, Waterside Press, Winchester, 1996, pp. 20–46.

[31] Only 6 per cent of the far smaller number of suspects proceeded against for murder or manslaughter in England and Wales in 1992 were under eighteen years of age. In that year a total of 669 persons were indicted for homicide (murder, manslaughter, or infanticide), of whom 497 were convicted. Home Office, *Criminal Statistics, England and Wales 1993*, Cm. 2680, HMSO, London, 1994, p. 85.

[32] *Economist*, 15 Oct. 1994, p. 23.

from a fearful, sometimes vindictive, public. To be tough on crime had become transformed from slogan to electoral necessity. Politicians of contrasting views could not afford to allow their opponents to occupy the high ground unchallenged, so they too joined in the chorus of rhetorical toughness. The transfer of such a powerful current of popular opinion into federal legislation that was workable and preserved the principles of justice was to be a severe test of America's political institutions.

III

Before embarking on a detailed study of the content and politics of the legislation on violent crime control and law enforcement enacted by the 103rd Congress, it will be helpful for readers unfamiliar with the American system of justice to comprehend its distinctive features. First there are the separate, although overlapping, federal and state criminal jurisdictions in the United States. Historically the responsibility for detecting, prosecuting, and punishing crimes lay with each individual state, not with the federal government. That responsibility remains today, with some 95 per cent of all prosecutions for violent crimes being tried in state courts. If offenders are convicted and sentenced to a term of imprisonment they are confined in a local jail or state-run prison. Throughout the twentieth century, however, the criminal jurisdiction of the federal courts, and the procedural provisions imposed by Congress (e.g. on wire-tapping and powers of search and seizure) have been greatly enlarged. Laws intended to curb the misuse of narcotic and other dangerous drugs, and to penalize those who trade in or use them, have been the main cause in recent years, although the expansionist trend was clear enough before.

Federal offences accumulated steadily from the early years of the century onwards: breaches of immigration laws, customs violations, tax frauds, crimes committed on the high seas, and subsequently in the air. Then came laws aimed at regulating the social evils, as they were seen at the time, of gambling, child labour, and prostitution, followed by prohibition of the sale of liquor in the 1920s and 1930s. The earlier enactments fell clearly enough under the heading of offences against the regulations necessary for the conduct of a modern federated state. Later regulatory legislation relied upon the device of prohibiting inter-state transportation, rather than inter-fering directly with local activities, so bringing into play the com-merce clause of the Constitution. However, the legislators in Washington had to tread with care, for the doctrine of states' rights emphatically included the right to make and enforce the laws to be observed in their own state on all matters not specifically reserved to the federal government. Federal courts were able to try only those classes of case designated to be within their jurisdiction by federal law. Everything else fell within the jurisdiction of the state systems.[33]

The expansion of the federal criminal jurisdiction and the emer-gence of a national system of criminal justice were made possible, if not inevitable, by advances in technology, particularly in rail and air transportation. As Lawrence Friedman has pointed out, the shrinking of distance coincided with economic developments and the electronic news media to make a reality of the national ideal implicit in the concept of federalism. As the years passed state boundaries were of less and less significance in determining the way of life of millions of Americans. Many crimes became inter-state; criminals too had 'wheels and wings'.[34] Not only offending by indi-viduals but also large-scale organized crime was mobile and not confined within state boundaries. Nor, it was contended, should be the law enforcement agencies of federal government, most notably the Federal Bureau of Investigation (FBI).[35] Responding to these developments, the number of federal offences multiplied rapidly. Drugs, stolen goods and merchandise of every sort, securities, and money frequently crossed state lines, calling for combined action by enforcement authorities and the ability to prosecute offenders in

[33] The jurisdiction and organization of the federal and state court systems are clearly described in L. Baum, *American Courts: Process and Policy*, 2nd edn., Houghton Mifflin, Boston, 1990, pp. 21–54.

[34] L. M. Friedman, *Crime and Punishment in American History*, Basic Books, New York, 1993, pp. 266–7. Chapter 12 is a finely written historical account of the development of a national system of criminal justice and its limitations. Lawrence Friedman is Marion Rice Kirkwood Professor of Law at Stanford University.

[35] The Bureau of Investigation, later renamed the Federal Bureau of Investigation, was established by the Attorney General in 1908 as part of the Department of Justice. The status and influence of the FBI grew under the long period as director of J. Edgar Hoover from 1924 until his death in 1972. Today it is the principal investigative arm of the Department of Justice and is charged with gathering and reporting facts, locating witnesses, and compiling evidence in cases involving the federal jurisdiction. Priority areas are organized crime, drugs, counter-terrorism, white-collar crime, foreign counter-intelligence, and violent crime.

federal district courts. Driving stolen motor vehicles across state lines and dealing in stolen vehicles that had moved from one state into another had been federal offences since 1919. Following the outcry over the Lindbergh baby case in 1932, kidnappers who had taken victims held for ransom or reward over state boundaries became subject to federal investigation and prosecution.[36]

To non-Americans it seems strange that the inter-state commerce clause of the Constitution should have been pressed into service to facilitate and validate the growth of the federal criminal jurisdiction. In enumerating the powers granted by the people to their government, the Constitution conferred on the Congress the power to regulate commerce with foreign nations 'and among the Several states'.[37] In the formative years of the Republic, national control was needed to prevent unneighbourly trade rivalries between the states, such as the imposition of tariffs on imports by one state from another and retaliatory action. The commerce power did much to create national markets but, as construed by the Supreme Court, it also became a prime source to justify the exercise of national authority and to restrain state action. Although the connections between the historical purposes of the clause and its modern applications were often tenuous,[38] the increasingly intense

[36] *Crime and Punishment in American History*, pp. 265–7.

[37] Article 1, Section 8.

[38] The commerce power was invoked for the purpose of banning racial discrimination in places of public accommodation under Title II of the Civil Rights Act of 1964 (Pub. L. 88–352, 78 Stat. 243), a landmark in American history. For the purposes of Section 201 commerce meant travel, trade, traffic, commerce, transportation, or communication among the several states, or between the District of Columbia and any state. Inns, hotels, motels, and other establishments providing lodgings for transient guests were brought within the ambit of the statute, as were restaurants and other facilities principally engaged in selling food for consumption on the premises where a substantial portion of the food was supplied from outside the state. Places of public accommodation included gasoline stations, motion picture houses, theatres, concert halls, sports arenas and stadiums, and other places of exhibition or entertainment. The constitutionality of these provisions was upheld by the Supreme Court in *Heart of Atlanta Motel* v. *United States*, 85 S. Ct. 348 (1964) and *Katzenbach* v. *McClung*, 85 S. Ct. 377 (1964). During the Senate hearings on the Bill in 1963 the Attorney General, Robert Kennedy, argued that the scale of racial discrimination in the South amounted to an injustice that needed to be remedied: 'We have to find the tools with which to remedy that injustice.' In the Administration's judgment the commerce clause provided the most apt constitutional tool. To some commentators, as to sceptical members of the Senate Committee on Commerce, it was straining the meaning and purpose of the 'affecting commerce' rationale to make it the basis of civil rights legislation which would have been better addressed by way of the Fourteenth Amendment. See G. Gunther, *Constitutional Law*, 12th edn., University Casebook Series, The Foundation Press, Westbury, NY, 1991, pp. 145–51.

searches for constitutional justifications amongst the powers expressly granted by the Constitution, in the words of one scholarly critic, have made the commerce clause 'a frequently attractive and often hospitable base for the assertion of regulatory authority'.[39]

While contained within the parameters of the Constitution, the division of authority between federal and state government fluctuated according to the needs of the time and how they were interpreted by the political leaders who reached the highest elective office. In the era of John F. Kennedy, federal power was directed towards obtaining for blacks the basic legal and political rights enjoyed by white Americans. The 'Great Society' measures promoted by Lyndon Johnson went further, recognizing that the life chances for black Americans were diminished by the incidence of poverty, sub-standard living conditions, especially in the inner cities, and lack of educational and employment opportunities. The determined resistance mounted by the defenders of states' rights in the courts failed, but it was not long before the neo-conservative attitudes of the next era once again adjusted the federal–state balance. When exposing his vision of a 'new federalism', a term used also by President Johnson to convey an opposite meaning, President Reagan proclaimed his intention to restrict the activities of federal government by reducing or eliminating a large number of social welfare and other programs, the cuts falling mainly on federal aid to state and local governments.[40] The objective was not simply to bring down the high level of public expenditure and its adverse effect on the American economy, but:

. . . because he judged these activities to be inefficient, unnecessary, and sometimes positively harmful. He also claimed that they were improper under the Constitution—not so much in the strict sense that they violated

[39] Gerald Gunther, William Nelson Cromwell Professor of Law at Stanford University and biographer of Judge Learned Hand. Ibid. p. 93. *Learned Hand: the Man and the Judge* was published by A. Knopf, New York, in 1994.

[40] In the opening chapter of *To Make a Nation* the political scientist Samuel Beer contrasts the attitudes towards federalism and the use of federal authority by Presidents Johnson and Reagan. The remainder of the book consists of a lively excursion into the history of ideas to support the theory of federalism as a unifying national force and to refute the notion that the Union was no more than a compact between states. The distinction is an important one in practice since the national theory allows a more generous view to be taken of the powers and responsibilities of the federal government than does the compact view. S. H. Beer, *To Make a Nation: The Re-discovery of American Federalism*, Harvard University Press, 1993.

specific provisions of our fundamental law as in the larger philosophical and historical sense that they offended against the true meaning of the document . . . accordingly, President Reagan promised to 'restore the balance between levels of government'.[41]

If President Clinton's policies fell short of the more sharply defined goals set by Johnson and Reagan, appearing at times to steer an erratic course between the polarities, on certain issues, healthcare and crime being his legislative priorities for the 103rd Congress, he showed that he was ready to use federal power and executive authority to act upon what he identified as a clear expression of the national will.

Apart from the federal/state duality, there are countless dissimilarities between American and British legislative institutions.[42] Congress and Parliament define their law-making duties in ways that seem to get further apart as the years pass, while British and European political institutions get closer. At each stage American contrasts stand out boldly: how and from where initiatives arise; the relative ease in introducing legislative proposals; the absence of executive control over the legislature; public hearings by the relevant committees or subcommittees of Congress; the building of coalitions to support or oppose bills before, during, and after they reach the floor of the Senate or House of Representatives; the readiness to add or discard large and important provisions while the legislation is under active consideration; the machinery to reconcile bills passed by each chamber but with separate content; and the presidential veto.

The turbulent political forces coursing through the channels of such a diverse structure are constrained by rigid procedural rules

---

[41] S. H. Beer, *To Make a Nation: The Re-discovery of American Federalism*, Harvard University Press, 1993, p. 2.

[42] In the introduction to a comparative study first published in 1972 two well informed British authors remark that despite a shared heritage the two greatest legislatures of the free world are 'separated by a width of incomprehension, an Atlantic of the mind, which prevents each from benefiting from the acquired wisdom of the other'. K. A. Bradshaw and D. A. M. Pring, *Parliament and Congress*, revised and updated edn., Quartet Books, London, 1981, p. 1. Sir Kenneth Bradshaw was Clerk of the House of Commons 1983–7, his co-author being Clerk of Committees 1976–87. The reasons why American federal statute law differs fundamentally from English statute law are attributed by P. S. Atiyah and R. S. Summers to the many vital respects in which the legislative process in Congress differs from that in Parliament. See *Form and Substance in Anglo-American Law*, Clarendon Press, Oxford, 1987, pp. 306–15. Patrick Atiyah was Professor of English Law at Oxford 1977–88.

and seniority, rather than by party discipline and ministerial authority as at Westminster. Members of the Cabinet are chosen by the President from outside the Senate or House. They are not directly accountable to the elected representatives in Congress as ministers are to Parliament. Cabinet members, and other holders of senior posts in the Administration, appear before Senate committees for their appointments to be confirmed and, once appointed, visit Capitol Hill only to be questioned by committees of either House on some aspect of the Administration's policies or decisions, or to lobby for support. An overview is that while it is much easier to start bills in Congress than in Parliament, it is far harder to bring them to completion in anything like their original form.

The separation between the executive and the legislature, at state as well as federal level, is absolute, in practice as well as in constitutional design. There is no question of the executive dominating the legislative branch of government in the way it does in Britain, even when the President's party has a majority in the Senate and the House. In the first two years of President Clinton's term he had that advantage but, as we shall see in the narrative which follows, it was no easier for him to get his policy aims enacted than for his immediate Republican predecessor in office, George Bush.

Since power is fragmented, and party discipline ineffective, the progress of legislation through Congress is unpredictable and prone to outside pressures. Local allegiances count for much, particularly in the House of Representatives where Congressmen have to face their electorates every two years. No representative can afford to distance himself from the views of constituents without risking the loss of electoral support. He must be seen and heard, regularly and articulately, advancing their interests in Washington. For these reasons cross-party alliances come together on specific issues. An instance can be found in the conflicting reactions to the policy of enlarging federal controls on firearms exemplified in the voting record of Congressmen from the run-down inner-city areas of the industrialized states, and the rural and farming regions of the South and West. Typically the Republican supporters of gun control in the House of Representatives came from urban or suburban districts with high rates of violence and street crime, whereas a large proportion of the Democratic opponents represented rural districts. On issues of this sort, where local attitudes are deeply entrenched, there is always potential for the opinions of local voters to override party affiliation and the national leadership in Congress.

No introduction to the scrutiny of the passage of a particular legislative enactment would be complete without concentrating attention upon of the role and influence of organized interest groups. A multitude of groups dedicated to promoting the entire spectrum of current policy preferences are at work at the grass roots. They are instrumental in bringing local opinion, or factions of local opinion, to bear on elected representatives. Moreover, as politicians need to raise financial support for their costly election campaigns, national interest groups and political action committees can and do play a crucial part in helping or impeding a candidate's return to Washington, and on voting behaviour once there. The sums of money now involved in campaign finance are huge. In the Congressional mid-term elections held in November 1994 the Federal Election Commission estimated that over half a billion dollars was spent on campaigns. Candidates were left with an estimated debt of more than $70 million.[43] Although during the campaign it was a Republican theme to castigate the Washington elite, with lobbyists being described as a blight on the political process, it was not long before they and their clients were being solicited by a noticeable number of the newly elected Congressmen to make donations to repay campaign debts.[44]

Those who provide the money are not philanthropists. They expect something in return from those who are elected. Both are keenly aware that candidates who fail to raise money to finance an effective campaign are those who are most likely to fail at the polls. The horde of spokesmen and lobbyists who cluster around the Capitol, seeking access to legislators and working to advance the interests of major national associations, labour unions, special interest groups, US and foreign companies, and many other corporate or individual interests are an enduring part of the political system. Whether or not regarded as a blight, the rapidity with which lobbyists established links with members of the first Congress for forty years to be dominated by the Republican Party showed that the rules of the game had not changed. Only some of the players.

---

[43] *The Washington Post*, 25 Mar. 1995.
[44] *The New York Times*, 20 Mar. 1995.

At a more elevated level of constitutional discourse, Congress is, and has been for many generations, a stronghold of particular interests of every sort. Presidents and party leaders may initiate proposals of general application which they regard as being in the national interest, but they are well aware of the truth of the dictum that 'Congress is a centre of resistance to actions in the general interest and an initiator of actions to benefit partial interests'.[45] Hence a state of disharmony between the White House and the legislators on Capitol Hill is unavoidable and, on one view, is integral to the healthy functioning of American democratic institutions.[46]

The statutory restrictions on the manufacture, transfer, and possession of certain firearms contained in the Violent Crime Control and Law Enforcement Act of 1994 afford a classic case-history of the interplay between interest group pressures and law-making. Like the gun control proposals in the crime bills that failed to make headway in the 101st and 102nd Congresses, these provisions, central to the President's appeal to the national public, were subjected to intense and sustained opposition from one of the most formidable, feared, and well financed of all interest groups, the National Rifle Association (NRA). The impact of the NRA will be noted, and the sources of its political strength explored, at the successive stages of the 1994 legislation.

In contrast, the influence of another organized group, drawing its support and legitimacy from a very different constituency, was evident in the rooted hostility of the Congressional Black Caucus (CBC) in the House of Representatives to the punitive orientation of the legislation, and in particular to the extension of the death penalty to a long list of federal offences. Members of the Caucus were convinced that the death sentences which were passed in those states where capital punishment was lawful discriminated against black people. Many of them shared with the voters who had sent them to Congress a deep distrust of the police, the prosecutors, and the courts, all of which were believed to be biased against them. These were far from the only organized interests brought to bear

---

[45] V. O. Key, *Politics, Parties, and Pressure Groups*, 5th edn., Thomas Y. Crowell, New York, 1964, p. 661.

[46] In *Congress and the Presidency*, 4th edn., Prentice-Hall, 1986, Nelson Polsby argues that the diversity of power centres in American politics, and the differences in their accessibility to different interest groups, serve to keep the political system open and responsive (p. 10). Professor Polsby is Director, Institute of Governmental Studies, University of California at Berkeley.

during the passage of the 1993/4 legislation on crime, but they were two of the most prominent.

IV

Twenty-five years earlier, in 1968, another Democratic controlled Congress had passed another omnibus crime bill,[47] although with little more than lukewarm support from the Johnson Administration. It contained some watered-down restrictions on the sale and purchase of firearms which were strengthened a few months later[48] in the aftermath of the assassinations by shooting of Martin Luther King and Senator Robert Kennedy. Thereafter the Democratic preference, apart from some of the more conservative Southern Democrats, was to adddress the causes of crime committed within state jurisdictions, rather than to convert various crimes against state laws into federal offences. Richard Nixon, who succeeded Lyndon Johnson as President in 1969, campaigned against Hubert Humphrey on a law and order platform, amongst other matters. At least for Presidential politics, and to some extent for Congressional politics, crime was largely a Republican issue for the next two decades.

During the late 1960s and early 1970s some Southern Democrats in the Senate, led by Senator John McLellan of Arkansas, espoused the cause of reforming and recodifying federal criminal law, gaining the support of some Republican Senators. A National Commission, with McLellan and other members of Congress included in the membership, was established under the chairmanship of former Governor Edmund Brown of California which produced a final report in 1971.[49] A new and comprehensive code was proposed to replace Title 18 of the United States Code, comprising a reclassification of virtually all federal penal statutes, together with the rules for interpreting them and the procedures for imposing sanctions for their violation. Important areas of judge-developed law were incorporated into associated statutory provisions, thus

---

[47] Omnibus Crime Control and Safe Streets Act of 1968. Pub. L. 90–351, 82 Stat. 197.

[48] Gun Control Act of 1968. Pub. L. 90–618, 82 Stat. 1213.

[49] National Commission on Reform of Federal Criminal Laws, *Final Report*, US Government Printing Office, Washington, DC, 1971.

providing for the first time a single, basic source of federal criminal law.[50]

Although the Executive branch, in the shape of Nixon and his Attorney General, John Mitchell, responded positively, institutional inertia had to be guarded against within the Department of Justice during the long drawn-out consideration of the necessary legislation by the Senate and, to a lesser extent, the House of Representatives. Like many other codification proposals, including those sporadically attempted in England and Wales,[51] when the general arguments for simplicity, rationality, consistency, and accessibility encountered the political controversies which legislators saw arising out of the detailed proposals the trouble began. A bill introduced in the Senate came under attack from both left and right, with the deletion being sought of its two most divisive sets of proposals: those involving defences to criminal conduct and those involving a series of provisions on espionage and the disclosure of classified information. Shorn of these controversial

---

[50] *Report to the Attorney General on Federal Criminal Code Reform*, p. 145. This government document was transmitted to the Attorney General of the United States in January 1989 by the Office of Legal Policy at the Department of Justice. Its author, Ronald L. Gainer, held several senior positions in the Department of Justice between 1963 and 1989, and had been closely involved in criminal law reform and the supervision of the Department's effort to achieve the enactment of a new federal criminal code. The report was reprinted in full (without its appendices) in 1 *Criminal Forum*, 99 (1989). It is a source document of great interest and value. An account from a different perspective has been provided by K. Stith and S. Y. Koh, 28 *Wake Forest Law Review*, 223 at 231–2 (1993). See n. 66 below.

[51] In its introduction to a report on the codification of the criminal law the Law Commission commented that attempts to codify the criminal law of England and Wales had a long but chequered history. The efforts made in the nineteenth century between 1833 and 1982 are summarized in *A Report to the Law Commission, Codification of the Criminal Law* (Law Com. No. 143), HC 270, HMSO, London, 1985, pp. 1–3. For a fuller treatment see Sir L. Radzinowicz and R. Hood, *A History of English Criminal Law and its Administration from 1750*, vol. 5, The Emergence of Penal Policy, Stevens, London, 1986, reprinted in paperback by Oxford University Press in 1990, pp. 723–40. In 1989 the Law Commission published a draft code setting out virtually the whole of the law relating to indictable offences in an accessible, comprehensive, and consistent form: *A Criminal Code for England and Wales* (Law Com. 177), vols. I and II, HMSO, London, 1989. Since then, the Commission has had the objective of enacting separate bills, the first of which codifies the law of non-fatal injuries to the person, together with a number of general principles and defences that apply throughout the criminal law. For a discussion document see Law Commission Consultation Paper No. 122, *Legislating the Criminal Code: Offences Against the Person and General Principles, a Consultation Paper*, HMSO, London, 1992; for proposals and a draft Criminal Law Bill see *Legislating the Criminal Code: Offences Against the Person and General Principles* (Law Com. 218), Cm. 2370, HMSO, London, 1993.

features, but with the addition of a sentencing commission to set detailed guidelines for the imposition of sanctions on federal offenders, a revised bill was the subject of floor debate in the Senate over a period of eight days in January 1978. In the upshot it was passed by a vote of 72 votes to 15.

In the House some far-sighted and sophisticated Democrats, Don Edwards of California and Robert Kastenmeier of Wisconsin among them, did not share the Senators' optimism about the advantages of a sentencing commission. Although no action was taken on the Senate bill in the 95th Congress, the House of Representatives set to work diligently on preparing its own bill. In the 96th Congress, after the House Subcommittee on Criminal Justice had held numerous hearings and met in over one hundred sessions, a bill was reported that only partially recodified federal criminal statutes and made limited changes to sentencing procedures.[52] It too failed to make progress.

Later legislative initiatives were no more successful, while opposition outside Congress mounted. Criticism from civil liberties groups was intense and prolonged. In support of recodification it was explained that many of the criticisms of provisions in the draft code were misguided as they were no more than counterparts of current law. Yet some controversial accretions had formed around the original framework during the years of Republican Administrations, and there was ineradicable suspicion that anything backed by Nixon and Mitchell was unlikely to further the cause of civil liberties. From another quarter the voices of indignant moralists were heard. A number of conservative organizations, including religious organizations, expressed alarm at what they perceived as the code's unduly lenient approach towards pornography, sex offences, prostitution, and drug trafficking. At the same time it was critized for being excessively severe towards corporate crime. It was not altogether a caricature to observe that their complaints added up to an indictment that the code would permit vice to flourish while hounding innocent businessmen into bankruptcy or prison.[53]

Codification efforts were abandoned by Congress in 1982 after more than a decade of inconclusive legislative deliberation. Apart

[52] Stith and Koh, *28 Wake Forest Law Review*, 235, (1993).
[53] Gainer, *Report to the Attorney General on Federal Criminal Code Reform*, p. 171.

from the merits or demerits of its content, a draft criminal code was singularly ill-suited to the ways of Congressional law-making. The essence of the code was its intended consistency, harmony, and structure.[54] The familiar tactic used to progress legislation through Congress of producing multiple proposals as a basis for compromise was simply not available. Nor could the code survive being broken up into separate pieces from which legislators could pick and choose. In the end the piecemeal approach prevailed. Although no further action was taken to renew the objective of codification, certain segments taken from the earlier bills were incorporated in an anti-crime package which was enacted in late 1984 as the Comprehensive Crime Control Act.[55] The whole of the code bill's sentencing provisions, originally regarded by McLellan as a sweetener to liberal opinion,[56] were included, together with proposals permitting the pre-trial detention of dangerous offenders, sections governing the disposition of insane or incompetent defendants, and the extension of wiretap authority.[57]

The sentencing regime approved by the 98th Congress in 1984 required the abolition of the US Parole Commission and the ending of the discretionary power, exercised since 1910, to determine the suitability for release of selected inmates from federal prisons on licence. In its place, a Commission appointed by the President was charged with devising and promulgating a system of sentencing guidelines binding on trial judges in the federal courts. At least three of its members had to be federal judges selected from a list of six judges recommended by the Judicial Conference of the United States.[58] Sentences would be calculated on a graduated scale

---

[54] Ibid., p. 156. [55] Pub. L. 98–473, 98 Stat. 1976.

[56] Stith and Koh, 28 *Wake Forest Law Review*, 232, (1993).

[57] Gainer, *Report to the Attorney General on Federal Criminal Code Reform*, pp. 174–5.

[58] The judicial and the non-judicial members of the US Sentencing Commission required confirmation by the Senate. Although the Department of Justice maintained that the executive functions of an independent sentencing commission set up in the judicial branch of government violated separation of powers principles, and others argued that Congress had granted the Commission excessive legislative discretion, the Supreme Court upheld the constitutionality of its location in the judicial branch. In a rare claim that Congress had improperly delegated its powers to an agency composed in part of federal judges, the Court decided that in creating the Sentencing Commission, an unusual hybrid in structure and authority, Congress had neither delegated excessive legislative power nor upset the constitutionally mandated balance of powers among the coordinate Branches. Judges served on the Commission not in their judicial capacity but because of their appointment by the

according to the gravity of the offence and the offender's prior criminal record. The discretion of the trial judge would be limited to selecting a sentence within a range in which ordinarily the maximum would not exceed the minimum by more than the greater of 25 per cent or six months. The period of time spent in custody would no longer be capable of being shortened by discretionary release on parole, all sentences in future being basically determinate. A prisoner would be released at the end of the sentence passed by the court, reduced only by any credit earned by good behaviour while in prison.

Few of the original proponents believe that events since the commencement of the system of guidelines in 1987 have brought the benefits they had hoped to see. Judicial discretion has been curtailed, but the disparities and uncertainties in sentencing which the reforms sought to eliminate have been replaced by other and less obvious sources of disparity and uncertainty. Plea bargaining transfers power to the prosecutor and determines the offence for which the offender is actually sentenced, and hence the penalty.[59] Although the guidelines are almost universally unpopular amongst federal trial judges, some follow them scrupulously while others, regarding them as unjust, treat them with less reverence. The operation of the system has been criticized as harsh, mechanistic, and excessively rigid. It has led to widespread judicial distress, some outspoken opposition, and a rising level of non-compliance.[60] Both the legislation and the US Sentencing Commission have been blamed for an outcome that is plainly unsatisfactory to all parties. By February 1992, at a symposium held at the Yale Law School to

President under the terms of the Act. *Mistretta* v. *United States*, 109 S. Ct. 647 (1989).

[59] For a detailed study of the use of prosecutorial discretion in charging and plea bargaining under the guidelines see I. H. Nagel and S. J. Schulhofer, 'A Tale of Three Cities: an Empirical Study of Charging and Bargaining Practices under the Federal Sentencing Guidelines', 66 *Southern California Law Review*, 501, (1992). Dr Nagel was a member of the US Sentencing Commission at the time of publication, although the article expresses her personal views. Professor Schulhofer is Director of the Center for Studies in Criminal Justice at the University of Chicago School of Law. In 'Plea Bargaining as Disaster', 101 *Yale Law Journal*, 1979, (1992), Schulhofer advocates the abolition of plea bargaining.

[60] For a critical analysis of why the federal Sentencing Commission and its guidelines have been so much less successful in operation, and accepted by so far fewer practitioners, than their state counterparts, see M. Tonry, *Sentencing Matters*, Oxford University Press, New York, 1996, p. 84. Failure of management is a factor trenchantly documented on pp. 84–9.

deliberate upon what should be done, there can have been no room for dissent from the proposition that when a penalty structure offends those charged with the daily administration of the criminal law, causing tension between the judge's duty to follow the written law and the judge's oath to administer justice, it is time for corrective action to be taken by the judiciary, the Sentencing Commission, and Congress.[61]

The problems encountered in devising a workable framework for sentencing guidelines were compounded in the later 1980s by an over- reliance by legislators on fixed sentences for persons convicted of the possession of drugs as well as dealing in them. The mandatory minimum terms of imprisonment prescribed by statute filled the prisons with relatively low-level drug offenders. For example, in 1993 approximately 3,500 defendants were sentenced to terms of imprisonment in the federal system under mandatory minimum laws for the possession of crack cocaine. The average sentence was more than five years.[62]The sentences for trafficking were longer than the median penalties for armed robbery, kidnapping, or extortion and were hard to reconcile with the painstakingly constructed mathematical matrix relating offence seriousness and previous record to a scale of penalties across the whole range of criminal offences.[63] Nor did the politically mixed parentage of the sentencing reforms in Congress help to make remedial action on agreed lines a realistic possibility.

In the early stages of policy formulation the desire to reduce disparities between sentences for similar offences in the interests of fairness and justice was impeccably liberal in origin. That impetus carried through to the idea, pioneered by a federal judge for the Southern District of New York, Marvin E. Frankel, of a sentencing

[61] The symposium papers, together with abstracts and a summary of the proceedings, were published as a special edition of the *Yale Law Journal*, vol. 101, 1681–2075 (1992). The opening paper by Professor Daniel Freed, an authority on sentencing and Editor of the *Federal Sentencing Reporter*, is a thorough and objective analysis of federal sentencing in the light of experience in operating the guidelines. The conclusion referred to above is taken from his article at p. 1687.

[62] *Hearings before a Subcommittee of the Committee on Appropriations, House of Representatives*, 103rd Congress, 2nd Sess., p. 29, 9 Mar. 1994. Justice Kennedy described these penalties as 'very, very harsh and severe sentences'.

[63] See H. Scott Wallace, 'Mandatory Minimums and the Betrayal of Sentencing Reform', 40 *Federal Bar News and Journal*, 158, (1993). A former Counsel to the Senate Judiciary Subcommittee on Juvenile Justice, the author was Legislative Director of the National Association of Criminal Defense Lawyers 1985–92.

commission to make rules or guidelines that would confine the discretion of individual (and often highly individualistic) judges.[64] A few liberal Democrats took up the cause in the Senate, and support for legislation began to grow in the late 1970s and early 1980s. Bills introduced by Senator Edward Kennedy (Dem. Mass.) were linked at first to the codification project being promoted by McClellan and other Senators more conservative in outlook than Kennedy. It was this that led him into an improbable alliance with his successor as chairman of the Senate Judiciary Committee, the veteran Republican (originally Democrat) Senator from South Carolina, Strom Thurmond. When the Republicans took control of the Senate in 1981 it was Thurmond who sponsored an omnibus anti-crime measure which included the Sentencing Reform Act.[65] The contents were virtually identical to a separate bill introduced by Kennedy. After some unorthodox manoeuvres in the closing stages the Senate bill, with the sentencing provisions attached, was passed by the House of Representatives and signed into law by President Reagan on 12 October 1984.[66]

Before then, however, a series of compromises with conservative opinion had been made over four successive Congresses. None of them was destructive of the original idea, but taken cumulatively they were hostages to fortune. As was so noticeable in the proceedings on the later crime bill in 1993–4, there is an engrained reluctance in the legislative process to abandon accommodations previously reached by hard bargaining. In this way the finishing point in one session of Congress tends to be the starting point for the same issue in the next.[67] Over a nine-year span, sentencing reform had begun its Congressional life as a free-standing measure; had been joined to the bill intended to reform and codify federal

[64] 101 *Yale Law Journal*, 2045 (1992). Marvin Frankel gave the keynote address at the Yale symposium referred to in n. 61 above. His book, *Criminal Sentences; Law Without Order*, Hill and Wang, New York, 1973, was a powerful and influential critique of indeterminate sentencing powers.

[65] Chapter II of the Comprehensive Crime Control Act of 1984, *op. cit.*, may be cited as the Sentencing Reform Act of 1994 (98 Stat. 1987). Section 217 amended the US Code by adding a new Chapter 58 on the Sentencing Commission (28 USC § 991).

[66] K. Stith and S. Y. Koh, 'The Politics of Sentencing Reform: The Legislative History of the Federal Sentencing Guidelines', 28 *Wake Forest Law Review*, 223, (1993). Kate Stith, a Professor at Yale Law School, is conducting a wider study of the federal sentencing guidelines of which this episode of legislative history forms a part.

[67] Ibid., p. 286.

criminal law; had been detached from it to stand alone once more; and finally had been joined to the Reagan Administration's anti-crime proposals enacted in 1984.

It was an ominous portent that the expectations of the two most significant backers of sentencing reform should have been so far apart in their aims. Whereas Kennedy insisted that guidelines were needed because federal sentencing practices, arising out of untrammelled judicial discretion, had become 'a national disgrace', Thurmond was looking forward to a Commission that would issue guidelines and policy statements which had teeth, and would not necessarily approach offences and offenders from 'the lenient perspective'.[68] Looking back a decade later, Michael Tonry encapsulated the underlying cause of the travails of the Sentencing Commission and the guidelines it promulgated in a single lapidary sentence: '. . . the federal sentencing commission legislation was formulated and agreed on in one political era, in which Judge Frankel's ideas were widely shared, but implemented in a different era in which they had little influence.'[69]

V

During the Reagan and Bush years at the White House the penal climate became progressively more punitive. The Republican takeover of the Senate and the subsequent passage of the 1984 Act began a process that was to be repeated many times: the introduction of a crime bill, pushed by Republicans and resisted, although out of political caution not usually killed, by Democrats in Congress. Whether talked up by politicians or for other reasons, there were visible signs that popular opinion was hardening. Debates about whether or not harsher penalties deterred were overtaken by the demand for retribution. An ideology, encouraged by the Administration, took hold that the public would be safer and better protected from the risk of victimization by incarcerating those who had offended against them for as long a time as possible. A single statistic bears out the results of the 'get tough on crime' policy. Between 1975 and 1989 the average prison time per

[68] Ibid., pp. 261–2.
[69] *Sentencing Matters*, op. cit., p. 12. The contextual explanation is developed further at p. 89.

violent crime tripled.[70] Yet, in spite of a record number well in excess of one million people in prison or jail,[71] the incidence of violent crime stuck obstinately at levels which were not only the highest in the Western world but, more relevant to domestic politics, beyond the tolerance of the American public and their elected representatives.

Thus a self-perpetuating cycle was established. To be tough on crime was a political necessity. Toughness on crime meant embracing demonstrably punitive measures, and ignoring a substantial body of public opinion research that indicated significant potential support for programs of prevention, treatment, and alternative sentencing. It meant building more prisons and ensuring that more offenders were sent to them for longer periods as a consequence of mandatory prison sentences. Some were career criminals and repeat violent offenders who were an evident threat to the public. However, others caught in the net, low level drug offenders being an obvious and numerous example, were not. The attraction of mandatory minimum penalties for legislators was straightforward. Politicians were powerless to effect the actual sentences imposed on particular offenders, although they could and did influence by their rhetoric policy decisions on levels of penalty set by sentencing commissions. Where there were no sentencing guidelines in state courts,

[70] A. J. Reiss, Jr. and J. Roth, *Understanding and Preventing Violence*, Report of the National Academy of Sciences Panel on the Understanding and Control of Violence, National Academy Press, Washington, DC, 1993, p. 6.

[71] Out of a general population in the United States of 248,710,000 in 1990, 1,179,694 persons were incarcerated in federal or state prisons and local jails, a rate of 474 per 100,000 of the population. L. W. Jankowski, *Correctional Populations in the United States, 1990*, Bureau of Justice Statistics, US Department of Justice, Washington DC, 1992, Tables 2.1, 2.3, 5.6; and Bureau of the Census, *Statistical Abstract of the United States*, 1992, US Government Printing Office, Washington, DC, 1992, Table 16. By 1992–3 the total number of inmates had increased to 1,339,695, giving an incarceration rate of 519 per 100,000 of the population. M. Mauer, *Americans Behind Bars: The International Use of Incarceration, 1992–1993*, The Sentencing Project, Washington, DC, 1994, Table 1. The comparable rate for England and Wales was 93 per 100,000 of the population. By the end of 1994 the number of persons in custody exceeded one and a half million. The total number of prisoners under the jurisdiction of federal or state correctional authorities was 1,053,738 at the year end 1994. Inmates held in local jails, operated by counties and municipalities and administered by local government agencies, are counted on 30 June each year. The number of jail inmates reached a record level of 490,442 on 30 June 1994, making an overall total of 1,554,180. About one-third are incarcerated in local jails, and two-thirds in state or federal prisons. Bureau of Justice Statistics, *Bulletin*, April and August editions, 1995, Office of Justice Programs, US Department of Justice, Washington, DC.

political rhetoric served to condition the environment in which judges across the nation, having seen the defendant in court, heard the evidence, and considered any relevant reports, duly passed what they judged to be the appropriate sentence to match the seriousness of the offence, but seldom disregarding the expectations of the public. Yet the legislators in Congress felt that they had to respond more decisively to the public mood. They had to act as well as talk. In criminal justice, as in much else, the only positive action open to legislators is to legislate. Even that, however, is hard to achieve and uncertain in outcome. Once adopted, the yardstick of toughness imposes inelastic constraints on the scope for legislative change in the future.

In the Anti-Drug Abuse Act of 1986[72] Congress explicitly adopted a sentencing approach that linked the punishment to the quantity and harmfulness of the narcotic substance. Mandatory minimum penalties were related to the amount of the drugs, rather than to the offender's role in the offence and degree of culpability. The justification for such an inflexible approach was that the punishment should reflect the damage done to society caused by the drugs handled by a particular defendant, irrespective of any personal or other circumstances. In short, the sentence was directed at the offence rather than the offender and his individual responsibility. Five- and ten-year minimum mandatory penalties were set for drug distribution or importation based on the quantity of any mixture or substance containing a detectable amount of the prohibited drug.[73]

Two years later, another Anti-Drug Abuse Act in 1988[74] tightened the screw, adding further mandatory minimums including one that was to cause the greatest of all sentencing disparities: a five-year minimum sentence on first conviction for the possession of crack cocaine exceeding five grams in amount.[75] Simple possession of other dangerous drugs including heroin and powdered cocaine, as well as less than five grams of crack cocaine on first conviction,

---

[72] Pub. L. 99–570, 100 Stat. 3207. [73] 21 USC § 841 (b) (1).

[74] Pub. L. 100–690, 102 Stat. 4181.

[75] Ibid., Sec. 6371 amending 21 USC § 844 (a). These examples, and others, of mandatory minimum penalties for drug offences are listed by Wallace in 'Mandatory Minimums and the Betrayal of Sentencing Reform', *op. cit.*, pp. 159–60. The five-year mandatory minimum was activated also by a second conviction for amounts exceeding three grams, or a third conviction for amounts exceeding one gram.

remained a misdemeanour with a mandatory penalty of no more than fifteen days imprisonment for a second offence. At the other end of the scale was a twenty-year mandatory minimum for drug offences forming part of a continuing criminal enterprise or using a weapon during a violent or drug-trafficking crime.[76] Mandatory sentences of imprisonment for life would be the fate of any offender with two or more prior state or federal drug felony convictions.[77] Attempts and conspiracies were made subject to the same mandatory penalties as completed offences.[78]

Federal judges complained that district courts were being flooded with minor drug cases formerly prosecuted in state courts where the penalties were generally lower for comparable offences.[79] In individual cases mandatory minimum sentences could be unjust and disproportionate, while the removal of all discretion from the court simply transferred its exercise from a public court-room to the privacy of a prosecutor's office. Judicial opinion could not have been expressed more plainly, nor more forcibly, than when two Supreme Court Justices, Souter and Kennedy, were invited to comment on the application of mandatory minimum sentencing at a hearing before a subcommittee of the House of Representatives Committee on Appropriations. Choosing his adjectives with precision, Justice Kennedy said that most judges in the federal system were of the view that mandatory minimums were an 'imprudent, unwise and often unjust mechanism for sentencing'. They took away from the judge the ability to differentiate among a group of defendants involved in a crime according to their degrees of culpability and responsibility.[80] Similarly the Chief Justice of the United States, William Rehnquist, told a conference that mandatory minimums frustrated 'the careful calibration of sentences, from one end of the

[76] Pub. L. 100–690, 102 Stat. 4181, Sec. 6481 and Sec. 6460 amending 21 USC § 848 (a) and 18 USC § 924 (c).

[77] Ibid., Sec. 6452, amending 21 USC § 841 (b) (1) (A).

[78] Ibid., Sec. 6470, amending 21 USC § 846.

[79] A report on mandatory minimum sentences in Feb. 1994 by the Department of Justice showed that 16,316 federal prisoners, amounting to 21 per cent of the total population in federal prisons, could be considered as low-level drug law violators with no record of violence and no previous jail-time. 17 per cent of federal drug prisoners were first-time offenders serving 5–10 year sentences for carrying quantities exceeding five grams of crack cocaine.

[80] *Hearings before a Subcommittee of the Committee on Appropriations, House of Representatives, op. cit.* p. 29.

spectrum to the other, that the guidelines were intended to accom-plish'.[81]

As a child of Congress the US Sentencing Commission was more restrained in its language, but the message was the same. In 1990 the Commission had been formally directed by Congress[82] to respond to a series of questions on the compatibility between guide-lines and mandatory minimums, the effect of mandatory mini-mums, and the options for Congress to exercise its power to direct sentencing policy through mechanisms other than mandatory min-imums. After a thorough review of all the available data, the Commission submitted a special report to the Congress in August 1991.[83] It noted that whereas over sixty criminal statutes contained mandatory minimum penalties applicable to federal offences, only four frequently resulted in convictions. Each of these related to drugs and weapons offences.

The report stated bluntly that despite the expectation that mandatory minimum sentences would be applied to all cases which met the statutory criteria of eligibility, the available data indicated that this was not the case. The lack of uniform application created unwarranted disparity in sentencing, and compromised the poten-tial of the guidelines to reduce disparity. In 35 per cent of cases where the defendant's behaviour 'strongly suggested' that a manda-tory minimum was warranted, defendants had pleaded guilty to offences carrying either non-mandatory or reduced mandatory penalties. Since the charging and plea negotiation processes were neither open to the public nor reviewable by the courts, honesty and truth in sentencing were compromised.

The data 'strongly suggested' that the disparate application of mandatory minimums appeared to be related to the race of the defendant, with whites more likely than non-whites to be sentenced below the applicable mandatory minimum, and to the circuit in which the defendant was sentenced. The differential application on the basis of race and circuit reflected the very kind of disparity and discrimination which the Sentencing Reform Act had been designed to reduce. Whereas the structure of the federal guidelines

---

[81] Quoted in 139 *Cong. Rec.* S. 15317 (daily edn. 8 Nov. 1993).

[82] Pub. L. 101–647, Sec. 1703; 104 Stat. 4845.

[83] United States Sentencing Commission, *Mandatory Minimum Penalties in the Federal Criminal Justice System*, Aug. 1991. The abstract that follows is taken from the Summary at pp. i–iv.

differentiated between defendants convicted of the same offence by a variety of aggravating and mitigating factors with a view to providing just punishment and proportional sentences, mandatory minimum sentences lacked any such distinguishing characteristics. Under the guidelines, offenders classified as similar received similar sentences. Under mandatory minimums, offenders apparently not similar nonetheless received similar sentences. The effect was unwarranted sentencing uniformity. The resort to mandatory minimums had generally been 'single-shot efforts at crime control intended to produce dramatic results'.[84]

The Commission concluded the summary of its findings with this comment:

Congress has ultimate authority over sentencing policy. The question is how Congress can best translate its judgment as to appropriate levels of sentence severity into sentences imposed. Our analyses indicate that the guidelines system established by Congress, because of its ability to accommodate the vast array of relevant offense/offender characteristics, and its self-correcting potential, is superior to the mandatory minimum approach. Congress has effectively communicated its policies on sentencing through the provisions contained in the Sentencing Reform Act and subsequent legislation. It has continuing oversight of the work of the Sentencing Commission through the statutory requirement that proposed guidelines and amendments to guidelines be submitted to Congress for 180-day review before they become effective. The Sentencing Commission is always open to guidance from the Congress through its established oversight mechanisms.[85]

It was not without irony that some of the criticisms, notably of inflexibility and prosecutorial discretion, were the same as those which had been directed at the Commission's own sentencing guidelines. Unlike the guidelines, however, mandatory minimum penalties lacked any mechanism for evaluating their impact or making adjustments. The result had been to magnify the existing weaknesses in the process of federal sentencing still further. There was no rational answer to the Commissioners' critique. The explanation was that mandatory sentencing had been taken up not as a result of any rational consideration of its likely effects, but as a symbolic gesture.

---

[84] United States Sentencing Commission, *Mandatory Minimum Penalties in the Federal Criminal Justice System*, Aug. 1991, p. iii.

[85] Ibid., pp. iii–iv.

American legislators are not alone in being motivated more by the immediate political pressures of public opinion and interest groups than by thoughtful assessment of the likely long-term results of their law-making. In England too, a leading member of the Government, Michael Howard, who as Home Secretary had responsibility for policies towards crime, told the Conservative Party Conference in October 1995 that he intended to bring forward proposals to enact mandatory minimum sentences for serious crimes. These would include a version of 'two strikes and you're out'. Anyone convicted for the second time of a serious violent or sexual offence would receive an automatic sentence of life imprisonment. His announcement, to a mass rally of party activists, was totally unexpected and appeared to fly in the face of American experience as well as peremptorily abandoning a long established principle of judicial decision-taking in sentencing.

One of the most telling objections to the policies aimed at countering the far-reaching evils of drug abuse in America in the 1980s and early 1990s is that the reduction of demand, accepted by a large majority of specialists in the field as well as by law enforcement officers as the most practical solution, was treated as too soft an approach to have any hope of winning more than token political support. Hence the concentration on reducing the supply of drugs, within the countries of origin and at the points of entry to the United States, as well as by stringent law enforcement at both federal and state level, designed to arrest, convict, and punish severely the largest number possible of those identified as being involved in drug trafficking.[86]

VI

The prologue to some of the most dramatic events of the 103rd Congress was set in the Rose Garden of the White House on 11 August 1993. During the presidential campaign Clinton had decided that, if elected, it would be a priority for his administration to bring forward an early crime bill. His strategy was to combine support for crime prevention measures, towards which he was sympathetic, with stronger penalties and law enforcement. It was a

[86] For an account of the strategies in the War on Drugs see Tonry, *Malign Neglect—Race, Crime and Sentencing, op. cit.*, pp. 116–23.

formula identical to that adopted by Tony Blair and the Labour Party in attempting to win back from the Conservative Government the initiative over the 1993–4 legislation on criminal justice. Such a combination, Clinton believed, would have popular appeal as well as being politically attractive to Democrats and their supporters in the urban areas where the needs were greatest and it was contended that too few resources had been directed towards the roots of the problems of crime before the harm occurred. Once installed at the White House, the President told the chairmen of the Judiciary Committees in the Senate and the House, Senator Joseph Biden (Dem. Delaware), and Representative Jack Brooks (Dem. Texas), both veterans of previous crime bill initiatives, that he wanted a bill drafted as soon as possible, building on the compromises reached in the Conference report on the Bush administration's crime bill which had been blocked in the Senate in its final stages. To this starting point he would add some new elements to give a greater emphasis to policing and prevention. On several occasions in the first six months of 1993 Clinton reminded Biden of his wish to see a draft without delay. From the outset he wanted the legislation to be introduced by the Congressional leadership rather than, as had been the practice under the Reagan and Bush Administrations, a bill drafted by the Department of Justice and sent to Congress by way of executive communication. The reasons lying behind this tactic will be explored later in the narrative when the scenario has become more familiar.

The President was accompanied at a 9.30 a.m. news conference by the Attorney General (Janet Reno), Biden, Brooks, and members of Congress from both parties. Representatives of States' Attorneys General, District Attorneys, and police organizations were also present. The first duty of any government, Clinton said, was to try and keep its citizens safe. Clearly, too many Americans were not safe. There was no longer the freedom from fear for all citizens that was essential to security and prosperity. When it was not possible to walk the streets of the cities without fear, then an essential element of civilization had been lost. To restore the rule of law on the streets it was necessary for the Administration to work with thousands of law enforcement officials who risked their lives every day, with the Mayors and the Governors, and the people who dealt with children before they became criminal. Politicians in Washington had to work together too. 'For too long, crime has been used as a way to divide Americans with rhetoric. . . . It is time to use crime as a way to unite Americans through action.' Thanking the Republican members of Congress who were present, the President called on Democrats and Republicans to work with the administration and the law enforcement community to craft the best possible crime legislation.[87]

One of the few specific policies announced was a community policing initiative. This meant having more police officers on the beat, patrolling the same neighbourhoods, and establishing relationships with the local community that would help to prevent crime. A first instalment to honour a campaign pledge to put 100,000 additional police officers on the streets would be the provision of $3.4 billion to make federal grants to state and local governments to increase police presence by up to 50,000 new officers. $150 million had already been made available to hire or rehire police officers, and the Labor Department was allocating funds to retrain newly discharged troops from the United States Armed Forces to become police officers.

The second policy, to which strong emphasis was given, was gun control: 'We must end the insanity of being able to buy or sell a handgun more easily than obtaining a driver's license.'[88] The Brady bill, which required a waiting period before the purchase of a handgun, was simply common sense. It was long past time for Congress to pass it, and if and when it did Clinton would sign the bill. There was no conceivable reason, he said, to delay action one more day. Nor would the effort against crime be complete if it did not eliminate assault weapons from the streets. No other nation would tolerate roving gangs stalking the streets better armed than police. 'Why should we do it? We shouldn't, and we ought to stop it.'[89] Finally, the President spoke about community boot camps for young people that he had worked on in Arkansas. He believed young people who were not yet hardened criminals deserved a second chance and that the discipline, training, and treatment which they would receive would help them to build a good life.

As Governor and a former Attorney General of a largely rural Southern state, Clinton needed no reminders of the risks he was

---

[87] 'Remarks Announcing the Anticrime Initiative and an Exchange With Reporters', 11 Aug. 1993, *Weekly Compilation of Presidential Documents*, 29: 32, 16 Aug. 1993, pp. 1602–4.

[88] Ibid., p. 1603.   [89] Ibid.

taking or the constituency to which he was appealing with his out-spokenness on gun control. Together with habeas corpus reform, by means of limiting petitions from prisoners on death row, which he also wanted to resuscitate, restrictions on the availability of firearms had been a prime cause of the failure of the Bush crime bill to pass the previous Congress. The Brady bill, named after James Brady, a former White House Press Secretary who had been wounded and severely incapacitated in an assassination attempt on President Reagan in 1981, had gained widespread public sympathy. However, it was vigorously opposed by the NRA and its allies, becoming one of the most contested issues in the country. Bills had been introduced in the 100th, 101st, and 102nd Congresses but none had succeeded.[90] As a Presidential candidate in 1992 Clinton had endorsed the attempts to pass the Brady bill. On his election the gun control movement had a sympathetic President in the White House for the first time since Johnson, who had come to office through the fatal shooting of his predecessor.

Where Clinton had executive authority to act, he did. On 11 August, timed to coincide with the announcement of the anti-crime initiative, he issued two directives under existing powers. The first was a memorandum addressed to the Secretary of the Treasury which opened the way to a ban on the import of assault-type pistols.[91] This action stemmed from proposals submitted to the Administration by the Center to Prevent Handgun Violence, the research, legal advocacy, and education affiliate of Handgun Control Inc., outlining a number of regulatory steps that could be taken to reduce gun violence by the Bureau of Alcohol, Tobacco and Firearms (ATF) pursuant to the Bureau's broad regulatory authority.[92] The Center had argued that assault-type pistols did not qualify for exemption from the ban on the importation of firearms under the Gun Control Act of 1968 as they were not 'suitable for or readily adaptable to sporting purposes'.[93]

[90] For the history of the Brady bill see R. M. Aborn, 'The Battle over the Brady Bill and the future of Gun Control Advocacy', 22 *Fordham Urban Law Journal*, 417, (1995). Richard Aborn, a former prosecutor with the Manhattan District Attorney's Office, has been President of Handgun Control Inc since 1992.

[91] Printed in *Weekly Compilation of Presidential Documents*, 29: 32, p. 1605.

[92] Center to Prevent Handgun Violence, *Proposals for the Clinton Administration to Implement New Gun Control Initiatives Without Passing New Legislation* (1993); cited in Aborn, 22 *Fordham Urban Law Journal, op. cit.*, 428–9.

[93] Pub. L. 90–618, 82 Stat. 1214; 18 USC § 922 (1).

The opening sentence of the second Presidential directive, also addressed to the Secretary of the Treasury, was: 'A major problem facing the Nation today is the ease with which criminals, the mentally deranged, and even children can acquire firearms.'[94] Gun-dealer licensing, which encouraged a flourishing criminal market in guns, was open to abuse. The memorandum stated that there were in excess of 287,000 federal firearms licensees, a great number of whom should probably not be licensed. The ATF estimated that only about 30 per cent were bona-fide storefront dealers. Probably 40 per cent of the licensees conducted no business at all and were simply persons who used the licence to obtain the benefits of trading interstate and buying guns at wholesale rates. The remaining 30 per cent engaged in a limited level of business, typically out of private residences. While the federal statute imposed no specific level of business activity required to qualify for a licence, many of the licensees were operating in violation of state and local licensing, taxing, and other business-related laws.[95] The Administration was committed to doing more than preventing the criminal market in illegal guns from continuing to flourish. Since all new firearms used in crime at some point passed through the legitimate distribution system, federal firearms licences represented the first line of defence. The ATF was instructed to improve the thoroughness and effectiveness of background checks in screening applications for dealer licences, including more reliable forms of identification such as fingerprints in order to assist in identifying any criminal or other disqualifying history. Six other requirements were specified with the aim of ensuring that only legitimate gun dealers were in the business of selling guns or holding licences.

A third proposal submitted by the Center to Prevent Handgun Violence was put into effect by the Secretary of the Treasury, Lloyd Bentsen, on 1 March 1994. On that date Bentsen announced the reclassification by the Treasury Department of combat shot-guns, including the Streetsweeper, Strike-12, and USAS-12, as destructive devices, thereby restricting their future sale.[96] Then on 27 May 1994, as part of the grant of most favoured nation status in trade

---

[94] *Weekly Compilation of Presidential Documents*, 29: 32, *op. cit.*, p. 1605.

[95] Ibid., p. 1606.

[96] Aborn, 22 *Fordham Urban Law Journal*, 429, (1995). A Streetsweeper is a revolving cylinder shotgun that fires twelve blasts in less than three seconds without reloading. Like the other two twelve-gauge shotguns, it fails the sporting purposes test in 18 USC § 925 (d) (3).

negotiations with China, the Administration was able to stop the import of Chinese guns that had been modified slightly in order to avoid the ban on the import of assault weapons, but which permitted certain non-sporting long guns.[97]

VII

In the week before the White House lawn party the Republican leadership in Congress had announced their own program. Some of the proposals were broadly bipartisan, such as increased federal aid for local law enforcement, while other policies, more punitive in intent, were familiar enough from the past: a greater emphasis on prison building; mandatory minimum penalties for crimes by gang members; and a restriction on the recourse to habeas corpus petitions by prisoners on death row challenging the lawfulness of their sentences under the Constitution, having exhausted appeals against their conviction in the state and federal appellate courts.[98] Unlike the Democratic version, the Republican proposal did not include any qualification standards for defence counsel in capital cases.[99] Two features of the Republican plans stood out. There was no mention of any need for gun control, while a new nostrum, life imprisonment for thrice convicted felons, popularly known as 'three strikes and you're out', made its first appearance on stage at Capitol Hill.

[97] Aborn, 22 *Fordham Urban Law Journal*, 429, (1995), pp. 429–30.

[98] In English law habeas corpus is an ancient writ, derived from the Royal prerogative, which enables challenges to be made in the High Court to the validity of a person's detention, whether in official or in private custody. Its scope as a post-conviction remedy in England and Wales has been strictly limited, since petitions by prisoners will normally not succeed if it can be shown that their detention results from a judgment by a competent court. The inherited 'privilege of the writ of habeas corpus' had a place in Article 1 of the United States Constitution, which specified the conditions in which it might be suspended. However, it was not until a post-Civil War statute in 1867 that federal habeas corpus became available as a remedy to any state prisoner held in custody in violation of the Constitution, laws, or treaties of the United States. For a historical survey of the growth and decline of habeas corpus, see G. Hughes, *Occasional Paper VIII*, Center for Research in Crime and Justice, New York University School of Law, 1990. Graham Hughes is a Professor of Law at New York University.

[99] Errors made by incompetent counsel account for a substantial proportion of wrongful or unconstitutional convictions in capital cases in state courts. In some 40 per cent of the cases reviewed by way of petitions for habeas corpus, federal courts have found that constitutional violations have occurred.

With the aim of passing an omnibus anti-crime bill by Thanksgiving, parallel bills were introduced in the House of Representatives (HR 3371) and the Senate (S. 1488) on 23 September 1993. Brooks and Biden were the sponsors. Much of the content of the two bills was similar, although there were some variations. Both authorized expenditure to enable states and local government to employ 50,000 more police officers; to develop local education and training programs to prevent crime, violence, and drug abuse in the schools; and to phase in drug treatment at federal prisons. The minimal, but nonetheless worthwhile, attempts to get to grips with the demand side of the drug problem were matched by authorizing expenditure to allow the Drug Enforcement Administration to take on more agents and staff to keep up the pressure on restricting the supply of narcotics.

Both measures extended the list of federal crimes punishable by death, including the murder of federal law enforcement officials, murder by federal prisoners or escaped prisoners, killings by terrorists, and rape, child molestation, and sexual exploitation of children resulting the death of the victim. The House bill extended the death penalty to sixty-four crimes and the Senate bill to forty-seven. In each case death was to be a maximum, and not a mandatory, penalty. The thorny issue of the long drawn-out series of collateral appeals by death row prisoners, which had divided liberals and conservatives within both parties, was whittled down to the compromise of permitting a single federal petition of habeas corpus to be filed within six months of exhausting regular appeals. Indigent defendants would be provided at all state proceedings with counsel meeting rigorous qualifications. The compromise had been hammered out in several months of negotiation between Reno, Biden, and the States Attorneys General and District Attorneys. Some defence lawyers had also seen parts of the proposed legislative language. Even before its publication, however, the formula had been sharply criticized as institutionalizing the diminution of civil rights for condemned prisoners which had resulted from a number of Supreme Court decisions. At the White House launch on 11 August Biden spoke confidently, and as it turned out prematurely, in describing the issue as 'Something the American public does not have much interest in, but has divided us. And we settled it.'[100]

---

[100] *The New York Times*, 14 Aug. 1993.

Another procedural controversy which had been before Congress on previous occasions, the admissibility of evidence obtained illegally, was omitted altogether.

Neither of the original bills authorized expenditure to add to the capacity of the federal prisons to house more convicted felons, although money would be provided for states to build some additional prison places for violent offenders. The Senate version encouraged states to develop military-style boot camps,[101] at one-third of the cost of traditional prisons, for younger non-violent offenders so releasing space in the prisons.[102] Other provisions included drug court programs, new offences of terrorism, sexual violence, and child abuse, kidnapping by parents, and action against youth gangs. Gun control was played in a low key. The House bill contained a waiting period for the purchase of handguns, and authorized expenditure to help states set up an instant check system to replace the period of waiting while checks were made on the bona fides of the purchaser.

Despite the President's forthright statements, the Senate bill went no further than enumerating a number of new penalties for gun crimes and the possession of explosives. The reason was that for tactical purposes Biden had decided the controversial issues of the Brady bill and a ban on assault weapons would be better handled

[101] In this context 'boot camp' means a correctional programme of not more than six months' duration requiring adherence by inmates to a highly regimented schedule that involves strict discipline, physical training, and work. There is also provision for education, job training, substance abuse counselling or treatment, and after-care. Both the terminology and the regime are borrowed from the Marines. Somewhere in the past new recruits to both the Navy and Marine Corps of the naval service were called boots. The description is now out of date, although the term is still applied to the basic training institution. Marine Corps boot camps have a demanding regime which aims to develop self-discipline and self-confidence in young recruits. It is not a correctional program. For this information the author is indebted to Major-Gen. J. Grinalds, USM (retired).

[102] In 1993 forty-one boot camp facilities were operated in twenty-six state correctional systems. In May of that year members of the English Prison Service Senior Management Programme visited a boot camp facility operated by the Maryland State Correctional Institution. Their impressions were published in 99 *Prison Service Journal*, 3 (1995). By then it was Home Office policy to open two institutions with similar regimes in England in 1996. On 18 Sept. 1995 the Home Secretary announced that a new, tough, and demanding regime for young offenders would be introduced. The regime would be based on some of the positive aspects of United States boot camps, together with other approaches that had been found effective in reducing reoffending. Young offenders would be selected by the Prison Service to take part in the new regime. Letter to author from Ann Widdecombe MP, Minister of State at the Home Office with responsibility for prisons, 10 Oct. 1995.

in separate measures which would not jeopardize the passage of the main crime bill. The Republicans' enthusiasm for a three-strikes law, a novelty not previously considered by Congress,[103] met no response at this stage. Nor was there any reference in either bill to racial justice, an issue of great concern to the Black Caucus and to some other liberal Democrats in the House. Several months later their insistence that the legislation must include provisions to combat any racial discrimination in the imposition of the death penalty was one of the two key issues that brought the crime bill to the edge of the abyss into which Bush's previous attempts had fallen. The other was the ban on assault weapons, also delayed for tactical reasons until the forces in Congress could be assessed and the necessary bargains forged to get the votes.

VIII

Let us pause here to take stock. On its introduction the anti-crime legislation was already a compromise. It was constructed from elements which had previously passed one or both Houses, or where the Congressional leaders believed the capacity for inter-party agreement existed. Yet significant policy differences remained between the mainstream Democrats, the Congressional Black Caucus and its sympathizers, and the conservative Democrats. On the Republican side too there were cross-currents. Both the Senate and the House contained Republican moderates whose support would be crucial to the passage of the legislation. Democrats had not abandoned faith in the potential for preventive programs, for young people and drug-abusers in particular, although care was taken to associate them with policies such as community-oriented policing to avoid the categorization of 'soft on crime'. The Republican leadership continued to press for stronger penalties, including mandatory minimum sentences and the building of new prisons, although the body politic did not seem any less threatened as a result of the dominance of these policies during twelve years of

---

[103] Many states already had recidivist statutes which called for life imprisonment after multiple convictions. Under federal law mandatory life imprisonment after two or more convictions was the penalty for certain serious drug violations and firearms offences. The novelty lay in the breadth of some formulations of the three-strikes policy, and the popular appeal of the link with baseball.

Republican administrations. Real as they were, these differences had not prevented coalitions from being formed before between moderate Republicans and the mainstream Democrats in the House, while in the more evenly balanced Senate tacit understandings had been reached on a variety of issues.

Consensus between relatively like-minded pragmatists in the two parties, however, would not be enough. Concessions unwelcome to the administration would have to be made to Republican hardliners, as well as to Democrat liberals, and to those in either party whose vision had been narrowed by the pursuit of special interests. Gun control was a rock on which the whole initiative could be wrecked. How different a picture from Westminster, where the idea that a bill presented to Parliament should incorporate policies emanating from the Opposition parties, and included in order to win their support for its passage, would be anathema to ministers and back-benchers alike. As we have seen in earlier Chapters, the adversarial nature of the parliamentary process encourages an all-or-nothing approach: all for the Government in power and nothing for the Opposition, with any but the most minor amendments made to bills contrary to the Government's intentions being treated as damaging defeats. If compromise in the passage of legislation is notably lacking in Parliament, it is the lifeblood of law-making by Congress.

6

Symbolism and Reality

I

Within weeks of its introduction there was a divergence between the House of Representatives and the Senate over the handling of the anti-crime legislation. While Senator Biden continued with a broad-brush bill, working to gain sufficient support in the Senate for its main proposals, Representative Brooks took another course. Unable to persuade liberals on the Judiciary Committee to adopt the omnibus bill, which they regarded as too harsh, he switched to the tactic of moving a series of smaller bills, including the Brady bill and ten other less contentious subjects. Action was deferred on the most controversial items, such as extensions to the federal death penalty and revising habeas corpus procedures, on the grounds that both liberal and conservative law-makers needed more time to debate those issues. Brooks was not willing, he said, 'to see important, innovative crime prevention programs like cops on the beat be deferred at a time when the American public is clamoring for us to provide more protection against violent acts'.[1]

By the end of November 1993 the House of Representatives had approved eleven single subject bills. These covered: federal drug treatment; youth gangs; state drug treatment; community policing; the Brady bill (HR 1025); prison alternatives; a youth handgun ban; crimes against women; crimes against minors; kidnapping by parents; and control over child-care providers. The last two (HR 3378 and HR 1237) quickly passed the Senate and were signed into law by the President on 2 December and 20 December.[2]

---

[1] 1993 *Congressional Quarterly (CQ) Almanac*, Vol. XLIX, Washington, D.C., 1994, p. 298.

[2] The International Parental Kidnapping Act of 1993 (Public Law 103–73, 107 Stat. 1998) made it a federal crime for a parent to kidnap a child under the age of sixteen from his custodial parents and to remove the child from the United States. The National Child Protection Act of 1993 (Public Law 103–209, 107 Stat. 2490) established criminal background checks for child-care providers.

The slow progress in the House meant that the objective of getting the main legislation enacted before the end of the 1st Session of the 103rd Congress could not be realized. There were two main causes: liberal disillusion with the direction in which the legislation was developing, and obstruction by the Congressional Black Caucus (CBC). Penal reformers had been encouraged earlier in 1993 by the overtly pro-prevention stance taken by Janet Reno, and expounded in a series of high profile speeches around the country during her first months in office as Attorney General.[3] Public reaction generally had been supportive and, although previously little known, she had become recognized as a popular and respected member of the administration. As described in the last Chapter, the federal judiciary, many of them Republican appointees, were highly critical of the disparities and injustices resulting from mandatory minimum sentences in practice, while corrections officials, state legislators, and a cross-section of criminal justice professionals were questioning the penal rationale and heavy burden of financial cost of continuing to build prisons as a solution to crime. To liberals it seemed that the ground was prepared and the climate receptive for the consideration of alternative policies to ever-harsher penalties and the reliance on incarceration as the main planks of anti-crime policy.[4]

If the Administration's initial approach, with the accent on policing, additional funds for prisons, the death penalty, boot camps, and drug treatment was a disappointment, it was soon eclipsed by the reaction to the bill by members of Congress. In each House, but the Senate especially, legislators vied to out do each other and to impress their intended audiences with demonstrations of the toughness of their attitudes. Speech after speech, amendment after amendment, called for more punitive policies, without regard to their likely effect. The Senate held no hearings, although a number of the proposals had been the subject of previous testimony. It was

---

[3] Janet Reno's nomination as the first woman to serve as Attorney General of the United States was confirmed by a unanimous vote in the Senate on 11 Mar. 1993. One of the themes of her early speeches was that pre-natal care was more important than prisons in controlling crime.

[4] For a well informed account of the passage of the legislation, and the collapse of the hopes of liberal reformers, see M. Mauer, 'The Fragility of Criminal Justice Reform', 21 *Social Justice*, 14–29, (1995). Marc Mauer is Assistant Director of the Sentencing Project in Washington, DC. The project was established in 1986 as a national non-profit organization to promote sentencing reform.

when Brooks attempted to impose the same procedure in the House that Democrats belonging to the CBC demanded a slowing down to allow a fuller public review of the proposals before any floor votes were scheduled.

The CBC was a cohesive force in the House of Representatives, and one to which the Democratic leadership had to pay close attention. Positioned on the party's left wing, its membership and influence had expanded steadily since its formation in 1970 with a membership of nine. The numbers had grown to about twenty by the mid-1980s, mainly concentrating on civil rights issues and sanctions against South Africa.[5] The 1992 elections which brought Clinton to the White House increased the strength of the caucus from twenty-six to thirty-eight Democratic Representatives. The nominal Congressional membership was forty, including a lone Republican, who seldom agreed with the caucus and was often shut out of its meetings,[6] and one Democratic Senator.[7]

The intersection of race, economics, and criminal justice policies[8] subjected black Congressmen to electoral pressures which were not shared by other legislators. While there was some awareness on Capitol Hill that the increased rates of incarceration had led to a costly quadrupling of prison populations over the two decades since the early 1970s, special interest pressures on elected representatives in their districts for the lesser use of imprisonment were minimal. However, in the mainly black districts the situation was markedly different. Whereas in the decade 1973–82 the proportion of African–American males in custody moved in step with the increase in custodial populations overall, a sharp escalation occurred in the mid-1980s. During that period drug offenders began to account for a progressively larger share of prison admissions, with African-Americans making up an ever larger share of drug convictions.

Between 1983 and 1993 the number of incarcerated drug offenders rose by 510 per cent, the majority of them being low-income African–Americans.[9] In 1990 the remarkable statistic had been published, and attracted much comment, that one in four African-

---

[5] 1993 *CQ Almanac*, p. 17.   [6] Ibid.
[7] Carol Moseley-Braun, Junior Senator for Illinois.
[8] Mauer, 21 *Social Justice, op. cit.* 19.
[9] For example, in 1992 African-Americans and Hispanics represented 89.7 per cent of all sentences to state prisons for drug possession offences. M. Mauer and T. Huling, *Young Black Americans and the Criminal Justice System: Five Years Later*, The Sentencing Project, Washington, DC, 1995, p. 13.

American males in the age group 20–29 was under some form of criminal justice supervision (in prison or jail, or on probation or parole) on any given day. Five years later the situation had worsened still further. From an examination of the data for 1994, and using the same methodology, it was calculated that almost one in three (32.2 per cent) of young black men in the same age group was under criminal justice supervision on any given day. The cost of criminal justice control for these 827,440 young African-American males was about $6 billion per year.[10] The fact that homicide was the leading cause of death among young black men was noted in the previous Chapter.

It was not only penal reformers who identified a vicious cycle with no clear resolution in sight. As Marc Mauer has pointed out, with the decline of manufacturing jobs in many parts of the country the urban economy and opportunity structure for the generation reaching adulthood changed. The limited availability of economic opportunities, combined with the lure of the drug trade and its financial rewards, resulted in unprecedented levels of criminal justice control over young black males.[11] The resulting polarities of opinion were equally ominous, with many African-Americans regarding the system of justice as irremediably biased against them, and many white Americans believing that crime is linked to race and ethnicity.

In the spring of 1993, when the Democratic and Republican leaderships were working on their crime bills, staff from the offices of several members of the CBC began meetings to develop an alternative bill. Advisers were called on to assist, and a comprehensive 280-page bill 'to prevent crime and to reform the criminal justice system to make it more fair' (HR 3315) was introduced in the House of Representatives on 19 October 1993. The declaratory findings printed at the start sounded several themes that were to be reiterated throughout the coming months. It was stated that:

> (6) many measures included in what is usually called a crime bill (more penalties, more Federal crimes, longer prison sentences) do nothing to reduce crime and polarize and shift the focus and resources away from

---

[10] M. Mauer, *Young Black Men and the Criminal Justice System: A Growing National Problem*, The Sentencing Project, Washington, DC, 1990; and *Young Black Americans and the Criminal Justice System: Five Years Later*, ibid., p. 1.

[11] Mauer, 21 *Social Justice, op. cit.*, 19–20.

strategies that have proven to be more effective in addressing crime and violence;

(7) law enforcement professionals agree that the solutions to the Nation's crime and drug problems will be found in crime prevention measures that include drug treatment, early childhood intervention programs, full funding for Head Start programs and the Women, Infants and Children Program, rehabilitation and alternatives to incarceration, community policing, and family support programs, as well as in programs to rebuild communities through education, employment, and housing . . .

(9) there is a sense of distrust and a widespread perception in many communities, particularly among people of color, that the criminal justice system values victims differently and is at times fundamentally unfair to criminal defendants of color;

(10) the perception and reality of racial bias in the workings of the criminal justice system is deeply corrosive of one of the most important institutions in our society and the perception of unfairness robs the criminal justice system of the respect and credibility it must have to achieve its goal of keeping the public safe and maintaining law and order;

(11) reform of the criminal justice system is necessary to restore the credibility and respect that have been undermined by racism, excessive and disproportionate prison sentences, abusive police practices and civil forfeiture practices . . .

HR 3315 placed greater emphasis on prevention and alternatives to incarceration than did the Brooks/Biden versions. It aimed to reduce the much criticized disparity in sentencing for crack-cocaine and powdered cocaine drug offences; it abolished minimum mandatory sentences; and it put forward less restrictive habeas corpus reforms. A substantial part of the bill dealt with firearms, incorporating a waiting period to enable checks to be made on the intending purchaser before the sale of a handgun; and a non-retrospective prohibition on the sale or possession of certain semi-automatic assault weapons. Licensed dealers would be subjected to more effective regulation. The bill contained no new death penalties, concentrating instead on measures to counter racially discriminatory capital sentencing which would narrow its implementation. The latter proposals were cited as the Racial Justice Act of 1993.

The bill attracted twenty-four named sponsors, not all of whom were members of the CBC. It was well received in the press: *The Washington Post* commented in an editorial that it was a counterweight for those who had reservations about the leadership proposals.[12] With the endorsement of the Congressional Hispanic Caucus, the combined caucuses represented almost sixty votes, a sizeable proportion of the Democratic majority in the House. The CBC bill became a rallying point for organized opposition to much of the content of the Brooks bill and to the fast-track treatment sought by the Democratic leadership. The chairman of the Subcommittee of the Judiciary Committee on Crime and Criminal Justice, Representative Charles Schumer (Dem., New York), initially opposed holding hearings on the bill. Ultimately, however, he acceded to the CBC's request, which culminated in two full days of hearings on 22 and 23 February 1994.

Over the entire period that the anti-crime legislation was before the 103rd Congress, the most significant positive achievement of the supporters of the CBC bill was to sustain a higher level of funding for prevention programs than would otherwise have been enacted. Their influence was crucial during the early negotiations on the Democratic proposals, and later in maintaining programs which might otherwise have been eliminated or cut back more than they were. While the most publicly visible opposition to the leadership bill in the final post-conference stages, which divided members of the CBC, centred upon the absence of the racial justice provisions, there remained until the end some who refused to abandon their objections of principle to what they regarded as the too heavily punitive orientation of the legislation as a whole.

II

On one issue at least, the CBC, the mainstream Democrats in the House of Representatives, and the Administration saw eye to eye. The Brady bill had been passed by the House on 10 November 1993, the voting being 238 yeas to 189 nays.[13] The result was almost identical to a floor vote on a slightly different version of the bill in the 102nd Congress, which had passed the House of

[12] *The Washington Post*, 22 Oct. 1993.

[13] 139 *Cong. Rec.* D 1291 (daily edn. 10 Nov. 1993). All references to the *Congressional Record* are to the edition published daily reporting the public proceedings when one or both Houses are in session. The revised and bound edition is not available until some years later. As at 1 Jan. 1995 the most recent bound volume reports proceedings in Oct. 1989.

Representatives by 239–186.[14] Then, as later, the problems lay in the Senate. Although in somewhat altered form the bill was passed by the Senate in June 1991,[15] it had been obstructed when there had not been enough votes to end the debate on the report of the House-Senate Conference Committee reconciling the differences between the respective bills.[16]

Once again, having passed the House with relative ease, the Brady bill ran into a determined filibuster on the floor of the Senate in November 1993. The Administration made strenuous efforts to break the impasse: the Attorney General, accompanied by Mrs Brady,[17] lobbied Senators in person on Capitol Hill, backed up by Vice-President Gore with telephone calls. The NRA, arguing that the bill posed no threat to criminals while inconveniencing the law abiding, was engaged simultaneously in furious lobbying. On Friday 19 November, after a vote approving the main crime bill package, opponents of gun control twice defeated motions to close the debate on the Brady bill[18] and the prospects looked bleak. Over the weekend the indications of public sentiment in favour of the measure began to undermine the resolve of some of the Congressional opponents to the waiting period for the purchase of a handgun. Although the conference report was passed by the House on Monday, 22 November by 238 votes to 188,[19] it was stalled again in the Senate. By then, however, tense negotiations were taking place behind the scenes between Biden and Robert Dole (Kansas), the Senate Republican Leader. The majority of Democrats and a smaller number of Republican Senators wanted to see the bill passed, but the Republican leadership continued to obstruct.

On 24 November Dole dropped his opposition when the Democratic leadership agreed to let the Senate consider legislation

[14] 137 *Cong. Rec.* H 2879 (daily edn. 8 May 1991).

[15] 137 *Cong. Rec.* S 9086 (daily edn. 28 June 1991).

[16] For the history of the Brady bill in the 100th, 101st, and 102nd Congresses see R. M. Aborn, 22 *Fordham Urban Law Journal* 417 at 420–5 (1995).

[17] Sarah Brady became Chairman of the Board of Handgun Control, Inc. in 1989 and also chaired its associated Center to Prevent Handgun Violence.

[18] On each vote to close the debate there was a majority of 57 to 42, 139 *Cong. Rec.* S 16332–3 and S 16417 (daily edn. 19 Nov. 1993). Under Senate Rules 60 votes are required to end the debate and invoke closure. It is this rule which facilitates filibusters in the Senate, since more votes are needed to end the filibuster than the simple majority required to pass a bill or an amendment. There is no parallel procedure in the House of Representatives.

[19] 139 *Cong. Rec.* H 10907–8 (daily edn. 22 Nov. 1993).

to modify the bill the following year. This modest, and essentially face-saving, concession would make possible the phasing out of the waiting-period requirement in two years, provided that by then the national computerized checking system had reached a certain level of accuracy.[20] With that settlement, the conference report was accepted and the bill passed after some brief remarks on 24 November. Few Senators were present in a chamber emptied by the Thanksgiving holiday. The two Leaders, George Mitchell (Maine) for the Democratic majority and Dole for the Republican minority, pronounced the measure adopted by unanimous consent on a voice vote. Dole was magnanimous: 'After a long, long, hard fight, Jim Brady has won. . . I believe all of us will feel better to have this issue behind us. There will be other issues, maybe other gun issues, but at least as far as the Brady bill is concerned it has now passed.'[21] The Senate then adjourned until 25 January 1994.

The following week, in the East Room at the White House, the President signed the bill into law on 30 November. It was a genuinely moving ceremony, far removed from the normal run of reportable happenings orchestrated by the Administration or its opponents. Seated in a wheel chair beside Clinton was James Brady, who all those years ago had stood beside another President when both were shot. 'How sweet it is; how long it took' was Brady's subdued comment. Clinton was more forceful. Thumping the lectern for emphasis, he recalled his own upbringing:

I come from a State where half the folks have hunting and fishing licenses. I can still remember the first day when I was a little boy out in the country putting a can on top of a fencepost and shooting a .22 at it. I can still remember the first time I pulled a trigger on a .410 shotgun because I was too little to hold a .12-gauge. I can remember these things. This is part of the culture of a big part of America.

. . . We have taken this important part of the life of millions of Americans and turned it into an instrument of maintaining madness. It is crazy. Would I let anybody change that life in America? Not on your life. Has

[20] The requirement in the Act was that thirty months after its enactment the Attorney General must make a determination as to whether the national instant-check system was operational. It would be deemed to be operational when at least 80 per cent of current criminal history records nationwide were available on the system. Once the instant-check system met the statutory standard, the Attorney General must certify it to be operational. At that stage gun dealers would be required to consult the instant-check system before any firearm sale took place, and the waiting-period requirement would cease to have effect.

[21] 139 *Cong. Rec.* S 17091 (daily edn. 24 Nov. 1993).

that got anything to do with the Brady bill or assault weapons or whether the police have to go out on the street confronting teenagers who are better armed than they are? Of course not.[22]

Exacerbated by the unremitting hostility of the NRA, gun control had become one of the most enduring and highly politicized of all crime policy issues. The 1993 Act[23] only delayed and did not ban the possession of handguns, allowing five working days for law enforcement authorities to check the background of every intending handgun purchaser for evidence of a criminal or mentally unstable past. Even with such limited scope, it was the first restriction of the general availability of firearms to be enacted by Congress for twenty-five years.[24] In 1968, the year of the assassinations by shooting of Martin Luther King and Robert F. Kennedy, the Administration had tried to introduce a ban on the sale by mail order of rifles and shotguns. The proposal was not acceptable to Congress, neither House being willing to go further than prohibiting the shipment or transportation of handguns and ammunition in interstate or foreign commerce, other than by licensed importers or dealers, and the purchase over the counter of handguns by non-residents of the state. Rifles and shotguns were exempt.

The Omnibus Crime Control and Safe Streets Act[25] was signed by President Johnson on 19 June 1968. Public opinion was so shocked, however, at the murder two weeks before of Robert Kennedy, a Senator and Presidential aspirant at the time of his death, that within a few months a second and more restrictive law was enacted. The Gun Control Act of 1968[26] removed the exemption of rifles and shotguns and prohibited the sale of handguns or ammunition to young people below the age of twenty-one. The Act

---

[22] 'Remarks on Signing the Brady Bill', 30 Nov. 1993, *Weekly Compilation of Presidential Documents*, 29: 48, 6 Dec. 1993, p. 2478.

[23] The Act was named in James Brady's honour as the Brady Handgun Violence Prevention Act of 1993 (Public Law 103–59, 107 Stat. 1536).

[24] Prior to 1993 nothing in federal law prevented an individual from obtaining a firearm by simply filling out a form stating that the potential purchaser was not a felon, had never been dishonourably discharged from a branch of the Armed Services, was not under indictment, nor a fugitive. No verification was required of the information given. Some states had more stringent requirements, and at the time of the passage of the Brady bill twenty-two states required some form of background check for would-be handgun purchasers. Aborn, 22 *Fordham Urban Law Journal* 417, 418 (1993).

[25] Pub.L. 90–351, 82 Stat. 197.   [26] Pub. L. 90–618, 82 Stat. 1213.

also specified certain high-risk categories of person, including drug-abusers, who were declared ineligible to purchase firearms. In his remarks on signing what he described as 'the most comprehensive gun control law ever signed in this Nation's history', Johnson added that Congress had not carried out all the requests made of them by the Administration. He had asked for the national registration[27] of all guns and the licensing[28] of those who carried them.[29] He continued:

If guns are to be kept out of the hands of the criminal, out of the hands of the insane, and out of the hands of the irresponsible, then we just must have licensing. If the criminal with a gun is to be tracked down quickly, then we must have registration in this country.

The voices that blocked these safeguards were not the voices of an aroused nation. They were the voices of a powerful lobby, a gun lobby, that has prevailed for the moment in an election year.

. . . We must continue to work for the day when Americans can get the full protection that every American citizen is entitled to and deserves—the kind of protection that most civilized nations have long ago adopted. We have been through a great deal of anguish these last few months and these last few years—too much anguish to forget so quickly.[30]

In his sixth and last annual message to Congress on the State of the Union, President Johnson repeated the same message with a vehemence not heard again from an occupant of the White House for more than two decades. As he left the Office of the Presidency, he said, one of his greatest disappointments was the failure to secure passage of a licensing and registration Act for firearms. If such an Act had been passed, he believed that it would have reduced the incidence of crime.[31] Although Johnson, so experienced in the ways of Congress,[32] had looked forward to further restrictions on the availability of firearms at 'not too distant a date', the next action taken by Congress did not come until 1986. When it did, the legislation amended, and for the most part weakened, the provisions of

[27] Registration means keeping records of the transfer or ownership of a specific handgun or firearm.

[28] Licences or permits issued to individuals to entitle the holder to purchase, receive, or possess a handgun or firearm.

[29] 'Remarks upon Signing the Gun Control Act of 1968', 22 Oct. 1968, *Public Papers of the Presidents of the United States, 1968–69*, Book II, US Government Printing Office, Washington, DC, 1970, p. 1059.

[30] Ibid., pp. 1059–60.   [31] Ibid., p. 1266.

[32] Lyndon Johnson was a US Senator from Texas 1948–61, and Minority or Majority Leader in the Senate 1953–61, before becoming Vice-President in 1961.

the Gun Control Act. The Firearm Owners' Protection Act of 1986[33] restored the exemption of rifles and shotguns from the interstate trade prohibition, although retaining the ban on interstate sales of handguns. It also narrowed the definition of who needed to obtain a licence to sell firearms and relieved ammunition dealers of record-keeping requirements.

As its name implied, the 1986 Act stood as a monument to the NRA. In many ways it marked the high point of its influence. For years the NRA had campaigned against the hated Gun Control Act. By its own account it spent an estimated $1.6 million working to overturn the Act, a figure which excluded campaign contributions. The money was spent on advertisements, direct mailing, lobbying, and other expenses. In addition, Federal Election Commission records showed that through its Political Victory Fund the NRA spent a total of $1.7 million on the Congressional elections to the Senate and House of Representatives in 1986.[34] Although there were other and deeper factors at work besides campaign finance, an independent analysis of the voting on the legislation indicated that 80 per cent of those legislators who voted with the NRA position had received campaign contributions from the Association or its affiliated organizations, while 80 per cent of those who voted against had not received any NRA support.[35] The legislation in 1986 was signed by President Reagan, a lifetime member of the Association, who symbolized in his own person and political ideology many of the values to which it appealed so emotively.

The disabled James Brady and his wife Sarah, a skilled campaigner and former worker for the Republican party, had crusaded tirelessly throughout the 1980s and a waiting period was incorporated in the 1988 drugs and anti-crime bill. It did not succeed in getting the approval of the House, although the Anti-Drug Abuse Act of 1988,[36] which contained some general criminal and law enforcement provisions, required the US Attorney General to develop a felon identification system. Another Act of 1988, the Undetectable Firearms Act,[37] aimed to regulate plastic guns by

---

[33] Pub. L. 99–308, 100 Stat. 449 (McClure-Volkmer Amendments).

[34] O. S. Davidson, *Under Fire: the NRA and the Battle for Gun Control*, Henry Holt, New York, 1993, p. 80. See also J. Sugarman, *National Rifle Association: Money, Firepower and Fear*, National Press Books, Washington, DC, 1992.

[35] The data was compiled by Common Cause. See Davidson, *Under Fire: the NRA and the Battle for Gun Control, op. cit.*, pp. 79–80.

[36] Pub. L. 100–690, 102 Stat. 4181.   [37] Pub. L. 100–649, 102 Stat. 3186.

banning the manufacture, import, possession, and transfer of firearms not detectable by security devices. The following year the Brady bill was reintroduced by Democrats in both chambers, only to see it founder in Senate Judiciary Subcommittee hearings. In 1990 the gun lobby beat back three separate attempts to enact further restrictions on firearms, including a ban on assault weapons and a seven-day waiting period before a person could buy a handgun.

Financial contributions to candidates in the 1990 Congressional elections were thought likely to have strengthened the hand of the NRA in the 102nd Congress, although the proponents of gun control were making some headway. According to the Federal Election Commission's figures, the NRA spent $916,135 on 1990 campaigns. By comparison, the fledgling but increasingly effective counter-lobby, Handgun Control Inc. (HCI), spent $178,882.[38] Both chambers voted for the handgun waiting period in 1991 by comfortable majorities: 239–186 in the House on 8 May, and 67–32 in the Senate on 28 June.[39] Yet when the anti-crime bill of which it was part reached the final stage, it was lost when the Senate failed to adopt the conference report. Two further efforts were blocked in the Senate the following year, in March and October 1992.

III

Although polls consistently indicated that the advocates of gun control had the majority of public opinion on their side, HCI and others had a hard task in competing with the relentless political pressures generated by the gun-rights activists. Fear of political intervention in elections by the NRA or its supporters against legislators who had advocated gun control in Congress was well founded, as was demonstrated in the mid-term elections in November 1994. There was also an authentic populist strain of

[38] *Congress and the Nation*, vol. VIII, 1989–92, Congressional Quarterly, Washington, DC, p. 765. Handgun Control Inc. was founded in 1974, and its associated Center to Prevent Handgun Violence in 1983.

[39] The party breakdown of the voting in the House was Democrats: 179 for and 83 against; Republicans: 60 for and 102 against; Independent: 1 against. In the Senate the voting was Democrats: 48 for and 8 against; Republicans: 19 for and 24 against. 137 *Cong. Rec.* H 2879 (daily edn. 6 May 1991) and 137 *Cong. Rec.* S 9086 (daily edn. 28 June 1991).

opinion upholding the NRA campaign. As crime, and especially violent crime, became so pervasive, a deep-rooted commitment to what was claimed to be the inalienable right of Americans to keep and bear arms was strengthened. Arguments about the ownership and, if called for, the use of guns to protect persons and property merged with a righteousness attached to the possession of firearms for farming, hunting, and sporting purposes.

None of this had much to do with the post-colonial right, indeed duty, of the citizenry to keep and bear arms to avoid the dangers of depending on a standing army for the defence of the new states.[40] But the assertion of a constitutional right, however remote the connection with modern life, added a sense of legitimacy to a personal need keenly felt. More than that was the conviction lodged in the minds of some of the true believers that their constitutionally conferred right justified holding firearms in order to check the excesses of an arbitrary government if its actions encroached on the fundamental freedoms of the populace.[41] Claims of the ultimate right of an armed citizenry to overthrow an oppressive and tyrannical government read better in the pages of law journals than they seemed after the emergence of the new-style citizen militias which came to public notice following the bombing of a federal office building in Oklahoma City in April 1995 with a death toll of 168 people including 19 children.

Two hundred years after the Bill of Rights the constitutional position can be stated briefly since it is a matter of settled law. The wording of the Second Amendment of the Constitution of the United States reads: 'A well regulated Militia, being necessary for the security of a free State, the right of the people to keep and bear

---

[40] *To Keep and Bear Arms: The Origins of an Anglo-American Right* by Joyce Lee Malcolm, Harvard University Press, Cambridge, Mass. and London, 1994, is an academic dissertation tracing the evolution of the right of citizens to have weapons from its roots in seventeenth-century England to its inclusion in the American Bill of Rights. The author's thesis that the right to keep and bear arms extended to private use as well as the defence of the state in well regulated militias was challenged by Garry Wills, 'To Keep and Bear Arms', *New York Review of Books*, 21 Sept. 1995, pp. 62–73 at p. 66. Wills also took to task the authors of some law journal articles justifying individual gun ownership on the basis of the Second Amendment. Replies to his arguments were published in *New York Review of Books*, 16 Nov. 1995, pp. 61–3.

[41] G. Wills, 'The New Revolutionaries', *New York Review of Books*, 10 Aug. 1995, pp. 52–5. A 'definitive manual for preserving your right to keep and bear arms' was published by W. R. LaPierre: *Guns, Crime, and Freedom*, Harper Perennial, New York, 1995. Wayne LaPierre is Executive Vice-President of the NRA.

Arms, shall not be infringed.' Relying on the last part of the Amendment, the NRA and other opponents of legal restrictions on the availability of firearms claim that gun control legislation is unconstitutional in that it violates a fundamental right to keep and bear arms conferred by the Second Amendment. The courts have taken a different view. As long ago as 1876 in *US* v. *Cruikshank*[42] the Supreme Court held that the right to keep and bear arms was not a right granted by the Constitution; that it was not dependent on the Constitution for its existence; and that the right of the citizen was protected only to the extent that the right to hold a firearm was necessary for states to maintain well regulated militias.[43] Eschewing selective quotation, in *US* v. *Miller* in 1939 the Supreme Court decided that the obvious purpose of the Second Amendment was 'to assure the continuation and render possible the effectiveness' of the militia. The Amendment 'must be interpreted and applied with that end in view'.[44] In 1980, upholding a federal statute prohibiting a felon from possessing a firearm, the Court in *Lewis* v. *US* found no constitutionally protected liberties infringed by the law.[45]

In two other cases, not involving the Second Amendment, the Court affirmed that the modern equivalent of the eighteenth century militia is the National Guard.[46] In more than thirty cases since *Miller* was decided, lower federal and state courts have found that the Second Amendment guarantees no right to keep and bear a firearm that does not have some reasonable relationship to the preservation or efficiency of a 'well-regulated militia'. There has been unanimity in rejecting the contention that the Amendment

[42] 92 US 588 (1876); SC, 2 Otto, 542–69.

[43] For a balanced study of the historical perspective and judicial interpretation, see W. Freedman, 'Terminology and Meaning of the Second Amendment', in *The Privilege to Keep and Bear Arms: The Second Amendment and Its Interpretation*, Quorum Books, New York, Westport, Conn. and London, 1989, pp. 19–41.

[44] 59 S. Ct. 816, 818 (1939). The modern case-law is summarized in *The Second Amendment: Myth and Meaning*, a Legal Action Project published by the Center to Prevent Handgun Violence, Washington, DC. For a critical scholarly commentary, see S. Levinson, 'The Embarrassing Second Amendment', 99 *Yale LJ* 637 (1989).

[45] *Lewis* v. *US*, 100 S. Ct. 915, 921 (1980).

[46] *Maryland* v. *US*, 85 S. Ct. 1293 (1965), and *Perpich* v. *Department of Defense*, 110 S. Ct. 2418 (1990). The statute of 1792 establishing 'an Uniform Militia throughout the United States' was described as 'obsolete and worthless' by President Theodore Roosevelt in his First Annual Message to Congress in 1901, and was repealed in that year. 14 *Messages and Papers of the Presidents*, p. 6672. The National Defense Act of 1916 reconstituted the militias as the National Guard.

relates to the use of firearms for sporting purposes or self-defence. In summary, as the US Court of Appeals for the Eighth Circuit has written, the courts 'have analyzed the Second Amendment purely in terms of protecting state militias, rather than individual rights'.[47]

If any further judicial authority is needed it can be found in a letter from the retired Chief Justice of the Supreme Court, Warren Burger, to Sarah Brady. On 2 December 1994 he wrote:

I would like to take this opportunity to applaud the tireless efforts of the Center to Prevent Handgun Violence to educate the American public on the true meaning of the Second Amendment to our Constitution. Your battle to shatter the myth, perpetrated by the National Rifle Association and other groups, that gun control laws violate the Second Amendment's right 'to keep and bear Arms' is a worthy cause. I wish you well in your continued efforts.[48]

The lack of any national system of registration or licensing,[49] as urged by President Johnson, has led to the accumulation of a vast reservoir of firearms, estimated at 212 million in 1992,[50] and an ease of access to them unknown elsewhere. The average number of victimizations in which firearms were stolen was estimated at 340,700 per year over the period 1987–92.[51] Hence the dismal catalogue of aggression, fights, violent settlement of disputes, robberies, woundings, and above all killings of individuals or whole groups of people, which so often involved the use of guns. Clinton did not

---

[47] *US* v. *Nelson*, 859 F. 2d 1318 (8th Cir. 1988).

[48] Copy letter on file with author. Burger was already on record as condemning the NRA's interpretation as 'one of the greatest pieces of fraud, I repeat the word *fraud*, on the American public by special interest groups, that I have ever seen in my lifetime . . .' *Under Fire: the NRA and the Battle for Gun Control, op. cit.*, p. 136.

[49] By 1994 eleven states had some form of licensing or registration of handguns or firearms.

[50] The Bureau of Alcohol, Tobacco, and Firearms estimated that in 1992 approximately 212 million firearms were available for sale to, or were possessed by, civilians in the United States. The total was made up of approximately 72 million handguns (mainly pistols or revolvers), 76 million rifles, and 64 million shotguns. Most guns available for sale were produced domestically. No statistics are available on the number of assault weapons in private possession or available for sale. Congressional Research Service, Issue Brief: *Gun Control*, Library of Congress, Washington, DC, 9 Feb. 1995, p. 2. The population of the US in 1992 was 255,458,000. US Bureau of the Census, *Statistical Abstract of the United States: 1994* (114th edn.), Washington DC, 1994.

[51] The statistic refers to the number of incidents reported of firearm theft, not the number of guns stolen. Crime Data Brief, *Guns and Crime*, Bureau of Justice Statistics, Office of Justice Programs, US Department of Justice, Washington, DC.

exaggerate in castigating the virtually unrestricted availability for firearms as 'an instrument for maintaining madness'.

Inevitably, violent crimes involving firearms are more likely to be fatal than those involving other weapons, or no weapon at all. Very many crimes of violence are impulsive and committed on the spur of the moment. If a loaded firearm is to hand, or readily available, the consequences are incomparably more serious. In the previous Chapter it was noted that in 1993 nearly 70 per cent of the murders, 42 per cent of the robberies known to law enforcement, and a quarter of the reported aggravated assaults were committed with firearms. 16,189 Americans were murdered with guns that year; in 13,252 of these crimes a handgun was the weapon used. The total number of gun murders increased every year between 1988 and 1993.[52] Nor are firearm deaths confined to unlawful homicide. Legal intervention, suicides, and accidents take the totals higher still. In 1993 deaths caused by firearms were estimated to include 19,590 suicides, 1,740 accidents, and 460 of unknown provenance.[53]

In England and Wales the figures are tiny by comparison. In 1993 212 defendants were found guilty of murder.[54] Over the five-year period 1989–93 an average of 54 incidents of homicide initially were recorded each year in which the apparent method of killing was by shooting. The number of suspects found guilty of murder involving a shooting, as a percentage of all suspects found guilty of murder over the same period, varied betwen 7 and 14 per cent. As Table 9 shows, there was no evidence of an upward trend. In the five-year period 1984–8 there were on average 54.4 initially recorded homicides each year in which the apparent method of killing was by shooting, compared with 54.0 in 1989–93. The provisional figures for 1994 show no departure from the settled pat-

---

[52] *Crime in the United States 1993*, Uniform Crime Reports published by the Federal Bureau of Investigation, Department of Justice, US Government Printing Office, Washington, DC, 1994, p. 18. In 1988 firearms were the weapon used in 10,895 murders; by 1993 the total had risen to 16,189. In 1994 it declined to 15,456. *Crime in the United States 1994*, p. 18.

[53] The National Center for Health Statistics of the Public Health Service publishes annual data on firearm deaths based on reports from coroners in each state. Cited in CRS Issue Brief, *Gun Control, op. cit.*, p. 3. Since there is a wide disparity in the information that is entered on death certificates, the statistics cannot be taken as exact.

[54] The population of England and Wales in 1991 was 49,890,277, *Whitaker's Almanack*, 1994, p. 118. The most recent official census in the United Kingdom was taken on 21 April 1991. The next census is due in April 2001.

TABLE 9. *Fatal gun crimes: England and Wales, 1984–94*

	Currently recorded homicide involving shooting	Suspects found guilty of murder involving shooting	Suspects found guilty of murder involving shooting as a % of all suspects found guilty of murder
1984	61	25	15
1985	44	16	10
1986	47	17	8
1987	78	26	12
1988	42	12	6
1989	38	13	7
1990	58	26	14
1991	50	16	8
1992	52	14	7
1993	71	30	14
1994*	63	13	12

* As at 4 Aug. 1995. Proceedings pending for 25 homicides.
Source: Home Office.

tern. A significant difference is that whereas in England and Wales it is a criminal offence for a person to have in his possession, or to purchase or acquire, a firearm or ammunition without a certificate,[55] the licensing requirements of federal law in the United States are confined to persons engaged in the business of importing, manufacturing, or dealing in firearms, or importing or manufacturing ammunition.[56]

No one who has studied the statistics or who has first-hand experience of criminal behaviour can doubt that the strikingly disproportionate level of homicide and violent crime suffered by the United States is directly related to the possession and availability of guns. Over and over again the President drove the message home, often in its most vivid form. 'We cannot renew this country,'

[55] Firearms Act 1968, Sections 1 and 2. The Criminal Justice and Public Order Act 1994 increased the maximum penalty for possessing a firearm or ammunition without a firearm certificate, or a shotgun without a shotgun certificate, from three years to five years imprisonment.
[56] 18 USC § 923.

he declared in his State of the Union Address in January 1994, 'when 13-year old boys get semiautomatic weapons to shoot 9-year-olds for kicks.'[57]

IV

One of the smaller House bills (HR 3355), authorizing the provision of federal funds for community policing, became the vehicle for the legislation enacted many months later. Although stemming from a Clinton campaign pledge, it had won all-party support in Congress. It was, however, the most expensive element in the package and raised the question of how the extra money was to be found. The funding of costly new programs is a perennial problem of legislators, never more so than when, as in late 1993, Congress had just put in place caps on appropriations in endorsing the Administration's five-year deficit-reduction plan.

HR 3355, passed by voice vote of the House on 3 November, was sent to the Senate and placed on its calendar the following day. Senators meanwhile had been zealous in amending their omnibus bill, by now renumbered S. 1607, which they preferred to the piece-meal approach. In passing HR 3355 on 19 November the Senate struck out all after the enacting clause and substituted the text of S. 1607. The extent of bipartisan support for this tactic, and for the contents of the big bill, was shown in the vote of 95 yeas and only 4 nays. By then the question of financing the anti-crime proposals, in particular the grants for additional police, had been resolved, also to bipartisan satisfaction, by an unorthodox proposal in the course of a debate on the Senate floor on 4 November from the Chairman of the Appropriations Committee, Senator Robert Byrd (Dem., W. Virginia). Although normally critical of the practice of dedicating public expenditure for specific purposes, such as the 'fire walls' dismantled only shortly before that had protected defence and foreign aid spending, Byrd had been persuaded by the Majority Leader, Senator Mitchell, with the support of the Budget Committee Chairman, to allocate the savings anticipated from the Administration's plan to reduce the size of the federal workforce to a trust fund that could be used solely to finance the programs con-

[57] Address Before a Joint Session of the Congress on the State of the Union, 140 *Cong. Rec.* H 33 (daily edn. 25 Jan. 1994).

tained in the crime bill. The costs were substantial. Originally estimated at $5.9 billion, the total cost of the bill had risen with
enlargements to $9.6 billion over five years, before more than doub-
ling to $22.3 billion once the unexpected largesse had come into
view. The final cost of the bill as enacted was approximately $30.2
billion over six years.

A trust fund earmarked to provide federal aid for employing
more police and law enforcement officers, to make grants to states
to expand their correctional facilities for the confinement of violent
offenders, to experiment with boot camps, and to provide drug
treatment and prevention programs for young people and soon to
be released prisoners, was an unforeseen development.[58] Thence-
forth it was to be the cement which held together the diverse groups
in the Congress on the crime bill. What had made it possible?
Although never spelt out, the explanation had more to do with fiscal than criminal policy. In the plan to cut back the scale of federal
government masterminded by Vice-President Gore, savings in
excess of $20 billion had been identified as a result of reducing the
numbers in the federal work force by 252,000 over a five-year
period. Nothing had been said about how to handle the savings.
The general assumption had been that they would be used to reduce
the deficit, another prime aim of the Clinton Administration, but
no commitments had been made. Some observers, it was reported,
thought this somewhat casual. 'It's like leaving a $20 bill out there
on the counter expecting it will be there when you come back
tomorrow. Somebody's going to pick it up' was the comment of
one Senate aide.[59] The main reason it was picked up so swiftly by
the Democratic leadership in the Senate was a fear that the recently
approved caps on appropriations might be cut still further. The
idea of the trust fund had three advantages. It would keep the
spending caps where they were; it would ensure that the savings
were directed towards domestic spending, always advantageous for
the party in power; and it would thwart Republican taunts that
although the Democrats were now talking tough on crime, it was

[58] All grants carried a matching requirement. The federal share of a grant towards
any eligible state proposal for correctional facilities could not exceed 75 per cent.
Grants for public safety and community policing were subject to a similar matching
requirement, although the Attorney General was given power to waive, wholly or in
part, the necessity for a non-federal contribution to the costs of any program, project, or activity.

[59] *CQ Weekly Report*, 5 Mar. 1994, p. 549.

only talk and they were not prepared to find the money needed to fight crime more effectively.[60]

The crime bill absorbed much time on the floor of the Senate in November. Amendments to strengthen the laws on child pornography and enhance the penalties for hate crimes were agreed on November 4. On November 5, 8, and 9, the next three working days, the Senate approved a long list of amendments and rejected or held over others. Carjacking (the theft of an automobile when the driver is present) would be subject to prosecution as a federal crime whether or not a gun was used, and the death penalty would be available if death resulted from the commission of the offence. Federal penalties would apply to persons involved in the criminal activities of street gangs, the possession of a handgun or ammunition by juveniles, and the sale or transfer to a juvenile. Juveniles with parental permission to use guns for ranching, farming, hunting, target practice, or a course of instruction in the safe and lawful use of a handgun were exempted, as were juveniles who defended themselves with a handgun against an intruder to their home. From the age of thirteen, juveniles prosecuted for serious crimes[61] or in possession of a firearm during the commission of the offence would be tried as adults. If found guilty they would build up criminal records in adult courts.

Political symbolism hung over the proceedings. Periodically it was acknowledged openly, as when the chairman of the Judiciary Subcommittee on Juvenile Justice, Senator Kohl (Dem., Wis.), whose amendment on the underage possession of handguns was agreed by a unanimous vote of 100–0,[62] said that only a small number of young people would be affected because the provision was limited to offences tried in federal courts, and not to the large majority tried in the state courts. Nevertheless, he believed there was 'a strong symbolism in the vote that says that kids are responsible for their action', adding 'It's more symbolic than it is real.'[63]

---

[60] Title XXXI of Pub. L. 103–322 created a Violent Crime Reduction Trust Fund 'into which shall be transferred . . . savings realized from the implementation of Section 5 of the Federal Workforce Restructuring Act of 1994 (Pub. L. 103–226).' The amounts to be transferred into the fund over a six-year period commencing with the start of the fiscal year 1995 were specified in Section 310001(b).

[61] Murder, attempted murder, assault with intent to commit murder, assault with intent to commit any felony, assault with a dangerous weapon with intent to do bodily harm. See 18 USC § 113 (a)–(c), 1111, and 1113.

[62] 139 *Cong. Rec.* S. 15425 (daily edn. 9 Nov. 1993).

[63] 1993 *CQ Almanac*, p. 296.

In another vote, also symbolic although appealing to a different interest group, an amendment by the liberal Senator Paul Simon (Dem., Ill.) to prohibit the death penalty for all young people under the age of eighteen failed on 8 November by 41 votes to 52.

Under federal law no person may be sentenced to death who was less than eighteen years of age at the time of the commission of an offence punishable by death. The federal exemption, however, did not effect the large majority of prisoners on death row who had been sentenced to death according to state law. Only five out of the total of 2,848 prisoners under sentence of death on 20 April 1994 had been sentenced under federal statutes.[64] In 1988 the Supreme Court ascertained that nineteen states had a statutorily authorized death penalty that did not include any minimum age, and that eighteen states had statutorily authorized minimum ages varying between sixteen and eighteen below which no defendant could be executed. In fourteen states there was no statutorily authorized death penalty. In *Thompson* v. *Oklahoma*[65] the Court decided by a majority of five to three that a capital sentence imposed on a defendant younger than sixteen at the time the crime was committed violated the Eighth Amendment prohibition of cruel and unusual punishments. Simon's amendment was aimed at prohibiting capital sentences being passed by state courts on defendants between the ages of sixteen and eighteen at the time of the crime, thus achieving parity in the administration of the death penalty between the federal and state jurisdictions.

At this stage in the Senate the habeas corpus reform proposal, on which Biden, a supporter of capital punishment, and Reno, who was opposed to the death penalty on principle, had worked together, was abandoned. Although a majority of legislators believed that the procedures which allowed so many prisoners condemned to death to spend ten years or more on death row were in urgent need of reform, there was insufficient consensus on the

---

[64] Bureau of Justice Statistics, *Sourcebook of Criminal Justice Statistics*, 1993, US Department of Justice, US Government Printing Office, Washington, DC, 1994. Tables 6.108 and 6.109.

[65] 108 S. Ct. 2687 (1988). In two cases in the following year the Supreme Court decided that the imposition of capital punishment for a crime committed at sixteen or seventeen years of age did not constitute cruel and unusual punishment under the Eighth Amendment. *Stanford* v. *Kentucky* and *Wilkins* v. *Missouri*, 109 S. Ct. 2969 (1989). For a note on the constitutional implications of the decision in *Thompson* v. *Oklahoma* see 40 *Drake Law Review*, 195 (1991).

nature of the reforms required to remedy the situation. The formula included in the bill was to allow a state-sentenced capital prisoner to file a single federal habeas corpus petition within six months of final adjudication in the state courts. Secondary petitions would be limited to extraordinary circumstances involving the establishment of innocence or a constitutional defect in the sentence. States would be required to provide indigent capital defendants with qualified counsel at all stages of state proceedings, and federal grants would be made available to assist states with the extra costs of fulfilling the counsel requirements. This was the settlement arrived at in negotiation earlier in the year with the National District Attorneys Association and the National Association of Attorneys General. As the months passed, however, and hopes of speedy enactment faded second thoughts began to surface. Some of the state representatives, mainly those who feared that the agreed formulation was too liberal, began to express reservations. At the same time, the libertarian view was articulated in a series of editorials in several of the leading newspapers that the proposal was regressive and failed to create adequate procedures to avoid the possibility of miscarriages of justice. An articulate strain of purist opinion wanted to see the decisions of the Supreme Court narrowing the scope of habeas corpus reversed, and was critical of any measures which would codify in statute law a restricted application of the 'great writ'.

Biden's chosen ground, on this as on other issues, was centre left. By the time the bill was under consideration in the Senate he had become uneasy, and was no longer sufficiently confident of the result to put the proposal to the test of a floor vote. Nor could he afford to risk the possibility of a more conservative Republican inspired version passing. In negotiation, therefore, he dropped the habeas corpus reform proposal. In return for an agreement not to bring it back during the 103rd Congress, he obtained an undertaking from the Republican leadership that they would not obstruct the passage of the bill as a whole. Recalling the fate of the previous crime bill, this was a valuable objective to have secured. Biden's aim was to maintain the momentum and get the bill into conference without allowing the Republicans and sectional interests time to regroup. In the outcome the tactic was unsuccessful, not because of undue delays in the Senate, but because of the slower pace dictated by the CBC in the House of Representatives.

Some of the amendments passed by the Senate in the two and a half-week, tougher-than-thou bidding war in November[66] had heavy cost implications. Replying to criticism that the criminalization of gang activities would increase the burden on the federal courts, Dole pointed out that the amendment of which he was the sponsor authorized $100 million over five years to be spent on recruiting additional federal prosecutors. A further $100 million would be made available for a grant program to support work with juveniles and gang members. When his amendment was debated Dole, as Minority Leader, was fully aware of the potential of the trust fund proposal which had been agreed by a large majority the previous week.[67] Other successful Republican amendments included the extension of the death penalty to drug 'kingpins', those engaged in continuing criminal enterprises dealing in large quantities of illegal drugs. This provision had been added to the 1991 crime bill by the populist Senator D'Amato (Rep., New York), but had been omitted from the Biden bill. On its introduction in September, D'Amato had committed himself and other Republican supporters of the policy to pressing it again. The flavour of the rhetoric comes through even in the printed record:

I am outraged that despite all the talk of getting tough on crime, the administration has shown itself, in fact, to be soft on crime. By deleting two provisions that I added to the 1991 crime bill, the new bill will not be one that cracks down on crime, but one that gives criminals a break—a break they do not deserve and should not get . . . it cannot be wrong to require the death penalty for large-scale drug enterprises. Those who sell death, should receive death. How many people have to die before we come to the realization that we need a greater sanction against those who head the criminal drug enterprises . . . Killing people by selling them drugs has the same result as killing them with a gun. The death penalty for drug kingpins . . . provides the ultimate sanction. This is right and this is just. We should do no less.[68]

Two of the other amendments affected prisons and prisoners. In future all prisoners held in federal, state, or local prisons would be subject to the statutory ineligibility for Pell grants for higher education which hitherto had applied only to death-row and life

[66] 1993 *CQ Almanac*, p. 295.
[67] The vote in the Senate had been 94 yeas, 4 nays, and 2 absentees. 139 *Cong. Rec.* S 15070 (daily edn. 4 Nov. 1993).
[68] 139 *Cong. Rec.* S 12446 (daily edn. 23 Sept. 1993).

prisoners. The second amendment, of profound importance, would restrict the power of the federal courts to set population caps in prison overcrowding lawsuits, barring class actions in such cases, and limiting the remedies that a federal court might impose for conditions caused by overcrowding in violation of the Constitution.

V

The proper role of federal judges in litigation over prison conditions and overcrowding had been a matter of controversy for some years. The power to intervene, and the prudent use made of it by certain judges, Morris Lasker in the US District Court for the Southern District of New York being an outstanding example, had been instrumental in ameliorating the total degradation in many state-run prisons and local jails as a result of the rapidly escalating populations in custody. Even the opponents of judicial intervention did not deny that in most cases basic standards of amenity, regulation, and service had been improved as a result of federal court orders.[69] In one of the most conspicuous instances, the New York City jails, amongst the largest, most politically complicated, and distressed of all detention facilities, it was a paradox that a majority of the inmates (over 13,000 out of a total of over 15,000 inmates in 1990[70]) was made up not of convicted and sentenced prisoners being punished for their wrongdoing but of accused persons awaiting trial in detention. During two decades following a notorious outbreak of inmate riots and staff protests at the Manhattan House of Detention for Men, then as now popularly known as the Tombs,[71] it was the skilful handling of a potentially explosive situation by Judge Lasker that led to the intervention of the federal court in New York being pronounced 'an almost unqualified success'.[72]

[69] John J. DiIulio (ed.), *Courts, Corrections and the Constitution: The Impact of Judicial Intervention on Prisons and Jails*, Oxford University Press, New York, 1990, p. 291.

[70] E. S. Storey, 'When Intervention Works: Judge Morris E. Lasker and New York City Jails', in DiIulio (ed.), *Courts, Corrections and the Constitution, op. cit.*, p. 165.

[71] Between 1979 and 1983 the Tombs was completely gutted and rebuilt as a modern jail incorporating far higher standards than before. Ibid. p. 160.

[72] DiIulio, ibid. p. 7.

By the late 1980s judicial activism in cases of overcrowding had become commonplace throughout the United States. A survey published in 1988 found that there were major court orders on prisons and jails in forty states,[73] a total which declined to thirty-one by 1993.[74] Limits were set on capacity to check overcrowding, and a wide range of orders made to change and improve specific administrative practices. To oversee the implementation of the court orders, judges appointed special masters, monitors, or compliance co-ordinators. One unusual solution to the problems of enforcement came when a federal judge who had taken control of the entire Alabama prison system appointed the Governor of the State as temporary receiver, and ordered the Board of Corrections to transfer all its authorities and functions to the Governor. The state legislature then passed a law dissolving the Board and replacing it with a Department of Corrections directly under the Governor's control. When he left office in 1983 the court set up a four-member expert committee to oversee the system.[75]

It is not hard to see why the intervention of federal judges was often resented and sometimes resisted. The main practical objection was that additional capacity in the shape of building new prisons and jails, and making improvements at existing penal establishments, cost money. All of the money, in the years before federal grants became available, had to be found by state and local governments from budgets already commited to funding more electorally attractive services. If the extra capacity needed to meet the requirements of a court order was not forthcoming, then some existing prisoners might have to be released to reduce the pressure of overcrowding and to allow for the admission of newly sentenced offenders. Such a resort was even less popular than finding the money for building more prisons and jails. Moreover it was argued, with some truth, that by training, background, and outlook, judges were not qualified to supervise and manage prisons. The orders they made,

---

[73] M. M. Feeley and R. A. Hanson, 'The Impact of Judicial Intervention on Prisons and Jails: A Framework for Analysis and a Review of the Literature', ibid. p. 13.

[74] 139 *Cong. Rec.* S 15747 (daily edn. 16 Nov. 1993).

[75] J. J. DiIulio, 'Conclusion: What Judges Can Do To Improve Prisons and Jails', *op. cit.*, pp. 287–8. For a compelling narrative account of the judicial-inspired reforms in Alabama's penal institutions, see L. W. Yackle, *Reform and Regret*: *The Story of Federal Involvement in the Alabama Prison System*, Oxford University Press, New York, 1989.

and the officers they appointed to supervise compliance with their orders, might make things worse rather than better by destabilizing precarious prison cultures. Some critics believed that once institutional authority was undermined by external intervention tension increased, leading to prisons becoming more unruly and violent. Other studies, however, indicated that while short-term disruption might result, court decrees did not lead to continuing problems of inmate unrest and violence.[76]

At another level, leaving practical issues to one side, there were the rival claims of judicial activism and judicial restraint. The conflict was not confined to intervention in the prisons and jails, but was part of a wider ideological clash of opinion over the constitutional propriety of judges making and implementing public policy. The breadth and detail of the involvement of the federal judiciary in initiating and supervising changes in penal administration was on a scale that some commentators regarded as second only to the courts' earlier role in dismantling racial segregation in the public schools.[77]

The legal basis for intervention was the prohibition against the infliction of cruel and unusual punishments in the Eighth Amendment to the Constitution. While only the most extreme would argue that protection against cruel and unusual treatment should not extend to prisoners, there were some large and unresolved questions. First was the status of class actions, brought not by an individual inmate as plaintiff, but by or on behalf of a group of inmates subject to similar conditions at a particular institution. Then there was the provision of remedies. Where a court found that conditions had violated the Eighth Amendment was it entitled to prescribe a ceiling on the size of the inmate population? And did the need to see that court orders were complied with justify the intrusive assumption of a management role?

These were questions which were bound eventually to be considered by Congress. In 1989 a fruitless attempt was made in the Senate to limit judicial intervention in prisons and jails by means of restricting judicial remedies for prison overcrowding. In the debates on the crime bill in November 1993 some of the proponents tried again, this time successfully. One of the most conservative members of the Senate, Jesse Helms of North Carolina, supported

---

[76] Feeley and Hanson, *op. cit.*, p. 25.   [77] Ibid. p. 13.

by Senator Gramm (Rep., Texas), moved an amendment in the course of the general floor debate on 16 November. It provided that a federal court should not hold prison or jail crowding unconstitutional under the Eighth Amendment, except to the extent that an individual plaintiff inmate proved that the crowding caused the infliction of cruel and unusual punishment of that inmate. The relief in such a case should extend no further than was necessary to remove the conditions that were causing the cruel and unusual punishment of the plaintiff inmate. As to inmate population ceilings, the amendment stated that 'A Federal court shall not place a ceiling on the inmate population of any Federal, State, or local detention facility as an equitable remedial measure for conditions that violate the eighth amendment unless crowding is inflicting cruel and unusual punishment on particular identified prisoners.'[78]

The short debate on remedies for prison overcrowding did not show the Senate at its best. Helms's rhetoric was addressed directly at the voters in his home state, with no acknowledgement of the wider constitutional implications. All over America, he declaimed, innocent citizens were being murdered, raped, robbed, and beaten by violent felons who had been turned loose on society by federal judges after they had served only a fraction of the prison terms received for other crimes. In North Carolina more than 26,000 prisoners had been given early release the previous year, including eighty-eight felons convicted of murder and thirty-seven rapists. They had been 'set free because prison cells were not quite large enough to suit some Federal judge'.[79] He cited examples of two young police officers and other victims from his state 'whose lives had been snuffed out by violent felons returned to the streets by the Federal courts'.[80] Senator Graham, a centrist Southern Democrat and former Governor of Florida, with greater knowledge of release procedures, was more restrained in his language, but he too asserted that the effect of judicial intervention had been to return serious offenders to the streets in order to find bed-space for those admitted to the institution. His concern was that the pattern of federal court orders relative to prison construction, operation, and population had been setting increasingly high standards that went far beyond those necessary to ensure that the constitutional

---

[78] The amendment was printed as No. 1159 in 139 *Cong. Rec.* S 15619 (daily edn. 10 Nov. 1993) and reproduced as Section 20409 of Pub. L. 103–322, 108 Stat. 1827.
[79] 139 *Cong. Rec.* S 15749 (daily edn. 16 Nov. 1993).   [80] Ibid.

prohibition of cruel and unusual punishment was not violated. He particularly objected to the federal government using the Eighth Amendment to impose standards on state prisons and local jails that were higher than those maintained in its own penal institutions.[81]

It was left to Biden, opposing the amendment, to point out that it would introduce changes in the relationship between Congress and the courts that required more thorough consideration. Thirty minutes of debate on the Senate floor was not an appropriate airing.[82] Although opinion amongst constitutional scholars was not unanimous, he believed that the weight of authority supported his contention that the amendment might be an unconstitutional encroachment on the separation of powers. It aimed to restrict the authority of the federal courts to interpret a part of the Constitution, and limited the courts' remedial powers. In his view, the amendment was infirm in both respects. The drafting meant that courts presiding over class-action lawsuits would not be permitted to hold that prison overcrowding violated the Constitution, unless the court made particularized findings of cruel and unusual punishment respecting an individual plaintiff. If the Senate adopted the amendment it would in effect be stating that the federal courts, which since *Marbury* v. *Madison* in 1803[83] had been considered to be the final arbiters of what the Constitution requires, might not make determinations of what is or is not constitutional with respect to Eighth Amendment litigation over prison crowding.

As its promoters intended, the Helms amendment would prevent a court which found system-wide constitutional violation from remedying the infirmity, even if the court believed that to be the correct action. Biden said that this flew in the face of national history and understanding of the courts' role in the constitutional system.[84] The proposal did more than merely telling the courts that they might not fashion a specific remedy for a constitutional violation; it sought to define the limits of the law under the Constitution. It prescribed that a federal court might not hold that certain prison conditions violated the Constitution unless the claim was brought

[81] 139 *Cong. Rec.* S 15747 (daily edn. 16 Nov. 1993).

[82] Ibid., S 15749.

[83] 1 Cranch (5 US) 137. Marshall CJ's judgment is reproduced in G. Gunther, *Constitutional Law*, 12th edn., Foundation Press, Westbury, New York, 1991, pp. 3–10.

[84] 139 *Cong. Rec.* S 15748 (daily edn. 16 Nov. 1993).

by an individual plaintiff, even where other aspects of the case were properly before the court. If a class of plaintiffs demonstrated pervasive unlawful prison conditions, the court would be prevented from finding such conditions unlawful and providing a remedy. The effect of the amendment would be to restrict the ability of the federal courts to remedy cruel and unusual punishment caused by prison overcrowding. 'Deny the remedy, you deny the right.'[85] Congress had never granted a federal court subject-matter jurisdiction over a particular class of claims and then stripped it of its right to fashion a particular remedy. Consequently, the Supreme Court had not ruled on the question of whether Congress improperly encroached on the judicial power by restricting the ability of the federal courts to provide appropriate remedies for constitutional wrongs.

Elegant and powerful as it was, Biden's reasoning, paraphrased above, failed to convince. Electoral politics, the attraction of seemingly tough and decisive measures, rooted in what was perceived by Senators as the weight of popular opinion, were against him. The following morning, 17 November, a motion to table the amendment, blocking its progress, was defeated by 68 votes to 31.[86] The amendment survived the remaining stages in both Houses and the following year was passed into law as Section 20409 of Public Law 103–322.[87] While Congress has a recognized power to define or alter the jurisdiction of the federal courts, it is unlikely to be long before such a direct instruction to judges as to how they must interpret the Eighth Amendment, and the remedies available, is reviewed by the Supreme Court.

VI

A turning point in the long drawn-out controversy over firearms came on the floor of the Senate on 9 November. Republican hardliners had proposed to increase mandatory minimum penalties for the use of a gun in the commission of a crime of violence or drug-trafficking crimes. They wanted mandatory terms of not less than ten years' imprisonment for the possession of a firearm during the commission of such a crime; twenty years for discharging it with

---

[85] Ibid. The maxim was cited by Biden at S 15749.
[86] 139 *Cong. Rec.* S 15817 (daily edn. 17 Nov. 1993).   [87] 108 Stat. 1827.

intent to injure another person; and life imprisonment or the death penalty for murder involving a firearm. To this amendment was attached the proposal that the federal penalties specified, including the death penalty, should apply also to offences committed within state jurisdictions where the firearm involved had moved at any time in interstate or foreign commerce. In such cases state prosecutors would decide whether to seek federal jurisdiction. Biden warned the mover, Senator D'Amato whose emotive rhetoric has already been noted, that this could lead to clashes with US Attorneys and to the federal death penalty being sought in cases where the law in the state in which the killing occurred did not allow capital punishment. 600,000 handgun crimes were committed each year, and under the amendment they would all be federalized.[88] Ignoring the objections by the federal judiciary, on record since a similar attempt had been made in the 102nd Congress, the amendment was approved by a majority of 58 yeas to 42 nays, with the underlying amendment agreed by voice vote.[89]

On 19 September 1991 the Chief Justice, William Rehnquist, in his capacity as Presiding Officer of the Judicial Conference of the United States, had written to Brooks to convey the opposition of the conference to legislation that would provide for federal jurisdiction over offences traditionally reserved for state prosecution. He enclosed a statement summarizing the objections, and the reasons for expressing them. During the proceedings on the crime bill in the 103rd Congress both Rehnquist and the chairman of the Executive Committee of the Judicial Conference, Chief Judge John Gerry, reiterated the misgivings of the judges towards the proposed expansion of the role of the federal courts in the administration of criminal justice. The statement read:

FEDERALIZATION OF STATE PROSECUTIONS: POSITION OF THE JUDICIAL CONFERENCE OF THE UNITED STATES
The Judicial Conference of the United States opposes legislation adopted by the Senate which would expand federal criminal law jurisdiction to encompass homicides and other violent state felonies if firearms are involved. Such expansion of federal jurisdiction would be inconsistent with

---

[88] 139 *Cong. Rec.* S 15391 (daily edn. 9 Nov. 1993). In a later debate Biden revised the estimate to over 900,000 violent crimes in 1992 which, according to the Department of Justice, had been committed at a state and local level by offenders armed with handguns. 140 *Cong. Rec.* S 6091 (daily edn. 19 May 1994).

[89] 139 *Cong. Rec.* S 15409 (daily edn. 9 Nov. 1993).

long-accepted concepts of federalism, and would ignore the boundaries between appropriate state and federal action.

The addition to federal jurisdiction of virtually any crime committed with a firearm that has crossed a state line will swamp the federal courts with routine cases that states are better equipped to handle, and will weaken the ability of the federal courts effectively to deal with difficult criminal cases that present uniquely federal issues.

Not only will *bona fide* federal criminal prosecutions suffer if the Senate's expansive firearms provisions are adopted, but federal courts, overburdened by criminal cases, will be unable to carry out their vital responsibilities to provide timely forums for civil cases.[90]

With the furies gathering, the omens were hardly favourable when later on 9 November Senator Dianne Feinstein (Dem., Calif.) moved to amend the bill to include a ban on the manufacture, transfer, or possession of nineteen specified types of assault weapon. Although the policy was fervently supported by Clinton, and had been raised in Congress before, the ban had not been included in the original bills introduced in either chamber. Unlike his counterpart in the House, Representative Brooks, Biden was a staunch supporter of gun control. However, he was apprehensive lest the intense controversy surrounding the assault weapons proposal should imperil the chances of the main bill being agreed. Moreover, the Brady bill was still outstanding, having been passed by the House, and was currently awaiting action by the Senate. Mrs Feinstein, a long-time campaigner against crime in California, remained resolute and would not be put off. Her proposal was confined to military-style weapons that could have no legitimate sporting or hunting use and were ill-suited for personal protection. It was estimated that as many as one million were in circulation. The ban, which had a life of ten years, did not apply to existing weapons lawfully possessed before the date of enactment, and specifically exempted more than 650 types of manual and automatic guns used for sports and hunting. The naming of the actual weapons which would be included and excluded was an effective counter to the allegation that the legislation would deprive law-abiding citizens of their favourite guns.

Feinstein began her speech with a reference to the state of general public opinion, and later listed the names of fifty-three organizations which endorsed a ban on assault weapons. They included

---

[90] The text was printed in 140 *Cong. Rec.* S 6090 (daily edn. 19 May 1994).

the National Association of Police Organizations and the Fraternal Order of Police, as well as the American Bar Association, the National Association for the Advancement of Colored People (NAACP), the US Conference of Mayors, medical associations, labour unions, and religious bodies.[91] The amendment, she said, dealt with:

. . . a problem that 66 per cent of all American citizens want addressed. Asked in a recent poll, 'Would you favor a law banning the manufacture, sale, and possession of semiautomatic assault guns such as the AK-47,' 66 percent said yes; only 30 percent said no. There is no reason for weapons of war to be used freely on the streets of America—where they are weapons of choice for every assassin, terrorist, gang member, drug syndicate, drive-by shooter, Mafioso, or grievance killer.

The most troubling of these categories is the grievance killer, someone who takes out their wrath on anyone who happens to be around—children in a school yard or a swimming pool or walking down a street; workers in offices or post offices; innocent people eating hamburgers in a restaurant; or the grandmother watching television in the privacy of her own living room, when a high velocity bullet from a semiautomatic assault weapon comes through the wall and pierces her chest. I believe it is time to stop the sale, the manufacture, and the possession of more semiautomatic assault weapons on the streets of America.[92]

Each of the examples was based on a factual incident, several of them having occurred in the Senator's home state. A lone gunman had gone to a law firm in San Francisco earlier in 1993 carrying two assault weapons and more than 500 rounds of ammunition. He opened fire and killed eight people. Six others were wounded. At a McDonald's outlet twenty-one people eating burgers had been killed, and nineteen more wounded, by a man armed with an assault weapon, a shot-gun, and a pistol. Another gunman, described as a 'dangerous drifter with an assault weapon', had walked into a schoolyard in Northern California and fired 106 rounds of ammunition. Five small children were killed and twenty-nine injured.[93] What had in the past, said Feinstein, been regarded

---

[91] The full list of organizations endorsing a ban on assault weapons was printed in 139 *Cong. Rec.* S 15449 (daily edn. 9 Nov. 1993).

[92] Ibid., S 15429.

[93] Most of the victims in the shooting at Stockton, California in Jan. 1989, and all of the dead children, were immigrants from Cambodia or South Vietnam. A powerful narrative description of this incident forms the introduction to Davidson, *Under Fire: the NRA and the Battle for Gun Control, op. cit.*, pp. 3–19. The assault weapon used had been bought openly over the counter shortly before the massacre.

as shocking episodes because of their randomness and multiple victims were now becoming the norm. Some senators had the audacity to argue that because more people might have been killed by the shotgun than by the assault weapon in the McDonald's shooting, the incident bore out their maxim that it was people who killed, not guns. Feinstein replied eloquently. While semiautomatic weapons were not in themselves responsible for the large number of deaths, their availability for sale over the counter in all save four states offered to the deranged killer or the grievance killer the possibility of taking out a whole room of people without having to reload. Yes, she admitted: 'guns do not fire themselves, nor however, do they thrust themselves into the hands of the distraught, the deranged and the disaffected. They have to be bought or stolen.'[94]

Later in the debate, an unwise remark, by a speaker opposed to the amendment, that the Senator from California needed to become 'a little more familiar with firearms', gave Feinstein an opening for a devastating riposte: 'I am quite familiar with firearms. I became mayor as a product of assassination . . . They found my assassinated colleague and you could put a finger through the bullet hole.'[95]

Passionate emotions were expressed on both sides of the argument and little quarter given. When the vote came it was taken not on the merits of the issue but on a procedural motion which would prevent the amendment making any further progress. The result was bound to be close. In the end a tie was averted only when one Democratic Senator, who had opposed an assault weapons ban in 1991, switched his vote, so keeping alive Feinstein's ability to offer her amendments.[96] After much negotiation behind the scenes, the Senate resumed its consideration of the Feinstein amendment on 17 November. There was no debate, but five Republicans changed sides to support the ban. The amendment was consequently agreed by 56 votes to 43, with one Senator absent.[97] The contest was not over, for the reaction of the House of Representatives could not be forecast with any confidence, but a significant step towards sanity had been taken.

[94] Ibid., S 15431.
[95] Ibid., S 15456. Dianne Feinstein became 38th Mayor of San Francisco in Nov. 1978 after the deaths by shooting at the City Hall of the Mayor, George Moscone, and the Supervisor, Harvey Milk.
[96] The vote for tabling the amendment was lost by 49 votes to 51. Ibid., S 15461.
[97] 139 *Cong. Rec.* S 15816 (daily edn. 17 Nov. 1993).

VII

Of all the diverse proposals that eventually found a place in the 355 pages of Public Law No. 103–322, none was more genuine a product of the demands of populist sentiment than mandatory sentencing to life imprisonment for repeat offenders on their third conviction in court, if previously convicted on separate occasions of two or more serious felonies, or one or more serious felonies and one or more serious drug offences. Whereas the first two convictions could be in either a federal or a state court, the third conviction, which activated mandatory life imprisonment, had to be in a federal court. That outcome still lay ahead. By November the Senate bill as amended contained some mandatory penalties for repeat offenders convicted of certain serious crimes which were variants of the three-strikes policy. However, they were limited to specified offences, as were the penalties up to imprisonment for life to which recidivists were liable under existing federal and state law. The tidal wave from the West, sweeping all before it with the slogan borrowed from baseball: 'three stikes and you're out', had not yet engulfed the Administration and Congress.

The origins were located far away in the State of Washington on the West Coast. It was rumoured that an advertising agency had come up with the catchy slogan linking the punishment of criminals, for which the public craved, to the sport which the public loved. At first the campaign was localized and low-key. The aim was to get the policy on repeat offenders onto the ballot as an initiative. The objective which had failed in 1992 was achieved by a 76–24 per cent margin the following November when the NRA and the Washington Citizens for Justice stepped in to help. The result was proclaimed by the NRA as a people's victory and a defeat for soft-on-crime politics.[98]

It was California, however, the seed-bed of regressive penal policies that had led to a population of 200,000 adults confined in state prisons and jails,[99] which provided the springboard to a national

[98] LaPierre, *Guns, Crime, and Freedom, op. cit.*, p. 107.

[99] For *The Christian Science Monitor*, 11 Apr. 1994, Franklin Zimring supplied an expert criminological analysis of the likely consequences of the three-strikes policy, combining it with a trenchant political attack: 'Fear of violent crime always presents an opportunity for demagogues.' The number of inmates in California's prisons and jails had multiplied fourfold since 1980, a rate of increase well in excess

audience. In the autumn of 1993 a campaign had been launched to put a version of three-strikes law on the ballot at the elections the following year as an initiative for popular vote. Political support was initially relatively low, being limited to the NRA and some of the state's more conservative politicians.

The catalyst which transformed the situation was a dreadful event: the abduction in October from her mother's home in a middle-class neighbourhood, and subsequent murder by strangulation, of a twelve year-old girl, Polly Klaas. The man charged with her killing had a lengthy criminal record and had been released from prison only three months earlier. He had served eight years of a sixteen-year sentence for kidnapping and robbery, being released under state rules as he had worked well and been of good behaviour while in prison.[100] The public outrage was made up of a mixture of anger, fear of victimization, sympathy for the victim and her family, and incomprehension that such a potentially dangerous repeat offender should have been allowed out of prison after serving no more than half the sentence imposed by the court. In the same way as the murder of an even younger child, Jamie Bulger, who had been killed by two boys in England the same year, it was the personal circumstances of a tragedy attracting massive national media coverage that was the stimulus for an unstoppable surge of opinion carrying far beyond the boundaries of the state.

Before continuing the narrative, a brief digression on the place of referenda and popular votes in certain American states may be in order. Throughout most states of the Mid and Far West, California amongst them, a system of direct legislation coexists alongside the more familiar processes of representative government.

---

of that in the next three largest states: New York, Texas, and Florida, all of which had high rates of offending.

[100] Because of a soaring rate in the California prison population, credit for 'good time' authorized the early release of inmates from prison once they had served half their sentence. No parole board had granted Richard Allen Davis discretionary parole after a hearing. For an illuminating account of his progress through the penal system see J. Toobin, 'The man who kept going free', *The New Yorker*, 7 Mar. 1994, pp. 38–53. Although the alleged assailant was arrested within weeks, and charges against him filed on 7 Dec. 1993, two years later the trial of Davis had still not begun. After efforts had been abandoned to select a jury in Sonoma County where the killing occurred, protracted negotiations took place to find an alternative location offering a greater prospect of a fair trial. On 5 Feb. 1996 the trial of Davis for the murder of Polly Klaas opened at the Santa Clara County Superior Court in San Jose.

Access to the electorate by way of legislative initiatives and popular referenda on laws or policies, especially if there are any constitutional implications, goes back to the progressive era at the turn of the nineteenth and twentieth centuries. The notion was that the citizens themselves should have the opportunity to participate directly in the law-making process, unmediated by elected representatives. During the last two decades direct legislation has become an important feature in more than fifteen states, and can influence political agenda-setting for the entire nation.[101] Since the 1970s California has been one of the most initiative-prone states. A new industry has grown up, with initiative campaigners spending large sums on employing professional managers, petition circulators, media consultants, and pollsters. Over two decades the industry has expanded to include litigation, direct-mail fund-raising, and petition signature collection.[102]

Because of its size, its wealth, and the heterogeneous nature of its vast and ethnically mixed population[103] California has acquired many of the characteristics of a nation within a federal union. Its political culture and way of life are quite distinct from the neighbouring states. The high proportion of immigrants from other parts of the United States, as well as across the Mexican border and the Pacific, has meant that there is little sense of shared history or tradition. In its eagerness to embrace new ideas California has invigorated, but also at times irritated, the American body politic. Directly, through the presence in Congress of fifty-two elected members of the House of Representatives (as well as its two Senators), and indirectly, through popular ballots, the media, and business, professional, intellectual, and special-interest channels, ideas germinated in California tend to be dispersed more widely, and taken up more readily, than those from elsewhere.

So it was with three strikes, a paradigm of populist policy appearing to offer a simple and clear-cut solution to an intractable

[101] D. B. Magleby, 'Direct Legislation in the American States' in D. E. Butler and A. Ranney (eds.), *Referendums around the World: The Growing Use of Direct Democracy*, Macmillan Press, Basingstoke and London, 1994, p. 218. David Magleby is Professor and Chairman of the Department of Political Science at Brigham Young University.

[102] Ibid., p. 234.

[103] The estimated resident population of California in 1993 was 31,211,000. US Bureau of the Census, *Statistical Abstract of the United States: 1994* (114th edn.), 1994, *op. cit.*, p. 27.

problem of high visibility. By 1 May 1994 the National Conference of State Legislatures reported that ten states had adopted variants of California's three-strikes law, rising to fourteen by the end of 1994. After much choppy water had flowed under the bridge, when the votes on the initiative were counted in the California ballot, coincident with the mid-term November elections to Congress, the three-strikes law, which had been effective since March 1994, was endorsed by a majority of almost three to one. 72 per cent of the voters were for and 28 per cent against.

The fact that populist policies should be supported by popular votes is hardly surprising, although not necessarily inevitable; miscalculations can be made of the public mood. There is a critical distinction to be drawn between the condition of latent opinion, as measured by a ballot of all the voters, and its political effect when mobilized. As already noted, public opinion was consistently favourable towards gun control, although not overwhelmingly so. The proportion of two to one claimed by Senator Feinstein reflected the findings of numerous opinion polls. More relevant to direct legislation was a successful initiative in Maryland approving handgun registration in 1988, despite a campaign by the NRA which spent $8 million opposing it.[104] That episode showed that the influence of the NRA derived not from majority support nationally, but from its effective mobilization of the minority, and the pressure applied by its strongly motivated supporters on elected politicians. Organization, and the intensity of commitment, can count for as much or more than numbers in influencing legislators.

Unlike the controversy over gun control, where the battle-lines had been drawn many years before, three strikes, although not essentially a new policy, had the quality of novelty. Its appeal suited it to the NRA's diversionary strategy to deflect public attention away from the gun issue towards penal policy, leading to a contribution of $90,000 to the campaign in support of the California initiative. The California Correctional Peace Officers' Association, which stood to gain from the creation of an estimated increase of 18,000 prison officers jobs by 2027, gave $101,000. The largest sum came from a wealthy individual running for election at the same time as the November ballot on the three-strikes initiative (Proposition 184). Michael Huffington, a member of the House of

---

[104] Magleby, *op. cit.*, p. 242.

Representatives and Dianne Feinstein's Republican opponent to represent California in the US Senate, donated $300,000.[105] Apart from the correctional officers there were few vested interests involved, and it is noticeable that most law enforcement officials were less ardent than legislators in their enthusiasm for the policy. The criminals had no say, and when the voices of criminologists and policy analysts were raised, they were drowned by the hubbub and their warnings ignored. The reality was that the message conveyed by three strikes, apparently so simple a formulation, was an extraordinarily powerful one. It offered, simultaneously, a response to the moral outrage of many voters, while holding out the potential for greater personal protection. It was to prove an irresistible combination to the majority.

VII

The Governor of California, Pete Wilson, never slow in responding to the clamour of public opinion and with re-election looming in 1994, had already taken up the crime issue as an integral part of his appeal to the electorate. He exhorted voters to adopt the three-strikes proposal as a memorial to Polly Klaas. On 7 March the Governor chose the broadest of five different versions of three strikes offered by the legislature, discarding a proposal drafted by the California Association of Prosecutors, which he regarded as being too soft on crime. Sources as diverse as the Los Angeles District Attorney and the Earl Warren Legal Institute at Berkeley estimated that the resulting law would increase the sentences of some 25,000 offenders a year, 70 per cent of them convicted of non-violent crimes,[106] and a majority not multiple recidivists. In contrast, the federal version passed by Congress later in the summer was expected to effect no more than a few hundred convicted offenders each year.[107]

While the first two strikes under the 1994 California law accrued

[105] *Sacramento Bee*, 26 Sept. 1994. Contributions recorded as at 30 June in support of three strikes amounted to $880,000, compared with $12,000 raised in contributions by those opposed to Proposition 184.

[106] See Los Angeles County District Attorney, Gil Garcetti, as reported in *The Sacramento Bee, op. cit.*, and F. Zimring, *op. cit.*

[107] In the outcome it was well below this estimate. See Ch. 8.

for serious felonies only,[108] the offence that triggered the life sentence could be any felony. The new law also doubled the minimum required sentence for the second strike. For second- and third-time offenders the sentences had to be served in prison, rather than in jail, low security rehabilitation centres, or on probation. The 'good time' credit prisoners could earn for good behaviour was reduced to 20 per cent, having been raised from a third to a half in 1983. Presented as a technical change, and attracting little notice at the time, the increase to 50 per cent 'good time' made a mockery of the boasted punitiveness of determinate sentencing. The reason for its introduction had been the sharp rise in the state prison population which had reached 130 per cent of capacity in 1982.[109] Although three-strikes rhetoric implied a life sentence without possibility of parole, the wording of the statute mandated an indeterminate term of imprisonment in a state prison for life, with prescribed minimum terms. A three-times convicted felon would have to serve a term not less than the greatest of three times the term otherwise provided as punishment for each current felony conviction subsequent to the two or more prior felony convictions, with a minimum of twenty-five years' imprisonment in a state prison, or the term determined by the court for the underlying conviction, including any applicable enhancement or punishment provisions.[110]

The fact that the third offence included such non-violent and frequent crimes as the possession of hard drugs, auto-theft, and house burglary opened the way for widespread criticism on financial as well as penal grounds. Even the Klaas family publicly questioned the Governor's judgment in signing a law that shifted the focus away from violent crime, and the girl's father became a public critic of the policy. However, crime control was a bitterly contested partisan issue in the coming electoral campaign, and Wilson could not afford to let his opponent claim to be as tough as he was in speech, attitudes, and policies. When the November elections were held in

---

[108] The definition of serious crimes in California law includes virtually all violent crimes which involve injuries to victims or in some cases threats with a deadly weapon. Other offences may fall within the serious category where there is a potential for injury to victims.

[109] See John Van de Kamp, Attorney General of California, 1983–91, quoted in the *New Yorker* article, *op. cit.*, at p. 46.

[110] Legislative Counsel's Digest, appended to Act AB 971 to amend Section 667 of the California Penal Code, passed by the California legislature and approved by the Governor on 7 Mar. 1994.

California, not only Governor Wilson, a Republican, but Senator Feinstein, a Democrat and the victor in persuading Congress to impose the ban on assault weapons, were candidates for re-election. Both were politicians of stature. They stood their ground, fended off vituperative criticism from those antipathetic towards them, and both were re-elected.

Also on the ballot, as Proposition 184, was the original initiative which had provided the California legislature with the impetus to take up the three-strikes proposal. The text of the initiative and the law passed in the wake of the killing of Polly Klaas were very similar. If the voters approved the initiative they would be ratifying the legislature's action; if they rejected it they would be sending a message that the law should be reconsidered, and possibly amended in favour of one of the competing alternatives.[111] An impartial and comprehensive analysis of the benefits and costs of the three-strikes law carried out by researchers at RAND and published in September 1994[112] indicated that certain alternatives could reduce crime almost as much, but at lower cost. Benefits were expressed in terms of quantifiable crime reduction, and costs defined as the expenditures required to implement the new law by the component parts of the criminal justice system. As a glimpse of the future it made sombre reading.

The findings of the RAND study derived from analytical models predicting how populations of offenders on the street and in prison would change under the new law and under various alternatives. From these populations future crime rates and costs were estimated.[113] The most impressive finding was that if fully implemented the new law would reduce serious felonies committed by adults in California to 22–34 per cent below the projected incidence under the previous law. About one-third of the felonies eliminated would be violent crimes, such as murder, rape, and assaults causing great bodily injury. The other two-thirds would be less violent but still serious, felonies including less injurious assaults, most robberies, and burglaries of residences. The qualification that the forecast

---

[111] *RAND Research Review*, Vol. XVIII, No. 2, 1994, p. 5.

[112] P. W. Greenwood, C. P. Rydell, A. F. Abrahamse, J. P. Caulkins, J. Chiesa, K. E. Model, S. P. Klein, *Three Strikes and You're Out: Estimated Benefits and Costs of California's New Mandatory-Sentencing Law*, RAND, Santa Monica, CA, 1994.

[113] For a technical explanation of the construction and operation of the models see pp. 10–16, and Appendices C, D & E, pp. 48–68, ibid.

applied only to serious felonies committed by adults was significant since juveniles, who were excluded from the three-strikes
law, accounted for about one-sixth of all violent crime in the
state.[114]

The benefits to society of a reduction in crime on this scale called
for no elaboration. But what would be the financial cost and how
did it compare with alternative policies? The RAND study estimated the extra costs of the three-strikes law, if implemented in full,
at between $4.5 and $6.5 billion per year in current dollars above
what would have been spent had the previous sentencing law
remained in effect. Some police and court costs would be saved by
closing the revolving door on repeat offenders, but they would be
outweighed by the far larger costs of additional prison construction
and operation. Over most of the twenty-five year projection period
the full three-strikes law would require more than double the available number of prison places.[115]

Were there any alternatives which would achieve a substantial
part of the benefits, but at lower cost? Four were postulated. They
were: to eliminate the third-strike provision but leave the other elements undisturbed; to confine the third-strike provision to violent
offences only; to be harsher on violent felons but more lenient on
others; and to abandon the three-strikes approach entirely and
guarantee instead that offenders convicted of serious felonies would
serve the full term of a prison sentence, without any discount for
work time or good behaviour. Each of these alternatives would be
less costly than the three-strikes law, but all save the last would also
be less effective in reducing crime. In each case, however, the cost
would decrease more steeply than the effectiveness. The limitation
to a second strike would be 85 per cent as effective, so establishing
that only 15 per cent of the total crime reduction attributed to the
three-strikes policy would come from the third strike, the feature
that had so dramatically caught the imagination of the public. The
guaranteed full term alternative, again with the crucially important,
and possibly unattainable,[116] caveat 'if implemented in full', would
be just as effective as the three-strikes law, but at substantially
lower cost.

---

[114] Ibid., p. xii and n. 1.   [115] Ibid., p. 25.
[116] The facility for convicted prisoners to earn remission of part of their sentence
for good work and co-operation with disciplinary regulations is regarded by many
prison administrators as an essential management tool for the maintenance of order.

The very high cost of the California three-strikes law, and the wasteful use of resources in locking up older offenders, many of them convicted of less serious felonies, until well after the time when they might be expected to have retired from their criminal careers, put a question mark against whether the policy would ever be implemented in full. Where was the money to come from? On the basis of the RAND calculation that over the next twenty-five years the new sentencing law would prevent something of the order of 340,000 serious crimes being committed each year, the additional cost would be roughly $5.5 billion annually. This expenditure represented about $16,000 per serious crime prevented. The guaranteed full prison term alternative could prevent the commission of a similar number of serious crimes for an additional expenditure of about $4.4 billion annually, representing a lesser cost per crime prevented of about $13,000.

Unusual as it is to have the cost of crime prevention quantified with such precision, it was beyond the reach of a computerized model to reconcile imponderable social values and financial cost. Neither did the authors of the survey find it possible to make any projections of economic savings resulting from lower medical costs and insurance premiums, nor reduced property losses from businesses and domestic residences. What were brought into the balance, however, were those publicly funded services which would have to be given up, or cut back, to find $5.5 billion annually from the state budget. The assumptions made in the RAND research were that tax increases of the order of $300 per year from the average working person to finance the three-strikes policy were unlikely to be forthcoming, and that borrowing as a long-term source of revenue on this scale would be impractical. Once the focus is directed towards current spending it immediately becomes evident how little flexibility there is for reductions.

The largest head of state expenditure in California, K-12 education (from kindergarten to twelfth grade), is mandated as a result of a popular initiative written into the state constitution by the voters. Minimal levels of funding are required and, because school enrolments are forecast to grow at a faster rate than the tax base, the percentage of the state budget devoted to K-12 education by the year 2002 is estimated to increase from 36 to 47 per cent. Health and welfare, amounting to 35 per cent in 1994; higher education at 12 per cent; corrections at 9 per cent; and other government expenditures, also at 9 per cent; are all under pressure. Of these headings the two most vulnerable are those which have been declining as a proportion of overall expenditure in recent years: higher education, down from 17 per cent to 12 per cent over the last twenty-five years; and other government services, including pollution control, park and other natural resource management, workplace safety assurance, and insurance industry regulation, which have fallen from 12 per cent of state expenditure in 1980 to 9 per cent in 1994. Corrections, which have risen threefold since 1980 to 9 per cent of the total budget in 1994, are estimated to double again to 18 per cent by 2002 to pay for the cost of three strikes.

It would be a dispiriting outcome, to say the least, if the only practical way to finance the theoretical maximum level of crime reduction was to cut back on total spending on higher education, including the great University of California, and other services by more than 40 per cent over the next eight years. Yet this is the prospect held out by the RAND study.[117] If the three-strikes law remains in force unamended, by 2002 the state government will be spending more money keeping people in prison than putting people through college. The probability, however, is that the legislators who voted so fervently for three strikes will find it far less politically attractive to fund its implementation in full. Developments may yet emerge which will avoid the most drastic outcomes, but only by accepting a lesser degree of crime protection than public opinion has been encouraged to anticipate. After the party comes the reckoning.

IX

Unintended effects elsewhere in the criminal justice system often follow hard on the heels of the implementation of populist-inspired legislation. Some of the trends take time to identify and measure; others are more immediately apparent. In the early months of 1995 two reports emanated from public sources in California, both telling the same story. A survey by the Legislative Analyst's Office for the State of California reviewed information collected over the first eight months operation of three strikes from local prosecutors,

[117] Greenwood et al., p. 34.

public defenders and defence counsel, county jails, the State Board
of Corrections, judges and trial court administrators, the State
Judicial Council, and the Department of Corrections.[118] The survey indicated that large numbers of cases were being prosecuted
under the three-strikes provisions. At the end of August 1994, six
months after enactment, more than 7,400 second- and third-strike
cases were filed. Los Angeles County, which generally accounted
for up to half of the state's criminal justice workload, indicated that
at the end of November more than 5,000 second- and third-strike
cases had been filed with the courts.

The usually hidden significance of plea bargaining was starkly
revealed by the statistic that prior to the enactment of the three-
strikes law about 94 per cent of all felony cases statewide were disposed of through plea bargaining. Given the much longer sentences
that defendants would face if convicted of a second- or third-strike
offence, it was hardly surprising that public defenders and criminal
defence attorneys were advising their clients to refuse to plea bargain and take their cases to jury trial. As a result of the drop in plea
bargaining in many jurisdictions a steep increase was forecast in the
number of jury trials. In Los Angeles County the District Attorney
estimated that jury trials would increase from 2,410 in 1994,
roughly the number handled annually since 1992, to 5,875 in 1995,
an increase of 144 per cent. More than half of the increase was
expected to be third-strike cases. In San Diego County the estimated increase was 300 per cent, and in Santa Clara County nearly
200 per cent. Because so many more cases were going to trial there
was an accumulation in the backlog of cases. This meant that some
District Attorneys were prosecuting fewer misdemeanour cases.

The impact on civil cases was likely to be even more marked. In
October 1994 no civil cases were being tried in three of Los Angeles
County's ten Superior Court districts. In addition, more than half
of the fifty court-rooms in the central district that were normally
used for civil cases were being diverted to criminal trials. By early
1995 the Los Angeles Superior Court anticipated that sixty of the
120 judges currently hearing civil cases would be redirected to criminal cases. The County estimated that in 1995 two-thirds to three-
fourths of all court-rooms would be devoted to criminal trials. The
displacement of civil litigation is likely to have far-reaching effects

[118] Legislative Analyst's Office, *Status Check*, 6 Jan. 1995, State of California,
Sacramento.

on the institutions of civil justice, possibly diverting cases to alternative forums for settlement such as arbitration or private judging.

More criminal cases coming to trial meant more pre-trial detention in County jails. Because offenders charged under the three-strikes law faced long prison sentences most counties had set bail for second-strike defendants at twice the usual amount, and refused bail altogether for third-strike defendants. By the end of 1994 Los Angeles County estimated that more than 1,000 three-strikes inmates were housed in its jails awaiting trial. Other counties were forecasting the need for additional accommodation to house three-strikes defendants in local jails pre-trial. Since third-strike offenders faced the possibility of life in prison if convicted, they were treated as high security inmates who had little to lose by assaulting staff or other inmates or attempting to escape. High security inmates called for closer supervision at higher cost than the general jail population. As a result of court-ordered population caps or federal mandates limiting jail overcrowding, the amount of available space in the jails was strictly limited.

The institutions containing 70 per cent of California's total supply of jail places were capped by court order. The only way to keep populations down and make room for new arrivals was to release sentenced inmates. Before the enactment of three strikes, sentenced offenders in Los Angeles County generally served about two-thirds of their sentence before being released. After implementation, the percentage of the sentence served fell to about 45 per cent. Before three strikes the County's jail population consisted roughly of 60 per cent sentenced offenders and 40 per cent pre-trial inmates. After, the proportions reversed to 30 per cent sentenced offenders and 70 per cent pre-trial offenders. This outcome was directly contradictory to the intentions of those stentorian advocates of 'truth in sentencing' who had so enthusiastically supported the policy of three strikes.

What were the criminal and personal characteristics of the offenders so far convicted and sentenced under three-strikes law? The data in the survey showed that at the end of November 1994 there were 2,912 persons in state prisons having been convicted of a second-strike offence, and 63 convicted of a third strike. The low number of third-strike offenders was attributed to the large group of offenders going to trial and the backlog in those cases reaching the courts. Approximately 17 per cent of the second-strike

offenders had been convicted of violent offences including robbery
and first-degree burglary, and the remainder of lesser offences, the
main categories being possession of a controlled drug or petty theft
with prior intent. The majority were male, 48 per cent were in their
twenties, 33 per cent in their thirties, and 9 per cent aged less than
twenty. 37 per cent were black, 33 per cent Hispanic, and 26 per
cent white or another race. The report commented that these proportions were roughly comparable to the state's overall prison population. Of the third-strike offenders, who faced a minimum
sentence of 25 years to life in prison, 20 of the 63 had been convicted of a serious or violent offence. The largest category was possession of a controlled drug.

And so it goes on. What seems on the political platform to be a
straightforward increase in penalties for the most dangerous of
criminals has consequences that run right through the system of
justice. Another report in March 1995[119] came from the 3 Strikes
Impact Subcommittee to the County of Los Angeles Countywide
Criminal Justice Coordination Committee. It confirmed that
although the law had been in effect for only one year, the data
showed that the justice system was 'seriously out of balance' and
that the primary cause was the number of strike cases which were
going to trial. They were staying in the system longer and costing
more to handle. Virtually every level of criminal justice from the
point of arrest to completion of sentence was being impaired. In his
covering letter the Chairman of the Subcommittee[120] said that 'As
strike cases increasingly demand greater and greater resources, the
system's capacity to handle other workload, such as the processing
of civil cases, minor felonies and misdemeanours, will dramatically
decline. These collateral impacts of three strikes may be almost as
significant as the direct impacts.'[121]

[119] 'Preliminary Report on the impact of the 3–Strikes Law on the Los Angeles
County Justice System', 15 Mar. 1995.
[120] Judge James Bascue, Supervising Judge, Criminal Division, Los Angeles
Superior Court.
[121] Report of 3 Strikes Impact Subcommittee, *op. cit.*, p. 2.

7

Partisanship and Compromise

I

By the time the legislators returned to Washington for the 2nd Session of the 103rd Congress in late January 1994 they had seen concern about crime climb in the polls and had been reminded of its compelling importance to their electorates. As at Westminster, when MPs had brought back from their constituencies after the Easter Recess the same year a determination to compel the Government to act on violent videos, so did Representatives declare that legislation on crime was a top priority.[1] The President echoed the popular sense of urgency. In his State of the Union Address Clinton characterized the problem of violence as an American problem without any partisan or philosophical element. He admonished members of Congress 'to find ways as quickly as possible to set aside partisan differences and pass a strong, smart, tough crime bill'.[2] In endorsing the three-strikes law, and mentioning Polly Klaas by name, he drew the longest ovation for his speech. The rapidity of Clinton's conversion to the policy of three-strikes owed more to the promptings of his private pollsters than the caution of the Department of Justice.[3] Biden for one was taken by surprise, having only shortly before dismissed the three-strikes policy as 'wacky'.

Despite the stirring language, what was smart and what was tough were linked only in rhetoric. In practice there were bound to

[1] *CQ Weekly Report*, 29 Jan. 1994, p. 171.
[2] Address Before a Joint Session of Congress on the State of the Union, 140 *Cong. Rec.* H 33 (daily edn. 25 Jan. 1994).
[3] Stanley Greenberg, a White House pollster, was reported in Aug. 1994 to have advised Democratic candidates campaigning for the mid-term elections in November to concentrate on the passage of three-strikes. No other accomplishment, he claimed, came close to it in showing how the Administration was giving a central place to crime. *The New York Times*, 5 Aug. 1994.

be conflicts. The dilemma was illustrated with embarrassing clarity by the Deputy Attorney General, Philip Heymann, an experienced criminal lawyer and administrator who had served four previous Attorneys General at the Department of Justice.[4] On the day before the State of the Union speech Heymann announced his resignation, citing differences in management style with the Attorney General, Janet Reno. However, as became only too clear at a news conference called when vacating office on 15 February and in later public statements, he had become disenchanted with the way the Administration had responded to public pressures and the legislative compromises required by Congress. Accepting that the omnibus crime bill passed by the Senate and awaiting consideration by the House had many useful provisions, he said that the ones getting most attention showed a legislature 'swept far from common sense by the heavy winds of political rhetoric about crime'. In an article for *The Washington Post* Heymann wrote:

The reason the Congress does these things and President Clinton supports them is, of course, straightforward. Fear is a powerful emotion in constituents. Pretending to retaliate fiercely against the source of fear has been politically popular in every country for a very long time. There is less of a market for real remedies than for patent medicines. Thus, there are dozens of new death penalties in the Senate bill, but they are largely irrelevant to any realistic law enforcement effort. They sound tough, and we as a nation are very sick of violence. The only problem is that the prescription won't improve the patient's condition.[5]

He was equally scathing about the populist motivation behind three-strikes; the unintended effects of previous Congressional attempts to control drug abuse by setting minimum mandatory sentences of imprisonment in federal prisons for drug dealing; and the D'Amato amendment for blurring the lines between state and federal law enforcement. In a press interview the previous week Heymann had elaborated on the conflict between toughness and smartness:

---

[4] A Harvard Law School Professor and Director of its Center for Criminal Justice, Heymann had been Assistant Attorney General in charge of the Justice Department's Criminal Division during the Carter Administration, 1978–81. He had also served as Senior Counsel to Common Cause and an associate Watergate special prosecutor.

[5] *The Washington Post*, 27 Feb. 1994.

Crime is one of the great political issues in most Western democracies. It generally breaks down along partisan lines. We're seeing a time when it's being handled in a nonpartisan way, with both parties competing to be as firm and tough on crime as they can be. I don't have any objection to that, but you can't be both the toughest and the smartest.

President Clinton said he wanted to be tough but smart. If you want to be decently smart and exercise some common sense, you can't be tougher than anybody who's competing for toughness. The toughest guy will say one strike, and you're out. Or the toughest guy will say, build 10 times more prisons.

So the difficult trick is how to be smart as well as tough in a political environment that rewards toughness more than smartness. The reason for that is it takes a little while to explain why one thing's smart and the other thing isn't. It doesn't take any time at all to explain why one thing's tougher than the next.[6]

Heymann spoke generously of Reno's ability to change the way people talked about violence by adding the prevention dimension, instancing her interest in child development. However, at the Justice Department she had been hampered by lack of familiarity with the workings of the federal system of government. She had come in as, and in many ways continued to think like, the chief prosecutor of a major urban area.[7] On matters of criminal policy, communications between the White House and the Department of Justice were too informal, without any clearly established structure at either end. The Associate Attorney General, Webster Hubbell, another outsider who had been brought to Washington by Clinton,[8] acted as the main point of contact, but he was no substitute for the regular consultation needed to ensure that policies were developed in a systematic way in the Department with an awareness of the views of the White House at each stage. The delay in getting an Attorney General into post further inhibited the Department's role at the formative stage when decisions were being taken on the scope of the legislation. Reno had not been the President's first choice, two earlier nominees having dropped

---

[6] *The Los Angeles Times*, 20 Feb. 1994.   [7] Ibid.

[8] The appointment of Webster L. Hubbell as Associate Attorney General was approved by the Senate on 28 May 1993. A close friend of President Clinton from Arkansas, and a partner in the same law firm as Hillary Rodham Clinton, Hubbell resigned abruptly on 14 Mar. 1994 amid allegations that he had overcharged his law firm. He was subsequently sentenced to twenty-one months' imprisonment for defrauding the firm.

out.[9] As a consequence there had been a two-and-a-half-month interregnum until her confirmation by the Senate on 11 March 1993. During this period the Department was left in the hands of Stuart Gerson, a Republican appointee of the Bush Administration.[10]

Even without these organizational and personal weaknesses, it is unlikely that the Department of Justice would have been able to accomplish much more than fine tuning in the preparation of the legislation. Many of the detailed provisions had been a long time in the making and were the product of previous compromises. As already noted, Clinton made known to Biden and Brooks his intention to depart from the practice of his Republican predecessors who had sent draft bills prepared by the Administration to Congress by way of an executive communication. The alternative of a single crime bill or, if that was not feasible, broadly similar bills sponsored by the two Judiciary Committee chairmen, building on the report of the conference on the Bush crime bill which had failed to pass the Senate in October 1992, appeared to hold out the promise of swift passage of an electorally attractive measure by a Congress in which the Democrats had a majority in each chamber. Clinton was not the first, or last, election winner to feel a compulsion to produce quick results. The Republicans, after gaining control of both Houses in the Congressional elections in November 1994, similarly committed themselves to an ambitious legislative programme for action in the first hundred days of the 104th Congress.

The strategy averted the prospect of lengthy and potentially divisive pre-legislative negotiations between at least four participants. In addition to the White House and the Justice Department, with inadequate co-ordinating machinery in place, there were two powerful factions in the Democratic Party in Congress: the moderate mainstream, with Senator Biden in the lead, and the more ideologically committed liberals, epitomized by Senator Howard Metzenbaum of Ohio and Representative Don Edwards, Dean of the California delegation in the House. On the liberal wing the Congressional Black Caucus stood as a cohesive and influential

[9] Zoe Baird, Vice-President and General Counsel, Aetna Life and Casualty 1990–, and Kimba Wood, Judge of the US District Court for the Southern District of New York 1988–.

[10] Assistant Attorney General in charge of the Civil Division, Department of Justice, 1989–93; Acting Attorney General, 1993.

grouping with its own agenda. The Attorney General, with her reserved style and deliberative cast of mind, had little time to make her mark on Capitol Hill. In any event Reno was awkwardly placed, being on record as pro-gun control, opposed to the death penalty, and supportive of social programmes aimed at addressing the root causes of crime. To a legislature so attentive to special interests and popular opinion, such clear-cut beliefs could too easily be caricatured as liabilities.

The reasons for the lack of progress in the House of Representatives and the substantial additions made by the Senate in the autumn of 1993 were described in Chapter 6. By the opening of the 2nd Session members of the Democratic caucus in the House were still at odds on several of the key issues after the President had addressed the joint session of both Houses of Congress at the end of January 1994. Keenly aware of the expectations of their constituents, most of them wanted to make progress, although not at any price. Brooks was in no hurry. A crusty and irascible Democrat of the old school from Texas, he was in his forty-second, and as it turned out last, year in Congress. At the age of seventy-one and in failing health, he was no great enthusiast for crime control legislation, having seen so many attempts founder in the past, and was accustomed to moving cautiously. Moreover, he was out of step with a majority of Democrats on the Judiciary Committee in being opposed to gun control on which he wanted a vote on a separate bill later. Brooks was sceptical of the Senate's proposal for a trust fund to pay for community policing and other programmes, and ensured that it was omitted from the House bill. Although his seniority, second in a House of 435 Representatives, still conferred power, by March the effective leadership on the bill had come to be shared in an uneasy partnership with the chairman of the Crime and Criminal Justice Subcommittee of the Judiciary Committee, Charles Schumer.

Representing an inner city Congressional District, Brooklyn in New York, Schumer was a contrast to Brooks in almost every sense. At forty-three he was energetic, ambitious, and publicity-conscious. He was more liberal in outlook, although prepared to compromise when necessary to achieve results. He also had the advantage of being a good friend and political ally of Leon Panetta, named as Chief of Staff at the White House at the end of June. Although some of the larger issues, such as grants to states or multistate alliances to help them build prisons or expand existing facilities, and racial justice and death row appeals, were the province of other subcommittees, the lion's share fell to Schumer's subcommittee to mark up. It was a formidable agenda: the extension in the number of federal crimes to which the death penalty would apply; mandatory sentencing and three-strikes; the trial of juveniles aged thirteen and older as adults for certain violent crimes; community services to reduce crime; and, most controversial of all, the ban on assault weapons. On 10 and 11 March the three House Judiciary subcommittees tackled the main proposals. Several of the key features were approved, although often in an amended form, including more than fifty new federal death penalty offences, aid from federal funds for state prison construction, the prosecution of juveniles as adults in certain circumstances, and a range of youth and community programmes designed to prevent crime.

II

That so potentially bothersome an issue as three-strikes was resolved with so little difficulty owed much to the improved liaison between the Administration and the Congress. Responding to representations by the Democratic leadership, Clinton had sent a member of the White House staff to the Justice Department with a mandate to co-ordinate the Administration's position on the new issues which continued to arise over the crime legislation. Although only in his early thirties, Ronald Klain was ideally fitted for the job.[11] Two years' clerking for Justice Byron White at the Supreme Court had been followed by appointment at the unusually early age of twenty-seven as Chief Counsel to the Senate Judiciary Committee. There, under Biden's chairmanship,[12] he had a hand in the evolution of the crime bills of the early 1990s which had come to nothing. Joining Clinton's campaign staff for the Presidential

---

[11] For an informative profile of Ronald Klain and some other younger Administration office holders see R. Shalit, 'The kids are alright', *The New Republic*, 18 and 25 July 1994, p. 23.

[12] Senator Biden became Chairman of the Judiciary Committee after the Democrats won a majority in the Senate at the 1986 election. He was succeeded as chairman by the ranking Republican Senator, Orrin Hatch of Utah, after the 1994 elections to the 104th Congress.

election, Klain had helped to develop the community policing project. At the White House he was put in charge of judicial appointment evaluations in the office of the Counsel to the President. His keen political instincts, first-hand knowledge of Clinton's methods, access to the President and his advisers, and experience of Congressional law-making were exactly the qualities absent from the Attorney General's Office. At the Department of Justice he was located strategically in Reno's office with the title of Counselor. Fortunately they had struck up a good working relationship dating from the time of her confirmation, and Reno had invited him to join her staff soon after. At that stage, however, he could not be spared from his judicial selection duties. By February, with discontent growing over the handling of the crime bill, the President was ready to agree to Klain's transfer 'to have a voice singing off our song book'.[13] The impact was immediate. 'Before [Klain] came over', one House Democrat was quoted as saying, 'you couldn't get the Administration to move on any of those issues. Justice and the White House weren't talking and didn't trust each other. Everyone would "yes" you. Nothing would happen.'[14]

Three-strikes was an issue well suited to Klain's presentational and political skills. It chimed with his mission to associate Clinton with a strong anti-crime position. It had attracted widespread public support. However, officials at the Justice Department were aware that in its more extreme manifestations three-strikes had the capacity to back-fire on the Administration. The unintended consequences of mandatory sentencing in terms of non-selectivity of offenders, cost, and the effects on prosecutors, courts, and prisons were only too familiar. The crucial decisions turned on the definition of a strike. Should it include offences against property or should it be confined to offences involving drugs or violence? If violent offences only, should all offences against the person qualify, or only the most serious offences? What should be the definition of seriousness? Would the public perception permit the exclusion of drug offences? How was a repeat offender, the 'career criminal' of popular legend, to become eligible to play in this game of criminal baseball? Apart from drug offences, relatively few crimes are tried in the federal District Courts. However, recidivism pays little regard to the jurisdiction under which the defendant is prosecuted.

---

[13] *The New Republic, op. cit.*, p. 25.   [14] Ibid., p. 23.

If the legislation was to have any practical meaning was it necessary to treat as strikes previous convictions in state courts, and if so, for what offences? Should there be a provision allowing the release from prison of convicted three-strikes inmates over the age of sixty who were sick or no longer dangerous?

Heymann was quoted as saying that he did not think anybody in the Justice Department knew about the three-strikes proposal before Clinton mentioned it in the State of the Union.[15] Klain came to the Department determined to prioritize action on the President's announcement. He was fortunate in that there were no existing decisions to accept or repudiate. The objective was straightforward and expedient: to gain the political kudos without paying an undue price. With the support of the like-minded Schumer, whose subcommittee would need to endorse the Administration's proposals, and working closely with his old colleague Cynthia Hogan, by now Chief Counsel of the Senate Judiciary Committee,[16] Klain evolved a minimalist approach. So long as the White House language was preserved, the three-strikes law could be narrowly defined, concentrating on incarcerating the genuinely dangerous and incorrigible offenders, safeguarding federal resources, and respecting the right of states to prosecute and sentence those convicted of committing crimes within their jurisdictions. It was a remarkable indication of the skill and political judgment represented in the drafting that, once the preferred formulation had been agreed by the House subcommittee, the three-strikes proposal, for all its high profile, attracted so little controversy or even debate in Congress.

The wording which in due course was enacted as Section 70001 of Public Law 103–322[17] provided that a person convicted in a court of the United States (i.e. a federal court) of a serious violent felony should be sentenced to life imprisonment if the person had been convicted on separate prior occasions either in a federal or state court of two or more serious violent felonies, or one or more serious violent felonies and one or more serious drug offences. A serious violent felony was defined as a federal or state offence of murder, manslaughter other than involuntary manslaughter, assault with intent to commit murder or rape, aggravated sexual

---

[15] J. Rosen, 'Crime bill follies', *New Republic*, 21 Mar. 1994, p. 24.
[16] *The New Republic*, *op. cit.*, 18 and 25 July 1994, p. 25.
[17] 108 Stat. 1982.

abuse and some other serious sex crimes, kidnapping, aircraft piracy, robbery involving the use or threat of a firearm or other dangerous weapon, extortion, arson posing a threat to human life, firearms use, and certain offences of carjacking. Attempts, conspiracy, or solicitation to commit any of the designated offences would qualify as strikes.[18]

Robbery, where no firearm or other offensive weapon was used or threatened and the offence did not result in death or serious bodily injury, and arson, where the offence posed no threat to human life and the defendant reasonably believed that his act posed no such threat, were specifically excluded.[19] Serious drug offences, which did not qualify for the third strike, were those defined in existing federal or state law of manufacturing, distributing, or dispensing certain quantities of drugs, or possessing them with the intent to do so; and committing a narcotics felony which was part of a continuing series of narcotics crimes in which at least five persons engaged in drug-dealing were supervised and substantial revenue was derived.[20] Although no one could forecast with any confidence the total number of persons likely to be sentenced to mandatory life imprisonment by federal courts under this carefully drawn formulation, the estimate of the Justice Department, based on statistics maintained by the US Sentencing Commission, was in the region of two hundred per year. The Bureau of Prisons could breathe again.

Despite the political imperative of making a gesture on three-strikes, the impact of mandatory sentencing was a mounting cause of concern within the Department of Justice, as well as to some members of Congress. In February 1994 a report prepared by the Deputy Attorney General's office, with the assistance of the Bureau of Prisons, analysed in detail the effects of mandatorily sentenced low-level drug offenders in the federal prisons. The work had been completed the previous August but release of the findings had been delayed, in Heymann's belief because of apprehension in the White House that its contents might be misconstrued.[21] Since 1980 the

---

[18] 108 Stat. 1983.   [19] 108 Stat. 1984.

[20] The qualifying offences were those punishable under Section 410(b)(1)(A) or 408 of the Controlled Substances Act (21 USC § 841(b)(1)(A), § 848) or Section 1010(b)(1)(A) of the Controlled Substances Import and Export Act (21 USC § 960(b)(1)(A)), or an offence under state law which would have been punishable under those statutes if prosecuted in a federal court.

[21] *The New Republic, op. cit.*, 21 Mar. 1994, p. 23.

population in the federal prisons had more than tripled, from 24,000 in 1980 to more than 90,000 in December 1993. Much of the increase was due to far longer mandatory minimum sentences for drug-law violations and offences involving firearms. 60 per cent of inmates in federal prisons were drug offenders compared with 18 per cent in 1980.

The report showed that 16,316 prisoners, amounting to 36.1 per cent of all drug-law offenders in the federal prison system, and 21.2 per cent of the total sentenced population, could be considered as low-level drug offenders. The criteria were: no recorded current or prior offences of violence, no involvement in sophisticated criminal activity, and no prior commitment.[22] The average sentence of this group of prisoners with relatively low levels of criminality was 81.5 months. Under federal sentencing guidelines this meant that the individuals would serve on average at least five and three-quarter years before release from prison. 42.3 per cent of low-level drug offenders were couriers or played peripheral roles in drug trafficking.[23] Drug quantity was the dominant determinant of sentence lengths, and defendants with minor functional roles received sentences that overlapped with those of defendants playing much more significant roles.[24]

In the Senate a bipartisan coalition formed between Democrats and Republicans, on grounds of fairness (Senators Simon and Kennedy) and pragmatism (Senator Thurmond) to promote the notion of a 'safety valve'. This was a device to leave existing mandatory sentencing laws in place, but to allow low-level, non-violent, and first-time offenders to be sentenced under the federal sentencing guidelines rather than the mandatory requirements. Schumer, adept at the interplay of politics and substance in law-making, was attracted by the idea. He proposed a variation to the House Subcommittee on Crime and Criminal Justice which would waive the mandatory minimum sentencing requirements for first-time, low-level drug defendants if they had co-operated with the government in providing information about the offence or offences with which they were charged.

Initially the White House was uncertain whether to give the proposal its support, but shortly after Klain's arrival at the Justice

[22] *An Analysis of Non-Violent Drug Offenders with Minimal Criminal Histories*, US Department of Justice, Washington, DC, 1994, Executive Summary, p. 2.

[23] Ibid., p. 3.　　　　　　　　　　　　　　　　　　　　　[24] Ibid., p. 4.

Department the Administration came out in favour of the safety valve. By June, a detailed commentary containing the views of the Department sent to Brooks and Biden by the Attorney General urged the conferees to adopt an exception to drug law mandatory penalties for certain low-level, non-violent offenders without serious records. Although not going so far as to agree that the proposal should be retroactive and applied to inmates already serving a prison term, the House proposal was commended as 'a sound step toward insuring that our limited Federal prison space is used to incarcerate violent and dangerous offenders for the long sentences they deserve'.[25] It was the language of Thurmond rather than of Kennedy, the two former Senate Judiciary Committee chairmen who had worked together on the sentencing guidelines ten years before,[26] but nevertheless it was a first step towards a reform that was overdue on grounds of principle as well as practicality.[27] Although never publicly acknowledged, there was a tacit understanding that the safety valve was a counterweight to give something to those liberal Democrats who were unhappy about the extension of mandatory sentencing implicit in three-strikes.

III

The full House Judiciary Committee met on 14 March and approved thirteen separate anti-crime bills dealing with death

---

[25] Annex to letter from the Attorney General, Janet Reno, to the Hon. Jack Brooks, Chairman, Committee on the Judiciary, US House of Representatives, 13 June 1994, p. 25.

[26] See Ch. 5.

[27] The 'safety valve' provision was enacted as Section 80001 of Pub. L. 103–322, 108 Stat. 1985. The section limited the applicability of mandatory minimum penalties in certain defined cases of offences under the Controlled Substances Act (21 USC § 841, § 844, § 846) and Controlled Substances Import and Export Act (21 USC § 961, § 963). To qualify for sentencing under guidelines promulgated by the US Sentencing Commission without regard to any statutory minimum sentence, the defendant had to satisfy five requirements. These were: that he had no more than one criminal history point on his record; that no violence had been used or threatened, nor had any firearm or other dangerous weapon been in the defendant's possession; that the offence did not result in death or serious bodily injury to any person; that the defendant was not an organizer, leader, manager, or supervisor of others involved in the offence, nor engaged in a continuing criminal enterprise; and that he had truthfully provided the Government with all information and evidence concerning the offence or offences. As a result of negotiations at the final stages to save the crime bill, the provision was to be prospective and not retrospective, with a minimum sentence of 24 months.

penalty sentencing and appeals, insurance fraud, violence against children, sexual abuse of children, community crime prevention programmes, crime victim protection and compensation, repeat offenders (the three-strikes policy), mandatory minimum sentencing, and trying juveniles as adults. Subsequently these bills were combined into a single bill (HR 4092). The debate on the floor of the House began on 13 April and continued over two weeks. Most of the provisions in HR 4092 were retained, with the exception of the habeas corpus reforms which had already been dropped by the Senate. The bill was passed on 21 April by 285 to 141 votes, renumbered HR 3355, and sent to a conference of representatives of each chamber to resolve the differences between the versions passed by the House and the Senate.

One outstanding issue was omitted from the House bill passed on 21 April. The ban, agreed by the Senate in November, on the manufacture, transfer, and possession of nineteen semi-automatic assault weapons had been held over for fear it would jeopardize agreement on the other provisions of the House anti-crime package. Two weeks later, on 5 May, in an atmosphere of high drama, another bill (HR 4296) incorporating a similar prohibition was passed by a majority of 216 to 214 votes, with two abstentions.[28] One Democrat, who had cast his vote against the ban, reversed it while the vote was being taken on the floor of the House, explaining that his original vote had been based on a misunderstanding. Representative Andrew Jacobs (Indiana) thought that he would have another chance to vote against the large magazines on assault weapons, but when he realized he was mistaken he switched his vote. Another Representative did the same. Moments afterwards the last three undecided members cast their votes: two in favour and one against. Brooks voted against, as did 76 other Democrats, while Schumer, after intense lobbying, won the support of 177 Democrats. Republican members of the House were divided: 137 voting against the measure, with 38 Republicans and one independent supporting it.

The result had been impossible to predict. Even as he watched the voting Schumer expected to lose. In his comments immediately afterwards he said that Clinton's support had been invaluable. The President had telephoned members until midnight the previous day,

---

[28] 140 *Cong. Rec.* H 3116 (daily edn. 5 May 1994).

and had resumed his calls in the morning, continuing until the vote was taken. Clinton himself told reporters of a conversation with a Democrat who had been a longtime supporter of the NRA: 'After I hung up the phone—that was right at the beginning of the vote—I said: You know, we might just pull this off.' He recognized that it had taken 'extraordinary courage' by the members of the House who had stood up for the national interest.[29]

The President was not the only Cabinet member to put his shoulder to the wheel. The Treasury Secretary Lloyd Bentsen, formerly a Senator from Texas and Democratic nominee for the Vice-Presidency in 1988, was recruited after his services had been offered by his Chief of Staff, one of the same cohort as Klain. As a gun owner well known and respected in Congress, Bentsen was able to provide cover for other gun owners who wanted to vote for the ban, but feared political repercussions from the NRA. In the pursuit of wider exposure in the press than he was receiving, Joshua Steiner, his Chief of Staff, saw a role for Bentsen in helping to sell the Administration's crime package. No longer dependent on electoral support in Texas, where to be pro-gun control was regarded as certain death at the polls, the ex-Senator agreed. Steiner coordinated a public relations initiative to portray the old Congressional warrior in a new light, making sure that he had an assault weapon in his hand and was accessible to photographers every day for a week. 'It would really be very useful' he ruminated 'for Bentsen to be seen going up the stairs of the Capitol, flanked by police officers. We ended up bringing in a group of police officers to line the steps of the Capitol. Bentsen and Schumer came down, shaking hands and schmoozing. It made for great visuals on TV. It made the front page of *US Today*.'[30]

Paradoxically, electoral intervention, the NRA's strongest card, may have lost them the vote. Douglas Applegate (Dem., Ohio), previously one of the Association's firmest backers, had voted for the Brady bill the previous year. After eighteen years' membership, he was retiring from the House of Representatives at the end of the 103rd Congress. When his chief aide sought to replace him, the NRA endorsed his opponent in the primary who won. Applegate was reported as telling friends in his home state that the gun lobby had distorted his record after years of loyalty, and that his vote for

[29] *The New York Times*, 6 May 1994.
[30] *The New Republic*, 18 and 25 July 1994, p. 31

the ban on assault weapons was partly in protest.[31] From a different quarter, the Congressional Black Caucus put pressure on
another past supporter of the NRA, a Democrat from Georgia, to
vote with them for the ban, and eventually he did.

IV

Throughout June and July the CBC occupied centre-stage in the
proceedings on the crime bill. The wrong done to African–
Americans which, as seen by the caucus, most urgently needed
righting in the legislation was racially discriminatory capital sentencing. Although previously raised in debates on the 1988 legislation, no proposals had been brought forward by the
Administration, nor did they feature in the original bills introduced
in either chamber. However, racial justice was one of the principal
components of the alternative crime bill (HR 3315) introduced in
the previous October by the CBC, with support from some influential non-black Democrats.[32] At a later stage, as a result of pressure from the caucus, it was incorporated in the House version of
the bill that went to the conference. For many black and Hispanic
representatives it was the top priority. To them, as to other legislators, symbolism was all-important.

Resentment over the imposition of the death penalty, especially in
the Southern states, had been building up for a long time. The argument advanced by some scholarly critics,[33] as well as by black
activists, was that sentencing for homicide was unduly influenced by
the race of the defendant and/or the race of the victim. Statistics on
disparities in sentence were marshalled to support the contention
that capital sentencing, in Georgia at least, was administered in a
way that was racially discriminatory and in violation of the Eighth

---

[31] *The New York Times*, 6 May 1994.

[32] Sponsors included Reps. Patricia Schroeder (Dem., Colorado) and Don
Edwards (Dem., California). First elected in 1972, Mrs Schroeder was the longest-
serving woman member of the House of Representatives in the 103rd Congress.
Edwards was Chairman of the Subcommittee on Civil and Constitutional Rights of
the House Judiciary Committee.

[33] See R. L. Kennedy, '*McCleskey* v. *Kemp*: Race, Capital Punishment and the
Supreme Court,' (1988) 101 *Harvard Law Review*, 1388; B. K. Landsberg, 'Race and
the Rehnquist Court', [1992] 66 *Tulane Law Review*, 1288–96.

and Fourteenth Amendments of the US Constitution.[34] The issue came to a head in 1986 when the Supreme Court considered an appeal by a death row prisoner named McCleskey.[35] The statistical disparity between the treatment of whites and non-whites had already been before the Court in an earlier challenge in 1976.[36] In a case brought by unsuccessful black applicants for employment as police officers by the District of Columbia, the Court held that although invidious discrimination on the basis of race was unconstitutional, it did not follow that a law or other official act was unconstitutional solely because it had a racially disproportionate impact, regardless of whether it reflected a racially discriminatory purpose.[37]

In its finding on McCleskey's petition the Court rejected the constitutional significance of racial disparities in the imposition of the death sentence, upholding Georgia's death penalty statute, and finding that the statistics alone were not sufficient to show purposeful discrimination in the adoption, maintenance, or administration of the death penalty statute. Delivering the opinion of the majority, Justice Powell accepted the existence of a discrepancy that appeared to correlate with the race of the victim, and assumed the statistical validity of a study used in support of McCleskey's claim.[38] However, he observed: 'our assumption that the Baldus

---

[34] The Eighth Amendment prohibits the infliction of 'cruel and unusual punishments'. Section 1 of the Fourteenth Amendment provides that no state shall '. . . deprive any person of life, liberty, or property, without due process of law; nor deny to any person within its jurisdiction the equal protection of the laws'.

[35] *McCleskey* v. *Kemp*, 107 S. Ct. 1756 (1987). McCleskey had petitions considered by the Supreme Court on three separate occasions before his execution in 1991. He had been convicted of the murder of a police officer in the course of an armed robbery in 1978 and sentenced to death. He had been on 'death row' ever since.

[36] *Washington* v. *Davis*, 96 S. Ct. 2040 (1976).

[37] Ibid., 2041, and White J. delivering the opinion of the Court at 2047.

[38] The US District Court, after holding an evidentiary hearing, had rejected as flawed the findings of the studies by Professors Baldus, Woodworth, and Pulaski. The studies were published under the titles 'Monitoring and Evaluating Contemporary Death Sentencing Systems: Lessons from Georgia', 18 *University of California, Davis, Law Review*, 1375 (1985), and 'Arbitrariness and Discrimination in the Administration of the Death Penalty: A Challenge to State Supreme Courts', 15 *Stetson Law Review*, 133 (1986). The judicial critique of the studies is summarized in 107 S. Ct. 1756 (1987) at 1764–6. The Court of Appeals nonetheless assumed the validity of the studies, and addressed itself to the constitutional issues. The Supreme Court followed the same course. The main finding upon which McCleskey relied was that defendants charged with killing white victims in Georgia were 4.3 times more likely to be sentenced to death than defendants charged with killing black victims. There was no statistically significant evidence to support the claim of discrimination on the basis of the race of the defendant.

study is statistically valid does not include the assumption that the study shows that racial considerations actually enter into any sentencing decisions in Georgia.'[39] The court held that the statistics did not prove, nor did they claim to prove, that race entered into any capital sentencing decisions, or that race was a factor in McCleskey's particular case.[40] Despite a widespread perception to the contrary, especially in black communities, the study did not show any markedly disproportionate link between an offender's race and the likelihood of his being sentenced to death.[41]

To circumvent the requirement of proof that a legislature, prosecutor, judge, or jury had acted with racially invidious and discriminatory motives, the CBC drafted the racial justice title which formed part of HR 3315. Finding words to express in law the strength of their conviction, and of others who shared it, had not been easy. There was a conceptual difficulty to be overcome in that the circumstances of each case were different and that no one case could be compared with another. The drafting of what was cited as the Racial Justice Act was amended over the months that it was in the House of Representatives, but the aim was to acknowledge the need for justice to be done by providing a remedy for a defendant who could show that the facts of his case fitted a pattern of racial disparity. Prosecutors, some of the more vocal of whom lost little time in declaring their opposition to the proposal, would have a chance to rebut claims of racial bias, with the decision being made by the judge on the preponderance of the evidence. The provision would apply to past as well as future cases.

In the final version, the opening section stated that 'No person shall be put to death under color of State or Federal law in the execution of a sentence that was imposed based on race'. An inference that race was the basis of a death sentence would be established if valid evidence was presented demonstrating that, at the time the death sentence was imposed, race was a statistically significant fac-

---

[39] 107 S. Ct. 1756 (1987), 1766, n. 7.

[40] Ibid., Powell J. at 1776. The reasoning was rejected in a dissenting opinion by Brennan J. at 1783.

[41] John C. Jeffries, *Justice Lewis F. Powell, Jr.*, Scribner's, New York, 1994, p. 438. This excellent biography contains an informative account of *McCleskey's* case and a discussion of the causes of the excessive delays and repetitive resort to the federal courts in capital cases. In 1989 a committee chaired by Lewis Powell after his retirement from the Supreme Court reported that the average delay between sentence and execution in death penalty cases exceeded eight years.

tor in decisions to seek or impose the sentence of death. Evidence relevant to establish such an inference might include evidence that death sentences were being imposed significantly more frequently in the jurisdiction in question upon persons of one race than on persons of another race. If statistical evidence was presented to establish an inference that race was the basis of the sentence of death, the court would be required to determine its validity and whether it provided a basis for the inference.

The evidence would have to take into account, to the extent it was compiled and made publicly available, evidence of the statutory aggravating factors of the crimes involved, including comparisons of similar cases involving persons of different races. In seeking to rebut an inference the prosecution would have to show that the death penalty was sought in all cases fitting the statutory criteria for the imposition of the death penalty. It could not rely on mere assertions that it did not intend to discriminate, or that the cases in which death was imposed fitted the statutory criteria. An additional procedural precaution had been designed to reinforce the protection against discrimination in the imposition of the death penalty. The effect would be that in a hearing before a jury, having been instructed by the judge before returning their finding, each juror would be required to sign a certificate that no consideration of the race, colour, religious beliefs, national origin, or sex of either the defendant or any victim had influenced him or her in reaching a decision.

On 20 April, the day before the House omnibus bill (HR 3355) was passed, an attempt to strike out the Racial Justice Act was narrowly defeated by five votes. The voting was 212 for the amendment, 217 against, with nine not voting.[42] Over the previous months opposition to the racial justice provision had been spreading. The National Association of Attorneys General, the National District Attorneys' Association, and the American Legislative Exchange Council, a body representing state legislators, had all come out against it. Most Republicans and a sizeable group of Democrats supported the amendment by Rep. Bill McCollum (Florida), the ranking Republican on the International Law, Immigration and Refugees Subcommittee of the Judiciary Committee, who argued that the Racial Justice Act would create an

---

[42] 140 *Cong. Rec.* H 2533 (daily edn. 20 Apr. 1994).

inference of racial discrimination on the basis of death penalty statistics. That inference was one the prosecutor would have to overcome.[43] The result would be to undermine the death penalty,
establish racial quotas for capital punishment, and lead to more litigation and delays in death-row cases. During the floor debate some
speakers offered evidence of disparity in sentencing which suggested that if the racial justice provision passed no state would be
able to inflict the death penalty, either upon those already on death
row or upon those subsequently convicted, because of the statistical significance of the race of the victim. Once the taint had been
established how could it ever be purged? Thus in the minds of
many, inside the Congress and outside it, the specific issue of
racially discriminatory capital sentencing became joined to the wider
controversy over the morality and constitutionality of the death
penalty.

The lack of voting power of the Black Caucus in the Senate (one
Senator) meant that its direct influence was minimal compared with
the House. The Democratic leadership, Mitchell and Biden, was
sceptical and had other more pressing priorities on the crime bill.
Nor had the President given any indication of his own position,
beyond repeating his campaign statement that he supported capital
punishment, and as Governor of Arkansas had on occasion implemented the death penalty. Thereafter the White House remained
silent. On 11 May it came as no surprise when Senators passed a
resolution, by 58 votes to 41 with one abstention, urging their conference negotiators to reject the racial justice provision.[44] In conference the Racial Justice Act was the major bone of contention,
taking up much time. In June some mild encouragement was
received when Reno and other Administration officials, who had
been noncommittal hitherto, said they favoured a compromise that
would counter any racial bias in sentencing without impairing the
implementation of the death penalty. That, however, was a circle
that could not be squared. On the other side was such indomitable
opposition as Senator Thurmond, who threatened to filibuster the
entire bill if the racial justice sentencing provision remained in the
House-Senate conference report.

As time began to run out for the bill to complete its passage by
the August recess, a realization took hold that several other impor-

---

[43] 140 *Cong. Rec.* H 2529.
[44] 140 *Cong. Rec.* S 5526 (daily edn. 11 May 1994).

tant items were being held hostage to the Racial Justice Act. Although a majority of the CBC members remained adamant that they would not vote for a bill which omitted the racial justice title, some cracks began to appear in its united stand. By July some caucus members found that they could after all support the total crime package, even without racial justice, because it contained substantial money for prevention programmes in the urban areas which they represented. Others cited their outright opposition to capital punishment as a reason why they could not vote for the overall bill, with its extension of the death penalty to many more offences, whether or not it included racial justice provisions.[45] But race and politics are an explosive mixture and the situation, by now becoming critical, called for delicate handling.

Who was going to tell the Black Caucus that the Racial Justice Act was doomed and would have to be dropped? The House leadership was apprehensive, with good reason as events were to show, that the CBC might join forces with the Republicans to block the procedural vote necessary to take the conference report to the floor of the House. If this happened the bill would be held up, and possibly lost owing to the limited amount of legislative time remaining. The President too was awkwardly placed. He had come to Washington with the support of many black voters and to an extent stood for their aspirations. Moreover, he badly needed the votes of the CBC and the Hispanic Caucus for his health-care legislation and other issues. Clinton had said that he would sign a crime bill with or without a racial justice provision, but he could not afford to put at risk the entire legislation. So it was Biden who was left holding the short straw. He conveyed the message to the CBC, courteously but firmly, that there was no prospect of the racial justice provisions passing the Senate, however modified. It was time to move on if the remainder of the bill, by now dangerously delayed, was to become law. If it did not, and failed as the Republican efforts had failed, they would all be the losers.

Shortly after the deed was done, and an unsuccessful appeal had been made to the White House, a mournful chairman of the CBC, Kweisi Mfume (Dem., Md), informed a news conference on 14 July that the Administration had given up efforts to find an acceptable version of the proposals on which his members had set such store.

---

[45] *The New York Times*, 14 July 1994.

The tone was one of disillusion: 'We have negotiated in good faith. I'm afraid I cannot say the same for all the negotiations we have had with the White House.'[46]

The unmistakable signal that the Racial Justice Act would be jettisoned cleared the outstanding impediments to reaching agreement in the conference. Some major unresolved issues remained: the ban on assault weapons being non-negotiable for some but not all Democrats in the Senate, and the practical imperative of deleting the sweeping Republican amendment federalizing gun crimes and drastically increasing the mandatory penalties for drug trafficking and violent crimes where a firearm was involved (the D'Amato amendment).

V

Conflicting attitudes towards crime prevention, and the political patronage that can accompany the distribution of federal grants, constituted another stumbling-block to agreement. Conservative ideology was suspicious of crime-prevention programs which were looked on as a branch of a prodigal system of social welfare on which successive governments had spent lavishly and to little effect. The liberal assumption that potential or actual offenders could be steered away from a life of crime by targeted government initiatives aimed at altering their environment was subjected to caustic analysis by conservative think-tanks which related the huge expenditure on welfare spending, an increase of 800 per cent in real terms between 1960 and 1990, to a tripling in the number of felonies per capita over the same period.[47] The fact that the same criticism could be made of incapacitation as a penal sanction was left unsaid.

The extremes of opinion were displayed in the House floor debate on HR 4092 on 21 April. Democrats warmly commended innovative prevention programs which were devoted towards providing youth with employment, education, and recreation as alternatives to crime and violence. The bill authorized a total expenditure of about $7 billion in federal grants to fund a variety of programs intended to prevent crime. An 'Ounce of Prevention'

---

[46] *CQ Weekly Report*, 16 July 1994, p. 1935.

[47] The Heritage Foundation, *Issue Bulletin*, No. 201, Aug. 1994 summarizes the basis of these calculations.

Council was to be set up, comprising in its membership several Cabinet officers and other officials of the executive branch of government nominated by the President. The new body would make grants for certain specified purposes: summer and after-school programs, mentoring and tutoring programs, substance-abuse treatment, and job placement. If requested by the relevant Council member, it could co-ordinate other programs and advise communities and community-backed organizations seeking information about the development of crime prevention, integrated program service delivery, and grant simplification.

Representative Bruce Vento (Dem., Minn), the co-author of some provisions on urban recreation and at-risk youth which had passed the House as a free-standing bill on 22 March before being added to HR 4092, said that his proposal to amend and strengthen existing legislation had attracted the support of over fifty national organizations. In 1978 Congress had enacted a program to help distressed urban areas develop recreational opportunities. Matching grants were made to economically distressed cities for repair of park and recreational facilities, and for innovative recreation-based programs for youth. It had been proven to be effective, but in recent years the available funds had fallen well short of the number of applications from cities which had matching funds and were ready to go. The new provisions were intended not only to provide more adequate federal funding but also to maximize cost-efficiency and program effectiveness. They recognized the important role that urban recreation played in developing positive values in young people and keeping them away from crime. Grants would be authorized to urban areas with a high prevalence of crime to expand park and recreation facilities for at-risk urban youth. They would enable facilities to be rehabilitated, improvements to be made to increase the security of urban parks, and support to be given to successful existing programs.

Vento claimed that urban recreation had been grossly neglected as a national priority over the previous decade. Ironically, opportunities for low and middle-income urban residents had declined at the same time as private health clubs had proliferated for higher-income residents. Urban dwellers, especially those in economically distressed communities, were the most dependent on public parks and recreation programs. Testimony had been provided by the police as well as by city park directors and boys' and girls' club organizers about the effectiveness of urban recreation programs as a crime prevention measure. He stressed that 50–60 per cent of all crime in the United States was committed by young offenders between ten and twenty years of age. If they could be reached before turning to a life of crime, dollars and lives would be saved.[48]

This speech, bringing into relief the operation of a program in which a Congressman had a particular interest, was matched by other advocates of the crime prevention proposals contained in the bill. In the final words spoken before the bill as amended was read a third time, Vento went wider. In a fervent expression of the liberal outlook, he said:

Some provisions in the measure and the votes of the House concern me. They demonstrate that significant misunderstandings exist regarding the antisocial behavior and the criminal justice system. Federalizing a crime is not an automatic solution. The death penalty in my view is an admission of frustration not a solution. So often our society in modern America is insulated and isolated. There does not appear to be much empathy or understanding of the social conditions and plight of significant populations and sectors of our society. The dehumanizing, antisocial behavior of the criminals and inexplicable actions should be met by the reason of law deliberation not retribution.[49]

However noble the purpose, the truth is that the diversion of federal funds to particular localities also confers political advantage upon those who can take the credit. Naturally this is unwelcome to their political opponents who are seldom slow to invoke the idiom of the pork barrel, so enduring a feature of American political life. A vivid passage in a speech during the same debate by a confrontational conservative, Jim Bunning (Rep., Kentucky), used traditional language to bring out the degree of patronage the bill would confer on the Democrat sponsors of the many funding programs: 'The bill before us is still far too soft and full of pork. In fact, it is so full of pork that I am surprised that it did not squeal and run out of the Chamber when it was brought to the floor. Once again, Members with pet projects that could not pass on their own have larded on the pork in a bill that they are certain will pass because it carries the "crime bill" label.'[50]

The same charge was later to be directed at Brooks when it emerged that a proposed criminal justice center at his Alma Mater,

---

[48] 140 *Cong. Rec.* H 2604–5 (daily edn., 21 Apr. 1994).
[49] Ibid., H 2605.   [50] Ibid., H 2603.

Lamar University in Texas, was to be established with the aid of a federal grant of $10 million. In his speech Bunning declared that even the pork would not be so bad if the rest of the bill 'truly returned deterrent power to the justice system'. Criminals and victims alike should be certain that the justice system would provide a sure, swift, and severe punishment for criminal behaviour. The American people were fed up with a system of justice that was kinder to criminals than to the victims of crime, and so was he. When he had gone home to Kentucky for the district work period at Easter the people who had come to his open-door meetings told him that they did not think they should have to wait for a violent criminal to get a third conviction before he was locked away for good. They were right. The average law-abiding citizens of Kentucky, and of the nation, deserved to be protected from the human predators that the criminal justice system had consistently returned to the streets to commit more and more criminal acts. Bunning urged the House to defeat the bill and to come back with one which would let the people know that 'we are on their side, not the criminals.'[51]

VI

By the time the conference had produced its report on 28 July there were warning signs that the final version of the bill could not expect an easy acceptance by the House of Representatives. The racial justice provisions had been eliminated, as had the D'Amato amendment extending federal jurisdiction over almost all crimes involving the use or threat of force against a person or property in which the offender had a firearm. In a covering letter forwarding the comments of the Administration on the crime bill Reno had strongly opposed these provisions. If put into effect they would largely obliterate the distinction between federal and state criminal jurisdiction. She continued:

They represent a false promise of action in fighting violent crime—a promise that will not be realized, given limited Federal resources—and divert attention from our critical Federal role in the fight against violent and drug crime.

[51] Ibid.

Extending Federal jurisdiction over hundreds of thousands of local offenses, which state and local law enforcement is generally best-situated to deal with, will not increase the public's security against these crimes. At best, these provisions would be ineffectual—at worst, they would divert Federal resources from dealing with the distinctively Federal matters and interstate criminal activities that Federal law enforcement is uniquely competent to handle.[52]

Despite the overwhelming volume of criticism which the federalization of violent crimes involving firearms had attracted, on grounds of principle as well as practice, the proposal was one which touched a responsive chord in the hearts of the more conservative Republicans inside and outside the Senate. Rejection by the conference was not the last that was heard of it. The ban on assault weapons survived unchanged, with a majority of the elements making up the House crime prevention package being accepted, although their total cost was $7.6 billion (including drug courts and violence against women), compared with the Senate prevention programs amounting to about $4 billion. Conversely, the conference accepted the higher Senate figure of $8.8 billion for hiring 100,000 extra police officers in preference to the original House proposal of 50,000 extra police at a cost of $3.5 billion. The combined effect of these changes, together with some other additional items, was to drive the overall cost of the bill up to $33.5 billion. This figure compared with the pre-conference cost of the Senate bill passed in November 1993 at $22.3 billion, and the House Bill which followed in April 1994 at about $28.0 billion.

Deep as were the divisions between members of the House on the merits of the more controversial provisions, there was a wider political perspective against which the next scene was to be played. Clinton's plan to reform health-care, the centrepiece of his Administration's legislative priorities, was in deep trouble and unlikely to make further progress before the mid-term Congressional elections in November. The Republican leadership was determined to exploit to the full every legislative issue to demonstrate that they had now obtained the upper hand, despite the Democrats' much-vaunted triumph in gaining control of the Presidency, as well as retaining a majority in both Houses of Congress in 1992. If the Republicans could win on crime control, as well as thwarting health-

[52] Letter from the Attorney General to the Hon. Jack Brooks, *op. cit.*, 13 June 1994, p. 10.

care, they could ridicule the President as weak and ineffective, so boosting their campaign platform for the November elections. Thus, to deny Clinton the credit he might derive from signing the crime bill was a prime objective of national politics.

The conflict of loyalties facing the Republicans who supported the bill was acute. For most, the motivation was a non-party conviction of the need to grasp the first real opportunity for a quarter of a century to make a start down the long road of restricting the availability of firearms which had so fatally aggravated the intolerable level of violent crime in America. Feeble as party discipline normally is in Congress, intense pressure was applied to prevent Republican defections in the House. On 9 August the Republican National Committee hand-delivered copies of a proposed resolution condemning any Republican Representatives who backed the assault-weapons ban and threatening to deny them electoral funding. One of the few who continued to stand firm on gun control was Christopher Shays (Rep., Conn.). A moderate Republican representing an urban district on the East Coast, and Co-Chair with Mfume of the Congressional Urban Caucus, Shays cited a barrage of negative calls in his district which he believed were orchestrated by the NRA.[53]

The Speaker, Thomas Foley (Dem., Wash.), deferred by one week the procedural vote needed to bring the conference report on the bill to the floor of the House. His foreboding was born out when on 11 August, beyond the date when members of Congress had expected to depart for their Summer Recess and the anniversary of Clinton's first unveiling of the legislative proposals in the Rose Garden at the White House, the motion was defeated by 210 to 225 votes.[54] Every House member cast a vote; a rare occurrence. The normally low-key Foley, leaving the chair to make a speech from the floor closing the debate, had pleaded: 'Let us not be a helpless giant in response to the demands and concerns of our people. Let us respond to their most deeply felt needs and concerns. The society that cannot protect the physical security of their citizens is a pretty useless society whatever else it can accomplish.'[55] It was, he said, unusual for the Speaker to vote. It was a tradition of the House. But, like everyone else, he had the right to vote and intended to exercise it in voting for the rule and for the bill.

[53] *CQ Weekly Report*, 13 Aug. 1994, p. 2341.
[54] 140 *Cong. Rec.* H 7960 (daily edn. 11 Aug. 1994).   [55] Ibid.

As at the previous critical stages in the bill's progress, the White House took an active part in lobbying for support. The Chief of Staff, Leon Panetta, a long-serving Congressman before joining the Cabinet as Director of the Office of Management and Budget in 1993,[56] was on hand to cajole his former colleagues, and a command post was set up by the Democratic Whips in a room off the chamber with an open line for the President to speak personally to any waverers. Republicans who had voted for the assault-weapons ban, and for the House version of the bill, were contacted direct. According to White House staff, Clinton called more than fifty members of the House on 10 and 11 August. One of them, a freshman from New York,[57] said that he had received a telephone call on the afternoon of the vote. The President did not offer any deals or inducements, but had stressed the importance of preserving their common stance on assault weapons.[58] At the same time, the Congressman was conscious of the insistence by the Republican leadership for a unity vote which they argued could be justified, in part at least, as a protest against the way in which the Democratic majority had manipulated procedural rules to their advantage in the past. In the end he, and all save eleven Republican supporters of the bill, voted with their party.

More ominous for the Administration was the total of fifty-eight Democrats who defied their leadership by preventing the bill from coming to the floor. Most of the dissentients were rural conservatives opposed to the ban on assault weapons. To take any other political position, said one of them, would be 'just like putting a gun in your mouth in rural Texas'.[59] Eleven others were members of the CBC, acting on principle in withdrawing their support from a bill that extended the death penalty to many additional offences while omitting the Racial Justice Act.

In the immediate aftermath of the defeat there was no unanimity amongst the Democratic leadership on the action necessary to

---

[56] Leon Panetta had been elected to the 95th-103rd Congresses as a representative of the 17th District of California, 1977–93, and was a former chairman of the House Budget Committee.

[57] Rick A. Lazio was first elected to the House of Representatives for the 2nd District of New York in 1992.

[58] *CQ Weekly Report*, 13 Aug. 1994, p. 2341.

[59] Rep. Charles Wilson (Dem., Texas), as quoted in *The Washington Post*, 12 Aug. 1994.

save the bill. As Schumer put it: 'there is no Plan B'.[60] All were agreed that the political stakes were too high to let the bill die, but time was running out and it would have to be brought back within the next two weeks at the outside if there was to be any chance of reversing the vote. The White House was in favour of trying again with the same bill after a few days drumming up public support. However, the House leadership felt that concessions would have to be made, if necessary even on the hard-fought ban on assault weapons. To those accustomed to the ways of Congress nothing was sacrosanct in the pursuit of compromise. After a post-mortem on 12 August the House Majority Leader Richard Gephardt (Dem., Missouri) indicated that Democrats would probably not return to the floor with an identical package. 'My sense is there need to be adjustments in the bill', he said, 'it would not be sensible to go back with the same bill.'[61]

At one remove from the setback, Biden was confident that the Senate would accept the conference report and pass the bill. The course he advocated was not to change the bill but to change eight votes in the House. Both Biden and Brooks rejected the idea of reopening the conference. After the vote Brooks commented: 'I don't think the conference can meet any more. It's too fragile.'[62] Schumer took the same line, warning that reopening the conference even on minor issues could open up the whole bill to renegotiation and would probably spell its doom.[63] The unpalatable choice had to be faced either to make compromises with the conservative Democrat rebels, mainly from the South and West, which would almost certainly mean abandoning the assault-weapons ban, or to try to find the extra votes from among the ranks of the moderate Republicans.

VII

Clinton himself decided the issue. Foley and Gephardt, the two most experienced and influential Democratic members of the House, called on him to urge that assault weapons be taken out of

---

[60] *CQ Weekly Report, op. cit.*, p. 2342.   [61] Ibid.
[62] Brooks denounced a 'solid phalanx of the Republican Party' for an intent to kill the crime bill. *The Washington Post*, 12 Aug. 1994.
[63] *CQ Weekly Report, op. cit.*, p. 2343.

the main bill and voted on separately. The President was stubborn in his response. He refused to compromise on the ban which to him was an indispensable part of the bill. In a statement after the vote he stressed that majorities had been won in votes in both Houses on all of the separate elements in the bill, including gun control. It was, he said: 'especially disheartening to see 225 members of the House participate in a procedural trick orchestrated by the National Rifle Association, then heavily, heavily pushed by the Republican leadership in the House and designed with only one thing in mind, to put the protection of particular interests over the protection of ordinary Americans.'[64]

This was to be the theme of Clinton's appeal in a barnstorming campaign to rally public opinion to his cause. The following morning, 12 August, the President was up early. Speaking to reporters on the South Lawn of the White House at 8.12 a.m., he said:

We are going out now, the Cabinet, mayors of both parties, citizens of both parties all across this country, to say that this crime bill cannot die. Congress has an obligation to the American people that goes way beyond politics and way beyond party. The American people have said over and over this is their first concern. If we can't meet this concern, there is something badly wrong in Washington. And we are going today, starting now, to the National Association of Police Officers [sic] conference to carry this battle back. We are going to fight and fight and fight until we win this battle for the American people.[65]

The assault weapons ban consolidated the support of the representative police organizations behind the bill which was to be a significant factor in outmanoeuvring the NRA. At about 1.30 p.m. Clinton appeared on the platform of the National Association of Police Organizations' convention in Minneapolis. In a spectacular *coup de théâtre* he was flanked by the Republican Mayor of New York and the Democratic Mayor of Philadelphia. Rudolph Giuliani and Edward Rendell were both former US Attorneys, and

[64] Transcript of a statement by President Bill Clinton, the White House Briefing Room, 11 Aug. 1994. The opposition of the NRA was not confined solely to the issue of gun control. Their lobbyist was quoted as saying that the Administration had failed to get the legislation passed because 'Americans want precisely the opposite of what politicians offered them. We want prisons, not pork; police, not empty promises; crime fighters, not social workers.' *The Washington Post*, 12 Aug. 1994.

[65] 'Remarks on Crime Legislation on Departure for Minneapolis, Minnesota', 12 Aug. 1994, *Weekly Compilation of Presidential Documents*, 30: 32, 15 Aug. 1994, p. 1664.

as prosecutors were only too well aware of the consequences of the unlimited access to automatic weapons which could leave the police outgunned on the streets. Their cities moreover stood to benefit substantially from the enhanced law enforcement and crime prevention measures and funding in the bill. For Giuliani it was nonetheless a courageous gesture to agree to join the President in a public display of bipartisan support for his counter-offensive.

Shortly after Clinton had appeared on television the previous evening, Giuliani had telephoned the White House to ask if he could do anything to help get the legislation restarted.[66] The next day he was aboard Air Force One en route for Minneapolis, accompanying the President and discussing the prospects for lobbying some Republican Congressmen. Senator Wellstone and Representative Vento, both Democrats from Minnesota, also joined the Presidential party, while on the West Coast another Republican Mayor, Richard Riordan of Los Angeles, made up a trio of big-city Mayors who lost no time in coming out in support of the bill. Joined by the Mayors of Chicago, Seattle, Kansas City, and Louisville, Kentucky, they formed an important element in a strategy designed to subject legislators in Washington to the pressures of local opinion.[67]

Clinton used the police convention platform,[68] and the national television and media exposure it attracted, to claim that never before had there been a bill which had been endorsed by every major law-enforcement group in the United States. It would put 100,000 more police on the streets, make 'three-strikes and you're out' the law of the land, and provide more funds for prisons to house serious offenders. Handgun ownership by juveniles would be banned, as would the assault weapons that gangs and thugs deployed to outgun the police. However, the bill protected 650 specified hunting and sporting weapons, something the American people had not been told often enough. There were tougher

[66] *The New York Times*, 13 Aug. 1994.

[67] In a teleconference thanking the mayors on 26 Aug. the President remarked that Mayor Abramson of Louisville got the prize for making the most telephone calls, having made over 200 in support of the bill. *Weekly Compilation of Presidential Documents*, 30: 35, 5 Sept. 1994, p. 1722. The US Conference of Mayors collectively supported the legislation.

[68] The National Association of Police Organizations represented more than 160,000 law enforcement officers and 3,000 police unions and associations throughout the country.

penalties for violent crime, including the death penalty for killing an officer of the law in his line of duty. In addition, the bill contained prevention funds. It made his blood boil to hear people talking about pork when he had seen first-hand the impact of prevention programs on children. To applause, he dared his audience to find one person who knew anything about crime who was not for tougher punishment and more prevention.[69] That the police organizations were solidly behind his stance was demonstrated in the introduction by the Convention Chairman. 'The police of this country', he assured the President, 'are completely outraged by the House action . . . Without the aid and resources contained in this bill, we will be forced to continue to fight the war on crime with limited manpower, substandard equipment and outdated laws'.[70]

As Clinton kept up the pressure on public opinion, the search for votes continued in Washington. At first the target of winning over eight Republicans, or persuading some of the Democrats who had rebelled against their party leadership to change sides, seemed attainable. The President had been careful to respect the 'principled opposition' of the ten Democratic members of the CBC who had voted against the bill because of their conviction that the use of the death penalty was racially discriminatory. On Sunday 14 August, the day after making a national radio address from Camp David,[71] Clinton spoke at a morning service at a non-conformist church in a poor and racially diverse suburban area of Maryland. Addressing a predominantly black congregation his secular message was unchanged: that the American people had made it clear to Congress they wanted the crime bill, and he intended to see that they got it.[72] Early in the following week two members of the CBC, after a meeting at the White House, announced that, while still opposed to the extension of the death penalty and the omission of the racial justice provisions, they had decided to vote to allow the House to take up the crime bill as a whole. One of them, Representative John Lewis (Dem., Georgia), a veteran civil rights leader, was influential in the House as a deputy Whip and member of the Democratic

[69] 'Remarks to the Convention of the National Association of Police Organizations in Minneapolis', 12 Aug. 1994, *Weekly Compilation of Presidential Documents*, 30: 32, 15 Aug. 1994, p. 1666.
[70] *The New York Times*, 13 Aug. 1994.
[71] 'The President's Radio Address', 13 Aug. 1994, *Weekly Compilation of Presidential Documents*, 30: 32, 22 Aug. 1994, p. 1671.
[72] Ibid., p. 1672.

leadership. Later the same day a third black Democrat, as a result of a meeting with Reno, said that while he could not vote for the bill itself, he would support the procedural motion to move it to the floor.[73]

The balance of five votes needed to reverse the decision remained elusive. Nor could it be assumed that the eleven Republicans who had voted to get the bill to the floor would be willing to do so again. Their spokesman, Representative Shays, like the Democratic leadership in the House, was convinced that the Administration would have to consent to some concessions. Once the first flush of victory had subsided the Republican leadership took a more conciliatory attitude and was open to negotiations. Republican Congressmen, in the same way as their Democratic counterparts, were uneasy about returning to their constituents with an empty knapsack. The vote had been on a little understood procedural rule and there was sensitivity towards the force of public criticism that Congress was so rule-bound, and so in debt to special interests, that it was incapable of legislating to meet the evident concerns of the people. Although each side would blame the other for the failure to end a stalemate on crime which had prevailed for six years, Clinton's media blitz had established irrefutably in the public mind that it was he and his Administration who were doing everything in their power to get the crime bill passed, and the Republicans in Congress who were obstructing it. Moreover, Republican leaders were uncomfortable about being depicted as the tools of the gun lobby.

For these reasons, as the quest for individual votes continued, being directed especially towards certain Republican Representatives from New York where the power of the gun lobby was weak and that of Giuliani was strong, the objective of working towards bipartisan compromise began to take shape in the minds of the less committed on each side of the barricades. The Republican leadership, in the shape of Robert Dole in the Senate and Newt Gingrich (Rep., Georgia), the Minority Whip, in the House, while not themselves instrumental in initiating attempts to bridge the gap, had indicated they were willing to talk if the President wanted to meet them. They insisted, however, that the overall levels of spending, particularly on crime prevention and social programmes, would

---

[73] Rep. Cleo Fields (Dem., Louisiana). *The New York Times*, 18 Aug. 1994.

have to be cut back drastically if there was to be any hope of making progress. At this stage they would have been aware of signs that there was a growing number of potential defectors within their ranks. By the middle of the week about forty Republican moderates in the House had coalesced around a newcomer, Michael Castle, first elected to Congress as recently as 1992, but experienced as a former Governor of Delaware.[74] It was this group that hammered out a compromise with the Democrats to save the bill.

In its original form the plan was for an across-the-board cut of $3 billion, representing rather less than 10 per cent of the overall cost of the bill which was estimated at $33.5 billion. The reductions would not eliminate any program in full, and would fall equally on social spending, the cost of additional police officers, and grants for prison building. The plan averted the main burden of the cuts falling on crime prevention projects in the urban areas where the support of their mainly Democratic sponsors (including some members of the CBC) was needed to maintain the voting strength for the bill. At a news conference on 19 August Clinton indicated that he was willing to accept the plan. The bill that had come out of conference, he said, met all his criteria: the assault-weapons ban, the ban on handgun ownership by kids, tougher penalties, longer imprisonment, more prevention.[75] However, the total cost amounted to more than could be accommodated in the trust fund resulting from reducing the size of the federal bureaucracy. A cutback of 10 per cent had the virtue of bringing the cost to a level that could be contained in the trust fund, while maintaining the bill's fundamental integrity.[76] The plan did not, however, satisfy the Republican leadership. Dole's blunt comment was that they wanted the focus to be 'on cutting pork, not on cutting prisons or the police', with the main cuts being made from the social spending account.[77] Gingrich, more hawklike, was calling for reductions amounting to $5.5 billion, with a similar emphasis, as well as the reinsertion of Republican-backed sentencing measures.[78]

The even-handedness of the bipartisan approach towards the imperative of cutting back the overall cost of the bill did not sur-

[74] As a two-term Governor, Castle was precluded under state law from seeking re-election for a third term. In 1988 he had worked closely with Clinton, then Governor of Arkansas, in an effort to overhaul the federal welfare system.

[75] *Weekly Compilation of Presidential Documents*, 30: 33, *op. cit.*, pp. 1685–6.

[76] Ibid.   [77] *The New York Times*, 20 Aug. 1994.

[78] *CQ Weekly Report*, 20 Aug. 1994, p. 2449.

vive an all-night bargaining session between the various interest groups in the second conference which was hurriedly convened with representatives of the Senate on 19 August. While the willingness of the moderates to trim as much as $3.3 billion from the total was maintained, the sources from which the savings would have to come were changed pointedly. Hard-line Republicans succeeded in pushing up to $2.5 billion the reductions in social spending from the conference cost of $7.6 billion, with the remaining $800 million coming from reduced expenditure on prisons.[79] Other controversial issues continued to delay agreement on a package which had a realistic chance of success in getting the bill relaunched onto the floor.

A Democratic proposal that large numbers of low-level drug offenders, estimated at between 10,000 and 16,000 prisoners serving mandatory minimum sentences for possession and dealing, should become eligible for early release to make room for violent offenders, was strenuously resisted. Republicans argued that many of those who would be eligible for release were drug dealers and not merely users convicted of possessing relatively small amounts of drugs. A compromise was reached whereby the safety valve was preserved, but it was to be prospective not retroactive. Where the statutorily prescribed minimum sentence was five years, and the conditions were met, including co-operation in providing information about the offence or offences, the sentencing guidelines and any amendments to them should call for a guideline range in which the lowest term of imprisonment was at least twenty-four months. Another last minute proposal was a Republican attempt to amend the bill to enable judges to order the deportation of illegal aliens who had been convicted of criminal offences immediately on their release from prison. Democrats were apprehensive that this proposal would imperil the support the bill needed from the nineteen-strong Hispanic Caucus.

---

[79] 50 per cent of the total funds appropriated for prison construction, amounting to $7,895 million over six fiscal years, 1995–2000, was to be made available to states in the form of Truth in Sentencing Incentive Grants. To be eligible to receive such a grant a state would have to demonstrate that it had in effect laws which required that persons convicted of violent crimes served not less than 85 per cent of the sentence imposed, or was moving in that direction. The criteria specified in Section 20102 of Pub. L. 103–322 included increasing the percentage since 1993 of convicted violent offenders sent to prison; increasing the average time to be served in prison by convicted violent offenders; and increasing the percentage of the sentence served in prison by violent offenders.

VIII

The winds of compromise blew back into contention some proposals that had not won sufficient support in the earlier stages. While
there had been little dissent concerning the bulk of the measures
designed to combat violence against women: on the streets, in public transit and public parks, and as victims of domestic violence,
there had been a lack of unanimity over the approach towards
repeat sexual offenders. The final version of the bill included provisions increasing the level of penalties for sex crimes, instructing
the US Sentencing Commission to review and promulgate amendments where appropriate to the sentencing guidelines in cases of
sexual abuse and aggravated sexual abuse. The guidelines should
also be reviewed and amended to take account of the general problem of recidivism in cases of sex offences, the severity of the offence,
and its devastating effects on survivors. On penalties for repeat
offenders it was more specific, providing that after one or more
prior convictions for an offence punishable under the relevant
chapter of the United States Code, as amended by the Act, or under
the laws of any state relating to aggravated sexual abuse, sexual
abuse, or abusive sexual contact, the penalty would be a term of
imprisonment up to twice that otherwise authorized.

A further proposal directed towards so-called sexual predators[80]
had been added to the Senate bill (S. 1607) by Senator Gorton
(Rep., Washington), modelled on a similar law in his home state.[81]
There had been no opposition and the amendment had been
accepted by the managers of the bill on both sides of the Senate.[82]
The intention was to require a person who had been convicted previously of a sexually violent offence to register a current address

---

[80] The term 'sexually violent predator' was defined in Section 170101 of Pub. L.
103–322 as a person convicted of a sexually violent offence and who suffers from a
mental abnormality or personality disorder that makes the person likely to engage
in predatory sexually violent offences.

[81] Community Protection Act of 1990, 1990 Wash. Laws, ch. 3, §§ 101–1406, cod-
ified as amended in scattered sections of Wash. Rev. Code. For a note on the
Washington State law which permitted police to notify communities about sex
offenders residing nearby when the release of information was 'necessary for public
protection', see 108 *Harvard Law Review*, 787 (1995).

[82] 139 *Cong. Rec.* S 15311 (daily edn. 8 Nov. 1993).

with a designated state law enforcement agency.[83] A comparable proposal to promote the establishment by states of registration systems for convicted child molesters was included in the House bill. In its detailed comments prepared for the conference, the Department of Justice supported the enactment of the child molesters registration proposal, and favoured the concept of registration systems for violent sex offenders who preyed on adult victims. However, it wanted to see more definite criteria concerning the class of offenders who would be covered and the duration of registration requirements.[84] In addition to these reservations, vexatious questions arose in conference over privacy, the conditions for the release of information collected under a state registration program, and the risks of excessive community vigilance and informal sanctions.

Gorton's amendment would have enabled the designated state law enforcement agency to release information that was 'necessary to protect the public' from a specific sexually violent predator who was required to register. By a large majority of 407 to 13 the House instructed its conferees to accept the Senate language. Instead, what emerged from the conference was a composite section covering both child molesters and sexual predators, narrowing the release of information to law enforcement purposes and the notification of victims of the offender. Once again, as with the murder of Polly Klaas in California, another emotive and highly publicized killing of a child strengthened the demand for the substitution of wording which would allow notification to local communities of the address of sexual predators. In the interim it had become known as Megan's provision, after a seven year-old girl, Megan Kanka, who had been sexually assaulted and murdered by a neighbour in July 1994. Unknown to the residents of the New Jersey suburb in which he lived, the man charged with her killing had twice been convicted of other sex crimes.[85]

During the final stages of negotiation a potential swing voter, Representative Susan Molinari (Rep., NY), pressed hard for a basic change in the judicial process. She wanted evidence of previous charges of sexual offences to be admissible in evidence in court,

[83] A majority of states (38 in 1994) had statutes requiring sex offenders released from prison to register with local law enforcement agencies. 108 *Harvard Law Review*, 787 (1995).

[84] Annex to letter from the Attorney General to the Chairman of the House Judiciary Committee, 13 June 1994, *op. cit.*, p. 13.

[85] *The New York Times*, 17 Aug. 1994.

even if the defendant had not been convicted of the offence. Democrats objected both on grounds of civil liberties and because a procedural change on these lines would have little effect as so few sexual crimes were tried in the federal courts. One of the most experienced city prosecutors, Linda Fairstein, Director of the Sex Crimes Unit in Manhattan,[86] commented that sex crimes committed within the federal jurisdiction accounted for only between 3 to 5 per cent of all sex crimes that go to court. It was more important, in her view, to finance programs to train investigators and prosecutors in this field.[87] In the meantime Molinari had obtained an encouraging response from a surprising quarter. She said that when she had talked to Clinton on the telephone he had expressed his disappointment that two items had been dropped from the bill: the sexual predator notification provision and the provision that would make admissible in court, at the discretion of the judge, a defendant's prior charges of sexual offences. According to Molinari, Clinton had said that he would try and get them back.[88]

The Safe Streets for Women title contained some new grant programs intended to combat violent crimes against women and to make available federal funds to increase security in public transportation systems and to reduce the incidence of crime in national parks. Community programs on domestic violence, and preventive and educational programs, were included in another title on Safe Homes for Women. After the uproar over pork had subsided, the realization gained ground that of all the multifarious provisions on violent crimes and prevention, women and children were the quiet winners.[89] First introduced six years earlier, the Violence Against Women Act originally had been regarded as a radical package and a political hot potato. It had been backed consistently by Senator Biden, its original author in the Senate, but was unable to gain majority support. With the passage of time Republican as well as Democratic Congressmen began riding the wave of changing attitudes, seeing in it another issue where each could demonstrate their toughness on crime.[90] In this way, sufficient bipartisanship was generated to enable the proposals to be passed into law with little resistance.

[86] Linda A. Fairstein is an Assistant District Attorney in New York County and the Director of the Sex Crimes Prosecution Unit. She is the author of *Sexual Violence: Our War Against Rape*, William Morrow, New York, 1993.

[87] *The New York Times*, 21 Aug. 1994.

[88] Ibid., 17 Aug. 1994.   [89] Ibid., 25 Aug. 1994.   [90] Ibid.

IX

The expectation of a vote on the bill on Saturday 20 August drew an estimated 6,000 people to the Capitol.[91] Throughout the day batches of visitors were ushered into the Gallery of the House where they sat patiently overlooking an empty chamber. But the culminating stages of the negotiations over the compromises needed to attract the forty Republican moderates without losing a significant number of Democrat votes were not yet complete. The bargaining in the second conference which had begun in earnest at 2.00 p.m. on Friday did not end until 3.15 a.m. on Sunday 21 August. During a chaotic series of meetings between different groups in different rooms the main impediments to agreement were eliminated one by one. The criminal justice center in Brooks's district in Texas had become a symbolic sacrifice demanded by even the most moderate Republican. It was of little importance to the Administration, but to the House leadership Brooks's seniority as chairman of the Judiciary Committee and his influence with conservative Democrats remained factors that could not readily be overlooked. In vain it was argued, by Foley among others, that two studies had verified the necessity for the center. It would be a training academy for federal, state, and local corrections officers. The prisons and jails in the region housed a total of 20,000 inmates, and the proposed center would provide training for more than 7,000 corrections officers. To Republicans, and even some Democrats, however, it was seen as pure pork that had to go. Gingrich had made it abundantly clear that he would agree to no negotiated compromises whatever until it was removed.[92]

By then Brooks was alienated from the process of negotiation and compromise. A prickly character, who had seen countless bills obstructed before, he had lost all remaining appetite for seeking consensus, either within his own party or with the Republicans. Did he, perhaps, have a premonition of what was to come, for him and for other Democrats, in the Congressional elections only eleven

---

[91] The chief doorman at the House gallery said the number was two to three times higher than on a normal weekday, and that a similar total of visitors came again the next day when the debate was in progress. *The New York Times*, 22 Aug. 1994.

[92] Ibid., 17 Aug. 1994.

weeks away?[93] Biden, although senior in the Senate, was a younger man who treated Brooks respectfully, whenever possible making a point of coming to see the Congressman at his House Office Building to discuss business on the bill. The same tactfulness had not been displayed by Schumer. Relationships between Brooks, Chairman of the Judiciary Committee, and the most powerful of his subcommittee chairmen had been strained from the start. In the final stages they broke down completely. Brooks retired to his room, a brooding presence who played no further decisive role as the political drama neared its climax. After the defeat over the vote on the rule, the Congressional leadership on the handling of the bill passed to Foley, the Speaker of the House; Gephardt, the majority leader; Biden, from the Senate; and Schumer. For part of the time they were joined by Panetta from the White House. Of these, it was the last named who broke the news to Brooks that the $10 million federal grant to the Lamar University project would have to be dropped.

Another Texas program, also labelled as pork by suspicious Republicans, was a $1 million grant for a centre to retrain laid-off military workers for new careers in drug-abuse treatment. Inoffensive as this seemed, hackles only rose when it was noticed in the febrile atmosphere of the negotiations at 2.00 a.m. on the Sunday morning that it was to be located at Huntsville, Texas. Huntsville was in the district of another Democrat Representative, Charles Wilson, adjoining that of Brooks, who had been responsible for its insertion into the bill.[94] It too was peremptorily deleted from the slimmed-down bill which exhausted legislators strove to achieve.

When the second conference finally reached agreement on its report, two votes took place on the afternoon and early evening of Sunday 21 August. The first was a procedural motion to bring the bill to the floor of the House. This time it was agreed by 239 to 189 votes, with 7 not voting.[95] 196 Democrats, 42 Republicans, and 1

---

[93] After 42 years in the House of Representatives, Jack Brooks was defeated by the Republican candidate in the 9th District of Texas in the mid-term elections on 8 Nov. 1994. Despite many years of steadfast opposition to gun control, the gun lobby intervened against him because of his support for the crime bill. Three decades earlier, as a member of Congress, he had been riding in the motorcade in Dallas when President Kennedy had been shot and killed.

[94] *The New York Times*, 22 Aug. 1994.

[95] 140 *Cong. Rec.* H 8967–8 (daily edn. 21 Aug. 1994).

Independent voted yea; 55 Democrats and 134 Republicans voted nay. After more than two hours of further debate, a second vote followed in which the House agreed to the conference report and sent the bill as amended to the Senate. The number of Republican supporters held in the forties, with the total number of Democrats voting against their party increasing to 64. Nevertheless, the final result was a clear enough demonstration of the collective desire of the House of Representatives to pass a crime bill which had seen such expenditure of time, energy, speech-making, and arduous negotiation. On the bill itself the voting was 235 for, 195 against, not voting 5.[96] 188 Democrats voted yea, joined by 46 Republicans and 1 Independent. 64 Democrats and 131 Republicans voted nay.

The ban on military-style assault weapons and copycat versions was preserved unchanged in substance, with ammunition clips for existing weapons being limited to ten bullets. The extension in the number of federal crimes punishable by death and the procedures for carrying out the death penalty were maintained, but unaccompanied either by the habeas corpus reforms so dear to the conservative right or the racial justice provisions sought by liberals and the Black Caucus. No last-minute challenge emerged to three-strikes. Once accepted by Clinton as part of the balanced package he wanted to present to the American public, soon to be voters in the November elections, it had become a shared orthodoxy. The total cost of the bill was cut back to $30.2 billion over six years, representing about 10 per cent less than the bill which had been reported by the first conference of both Houses. It was still a huge increase on the original cost of the legislation introduced into the Congress the previous year, which had been estimated at $5.9 billion. Prevention programs totalled $6.9 billion, law enforcement $13.5 billion, and prisons $9.8 billion.

The late run of enthusiasm for counter-measures aimed at sexual offenders was sustained. The content of the title on crimes against children and the registration of sexually violent offenders was amended to give access to community groups as well as law enforcement officials to the criminal histories of repeat offenders. Persons classified as sexually violent predators would have to register with state law enforcement officials for the rest of their lives

---

[96] Ibid., H 9005.

or until declassified as a sexual predator,[97] notifying officials of their address at regular intervals. The information could then be shared with community officials. This concession to Republican opinion, fanned by the public outrage at the death of Megan Kanka, was described by Senator Gorton's colleague from Washington, Rep. Jennifer Dunn, in the House of Representatives in these words:

Ten days ago I rose to complain about bogus language that supposedly allowed local police to notify a community when a sexual predator was released into their midst. After nearly 4 hours of tough negotiations, we conferees finally succeeded in reinserting true community notification language that should have been there in the first place—language that had been approved by 407 Members of the House, and unanimously accepted in the Senate. No question, this is one small victory for the women and families in this nation.[98]

Another last minute addition sailed even closer to the rocks marking the outermost boundaries of justice. Molinari's energetic lobbying, unexpectedly made easier by the President, resulted in a provision that when a defendant was accused in a federal court of an offence of sexual assault, evidence of the commission of another offence or offences of sexual assault would be admissible, whether or not a conviction had resulted. Such a significant departure from the longstanding rules of procedure intended to safeguard persons accused in a criminal trial caused Biden to remark despairingly that 800 years of Anglo-Saxon jurisprudence had been turned on its head.[99] The Judicial Conference of the United States, to which the amended Federal Rules of Evidence were referred, was more explicit in its criticism.

In a report submitted to Congress in accordance with Section 320935 of Pub. L. 103–322,[100] the Judicial Conference pointed out

[97] A determination that a person was no longer a sexually violent predator would be made by the sentencing court after receiving a report by a state board composed of experts in the field of the behaviour and treatment of sexual offenders.

[98] 140 *Cong. Rec.* H 8964 (daily edn. 21 Aug. 1994).

[99] *The New York Times*, 25 Aug. 1994.

[100] 108 Stat. 2135. The section added three new rules of evidence to the Federal Rules of Evidence. Implementation was delayed for 150 days after the enactment of the Act to enable the Judicial Conference of the United States to transmit to Congress a report containing recommendations for amending the Federal Rules of Evidence as they affected the admission of evidence of a defendant's prior sexual assault or child molestation crimes in cases involving sexual assault and child molestation. 108 Stat. 2137.

that the provisions would apply to both civil and criminal cases. Accordingly, they had been reviewed by the separate Advisory Committees on criminal and civil rules of evidence. Having solicited comments, the report stated that 'the overwhelming majority of judges, lawyers, law professors, and legal organizations who had responded'[101] were opposed to the new rules. The principal objections were that the rules would permit the admission of unfairly prejudicial evidence and that they contained numerous drafting problems not intended by their authors. The Advisory Committees agreed, adding that the new rules were unsupported by empirical evidence and could significantly diminish the protections that safeguard accused persons in criminal cases and parties in civil cases against undue prejudice. These protections formed a fundamental part of American jurisprudence and had evolved under longstanding rules and case-law.

A significant concern was the danger of convicting a criminal defendant for past, as opposed to charged, behaviour or for being a bad person. Because prior bad acts would be admissible even though not the subject of a conviction, mini-trials within trials concerning those acts would result when a defendant sought to rebut such evidence.[102] Many of the comments received had argued that the rules as drafted were mandatory, i.e. that such evidence would have to be admitted regardless of other rules of evidence such as the hearsay rule. If the critics were right, the new rules would free the prosecution from rules that applied to the defendant, giving rise to serious constitutional implications.[103]

The Advisory Committees, unanimous except for the representatives of the Department of Justice, concluded that the new rules would permit the introduction of unreliable but prejudicial evidence, and would complicate trials by causing mini-trials of other alleged wrongs. The Standing Committee endorsed the conclusion, and recommended Congress to reconsider its decision on the policy embodied in the new rules in Section 320935. In its formal report the Judicial Conference drew attention to the 'highly unusual unanimity of the members of the Standing and Advisory Committees, composed of over forty judges, practising lawyers, and academicians' in

---

[101] *Report of the Judicial Conference of the United States on the admission of character evidence in certain sexual misconduct cases*, Feb. 1995, p. 2.
[102] Ibid.   [103] Ibid., p. 3.

taking the view that the new rules were undesirable.[104] Indeed, the only supporters were the representatives of the Department of Justice. If Congress would not reconsider its decision on the policy questions an alternative draft of the rules had been prepared which would correct ambiguities and possible constitutional infirmities, yet still effectuate Congressional intent.

Despite the strength and uniformity of the judicial recommendation no action was taken by Congress within the prescribed period, with the result that the new rules of evidence as set out in Section 320935 became effective on 9 July 1995. Although representatives of the Judicial Conference continued to try to persuade Congress to adopt the alternative rules which had been recommended,[105] their ability to achieve changes when faced with a resistant, or disinterested, Congress was limited. The constitutional position is that, whereas Congress has authorized the federal judiciary to prescribe the rules of practice, procedure, and evidence for the federal courts, such authority is subject to the ultimate legislative right of the Congress to reject, modify, or defer any of the rules.[106]

[104] *Report of the Judicial Conference of the United States on the admission of character evidence in certain sexual misconduct cases*, Feb. 1995.

[105] Letter from J. K. Rabiej, Chief, Rules Committee, Support Office, Administrative Office of the United States Courts, Washington, DC, 31 July 1995.

[106] See *The Federal Rules of Practice and Procedure*, A Summary for Bench and Bar, Administrative Office of the US Courts, Oct. 1993.

8

Ending the Insanity

I

The closing scene could have been portrayed as the finale of a compelling action drama, were it not for the gravity of the consequences
when the elected representatives of a legitimate democracy were in
the throes of arriving at such a long drawn-out conclusion. It was fitting that the decision lay with the United States Senate, where 100
Senators, some far-sighted and others with their gaze directed single-
mindedly towards the imminent mid-term elections, had the last
word on the legislative measure which had consumed so much time
over two sessions. The President sensed that the Senate was more
than simply a final fence to be surmounted in the steeplechase that
law-making in Washington had proved to be for his Administration.
Senators needed to be treated with respect and encouraged to take a
statesmanlike view. As the 103rd Congress neared its end he urged
them to reach agreement without delay on the remaining issues, giving less weight to the specific provisions of the crime bill, to be
accepted or rejected as part of the give-and-take of partisan politics,
and more to the need for a demonstrable response by President and
Congress alike to the heartfelt desires of millions of Americans to see
the power and wealth of the nation's government purposefully
directed towards combating the destructive anti-social forces which
so adversely affected the quality of their lives. It was true that
Clinton badly needed the bill to pass for his own credibility; especially as health-care, his other main legislative priority, was founder-
ing and unlikely to become law. Such factors, however, did not
conflict with the persuasiveness of his wider democratic message.

The day after the House vote, these considerations found expression in a letter sent personally by the President to each Senator on
22 August. The text is reproduced in full.[1]

---

[1] *Weekly Compilation of Presidential Documents*, 30: 34, 29 Aug. 1994, p. 1701.

Dear _____

This week, the Senate has an historic chance to move us beyond old labels and partisan divisions by passing the toughest, smartest Crime Bill in our nation's history.

I want to congratulate members of Congress in both houses and both parties who have reached across party lines and worked in good faith to produce this Crime Bill. This isn't a Democratic Crime Bill or a Republican Crime Bill, and it will make a difference in every town, every city, and every state in our country.

The Crime Bill produced by House and Senate conferees and passed yesterday by Democrats and Republicans in the House achieves all the same objectives as the bipartisan Crime Bill which the Senate passed last November by a vote of 95 to 4.

Many of the central provisions of this Crime Bill were included in the Senate bill:

—Nearly $9 billion to put 100,000 new police officers on our streets in community policing;

—An additional $4.6 billion for federal, state and local law enforcement (a 25% increase above the Senate bill);

—$9.9 billion for prisons (a 30% increase above the Senate bill), coupled with tough truth-in-sentencing requirements that will shut the revolving door on violent criminals;

—Life imprisonment for repeat violent offenders by making three-strikes-and-you're-out the law of the land;

—Federal death penalties for the most heinous of crimes, such as killing a law enforcement officer;

—A ban on handgun ownership for juveniles;

—Registration and community notification to warn unsuspecting families of sexual predators in their midst;

—A ban on 19 semiautomatic assault weapons, with specific protection for more than 650 other weapons; and

—Innovative crime prevention programs, such as the Community Schools program sponsored by Senators Danforth, Bradley, and Dodd, and the Violence Against Women Act sponsored by Senators Biden, Hatch, and Dole.

One of the most important elements of this Crime Bill is the creation of a Violent Crime Reduction Trust Fund, which ensures that every crime-fighting program in the bill will be paid for by reducing the federal bureaucracy by more than 270,000 positions over the next six years. The idea for the Trust Fund came from Senators Byrd, Mitchell, Biden, Gramm, Hatch, and Dole, and the Senate approved it by a vote of 94 to 4. The Trust Fund will ensure that the entire Crime Bill will be fully paid for, not with new taxes, but by reducing the federal bureaucracy to its lowest level in over 30 years.

The Senate led the way in passing these important anti-crime proposals last November, and I urge you to take up this Crime Bill in the same bipartisan spirit that marked that debate. The American people have waited six years for a comprehensive Crime Bill. It's time to put politics aside and finish the job. After all the hard work that has gone into this effort by members of both parties acting in good faith, we owe it to the law-abiding citizens of this country to pass this Crime Bill without delay.
Sincerely

Bill Clinton

A new procedural challenge faced the bill in the Senate. The device of setting up a trust fund, financed by savings made in the reduction of the federal workforce, had not been approved by the Senate's Budget Committee as required by the Congressional Budget Act 1974. There was power to waive the rule, but the Act provided that such a waiver required sixty votes out of the total membership of 100. Although the Democrats had a majority in the Senate, they held only fifty-six seats. Thus the procedural hurdle was far more formidable than the simple majority needed to accept the conference report. Over four hot summer days, well into the normal vacation period, Republican obstructionists mounted a last assault. The ranking Republican on the Judiciary Committee, Senator Hatch of Utah, led the charge, backed by Senator Gramm, a dedicated opponent of the Administration's economic policies and a leader on budget issues in the Senate. They were reinforced by Senator Domenici (Rep., New Mexico), another strong critic of what he condemned as the Democrats' propensity to high spending and the escalating federal budget deficit. As a member of both the Appropriations and the Budget Committees, it was Domenici who raised the crucial point of order against the conference report on the ground that it contained matters within the jurisdiction of the Senate Budget Committee which had not been considered as required by Section 306 of the Budget Act. Senator Mitchell, the Majority leader, then moved to waive the Budget Act to allow consideration of the conference report.[2]

On the previous day the Minority leader, Senator Dole, had objected to the inaccuracy of a *New York Times* heading 'Dole Seeks Measure Without Weapons Ban, Asserting He Has Votes to Block Bill'.[3] Mindful of the sensitivity of national public opinion

---

[2] 140 *Cong. Rec.* S 12499 (daily edn. 25 Aug. 1994).
[3] 140 *Cong. Rec.* S 12391 (daily edn. 24 Aug. 1994).

on gun control, he maintained that the argument was not about guns but about unjustified discretionary spending. Republicans were looking for changes and he had given a list of proposed amendments to the Majority leader. They were not set on wrecking the bill or preventing the Congress legislating on crime. The American people, he said, expected Senators to protect their interests: their interests in crime and their interests in the way their money was spent.[4] Behind these high-flown sentiments lay a straightforward power-struggle embracing the familiar ingredients. At this late stage any further delay, caused by reopening the bill to amendments likely to be unacceptable to the House, meant that it would be lost. An undeclared sub-plot was that if the point of order tactic was successful, and the version of the bill before the Senate invalidated as a result, it would be substituted by an earlier version before the trust fund device had been added. The text of that bill did not contain the ban on assault weapons which had been inserted by Feinstein's amendment on 17 November 1993. The opponents of gun control realized they could not win on that issue alone. Delay offered the only chance of averting the prospect of defeat.

As an experienced and skilful manager of legislative business, Dole had taken care to omit assault weapons entirely from a list of ten amendments which he offered to the Democratic leadership. The Republican amendments concentrated on deeper cuts in the cost of prevention programs, and toughening penalty provisions. Mitchell and Biden, having by then obtained indications of support from three Republican Senators, retaliated with the counter-offer of a single amendment of their own. This would have stripped the bill of all prevention programs, except those involving domestic violence and anti-drug treatment in prisons. Knowing that it would fail on a floor vote, and noting the absence of any mention of penalties, the Republican leadership rejected it out of hand. This was enough to win over an independent-minded Republican, Nancy Kassebaum, Dole's colleague from Kansas. In a written statement shortly after the leadership's decision was announced she expressed her disappointment that the offer of an additional $5 billion cut in social spending had been rejected. On balance she now believed that the positive aspects outweighed the negative.[5] Soon

---

[4] 140 *Cong. Rec.* S 12392.

afterwards she was joined by another Republican Senator, John Chafee of Rhode Island. With five out of the total of forty-four Republicans ready to change sides, it looked as though Mitchell had the votes he needed to beat off the challenge on the Budget Act waiver, provided there were no defections on his own side. Both factions being aware of the urgency to reach a decision, the Senate voted on 25 August to accept the motion to waive the requirement of the Budget Act. The necessary votes were gained, with one to spare: 61 Senators voted for the motion and 39 against.[6] The required three-fifths majority having been obtained, the point of order fell.

An analysis of the vote by party allegiance shows the cross-currents which distinguish the key Congressional decisions on legislation so sharply from those at Westminster. Fifty-five of the fifty-six Democrats voted for Mitchell's motion, and one against. Richard Shelby of Alabama, a wayward conservative Democrat, joined thirty-eight Republicans in opposing the waiver.[7] However, six Republicans, including Arlen Specter of Pennsylvania, who within months was a candidate to seek the Republican nomination for the next Presidential election campaign, voted with the Democrats. On a second vote to close the debate later in the evening a consistent opponent of the death penalty, Russell Feingold (Dem., Wis.), joined Shelby in voting against the bill, while a seventh Republican Senator broke ranks to support it. Another Republican did not participate in the final vote. The outcome was that the Senate approved the report of the second conference on the bill, as amended by the House of Representatives, by 61 votes to 38.[8] It then adjourned for a foreshortened recess until 12 September.

The eventful passage of the legislation launched a full year earlier was finally complete. After the procedural vote Mitchell and Biden praised the courageousness of the dissident Republicans and credited Clinton's steadfastness on the assault weapons ban as a key factor in preserving the most politically hazardous of the bill's objectives. Dismissing Republican protestations to the contrary, Biden said that the issue had been 'guns, guns, guns, guns and

[5] *The Los Angeles Times*, 26 Aug. 1994.

[6] 140 *Cong. Rec.* S 12557, (daily edn. 25 Aug. 1994).

[7] The day after the results in the mid-term elections, Shelby joined the Republican ranks in the Senate.

[8] 140 *Cong. Rec.* S. 12600 (daily edn. 25 Aug. 1994).

guns'.[9] Mitchell added a cautionary rider. Despite the NRA's defeat, he said, it should not be assumed that it had lost its clout: 'An organization that can wield such enormous power with such an unpopular issue cannot be discounted.'[10] To comprehend how the NRA came to nail its colours to the mast of such an extreme example of defending gun owners' rights as retaining the right of private individuals to purchase deadly weapons designed for military purposes, it is necessary to have some insight into the origins, beliefs, and methods of one of the most politically assertive of all single-issue interest groups in America.

II

The intensity of belief which characterizes so many NRA activists is rooted in habitual populist fears that the government is set on taking away basic freedoms. This belief transcends the traditional objectives of the NRA which were to encourage accurate rifle-shooting, both as a competitive sport and as training for military reservists, and to further the legitimate use of firearms for hunting and farming purposes. In the early years, following the formation of the Association in 1871, it concentrated on sponsoring target-shooting competitions on its own rifle ranges on Long Island and elsewhere, in order to provide riflemen with an incentive to improve their skills and foster military preparedness.[11] Connections, never to be entirely severed, were forged with arms and ammunition manufacturers, and it was political lobbying that secured funding from the New York state legislature for the purchase of the land and the construction of the Long Island range. After a decline of interest in target-shooting during the latter part of the nineteenth century, Congress established a National Board for the Promotion of Rifle Practice at the instigation of the NRA in 1903. One-third of the Board's officers were trustees of the National Rifle Association, and following a change in the law in 1905 surplus military firearms and ammunition were made available at cost, and later given away free, to rifle clubs sponsored by the NRA.[12]

[9] *The Washington Post*, 26 Aug. 1994.   [10] Ibid.
[11] Davidson, *Under Fire, op. cit.*, p. 23. The account of the origins of the NRA that follows draws on ch. 2, 'The Early Years'.
[12] Ibid., pp. 27–8.

Between the two World Wars NRA members continued to enjoy the exclusive privilege of purchasing weapons at cost. The membership flourished, tripling between 1945 and 1948 as a result of servicemen joining the Association on post-war demobilization. By the mid-1950s, with a national membership of about 300,000, the goal had shifted away from military preparedness to preserving the interests of sportsmen and hunters. In 1958 the aims of the NRA, as boldly stated for all to see on the facade of its new headquarters building in Washington, were 'Firearms safety education, marksmanship training, shooting for recreation'.[13]

The politicization of the NRA, although always present in its culture, did not become the dominant strain until after a palace revolution in 1977. In that year the old guard previously in control of the Association was summarily displaced. Its policy was to consolidate the strength and reputation of the NRA as the national representative body for hunters and target-shooters. A future was envisaged in which the NRA would expand its role beyond the encouragement of safe shooting to teaching outdoor skills such as camping, survival training, and environmental awareness, for which 37,000 acres of land had been purchased in New Mexico. The ambitious plan for a National Outdoor Center was the last straw for the militant wing of the NRA. The 1968 gun-control legislation, described in Chapter 6, had strengthened the hands of an activist group of hard-liners who were convinced that the priority should be the single-minded lobbying of legislators to prevent the erosion of the cherished right to bear arms. Not for them the boy scout-like activities of the leadership they overthrew. What mattered above all else was to curb the menace of federal regulatory control of firearms.

The ideology of the Reagan era favoured the militants of the NRA. The accent on self-reliance, personal responsibility, and less government chimed with the fundamentalist message they preached. The imagery of rugged individualism, the pioneer striding westwards towards the setting sun with his dog at his heels and his gun on his shoulder, was one that appealed alike to a fast-growing NRA membership and to the voters who flocked to the Republican standard. In 1983, for the first time in its history, a serving President of the United States came to an NRA Annual

---

[13] Ibid., p. 29.

Convention. Speaking at the Annual Members banquet, with 1,000 more people watching on closed-circuit television in an overflow hall, Ronald Reagan expressed his 'pride and pleasure' at being the guest of his fellow members of the NRA. It did his spirit good, he said, 'to be with people who never lose faith in America, who never stop believing in her future, and who never back down one inch in defending the constitutional freedoms that are every American's birthright'.[14] Remarking on the 'great respect' in which the 'fine, effective leaders' of the NRA were held in Washington, the President continued: 'Being part of this group, you know that good organizations don't just happen. They take root in a strong body of shared beliefs. They grow strong from leadership with vision, initiative, and determination to reach great goals. And what you've accomplished speaks for itself—more than 2½ million members, and the NRA's getting stronger every day.'[15]

The references to never backing down one inch in the defence of constitutional freedoms and the bond of shared beliefs illustrated Reagan's knack of putting into words what his audience felt deeply and wanted to hear from their President. Fortified by the reassuring presence of a soulmate at the White House, the NRA stepped up its political activities during the 1980s. National advertising campaigns were launched to boost the total membership and improve the Association's image by portraying its members as decent and upright citizens, dedicated to responsible gun use. The underlying message throughout was that to confiscate the weapons of such wholesome persons (which had never been proposed) would be unthinkable, an abuse of power, and a step down the road to an authoritarian state.

The lobbying wing, known as the Institute for Legislative Action, maintained the pressure on legislators, reinforcing voluntary persuasion with sanctions. Intervening directly in Congressional and state elections, the NRA and its allies supported selected candidates, either by contributing money directly to their campaigns or by providing advertising, mailings, or organizational resources. Candidates unsympathetic to the cause were virulently opposed. Although empirical evidence was hard to come by, exit polls and

---

[14] 'Remarks at the Annual Members Banquet of the National Rifle Association in Phoenix, Arizona', 6 May 1983, *Public Papers of the Presidents of the United States*, 1983, Vol. 1, US Government Printing Office, Washington DC, p. 659.
[15] Ibid., p. 660.

the first-hand experience of elected representatives tended to verify the ability of the NRA to influence the results of certain contests by bringing the single issue of the rights of gun owners to the forefront. Thus it was more than NRA self-promotion that had caused it to become renowned for the effectiveness of its lobbying and feared for the potential consequences of its electoral intervention.

The fervour of the activists' beliefs left little or no room for compromise. In their minds there was no middle ground. Congressmen and Senators were either with them or against them. Those in the first category could look forward to electoral support and were encouraged to obstruct all attempts to restrict the availability of firearms. Those in the second category were treated as enemies, lacking in determination to stand up for fundamental freedoms, and unfit for the responsibilities of law-making. As the NRA was fond of reminding waverers, no politician mindful of his career would want to challenge its legitimate goals.[16]

III

A combination of factors came together in the early 1990s to weaken the hold of the gun lobby on the makers of public policy. The widespread revulsion towards violent crime, so often aggravated by the use of firearms, continued to grow. Horror story after horror story was featured in the headlines and the electronic media. The public memory may have been short but the cumulative impact was more enduring. The repeated assertion of the NRA that it was criminals who killed, not guns, failed to explain some of the most notorious incidents. Like much else in populist culture, the claim was based on a stereotype of the professional criminal which did not correspond with the reality of many of the deranged, disaffected, or intoxicated individuals who had killed, sometimes on a mass scale, with firearms bought over the counter.

The frequency of accidental and non-accidental deaths and other injuries in the home involving firearms was another factor which had led to the medical profession becoming increasingly vocal on the need for preventive action. The American Academy of Pediatrics co-operated with the Center to Prevent Handgun

[16] Davidson, *Under Fire, op. cit.*, p. 39.

Violence to publicize the alarming fact that every day fourteen young people under the age of twenty were killed, and many more wounded, by guns. The risk of suicide was five times higher, and of domestic homicide three times higher, if a firearm was available in the home.[17] A survey of 800 adult gun owners residing in the United States, carried out in 1994 for the Harvard Injury Control Center and published in the *Journal of the American Medical Association*,[18] found that one-fifth kept loaded weapons in their homes and did not lock them up. One in seven of gun owners with children kept firearms loaded and unlocked. After a review of the literature the authors concluded that many firearms fatalities were not premeditated. Lethal assaults frequently occurred during arguments, often domestic, when one or both parties had ingested alcohol. Individuals who had taken their own lives had often done so when confronting a severe but temporary crisis. Morbidity and mortality associated with unintentional shootings involving children were often the result of spontaneous happenings that occurred when children found and played with a loaded gun.

Further data established that a high proportion of homicides were killings by family members or friends in the course of quarrels or violent altercations. Disputes between family members or intimates in New York City were twenty-three times more likely to result in death if a firearm was present at the scene.[19] Firearms were the cause of death for 49.6 per cent of all homicides in the home in New York City in 1990 and 1991, and 80.3 per cent of those on the streets.[20] The fact that nearly half of all domestic homicides were the result of shooting supported the results of a previous study which showed that guns kept in the home increased the risk of

[17] 'Keep your Family Safe from Firearm Injury', brochure published by the American Academy of Pediatrics/Center to Prevent Handgun Violence, 1994.

[18] D. Hemenway, S. Solnick, D. Azrael, 'Firearm training and storage', *Journal of the American Medical Association* (1995), 273: pp. 46–50. The authors are at the Harvard School of Public Health, Boston, Mass.

[19] K. Tardiff, P. Marzuk, A. Leon, C. Hirsch, M. Stajic, L. Portera, N. Hartwell, 'A Profile of Homicides on the Streets and in the Homes of New York City', *Public Health Reports* (1995), 110: pp. 13–17. Data was collected from the files of the Chief Medical Examiner of New York City who has responsibility for the certification of unnatural deaths in the five boroughs of the city. All deaths occurring in the calendar years 1990 and 1991 and certified as homicides were eligible for the study. Dr Tardiff is Professor of Psychiatry at Cornell University Medical College, New York City.

[20] Ibid., p. 13.

homicide by a family member or intimate acquaintance rather than conferring protection against intruders.[21]

Domestic homicides failed to fit the caricature of the career criminal; nor did the instinctive resort to firearms as a way of resolving some of the most mindless disputes outside the home. In vivid form this was seen in the number of young men roaming city streets armed with semi-automatic weapons ready to shoot each other if provoked by behaviour they regarded as disrespectful, or because of gang affiliations. Sometimes strangers were killed accidentally.[22] The relevance of the public health data, and the extent of the heightened risks of domestic homicide, suicide, and unintentional injury to children and adults were brought home by the Department of Justice statistic that in 1993 nearly half of all US households (49 per cent) contained one or more firearms.[23]

In an attempt to counter this situation, one of a set of national health promotion objectives adopted for the year 2000 by the US Department of Health and Human Services was a 20 per cent reduction in the proportion of people who possess weapons that are 'inappropriately stored and therefore dangerously available'.[24] The unambiguous wording of this official publication aimed at improving national standards of public health is worth noting:

The impulsive nature of many homicides and suicides suggests that a substantial portion of those events might be prevented if immediate access to lethal weapons was reduced, in particular through appropriate storage of guns and ammunition. More than half of the 20,000 homicide victims in the United States each year are killed by persons they know. In many instances, these homicides are committed impulsively and the perpetrators are immediately remorseful. Similarly, a substantial proportion of the Nation's 30,000 suicides each year are committed impulsively. Impulsive suicide without concomitant clinical depression appears to account for a particularly large proportion of youth suicides. Homicide and suicide attempts are more likely to result in serious injury and death if lethal

---

[21] Ibid., p. 16 and A. Kellermann et al., 'Gun ownership as a risk factor for homicide in the home', *New England Journal of Medicine* (1993), 329: pp. 1084–91.

[22] K. Tardiff et al., ibid., p. 16.

[23] Bureau of Justice Statistics, *Sourcebook of Criminal Justice Statistics*, 1993, US Department of Justice, US Government Printing Office, Washington, D.C., 1994, p. 203, tables 2.57 and 2.58. The estimate is likely to be understated as individuals who own guns illegally may be reluctant to admit to ownership.

[24] U.S. Department of Health and Human Services, *Healthy People 2000: National Health Promotion and Disease Prevention Objectives*, US Government Printing Office, Washington DC, 1990, p. 236.

weapons are used. Firearms are both the most lethal and the most common vehicle used for suicide and homicide, accounting for approximately 60 percent of these violent deaths each year.[25]

While safer storage of firearms would certainly reduce the risk of misuse, some gun owners, female as well as male, fear that it would inhibit the immediate access to their weapon needed for purposes of self-defence. Here again the evidence is salutary. A comprehensive study, based on National Crime Victimization Survey data for the period 1987–90, showed that crime victims very rarely used firearms for self-defence.[26] Only in 0.18 per cent of all crimes recorded by the NCVS, and in 0.83 per cent of violent offences, was a gun used against an offender. While firearms should not be ruled out as a protection against crime, the conclusions of the study were that criminals faced little threat from armed victims. The probability of armed resistance was not zero, but given that about half of all US households owned a gun armed self-defence was extremely uncommon. Compared with the risks of wrongful or accidental use of guns kept in the home by family members or acquaintances, the findings of the survey raised questions about the crime-related costs and benefits of civilian firearm ownership.[27] Nor did the survey find any evidence that the possession of firearms has a measurable deterrent effect on potential offenders.

If any more evidence is required to establish that the ease of access to firearms is a crucial determinant in the relative risk of death from homicide, there is a convincing example to be found in the Pacific North-West. No more than 140 miles apart, but separated by the border between the United States and Canada, are the two large cities of Seattle and Vancouver. There are many similarities between them: in levels of schooling and median annual incomes; in rates of unemployment; and in cultural values and interests. At the time of a detailed study carried out on the basis of data available for 1980–6, both cities had large white majorities.[28]

[25] US Government Printing Office, Washington DC, 1990, pp. 236–7.

[26] D. McDowall and B. Wiersema, 'The Incidence of Defensive Firearm Use by US Crime Victims, 1987 through 1990', *American Journal of Public Health* (1994), 84: pp. 1982–4. The authors are with the Violence Research Group at the University of Maryland, College Park.

[27] Ibid., p. 1984.

[28] J. Sloan, A. Kellermann, D. Reay, J. Ferris, T. Koepsell, F. Rivara, C. Rice, L. Gray, and J. LoGerfo, 'Handgun Regulations, Crime, Assaults, and Homicide: A Tale of Two Cities', *New England Journal of Medicine* (1988), 319: pp. 1256–

Seattle had larger black and Hispanic minorities, and Vancouver a larger Asian population. Rates of burglary and robbery were comparable, as were overall rates of criminal activity. However, the rate of assaults involving firearms was seven times higher in Seattle than in Vancouver. The relative risk of death from homicide, adjusted for age and sex, was again significantly greater in Seattle, virtually all of the excess risk being explained by a 4.8–fold higher risk of being murdered with a handgun.[29]

The contrast between the two cities lay in the markedly different approaches to handgun control. Whereas in Vancouver all legal purchases of handguns required a restricted weapons permit, in Seattle handguns could be purchased over the counter legally for purposes of self-defence in the streets or at home. After a thirty-day waiting period a permit could be obtained to carry a handgun as a concealed weapon. The recreational use of handguns was minimally restricted. There was an inevitability about the finding that firearms were far more commonly owned, and accessible, in Seattle than in Vancouver. In Canada as a whole, with stricter regulation, the rate of handgun ownership was estimated to be only about one-fourth of that in the United States. The conclusion of this meticulously fair analysis of the rates of homicide in two largely similar cities was that the modest restriction on the citizens' access to firearms in Vancouver, especially handguns, was associated with the lower rates over a six-year period. It was not explained by any differences between the communities in aggressiveness, criminal behaviour, or response to crime. The inference was that a more restrictive control of handguns might be expected to reduce national homicide rates.

62. This important survey, together with some of the other studies referred to above, was funded by the Centers for Disease Control and Prevention (CDC), part of the Department of Health and Human Services. In August 1995 it was reported that the NRA was calling for the research program on firearms injuries and deaths to be 'disbanded, defunded, and taken completely apart'. Its Director of Federal Affairs fulminated that there was nothing important about the research; nothing objective about the analysis; and that the mission was to distort issues relating to firearms. Violence should be treated as a criminal justice issue and not a public health problem. *The Lancet* (1995), 346, pp. 563–4.

[29] The homicide rate for Seattle in the 1980s was not unduly high by American standards, being consistently between half and two-thirds of the rates reported for Chicago, Los Angeles, New York, and Houston. See the Uniform Crime Reports compiled by the Federal Bureau of Investigation and published annually by the US Department of Justice. Conversely, Vancouver was by Canadian standards experiencing disproportionately high rates of homicide over the same period, being two to three times higher than those reported for Ottawa, Toronto, and Calgary. Ibid., p. 1259.

IV

To take advantage of the signs of climatic change, the incoming tide of opinion had to be channelled and directed towards specific targets if the thrust of public policy was to be intensified. The agent of change, gathering in public opinion and bringing it to bear on legislators, was Handgun Control, Inc. (HCI). From modest beginnings in 1974, HCI had enrolled a membership of some 8,000 across the country by 1980. In the belief that legislation alone would be insufficient to curb gun-related violence, the Center to Prevent Handgun Violence was set up in 1983 to promote education and research. A legal advocacy component was added later, and came to have a high priority as a means of bringing about the most rapid changes. In 1985 Sarah Brady, wife of the former White House Press Secretary James Brady, joined, subsequently becoming chairman of both HCI and the Center. By 1994, when the crime bill was before Congress, HCI had a paid-up membership of 450,000 and claimed over one million supporters. This total was made up of members past and present and others who had expressed their support in a variety of ways.

At election time, which had seen the NRA's influence at its peak in the past, HCI also began to campaign vigorously. Receipts for the 1991–2 electoral cycle amounted to $1,101,072 with an expenditure of $938,210. Campaign contributions amounted to $154,862 of which $135,112 went to Democrats and $19,750 to Republicans.[30] Comparable statistics in the same year for the NRA showed a stated membership of 2.8 million (the basis of the calculation not being disclosed) with receipts of $5,971,253. Expenditure totalled $5,708,327, with contributions from its Political Victory Fund amounting to $1,738,446. Of this $1,098,354 went to Republican candidates and $635,142 to Democratic candidates.[31]

As those statistics indicate, HCI, although still smaller and less wealthy than the NRA, was by no means an insignificant competi-

[30] *Almanac of Federal PACs: 1994–5*, Amward Publications, Arlington, Va., 1995, pp. 206–7.

[31] Besides contributing directly to candidates for federal, state, and local office, the NRA Political Victory Committee also engaged in 'independent' expenditure activities on behalf of candidates it supported. A candidate's position on gun control was the sole basis for determining an NRA endorsement and NRA/Political Victory Fund campaign gift. Ibid.

tor. By 1993 the published annual financial statement for HCI showed a total revenue of $8,055,830, of which $5,553,105 was spent on program services (legislation and adjudication, public education, membership services, and political action) and $2,645,796 on supporting services (management and general, membership development, and fund-raising). Equally important was the powerful symbolism of the crippled James Brady, campaigning from a wheelchair often pushed by his indomitable wife. Republicans both, the Bradys were not merely figure-heads but skilful and determined publicists to whom the media responded positively. With an active and highly motivated leadership, HCI established national headquarters in Washington DC, with offices in New York, Los Angeles, Chicago, San Francisco, and San Diego. By the time the crime bill was introduced in Congress in 1993, the NRA no longer had the field to itself on the gun issue. A formidable opponent, using the techniques of political activism, applying pressure to the same legislators and, ominously for the NRA, with access to the White House, had entered the arena on the other side.

The inability of the NRA to make any move that could be interpreted as an ideological softening of its position, the 'not an inch' strategy which had been commended by Reagan, accelerated the pace of its declining support amongst those who might be expected to have been counted amongst its natural allies. To the police and many law enforcement officers the outright refusal by the NRA to contemplate any restrictions on the availability of military-style assault weapons was unacceptable and indefensible. Worse still, on the streets and in other emergency situations it left policemen at a disadvantage in the firepower at their disposal. The remarks of Robert Morgenthau, District Attorney for Manhattan, were symptomatic of prosecutors and big-city law enforcement officers across the nation: '. . . we must enact strong Federal gun control legislation. By itself, no state or city can control the spread of illegal guns. Federal leadership and laws are required. Current law bans the importation of assault weapons, but not their manufacture or distribution within our borders. It is small solace to police officers that the weapons overpowering them are made in America.'[32]

Nearly a year after its introduction, after many hesitations and compromises, Congress had enacted the most extensive gun control

---

[32] *The New York Times*, 10 Nov. 1993.

legislation for quarter of a century. The Brady Handgun Violence Prevention Act (Pub. L. 103–159) and the Violent Crime Control and Law Enforcement Act (Pub. L. 103–322) contained between them six substantive changes in the law restricting the availability of firearms or ammunition, as well as enhanced penalties for a number of crimes involving firearms or explosives. The laxness in the licensing procedures for gun dealers, which already had attracted executive action by the Administration, was tightened up. The firearms provisions contained in Title XI of Pub. L. 103–322 ran to twenty-five pages[33] and are summarized in Appendix C to this Chapter.

The highly publicized five-day waiting period to enable checks to be made on the intending purchaser of a handgun (the Brady bill) had by 1991 won the public support of all living ex-Presidents of the United States: Nixon, Ford, Carter, and Reagan, the last-named being a great prize won over by Sarah Brady. In addition to the restrictions on the manufacture, transfer, and possession of certain semi-automatic assault weapons,[34] Pub. L. 103–322 made four other important changes. They were: a ban on large-capacity ammunition-feeding devices;[35] a prohibition against the possession of a handgun or ammunition by, or the private transfer of a handgun or ammunition to, a juvenile (subject to certain exemptions);[36] a prohibition against the disposal of firearms to, or the receipt of firearms by, persons who had committed domestic abuse;[37] and a prohibition against transactions involving stolen firearms which had moved in interstate or foreign commerce.[38] The gun-dealer licensing provisions of the Act[39] went further and gave the force of statute law to the directive issued by the President the previous year in an effort to reduce the number of persons dealing in firearms who need not be licensed. In future all applications for licences would have to be accompanied by photo-identification and fingerprints. It would be a condition of the licence to conduct the business in compliance with the requirements of state and local law.[40]

---

[33] Title XI on Firearms had five subtitles: A. Assault Weapons; B. Youth Handgun Safety; C. Licensure; D. Domestic Violence; E. Gun Crime Penalties. 108 Stat. 1996–2021.

[34] Sec. 110102; 108 Stat. 1996–8.   [35] Sec. 110103; 108 Stat. 1998–9.
[36] Sec. 110201; 108 Stat. 2010–12.   [37] Sec. 110401; 108 Stat. 2014–15.
[38] Sec. 110511; 108 Stat. 2019.   [39] Secs. 110301–7, 108 Stat. 2012–14.
[40] Sec. 110302, 108 Stat. 2013.

Another straw in the wind, indicative of changing attitudes amongst manufacturers, came in November 1993 when Black Talon handgun ammunition was withdrawn from sale to the public. This bullet, which with others had come to the critical notice of Senator Moynihan (Dem., New York),[41] was designed to split open into six prongs on entering the body. These then spun and were especially destructive of the organs in the area of the body entered.[42] According to the manufacturer, the decision had been taken because Black Talon ammunition was becoming a focal point for broader issues that were well beyond their control. The controversy threatened the good name of Winchester which had stood for the safe and responsible use of arms and ammunition for 125 years.[43]

Moynihan's campaign, pursued for several years, differed from other protagonists of gun control in that it was based on a single causative factor which he encapsulated in a parody of the NRA slogan: guns don't kill people, bullets do.[44] Unlike firearms which had a long life, measured in decades, generations, or even centuries, ammunition had a far shorter finite life. Moreover, while the supply of handguns in existence could last for two centuries, there was only a four-year supply of ammunition. Since 1918 manufacturers of ammunition had been taxed, and since 1938 the Bureau of Alcohol, Tobacco and Firearms required a licence to manufacture. In supporting the efforts to control access to handguns, Moynihan recognized that with an estimated 200 million in the United States, and between one million and 1.7 million handguns in the City of New York alone,[45] the problem was not going to go away. His argument that the availability of ammunition, particularly in its most lethal forms, should be subjected to greater restriction and higher taxation was both convincing and persistently maintained.[46]

---

[41] Daniel Patrick Moynihan, formerly a Harvard Professor, served as US Ambassador to India 1973–5, and as Permanent Representative to the United Nations 1975–6. US Senator for New York State since 1977.

[42] 139 *Cong. Rec.* S 16931 (daily edn. 22 Nov. 1993).

[43] *Winchester Ammunition Press Release*, 22 Nov. 1993, printed in the *Congressional Record* for the same date. Ibid.

[44] Ibid., S 16932.   [45] Ibid.

[46] A note in 108 *Harvard Law Review*, 1679 (1995) on the premise that bullet-related injuries were increasingly viewed as a serious public health problem, instead of a crime problem, argued that ammunition manufacturers should be subjected to a form of absolute liability for all injuries caused by bullets they had manufactured.

By the time the crime bill was signed into law by the President in September 1994, public health and epidemiological approaches[47] towards counteracting the epidemic of gun crime had conjoined the more familiar approaches towards the rational formulation of policy. As we have seen, however, policy towards gun crime was dictated less by rational considerations than by an irrational belief, intensely held, that the federal government wanted to confiscate people's guns. It was this dogma, cultivated by the NRA and rooted in mistrust of a distant and interfering government, which had facilitated political mobilization.[48] Once mobilized, it was the special-interest groups dedicated to preserving the rights of gun owners who set the parameters beyond which legislators strayed at their peril. Senator Mitchell's forecast that the NRA had not lost its clout as a result of the defeat in Congress was soon borne out by events. Only weeks later the NRA sought retribution at the polls. 'This year', the NRA's chief lobbyist Tanya Metaksa proclaimed, 'it's payback time—time to reward our friends and punish our enemies.'[49]

Democratic casualties in the mid-term Congressional elections on 8 November included Jim Sasser, Chairman of the Senate Budget

[47] The epidemiological approach to gun control means an examination of all the elements of human behaviour, as well as the mechanical instruments, that form the causative factors of gun violence. Interventions are then designed to address all of the causative factors. The composite strategy adopted by HCI offered the prospect of a greater chance of reducing assaultive behaviour than concentration on a single issue. (Letter from Richard M. Aborn, President, Handgun Control, 16 Oct. 1995.)

[48] The controversy over abortion is another issue on which feelings ran deep. The findings of a large-scale citizen-participation survey show that pro-choice and pro-life views are polarized at the extremities of a scale indicating degrees of intensity of opinion. Although opinion on abortion is clustered at the ends of the issue continuum, it is not balanced. More than twice as many respondents registered extremely pro-choice views as registered extremely pro-life views. Yet the impact of those holding pro-life attitudes on political activity is more than twice as great as those holding pro-choice attitudes. The effect of education is to bring in an activist population which is more pro-choice, whereas the effect of religious factors is to enhance the number of pro-life activists. See S. Verba, K. L. Schlozman, and H. Brady, *Voice and Equality: Civic Voluntarism in American Politics*, Harvard University Press, Cambridge, Mass., 1995, pp. 400–5. The survey did not measure attitudes towards gun control, although there appear to be parallels between the intensity of pro-life attitudes towards abortion and the strength of feeling about the rights of gun owners. In both, the minority is more politically active than the majority.

[49] *The Wall Street Journal*, 2 Nov. 1994. Over the previous weeks the US Federal Election Commission records showed that the NRA had put more than $1 million into House and Senate election campaigns, the bulk of it for radio and television advertising.

Committee, in Tennessee[50] and two of the most prominent members of the House of Representatives. Thomas Foley in Washington was the first Speaker of the House to be defeated in the twentieth century, and in Texas Jack Brooks went down to defeat after forty-two years in Congress. In each case there were other factors besides the hostile intervention of the NRA, notably the compelling forces which swept the Republicans to a victory of landslide proportions nationally.[51] Yet the NRA and its associates, such as Gun Owners of America, which opposed Brooks, were skilled at picking contests where they could make a difference. For Brooks, more than any-one else, there was cruel irony in his political career ending in this way, since he had long been an outspoken opponent of gun con-trol. Nevertheless, the fact that he had voted, however reluctantly, for the crime bill containing the ban on assault weapons and other restrictions on firearms was enough to condemn him in the eyes of the unforgiving zealots who were determined to make a public dis-play of undiminished strength.

No accurate measure exists of the impact of the gun-control issue on the results of individual elections. But at the heart of govern-ment there were no doubts. In his State of the Union Address in January 1995 the President said:

The last Congress passed the Brady Bill and the ban on 19 assault weapons. I think everybody in this room knows that several members of the last Congress who voted for the assault weapons ban and the Brady Bill lost their seats because of it. Neither the bill supporters [nor] I believe anything should be done to infringe upon the legitimate right of our citi-zens to bear arms for hunting and sporting purposes. Those people laid down their seats in Congress to try to keep more police and children from laying down their lives in our streets under a hail of assault weapons' bul-lets. And I will not see that ban repealed.[52]

---

[50] *The New York Times* reported on 7 Nov. 1994 that the NRA had targeted Sasser, spending more than $350,000 in an independent effort to prevent his re-elec-tion to the Senate.

[51] The Democrats lost control of the Senate and the House of Representatives, where there had been a Democratic majority for forty years. The Republicans had not controlled both Houses of Congress since 1954.

[52] 141 *Cong. Rec.* H 587 (daily edn. 24 Jan. 1995).

V

In striving to accomplish a 'more perfect Union',[53] balancing the rights of individuals and minority groups against the requirements of an orderly society, there needs to be some facility for the correction of error. The latitude permitted by the interpretation of the Constitution and the evolution of a participatory political system have enabled mistakes to be identified and corrections made. Controversy and hesitation have often marked the transitional phases of American legal history, yet the recognition of error has been a necessary precursor to changes of direction in public policy. This is the reality now facing law-makers. The policies which have been implemented over the last decade in response to levels of violent crime, especially gun crime and drug-related crimes of violence that so far exceed the experience of other developed industrialized societies, have been, to put it bluntly, shown to be mistaken.

A mistake is made if public policy fails to achieve its intended effects. Public expectations are raised, and then dashed. Confidence in the ability of government to lead the nation towards attainable objectives for betterment suffers. Human as well as material resources are wasted. Individual injustice, distortions of process, and indefensible anachronisms in the system of criminal justice are the legacies of misdirected policies. If it is objected that so critical a verdict ill becomes an observer from another country, my answer must be that those who stand further away from a mountain can sometimes see its shape more clearly than those who live on it.

The underlying reasons why the incidence of violent crime in America is so high lie outside the scope of this study. The focus is upon the policy responses to a social epidemic which has debilitated large parts of American society. That the violence is concentrated in certain geographical areas and amongst certain groups defined

[53] The Preamble to the 1787 US Constitution reads: 'We the People of the United States, in order to form a more perfect Union, establish Justice, insure domestic Tranquility, provide for the common defence, promote the general Welfare, and secure the Blessings of Liberty to ourselves and our Posterity, do ordain and establish this Constitution for the United States of America.' For a comparative study, including the modern texts of the constitutions of the United Kingdom, United States of America, Federal Republic of Germany, Fifth French Republic, and the Russian Federation, as well as the basic institutional provisions of some European conventions and treaties, see S. E. Finer, V. Bogdanor, and B. Rudden, *Comparing Constitutions*, Clarendon Press, Oxford, 1995.

by age and ethnicity has not contained a more widespread sense of danger and fear. The general perception of crime has unleashed exceptionally potent forces of populist opinion, based more often than not on anger, resentment, and a demand for vengeance. The ideals of behavioural reform and improvement inherent in the term 'corrections' have given way to the desire to punish offenders and to protect the public from victimization. Death-penalty statutes are in the ascendant, although relatively few executions have been carried out. The opportunities for many years' delay stem from the demands of due process that execution should be stayed until all avenues of appeal have been exhausted and petitions considered and rejected.[54]

Understandable as these reactions are, they are infirm foundations for sound policies. Ignorance of the wide variety of circumstance and culpability which characterize criminal offending has to be met with explanation and analysis. There are no short cuts and no ultimate solutions just beyond reach. Violent crime must be distinguished from property crime and the interconnections carefully studied. The fact that opinions are so strong does not mean that they should be accepted as the guiding light for legislation without critical evaluation.

At every point in the American system of law enforcement the pressure of public opinion makes itself felt. The police, the prosecution, the judges, juries, and corrections officials are all conscious of public expectations. State governors and administrators grapple with intractable practical issues such as the avoidance of undue delay in prosecuting defendants, the relative costs of alternative forms of containment if custodial sentences result, the funds available for building and operating prisons, and the need to maintain security, order, and adequate standards within them. Federal

---

[54] In deciding a series of appeals from Jamaica and other West Indian states on the legality of long-delayed executions, the Judicial Committee of the Privy Council laid down a period of five years after which there would be strong grounds for believing that the delay in carrying out a sentence of death would constitute inhuman or degrading punishment or other treatment. The leading case is *Pratt* v. *Attorney-General for Jamaica* [1994] 2 AC 1. In March 1995 Justice Stevens cited the Privy Council cases in a memorandum on the denial of a petition to the Supreme Court for a writ of *certiorari. Lackey* v. *Texas*, 115 S. Ct. 1421 (1995). Justice Breyer agreed with Justice Stevens that the question of whether executing a prisoner who had already spent seventeen years on death row violated the Eighth Amendment's prohibition against cruel and unusual punishment was both important and undecided.

judges see the inequities that can result from a legislative framework which denies them the ability to punish individual offenders according to the principles of just deserts and proportionality upon which the sentencing guidelines are based. It seems extraordinary that the flaws in the system of federal guidelines dating from the sentencing reforms of 1984, which had become so unpopular with the judiciary, could be compounded by later statutory enactments. But that is what has happened.

In a recent study of mandatory penalties[55] Michael Tonry brings out the full extent to which they are seen as symbols by the elected representatives who have espoused them. They want to reassure the public generally, he writes, that their fears have been noted and acted on. They do so by making promises that the law can at best imperfectly and incompletely deliver. Instrumental arguments against the effectiveness of mandatory penalties, and normative arguments about injustice, fall on deaf ears.[56] Once the votes are cast, elected officials move on to other issues. However, the judges, the prosecutors, defence counsel, and many others have to live with the consequences. They must keep the courts functioning, and it should come as no surprise that they sometimes devise ways to avoid the application of laws which they believe to be uncommonly harsh. Elected officials, Tonry concludes, should become more responsible about crime-control policy, and should balance any need which they feel to make symbolic and rhetorical statements during the passage of legislation with well established knowledge of how mandatory sentences operate in practice.[57]

The accumulation of professional knowledge and expertise has often acted as a brake on the cruder forms of populist-inspired legislation, whether federal or state. Yet in the Congresses of the late 1980s and the early 1990s professional expertise has been at a discount in penal policy-making. The same phenomenon has been observed in England. Of all the lessons to be drawn from dissecting the 1994 crime legislation, the first is the way in which so many of the provisions which found their way into law derived from the perceived demands of local, sectional, or national public opinion rather than from practical experience or any detectable body of coherent principle. The pattern was not confined to crime, nor to those proposals put forward by Congressmen or Senators. On sev-

---

[55] *Sentencing Matters, op. cit.*, 1986, pp. 134–64.   [56] Ibid., p. 160.
[57] Ibid., p. 161.

eral important issues, policies originating from or taken up by the Administration owed more to the pollsters advising the White House than to the expertise of the Department of Justice. On occasion, however, it was the professionals who had the last word.

Nowhere was the gap between legislative rhetoric aimed at the general public and unpublicized post-enactment effect wider than in the federal three-strikes provision. The formulation worked out with such care by the Department of Justice, and the definition of what constituted each of the three strikes necessary to activate mandatory life imprisonment for persons convicted of certain felonies, was deliberately narrow. The fact that the third strike had to be a conviction for a serious violent felony in a court of the United States when only some 5 per cent of all felony convictions were in the federal district courts,[58] meant that the total number of offenders sentenced under the provision in Section 70001 was likely to be relatively small. Who, though, could have anticipated that by July 1995, ten months after enactment, as few as sixteen federal third-strike cases should have been brought in ten districts?[59] Accepting the probability that the enactment of three-strikes statutes by fourteen states[60] may have contributed to this minimal outcome, there is a sharp contrast between the negligible numbers of such cases prosecuted in the federal courts and the dislocation caused by the policy of the same name to the entire process of criminal justice in California.

Below the surface of the legislation, ideological currents ran strongly. Apart from gun control, the mechanism by which additional federal funding was to be made available to the states for prison construction and operation was conditional on the acceptance of the so-called 'truth in sentencing' objective that violent offenders should serve 85 per cent of their sentence in custody. Whether or not this policy would lead to a reduction in the

[58] In 1992, the most recent year for which data are available, 95 per cent of all felony convictions occurred in state courts. P. Lane, *Felony Sentences in State Courts 1992*, Bureau of Justice Statistics, US Department of Justice, Washington DC, 1994.

[59] Information provided by US Department of Justice, Criminal Division; letter of 27 July 1995.

[60] As of April 1995, fourteen states had their own versions of a three-strikes provision in effect. They were: California, Colorado, Connecticut, Georgia, Indiana, Kansas, Louisiana, Maryland, New Mexico, North Carolina, Tennessee, Virginia, Washington, and Wisconsin. Other states were considering enacting similar provisions. D. Hunzeker, *State Sentencing Systems and Truth in Sentencing*, National Conference of State Legislatures, Denver, Co., 1995.

incidence of violent crime, and if so the projected costs and savings, mattered less than its appearance as a seemingly tough approach in tune with the public mood. In other parts of the Act, for example the intention to curtail the power of the federal courts to regulate overcrowding in state prisons and local detention facilities; the notification requirements of the addresses of released sexual predators; and the admissibility in evidence of the commission of previous offences of sexual assault where no conviction had resulted; longstanding case-law and procedural rules designed to protect persons in the criminal process accused but not convicted were abruptly swept aside. Should these be interpreted as early indications of a wider shift away from the canons of due process towards what are seen as the imperatives of crime control?

With the exception of the prevention programs, little concern was displayed during the passage of the Act for the traditional American values of fairness, economic efficiency, and the social consequences of governmental action. That outcome may have resulted as much from a gradual lessening of the hold of liberal idealism on the centre ground of politics and law-making as a deliberate move towards the political right. Taken as a whole, few law-makers would have been able to agree on where to place the Act on a graduated ideological spectrum. Appearances were all-important. The practical application of such a varied collection of largely self-contained provisions will depend less on the reactions of the diverse audiences at which they were directed than on the myriad factors, predictable or otherwise, that will bear on their implementation. It is easy for legislators to overlook the truism, succinctly expressed by Judge Posner, that the criminal justice system is a machine comprising a set of interrelated and interacting parts, each of which has a function in maintaining the system. However, the parts are in the hands of different branches of government, and the American commitment to separation of powers keeps it that way.[61]

Ultimately, the new public law represented the sum of a series of political decisions, connected loosely by the requirements of compromise, on issues which had been propelled into the federal legislative arena by the force of special interests or their perceived popular appeal. As in previous Congresses, some issues remained

---

[61] 'The most punitive nation', *Times Literary Supplement*, 1 Sept. 1995, p. 4. Richard A. Posner is Chief Judge of the US Court of Appeals for the Seventh Circuit and Senior Lecturer at the University of Chicago Law School.

grid-locked, habeas corpus reform and racially discriminatory capital sentencing being prominent amongst them. While the 103rd
Congress did succeed in passing a comprehensive bill, which its
immediate predecessors had failed to do, it was unlikely in practice
to live up to its title of controlling violent crime. Despite the substantial extra funding authorized for state action, subject to the prescribed conditions being met, the vast bulk of criminal offences,
when and if detected, will continue to be prosecuted, tried, sentenced, and punished under state law by the individual states.[62] Yet
federal legislation, proposed if not always enacted, is the product
of an assumption now held on right and left alike that crime policy is the proper concern of national government. This is a comparatively new feature of American political life and one that in the
long run could be very important.

On the farther side of the mountain, and the more dangerous for
those attempting the ascent, the weather was brighter. It is incon-
testable that of all the provisions in the 1994 crime legislation the
most important, symbolically as much as in terms of their practical
effect, were those relating to gun control. To the NRA and the gun-
rights lobby it was a battle lost. Other voices, less strident and
apparently more reasonable, questioned the emphasis on gun control as a panacea that was bound to fail because of Americans' love
of guns and their utility for the purposes of deterrence and self-
defence.[63] The world-weary resignation implicit in this view came
close to accepting the fallacy promulgated sedulously by the NRA:
that the aim of the Administration's policy was the outright prohibition, rather than the regulation, of firearms held for legitimate
purposes.[64] Unschematic and unpredictable as had been the passage by Congress of the individual regulatory provisions, each of
them so patently justified on their merits, there had been a consistency of purpose from the outset: to restrict the ease of access to

---

[62] In 1993, 98 per cent of all felony cases filed occurred in state courts. *1993
Judicial Business of the United States Courts*, Administrative Office of the US
Courts, and *Examining the Work of State Courts, 1993*: Conference of State Court
Administrators, the State Justice Institute, the Bureau of Justice Statistics, and the
National Center for State Courts.

[63] Posner, 'The most punitive nation', *op. cit.*, p. 3.

[64] Thus Wayne LaPierre, chief executive officer of the National Rifle Association:
'Despite the rise of big government, Americans recoil at the thought of a police state.
Any plan to ban firearms, including the police-state tactics necessary to enforce it,
would be rejected out of hand by the American people.' *Guns, Crime, and Freedom*,
op. cit., p. 176.

deadly weapons. The degree of restriction was related to ascertainable risk factors such as the intrinsic dangerousness of certain firearms, e.g. assault weapons, and the age, state of mind, or previous misconduct of would-be purchasers of handguns.

For his handling of the issue credit must go to President Clinton.[65] He marked out his position on gun control at the start and saw it through to the end. It was a classic instance of a President positioning himself one step ahead of the general public, articulating and acting in accordance with their latent wishes in defiance of the demands of a louder, more politically active minority. On 11 August 1993, when first announcing the anti-crime initiative, Clinton had spoken of ending the insanity of it being easier to buy or sell a handgun than to obtain a driver's licence. On the same day he signed two Presidential directives aimed at reducing gun violence. He had stated explicitly that the effort would not be complete if assault weapons were not eliminated from the streets: 'No other nation would tolerate roving gangs stalking the streets better armed than the police officers of a country. Why do we do it? We shouldn't, and we ought to stop it.'[66] Twelve months later, in one of the most fiercely controversial of all policy areas, and with the equivocal consent of Congress, those legislative objectives had been achieved.

[65] In the short term at least it seemed as though this verdict was shared by the public. During the final stages of the crime bill, when Clinton had refused to compromise on the assault weapons ban, a *USA Today* poll indicated that confidence in the President's handling of crime jumped from 29 to 42 per cent. *CQ Weekly Report*, 20 Aug. 1994, p. 2450.

[66] *Weekly Compilation of Presidential Documents*, 30: 32, 16 Aug. 1993, p. 1603.

Appendix C *Violent Crime Control and Law Enforcement Act of 1994 Title XI—Firearms Provisions*

Subtitle A: Assault Weapons
This provision bans the possession, transfer, and manufacture (with some exceptions) of many semi-automatic assault weapons and ammunition-feeding devices holding more than ten rounds. It amends 18 USC § 924(c) increasing the mandatory minimum sentence to ten years' imprisonment for using such an assault weapon. The entire set of provisions will be auto-matically repealed (unless renewed) ten years after the effective date.

Subtitle B: Youth Handgun Safety
This provision renders as federal crimes (i) the possession of a handgun by a minor, and (ii) the transfer of a handgun to a minor. The penalty imposed for first-time juvenile violators is probation. The subtitle includes a set of wide-ranging exceptions to the prohibition, e.g. possession in the course of employment or instruction, or when defending against a burglar. It also permits proceeding against a juvenile violator under the delinquency laws.

Subtitle C: Licensure
Provisions under this subtitle tighten restrictions on the issuance and over-sight of federal firearm-dealers' licences. Also included are provisions that require dealers to respond within one day to a request for information con-cerning the disposition of any firearms, and that require a report within two days of any lost or stolen firearms.

Subtitle D: Domestic Violence
Two new offences are created. One provision makes it a felony to dispose of a firearm to any person knowing that the person is subject to a court order that restrains the person from harassing, stalking, or threatening an intimate partner of such person or such a partner's child, or engaging in conduct that would place the intimate partner in reasonable fear of bodily injury to the partner or his or her child. The court order must, however, have been issued after a hearing at which the prohibited person received actual notice, and must include a finding that the prohibited person

represents a credible threat to the safety of the intimate partner or child. The second provision prohibits individuals subject to restraining orders from possessing firearms.

The subtitle provides that any firearms seized from an individual who is the subject of a restraining order under either of the new provisions must be securely stored and returned to the offender upon the lapse or termination of the restraining order.

Subtitle E: Gun-Crime Penalties

The subtitle provides enhanced penalties for gun crimes and makes relatively minor improvements to the firearms statutes.

PART IV

Curbing Discretion

9

Life Sentences: The Defects of Duality

I

The preceding Chapters have shown the closer degree of control exercised over law-making by the executive branch of government in England than in the United States. As a generalization, it is true to say that ministers dominate the formulation of policy before legislation is introduced. Once proposals are before Parliament, backed by a highly effective system of party discipline, ministers determine its detailed content. When enacted, ministers, or more often officials acting on their behalf, are usually responsible for implementation. In America, by contrast, Congress plays a pivotal role. The President and his Administration may introduce legislative proposals and urge his party's supporters in Congress to support them. However, the weakness of party discipline and loyalties, and the strength of special interests combine to make it uncertain whether the proposals will be enacted and, if so, in what form. As we have seen, the eventual scope of the Violent Crime Control and Law Enforcement Act of 1994 (Pub. L. 103–322) was markedly different from what it had been on introduction.

In America greater protection exists for the individual from the provisions of legislative enactments, whether state or federal, since laws must conform to the requirements of the Constitution. The arbiter is the federal judiciary, and on major issues this means the Supreme Court of the United States. Infringements may be struck down or remedies provided. In the penal context, the Eighth Amendment prohibition on the infliction of cruel and unusual punishments is discussed above. The unsuccessful challenges under the Second Amendment to restrictions on the availability and possession of firearms were also noted in Chapter 6. Over the last three decades, however, the most important constitutional development in the administration of justice has been the heightened emphasis on equal protection and due process. These ideals were embedded in the second sentence of Article XIV amending the Constitution, one of the Civil War amendments dating from 1868. It reads: 'No State shall make or enforce any law which shall abridge the privileges or immunities of citizens of the United States; nor shall any State deprive any person of life, liberty, or property, without due process of law; nor deny to any person within its jurisdiction the equal protection of the laws.'[1]

Uplifting as it is, the wording of the Fourteenth Amendment has been characterized by leading constitutional scholars as a 'slippery, open-ended, protean' concept[2] which recognizes a number of broad protections that the Supreme Court has never succeeded in defining in any limited way. Nevertheless, in the opinion of Laurence Tribe its provisions have on various occasions been construed to affect many of the most important aspects of the nation's economic, political, and social life.[3] Although little used for three-quarters of a century after the Civil War, the Fourteenth Amendment became the vehicle for a revolution in procedural rights in the 1960s. The civil rights movement with its demand for equal treatment for black Americans was the major force for change, and the Supreme Court, under the leadership of Chief Justice Earl Warren,[4] the agent for change. The force was so great that it soon encompassed not only questions of racial equality but

---

[1] See S. E. Finer, V. Bogdanor, and B. Rudden, *Comparing Constitutions*, Clarendon Press, Oxford, 1995, p. 120. The reference to 'due process of law' repeated a phrase of the Fifth Amendment, one of the first ten amendments ratified in 1791: 'No person shall . . . be deprived of life, liberty, or property, without due process of law . . .' *Comparing Constitutions* is a recent and accessible handbook containing the texts of the US Constitution and all of its subsequent additions and amendments, as well as the current versions of the constitutions of France, the Federal Republic of Germany, and the Russian Federation. V. B. Bogdanor contributes an authoritative essay on the 'indeterminate, indistinct, and entrenched' constitution of the United Kingdom. He is Reader in Government at the University of Oxford, where Bernard Rudden is Professor of Comparative Law. Professor Finer, author of the original work, *Five Constitutions* (1979), died in 1993.

[2] L. Friedman, *Crime and Punishment in American History*, Basic Books, NY, 1993, p. 298.

[3] L. Tribe, *American Constitutional Law*, 2nd edn., Foundation Press, NY, 1988, p. 340. Laurence Tribe is Ralph S. Tyler Professor of Constitutional Law at Harvard University and has argued a number of cases in the Supreme Court.

[4] Attorney General 1939–42; Governor of California 1942–53; appointed Chief Justice of the Supreme Court of the United States in 1953. He served in that capacity until retirement in 1969. For an assessment of the influence of the developing constitutional doctrines during this period see A. Cox, *The Warren Court*, Harvard University Press, Cambridge, Mass., 1968.

a doctrine of due process arising out of a libertarian interpretation of the protection given to individual rights by the Constitution.

A thoroughgoing examination of the day-to-day administration of justice, carried out in the late 1950s by the American Bar Foundation with financial assistance from the Ford Foundation, revealed that each of the critical decision-points: the detection of the crime, arrest, prosecution, adjudication, and sentencing, involved a wide exercise of discretion.[5] The sequence of discretionary decision-taking, in the words of one informed commentator, was 'both hidden from the public and largely ungovernable by any standards or guidelines'.[6] It was the spirit of the age to scrutinize critically the repercussions on the quality of justice of decisions which might be arbitrary, capricious, or inconsistent. Seeing the opportunity to interpret the Fourteenth Amendment as a sword as well as a shield,[7] the Supreme Court did not hesitate to subject to judicial control many hitherto entirely discretionary decisions in the criminal process which had an impact on the rights, and by now the expectations, of the individual citizen. Most far-reaching of all, the new constitutional imperatives were applied to the customary practices of state and local criminal justice agencies, as well as to the agencies of federal government.

In England the doctrine of parliamentary sovereignty means that the intentions of Parliament as expressed in statute law cannot be set aside by the courts. However, this immunity does not extend to the actions of ministers or officials, either under powers conferred specifically by legislation or in the exercise of extra-statutory discretion. Although different in origin, the principle of judicial review of executive acts of government has effected a similar redistribution of governmental power in recent years. As a result of what in America would be regarded as a display of judicial activism, the higher courts have shown readiness to impose curbs on executive discretion. Three aspects of public policy in the 1990s illustrate a subtle sea-change in the relationships between the legislature, executive, and judiciary. The proposition is that in the administration of criminal justice, with particular regard to the lawfulness of

---

[5] D. M. McIntyre (ed.), *Law Enforcement in the Metropolis*, American Bar Foundation, Chicago, 1967, pp. vii–xi.

[6] S. Walker, *Popular Justice*, Oxford University Press, New York, 1980, pp. 218–19.

[7] Tribe, *American Constitutional Law, op. cit.*, p. 6.

its procedures, the English courts are moving in the same direction as that taken by the American judiciary. In two of the examples explored in the final Chapters of this volume, life sentences of imprisonment and criminal injuries compensation, the thrust of public policy has been altered by the need to avoid decisions or practices which have been or may be found by the courts to be tainted by illegality, irrationality, or procedural impropriety.[8] In the third, criminal appeals, it was the force of opinion following some notorious miscarriages of justice that brought about the removal of the Home Secretary's discretionary power, sparingly used, to refer cases to the Court of Appeal.

II

Let us begin with a summary of the legislation of 1990–1 which was described in detail in Volume 2 of *Responses to Crime*. When first introduced in the House of Commons the Criminal Justice Act of 1991 did not alter the situation of life-sentence prisoners. Despite a mounting chorus of parliamentary and judicial criticism of the way in which tariffs[9] were set and adjusted by ministers in private, and of the procedures for reviewing the cases of lifers on expiry of their tariffs, the original Bill went no further than reiterating the Home Secretary's power to release a life prisoner on licence, subject to the two existing fetters on his discretion. These were: an obligation to consult the Lord Chief Justice and the trial judge, if still available, and a favourable recommendation by the Parole Board. Without such a recommendation, the Secretary of State was not able to release a life prisoner. The power to initiate the process leading to release was retained by the Home Office since it is the Secretary of State who sets the date for the first review.[10]

[8] Lord Diplock's formal statement of the grounds for judicial review in *Council of Civil Service Unions* v. *Minister for the Civil Service* [1985] AC 374 at 408 is reproduced as Appendix 1 to Sir W. Wade and C. Forsyth, *Administrative Law*, 7th edn., Clarendon Press, Oxford, 1994, pp. 1012–14.

[9] The term 'tariff' is used to describe that portion of the life sentence, fixed after consultation with the judiciary, which must be served in custody in all save the most exceptional circumstances before release on licence can be considered. The tariff element is intended to reflect the requirements of retribution and deterrence, as distinct from any consideration of risk to the public.

[10] The decision on when to refer a case to the Parole Board for review was in effect reserved to the Secretary of State by Section 59 of the Criminal Justice Act

At this early stage in the narrative it is worth making the point that the term 'Secretary of State', which runs so easily off the tongue and sounds so impressive, may include junior Home Office ministers and officials acting on the Home Secretary's behalf. The Bill made no distinction between *mandatory* life prisoners, sentenced for murder as prescribed by Section 1 of the Murder (Abolition of Death Penalty) Act 1965, and *discretionary* life prisoners sentenced on conviction for other serious offences carrying a maximum penalty of life imprisonment. In practice, however, separate procedures had applied to the handling of discretionary life cases since 1987 as a result of the *Handscomb* judgment in the Queen's Bench Divisional Court.[11]

The paucity of provision for life prisoners contrasted with the introduction of sweeping changes in the arrangements for paroling prisoners serving determinate sentences of imprisonment. A greater degree of independence was conferred on the Parole Board, although falling short of the recommendations of a Review Committee under the chairmanship of Lord Carlisle of Bucklow which had subjected to detailed scrutiny the system of parole in England and Wales.[12] Their report was the first root and branch review since the inception of parole twenty years earlier. The terms of reference had enjoined the Committee to look beyond the operational defects which had resulted from piecemeal policy decisions to the wider question of the relationship between the sentences of imprisonment passed by the courts and the amount of time spent in custody by convicted and sentenced offenders. Legislative

1967. The increased reliance since 1983 on fixed, and originally undisclosed, tariffs for life-sentence prisoners has made this a most important administrative decision in the release procedures.

[11] *R. v. Secretary of State for the Home Department, ex parte Handscomb and others* (1988) 86 Cr. App. R. 59. In this case, brought by way of an application for judicial review, Watkins LJ considered the review procedures where a life sentence had been awarded at the discretion of the sentencing judge. He held that initial consultation with the judiciary on the period necessary to meet the requirements of retribution and deterrence should take place as soon as practicable after the imposition of the sentence, and should not be delayed for three or four years. The Secretary of State should not substitute his own views as to the requirements of retribution and deterrence for those expressed by the judiciary, which should take into account the notional equivalent determinate sentence less one-third remission. For a discussion of the implications of this judgment see *Responses to Crime*, Vol. 2, pp. 319–20, 322, 330.

[12] The Parole System in England and Wales, *Report of the Review Committee*, (Cm. 532), HMSO, London, 1988, pp. 75–7.

proposals based on Carlisle had been generally acceptable to informed penal opinion and, although modified in certain respects by the Government, neither House of Parliament saw any reason to dissent from the main outlines of the scheme. The result was a fundamental reform of the principles and practice regulating the early release of prisoners and young offenders serving determinate sentences of imprisonment,[13] but one that did not bear on life sentences.

The division of mandatory and discretionary life sentences of imprisonment into distinct categories, the primary cause of so many of the difficulties that have arisen subsequently, goes back only to 1983. Until then the cases of all life prisoners were considered by a Joint Parole Board and Home Office Committee which set the date for their first full review. The features of that procedure, and the reasons for abandoning it following a statement by Leon Brittan[14] as Home Secretary in October 1983, were recounted in Volume 2 of *Responses to Crime*.[15] Next came the *Handscomb* judgment and the policy changes made in consequence by the Home Secretary, Douglas Hurd, in July 1987. Since then continued pressure from Parliament, the domestic courts, and the European Court of Human Rights at Strasbourg has forced a series of further changes, calling to mind sailors desperately plugging leaks in a sinking ship.

The Government's intention to exclude life sentences from the Criminal Justice legislation of 1990–1 did not survive the Bill's passage through Parliament. Insistent political demands, especially evident in the House of Lords which had set up a Select Committee on Murder and Life Imprisonment in 1988, coincided with the need to comply with a judgment of the European Court of Human Rights in the case of *Thynne, Wilson and Gunnell* v. *United Kingdom*.[16] Applications by three British prisoners, each serving discretionary life sentences for serious offences of rape or buggery, had been before the Commission and Court of Human Rights since

[13] For a discussion of the reshaped arrangements for early release in Part II of the Criminal Justice Act 1991 see Martin Wasik [1992] Crim. L.R. 252.

[14] Sir Leon Brittan QC has been a Vice-President of the European Commission since 1989. He was Chief Secretary to HM Treasury 1981–3, Home Secretary 1983–5, and Secretary of State for Trade and Industry 1985–6.

[15] Chapter 7 of *Responses to Crime*, Vol. 2, is entitled 'Life Imprisonment: A Sentence Nobody Can Understand?', pp. 308–46. The author was chairman of the Joint Committee when it was disbanded.

[16] (1991) 13 EHRR 666. The facts of this case and a discussion of the implications of the Court's findings are included in *Responses to Crime*, Vol. 2, pp. 347–55.

1985. The basis of their claim was that Article 5(4) of the European Convention on Human Rights had been violated in that no judicial procedure had been available to determine the continued lawfulness of their detention after the expiry of their tariff periods, nor, in two of the cases, the lawfulness of their re-detention following release and recall to custody. Although the legitimacy of their original imprisonment, following trial and sentence by a competent court, was not at issue, their continued detention in the post-tariff period was open to challenge. It was a stick of the Home Office's own making, resulting from the distinction, ever more sharply drawn, between the penal element of a discretionary life sentence standing for retribution and deterrence (the 'tariff') and the preventive aim of protecting the public from risk of further offences of comparable seriousness being committed.

In ruling that the applicants were entitled to a periodic review of the legality of their continuing detention by a court, or by a tribunal with court-like characteristics, the Court said there was no evidence that the applicants would have regained their freedom had Article 5(4) not been violated. It is a familiar outcome of cases brought by prisoners that while administrative procedures found to be incompatible with the Convention have to be changed, the applicants themselves are not released from custody.

A series of all-party amendments to the Criminal Justice Bill in the House of Lords stemmed from the recommendations of the Select Committee which had reported two years earlier.[17] They provided (1) that in future no court should be required to sentence a person convicted of murder to imprisonment for life, and (2) that judicial procedures should govern both the setting of the length of the penal term contained within an indeterminate sentence of life imprisonment and the decisions on release or continued detention of life prisoners on expiry of the penal term. As a result, mandatory and discretionary sentences would be reunited and the need for separate procedural regimes eradicated. The proposed unified procedure corresponded closely with the essentials of due process. The trial judge would be required to give reasons in open court, both for imposing a life sentence in preference to a determinate sentence and for the length of a penal term to reflect retribution and deterrence. Such a term would not be open to revision by ministers, but would

---

[17] House of Lords, *Report of the Select Committee on Murder and Life Imprisonment*, (HL 78–I), HMSO, London, 1989, pp. 50–1.

be subject to appeal by either side. Release decisions at the expiry of the penal term would no longer be taken by ministers on undisclosed grounds and in private, but by a tribunal constituted as a court-like body in conformity with the case-law of the European Court of Human Rights. Procedural rules would enable a prisoner to appear before the tribunal; to make representations in person or to be legally represented; to know what was said about him; and to challenge reports and other information before the tribunal, the contents of which would be disclosed to him.

The legislative history of this provision: its passage through the Lords by substantial majorities; its overwhelming support by the higher judiciary and much informed opinion; and its rejection by the Government and their supporters in the Commons, apprehensive that any departure from the mandatory sentence for murder would be seen as a weakening of resolution to combat violent crime was related in the previous volume.[18] The eventual outcome, as so often, was a partial compromise. To go some way to meet the parliamentary pressures, and being aware that before long changes would have to be made to bring into line the handling of discretionary life sentence cases with the judgment in *Thynne*, the Government decided to introduce new procedures to provide for regular reviews, by a court-like body, of the need for continued detention of prisoners serving discretionary life sentences after the expiry of their tariffs.

The consequential legislation, incorporated in Section 34 of the Criminal Justice Act 1991, did not extend to mandatory life prisoners, who had not been applicants before the Court of Human Rights, on the ground that the lawfulness of their detention for life had been determined once and for all at the moment of sentence following conviction by a properly constituted court. Any subsequent release was regarded as a matter of mercy and privilege, not of right. In the eyes of ministers, an offender serving a mandatory life sentence had committed a crime of such gravity that he had forfeited his liberty for life without the necessity for judicial intervention. The presumption was that such an offender should remain in custody unless and until the Home Secretary concluded that the public interest would be better served by the prisoner's release than by his continued detention. In reaching his decision he would take

---

[18] *Responses to Crime*, Vol. 2, ch. 9, pp. 430–50.

account not just of the risk of further offending but 'how society as a whole viewed the prisoner's release at that juncture'.[19]

The practical result of the 1991 Act was to ameliorate the situation of one category of life sentence prisoner at the cost of hardening it for the other, larger category. The divide was deeper than before with newly formulated justifications being put on record to defeat arguments based on parallels between the two categories of life prisoner. So stiff and unyielding a stance left insufficient mobility even for a genuflection towards the idea of extending the principles of due process to mandatory lifers. The reluctant relaxation of discretionary power in one direction was accompanied by its bold reassertion in another.

III

Although the sentencing provisions of the 1991 Act came into effect on 1 October 1992, the changes inaugurated by the legislation in the arrangements for the early release of determinate sentence, discretionary life sentence, and mandatory life sentence prisoners were so extensive, and affected such large numbers of prisoners, that they were introduced in stages. It was not until two years later, in October 1994, that the Parole Board was able to report that all stages had been completed and that the new systems were in operation.[20]

For life sentence prisoners a dual system was created for the review of their cases and for reaching decisions on release or continued detention. Rather than setting up quasi-judicial tribunals modelled on the Mental Health Review Tribunals, or entirely judicial tribunals as recommended by the Lords Select Committee,[21] the Government decided that special panels of the Parole Board, chaired by a judge, should be adapted for the purpose of reviewing the cases of discretionary life sentence prisoners after the expiry of the term set by the trial judge. Each case is reviewed by a three-member panel of the Parole Board at an oral hearing held at the

---

[19] *Parl. Debates*, HC, 195 (6th ser.), cols. 309–10, 16 July 1991, *per* Angela Rumbold, then Minister of State at the Home Office.

[20] *Report of the Parole Board for 1994* (HC 531), HMSO, London, 1995, p. 1.

[21] *Report of the Select Committee on Murder and Life Imprisonment*, (HL 78–I), *op. cit.*, p. 48.

prison where the prisoner is serving his sentence. The chairman is invariably a judicial member of the Board. One of the other members will be an experienced psychiatrist.[22] Decisions are reached by a majority. The date for the hearing is fixed in conformity with the tariff. The prisoner is entitled to attend in person, to legal representation at the public expense, to see his dossier in advance, to speak for himself, and to call witnesses. Procedural rules, made by the Secretary of State in exercise of the powers conferred on him by Section 32(5) of the Criminal Justice Act 1991, regulate the conduct of the proceedings. Since 1994 hearings have been recorded, an innovation introduced after the Divisional Court had criticized the absence of a sufficient note of the proceedings.[23]

Within seven days of the end of the hearing the Parole Board gives a direction to release or not to release the prisoner serving a discretionary life sentence, together with written reasons. The decision must be complied with by the Home Secretary and his officials. If the direction is to release, they have a statutory duty to release the prisoner on licence. The decision is reached solely on the basis of the panel's view as to whether or not it is necessary for the protection of the public that the prisoner continue to be confined.[24] Recommendations other than to release may be, and often are, made on such matters as transfer to a prison of another category, the provision of psychiatric or other forms of treatment, a further review before the expiry of the statutory two-year period, or the

[22] According to Dr John Gunn, Professor of Forensic Psychiatry at the Institute of Psychiatry, it is an inescapable necessity in everyday psychiatry to make judgments about the dangers and risks which patients pose to themselves and to others. He makes the important point, often overlooked, that dangerousness is a subjective concept which is attributed to individuals partly on the basis of risks that can be calculated, but also on the basis of public fear resulting from their previous violent behaviour or criminal offending. The attribution of dangerousness is not necessarily a reliable guide to the statistical risk that an individual poses. Above all, it is not a medical diagnosis. Nevertheless, when inmates are being considered for discharge or release from hospitals or prisons there is a public demand for predictions as to dangerousness to which psychiatrists must respond. The feelings of victims, as well as relatives and neighbours, and the availability of supervision and support in the community are legitimate factors in the assessment of risk. J. Gunn & P. J. Taylor (eds.), *Forensic Psychiatry: Clinical, Legal and Ethical Issues*, Butterworth-Heinemann, Oxford, 1993, pp. 624–40.

[23] *Report of the Parole Board for 1994, op. cit.*, p. 4.

[24] In *R. v. Parole Board, ex parte Telling* the Divisional Court held that in reaching its decision the Parole Board must consider all the evidence, and should not be expected to rely exclusively on the evidence of psychiatrists in evaluating the risk to the public. *The Times* Law Report, 10 May, 1993.

inclusion of special conditions in the licence. Such recommendations are not binding on the Home Secretary but will carry weight.
Reasons are given to the prisoner for any recommendations made
as well as for the decision on release. If the Board does not order
the release of the prisoner on licence he is entitled to a further
review on the second anniversary of the preceding review.

Release was only directed in a minority of the cases heard by
Discretionary Lifer Panels of the Board (DLPs) in the final quarter
of 1992 and the calendar years 1993 and 1994. Out of a total of
forty-four cases considered in 1992, seven resulted in a direction of
release (16 per cent). In 1993 release was directed in fifty-four cases
out of 265 (20 per cent), and in 1994 in thirty-three cases out of a
total of 121 (27 per cent).[25] The largest group released in 1994 was
of offenders convicted of manslaughter. Others had been sentenced
to life imprisonment for sex offences, arson, or serious offences of
violence. The majority of those released were returned to the community from open prisons or pre-release hostels. All were released
on licence and liable to recall if the conditions of their licence were
breached. The terms of imprisonment served varied from five to
twenty-four years. The average term was fifteen years.[26] The unspoken fear of ministers that the floodgates would be opened if their
control was relaxed proved illusory.

The fact that such a sizeable group of prisoners released under
the new procedure had been convicted of one form of homicide
shows the narrowness of the dividing line separating their treatment
from offenders found guilty of another form of homicide. The law
on murder, and its application to the boundless variety of human
conduct resulting in a victim's violent and unnatural death, are
widely misunderstood. There are misconceptions about the true
nature of the offence and its relationship to other types of homicide. Convictions of manslaughter under Section 2 of the Homicide
Act 1957, which allows a plea of not guilty of murder by reason of
diminished responsibility but guilty of manslaughter, are a particularly common source of confusion. Contrary to the public assumption, not all crimes of murder are of such unique heinousness that

[25] *Report of the Parole Board for 1994*, Table 13, p. 34. The statistics for 1992
included the case of one prisoner subject to deportation where release was recommended but not directed. The fall in the case-load between 1993 and 1994 was the
result of having cleared a large group of prisoners who had immediate entitlement
to a DLP hearing when the new procedures were introduced in Oct. 1992.

[26] Ibid., p. 13.

the offender deserves to forfeit his liberty for the rest of his existence.[27] Some intentional killings, often those that receive the most
publicity, are truly heinous and deserving of the most severe punishment the courts have the power to impose. However, the common law definition of murder[28] embraces a wide range of unlawful
acts which fall short of the public image of murder.[29]

A soldier on patrol in West Belfast who opens fire at a stolen car,
believing a fellow soldier's life to be in danger, and kills a passen-
ger; a doctor who from humanitarian motives injects a terminally
ill patient in agony with a lethal dosage; and a battered wife who
kills her allegedly drunken and violent husband: each of these
offences has resulted in a conviction for murder or attempted murder. In the case of Dr Nigel Cox, a hospital consultant found guilty
of the attempted murder of an elderly patient in 1992, the conviction did not automatically attract a mandatory sentence. Owing to
the mitigating circumstances, the trial judge imposed no more than
a twelve-month suspended sentence. The other two defendants,
Private Lee Clegg and Sara Thornton, were less fortunate. Because
their actions fulfilled the elements of the crime of murder, the
defences of provocation and self-defence notwithstanding, each of
them received a mandatory sentence as the law required. Calls to
redefine these defences followed, but it was the inflexibility of the
mandatory penalty of life imprisonment which prevented the trial
judge in these cases, having heard the evidence and seen the witnesses and the accused in court, from exercising his sentencing discretion up to the maximum penalty permitted by statute.

---

[27] For a classic statement of the fallacy of the assumption that murder is a
uniquely heinous crime and the intrinsic injustice of the mandatory penalty, see
Committee on the Penalty for Homicide, *Report*, Prison Reform Trust, London,
1993, pp. 5, 21–3.

[28] In England and Wales it is murder to kill by an act intended either to kill or
to cause serious bodily harm. The courts have not defined intention, but if the jury
is satisfied that the defendant recognized that death or serious harm would be virtually certain to result from his voluntary act, then that is a fact from which intention to kill or to do serious bodily harm may be inferred, even though the defendant
may not have desired to achieve that result. *Nedrick* (1986) 83 Cr. App. R. 267, per
Lord Lane CJ. Murder is defined differently in Scotland.

[29] One of the most common misconceptions is that a person can be convicted of
murder only if he intends to kill. In practice a minority of defendants convicted of
murder have that intent. It is sufficient for the prosecution to prove an intention to
cause serious harm. If the death of the victim ensues, however unexpected, however
unintended, the offence is made out and the mandatory life sentence must follow.

It was not the end of the road either for Lee Clegg or Sara Thornton. Public concern and populist agitation has an effect on ministers, particularly when it is led by vociferous and propagandizing press coverage. The tabloids, as well as the conservative-oriented mid-market press, *The Daily Mail* and *The Daily Telegraph*, did not take up the campaign to free Private Clegg of the Parachute Regiment until more than three years after the shooting, at a time when an appeal to the House of Lords from the Court of Appeal in Northern Ireland was being planned.[30] Dismissing the appeal, in a speech with which the other Law Lords agreed, Lord Lloyd of Berwick said that under the present law, and on the facts as found by the trial judge, the soldier was guilty of murder and not manslaughter. He added that the point at issue was whether the mandatory life sentence for murder should be retained. That issue could only be decided by Parliament.[31]

Immediately after the dismissal of his appeal to the House of Lords an internal review of Clegg's case was put in hand by the Northern Ireland Office. The purpose of the review was to determine when his eligibility for release on licence should be considered by the Life Sentence Review Board,[32] there being no Parole Board in Northern Ireland. The power to release a Northern Ireland prisoner on licence rests with the Secretary of State, who is advised on such matters by a Life Sentence Review Board to which the case was referred for consideration with the minimum of delay. The Review Board's advice is confidential and is not disclosed.[33] The

[30] See Roy Greenslade, 'How the press freed Lee Clegg', *The Times*, 5 July 1995.

[31] *R. v. Clegg* [1995] 1 AC 482 at 500. The case is reported in [1995] Crim. L.R. 418 with a critical comment by Sir John Smith at 419–20.

[32] The Board is a non-statutory body established in 1983. It is chaired by the Permanent Under-Secretary of State at the Northern Ireland Office and includes in its membership other officials from the Northern Ireland Office, a prison medical officer, a consultant psychiatrist, and the Chief Probation Officer.

[33] The author wishes to acknowledge the assistance of Sir John Wheeler, Minister of State for Northern Ireland, in supplying detailed information on the legislation governing life sentence prisoners in Northern Ireland and the operation of the procedures for taking decisions on their release. Unlike in England and Wales, there is no fixed tariff set in the case of a mandatory life sentence for murder. The sentence is viewed in a holistic way with a number of factors influencing the period of imprisonment that any individual will serve. These factors include retribution, deterrence, risk, and public interest; all are considered relevant to various degrees throughout sentence. The same decision-taking procedures apply to mandatory and discretionary life sentences. (Letter of 16 Oct. 1995). The system is similar to the practice in England and Wales before the changes made in 1983, and has avoided many of the problems that have arisen since then.

pressure of public opinion was maintained at a high level, the campaign organizers claiming to have received two million letters of support. In reply to a Parliamentary Question, the Secretary of State for Northern Ireland, Sir Patrick Mayhew, informed the House of Commons that he had received over 4,000 letters and a number of petitions.[34] Once he had obtained the advice of the Review Board, and consulted the trial judge and Lord Chief Justice of Northern Ireland, Mayhew was able to reach a decision taking account of all the circumstances of the case. He had no hesitation. A licence was signed, and Clegg was released from Wakefield Prison on 3 July 1995.

Then came the Home Secretary's decision to refer Sara Thornton's case to the Court of Appeal, and her release on bail pending the hearing. This too owed much to vigorous campaigning, reinforced by press publicity. Earlier the same month, on 7 July 1995, the Criminal Division of the Court of Appeal had substituted a verdict of manslaughter for that of murder in the case of Emma Humphreys. At the age of seventeen she had been convicted of murder and sentenced to detention during Her Majesty's pleasure for killing a male partner who had subjected her to months of abuse, both mental and physical, beating her up on several occasions. Hirst LJ held that the trial judge had failed properly to direct the jury on the cumulative effect on the defendant of continuing cruelty and encouragement of prostitution, and the breakdown of the sexual relationship.[35] The judge had not given guidance on the stormy history behind the killing to enable the jury to decide whether the defendant had suffered the sort of provocation which would have caused a reasonable person to do as she did. Both cases had been supported by Justice for Women, a small but effective pressure group founded in 1991, which argued that the Home Secretary should review the cases of fifty women serving mandatory life sentences for killing their male partners after being subjected to violent abuse. Their contention was that a history of domestic violence, and its cumulative effects, had not been fully considered by the courts in these cases.[36]

When Sara Thornton's case was heard later in the year the Court of Appeal, Criminal Division, quashed her conviction for murder.

[34] *Parl. Debates*, HC, 258 (6th ser.) col. WA 698, 27 Apr. 1995.
[35] *R.* v. *Humphreys*, CA, unreported transcript, 7 July 1995.
[36] *The Times*, 29 July 1995.

Giving the reserved judgment of the Court on 13 December, Lord Taylor CJ said there was evidence that medical knowledge had progressed considerably since the hearing of her appeal in 1990. Further medical evidence raised the question of whether the battered woman syndrome might have affected her personality so as to constitute a significant characteristic that would be relevant for the jury to consider in regard to the defence of provocation. Since a judge should give directions to the jury on any factor which, on the evidence, was capable of amounting to a relevant characteristic, and since neither the characteristic of the appellant's personality disorder nor the element of the battered woman syndrome had been considered by the jury, doubt was cast on the verdict. As the Court of Appeal could not be sure that the verdict was safe and satisfactory[37] a retrial was ordered.[38] It was not what the appellant or the campaigners had hoped for, which was a reduction of her murder conviction to one of manslaughter on grounds of provocation. However, as we shall see in the next Chapter, the decision avoided the Appeal Court substituting itself for the jury as the judge of fact.

For every *cause célèbre* we can be sure there are other cases, unacknowledged and unpublicized, where the mandatory punishment of life imprisonment appears disproportionate to the nature and circumstances of the offence and the culpability of the offender. The outcomes cited above, each of which was greeted with criticism as well as approval, show the futility of trying to patch and mend a faulty structure that is beyond repair. In the case of *Clegg* it is hard to avoid the conclusion that the regular procedures were accelerated to produce a politically desirable result,[39] albeit one that would be unwelcome to a strand of sectarian opinion in Northern Ireland. The upsurge of interest in changing the law on murder, and the defences to murder, in response to these cases exemplified an attempt to rectify a recognized problem by

[37] Under Section 2(1) of the Criminal Appeal Act 1968 the test in deciding whether a conviction should be quashed or upheld is whether in all the circumstances of the case the conviction was unsafe or unsatisfactory.

[38] *The Times* Law Report, 14 Dec. 1995. In May 1996 a jury substituted a verdict of manslaughter for the original murder conviction.

[39] The Northern Ireland Office points out that *Clegg's* case was one of a total of forty-three cases since 1983 which, because of mitigating factors, had been referred to the Life Sentence Review Board earlier than at the normal ten-year stage. The earliest referral of a terrorist life sentence case was shortly before the five-year stage. Letter from Sir J. Wheeler, *op. cit.*, 16 Oct. 1995.

approaching it from the wrong end. The solution to the problem of unlawful killing illustrated in three of its many manifestations: the mercy killing by a humane doctor; the action of a soldier on duty in a dangerous situation;[40] the reaction of a battered wife which fails to meet the test of provocation, can be found in the concise wording of the Lords' amendment: that no court should be required to sentence a person convicted of murder to imprisonment for life.

IV

The objection to mandatory penalties, whether for murder or the wider range of offences to which mandatory minimums apply in the United States, is that to subject each individual offender to the same punishment, irrespective of the circumstances of the crime and the culpability of the defendant, will lead inevitably to inequity. Inequities are not confined to the length of time spent in custody, but extend also to procedural aspects. For mandatory life sentences the inequities are most clearly apparent at two points: the taking of decisions on release and, at an earlier stage, the setting of the tariff. Both have been subjected to critical scrutiny by the courts.

In the review process, as with the cases of discretionary life-sentence prisoners, the Parole Board is the functional mechanism. The procedure differs in a number of significant respects, the most important of which is that the Board only makes a recommendation, the final decision being taken by the Home Secretary. The first stage of the review is the preparation of detailed reports on the prisoner by the staff at the prison where he is held. Since the abolition in October 1994 of the Local Review Committees (LRCs) which met at each prison, the prisoner is interviewed by a member

[40] In a review of the Northern Ireland (Emergency Provisions) Act 1991, presented to Parliament by the Secretary of State for Northern Ireland in Feb. 1995 (Cm. 2706), a Queen's Counsel independent of Government, J. J. Rowe, advocated the abolition of the mandatory sentence for murder and stated his opinion that judges should have a discretion as to the sentence appropriate for the offence. The Lord Chief Justice of Northern Ireland had given the proposal his support, and the Lord Chief Justice of England had recently urged it. He also recommended providing a defence of excessive force in self-defence, or in the course of duty, which would reduce murder to manslaughter. After considering a report by an inter-departmental committee of civil servants set up in the light of the *Clegg* case, the Government decided against making any changes in the law on murder. *Parl. Debates*, HC, 275 (6th ser.), cols. 624–5, 19 Apr. 1996.

of the Parole Board who visits the prison for the purpose.[41] A report of this interview is submitted to the Board. The prisoner receives a copy and has an opportunity to make representations before his case is considered by a panel of the Board. The Probation Service supplies a home circumstances report, usually after a visit to the address at which the prisoner intends to live if released. A comprehensive dossier is prepared by the Lifer Section at Prison Department Headquarters and sent on to the Parole Board.

For mandatory life prisoners, a four-member panel of the Board consisting of a judicial member, a Chief (Deputy or Assistant Chief) Probation Officer, a psychiatrist, and an independent member normally reviews each case about three years before expiry of the tariff, and thereafter on dates recommended by the Board or set by the Secretary of State if the Board's recommendation is not accepted. The meeting is held in private, the prisoner is not present or represented, and until 1993 the dossier containing the reports was not disclosed to him. After considering the case on its merits a recommendation is made to the Home Secretary, who may not release a mandatory prisoner unless recommended to do so by the Board, but is not bound to accept the Board's recommendations. Recommendations may include a further review of the case after the transfer of the prisoner to open conditions, usually a prerequisite to release on licence.

Each year the Secretary of State rejects a proportion of the Board's recommendations. In 1991, the last full year before the Criminal Justice Act 1991 came into effect, the Parole Board recommended ninety-nine life sentence prisoners as suitable for release, on dates ranging from the immediate future to two years ahead, subject to good behaviour in the meantime. The Home Secretary accepted eighty recommendations for release and rejected twelve. The statistics do not reveal how many of these were mandatory and how many discretionary. The remaining seven were still

---

[41] By 1 Jan. 1995 the membership of the Parole Board for England and Wales had expanded to sixty-four. The purpose of the interview with the prisoner was twofold: to acquaint him with the parole procedure and to provide the panel who will review the case with clarification and, when necessary, elaboration of the prisoner's attitude towards offending behaviour, preconvictions, behaviour and progress in custody, release plans, risk of reconviction, and any other relevant considerations. *Report of the Parole Board for 1994* (HC 531), HMSO, London, 1995, p. 2.

under consideration at the year end.[42] By 1994, when the dual system was in operation, separate statistics were published which enabled mandatory cases to be distinguished from the discretionary cases decided by the Parole Board. In that year the Board recommended ninety-four mandatory life sentence prisoners for release. The figure represented 18 per cent of the total number of cases considered and compared with eighty-eight such recommendations in 1993 (21 per cent of the total considered). Of the ninety-four recommendations for release, the Home Secretary accepted forty-two and rejected six. The remaining forty-six were still awaiting his decision at the end of 1994. He accepted twenty out of the twenty-one release recommendations which were outstanding at the end of 1993.[43]

Until March 1993 mandatory prisoners were advised of the Home Secretary's decision but not given the reasons for it. The practice had been upheld by the Court of Appeal in *Payne* v. *Lord Harris of Greenwich and Another*[44] and prevailed thereafter. Since 1 April 1993 in accordance with a reply by the Home Secretary, Kenneth Clarke, to a Question for Written Answer in the House of Commons in December 1992[45] the dossier and any other papers before the Board have been disclosed to a mandatory prisoner in advance of the Board's consideration of his case so that he can base his written recommendations on the evidence to be considered by the panel. There is full disclosure, including reasons, of the Board's recommendations and the Home Secretary's decision. An unfavourable recommendation by the Board, or a decision by the Home Secretary not to accept a favourable recommendation, is subject to judicial review if tainted by irrationality or unreasonableness. In his Answer Kenneth Clarke said that he intended to bring the procedures applying to prisoners subject to mandatory sentences 'more closely into line' with those which since 1 October 1992 had applied to discretionary life prisoners.

The change in practice was prompted by some critical remarks in the Queen's Bench Divisional Court in *R.* v. *Parole Board, ex parte Creamer and Scholey*.[46] Referring to the distinction between

---

[42] *Report of the Parole Board for 1991* (HC 43), HMSO, London, 1992, p. 21.
[43] *Report of the Parole Board for 1994, op. cit.*, p. 13.
[44] [1981] 2 All ER 842.
[45] *Parl. Debates*, HC, 216 (6th ser.), cols. WA 218–19, 16 Dec. 1992.
[46] Reported in *The Independent*, 23 Oct. 1992.

mandatory and discretionary sentences, Rose LJ said that once it was accepted that both types of sentence had a tariff and possible risk element; that risk to the public was the sole justification for detention when the tariff period had been served; and that assessment of risk was in each case made by essentially similar procedures, it seemed to him that the requirements of natural justice should be the same in both cases. The Home Office settled the case before it went to the Court of Appeal by conceding the right of mandatory life prisoners to see the reports.

For many years it was Home Office policy to refuse to notify life sentence prisoners of the duration of their tariffs. They were nevertheless able to calculate them without difficulty from the date set for the first review by the Parole Board, normally three years before the expiry of the tariff. Long-term mandatory lifers with tariffs of more than twenty years were neither informed of the length of their tariffs nor were they able to calculate them. Their cases were reviewed automatically at the seventeen-year point and at intervals thereafter. In another case in 1992, *Secretary of State for the Home Department* v. *Walsh*,[47] the Court of Appeal upheld a judgment in the Divisional Court that in order to achieve fairness and equality of treatment between life prisoners the Home Secretary was under an obligation to disclose the tariff period to a discretionary prisoner with a tariff of more than twenty years. Practice was changed accordingly but, until compelled to do so by further declarations of the courts, the Home Office continued to resist extending the same policy to mandatory life prisoners with tariffs over twenty years, even though by then those with tariffs of less than twenty years were notified of their duration.[48]

As the frequency of applications for judicial review by life sentence prisoners was maintained, some of them supported by civil liberties groups,[49] the issues made their way up the judicial ladder

[47] (1993) 5 Admin. LR 138.

[48] On 30 Apr. 1993 Lord Merlyn-Rees (a former Home Secretary), Lord Scarman, and the author wrote jointly to the then Home Secretary, Kenneth Clarke, urging him not to await the outcome of further legal proceedings but to extend to those mandatory lifers who did not know their tariffs the same right as that of discretionary lifers with tariffs of over twenty years and mandatory lifers with tariffs of less than twenty years.

[49] In addition to the cases already cited see *R.* v. *Parole Board, ex parte Bradley* [1991] 1 WLR 134 (test of dangerousness); *R.* v. *Parole Board, ex parte Wilson* [1992] 1 QB 740 (discretionary life-sentence prisoners entitled to see reports in advance of Section 34 procedures coming into effect); and *R.* v. *Secretary of State for the Home*

to the Appellate Committee of the House of Lords. In May 1992 the Court of Appeal had gathered many of the strands together in judgments delivered by Glidewell LJ, Staughton LJ, and Farquharson LJ in *R.* v. *Secretary of State for the Home Department, ex parte Doody, Pierson, Smart and Pegg.*[50] *Handscomb* was reversed, the Court of Appeal holding that the Home Secretary was not required by law to follow the judicial tariff. Provided he had some good reason for doing so, he was entitled to set a tariff period which differed from the judicial recommendation. However, as the Home Secretary had adopted a policy of accepting the judicial view on the tariff for discretionary life prisoners he had probably created a legitimate expectation that the policy would continue to be applied. Since new procedures giving statutory expression to post-*Handscomb* policy were contained in Section 34 of the Criminal Justice Act 1991 due to come into force in October 1992, presumably there would be no departure from it in the meantime. Declarations were granted requiring the Home Secretary to afford to a prisoner serving a mandatory life sentence the opportunity to submit representations in writing before his tariff was set, and to be informed of the judicially recommended period and any other relevant expressions of judicial opinion.

The Home Secretary appealed against the judgment, so giving the House of Lords the first opportunity since *Findlay's* case[51] a decade earlier to review law and practice relating to life sentences and the way in which release decisions are reached. In June 1993 the screw was given another turn, the Appellate Committee adding a third declaration to the two already granted by the Court of Appeal, which were upheld.[52] Describing the decision in *Payne* v. *Lord Harris of Greenwich* as 'obsolete'[53] Lord Mustill, in a speech

Department and Another, ex parte Singh (Prem), The Times, 27 Apr. 1993 (prisoners sentenced as young offenders to be detained during Her Majesty's pleasure under S. 53(1) of the Children and Young Persons Act 1933 are entitled to see their reports).

[50] [1993] QB 157. For a summary of the judgments in the Court of Appeal, and their policy implications, see *Responses to Crime,* Vol. 2, pp. 321–4.

[51] *Re Findlay and others* [1985] 1 AC 318.

[52] *R.* v. *Secretary of State for the Home Department, ex parte Doody, Pegg, Pierson, and Smart* [1994] 1 AC 531.

[53] Lord Mustill dismissed its continued relevance summarily: 'Sound as it may well have been at the time, the reasoning of *Payne* v. *Lord Harris of Greenwich* cannot be sustained today.' [1994] 1 AC at 566.

agreed without amplification or qualification by the other four Law Lords, said that while the giving of reasons by the Secretary of State for setting out the tariff might be inconvenient, he could see no reason why it should be against the public interest. Indeed, rather the reverse. Comparing the position of the prisoner sentenced for murder with a discretionary life prisoner subject to an order under Section 34 of the Criminal Justice Act 1991, Mustill elaborated ringingly: 'He never sees the Home Secretary; he has no dialogue with him: he cannot fathom how his mind is working. There is no true tariff, or at least no tariff exposed to public view which might give the prisoner an idea of what to expect. The announcement of his first review date arrives out of thin air, wholly without explanation. The distant oracle has spoken, and that is that.'[54]

In the interests of greater openness in decision-making, the House of Lords made an additional order that the Home Secretary was obliged to give reasons for departing from the period recommended by the judiciary as the period which the prisoner should serve for the purposes of retribution and deterrence. Mustill said that the declarations should not be interpreted as the signal for a flood of successful applications for judicial review. They should be read in the context of the reasoning set out in his long and carefully argued speech. While discretionary and mandatory sentences of life imprisonment, having in the past grown apart, might now be converging, there remained a substantial gap between them. Any further assimilation was a task for Parliament. Despite his cautionary remark that it was 'quite impossible' for the courts to introduce a fundamental change in the relationship between the convicted murderer and the state through the medium of judicial review,[55] there was no doubt that *Doody* was an important step forward in procedural justice, the English equivalent of due process.

The court-induced policies of greater openness, particularly the obligation imposed on the Secretary of State and the Parole Board to give written reasons for their decisions, brought in its train more opportunities for challenges in the courts. In 1994 alone seven applications by way of judicial review were heard in the Court of Appeal or Divisional Court.[56] Two of the cases turned on the status of prisoners who had been transferred from a prison

---

[54] Ibid., 565.   [55] Ibid., 559.
[56] *Report of the Parole Board for 1994, op. cit.*, pp. 2–3.

establishment to a mental hospital for treatment after conviction and sentence.[57] The Divisional Court found that five prisoners who had received discretionary life sentences for serious sexual or violent offences, and one prisoner who had been sentenced to be detained during Her Majesty's pleasure for a murder committed when he was seventeen, did not forfeit their entitlement to benefit from the release procedures for discretionary life prisoners under Section 34 of the Criminal Justice Act 1991 because of their transfer to a mental hospital by order of the Secretary of State with a restriction direction. The Home Secretary's policy not to certify that such cases were eligible for review by the Parole Board was held to be unlawful.[58]

The Court of Appeal disagreed, allowing appeals by the Crown and setting aside the orders for declaratory relief granted by the Divisional Court. Rose LJ, in a judgment agreed by Butler-Sloss LJ and Sir Tasker Watkins,[59] said the fact that a person has more than one status does not necessarily mean that he can simultaneously exercise the rights attaching to each. Discretionary life prisoners who had been transferred to hospital and were subject to restriction had regular access to a Mental Health Review Tribunal. When returned to prison they were entitled to have their cases reviewed by a Discretionary Lifer Panel of the Parole Board once the tariff period had expired. There were striking similarities between the composition and procedures of the two bodies, each being chaired by a judge with a psychiatrist as a member. Both satisfied the requirement of the European Court of Human Rights in *Thynne, Wilson, and Gunnell* that continued detention was subject to the availability of a periodic judicial hearing. He saw nothing unjust or illogical in the existence of two separate codes which could not be triggered simultaneously, but each of which could be triggered at

---

[57] Before the Criminal Justice Act 1991 the practice had been for life-sentence prisoners who had been transferred from prison to hospital to be released on life licence rather than under Mental Health Act procedures. This was thought to provide greater protection to the public and to be consistent with the intentions of the sentencing court. See *Report of the Parole Board for 1985* (HC 428), HMSO, London, 1986, pp. 5–6.

[58] *R. v. Secretary of State for the Home Department, ex parte T and Others; R. v. Secretary of State for the Home Department, ex parte Hickey* [1994] 1 All ER 794.

[59] Lord Justice of Appeal 1980–93 and Deputy Chief Justice of England 1988–93. Judge of the High Court of Justice, Family Division 1971–4, Queen's Bench Division 1974–80. Senior Presiding Judge for England and Wales 1983–91. Awarded the Victoria Cross 1944.

an appropriate time so as to achieve a judicial hearing. Where two Acts apply, and a person is both a prisoner and a patient, the interplay between the Acts will depend on the particular circumstances of the case.[60] The court held that the respondents in the appeal were not entitled to exercise their right to be considered for release by the Parole Board while still in hospital. The appropriate route was via the procedures contained in the Mental Health Act 1983 and the Mental Health Review Tribunals.

While judicial review does tend to draw fine distinctions it can also isolate and concentrate attention upon broad aspects of policy and practice which may affect the situation of many people in the future. In another case brought by a discretionary life prisoner in 1994, *R.* v. *Parole Board, ex parte Lodomez*,[61] Leggatt LJ in the Divisional Court held that when directing the release of discretionary prisoners the Parole Board should be satisfied that the risk of reoffending was low enough to justify release. The argument was rejected that the Board was required to direct release unless the prisoner represented a substantial risk of committing offences dangerous to life or limb.[62] The decision to release a discretionary life prisoner rested with the Board alone, and it was entitled to take a decision contrary to the opinions of the report writer and both parties (the prisoner and the Secretary of State) if it concluded that the risk of reoffending was not sufficiently low to warrant release on

[60] *R.* v. *Secretary of State for the Home Department, ex parte Hickey (No. 1)* and *R.* v. *Secretary of State for the Home Department, ex parte H., F., B., and W.* [1995] 1 All ER 479 at 487–8.

[61] The case was reported, inadequately, in *The Times* on 3 Aug. 1994. The full judgment, as approved by the Court, is to be found in transcript CO 2761 of the case heard on 4 May 1994 in the High Court of Justice, Queen's Bench Division (Divisional Court).

[62] The volume of applications for judicial review means that successive judgments have put different emphases and different glosses on the case-law bearing on the proper discharge of the Parole Board's functions. Much legal argument has centred upon the degree of risk of reoffending as a ground for recalling a discretionary life sentence prisoner to custody or refusing to release one after the expiry of the relevant part (the fixed tariff) of his sentence. In reaching its decision the Board does not have to establish that there is a positive risk; rather, in its subjective judgment it must be satisfied that the resultant risk to the public will be no more than minimal. *R.* v. *Parole Board, ex parte Bradley* [1991] 1 WLR 134; *R.* v. *Parole Board, ex parte Lodomez (op. cit.)*; *R* v. *(1) Secretary of State for the Home Department (2) Parole Board, ex parte Evans* unreported, official transcript CO 2454, 2 Nov. 1994; *R.* v. *Parole Board, ex parte Watson* unreported, official transcript, CO 3104, 16 Oct. 1995. The author's thanks are due to T. Russell, Secretary of the Parole Board, for information about recent cases. Letter of 8 Nov. 1995.

licence. The Board's decision not to direct release was quashed, however, with costs awarded against the Parole Board on the grounds that the reasons given were grossly deficient. The Court directed that the case should be reheard by the Board as soon as was practicable.

The remaining applications in 1994, brought by two discretionary lifers[63] and two mandatory lifers,[64] contested the adequacy of reasons for decisions of the Board or recommendations to the Secretary of State. The judgments reasserted the Board's obligation to give reasons which were easily understandable and related to the main points at issue in individual cases.[65] Although English law at present does not recognize a general duty on the part of administrative bodies to give reasons for their decisions, the case-by-case approach is moving in that direction. Giving judgment in the Court of Appeal in 1995, Swinton Thomas LJ, a former member of the Parole Board, remarked that the Board had found 'the requirement

---

[63] *R. v. Parole Board, ex parte Gittens,* unreported transcript, 26 Jan. 1994, and *Lodomez,* (*op. cit.*).

[64] *R. v. Secretary of State for the Home Department, ex parte Pegg*, unreported transcript, 29 July 1994, and *R. v. (1) Secretary of State for the Home Department (2) Parole Board, ex parte Evans.* Life sentences remained a fertile field for applications for judicial review in 1995. In the last quarter of the year alone, cases heard by the Queen's Bench Divisional Court and Court of Appeal included *R. v. (1) Secretary of State for the Home Department (2) Parole Board, ex parte Norney and Others*, DC, official transcript CO 2092, 28 Sept. 1995 (new discretionary lifer cases to be referred to the Parole Board six months earlier than before); *R. v. Secretary of State for the Home Department, ex parte Chapman*, DC, *The Times* Law Report, 25 Oct. 1995 (reconsideration ordered of the tariff of a discretionary life sentence prisoner on grounds that no equivalent determinate sentence had been imposed for similar offences); *R. v. Dalton*, CA, *The Times* Law Report, 25 Oct. 1995 (right to appeal against the relevant part of a discretionary life sentence); *R. v. Secretary of State for the Home Department, ex parte Pierson*, DC, *The Times* Law Report, 29 Nov. 1995 (in revising the tariff of a mandatory life sentence prisoner the Home Secretary's discretion to increase the period was not absolute but had to be fair); appeal by the Secretary of State allowed by the Court of Appeal, *The Times* Law Report, 8 Dec. 1995. In his judgment the Master of the Rolls concluded, although not without misgiving, that the Home Secretary's decision in maintaining a tariff set in 1988 five years longer than the period recommended by the judiciary, despite the absence of the aggravating features previously relied upon, had not been shown to be unlawful on the ground of irrationality and ought not to be quashed.

[65] The giving of reasons had been the subject of inconclusive debate in Parliament, the Home Office, and the Parole Board during the 1970s, and amendments requiring reasons to be given were defeated in both Houses during the proceedings on the Criminal Justice Act 1982. For an account of an experiment conducted by the Board, and why it was abandoned in 1979, see *Responses to Crime*, Vol. 1, pp. 277–8, and *Report of the Parole Board 1979* (HC 651), HMSO, London, 1980, pp. 42–3.

to give reasons for a decision, most particularly a decision to refuse parole, concentrated the minds on the proper issues involved in the decision-making and imposed a very desirable discipline'.[66]

V

On 30 June 1995, the most recent date for which statistics were available at the time of writing, 3,273 prisoners were serving sentences of life imprisonment in Prison Service establishments in England and Wales. Of this total 3,176 were men and 97 were women. Close on 82 per cent of the overall life-sentence population were serving mandatory sentences for murder. The consistent pattern of annual growth in the life sentence population from 1,675 in 1981 to 3,273 in 1995 is shown in Table 10.[67] The broad picture is that the number of persons sentenced to life imprisonment has nearly doubled since 1981. In each year an increase has been recorded, both in the total number of persons serving a sentence of life imprisonment and in the number of mandatory life prisoners. When prisoners serving life sentences in Scotland and Northern Ireland are added it seems probable that in the early 1990s, before the expansion in membership which resulted from the overthrow of communist rule in Central and Eastern Europe, the United Kingdom accumulated a larger life-sentence population than the combined aggregate for all other member states of the Council of Europe.[68]

Information prised out of the Home Office by way of Answers to Parliamentary Questions reveals the effect of tariffs set by ministers on release decisions in the cases of mandatory life prisoners.

[66] R. v. *Mayor and Commonalty and Citizens of the City of London and another, ex parte Matson*, CA, unreported transcript, 18 Aug. 1995, p. 56. In this case the Court of Appeal quashed a decision by the Court of Aldermen of the City of London not to confirm the candidate who had obtained a majority of the votes in a properly conducted ward election without giving any reasons. In the judgment of Neill LJ fairness and natural justice required that the decision should not be allowed to go unexplained (p. 33).

[67] Table 10 updates Table 10 of *Responses to Crime*, Vol. 2, p. 346. There was an error in the number of male prisoners shown as serving a sentence of life imprisonment in 1991. The correct statistic should have been 2,800. The figure of 2,904 was for males serving life sentences in 1992.

[68] Not too much should be made of this argument owing to the unreliability of the data, although the claim of far more frequent recourse to life imprisonment in the UK than elsewhere in Europe is undeniably true.

TABLE 10. *Life sentence prisoners 1981–95[1]*

	Males	Females	Total	Mandatory	Mandatory % of Total
1981	1,626	49	1,675	1,274	76.1
1982	1,735	53	1,788	1,346	75.3
1983	1,767	55	1,822	1,377	75.6
1984	1,856	61	1,917	1,462	76.3
1985	1,991	60	2,051	1,591	77.6
1986	2,126	68	2,194	1,706	77.8
1987	2,265	74	2,339	1,824	78.0
1988	2,427	76	2,503	1,973	78.8
1989	2.592	85	2,677	2,131	79.6
1990	2.704	91	2,795	2,237	80.0
1991	2,800	96	2,896	2,318	80.0
1992	2,904	96	3,000	2,380	79.3
1993	2,990	105	3,095	2,509	81.1
1994*	3,081	111	3,192	2,618	82.0
1995*	3,176	113	3,289	2,705	82.2

[1] Population on 30 June each year of persons serving a sentence of life imprisonment (including detention during Her Majesty's pleasure and custody for life) in England and Wales.
* Provisional figures subject to correction.

Source: Home Office.

TABLE 11. *Mandatory life sentence prisoners released on licence having served fewer than ten years, 1990–5*

Years	Up to five	Five under six	Six under seven	Seven under eight	Eight under nine	Nine under ten	All under ten
1990	—	—	—	3	3	7	13
1991	—	—	2	1	4	9	16
1992	1	—	1	2	1	12	17
1993	—	—	1	1	3	1	6
1994	1	—	—	—	—	4	5
1995*	1	1	0	2	4	5	13

* Provisional figures subject to correction.
The statistics relate to prisoners sentenced to life imprisonment for murder first released on licence, other than on compassionate grounds, in England and Wales during the five year period, 1990–4. Time spent on remand in custody is excluded.

Source: Home Office.

Table 11 shows that over the six-year period 1990–5 only six prisoners sentenced to life imprisonment for murder, an average of one per year, were released on licence in England and Wales having served less than six years. The number of releases after six and before ten years are shown in the Table. The statistics exclude prisoners released for a second or subsequent time having been recalled to custody after a previous release on licence, and very occasional release on compassionate grounds such as terminal illness.

These figures call for critical examination. The first point to note is the sharp decline which occurred in 1993 and 1994. This shows the very significant statistical impact that discretionary decisions can have on a small control group. The dates coincide with Michael Howard's more stringent regime at the Home Office, but judicial recommendations on tariff and release may also have played a part. Then there is the principle of proportionality in punishment. While comparisons with determinate sentences cannot be exact, the tariff element in a mandatory sentence is a fixed penal sanction, specifically imposed in the interests of retribution and deterrence, the duration of which must be served in all save the most exceptional circumstances before any factors bearing on the prisoner's progress or future prospects can be considered. The scale of punishment is decided upon by ministers having received, but not necessarily accepted, recommendations from the judiciary. It can be assumed that prisoners convicted of murder with sufficient mitigating circumstances not to have merited a life sentence but for the mandatory penalty will attract the lowest tariffs. Some will be first offenders, with good prison reports and release plans, who will be strong candidates for release on licence as soon as the tariff period has expired. In other cases the risk of serious reoffending will justify continued detention beyond the tariff. But this factor is more common in discretionary than in mandatory cases, since the risk to the public is often the reason why a life sentence was passed in the first place.

The question arises of whether the requirements of fairness, and consequently lawfulness in public law terms, is satisfied by ignoring altogether any comparison between the tariff and the notional equivalent determinate sentence in mandatory cases. Although remission in its traditional form was abolished by the Criminal Justice Act 1991, no determinate sentence prisoner of good behaviour[69] now serves the full term of a sentence of imprisonment passed by the court. Long-term prisoners (defined as those serving sentences of four years or more) become eligible for release on parole half-way through their sentence if recommended by the Parole Board. For prisoners serving sentences of between four and up to seven years, the Home Secretary must accept the Board's recommendation. For sentences of seven years or more, the final decision remains in the hands of the Home Secretary. Although he may not release a prisoner in this category without a favourable recommendation from the Board, he is not obliged to accept such a recommendation. As soon as a prisoner has served two-thirds of his sentence, whether or not he has been the subject of a recommendation, the Secretary of State is obliged to release him. All long-term determinate prisoners, irrespective of whether they have been granted parole, remain under supervision until the three-quarter point is reached. If a further offence is committed after release but during the currency of the original sentence the whole of the unexpired portion of that sentence may be activated and added to any custodial sentence imposed for the further offence.

The contrast in the punishment accorded to the mandatory life prisoner is striking. Leaving aside the question of what the equivalent determinate sentence should be if the court were able to pass one for murder, the very operation of the parole system means that if the circumstances of the offence and the prisoner's subsequent behaviour and future prospects are such as would warrant release following first review, he may well serve twice as long in custody as a similarly low-risk long-term prisoner, who may also have been convicted of taking the life of another. Under the 1991 Act even the most hardened recidivist serving a long-term determinate sentence is entitled to be released after completing two-thirds of the punishment imposed by the court, whereas the mandatory lifer must serve the full penal term. In this respect he is also at a disadvantage compared with the discretionary lifer whose tariff (the 'relevant part' of the sentence intended to mark the seriousness of the offence) will take account of the parole entitlement on a notionally equivalent determinate sentence.[70]

---

[69] A short-term or long-term prisoner could serve the full term of a determinate sentence if awarded enough additional days for disciplinary offences under Section 42 of the Criminal Justice Act 1991.

[70] Section 34(2)(b) of the 1991 Act required the relevant part of the sentence to

Relating current practice to an individual case brings out the enormity of the difference. Let us return to the case of Dr Nigel Cox, the consultant rheumatologist, shortly afterwards restored to his post, who in September 1992 was tried in the Crown Court at Winchester and found guilty of the attempted murder of a terminally ill patient by giving her a lethal injection.[71] He received a twelve-month suspended sentence. If, on the facts and beyond reasonable doubt, the results of a post-mortem examination had shown the injection to have been the cause of the seventy year-old patient's death, it is probable that Dr Cox would have been charged with murder rather than attempted murder. If convicted, he would have received the mandatory penalty of life imprisonment, irrespective of the circumstances leading to his action. As it happened, the deceased patient had already been cremated before a complaint was lodged concerning Dr Cox's decision, and so there had been no opportunity for a post-mortem examination.

From the available data it appears that the mandatory life-sentence prisoners serving the shortest custodial terms between 1990 and 1994 were two prisoners released in 1992 and 1994, each having served between three and four years. Without a case-by-case analysis it is not possible to say what mitigating circumstances there were in these or other cases. However, given the known incidence of tragic domestic killings by persons of previous good character, such as women killing men who have maltreated them over a lengthy time, and of quarrels between friends after heavy drinking ending in violence with an intention to cause serious injury resulting in a bitterly regretted death,[72] it seems certain that there will have been a number of cases with strong mitigating circumstances. Even if, as is to be hoped, Dr Cox's case would have come at the lower end of the range, the conclusion is unavoidable that he would

be specified after taking into account the provisions for early release of short-term and long-term prisoners in Sections 32(2) and 35(1).

[71] Dr Cox's case attracted much informed comment. See Committee on the Penalty for Homicide, *Report*, pp. 7–8; and a memorandum submitted by the Law Commission in evidence to the House of Commons Home Affairs Committee, *Murder: Mandatory Life Sentences and the 'Year and a Day' Rule* (HC 214–II), Minutes of Evidence and Memoranda of Evidence, HMSO, London, 1995, pp. 111–12.

[72] More than half of all homicides in 1992 were committed in the course of quarrels or bouts of temper. Only 7 per cent were committed in furtherance of theft or gain. Home Office, *Criminal Statistics, England and Wales 1992* (Cm. 2410), HMSO, London, p. 69.

have served years rather than months in prison, and without any off-set for notionally equivalent parole. While the state of English law on murder, and the contrivance of a single mandatory penalty for an offence which covers so diverse a range of criminal acts and culpability of offenders, may share the blame, such imbalance should not be tolerated when the act was identical and the intention the same.[73]

VI

Provided that all avenues for relief in the domestic courts have been exhausted, and certain other conditions fulfilled,[74] a prisoner who claims that he has suffered the violation of a right protected by the European Convention on Human Rights[75] may pursue his complaint by way of an application to the European Commission of

[73] Germany is one of the very few other European countries which has a mandatory penalty of life imprisonment for murder. The Republic of Ireland and Cyprus are believed by JUSTICE to be the only others (HC 214–II, *op. cit.*, p. 99). The German definition of murder is narrower than in England: it requires proof of intention to kill and aggravating circumstances. The importance of the principle of proportionality between life imprisonment for murder and other custodial penalties has been recognized by the Federal Constitutional Court. In 1977 the Court held that life imprisonment could only be constitutional when the possibility of the offender's release was guaranteed by a statutorily prescribed review procedure which met constitutional standards of procedural fairness. In 1982 the German Penal Code was amended to provide for every life sentence to be reviewed after fifteen years by the court responsible for the execution of sentence. See D. van Zyl Smit, 'Taking Life Imprisonment Seriously', in E. Kahn (ed.), *The Quest for Justice*: Essays in Honour of M. M. Corbett, Chief Justice of the Supreme Court of South Africa, Juta, Kenwyn, 1995, pp. 312–13, 318–19. The same author has analysed the 1977 decision of the Federal Constitutional Court in 'Is Life Imprisonment Constitutional?—The German Experience', [1992] *Public Law*, 263–78. Dirk van Zyl Smit is Professor of Law and Dean of the Faculty of Law at the University of Cape Town.

[74] The conditions for a petition to be found admissible by the Commission are listed in *Responses to Crime*, Vol. 2, pp. 372–3.

[75] The Convention for the Protection of Human Rights and Fundamental Freedoms was signed in Rome on 4 Nov. 1950 by the original member states of the Council of Europe. By the end of 1994 there were thirty-three member states, rapid enlargement having resulted from the collapse of the Communist regimes in East and Central Europe. At its 95th Session on 10 Nov. 1994 the Committee of Ministers of the Council of Europe 'underlined their political will' to admit to membership eight more candidate states: Albania, Belarus, Croatia, Latvia, Moldova, the Russian Federation, the former Yugoslav Republic of Macedonia, and Ukraine, 'at the earliest possible date, according to the pace of their democratic development'. Council of Europe, *Information Sheet No. 35*: *Human Rights*, H. INF(95)2, Strasbourg, 1995, pp. 79–80.

Human Rights at Strasbourg. After a preliminary screening process carried out by the Secretariat, the Commission reaches a decision on admissibility. If it admits a petition it endeavours to promote a friendly settlement between the parties. If that fails, either the Commission or the government of any member state involved in the case may refer it to the European Court of Human Rights for a full judicial hearing. Member states have an obligation not to hinder the effective exercise of the right of individual petition, a provision of particular importance to sentenced prisoners and persons held in detention pending trial or for other reasons.[76] A substantial proportion of the total number of applications accepted each year come from persons in custody. Discretionary legal aid is available,[77] and some applications are supported, either *ab initio* or at a later stage, by one of the civil liberties organizations, notably JUSTICE (the British Section of the International Committee of Jurists) or Liberty (the National Council for Civil Liberties).

Constrained by limited financial and staff resources JUSTICE and Liberty have concentrated on assisting selected applications by prisoners which expose contested practical issues or questions of policy to external judicial scrutiny. If an application succeeds in establishing that a practice or policy violates an article of the Convention, there is a binding legal obligation on the government of the member state or other responsible public body to take the measures necessary to comply with the judgment of the Court.[78] In this way, through the medium of carefully selected test cases, the situation of many other prisoners besides the applicant will be affected. Sometimes an individual prisoner has the persistence to press on with an application on his own, either applying in person

[76] 384 out of the total of 2,944 applications (13 per cent) considered by the Commission in 1994 came from applicants detained or interned. That compared with 16 per cent in 1993, 13 per cent in 1992, 15 per cent in 1991, and 17 per cent in 1990. European Commission of Human Rights, *Survey of Activities and Statistics 1994*, Council of Europe, Strasbourg, 1995, p. 21.

[77] 34 per cent of the applications were introduced through a lawyer in 1994, a lower proportion of the sharply increasing annual total of cases than in 1993 (43 per cent), 1992 (51 per cent), 1991 (43 per cent) and 1990 (45 per cent). Ibid.

[78] The measures taken by the United Kingdom Government as a result of the finding of a violation of the Convention in the case of *Thynne, Wilson, and Gunnell* were reported to the Committee of Ministers of the Council of Europe and adopted at the 477th meeting of the Ministers' Deputies on 15 June 1992. Compliance took the form of the amendments incorporated as Section 34 of the Criminal Justice Act 1991, then before Parliament. Council of Europe, *Information Sheet No. 31: Human Rights*, H/INF (92)3, Strasbourg, 1994, Appendix 13, pp. 123–4.

or seeking a solicitor willing to represent him and brief counsel if the case gets as far as a hearing at Strasbourg. The facts of the case may be atypical, however, with features that make it less than ideally suited for the purpose of testing the application of policies or practice against the standards of the Convention.

So it was with the first application from an English mandatory life sentence prisoner, Edward Wynne, to be found admissible by the Commission. Wynne's case was highly unusual in that he was a maximum security prisoner, held in Category A conditions, who was serving two life sentences simultaneously. A mandatory sentence had been imposed following his conviction for murder in 1964. He was released on licence by decision of the Secretary of State in May 1980, but in January 1982 was found guilty of a second homicide. Because his state of mind at the time of the offence met the requirements of Section 2 of the Homicide Act 1957, Wynne was convicted of manslaughter and sentenced to a discretionary life sentence on the grounds of the extreme danger that he represented to the public. His life licence was revoked by the trial judge, thus reactivating the earlier mandatory sentence. To have the dual system of life imprisonment, already amongst the most complicated of national systems for the sentencing and punishment of offenders, combined in one person was a stiff test to the acumen of the jurists at Strasbourg.

As with the majority of cases brought by prisoners, Wynne's application turned on the interpretation of Article 5(4) of the Convention and the case-law that had accrued around it. Article 5(4) states that: 'Everyone who is deprived of his liberty by arrest or detention shall be entitled to take proceedings by which the lawfulness of his detention shall be decided speedily by a court and his release ordered if the detention is not lawful.'

Having declared the application admissible on 15 October 1992, and made an unsuccessful attempt to secure a friendly settlement, the Commission expressed the opinion in a report to the Court on 4 May 1993 that there had been no violation of the Convention. The finding was not unanimous; the report was agreed by ten votes to five. The next stage was a hearing before the full Court on 23 February 1994.[79] Wynne was represented by Edward Fitzgerald, a well respected member of the English Bar, experienced in arguing

[79] The proceedings before the Commission are reported in (1995) 19 EHRR 333 at 339.

life-sentence cases in the domestic courts and at Strasbourg. David Pannick QC appeared for the United Kingdom Government, supported by a Foreign Office legal counsellor and Home Office officials. He too had much experience of representing both applicants and HM Government in proceedings in Strasbourg. After the hearing by a Chamber composed of the President and twelve judges, including the British judge,[80] the Court deliberated in private. Judgment was reserved for delivery at a later date.

On 18 July the judgment was read out in open court by the President, Rolv Ryssdal of Norway, with eight judges present.[81] Rejecting the applicant's submission that it was the discretionary life sentence, imposed for the second homicide, which had been the real and effective basis for his detention since his conviction for manslaughter in 1982, and hence should govern the release procedures, the Court held that the legal basis for his detention was both the mandatory life sentence, which remained in force, and the new discretionary life sentence. The fact that he had committed a further offence in 1981, and was found to have been suffering from a mental disorder at the time, in no way affected the continued validity of the original sentence or its reactivation on his recall. The Court noted judicial comments to the effect that the theory and practice of the mandatory sentence were out of tune, and quoted Lord Mustill's observation in *Doody* that while the two types of life sentence might be converging, there was still a substantial gap between them.[82]

It was the opinion of the Court that in mandatory life sentence cases the release of the prisoner was entirely within the discretion of the Secretary of State, who was not bound by the judicial recommendation as to the length of the tariff, and who could have regard to other criteria than dangerousness in deciding on release. Against that background, the Court saw no cogent reason to depart from its finding in the case of *Thynne, Wilson, and Gunnell* v. *United Kingdom*[83] that the guarantee of Article 5(4) was satisfied in mandatory cases by the original trial and appeal proceedings. No additional right was conferred to challenge the lawfulness of continued detention, or re-detention following revocation of the life

---

[80] Sir John Freeland, Legal Adviser to the Foreign and Commonwealth Office 1984–7.

[81] (1995) 19 EHRR 333. The judgment of the Court is reported at 344.

[82] Ibid., 347.   [83] (1991) 13 EHRR 666.

licence. There were no new issues of lawfulness in Wynne's case to entitle him to review by a court or a court-like body. To grant a review of the lawfulness of his continued detention under the discretionary life sentence would be devoid of purpose, since he was also serving a mandatory life sentence and enjoyed no possibility of release until the Secretary of State considered it was in the public interest to release him.[84]

Although the judgment in *Wynne*, upholding the finding in *Thynne, Wilson, and Gunnell*, might seem to have closed off the route for successful appeals to Strasbourg by mandatory prisoners, attempts were being made by JUSTICE and others to open another avenue joining the main highway farther on. The distinction between the separate handling of mandatory and discretionary life prisoners had attracted so much attention that little notice had been taken of the existence of two other categories of indeterminate sentence: detention during Her Majesty's pleasure and custody for life. The first is the fixed penalty for children and young persons between the ages of ten and eighteen who are convicted in the Crown Court of murder or manslaughter.[85] Custody for life is the sentence imposed for murder committed by an individual between the ages of eighteen and twenty-one.[86] Detention orders under Section 53(1) of the Children and Young Persons Act 1933, as amended, are automatic in the case of convictions for murder. Detention during Her Majesty's pleasure is 'in such a place and under such conditions as the Secretary of State may direct'.[87]

[84] (1995) 19 EHRR 347–8.

[85] Children and Young Persons Act 1933, Section 53(1). The historical background to this Section is that it was one of a number of provisions designed to protect young offenders from the death penalty. Detention during His Majesty's pleasure as a sentence for children was introduced by Section 103 of the Children Act 1908, which provided that a person under the age of eighteen at the time of conviction should receive such a sentence instead of the death penalty. The sentence of detention during His Majesty's pleasure, as opposed to imprisonment, reflected the belief that children should not go to prison but should serve their sentence in institutions separate from adult offenders. That remains the practice to the present day. The author is indebted to Baroness Blatch, Minister of State at the Home Office, for this information. Letter of 28 Nov. 1995.

[86] Criminal Justice Act 1982, Section 8(1).

[87] Young people detained under Section 53 are held either in Young Offender Institutions or secure child-care establishments, including two residential centres maintained by the Youth Treatment Service of the Department of Health. Decisions about placements are made by the Home Office in conjunction with the Department of Health. Over the age of sixteen and a half, juveniles are usually allocated to Young Offender Institutions managed by the Prison Service, unless reports indicate

Detention under Section 53 is available for young offenders convicted of murder or manslaughter between the ages of ten to thirteen. Between the ages of fourteen and eighteen, detention is available under the same Section on conviction for certain additional offences which in the case of an adult carry a maximum sentence of fourteen years imprisonment or more (e.g. rape, robbery, arson, domestic burglary, buggery). For sixteen and seventeen year-olds the offence of indecent assault on a woman is added.[88]

Two cases raising the question of how sentences of detention at Her Majesty's pleasure for offences of murder should be categorized were declared admissible after oral hearings by the European Commission of Human Rights in 1994. The case of *Prem Singh*[89] had been considered by the domestic courts in the previous year. Sitting in the Divisional Court, Evans LJ had quashed the Parole Board's decision not to re-release Singh after he had been recalled to custody when his licence had been revoked. At the age of fifteen Singh had been convicted of the murder of a seventy-two year-old woman and sentenced to be detained during Her Majesty's pleasure in 1973. Seventeen years on, after completing the tariff part of his sentence, he had been released on licence in October 1990. A few months later, in March 1991, he was arrested and interviewed by the police in connection with alleged offences of obtaining by deception and threatening behaviour. The criminal charges were later dismissed when the judge refused to sign the indictments presented by the prosecution out of time. Before then Singh had been recalled to custody by the Parole Board, not solely on the basis of the criminal charges he was facing but because the circumstances

that they are immature or particularly in need of the kind of care and attention they would receive in a child-care establishment. On 6 Nov. 1992 there were 146 young people sentenced by the English courts, and subject to Section 53 orders, placed with the Youth Treatment Service or in a local authority children's home. Only seven of these were detained at Her Majesty's pleasure. No available statistics show how many inmates in Young Offender Institutions or adult prisons are still serving this sentence imposed on them when juveniles. Once allocated to the child-care system juveniles will normally remain there until release or until aged eighteen or nineteen when they will be transferred to a prison establishment to complete their sentence. This information was included in a memorandum submitted by the Home Office to the Home Affairs Committee of the House of Commons in connection with an inquiry into juvenile crime. Home Affairs Committee, Sixth Report, Session 1992–93, *Juvenile Offenders* (HC 441–II), HMSO, London, 1993, p. 36.

[88] Ibid., p. 28.

[89] *Prem Singh* v. *United Kingdom* (Application No. 23389/94). Report of the Commission adopted 11 Oct. 1994.

surrounding the alleged offences had demonstrated conclusively that the trust and openness necessary for his supervision in the community were lacking. When he made representations against his recall the Board had before it a number of reports from the Probation Service and the police, which he did not see.

On his subsequent application for judicial review in April 1993 the Divisional Court held that there had been a breach of the rules of natural justice because of the failure to disclose to the applicant all the reports placed before the Board. Evans LJ found that the applicant's status was that of a person whose continued detention could only be justified if the test of dangerousness, meaning an unacceptable risk of physical danger to the life and limb of the public, was satisfied.[90] The Board reviewed the case twice more, with disclosure of the documents. On the second occasion it recommended that Singh should be released subject to a six-month pre-release employment scheme. The recommendation was rejected by the Home Secretary and the reasons for his decision were notified to the prisoner in writing on 21 July 1994. By then he had served more than three further years in custody since his recall in 1991.

The basis of the application to the European Commission of Human Rights by a firm of Bristol solicitors acting on behalf of Prem Singh was that he had been unable to obtain a review by a court of the lawfulness of his continued detention at Her Majesty's pleasure under Article 5(4) of the Convention. The Parole Board panels which had considered his case lacked the court-like characteristics and powers of the discretionary lifer panels. Detention at Her Majesty's pleasure should be regarded as a wholly indeterminate sentence based on the special factor of youth. It should be assimilated with discretionary sentences for adults which the European Court of Human Rights had held to require judicial rather than executive control after the expiry of the punitive or tariff part of the sentence. The only justification for continued detention under an indeterminate sentence was the risk of further offending or dangerousness, which was a factor susceptible to change.

Although setting out both sides of the argument, that of the applicant and the Government's contention that detention at Her Majesty's pleasure should be equated with mandatory life impris-

---

[90] Transcript of unreported case in the Divisional Court, 20 Apr. 1993, p. 3.

onment for adults convicted of murder and was in effect the equivalent sentence imposed on juveniles, the unanimous report of the
Commission declaring the application admissible leant in favour of
the case presented by the applicant. Evans LJ's remarks were
quoted that detention orders made under Section 53(1) of the
Children and Young Persons Act 1933 were closer in substance to
the discretionary than the mandatory life sentence for murder, and
endorsed by the opinion of the Commission that the sentence
would appear 'to reflect an intention of imposing a distinct regime
of detention geared to the special considerations which apply in
dealing with very young offenders who are particularly dangerous
but who still have formative years ahead of them and may change
with maturation'.[91]

A second case, brought by JUSTICE on behalf of *Abed Hussain*,
was heard consecutively with Prem Singh's application.[92] The facts
were different, and Hussain's application was uncomplicated by the
recall procedures and decisions which were a feature of Singh's
case. The two applicants and the Government were represented by
the same Counsel as in *Wynne*, Edward Fitzgerald appearing for
both applicants and David Pannick QC for the United Kingdom
Government.

At the time his application was heard, Abed Hussain, a Pakistani
citizen born in 1962, had spent more than half of his natural life,
and all of his adult life, in custody. At the age of sixteen he was
found guilty of the murder of his two year-old younger brother. No
motive was established by the trial court and he was sentenced to
detention during Her Majesty's pleasure pursuant to Section 53(1)
of the Children and Young Persons Act 1933. Between 1986 and
1994 the Parole Board considered his case on four occasions, with
an application for judicial review between the third and fourth
reviews. On neither of the first two reviews did the Parole Board
recommend release. At the third review in December 1992 the
Board recommended that Hussain should be transferred to open
conditions, with a further review six months later. The Secretary of
State rejected the recommendation, directing that the prisoner
should remain in closed conditions, with a further review to take
place in March 1995. In accordance with the procedures then

[91] *Op. cit.*, para. 63.
[92] *Abed Hussain* v. *United Kingdom* (Application No. 21928/93). Report of the
Commission adopted 11 Oct. 1994.

prevailing, at none of these reviews did the prisoner see any of the reports before the Board. Neither did he have an opportunity to appear before the panel when his case was considered, nor given any reasons for the decisions taken. In June 1993 he applied for judicial review on the basis that he had not been shown the reports placed before the Board, relying on the case of *Prem Singh*.

The application was withdrawn after the Parole Board gave an undertaking in the High Court to reconsider Hussain's case immediately, and to disclose their dossier to him so that he could make informed representations with knowledge of its contents. Following the court review in January 1994, the Secretary of State accepted the Board's recommendation that he should be transferred to open conditions as the first step towards release, and the transfer took place in February 1994. His case was due to be reviewed again in the light of his progress in coping with open conditions in February 1996.

The later stages of this sequence of events overlapped with the opening moves at Strasbourg. Hussain's application to the Commission was introduced on 31 March 1993 and registered on 27 May. The Government was asked for, and submitted, written observations on the admissibility and merits of the application, to which Hussain replied. In April 1994 the Commission decided to hold an oral hearing on admissibility and merits consecutively with the case of Prem Singh. The hearing took place on 30 June 1994 when both applications were declared admissible. The Commission concluded in its report of 11 October, unanimously, that there had been a violation of Article 5(4) of the Convention on the grounds that neither applicant had been afforded the opportunity to obtain a review of the lawfulness of their continued detention by a body satisfying the requirements of the Convention.

After declaring the case admissible, the Commission placed itself at the disposal of the parties to see if there was any basis on which to secure a friendly settlement. The Government maintained its stance that detention during Her Majesty's pleasure should be equated with the term of mandatory life imprisonment for adults and was in effect the equivalent sentence imposed on juveniles. It was to be regarded as a sentence fixed by law because of the gravity of the offence. Mandatory sentences differed from discretionary sentences in their nature as well as in the applicable procedures. The determination of these issues was referred to the Court of

Human Rights to decide the merits. The cases of *Hussain* and *Singh*
v. *United Kingdom* were heard together on 27 September 1995.
Having deliberated in private on 28 September and 26 January
1996, the Court delivered judgment in both cases at a public session in Strasbourg on 21 February.

Counsel for the applicants argued that a sentence of detention
during Her Majesty's pleasure differed from the mandatory life sentenced imposed on adults in that it was not solely based on the
gravity of the offence, but took account of the age of the offender.
The principle that crimes committed by young persons should not
be punished as severely as the crimes of adults, in counsel's submission, was contained in all civilized penal codes. The purpose of
the sentence was not wholly punitive in character, but partly punitive and partly preventive. Consequently, detention under Section
53 of the Children and Young Persons Act 1933 was closer in its
indeterminacy and preventive objectives to a discretionary life sentence than to a mandatory life sentence for adults. For its part, the
Government contended that detention during Her Majesty's pleasure had an essentially punitive character and was imposed automatically on all juvenile murderers because of the gravity of their
offence, regardless of their mental state or dangerousness. This
explained why under the Criminal Justice Act 1991 the same release
procedures governed both mandatory life sentences passed on
adults, and sentences of detention during Her Majesty's pleasure
passed on juveniles. The same administrative procedures applied to
both categories, and once the tariff had elapsed not only a prisoner's dangerousness had to be considered, but also the acceptability of his release to the public, in order to maintain public
confidence in the criminal justice system.

The Court concluded that the central issue before it was whether
detention during Her Majesty's pleasure should be assimilated
under the case-law of the Convention to a mandatory or a discretionary sentence of life imprisonment. Noting that in its statutory
origins the expression 'during Her Majesty's pleasure' had a clearly
preventive purpose, and that the word 'life' was not mentioned in
the description of the sentence, the Court addressed itself to resolving whether the purpose of the sentence was such as to require that
the lawfulness of continued detention be examined by a court or
court-like body. Each of the applicants had been sentenced to be
detained during Her Majesty's pleasure because of their young

age. Their sentences contained a fixed punitive period and an indeterminate term of detention, which could only be justified by considerations based on the need to protect the public. These considerations, centred on an assessment of the applicants' character and mental state, had of necessity to take into account any developments in their personality and attitude as they grew older. Otherwise, the applicants would be treated as having forfeited their liberty for the rest of their lives; a situation which might give rise to questions under Article 3 of the Convention (inhuman punishment).

In its judgment[93] the Court found that the applicants' sentences after the expiry of their tariffs, were more comparable to discretionary life sentences than to mandatory life sentences in that new issues of lawfulness might arise in the course of detention (or re-detention after revocation of his life licence in the case of Singh), and the applicants were entitled under Article 5(4) to take proceedings to have these issues decided by a court or court-like body at reasonable intervals. Other than when constituted as Discretionary Lifer Panels for the purpose of reviewing the cases of discretionary life sentence prisoners under Section 34 of the Criminal Justice Act 1991, the Parole Board's lack of decision-making power did not satisfy the requirements of Article 5(4). That Article did not guarantee a right to judicial control of such scope as to empower a court or court-like body in considering all aspects of the case, including questions of expediency, to substitute its own discretion for that of the appropriate national decision-making body.[94] However, its review should be wide enough to bear on those conditions which, according to the Convention, are essential for the lawful detention of a person subject to a special type of deprivation of liberty. In a situation where a substantial term of imprisonment might be at stake, and where characteristics pertaining to the per-

---

[93] *Hussain* v. *United Kingdom* (55/1994/502/584) and *Singh* v. *United Kingdom* (56/1994/503/585). The unanimous judgment was read by the President of the Court on 21 Feb. 1996. The initial reports circulated by the Registrar of the Court, as cited here, are subject to revision before publication in the final form in the official *Reports and Judgments for 1996* (Carl. Heymanns Verlag, Cologne) and the EHRR series in the United Kingdom.

[94] The relationship between the European Court of Human Rights and the national decision-making bodies of the member states is a delicate one. When the Court has made a final ruling on a case it is up to the Committee of Ministers of the Council of Europe to supervise the execution of the judgment in accordance with Article 54 of the Convention.

sonality and level of maturity are of importance in deciding on a prisoner's dangerousness if released, Article 5(4) required an oral hearing in the context of an adversarial procedure involving legal representation and the possibility of calling and questioning witnesses. The Court decided that there had been a violation of Article 5(4) of the Convention in that neither applicant, after the expiry of the specified tariff period, had been able to bring the case of his continued detention during Her Majesty's pleasure before a court or similarly constituted body with the powers and procedural guarantees needed to satisfy that provision.

VII

Instrumental as the jurisprudence of the European Convention has been in inducing changes in public policy and administration throughout the United Kingdom,[95] the impact on life sentences has so far been limited to the decision-taking processes which determine the continued detention or release of offenders sentenced to indeterminate terms of imprisonment. The careful way in which the Commission and Court have closely adhered to the wording of Article 5(4) of the Convention has reflected an attitude derived from the insistence that recourse to the Strasbourg institutions should be a last, and not a first, resort: 'the last means of preventing or impairing an infringement of the rights of the individual.'[96] Until recently the English courts have had little opportunity to scrutinize the pervasive, but no more than lightly controlled, exercise of discretionary power in the hands of ministers. With strictly enforced discipline in the Commons, and the domination of ministers in the legislative process, the justification of parliamentary accountability had come to count for less and less. The emergence of judicial review has changed the picture significantly. The interface between the domestic courts and the European human rights institutions has been managed skilfully, on the whole steering clear of the chauvinistic displays of public hostility directed towards

---

[95] i.e. the three jurisdictions of England and Wales, Scotland, and Northern Ireland.

[96] European Court of Human Rights, *Speech delivered by Rolv Ryssdal, President of the Court, on the occasion of the first session of the year*, Cour. (94) 34, Council of Europe, Strasbourg, 1994, p. 2.

decisions of the European Commission at Brussels and the binding force of European Community law. But a decision by the Court of Human Rights in 1995, implemented by the Government only after protest, arising from the death of three members of an IRA active service unit who had been shot by the security forces before planting a bomb in Gibraltar, evoked a hostile response.

What of that other source of influence: informed or expert opinion, inside and outside Parliament? The events leading up to the establishment of a Select Committee of the House of Lords on Murder and Life Imprisonment in 1988 under the chairmanship of Lord Nathan are set out in the previous volume.[97] The evidence given to the Committee and the wide support which its subsequent report[98] received, were influential in the debates on the Criminal Justice Bill in both Houses in 1990–1, and contributed to the introduction of the new procedures governing discretionary life sentence prisoners. One of the most forthright critics of the involvement of ministers in the tariff setting process and the subsequent decisions was the then Lord Chief Justice, Lord Lane.[99] In his written evidence, later supplemented by oral evidence to the Select Committee, he declared: 'it is unsatisfactory, to say the least, that the length of a prisoner's stay in prison should be determined or partially determined behind the scenes by someone who has not heard any representations by or on behalf of the prisoner on grounds the prisoner does not know.'[100]

Soon after his retirement in 1992 Lane was invited by the Prison Reform Trust to chair an independent committee of inquiry to consider afresh the issues raised by the penalty for homicide in the light of the changes made in Part II of the Criminal Justice Act 1991. The invitation was accepted without hesitation, and a serving Lord Justice of Appeal, Sir Patrick Russell, agreed to join the Committee

[97] *Responses to Crime*, Vol. 2, pp. 330–7.

[98] House of Lords, Session 1988/9, *Report of the Select Committee on Murder and Life Imprisonment* (HL 78), Vol. 1: *Report and Appendices*, Vol. 2: *Oral Evidence, Part 1*, Vol. 3: *Oral Evidence, Part 2 and Written Evidence*; HMSO, London, 1989.

[99] Lord Chief Justice of England 1980–92; Judge of the High Court of Justice, Queen's Bench Division 1966–74; Lord Justice of Appeal 1974–9; Lord of Appeal in Ordinary 1979–80. Member of the Parole Board 1970–2 (Vice-Chairman, 1972). The Lord Chief Justice is the chief judge of the Queen's Bench Division of the High Court, which has criminal and civil jurisdiction in England and Wales. He ranks second to the Lord Chancellor in the judicial hierarchy.

[100] HL 78—II, *op. cit.*, p. 254.

at Lane's suggestion.[101] In commenting on the terms of reference Lane said that the mandatory life sentence was an anachronism that resulted in potential injustice. There was a need to ensure that sentencing of the most serious cases enjoyed the support of the public. The task was to draw up proposals which addressed the injustices and maintained the confidence of the public.

Throughout 1993 the Chairman was the most active member of the Committee and drafted much of the Report himself. Lane's personal stamp showed clearly in the opening paragraphs of the summary of conclusions printed at the start of the Report:

1. The mandatory life sentence for murder is founded on the assumption that murder is a crime of such unique heinousness that the offender forfeits for the rest of his existence his right to be set free.
2. That assumption is a fallacy. It arises from the divergence between the legal definition of murder and that which the lay public believes to be murder.
3. The common law definition of murder embraces a wide range of offences, some of which are truly heinous, some of which are not.
4. The majority of murder cases, though not those which receive most publicity, fall into the latter category.
5. It is logically and jurisprudentially wrong to require judges to sentence all categories of murderer in the same way, regardless of the particular circumstances of the case before them.
6. It is logically and constitutionally wrong to require the distinction between the various types of murder to be decided (and decided behind the scenes) by the Executive as is, generally speaking, the case at present.
7. Logically, jurisprudentially and constitutionally, the decision on punishment should be made in open court by the judge who passes sentence. He should be enabled to pass such sentence as is merited by the facts of the particular case, whether a hospital order, a determinate period of imprisonment or . . . life imprisonment.[102]

The Report referred to the 'unsavoury devices' that had been adopted to evade the difficulties posed by the mandatory life sentence. Manslaughter on grounds of diminished responsibility was the prime example. It was a device which was unpopular alike with

[101] The other members of the Committee were Sir Louis Blom-Cooper QC, Dr John Coker, David Faulkner, Edward Fitzgerald, Professor Terence Morris, Professor Elaine Murphy, Viscountess Runciman, and the author.

[102] Committee on the Penalty for Homicide, *Report*, Prison Reform Trust, London, 1993, p. 5.

the families of the victim and the psychiatrists who had 'the unhappy task of stating on oath their views on matters which are often on the fringe of their professional competence'. One of the considerations which had militated against change was a fear that the abolition of the mandatory sentence for murder would be regarded as a sign of weakness, of 'going soft on law and order', and of promoting the welfare of the criminal at the expense of the victim or potential victim. The Committee aimed to demonstrate that the opposite would be the case. A sentence of life imprisonment, if imposed at the discretion of the court, would have a meaning restored to it which was obscured at present. It would show that the offender had committed a crime of such heinousness that no finite term of imprisonment would be appropriate, or that the degree of risk of further serious offending was such that it was impossible to predict, from the standpoint of the safety of the public, when release would be justified.[103]

The Home Secretary, Michael Howard,[104] acknowledged receipt of an advance copy of the Report on 21 December 1993, saying that it dealt with very important matters about which strong views were held on both sides. He had no doubt that the public debate on the appropriate penalty for murder would continue, indeed the Report had generated great interest when it was published. His preliminary reaction was that he was not persuaded it would be right to remove the mandatory life sentence for murder, but that the Report deserved careful attention and he would respond more fully in due course.[105] A lengthy five-page letter addressed to Lord Lane, commenting on the conclusions one by one, followed on 23 May 1994. On the first seven conclusions, cited above, which had been widely reported in the press, the Home Secretary's reply indicated that public attitudes did indeed loom large in the thinking behind the Government's insistence that the mandatory life sentence be maintained:

These conclusions do not fully reflect the Government's view on the principle of providing a mandatory life sentence for murder. The Government regards murder as a *unique* offence and one which, as your report recog-

---

[103] *Committee on the Penalty for Homicide*, Report, Prison Reform Trust, London, 1993, pp. 5–6.

[104] Michael Howard had replaced Kenneth Clarke as Home Secretary in May 1993.

[105] Letter from the Home Secretary to Lord Lane, 21 Dec. 1993.

nises, has particular resonance among the public and significant implications for public confidence in the criminal justice system. There are of course different views about whether murder should be regarded as being of greater heinousness than other offences or as of unique heinousness. I cannot accept your judgement that the majority of murders, which are carried out by a murderer known to the victim in a fit of temper or a quarrel, are not 'truly heinous' but I accept that there is some strength in the argument that there are other appalling offences that can be committed, that do not result in death but which, in the particular circumstances in which they are committed are so serious that they must also be met by the most condign of punishments. It cannot be denied, however, that murder is unique in that it involves the deprivation of another person's life, with intent, at least, to cause them grievous harm. The taking of a person's life in such circumstances inevitably sets murder apart from any other offence and we should not be surprised that this is reflected in society's view of and reaction to such acts. It is on *this* basis that the Government believes it is right to mark the particular nature of the offence of murder with a mandatory sentence of life imprisonment and to provide in the case of murderers the particular safeguards afforded by the mandatory life sentence.

This does not mean that we do not recognise that the offence of murder covers a range of acts. As you know, the operation of the mandatory life sentence is in practice highly flexible. In considering the period to be served for retribution and deterrence the Home Secretary considers the advice of the trial judge and the Lord Chief Justice and the circumstances of the individual case. This procedure can lead to very different tariff periods being set in different cases. But the Government continues to believe for the reasons given above that offences of murder should be marked out by the imposition of the mandatory life sentence, and that the additional safeguards it affords should be provided . . .

Answering the criticism that it was wrong to allow the Home Secretary to decide on the period of time to be spent in prison to meet the needs of retribution and deterrence, Howard said:

I do not accept that it is constitutionally, or logically, wrong for the Home Secretary to take the final decision on the period to be served for retribution and deterrence in murder cases. Parliament has decided, for the reasons outlined above, that the punishment for the offence of murder should in all cases be a sentence of life imprisonment. That position has been tested by the domestic courts and is presently under consideration by the European Court of Human Rights. Parliament has also given the Home Secretary discretion to release a mandatory life sentence prisoner, subject to a requirement to have consulted the Lord Chief Justice and the trial judge where available and to have received a positive recommendation for release by the Parole Board.

As Home Secretary I am accountable to Parliament for ensuring that the public can have confidence in the criminal justice system. It is therefore entirely appropriate that I should have the final discretion to decide whether and if so when a murderer should be released from prison.

As far as making decisions 'behind the scenes' is concerned, as your report acknowledges, a great deal of progress has been made towards increased openness in all aspects of the operation of the mandatory life sentence including tariff setting for mandatory life sentence prisoners. Prisoners are now told and afforded opportunity to make representations on the judicial recommendation of the period they should serve for retribution and deterrence, as well as the Home Secretary's decision and any reasons for departing from that recommendation. That decision is, like any other, open to judicial review.

Although it contained nothing new, and rehearsed arguments that were to be repeated many times, the Home Secretary's reply was the fullest defence of the Government's position to date. The gist of it was repeated by the Minister of State in the Lords when amendments to the Criminal Justice and Public Order Bill were debated at the Committee and Report stages. Before then the Upper House had returned to the subject when a Private Member's Bill, introduced by Lord Ashley of Stoke, a former Labour MP, was debated on Second Reading on 8 February 1993. The only dissenting voice against the renewed attempt to give legislative effect to the Select Committee's recommendation that no court should be required to sentence a person convicted of murder to imprisonment for life came from the Government Front Bench.[106] With no more than a single objection, the later stages were completed and the Penalty for Murder Bill was passed and sent on to the House of Commons. No further progress was made, as is customarily the fate of Private Members' Bills. However, the arguments for reform had been restated and accepted by the Lords for a second time.

The Criminal Justice and Public Order Bill, which reached the Lords the following Spring, was a different matter altogether. It was a set-piece of Government policy which had been before the Commons for several months. Although amendments were pressed, with cross-bench and Conservative support, on a number of issues, secure training orders and the right of silence prominent amongst

[106] *Parl. Debates*, HL, 542 (5th ser.), cols. 479–504, 8 Feb. 1993.

them, the House had fought its battles and won important concessions from the Government on the Police and Magistrates Courts Bill earlier in the session. Because of its unreformed composition the Lords is generally cautious about resisting the will of the elected House too frequently, especially where confrontations concern crucial issues of Government policy. Ministers were not slow to point out to their supporters in both Houses that the mandatory penalty for murder was such an issue.

In the Commons no concerted cross-party effort had been made to amend the Bill in order to enact the proposals of the Lane Committee. When Lord Longford[107] raised the question in the Lords of the penalty for murder and the rights of life-sentence prisoners to a review of their sentence, during the Committee Stage on 23 May, there was a sense that the time was not right to press amendments to a vote. Apart from the Minister of State at the Home Office, Earl Ferrers, who replied, the other twelve speakers taking part in the debate had been unanimous in their endorsement of the reasoning and conclusions of the Select Committee and the Lane Committee. Two were former Law Lords,[108] and three spoke from the Government benches, two of them former members of Conservative Cabinets.[109] However, there was a realization that there was no possibility of the House of Commons or the Home Secretary accepting the change. The tone of pessimism caused one speaker from the Opposition Front Bench to hope that it might be the darkest hour before the dawn.[110]

Not long before, the Lords had debated the report of the Select Committee on Medical Ethics. The anguish of mercy killing had brought the penalty for murder and the perceived injustice of the mandatory life sentence within the purview of the Committee. The Committee came down against the creation of a separate offence of mercy killing, but strongly endorsed the recommendation of the previous Select Committee of the House that the mandatory life

---

[107] Veteran penal reformer and ex-Labour Minister. Chancellor of the Duchy of Lancaster 1947–8; Minister of Civil Aviation 1948–51; First Lord of the Admiralty 1951. Leader of the House of Lords 1964–8; Secretary of State for the Colonies 1965–6.

[108] Lord Simon of Glaisdale and Lord Ackner.

[109] Lord Carlisle of Bucklow and the author.

[110] Baroness Mallalieu QC, *Parl. Debates*, HL, 555 (5th ser.), col. 571, 23 May 1994.

sentence should be abolished.[111] At the conclusion of a debate on its Report in May 1994 the Chairman of the Select Committee, Lord Walton of Detchant, said he knew that the Lord Chancellor, who had spoken for the Government, would recognize that the comments he had made about the mandatory life sentence for murder in his speech had failed to persuade the House.[112] An editorial in the *Criminal Law Review* aptly remarked that the debate had 'turned into a contest between successive committee reports and an intransigent Government'.[113]

That there was no slackening of interest in the topic was shown by the decision of the Home Affairs Committee of the House of Commons to hold an inquiry into two issues relating to the crime of murder: the mandatory life sentence, and the 'year and a day' rule, in 1995. Lord Lane was once more in the forefront when, together with myself, he gave oral evidence at the opening session on 8 February.[114] The familiar arguments were repeated in reply to questions from members of what had the signs of being a Committee divided on party lines. Other witnesses followed from the Law Commission, the Penal Affairs Consortium, Victim Support, SAMM (Support After Murder and Manslaughter), the Association of Chief Police Officers, and the Police Federation. At the last session on 29 March 1995 the Home Secretary gave oral evidence, supported by Home Office officials.[115]

The Home Affairs Committee did not publish its Report on the main issue of the mandatory life sentence for murder until December, and then its recommendations contained a surprise. The Committee had a strong supporter of the Home Secretary's policies towards law and order in the chair, Sir Ivan Lawrence QC, and there was a majority of Conservative MPs in the composition of the

---

[111] *Report of the Select Committee on Medical Ethics* (HL 21–I), Session 1993/4, HMSO, London, p. 53.

[112] *Parl. Debates*, HL, 554 (5th ser.), col. 1412, 9 May 1994.

[113] [1994] Crim. L.R. 81.

[114] Home Affairs Committee, *Murder: Mandatory Life Sentences and the 'Year and a Day' Rule* (HC 214–II), Session 1994–95, HMSO, London, 1995, pp. 1–14. The volume contained the Minutes of Evidence and Memoranda of Evidence. In its Second Report entitled *Murder: the Year and a Day Rule* (HC 428) the Committee recommended the abolition of the common law rule that a person cannot be convicted of murder where death does not occur within a year and a day of the injury that caused it. In Dec. 1995 the Committee published its First Report on *Murder: The Mandatory Life Sentence* (HC 111), Session 1995–96.

[115] HC 214–II, pp. 60–71.

Committee. The tone of questioning at the public sessions when evidence had been given indicated an assumption, at least on the part of the Conservative members, that it was politically necessary to preserve the life sentence as the mandatory penalty for murder. Their concern with the public acceptability of the procedures surrounding it was reflected in a paragraph of the Report which stated: 'the major role given to the Home Secretary enables public opinion to be taken more clearly into consideration than does the alternative of leaving sentencing and release entirely to the judiciary and the Parole Board; . . . it allows for a greater degree of accountability for the decisions taken; and . . . it accordingly may give the public greater confidence in the criminal justice system.'[116]

In the next sentence, however, the Report recognized that this very feature, representing a strength to some, was regarded as a significant weakness by others who considered it to be wrong in principle.

The resolution of the dilemma advanced by the Committee was unorthodox. In what were described as preliminary conclusions the Committee recommended that the life sentence should be retained as the mandatory penalty for murder, but that the responsibility for setting the tariff and for taking decisions on release should be removed from the Home Secretary.[117] The procedures for assessing the danger to the public of releasing mandatory and discretionary life sentence prisoners should be aligned. The Committee was not aware of any direct evidence suggesting that Discretionary Lifer Panels had failed in their duty to protect the public from dangerous or unstable prisoners, and recommended that the Parole Board procedures for assessing the risk of releasing mandatory life sentence prisoners should follow the Discretionary Lifer Panel model.[118] The Committee had decided to solicit further evidence in writing on how to establish a system combining the retention of the mandatory sentence with the removal of the Home Secretary's role.[119] In May 1996, no insuperable practical difficulties having been identified, the Committee confirmed its preliminary conclusions.

---

[116] HC 111, p. xxvii.   [117] Ibid., pp. xxxv–vi.   [118] Ibid., p. xxxiv.

[119] Responding to an invitation from the Home Affairs Select Committee, I submitted a memorandum of further evidence on 22 Jan. 1996. With the addition of a short introduction, it was reproduced with only minor amendments in The *Criminal Law Review*. See Windlesham, 'Life Sentences: The Case for Assimilation' [1996] Crim. L.R. 250–4.

VIII

The eventual solution to such a long-running problem as the penalty for murder, and the way in which it is administered, will be a political one. The courts, the institutions at Strasbourg, the special interest groups, and much expert opinion will keep chipping away at what is fundamentally an unsound structure. Officials, whatever their personal views, must defend the policies of ministers. They have to be protective of ministerial power not for any reasons of principle, still less of sound administration, but for the simple reason that ministers believe that the general public reposes more confidence in their judgement on the release of prisoners convicted of murder than it does in a judicially constituted tribunal. The belief is based more on conjecture, or political instinct, than on any available evidence. The nearest analogy is the ending of exclusive executive control over the discharge of mental patients concerned in criminal proceedings and subject to restriction orders. Until 1983[120] the Home Secretary had the last word, but this power was successfully challenged in the European Court of Human Rights in *X* v. *United Kingdom*.[121] Unwelcome as it was to ministers at the time, the enhanced powers conferred on Mental Health Review Tribunals were implemented without uproar, or indeed any noticeable political embarrassment.[122]

The priority now is to persuade the last but most powerfully defended bastion in Parliament, the Government Front Bench in the Commons, of the merits of the argument and the need to make an effort to win over public opinion. The public acceptability criterion for release, as enunciated by Michael Howard,[123] should not

---

[120] The provisions in Schedule 1 of the Mental Health (Amendment) Act 1982, brought into effect on 30 Sept. 1983, were consolidated in the Mental Health Act 1983.

[121] (1982) 4 EHRR 188.

[122] Embarrassment from a different quarter was experienced when in an attempt to prevent the discharge of patients whom he regarded as dangerous, David Mellor, then a Home Office Junior Minister, prompted a Parliamentary Question from his own side of the Commons. *Parl. Debates*, HC, 84 (6th ser.), cols. WA 552–3, 30 Oct. 1985. In reply, he commented on the circumstances of an individual case, soon afterwards reinforcing his views by referring to another case in a press interview. The upshot was that he was summoned to appear and explain himself before the Council on Tribunals.

[123] In a policy statement by way of Written Answer to a Parliamentary Question in the House of Commons about how he would implement the House of Lords

be accepted as a barrier to an institutional reform supported by the large majority of those outside the Government who have familiarized themselves with the issue and comprehend the significance of what is at stake. The fact that popular opinion on the aptness of the mandatory life sentence for murder, irrespective of the circumstances, is not monolithic and indivisible was demonstrated by the cases of Dr Cox, Lee Clegg, and Sara Thornton, amongst others.

An alternative structure for release decisions exists and is working well. The Lords has twice agreed to legislation making life imprisonment the maximum rather than the mandatory penalty for murder. That policy gained the support of the Official Opposition in the Commons in the 1991 debates on the Criminal Justice Act of that year. A majority of the higher judiciary is in favour; three specialist committees have come to the same conclusion; as did the Law Commission in its evidence to the House of Lords Select Committee.[124] In 1993 a petition signed by over one hundred criminal justice practitioners was sent to the Home Secretary by the Bishop of Lincoln.[125] No less an authority than Kenneth Baker, who had defended the executive discretion of ministers so resolutely while Home Secretary in 1991, has since come round to the view that decisions on the length of time to be spent in custody by life sentence prisoners are 'essentially judicial, and better removed from the Home Secretary'. In his opinion, it is only a question of time before the system presently applicable to discretionary life prisoners is extended to the review of mandatory life sentence prisoners.[126]

judgment in the *Doody* case, the Home Secretary explained the way in which he used his discretion to release mandatory life sentence prisoners, and intended to do so in the future, in these terms: 'before any such prisoner is released on licence, I will consider not only (a) whether the period served by the prisoner is adequate to satisfy the requirements of retribution and deterrence and (b) whether it is safe to release the prisoner, but also (c) the public acceptability of early release. This means that I will exercise my discretion to release only if I am satisfied that to do so will not threaten the maintenance of public confidence in the system of criminal justice. *Parl. Debates*, HC, 229 (6th ser.), cols. WA 862–4, 27 July 1993. The introduction of a third phase, after punishment is complete and dangerousness no longer an issue, was criticized scathingly in the *Report* of the Committee on the Penalty for Homicide, *op. cit.*, p. 18.

[124] HL Paper 78–II, *op. cit.*, p. 170.

[125] In his capacity as Bishop to HM Prisons, the Rt. Rev. Robert Hardy wrote on 19 Apr. 1993 urging the Home Secretary to change the law in respect of mandatory life sentences and those awarded them.

[126] Kenneth Baker, *The Turbulent Years: My Life in Politics*, Faber, London, 1993, p. 433.

Once the final objective is achieved everything will fall into place. Life sentences for murder would become less frequent than they are now, being reserved for cases where there was a clear risk of repeat offending, or where the crime was so serious that no other sentence would suffice. Public opinion would recognize imprisonment for life as the most severe penalty permitted by law in a civilized state, appropriate for the gravest crimes committed by the most dangerous people. The artificial and relatively recent separation of mandatory and discretionary categories of offender, and the nomenclature, would disappear. The dual system, with its fearsome complexities, would be superseded. All life sentences would be passed at the discretion of the court and the Section 34 procedure would become standard. In very exceptional cases of murder, as with the existing non-murder offences, the trial judge would have the power not to apply Section 34.[127]

At the expiry of the tariff, or relevant part of the sentence, decisions on whether or not it is safe to release a life prisoner back into the community would be taken by a body independent of ministers with judicial characteristics. Continued detention after the expiry of the punitive period would be reviewed at regular intervals. New relationships between ministers and officials could be forged out of the contemporary Whitehall doctrines of functional devolution and delegation. The extent to which undisclosed political sensitivities on the part of ministers influence release decisions would be greatly diminished, if not completely eradicated. The resulting administrative procedures would enable the United Kingdom to conform more closely to the principles of natural justice reflected in the case-law of the European Convention. A sorry chapter in the history of English criminal law and its administration would be brought to an end.

[127] Lord Taylor CJ gave a Practice Direction in the Court of Appeal, Criminal Division, on 8 Feb. 1993 stating that although trial judges were not obliged by statute to make use of the provisions of Section 34 when passing a discretionary life sentence, they should do so save in the very exceptional case where the judge considers that the offence is so serious that detention for life is justified by the seriousness of the offence alone, irrespective of the risk to the public. [1993] 1 All ER 747. The wording closely follows the intention stated by Government spokesmen during the passage through Parliament of the amendment to the Criminal Justice Bill which became Section 34 of the Act. In effect there are currently three sorts of life sentences: mandatory life sentences; discretionary sentences to which trial judges choose to apply Section 34; and discretionary sentences to which Section 34 is not applied, or does not apply. See N. Padfield, (1993) 32 *Howard Journal of Criminal Justice*, 97.

Appendix D *Life Sentences: The Dual System 1995*

	Mandatory	Discretionary
Tariff ('Relevant Part') Setting	Known as tariff. Set by Home Office minister after consultation with trial judge and Lord Chief Justice. Prisoner is given opportunity to make representations.	Known as relevant part. Set by trial judge in open court. Length of relevant part can be appealed or referred by the Attorney General.
Timing of Reviews	First review 3 years before expiry of tariff. Subsequent reviews as set by Secretary of State taking into account Parole Board's recommendation.	First review 3 years before expiry of relevant part. Second review by DLP usually after expiry of tariff (in exceptional cases before). Subsequent reviews at 2-yearly intervals or earlier if Home Secretary so decides.
Review Procedures	Review by Parole Board panel. Dossier disclosed to prisoner. Interviewed by Parole Board member before panel considers case.	Review by DLP. Dossier disclosed to prisoner.
	Prisoner given opportunity to make written representations but does not attend panel. Outcome conveyed to prisoner in writing.	Prisoner can attend DLP hearing, be legally represented, and call witnesses. Written decision within 7 days of hearing.
Recommendations for Transfer to Open Conditions	Decision taken at ministerial level.	Decision taken at ministerial level.
Recommendations for Release	Decision taken personally by Home Secretary, following consultation with judiciary.	DLP have power to direct release.

	Mandatory	Discretionary
Recall	Decision taken at ministerial level, following a Parole Board recommendation. If not possible to consult Board, then case is referred to them as soon as possible after recall.	Decision taken at ministerial level, following a Parole Board recommendation. If not possible to consult Board, then case is referred to them as soon as possible after recall.
Representations following Recall	Prisoner has right to make representations against recall. Case then referred to Parole Board who may recommend immediate release. Such a recommendation is binding on the Home Secretary.	Prisoner has right to make representations against recall. Where he does so, case referred to DLP who may direct immediate release.
Review following Recall	Set by Secretary of State in light of Board's recommendation.	Statutory review 2 years after recall to prison unless Home Secretary decides earlier review is appropriate.

Source: Home Office memorandum of evidence submitted to the House of Commons Home Affairs Committee Inquiry into the mandatory life sentence for murder, 1995.

10

Criminal Appeals: An Orderly Reform

I

Acts of Parliament making changes in a branch of substantive law or administration are rarely attributable to a single source. More often the momentum needed to gain a place in the Government's legislative programme is generated from a multiplicity of sources. Yet in the session 1994–5 two legislative enactments altering component parts of the machinery of criminal justice could be so described. The first was the Criminal Appeal Bill announced by the Prime Minister at the start of the session on 16 November 1994[1] and published in February 1995. The second measure was the Criminal Injuries Compensation Bill, which is the subject of the next Chapter.

The origin of the legislation on criminal appeals can be dated with some precision. On 14 March 1991, after a hearing lasting for nine days, the Court of Appeal, Criminal Division, allowed the appeals against conviction of six men, known as the Birmingham Six, who had been convicted on twenty-one counts of murder following two bomb explosions in public houses in Birmingham in November 1974. Each of them had served over sixteen years of a mandatory life sentence in prison at the time of their release. In announcing the decision Lloyd LJ said that it had been taken in the light of fresh evidence which had become available since the previous hearing in the Court of Appeal, and that reasons would be given at a later date.[2] The same afternoon the Home Secretary, Kenneth Baker, came to the despatch box in the House of Commons to make a statement about the Government's response to the court's decision to quash the convictions of the six men. It was of fundamental importance, he declared, that the arrangements for criminal justice should secure the speedy conviction of the guilty

---

[1] *Parl. Debates*, HC, 250 (6th ser.), col. 33, 16 Nov. 1994.
[2] *R.* v. *McIlkenny and Others* (1991) 93 Cr. App. R. 287.

and the acquittal of the innocent. When that was not achieved, public confidence was undermined.[3] The Government fully recognized the seriousness of the issues raised by the outcome of the appeal and was resolved to see them properly addressed. A Royal Commission would be set up to review all stages of the criminal process. It would consider the investigation and pre-trial stages, as well as the role of expert witnesses and forensic scientists, and the reliability of scientific evidence.[4] The conduct of criminal trials, including the right of silence, and the duties and powers of the courts would be scrutinized.

Because of the evident failure of post-conviction remedies in the case of the Birmingham Six and other IRA-related incidents, emphasis was placed on the need for a thorough examination of appeal procedures and the investigation of alleged miscarriages of justice once appeal rights had been exhausted, including the functions carried out by the Home Secretary.[5] Replying to the comments made by by Roy Hattersley, the Opposition Home Affairs spokesman, Baker agreed that the present system, whereby he could refer a case back to the Court of Appeal for reconsideration, was not satisfactory.[6] The early indication that the Home Secretary did not seem inclined to cling to this discretionary power as tenaciously as to his control of life sentence prisoners was borne out when his successor, Kenneth Clarke, came to give evidence to the Royal Commission.

When Prime Minister, Margaret Thatcher did not approve of the recourse to a Royal Commission to review and make considered recommendations for changes in public policy. None had been established during her eleven-year premiership, and thirteen years separated the establishment of the Royal Commission on Criminal Justice in 1991 from its immediate predecessor, the Royal Commission on Criminal Procedure, which had been set up in 1978.[7] The fact that the subject-matter of the only two Royal Commissions over this lengthy period was so closely related underlined the political sensitivity of criminal justice and the desirability, when the opportunity allowed, to devise reforms on a non-party basis.

---

[3] *Parl. Debates*, HC, 187 (6th ser.), col. 1109, 14 Mar. 1991.

[4] Police malpractice and the unreliability of the scientific evidence were the two main grounds for setting aside the convictions of the Birmingham Six as both unsafe and unsatisfactory.

[5] *Parl. Debates*, HC, 187, *op. cit.*, col. 1110.   [6] Ibid., col. 1112.

[7] The recommendations of the Royal Commission on Criminal Procedure in 1981 (Cmnd. 8092) paved the way for the Police and Criminal Evidence Act 1984.

The choice of Lord Runciman as chairman came as a surprise, to him as well as to the informed public, but was generally well received. As a company chairman with unusually strong academic credentials he brought the qualities of practical experience, learning, and an open mind to the contentious issues of criminal justice.[8] He also had the advantage of being politically uncommitted. When the time came for Runciman to make his maiden speech in the House of Lords, in a debate to take note of the report of the Royal Commission, he did so from the cross-benches.[9] In some afterthoughts published in 1994 he said that the topic which he and his fellow Commissioners had found the most intellectually testing in the course of their far-reaching review was that of the grounds for further appeal after conviction where there might have been a miscarriage of justice.[10]

II

Law and executive discretion have been intermingled in successive attempts to find ways of rectifying the wrongful conviction of defendants accused of the more serious crimes in England and Wales. Before the novelty of a Court of Criminal Appeal in 1907, the Royal Prerogative of Mercy, exercised by the Home Secretary, provided an occasional remedy in the shape of a pardon for a convicted offender. But the procedure was arbitrary and uncertain in application, and the number of successful petitioners was strictly limited. If doubt was felt on a point of law the trial judge might reserve a case for further consideration by the Court of Crown Cases Reserved, established in 1848.[11] On findings of fact, however, upon which allegations of miscarriage of justice so often turn,

[8] Viscount Runciman of Doxford: Chairman, Walter Runciman plc, 1976–90; Andrew Weir and Co Ltd 1991–; President, General Council of British Shipping 1986–7. Fellow of Trinity College, Cambridge 1959–63 and 1971–; FBA 1975.

[9] *Parl. Debates*, HL, 549 (5th ser.), cols. 790–2, 26 Oct. 1993.

[10] *London Review of Books*, 10 Nov. 1994, pp. 7–11.

[11] The practice before and after 1848 is described in Sir William Holdsworth, *A History of English Law*, Vol. I, 7th edn., revised 1956, paperback edn. 1969, Methuen/Sweet and Maxwell, London, p. 217. See also 'Remedy by Appeal' in Sir L. Radzinowicz and R. Hood, *A History of English Criminal Law and its Administration from 1750*, Vol. 5, Stevens, London, 1986, and Clarendon Press, Oxford (paperback edn.), 1990, pp. 758–70. The paperback edition is titled 'The Emergence of Penal Policy in Victorian and Edwardian England'.

the verdict of the jury was supreme in deciding whether to convict or acquit. The justification was, and still is, that only the jury had seen the witnesses and the accused in the court, and heard the evidence and the arguments of counsel. At the conclusion of the trial the judge sums up the evidence and explains the law to the jury, but in contested cases it is they and not he who decide whether the defendant is guilty or not guilty of committing the offences charged.

The Act which established the Court of Criminal Appeal gave it power to set aside the verdict of the jury on the ground that it was unreasonable or could not be supported having regard to the evidence.[12] In 1966 the Court of Criminal Appeal ceased to exist[13] when its jurisdiction to hear appeals in criminal cases was transferred to the newly established Criminal Division of the Court of Appeal.[14] Practice remained unchanged, however, and the Court of Appeal, like its predecessor, was generally willing to quash a jury's verdict only when there was no evidence on which a reasonable jury properly directed could have convicted the defendant. Judicial doubts about the verdict were insufficient grounds for overturning it unless they could be supported by the presence of procedural defects. The doctrine was reiterated by Lloyd LJ giving the judgment of the Court of Appeal in the Birmingham Six case: 'Nothing in Section 2(1) of the Criminal Appeal Act 1968, or anywhere else, obliges or entitles us to say whether we think that the appellant is innocent. This is a point of great constitutional importance. The task of deciding whether a man is guilty falls on the jury. We are concerned solely with the question whether the verdict of the jury can stand.'[15]

[12] Criminal Appeal Act 1907, Section 4(1).

[13] An irreverent gloss on the origins of the unified Court of Appeal sitting in two separate divisions was provided by Lord Devlin, who had spent only a brief period in the Court of Appeal in 1960–1 on his way to the House of Lords from the High Court Bench: 'It was thought by some to be unseemly that criminal appeals should be determined by ordinary justices in the Court of Criminal Appeal, while civil appeals were heard by persons of superior rank, to wit, lords justices. The solution found was to abolish the existing court and create a new division of the Court of Appeal in which lords justices mingled with justices'. Patrick Devlin, *The Judge*, Oxford University Press, 1979, p. 151.

[14] Criminal Appeal Act 1966, Section 1(1) and (2). Two years later the Criminal Appeal Act 1968 consolidated certain enactments relating to appeals in criminal cases to the criminal division of the Court of Appeal, and thence to the House of Lords.

[15] *R* v. *McIlkenny and Others* (1991) 93 Cr. App. R. 287 at 311.

The right of a defendant to appeal against his conviction for an indictable offence tried in the Crown Court or its predecessors, which has existed since 1907, is circumscribed by two factors. First, he must obtain leave from a High Court judge who will need to be satisfied that there appears to be a serious question justifying examination by the Court of Appeal.[16] A large majority of applications fail at this stage. If leave is given the Court of Appeal, Criminal Division, will not rehear the witnesses who testified at the trial, and in most cases will refuse to consider the submission of fresh evidence. Under Section 2(1) of the Criminal Appeal Act 1968 an appeal against conviction would be allowed only if one or more of three specified criteria were met. These were: (a) that in all the circumstances of the case the conviction was unsafe or unsatisfactory; (b) that there was a wrong decision of any question of law; and (c) that there had been a material irregularity in the course of the trial. The majority of appeals were confined to ascertaining whether there had been procedural errors or misdirection by the judge in his summing up at the trial.[17]

There is also a right to appeal against the sentence imposed in the Crown Court. Until 1989 only the defence had the right to appeal against sentence. During the mid-1980s, however, public policy was shifting, and after several abortive attempts[18] a limited right to appeal against sentence was granted by Parliament to the prosecution in the Criminal Justice Act 1988. This took the form of enabling the Attorney General to refer a case, with leave, to the Court of Appeal if it appeared to him that the sentencing of a person in a proceeding in the Crown Court had been unduly lenient.[19] The qualification that the sentence passed by the Court should have been unduly lenient, and not merely lenient, was crucial, and the

[16] A small number of cases come directly to the Court of Appeal if the trial judge issues a certificate that the case is fit for appeal, or the appeal involves a question of law only, or it has been referred back to the Court by the Home Secretary.

[17] A research study for the Royal Commission on Criminal Justice analysed the first 300 appeals against conviction which were considered by the Court of Appeal in 1990. Of the cases received, just over one-third were allowed. Although the sample included a relatively wide range of different grounds of appeal, over 60 per cent were based on errors of the trial judge. These were also the most successful, as 43 per cent of such cases were allowed. *Research Study No. 17*, K. Malleson, 'Review of the Appeal Process', HMSO, London, 1993, pp. 7–8.

[18] See *Responses to Crime*, Vol. 1 (1987) pp. 17–19 and Vol. 2 (1993), pp. 20–7, 178–80.

[19] Criminal Justice Act 1988, Section 36(1).

Government's stated intention was that the power should be used sparingly.

The definition of what constitutes undue lenience has been considered by the Court of Appeal on a number of occasions, similarly from the standpoint of a restrictive approach.[20] An early interpretation by Lord Lane CJ in *Attorney-General's Reference No. 4 of 1989*[21] was that an unduly lenient sentence was one which fell 'outside the range of sentences which the judge, applying his mind to all the relevant factors, could reasonably consider appropriate'.[22] Lane said that even where it considered the sentence to be unduly lenient the Court of Appeal had a discretion as to whether to exercise its powers. Three years later his successor as Lord Chief Justice, Lord Taylor, went further. In *Attorney-General's Reference No. 15 of 1992*[23] he added, or made explicit, another test. Taylor said that the Court had to ask itself whether public confidence in criminal justice could be maintained if the public were aware of the circumstances of the case and the sentence which was passed. The inference was that the factor of public confidence was not to be left for politicians alone to decide.

Not surprisingly, in view of the changing penal climate and the disposition of the judiciary as well as the executive to take account of the anticipated public reaction, the prediction given by ministers to Parliament that no more than a dozen or so sentences would be referred in each year turned out to be too low. In the five-year period from 1 February 1989, when this part of the Criminal Justice Act 1988 came into effect, and 1 February 1994, a total of 140 references were made, of which 110 had reached the Court of Appeal.[24]

There is also a second tier of criminal appeals, to which much less attention is paid, and where the procedure is quite different. Following a conviction in the Magistrates' court, the accused has a right to appeal to the Crown Court, where all the evidence is heard

---

[20] S. Shute, *Prosecution Appeals Against Sentence: The First Five Years*, 57 MLR (1994) 745 contains a comprehensive review of the history of the prosecutorial right of appeal against unduly lenient sentences and its operation over the first five years, 1989–94. Stephen Shute is a Senior Lecturer in Law at the University of Birmingham.

[21] (1989) 11 Cr. App. R. (S.) 517.   [22] Ibid., at 521.

[23] (1993) 14 Cr. App. R. (S.) 324 at 327.

[24] Shute, *op. cit.*, 747. Of the remaining cases, sixteen were withdrawn by the Attorney General before being considered by the Court and fourteen were still outstanding.

and examined again and the prosecution once again has to prove the guilt of the accused.[25] It is an irony that the procedural rights of persons convicted of less serious offences are more favourable than the rights of those who may have been wrongly convicted of more serious indictable offences in the Crown Court. In 1994 the Crown Court dealt with 12,030 appeal cases from Magistrates' courts against conviction and 8,505 against sentence. Of these, 8,139 individual appellants had their appeal against conviction allowed and 3,946 had their sentence varied. The Criminal Division of the Court of Appeal heard 928 appeals from the Crown Court against conviction, of which 351 were allowed, and 2,027 appeals against sentence, of which 1,384 were allowed.[26]

The most difficult phase in any system of justice occurs when decisions have to be taken about what to do once post-conviction appeal rights are exhausted, but there are grounds for believing that there may have been a miscarriage of justice leading to a wrongful conviction. Separation of powers does not allow ministers to set aside the decisions of the courts, yet it is hard to see how appeals can be relaunched in the same court which has already heard and dismissed them, without undermining the finality of appeal procedures. The reconciliation contained in the Criminal Appeal Act 1968 was twofold. Under Section 7 the Court of Appeal had power to order a retrial if it appeared to the Court that the interests of justice so required, and if certain conditions relating to the offence for which the applicant is to be retried were fulfilled.[27] Under Section 17 of the same Act the Home Secretary had discretion to refer the case of a person convicted on indictment to the Court of Appeal. The case was then treated for all purposes as an appeal to the Court by that person.

The power to refer a case to the Court of Appeal for reconsideration did not extend to summary convictions in the Magistrates courts which had been upheld in the Crown Court, or not appealed

---

[25] J. Spencer, 'Criminal Procedure in England—A Summary of its Merits and Defects—the Outlines of the System', in M. Delmas-Marty (ed.), *The Criminal Process and Human Rights: Toward a European Consciousness*, Martinus Nijhoff Publishers, Dordrecht, 1995, pp. 74–5.

[26] Letter to the author from the Chief Executive of the Court Service, Michael Huebner, 23 Oct. 1995; published in the Official Report, *Parl. Debates*, HL, 566 (5th ser.), col. WA 108, 23 Oct. 1995.

[27] Sections 7 and 8 of the Criminal Appeal Act 1968 were amended by Section 43 of the Criminal Justice Act 1988.

against. In such cases the only remedy was a pardon under the Royal Prerogative of Mercy, recommended by the Home Secretary. The Royal Commission found that seventeen out of the total of nineteen free pardons granted in 1992 related to motoring offences, and two to convictions for failing to purchase a television licence.[28] The effect of a free pardon is to relieve a person so far as possible of all penalties and other consequences of the conviction. It does not expunge the finding of guilt. Recourse to the Royal Prerogative to override convictions on indictment in the Crown Court was 'extremely rare', being limited to cases where there were convincing reasons for believing that a person was innocent but where a reference to the Court of Appeal was not practicable, for example because relevant material was not admissible in evidence.[29]

The exercise of the Royal Prerogative is not confined solely to miscarriages of justice. It is also used very occasionally to grant special remission of all or part of a sentence of imprisonment, for example to reward prisoners who have given exceptional assistance to prison staff, the police, or the prosecution authorities. Relief of this kind is distinct from a free pardon, although both special remission and pardons result from discretionary decisions by the Home Secretary leading to the exercise of the Royal Prerogative by the Sovereign. Free pardon of a person convicted of an indictable offence does not automatically quash the conviction. What is imposed by the courts can be lifted only by the courts. The conviction stands unless and until it is quashed on a separate application to the Court of Appeal.[30]

The Home Secretary's ability to intervene in cases of alleged miscarriage of justice by making use of the power to refer a case to the Court of Appeal, either to obtain its opinion on a particular point or for further consideration of the whole case, has been limited more by custom than by statutory enactment. The wording of Section 17(1) of the 1968 Act was evidently intended to confer an unfettered discretion in stating that the Secretary of State may, at any time, refer the case of a person convicted on indictment to the Court of Appeal 'if he thinks fit' for either of these two purposes. Yet it became the established practice of successive Home Secretaries, and the officials who advised them, to treat the power

[28] The Royal Commission on Criminal Justice, *Report* (Cm. 2263), HMSO, London, 1993, p. 180, n. 3.

[29] Ibid., pp. 180–1.   [30] Ibid., p. 181.

to refer as an exceptional one, normally to be activated only when and if fresh considerations had come to light which were not before the court at the time of the trial.

In his second report on the *Maguire* case, published in December 1992, Sir John May, a retired Lord Justice of Appeal,[31] described the practice within the Home Office as operating within 'strict self-imposed limits', resting upon constitutional considerations.[32] These considerations were best expressed in evidence to his inquiry from an authoritative source. Douglas Hurd, by then the Foreign Secretary, had been away from the Home Office since October 1989 and was preoccupied with the demanding issues of foreign policy. However, as Home Secretary for the four preceding years he had been deeply involved in decisions on the handling of the cases of the Guildford Four, the Maguire family, and the Birmingham Six. In January 1987 he had decided to refer the case of the Birmingham Six back to the Court of Appeal, but not those of the Guildford Four or the Maguires which similarly turned on allegations of police malpractice and doubts over the validity of the scientific evidence. Shortly before he left the Home Office, Hurd had been responsible for appointing Sir John May to carry out a judicial inquiry into the circumstances surrounding the convictions of thirteen persons arising from a series of bomb attacks on public houses in Guildford and Woolwich in 1974. In the course of giving evidence to the subsequent inquiry he said:

a Home Secretary must never allow himself to forget that he is an elected politician, and that under our system the process of justice must be kept separate from the political process. It is open to others to say: 'If I were trying that case as a judge I would have given a different summing-up', or, 'If I had been on that jury I would have reached a different verdict', but it is not open to the Home Secretary simply to substitute his own view of the case for that of the courts. It would be an abuse of his powers if he were to act as though he or those who might advise him constituted some private court of law.

[31] Judge of the Queen's Bench Division of the High Court 1972–82; Lord Justice of Appeal 1982–9. Member of the Parole Board 1977–80 (Vice-Chairman 1980). Chairman: Inquiry into UK Prison Services 1978–9; University Commissioners 1989–95.
[32] Return to an Address of The Honourable The House of Commons dated 3 Dec. 1992 for a report of the inquiry into the circumstances surrounding the convictions arising out of the bomb attacks in Guildford and Woolwich in 1974 by Sir John May, *Second Report on the Maguire Case*, HC 296, HMSO, London, 1992, p. 49.

A different situation arises of course if new evidence or some new consideration of substance is produced, which was not available at the trial or
before the Court of Appeal. In any civilised system of justice there must be
a means whereby a case can be reopened so that new matters can be
assessed alongside the old evidence by due process of law. This distinction
between new evidence and differences of opinion about old evidence has
governed the way which my predecessors have used the power under section 17 of the 1968 Criminal Appeal Act to refer cases to the Court of
Appeal.[33]

As a novelist as well as a politician, Hurd had more of a feel for
the characters and events in contentious cases than most holders of
his office. He had shown himself to be no slave to Departmental
orthodoxy, yet his rationality led to his upholding the practice governing the reference to the Court of Appeal of cases of possible
miscarriage of justice which had been maintained by the Home
Office for many years. With hindsight, it is easy to ignore or belit-
tle the credibility of the conventional reasoning. It went like this.[34]
In exercising the power of reference conferred by Section 19 of the
Criminal Appeal Act 1907, and subsequent similar provisions, it
would have been wrong for Home Secretaries to have granted each
and every application for the exercise of that power. If some applications were granted but others refused, it was surely right for these
decisions to be reached in accordance with a criterion formulated
in general terms, so offering some guarantee against arbitrariness
or suspicion of favouring particular requests because of the support
they attracted rather than their intrinsic merits. There is plainly
room for argument over what the criterion should be; but the case
for the criterion actually adopted was cogently expressed by
Douglas Hurd in his evidence to the May Inquiry.

Once the requirement of new evidence, or some other consideration of substance which was not before the court of trial, was
shown to have obstructed for many years correction of the wrong-

---

[33] *Second Report on the Maguire Case*, HC 296, HMSO, London, 1992,
pp. 49–50. This extract repeats in part Hurd's statement in the House of Commons
on 20 Jan. 1987 explaining his decision to refer to the Court of Appeal the case of
the Birmingham Six, but not the Guildford Four or the Maguires. *Parl. Debates*,
HC, 108 (6th ser.), cols. 735–8, 20 Jan. 1987.

[34] The explanation that follows was provided by a retired senior civil servant with
long experience of the Criminal Policy Department at the Home Office. Although
slightly edited and abbreviated, the wording is unchanged. The exegis is one that
should be considered and weighed against the criticisms of the Home Office.

ful convictions of the Birmingham Six and Guildford Four it was no longer sustainable in its traditional form. It is reasonable to ask why the requirement was not modified earlier, when there was such strong pressure from eminent people for the cases to be sent for review. The trouble was that neither Home Office officials nor the eminent persons themselves could at that stage devise a better alternative. They seemed to be basing their arguments mainly on an 'intuition of innocence' which, however well founded in the cases in question, could hardly serve as the basis for the rational and consistent exercise of a statutory power.

May's conclusion was that neither the Court of Appeal, which lacked the necessary expertise to initiate let alone control investigations, nor the Home Office, was the right body to investigate alleged miscarriages of justice. He recommended that new independent machinery should be created to carry out the investigations and inquiries which the circumstances of a given case might call for. If, on completion of these investigations and inquiries, it appeared that a miscarriage of justice might have occurred, then the results should be referred back to the Court of Appeal. This recommendation was endorsed by the Royal Commission, to which May had been appointed as a member, after a thorough review of the appeal process supported by two research surveys designed to examine the practices of the Court of Appeal in order to determine how it interpreted and applied its powers.[35]

The fact that in his evidence to the Royal Commission the Home Secretary, Kenneth Clarke, had so readily acquiesced in the prospect of removing the Secretary of State's power to refer cases to the Court of Appeal under Section 17 of the Criminal Appeal Act 1968 and transferring it to a new body owed much to the strong lead that Hurd had given. In a letter to the author on 16 October 1995 Hurd paid tribute to the Home Office officials, and repeated his conviction that the power to refer was not an appropriate one for the Home Secretary:

I am sure that it is right to remove this particular responsibility from the Home Secretary for the reasons which I gave to Sir John May. The Home Secretary is particularly vulnerable as an elected politician to waves of opinion surging at his door. The team of Home Office officials dealing with

---

[35] Royal Commission on Criminal Justice, *Research Studies 17 and 18*: 'Review of the Appeal Process' and 'Information and Advice for Prisoners about Grounds for Appeal and the Appeals Process', HMSO, London, 1993.

this subject are dedicated and conscientious but I am clear in my own mind that these are not matters for a Government Department.

In the opinion of the Royal Commission it was neither necessary nor desirable that the Home Secretary should be directly responsible for investigating alleged miscarriages of justice as well as having ministerial responsibility for law and order and the police.[36] As their Report noted, the view that these responsibilities should be divided had been expressed by a former Home Secretary (Hurd) to Sir John May's Inquiry, and confirmed in oral evidence to the Royal Commission by the then Home Secretary (Clarke) and two of his predecessors (Roy Jenkins and Merlyn Rees).[37] Recommendations were made on how the proposed Criminal Cases Review Authority should consider the allegations put to it; what its relationship should be with the Government and the Court of Appeal; the composition and accountability of the new Authority; how it should select cases for further investigation; and what investigatory powers it would need.[38] It did not, however, formulate an alternative criterion for referring cases to the Court of Appeal, leaving the new Authority to devise its own rules and procedures.

III

The Home Office had been the focal point for formal complaints of miscarriage of justice throughout the twentieth century. Such complaints were not infrequent. The Royal Commission ascertained that in the early 1990s between 700 and 800 cases a year were received which were no longer before the courts and where it was claimed that there had been a wrongful conviction.[39] The rigorous nature of the sifting process was shown by the very small number of cases, between three and sixteen a year in 1989–95, which led to a reference to the Court of Appeal under Section 17. Moreover, these years were exceptional as they included the reference of several cases with more than one defendant arising out of the terrorist incidents of the early 1970s and the dubious practices of the

---

[36] Royal Commission on Criminal Justice, *Report*, Ibid., p. 182.

[37] Roy Jenkins was Home Secretary in the Labour Governments between 1965–7 and 1974–6. Merlyn Rees was Home Secretary in 1976–9.

[38] Royal Commission on Criminal Justice, *Report*, Ibid., pp. 182–6.

[39] Ibid., p. 181.

West Midlands Police Serious Crime Squad. The activities of this unit had given rise to ninety-one complaints about beatings, fabrication of evidence, and denial of access to lawyers before it was disbanded in 1989.[40] The statistical pattern of references over a seven-year period is shown in Table 12.

TABLE 12. *References to the Court of Appeal under Section 17(1)(a) of the Criminal Appeal Act 1968, 1989–95*

Year	Number of representations	Cases referred and number of defendants	Outcomes	
			Allowed	Dismissed
1989	568	3 (6)	3 (6)	nil
1990	731	7 (20)	7 (20)	nil
1991	714	10 (12)	10[a] (12)	nil
1992	763	8 (11)	5 (8)	3 (3)
1993	670	8 (9)[b]	4 (5)	2 (2)
1994	480	9 (12)[c]	4 (4)	nil
1995 (to Oct.)	529	18 (20)[d]	nil	nil

[a] Court ordered a retrial in one case: defendant later acquitted.
[b] 2 still outstanding at year end 1995.
[c] 5 (8) still outstanding.
[d] 18 (20) outstanding.

Source: Home Office.[41]

The discretion vested in the Home Secretary to recommend the exercise of the Royal Prerogative of Mercy, or to refer a case tried on indictment to the Court of Appeal, meant that the Division within the Criminal Policy Department of the Home Office, designated as C3, came to exercise a dominion over the entire range of alleged miscarriages of justice, great or small. The Division later assumed the additional responsibility for handling claims for financial compensation for wrongful conviction and establishing whether they met the criteria for eligibility contained in Section 133 of the Criminal Justice Act 1988.[42]

[40] C. Walker in C. Walker and K. Starmer (eds.), *Justice in Error*, Blackstone Press, London, 1993, pp. 10–11.
[41] *Parl. Debates*, HL, 566 (5th ser.), col. WA 105, 23 Oct. 1995, updated with additional data from the Home Office Research and Statistics Department.
[42] Section 133 provided that when certain conditions had been fulfilled,

The performance of C3 in advising the Home Secretary and in filtering the cases brought to his notice seldom escaped critical attention. The process was regarded externally as being remote and impersonal, insensitive, and rule-bound. Closer inspection revealed an organizational system characterized by a number of conflicting forces. The stated aim, as elsewhere in the Home Office, was to secure individuals' rights and freedoms under the law and to provide for the protection and security of the public.[43] However, the zeal with which this worthy ideal was pursued was inhibited by a deeply engrained culture, as well as by practical considerations. Although the correction of miscarriages of justice, depending as it did entirely before 1907 and in part since on the exercise of the Royal Prerogative of Mercy, was one of the traditional functions of the Home Office, in more recent times officials came to recognize that they lacked both the expertise and resources to make thorough investigations. The costs, which could be substantial, were normally met from its existing budget by the police force which had originally handled the case. It might be asked for further particulars or, at a later stage, to carry out a more detailed investigation. This request could be unwelcome to the police, and forces varied in their readiness to co-operate. The most serious allegations, including some arising out of the IRA's bombing campaign on the mainland, were referred to a separate police force for investigation, on occasion leading to misunderstandings as to where responsibility for meeting the consequential expenditure would lie.

In 1995 the culture of the Home Office was subjected to an internal appraisal which pulled no punches. While acknowledging the integrity of the staff, a Senior Management Review stated bluntly that the Home Office was seen as 'inward-looking, resistant to new ideas, too negative in its orientation, slow to deliver, remote from its services and insufficiently driven by outcomes or needs of client groups'.[44] The ability to meet the needs of client groups, in the managerial jargon used in the Management Review as elsewhere in

compensation should be paid to a person convicted of a criminal offence who had suffered punishment and whose conviction had subsequently been reversed, or who had been pardoned on the ground that a new or newly discovered fact showed beyond reasonable doubt that there had been a miscarriage of justice. The provision extended to Scotland as well as to England and Wales.

[43] Home Office, *The Government's Expenditure Plans 1995–96 to 1997–98 for the Home Office and the Charity Commission* (Cm. 2808), HMSO, London, 1995, p. 14.
[44] *The Times*, 22 June 1995.

Whitehall, was inhibited by the allocation of resources of staff and money. Although the conflict between needs and resources was not peculiar to C3, it nevertheless provides an insight into the self-imposed limits on the number of cases investigated, which was commented on by Sir John May, and the essentially reactive role which had become the accepted norm. For the purposes of public presentation a more convincing and defensible policy than what some of its critics had stigmatized as the rationing of resources to control demand was called for, and one which would withstand public and parliamentary scrutiny. Thus it was not just constitutional principle which lay behind the policy that the Home Secretary would normally only refer a conviction if there was new evidence or some other consideration of substance which was not before the trial court. As so often, fine sounding justifications based on principle, however sincere, do not always tell the whole story.

Prisoners are not well placed to prepare petitions which will catch the eye of Home Office officials. Prison libraries are supposed to contain basic texts on criminal law and procedure, as well as information about legal aid. However, research carried out for the Royal Commission found that only in few prisons was such material openly available to inmates.[45] This is contrary to the terms of a Circular Instruction listing the publications which should be included in all prison establishment libraries: it states that the publications should be 'readily available on open shelves to inmates'.[46] Where this is impracticable due to lack of space, a list should be prominently displayed in the library with a clear indication of how inmates may gain access to the publications.[47] Lay advice may be forthcoming from prison visitors, probation officers, or chaplains, and legal advice from defending solicitors who may continue to take an active interest in a case even after a conviction and unsuccessful appeal. The fact that the general standard of literacy amongst the prison population is low, with a sizeable group of inmates speaking no or only limited English, means that many petitions are incoherent and poorly presented and do not encourage further investigation.[48] Members of Parliament may take up pris-

---

[45] *Research Study No. 18, op. cit.*, p. 101.

[46] HM Prison Service, 'Prison Libraries: Provision of Certain Publications', C.I. 20/1992, para. 1.

[47] Ibid., para. 4.

[48] M. Mansfield and N. Taylor, 'Post-Conviction Procedures' in C. Walker and K. Starmer (eds.), *Justice in Error, op. cit.*, p. 164. Michael Mansfield QC is a

oners' grievances from time to time, but with a few notable exceptions they more often make non-committal inquiries on behalf of constituents than determined attempts to remedy possible injustices.

Dissatisfaction with Home Office practice was long-standing. In 1878, well before the Criminal Appeal Act 1907, in one of his less remembered novels, Anthony Trollope described the frustration of the father of a man unjustly convicted of bigamy in these terms:

. . . the letters from the (father) were long and well argued, whereas the replies, which always came by return of post, were short and altogether formal. Some assistant under-secretary would sign his name at the end of three lines, in which the correspondent was informed that as soon as the matter was settled the result would be communicated.

Who does not know the sense of aggravated injustice which comes upon a sufferer when redress for an acknowledged evil is delayed? The wronged one feels that the whole world must be out of joint in that all the world does not rise up in indignation.[49]

Although prompt replies are no more than a faint memory, the rest of the passage remained an apt comment more than a century after it was written. What had changed was the emergence of the mass media as a powerful agency in support of campaigns challenging disputed verdicts. The print media can promote a relatively high level of public interest for a time, but they rely on new developments and the activities of sympathetic family members, or well known personalities, to initiate reportable events if they are to maintain the pressure over a long haul. In terms of direct persuasion, the most effective influences on decision makers are thoroughly researched books and investigative television programmes, and the intervention of prominent public figures.

The cases of the Maguires and later of the Guildford Four were first taken up with ministers by the Archbishop of Westminster, Cardinal Hume, in 1979. Over the next decade he persisted in his representations, being joined in due course by two of the most esteemed of all judges, Lords Scarman and Devlin, as well as two former Home Secretaries. Roy Jenkins had been at the Home Office

leading criminal practitioner at the Bar who represented the Birmingham Six when their conviction was quashed by the Court of Appeal in 1991.

[49] *John Caldigate*, Oxford University Press, World's Classics edn., 1946, p. 545. The novel originally appeared in *Blackwood's Magazine*, April 1878–June 1879, and was published in three volumes in 1879.

at the time of the Guildford bombings, and Merlyn Rees was the Home Secretary with whom Hume had first raised his doubts about the validity of the convictions. Together with other documents, the Cardinal's exchange of correspondence with the Prime Minister, Margaret Thatcher, is printed in full in the *Second Report on the Maguire Case*.[50] The extracts from correspondence with ministers and submissions by officials constitute an unusually informative archive on the way in which consistent pressure can be brought to bear on ministerial decisions behind the scenes.[51] On the day that the convictions of the Birmingham Six were quashed by the Court of Appeal, Lord Jenkins of Hillhead, by then Leader of the Liberal Democrat peers, told the Lords he was convinced that without 'the dedicated conviction and moral authority of Cardinal Hume' it was very doubtful whether the miscarriages of justice would ever have been corrected. That was a disturbing thought.[52]

Jenkins also remarked that he had for some years been worried that the climate of the time had led to a range of unsafe convictions on a scale which could deal a grave blow to confidence in the judicial system.[53] To relate this comment to the failure of the review procedures, it should be noted that the restrictive attitudes which characterized the formal system for investigating possible miscarriages of justice were well entrenched before the outbreak of IRA-related bombings and other indiscriminate acts of organized violence in mainland Britain during the 1970s. The effect of these appalling incidents on public opinion was profound. The police came under intense pressure to find and arrest the perpetrators, as did the prosecution to bring them to trial and successful conviction.

Not for the first time in penal history, the sequence of events which subsequently unfolded was to bear out the truth of the maxim that the more horrific the incident, the greater the chance of a miscarriage of justice occurring. The existing procedures, designed to rectify wrongful convictions of individual defendants, were not suited to, and could not function adequately in the face

---

[50] *Op. cit.*, pp. 65–6.

[51] It is standing Whitehall policy to refuse to disclose the advice given to ministers by officials. The exceptional circumstances of Sir John May's judicial inquiry enabled him to see, and to obtain permission to publish in his report to the House of Commons (HC 296), submissions prepared by C3 for the Home Secretary, internal memoranda from the Forensic Science Service, letters to and from ministers, and notes of ministerial meetings.

[52] *Parl. Debates*, HL, 527 (5th ser.), col. 313, 14 Mar. 1991.   [53] Ibid.

of, organized mass terrorism. In retrospect, the factors which contributed to the enhanced likelihood of miscarriages can be clearly identified. They were: public outrage and lack of sympathy for the political cause; the frequency and severity of the incidents, many of them resulting in random casualties; and the particular difficulties in investigating such cases and bringing suspects before the courts.

IV

The bulwark upon which the Home Office relied to stem the tide of petitions was the requirement for the presence of significant new factors or considerations of substance, casting doubt on the rightness of the conviction, and which had not previously been before the courts.[54] Yet when the Royal Commission subjected this test to independent scrutiny the primacy accorded to the fresh evidence requirement did not survive. Although evidence and procedure could be seen as distinct features of a criminal trial, in practice the Court of Appeal sometimes fastened on procedural defects as a means of legitimating evidential unease.[55] The Commission urged that the Court should take a broad rather than a narrow approach in considering some awkward evidential questions. These included whether the evidence later adduced was available at the time of the trial; if so, whether there was a reasonable explanation for the failure to adduce it; the standard of credibility that should be adopted; what to do when a witness wished to change the evidence he gave at trial; and the allowance to be made for the competence of counsel in deciding on what evidence to call.[56]

Cutting through all the complexities, the main findings of the Royal Commission were straightforward. The Home Secretary's power to refer cases to the Court of Appeal under Section 17 of the Criminal Appeal Act 1968 should be removed. Allegations of miscarriage should be investigated by a body independent of both central government and the court structure. Where there were reasons for supposing that a miscarriage of justice might have occurred, the case should be referred by that body to the Court of Appeal.[57] The

---

[54] See the Prime Minister's reply to Cardinal Hume, 4 Aug. 1984, *op. cit.*, p. 66.

[55] Runciman, *London Review of Books*, 10 Nov. 1994, p. 8.

[56] Royal Commission on Criminal Justice, *Report, op. cit.*, p. 174.

[57] Ibid., pp. 182–3, and Recommendations 331 and 332 on p. 217.

overlapping and confusing grounds for appeal contained in Section 2(1) of the Criminal Appeal Act 1968 should be replaced by a single broad ground which would give the court flexibility to consider all categories of appeal. The question for the court to decide was whether a conviction 'is or may be unsafe'.[58]

The Royal Commission made 352 recommendations in its Report published in July 1993. The Home Secretary, Michael Howard, initially accepted around thirty of them in a speech at the Conservative Party Conference in October, including the setting up of a Criminal Cases Review Authority.[59] It was the sole gesture in the direction of penal reform in what was otherwise an overtly punitive speech. Yet despite the fact that the Home Office had several months to cogitate on how to implement one of the most conspicuous, widely forecast, and least controversial of the Commission's proposals, the Government strenuously resisted early legislation. The opportunity was there since a major bill on criminal justice and public order was in the final stages of preparation and was announced as a main plank of the Government's legislative programme in the Queen's Speech in November 1993. Ministers insisted, however, that while the Royal Commission's recommendation was acceptable in principle, no detailed scheme had been worked out and that further consideration was necessary before legislation could be brought forward.[60]

In introducing a debate on the Royal Commission's proposals in the House of Lords in October 1993, I argued that early action on the setting up of an independent review body to investigate alleged miscarriages of justice had an importance that transcended its function. It would be a touchstone of the Government's willingness to legislate at the earliest possible moment to atone for one of the blackest episodes in the modern history of English criminal law and its administration.[61] However, the sense of urgency which had

[58] Ibid. Recommendation 317 on p. 215 represented the view of a majority of the Commission's membership. A minority, led by Professor Michael Zander, wished to go further and give the Court of Appeal the power to order a retrial where there had been an error of law or procedure at the original trial, even though the defect could not be said to have made the verdict unsafe. Ibid., p. 233.

[59] *Conservative Party News*, 400/93. Extract from a speech by the Rt. Hon. Michael Howard QC, MP at the 110th Conservative Party Conference at Blackpool, 6 Oct. 1993, p. 9. The body corporate later established by Section 8 of the Criminal Appeal Act 1995 was named as the Criminal Cases Review Commission.

[60] *Parl. Debates*, HL, 549 (5th ser.), col. 783, 26 Oct. 1993.

[61] *Parl. Debates*, ibid., col. 781.

accompanied the setting up of the Royal Commission two and a half years earlier had dissipated. The climate of opinion had changed once more. The dramatic decline in confidence in the police and the legal system had been superseded by an atmosphere of near panic about the failure to prevent crime and to catch, convict, and punish criminals. As was pointed out in the debate, both of these contrasting concerns were valid.[62] Only when a higher proportion of the guilty are brought to justice and convicted, and wrongful convictions are thoroughly investigated and speedily corrected, will the system of criminal justice command respect.

The next step was the publication by the Home Office on 25 March 1994 of a discussion paper.[63] While accepting the main thrust of the Royal Commission's recommendations, the paper went further in outlining two additional proposals. In a statement on the same day Howard pointed out that his existing power to refer cases to the Court of Appeal included grounds of sentence as well as conviction.[64] It was proposed that a similar power should be available to the Criminal Cases Review Authority where there were doubts about the technical validity of the sentence, or where material not previously available to the court suggested that the sentence might have been based on substantially wrong information. The power would not be available for appeal against unduly lenient sentences, which would continue to be a matter for the Attorney General.

New arrangements were also envisaged for rectifying wrongful convictions in summary cases heard in the Magistrates' courts.[65] The current situation was that once existing appeal procedures had been exhausted, errors in summary cases could be corrected only by the exercise of the Royal Prerogative of Mercy. The Govern-

---

[62] Lord Alexander of Weedon QC, ibid., col. 792.

[63] Home Office, *Criminal Appeals and the Establishment of a Criminal Cases Review Authority: a Discussion Paper*, 1994.

[64] Home Office, *Press Release*, 63/94, 25 Mar. 1994. There was about one reference a year on grounds relating to sentence, normally on the basis that the sentence passed by the Crown Court and upheld on appeal may have been *ultra vires*, or on the ground that the sentence may have been based on substantially wrong factual information. Home Office, *Discussion Paper, op. cit.*, para. 30.

[65] In 1994 the Home Office was receiving approximately 100 representations a year about summary convictions. They ranged from cases which required significant investigation to others (the majority) in which the only question to be answered was whether late evidence supporting the defendant's case (e.g. a vehicle insurance document) was what it purported to be. Ibid., para. 33.

ment proposed that the Authority should have power to investigate such cases and refer them to the appropriate court for review. A procedure would be developed to allow summary cases which did not require investigation to be reviewed in the Magistrates' courts.[66] Both sets of proposals were included in the Bill when it was published, and in due course became law. The legislation applied in Northern Ireland as well as England and Wales, but not in Scotland.

One manifestation of wishful thinking did not survive. In its deliberations the Royal Commission had persuaded itself that the decisions of the Authority to investigate or not to investigate the cases put to it, and to refer or not to refer them to the Court of Appeal, should be placed beyond reach of judicial review.[67] Recommendation 340 stated unambiguously: 'There should be neither a right of appeal nor a right to judicial review in relation to decisions reached by the Authority.'[68] It was a goal that others had dreamed of, but which had hitherto proved unattainable. Despite the periodic frustrations of ministers and civil servants at having their actions found unlawful, and declarations made accordingly in the High Court, no statutory formula had been devised to make legislation judge-proof. Parliamentary efforts to curb or prevent judicial review had a long history: 'Ever since Coke, Holt and Mansfield laid the first foundations for judicial review the legislature has attempted to prevent those principles from being applied. Various formulae have been inserted into legislation with the intent of precluding judicial intervention. Little success has attended these efforts as the courts have time and again restrictively construed the legislation.'[69]

The Royal Commission offered no explanation for its recommendation that the decisions of the Criminal Cases Review

---

[66] The Government proposed a procedure for quashing erroneous convictions based on simple verification. An application would be made to the convicting Magistrates' court supported by the new evidence, and the Crown would be given an opportunity to indicate whether it wished to contest the application. If it did not wish to do so the Magistrates would be invited to quash the conviction. If the Crown disputed the new evidence there could be a trial before the Magistrates if the defendant had pleaded guilty originally, or a review in the Crown Court if there had been a summary trial. Ibid., para. 36.

[67] Royal Commission on Criminal Justice, *Report, op.cit.*, p. 184.

[68] Ibid., p. 218.

[69] P. P. Craig, *Administrative Law*, 3rd edn., Sweet and Maxwell, London, 1994, p. 600. Chapter 16 discusses the attempts to exclude or limit judicial review.

Authority should be exempt from judicial review. If an error of law had occurred it is hard to see why a decision of the Authority should not be examined by the courts so that it was not left unchecked. Similarly, if the Authority used its powers improperly, or failed to observe the requirements of rationality or procedural fairness, then consistency with decisions taken by other public bodies or officials (e.g. the Parliamentary Commissioner for Administration[70]) required that its actions should be subject to the same degree of judicial control.

The proposal perished at an early stage and was never presented to Parliament, and so the ingenuity of the draftsman was not put to the test. The only reference to judicial review in the Commons Second Reading debate on the Criminal Appeal Bill came in the winding up speech from the Government Front Bench when the Minister of State, David Maclean, virtuously declared: 'There will be no right of appeal as such from the Commission's decisions, but those decisions will be subject to the possibility of judicial review, as is proper in cases where liberty and livelihood may be at stake.'[71]

V

Although Taylor had endorsed the Government's contention that more time was needed for consultation and the preparation of legislation than would have been possible if new appeal provisions had been included in the Criminal Justice and Public Order Bill on its introduction in December 1993, the Lord Chief Justice became increasingly restive as it appeared that ministers were reluctant to commit themselves to legislating in the 1994–5 parliamentary session either. In the event, the Criminal Appeal Bill did not feature in the Queen's Speech in November 1994, sixteen months after publication of the Royal Commission's Report. It was rescued, however, by the omission at a late stage of another and larger proposal, the planned privatization of the Royal Mail. This left space in the legislative programme for the addition of a number of smaller and

---

[70] Colloquially known as the Ombudsman. For a discussion of the Parliamentary Commissioner's powers and matters excluded from his jurisdiction, e.g. the investigation of crime, the exercise of the prerogative of mercy, and the protection of national security, see Craig, ibid., pp. 127–41.

[71] *Parl. Debates*, HC, 256 (6th ser.), col. 108, 6 Mar. 1995.

less controversial measures. One of these was criminal appeals. In the course of his speech in the Debate on the Address the Prime Minister said that the Government intended to introduce a bill, following its acceptance of the Royal Commission's recommendation, that a new body should be set up to consider possible cases of miscarriage of justice.[72]

During the Home Affairs and Environment day of the Debate on the Address, the Home Secretary gave a brief outline of the forthcoming legislation and expressed the hope that it would be carried through with all-party support.[73] The Opposition Front Bench Spokesman, Jack Straw, welcomed the intention to legislate which reflected long-standing Labour policy to establish an independent review authority. The Opposition had backed a Home Affairs Select Committee Report in 1982, and produced its own detailed report in 1990.[74] The replacement of Home Office officials and ministerial discretion by the proposed new body was a major step forward. Of itself, however, it would not be a magic wand. How it operated, whether it would be seen as independent, and what powers it exercised would be of critical importance. While indicating that the Opposition would co-operate in the passage of the Bill, Straw forecast what was to become one of the few strongly argued points of difference: the arrangements for the supervision and execution of investigations into alleged miscarriages. In the judgement of the Opposition, he said, there would be cases in which it was essential for public confidence that such investigations should be independent of the police.[75]

The Bill was published in February and received an unopposed Second Reading in the House of Commons on 6 March 1995. Howard made no apology for 'refusing to rush into legislation'.[76] It contained, he claimed, the most significant changes to the structure of the criminal appeal system for almost thirty years. He and the Secretary of State for Northern Ireland had thought it right and necessary to consult in detail about the proposals, and had benefited greatly from the opinions and advice of many who worked in the criminal justice system and beyond.[77] The Bill was in three main parts. Part I clarified and strengthened the powers of the respective

---

[72] *Parl. Debates*, HC, 250 (6th ser.), col. 33, 16 Nov. 1994.
[73] *Parl. Debates*, HC, 250 (6th ser.), col. 238, 18 Nov. 1994.
[74] Ibid., col. 252.
[75] Ibid., col. 253.
[76] *Parl. Debates*, HC, 256 *op. cit.* col. 23, 6 Mar. 1995.
[77] Ibid.

Courts of Appeal in England and Wales and in Northern Ireland; Part II established a new Criminal Cases Review Commission (rather than Authority, the term used by the Royal Commission) setting out its functions and powers; and Part III extended the powers of the Magistrates' courts to reopen cases to rectify mistakes.

The emphasis in Straw's speech, echoed by other MPs, was directed towards the provision that whereas the new statutory commission would have the responsibility of determining the main lines of inquiry and of supervising the investigations, the actual work of investigation would be carried out by operational police officers. The investigating officers would be appointed at the discretion of the Criminal Cases Review Commission, either from the police force initially responsible for investigating the crime or from another force. The Commission would not have its own central investigatory unit. In the opinion of the Government, relying on the Runciman Commission's conclusion, there was 'no practicable alternative to the police carrying out the investigations'[78], given the size and scope of the inquiries which sometimes had to be made and the resources and expertise required. To the critics, this scheme of things was too close to previous Home Office practice, and would suffer from the same handicap as the Police Complaints Authority which had been drawn on as a model. Despite the dedication and commitment of that Authority's staff and members, to which Straw paid tribute, the unpalatable truth was that public confidence had not been earned because of a deep-rooted suspicion that justice would not be done when the police were investigating themselves.[79]

To Chris Mullin,[80] the Labour MP who had campaigned so persistently, and ultimately effectively, for the release of the Birmingham Six, the failure to incorporate an independent element in the investigatory process was potentially 'a fatal flaw' in the new arrangements. His extensive experience of police inquiries, of which he gave the House a sample, caused him to reject the Royal Commission's 'rather reluctant conclusion' that there was no practicable alternative.[81] At the least, he urged that the new statutory

---

[78] Royal Commission on Criminal Justice, *Report, op. cit.*, p. 186.

[79] *Parl. Debates*, HC, 256 (6th ser.), col. 33, 6 Mar. 1995.

[80] MP for Sunderland South 1987–. Journalist and author of *Error of Judgement: the Birmingham Bombings*, Chatto and Windus, London, 1986; revised edn. 1990. Editor, *Tribune*, 1982–4.

[81] *Parl. Debates*, HC, 256 (6th ser.), col. 47, 6 Mar. 1995.

Commission should have a reserve power which would enable it to order investigations by people who were not police officers if it appeared that the police were not trying hard enough. He cited in support a letter from Cardinal Hume, published in *The Times* that day, which suggested that the powers available for the Commission to direct and supervise inquiries were unduly limited.[82]

The doubts continued to be expressed throughout the Bill's passage through Parliament, but the Government remained adamant. Its stand was essentially pragmatic: that only the police had the necessary skills and resources to make the investigations; that officers from another force could be brought in when it was undesirable for a force to investigate the conduct of its own officers; and that while attractive in the abstract, a central unit of investigators drawn from outside the ranks of the police would lack police powers and would not be subject to police discipline during investigations. Moreover, the demand for the larger and more complex investigations was likely to fluctuate, making it difficult to establish a unit of optimum size. The likelihood was that at times such a unit would be unable to meet the demand, while at other times it would be under-used. These are the axioms of bureaucratic organization and, as is often the outcome, they carried the day.

The Committee and later stages of the Bill in the Commons were uneventful. Five mornings were spent in Standing Committee between 21 March and 4 April, a total of eleven hours and nineteen minutes (see Table 13). The desire of the Opposition to see the Bill become law as soon as possible combined with a Government-in-waiting mind-set of the Labour Party to create an atmosphere that was more co-operative and constructive than was sometimes apparent. All the amendments made in Committee or at Report Stage were Government amendments, many of them to correct poor drafting. A statistical summary is shown in Table 14. On occasion, as is customary in the prudent management of legislation, Home Office junior ministers undertook to look again at a few points of detail put forward by the Opposition in Committee to see if they could be met by a Government-sponsored amendment on Report. Civil servants are sometimes sceptical about the merits of such changes, but there is no doubt that a degree of elasticity helps to expedite the passage of Government-sponsored Bills.

[82] *The Times*, 6 Mar. 1995.

TABLE 13. *Criminal   Appeal   Bill   1994–5*:
*House   of   Commons   Standing   Committee,
hours of sitting*

	Morning hrs./mins.
21 March 1995	2.12
23 March 1995	2.16
28 March 1995	2.01
30 March 1995	2.26
4 April 1995	2.24
Total time:	11 hours 19 mins
There were no afternoon or evening sittings.	

Source: Public Bill Office, House of Commons.

TABLE 14. *Criminal   Appeal   Bill   1994–5*: *new   clauses   and   amendments tabled in the House of Commons*

	(a) No. tabled		(b) No. made		(c) Origin
	New Clauses	Amendments	New Clauses	Amendments	
Standing Committee	7	109	—	28	All amendments made were Government amendments
Report stage	18	46	—	7	As above

Source: Public Bill Office, House of Commons.

The importance of the Commission having its own investigative capacity continued to be the issue most persistently pursued by the Opposition, both in Standing Committee and on Report. Several variations were put forward: that there might be a standing central unit of investigators directly employed by the Commission; or that it might maintain an in-house team of seconded police officers; or that it should have a reserve power to instigate and carry out investigations from time to time using suitably qualified staff. The Bar Council recommended that the Commission should be empowered to appoint its own employees as investigating officers. In a widely circulated brief JUSTICE contended that a core investigating team was needed for the investigations to be truly independent. However thorough and competent, serving police officers, sometimes drawn from the same force as the officers whose conduct was under investigation, would be bound to approach their task through the eyes of police officers. Complete objectivity and a fresh approach would be hard to achieve. None of these arguments prevailed. The response of ministers was unyielding, and there was no deviation from their previous stance.

VI

In the course of its scrutiny of the Bill, the Standing Committee performed a useful function by concentrating attention on a provision which had hitherto attracted little comment. The Home Secretary's power to refer a sentence as well as a conviction to the Court of Appeal had been used only occasionally. Ministers received representations on about fifty cases a year, either on grounds of sentence alone or on both sentence and conviction. On average no more than one or two sentences were referred each year to the Court of Appeal under Section 17 of the Criminal Appeal Act 1968. The Government had to decide how to deal with these cases in the legislation, in the absence of any recommendation by the Royal Commission. There were three options: to leave the Home Secretary with the power to refer sentences to the courts; to provide extended grounds of appeal to the courts; or to transfer the function to the Criminal Cases Review Commission.[83] The decision was that the new Commission should be given responsibility for investigating possible wrongful sentences and referring such cases to the courts. Maclean was eloquent in explaining why the option of leaving the power with the Secretary of State had been rejected:

There were several reasons. First, we thought it inappropriate to leave the function with the Secretary of State when his other powers—to refer convictions—were being removed. We think it right that the Secretary of State should withdraw from that aspect of alleged miscarriages of justice. It seems, then, to make sense and to be right to withdraw him from his role

[83] *Parl. Debates*, Standing Committee B, Criminal Appeal Bill, Fourth Sitting, col. 109, 30 Mar. 1995.

in relation to sentence referrals. To keep the power where it is now would have resource implications and would create some problems.

Representations of the kind we are discussing sometimes require investigation, and those investigations require resources. Difficulties would inevitably arise where the representations received covered both the conviction and the resulting sentence. The situation could arise in which both the Secretary of State and the commission were investigating a case simultaneously with all the duplication of effort and necessary expenditure that would bring. That would be nonsensical.[84]

These arguments, embracing both principle and administrative tidiness, did not convince Opposition members. They looked beyond the intention of the change to what might happen in practice. In seeking to resolve a small problem, Mullin said, the Government was in danger of creating a larger one.[85] Very few people indeed were aware of the existence of a power to refer sentences. He had taken a close interest in miscarriages of justice for several years and he did not know about it. Once it appeared in legislation, and the Commission started its work, the trickle of applications could swell rapidly into a flood which might engulf it. Although fully debated, the Opposition amendment was not pressed to a vote in Standing Committee. It was withdrawn, but with a warning that it would be raised again on the floor of the House at the next stage. The inference was that there would be an attempt to obtain all-party support in the interim.

On 26 April the Bill, as amended in Committee, was considered on Report, followed by Third Reading on the same day.[86] Howard did not speak himself, causing Mullin to comment that there was a feeling the Government's heart was not entirely in the Bill. It was one of the few pieces of Government legislation on which the Opposition was keener than the Government.[87] After a two-hour debate an Opposition amendment giving the Commission a reserve power to take an investigation out of the hands of the police and transfer it to an independent investigator nominated by the Commission was defeated on a whipped vote, with 239 MPs voting for and 267 against.[88] Later amendments extending the new system to Scotland; making the Commission responsible for defraying the expenses of the police in carrying out inquiries (a matter of concern

[84] Ibid., cols. 109–110.   [85] Ibid., col. 116.
[86] *Parl. Debates*, HC, 258 (6th ser.) cols. 860–952, 26 Apr. 1995.
[87] Ibid., col. 860.   [88] Ibid., cols. 889–93.

to the Association of Chief Police Officers); and including on the face of the Bill a definition of the word 'unsafe' in the grounds of appeal, fared no better.

Another Opposition amendment enabling the Government to retain the Commission's power to consider sentences as well as convictions, but to delay implementation for at least twelve months and thereafter only to be brought into effect if approved by resolution of both Houses of Parliament, was resisted by the Government. While accepting that the Opposition's motives in raising the issue again were genuine, Maclean believed them to be misguided. In his view the best solution to the residual problem of what to do about sentences after the abolition of the Secretary of State's power to refer convictions to the Court of Appeal was that contained in the Bill. It was the most sensible and cost-effective.[89] A large work-load arising from representations about wrongful sentences after normal appeal rights had been exhausted was not envisaged. The amendment was negatived without a division.

To take account of the evident worry about undue reliance on the police, a set of amendments were inserted in the Bill by all-party agreement which aimed to strengthen the supervision and oversight by the Commission of police inquiries. These conferred on the Commission specific powers relating to the dismissal of an unsatisfactory investigating officer; to receive from the investigating officer not simply a report of his findings but also the evidence on which it was based; and to take any steps considered appropriate by the Commission for supervising the inquiries made by an investigating officer.[90] After some brief concluding remarks the Bill was read a third time and passed on to the Lords.

VII

The participation of some of the most senior judges in the country in the legislative as well as the judicial work of the House of Lords, a constitutional anomaly unthinkable in the United States, means that bills affecting the powers of the courts can expect to attract close and expert scrutiny. On Second Reading Lord Taylor, having been consulted by the Government during the preparation of the

[89] Ibid., col. 944.
[90] Criminal Appeal Act 1995, Sections 20(5), 20(7), and 20(4).

Bill, gave it a general welcome. In doing so, he explained that he spoke not only for himself but with the concurrence of a group of judges who had great experience, both in the practice of the criminal law and in the Criminal Division of the Court of Appeal, whom he had consulted on the policy of the Bill and its detailed provisions.[91]

At the heart of any appeal system, Taylor said, was the test to be applied when deciding whether a conviction should be quashed or upheld. He supported the wording contained in the Bill, that the test should be whether or not the conviction was unsafe. The test was concise, just, and comprehensible to the ordinary citizen without narrowing the existing grounds of appeal. He saw no merit in the formulation recommended by the Royal Commission that a conviction should be quashed if it 'is or may be unsafe'.[92] Brushing aside the anxieties expressed by JUSTICE that the omission of the words 'or may be' would narrow the grounds of appeal, Taylor said that the implication of doubt was already inherent in the word 'unsafe'. A conviction that may be unsafe, he declared robustly, is unsafe.[93] He 'very much supported' the setting up of an independent body to investigate alleged miscarriages of justice and was delighted when, seemingly at the last moment, time had been found by the Government to include the Bill in its current legislative programme.

The Commission's power to refer sentence cases to the Court of Appeal caused Taylor 'some disquiet'. He mentioned the apprehension expressed in the Commons that the Commission might in its early years receive a great number of applications on grounds of sentence, leaving it struggling to cope with the inherited case-load of allegedly flawed convictions which was what the Commission was essentially about.[94] He also anticipated what was to become the major challenge to the Bill in the Lords: the lack of a right to appeal against the trial judge's recommendation of the minimum term to be served when imposing a mandatory life sentence on conviction for murder.

The Law Lords, sitting and retired, were out in force during the passage of the Bill. Apart from Taylor, six of them took part in the

---

[91] *Parl. Debates*, HL, 564 (5th ser.), col. 311, 15 May 1995.

[92] Royal Commission on Criminal Justice, *Report, op. cit.*, p. 215.

[93] *Parl. Debates*, HL, 564, *op. cit.*, col. 311.   [94] Ibid., col. 312.

debates in Committee and on Report.[95] They were supplemented by five Queen's Counsel,[96] a prominent solicitor,[97] two former Chairmen of the Parole Board,[98] and the Chairman of the Royal Commission on Criminal Justice.[99] At the age of 83, one of the most esteemed judicial luminaries of an earlier era was the mover of two amendments. For years Lord Scarman had worked with Cardinal Hume and others to persuade the Home Secretary, the courts, and public opinion that there had been a grave miscarriage of justice in the convictions arising out of the bomb attacks at Guildford and Woolwich in 1974. Now, like Mullin in the Commons, Scarman experienced the satisfaction of having a say in the shape of the legislation which he had done so much to bring about.

Scarman's initial amendment was debated during the first day in Committee on 8 June. It was designed, he said, to achieve a principled answer to an awkward problem. The problem arose in those cases where the Court of Appeal received admissible evidence which it considered was capable of belief. In such appeals one would expect the Court of Appeal either to allow the appeal or to order a retrial. But if a re-trial was impracticable or undesirable, should the Court of Appeal be able to decide the question of fact against the appellant and dismiss the appeal?[100] The Royal Commission had correctly identified the awkward issue in such cases, pointing to the danger of the Court of Appeal usurping the function of the jury and reaching decisions on evidence which had not previously been available at the trial. It had gone on to conclude, however, that where a retrial was impracticable or otherwise undesirable there was no sensible alternative to the Court of Appeal deciding the matter for itself.[101] Scarman disagreed. He reminded the Committee of Lord Devlin's horror at the desertion of trial by jury as the principle for dealing with indictable cases when the Court of Appeal entered the lists itself as the judge of fact.[102]

---

[95] Lords Ackner, Bridge of Harwich, Lane, Lowry, Roskill, and Scarman.
[96] Lords Alexander of Weedon, Campbell of Alloway, Hutchinson of Lullington, Baroness Mallalieu, and Lord Renton.
[97] Lord Mishcon.   [98] Lord Harris of Greenwich and the author.
[99] Viscount Runciman of Doxford.
[100] *Parl. Debates*, HL, 564 (5th ser.), col. 1496, 8 June 1995.
[101] Royal Commission on Criminal Justice, *Report*, *op. cit.*, p. 175.
[102] *The Judge*, *op. cit.*, pp. 148–76. Chapter 5 included a revised version of a lecture delivered at Oxford entitled 'Sapping and Undermining'. In it Lord Devlin

The argument was a sophisticated one; perhaps too sophisticated for what was predominantly a lay audience, despite the presence of such a well qualified legal contingent. In abridged form it was as follows. Where there is fresh evidence, capable of belief and admissible, which was not available at the trial, the verdict in the Crown Court, and so the resulting conviction and sentence, will be unsafe because it was founded only on part of the evidence, and the jury had no cognizance of the new evidence. If the Court of Appeal subsequently decided the question of fact against the appellant, its finding would not make the original verdict safe. It would remain an unsafe verdict unless and until there was a jury verdict based on all the evidence. That could be achieved by a retrial. If there was no retrial, it could not be achieved. The end result would be a conviction based on an unsafe verdict which went only to part of the evidence, and a finding of fact by the Court of Appeal on evidence never seen or heard by the original jury. Guilt would have been established not by a jury but by an appellate court.[103]

Scarman saw that feature as the first lack of principle which he said had been present in case-law since the judgment in *Stafford* v. *DPP*.[104] In that case the House of Lords in its judicial capacity held that when the Court of Appeal decides whether or not to set aside a conviction in the Crown Court on the ground that in all the circumstances it is unsafe or unsatisfactory, it should consider the weight of the fresh evidence, concerning itself not so much with the question of the effect it might have had on the jury had it been available at the trial. While such an approach might be a convenient one, the ultimate responsibility for allowing or dismissing the appeal rested with the Court of Appeal alone.[105]

A further lack of principle could be seen in the effect on the burden of proof. When deciding a new question of fact, that is a decision based on facts not known to the jury at the original trial, the

criticized vigorously the decision of the House of Lords in *Stafford* v. *DPP* which allowed men and women to be kept in prison for serious crime otherwise than upon the verdict of the jury (ibid., p. ix).

[103] *Parl. Debates*, HL, 564, *op. cit.*, col. 1497.

[104] [1974] AC 878. In a later case, *R.* v. *Chard* [1984] 1 AC 279, the House of Lords held that a convicted person whose case had been referred to the Court of Appeal under Section 17 of the Criminal Appeal Act 1968, and who had thus become an appellant, was entitled to argue all questions of fact and law that arose in the case, whether or not they were connected with the reasons for the reference set out in the Secretary of State's letter.

[105] See Viscount Dilhorne in *Stafford* v. *DPP*, ibid., 906.

Court of Appeal automatically reverses the burden of proof. In an appeal against a conviction the appellant goes first and puts his case. The Crown, the prosecutor, responds. When new facts are considered by the court and a ruling made upon them the defendant has to prove his case on the new facts. He goes first. The Crown answers. No doubt he has a reply, but he has to make the going. Where, asked Scarman, had the presumption of innocence gone?[106] The appellant is attempting to establish a defence, whereas in the court of first instance the evidence would be led by the Crown. The accused would have the benefit of the presumption of innocence, and the burden of proof would rest on the Crown. Whenever the Court of Appeal hears new evidence and decides to dismiss the appeal, confusion and injustice are likely to arise unless it is made absolutely clear that in fresh evidence cases where it is impracticable or undesirable to order a new trial the Court of Appeal's duty is to allow the appeal and quash the conviction. That was the purpose of his amendment. Scarman looked to past experience as well as to the principles of justice, citing the wrong decision which had been reached on the facts when new evidence had been adduced before the Court of Appeal which had never been seen or heard by the jury in the trial of the Guildford Four. The result was that the appellants had spent another fifteen years in gaol before they were vindicated.[107]

Replying for the Government, the Minister of State at the Home Office, Baroness Blatch, who admitted to speaking as a 'total lay person', argued that the effect of the new clause would be to require the Court of Appeal to allow an appeal against conviction whenever it decided to receive fresh evidence which could render the conviction unsafe, without considering whether the evidence in the court's view did render the conviction unsafe. The Government did not agree that the Court of Appeal was never in a position to assess the weight of new evidence in the context of the evidence heard by the jury. Over many years it had shown itself capable of performing that function wisely and fairly. The power to order a retrial was available to the court in fresh evidence cases, but sometimes a retrial would simply not be possible. There was also a possibility that the new evidence on which the appellant relied might be rebutted by other new evidence adduced by the prosecution. In

[106] *Parl. Debates*, HL, 564, *op. cit.*, col. 1497.   [107] Ibid.

such cases it was not unreasonable for the court to have a power to assess the strength of the new evidence, rather than a duty to allow appeals automatically without any consideration of their merits.[108] She hoped that the amendment would not be pressed.

Scarman confirmed that he did not intend to divide the Committee. He wished the Government to bear in mind the 'extraordinary importance' of the points which had been raised. In his view, what the Royal Commission regarded as the sensible alternative, namely the arguments of convenience, should not prevail over the arguments of principle which he had put before the Committee.[109] It was a clarion call, but the prevailing tide of opinion meant that it was unlikely to be answered.

VIII

The following week Scarman lent his authority to an amendment debated on the Second Committee day, 12 June. This time the issue was one which more than any other had preoccupied both the Commons and informed debate inside and outside Parliament. It was the vexed question of the relationship between the newly established Commission and the police. The importance of the Commission being independent of the police, as well as of government and the courts, was not disputed. Like others, Scarman believed that occasional, possibly sensational cases might arise in the future, as they had in the past, where the role played by the police required that the Criminal Cases Review Commission should be seen publicly to act firmly and independently, conducting the investigation itself and appointing its own investigating officer.

The objections seemed to come down to cost, to the powers of the investigators, and to what a former minister, Lord Rodgers of Quarry Bank,[110] aptly called the orthodoxy of government. By this he meant the reluctance shown by ministers and their departments when called upon to find a way of changing course to achieve new

---

[108] *Parl. Debates*, HL, 564, *op. cit.*, cols. 1499–1500.

[109] Ibid., cols. 1501–2.

[110] William Rodgers: General Secretary of the Fabian Society 1953–60; MP for Stockton-on-Tees 1962–74 and Teesside, Stockton, 1974–83 (1974–81 Labour, 1981–3 SDP). Minister of State: Board of Trade 1968–9; Treasury 1969–70; Ministry of Defence 1974–6. Secretary of State for Transport, 1976–9. Vice-President, Social Democratic Party, 1982–7.

objectives. In declining to depart from the tramlines of past proced-ure, both the officials who had advised on a particular course and ministers who had adopted their advice felt protected from poten-tial criticism. Should they be called to account, they could then reply 'We simply followed precedent. We followed the practice that had been found adequate before.'[111]

Although three months had passed since the Second Reading of the Bill in the Commons, the Government had not brought forward any convincing arguments to sustain their main objections of cost and the necessity for police powers. There appeared to have been no detailed analysis of the comparative costs of investigation, or if there had been its conclusions had not been revealed. Investigations by the police were very expensive, and chief police officers were known to be unhappy about meeting the additional costs from their existing cash-limited budgets. In the response by the Association of Chief Police Officers (ACPO) to the Home Office Discussion Paper, the chief officers said that within individual forces there was a shortage of officers of sufficient rank and experience to undertake such investigations. They noted that the small number of larger forces were likely to be undertaking a number of inquiries, which might involve two forces simultaneously investigating one another. Such a situation, the ACPO observed laconically, was 'not likely to enhance the credibility of the result'.[112]

At that stage the chief officers had proposed the establishment of a central unit, within the Commission and independent of police forces, which could carry out or manage complex or controversial investiga-tions. It also favoured a seconded team of officers from a different force to investigate some cases, particularly if police misconduct was alleged.[113] Later, when the legislation was before Parliament, minis-ters claimed that ACPO had changed its mind and had indicated sup-port for the procedure outlined in the Bill. Nevertheless, the initial reaction on the record showed that those senior police officers with first-hand experience of such investigations, and paying for them, saw the issue in a different light from the Government.

Nor did the objection that only the police possessed the powers needed to carry out investigations stand up well when subjected to

[111] *Parl. Debates*, HL, 564, col. 1596, 12 June 1995.
[112] JUSTICE, 'Criminal Appeal Bill briefing for Report Stage, House of Lords', May 1995, p. 4.
[113] Ibid.

detailed scrutiny. In moving an amendment enabling the Commission to appoint its own investigating officer to carry out inquiries, Scarman said that under the Bill the Commission could call for documents to be produced which were in the possession of a public body. It could retain those documents and take copies of them. The Commission also had ordinary powers to ask questions and to ask people to help it with its inquiries. Under a subsequent amendment, the Commission would be able to obtain a warrant requiring private persons to produce documents in their possession. More important still, the same amendment contained the suggestion that a power should be given to magistrates to issue a warrant allowing the Commission to enter premises, to search for documents, to take possession of them, and to copy them.[114] Legislation could be framed to ensure that adequate powers were provided for non-police investigators, answerable to the Commission, to carry out effective inquiries. A possible model was the powers conferred upon Department of Trade and Industry inspectors investigating financial wrongdoing under the Companies Act 1985.

Lord Runciman, one of the sponsors of Scarman's amendment, said that the issue had been considered carefully by the Royal Commission. In its recommendation on investigatory methods and powers[115] the Royal Commission was not proposing the creation of a kind of Pinkerton's army of police directly employed by the new review authority. In the great majority of cases the powers which the Bill provided for the review body to supervise investigations carried out by a police force would be all that was needed to enable it to place before the Court of Appeal its conclusions as to whether that court should consider if a miscarriage of justice might have taken place. In the rare cases where the review body, or in practice the case controller, had reason to think that the interests of justice required an independent investigator directly employed by the review body to be put onto a particular investigation, he could not see an argument against.[116]

No peer, either on the Conservative benches or elsewhere in the House, having spoken against the amendment, indeed the authori-

---

[114] *Parl. Debates*, HL, 564, *op. cit.*, cols. 1592–3.

[115] Recommendation 348 of the Royal Commission Report was that 'The possibility of the Authority, or police officers undertaking investigations under its direction, being given additional powers should be kept under review'. *Op. cit.*, p. 218.

[116] *Parl. Debates*, HL, 564, *op. cit.*, col. 1594.

tative Lord Alexander of Weedon having sent a message of unqualified support for it via Runciman, Baroness Blatch was left to defend the Government's stance unaided. In the most closely argued rejoinder yet heard she said it was intended that there should be three or four people on the Commission's staff with investigative experience. There was no reason why they should not be police officers on secondment, but the Government believed that such people would be best used in assisting the Commission to plan, direct, and supervise investigations by the police and others rather than conducting investigations themselves. It was a significant departure from the current arrangements that the police would be working under the active direction and supervision of the Commission. That, and the power to insist on an inquiry by an outside force, provided the necessary independent element in such investigations. The difficulty about complex and rare cases was that those were just the cases in which police expertise was needed. Their knowledge was necessary if such cases were to be investigated properly.[117]

While acknowledging that the Minister had done her best to try and meet the various points which had been raised, Scarman asked why the Government would not trust the Commission with a reserve power? Nobody urging the necessity for the amendment was motivated by distrust of the police. One had only to think of some of the miscarriage of justice cases which had been revealed and dealt with as a result of police inquiries. Surely the new review body, coming into existence as a result of the recommendation of the Royal Commission, could be trusted to handle a reserve power in such a way that in an unusual case where the police might be an interested party the public could see there had been an absolutely independent inquiry? It might be a long time before such a case would arise, but that one day there would be one he was certain.[118] The amendment was then put to the vote and defeated by 76 to 68 votes. The majority was secured by just enough back-benchers on the Government side summoned on a strong whip.

IX

Even the Tory loyalists were insufficient in number or motivation to rebuff a determined and judicially led bid to amend the Bill at

[117] Ibid., cols. 1600–1.   [118] Ibid., col. 1604.

Report Stage. The proposal to provide a right of appeal against the minimum term recommended by the trial judge in mandatory life sentence cases had been ventilated by Taylor on Second Reading, and thoroughly debated in Committee on 8 June on an amendment moved by Lord Ackner. On that occasion the amendment, having built up a powerful head of steam, was withdrawn without a vote due to the coincidence that there was an application pending for leave to appeal to the Appellate Committee of the House of Lords in a case turning on a related point.[119]

By the time the Report Stage was reached on 26 June the application had been refused, so enabling sitting as well as retired Law Lords to express their opinions by voting or speaking. Ackner opened the debate by quoting an aphorism of Lord Atkin half a century earlier, that convenience and justice were seldom on speaking terms.[120] Ackner's premiss was that whereas the amendment was founded on the requirements of justice, the Government's opposition was dictated by convenience. There was truth in his assertion, although the conflict went deeper. Beneath the intricacies surrounding the administration of mandatory life sentences, understood by so few, lay an unresolved question at the heart of penal policy. Life sentences are misleadingly named. They are not and never have been, other than in very occasional cases, sentences of imprisonment for the remainder of an offender's natural life. In their current form they are indeterminate sentences encompassing a fixed term.

The crucial question was who should determine the duration of the fixed term: the executive or the judiciary? Chapter 9 described how Section 34 of the Criminal Justice Act 1991 emerged as a compromise solution, accepted with great reluctance by the Government, to the dispute over the handling of life sentence cases. The Section applied only in those cases where life imprisonment was imposed at the discretion of the court for serious offences apart from murder. The list included convictions for manslaughter under Section 2 of the Homicide Act 1957,[121] other manslaughters, cer-

---

[119] *R.* v. *Leaney*, *The Times* Law Report, 12 Apr. 1995, and [1995] Crim. L.R. 669.

[120] *General Medical Council* v. *Spackman* [1943] AC 638.

[121] Under Section 2 of that Act persons charged with murder may be convicted of the lesser offence of manslaughter if the defendant's abnormality of mind is such as to impair substantially his mental responsibility for his acts and omissions in doing or being party to the killing. The defence of diminished responsibility applies

tain explosives offences, armed robbery, arson, and rape. In such cases the quantum of punishment, i.e. the duration of the fixed term (or 'relevant part' in the words of the Act) was decided by the judge in open court after representations by counsel on behalf of the defendant. The resulting court order was subject to appeal, with leave, to the Court of Appeal. Decisions to release or retain in custody at the expiry of the fixed term were taken not by a court but by a court-like tribunal in the form of a special panel of the Parole Board, chaired by a judicial member, and meeting the requirements of the European Convention of Human Rights.[122] The Home Secretary was bound to accept and act upon a decision to release once the Parole Board was satisfied that it was no longer necessary for the protection of the public that the prisoner should be confined.

No similar process applied to prisoners who had been convicted of murder and sentenced to mandatory life imprisonment. Then, subject to certain procedural constraints on the use of his executive discretion, the Home Secretary decides on the length of the penal term. Before setting the tariff he considers the views of the trial judge and the Lord Chief Justice on the period of time necessary to satisfy the requirements of retribution and general deterrence. The expression of these views can take one of two forms. Under Section 1(2) of the Murder (Abolition of Death Penalty) Act 1965, in passing a life sentence of imprisonment following conviction of murder the trial judge may make a formal recommendation in open court as to the minimum period which should be served before the possibility of release arises. The power has been little used, being reserved in the main for cases of exceptional wickedness or notoriety which have attracted great public interest, and where long terms have been recommended.

The usual practice since the 1983 changes has been for the trial judge to complete a report after the conclusion of each case, stating his view on the appropriate tariff. The report is then sent on to

only to murder and is a device often used to avoid the inflexibility of the mandatory life sentence. On conviction under this Section, the sentencing court may select the penalty most appropriate to the circumstances of the offence, be it life imprisonment, a determinate sentence of imprisonment, a hospital order, or some other disposal.

[122] For the legislative history of this provision see *Responses to Crime*, Vol. 2, pp. 443–50. The operation of the dual system for the review of life sentence prisoners is described in Chapter 9 above.

the Lord Chief Justice who, not having been present in court and having little more to rely on than a short summary of the case, adds his own comments and forwards it to the Home Secretary. Conventionally, the judicial advice has been given behind the scenes and in private. Since the decision of the Appellate Committee of the House of Lords in the case of *Doody and Others*[123] the advice must now be disclosed to the prisoner before the Home Secretary reaches his decision on the tariff, so that the prisoner's representations may be taken into account before a decision is reached. Should the Home Secretary depart from the period recommended by the judiciary he must give his reasons for doing so.

In mandatory cases, therefore, while the judiciary has the function of recommending what the penal element should be, the Home Secretary has the power to decide. Since Howard and his attendant ministers had made it abundantly clear that they had no intention of relinquishing any further measure of control over life sentence prisoners, the legitimacy of the tariff-setting process was skilfully protected by officials in their briefing. Although the effect of Ackner's amendment would not negate the distinction between judicial recommendation and ministerial decision, it was seen as a threat to be resisted at all costs.

Throughout the 1990s criticism of the dual system persisted. Time and again cases came before the courts by way of judicial review which resulted in encroachments of the Home Secretary's originally unfettered discretion. For example, the fiction that the recommendation as to tariff was confidential between the trial judge and the Home Secretary could be maintained no longer. While it had some validity in the pre-tariff era, when it was the custom for the judge to write a personal letter to the Home Secretary at the conclusion of a murder trial, the formal procedures adopted for setting the tariff since 1983 had led the House of Lords to declare in *Doody* that the judicial recommendation should be disclosed to the prisoner and those advising him in advance of the Home Secretary's decision. Once the aura of secrecy implicit in the previous arrangements had been breached there seemed no reason why the trial judge should not state his recommendation in open court, having heard submissions on behalf of the defendant. This was the course favoured by Taylor.

---

[123] *R. v. Secretary of State for the Home Department, ex parte Doody, Pegg, Pierson, and Smart*, [1994] 1 AC 531.

Speaking on 8 June in the first debate on Ackner's amendment in Committee in the House of Lords, the Lord Chief Justice explained that he had in mind issuing a practice direction analogous to that which he had given following the enactment of Section 34 of the Criminal Justice Act 1991.[124] In that direction he had stated that although trial judges were not obliged by statute to make use of the provision of Section 34 when passing a discretionary life sentence, they should do so in all save very exceptional cases. The practice followed thereafter in the generality of non-murder cases was for the trial judge to state in open court what he considered the minimum period ought to be.

As regards mandatory sentences, if the amendment was carried Taylor intended to issue a similar practice direction saying that judges should implement Section 1(2) of the Murder (Abolition of Death Penalty) Act 1965 at the conclusion of all murder trials, save perhaps in some very exceptional cases. The effect would be that in almost all cases of murder the judge would invite comments from defending counsel as to the length of the period he should recommend. He would then make his recommendation, which would be open to appeal in the same way as under the Section 34 procedure.[125] On appeal, it would be dealt with by three judges in a division presided over by the Lord Chief Justice so as to achieve consistency. In that way everything would be done openly, and the behind-the-scenes reporting done away with in the case of mandatory life sentences as it had been already in the case of discretionary life sentences.

Taylor revealed that he had discussed his proposal with the Home Secretary. Howard's reaction had not been enthusiastic, even though he had been assured it would not alter his power to decide the minimum period to be served by a mandatory life sentence prisoner.[126] The procedure would not only be more open, but Taylor believed it would have a better chance of achieving a fair result, with three judges in the Court of Appeal having an opportunity to review the recommended penal element. The need had been demonstrated shortly before in the case of *R.* v. *Leaney*. In that case the trial judge, in sentencing the defendant to life imprisonment, had

---

[124] *Parl. Debates*, HL, 564, col. 1480, 8 June 1995.
[125] This course of action had been urged in a powerfully argued commentary on the case of *R.* v. *Leaney* in the *Criminal Law Review*, [1995] Crim. L.R. 670–1.
[126] *Parl. Debates*, HL, 564, col. 1479, 8 June 1995.

made a formal recommendation under the Murder (Abolition of Death Penalty) Act 1965 that the convicted person should serve a minimum of twenty years on the ground that the offence was racially motivated. He also regarded Leaney as a continuing danger to the public. The defendant sought leave to appeal against the recommendation. The Court of Appeal, presided over by the Lord Chief Justice, was not satisfied that there was an element of racism nor that Leaney was a continuing danger. It concluded that the twenty-year recommendation was excessive. However, it further concluded, after reviewing the case-law, that it had no power to interfere with the recommendation because it was not a sentence for the purpose of the Criminal Appeal Act 1968. In refusing leave to appeal, the court wished to draw attention to the anomalous distinctions between the provisions and practices relating to mandatory and discretionary life sentences which ought to be considered by Parliament as a matter of urgency.[127]

The combination of the amendment and the proposed practice direction had the advantage of simplifying at least one aspect of the complex procedures applicable to mandatory life sentences: the two different forms of judicial recommendation would be unified. Under such a regime recommendations in all save very occasional cases would be made in open court and would be appealable. If it was argued, as it was by the Government, that it was not appropriate for a right of appeal to be available when a judge was making a recommendation rather than deciding on a sentence, Taylor countered by pointing out that Parliament had conferred just such a right on the judiciary in deportation cases. He said that when a judge makes a recommendation for deportation it is not binding on the Home Secretary. It remains only a recommendation. Yet the statute provides a right of appeal in respect of that recommendation.[128]

The Government's reply was that mandatory and discretionary life sentences are different in kind. In discretionary sentence cases

---

[127] Lord Ackner, ibid., cols. 1471–2, and [1995] Crim. L.R. 669.

[128] Ibid., col. 1479. This point was never answered in the Lords, although in the Commons Howard drew the distinction that a judicial recommendation to deport was part of an order of the court. Unless such a recommendation is made the Secretary of State cannot deport on the ground that the person concerned has been guilty of a criminal offence. There may, however, be other grounds on which he can deport without a recommendation. *Parl. Debates*, HC, 263 (6th ser.), col. 1361, 17 July 1995.

the judge specifies in open court what should be the penal element in the sentence. The determination of the 'relevant part' of the sentence has the status of an order of the court and specifies the minimum period to be spent in detention. Ministers have no power to substitute their own views and consequently it is entirely right that there should be an appeal against the setting of the penal element. By contrast, the decision on tariff in mandatory sentence cases lies with the Home Secretary. The legal position had been set out in the *Doody* judgment by Lord Mustill, who had said that Parliament had not by statute conferred on the judges any role at the time when the penal element of a mandatory sentence was fixed.[129]

Baroness Blatch argued that the trial judge makes a recommendation on the basis of the evidence heard in court and having made an assessment of the prisoner. The Lord Chief Justice sees every case on paper, and can confirm the recommendation or offer a different view as he thinks fit. The Home Secretary regarded such advice as very valuable. It was subsequently made available to the prisoner who was invited to make representations. If, after considering the judicial view and the prisoner's representations, the Secretary of State decided in the public interest that a tariff higher than that recommended was required for deterrence and retribution, the prisoner was given detailed reasons for the decision. Those reasons were open to judicial review. In this process the trial judge was no more than an adviser, and in the view of the Government it was inappropriate to erect an appeal mechanism to deal with that advice, which formed only one part, and not the most significant part, of the tariff-setting process.[130]

What was left unsaid in the exposition of such an apparently rational and methodical process was that each step had been fought tooth and nail by the Home Office. Only the cornerstone of the Secretary of State's power to decide on the tariff for mandatory life sentence prisoners survived as the last relic of the arbitrary structure devised and introduced in 1983. The elaborate edifice of a separate procedure for the sentencing, review, and release of prisoners serving life sentences for grave offences apart from murder had been created as a result of setbacks suffered by the Government on two fronts. At home, there had been a report by an all-party Select Committee of the House of Lords leading to an

---

[129] *Parl. Debates*, HL, 565 (5th ser.), col. 548, 26 June 1995.
[130] Ibid., cols. 547–52.

extended clash between the two Houses during the criminal justice legislation in 1991. Coincidentally, at Strasbourg the European Court of Human Rights held that the continued detention of discretionary life sentence prisoners after the expiry of the penal term should be decided not by ministers, but by a court or a tribunal with court-like characteristics. Nor had the domestic courts been passive. A series of judicial review cases had superimposed constraints on the decision-taking process both for mandatory and discretionary cases. Virtually all of them had initially been resisted by the Government, although now presented as integral parts of a coherent and defensible whole.

Despite these limitations, the Minister of State put up a doughty fight, but she did not succeed in persuading the Lords to override the weight of expert opinion. In addition to Ackner and Taylor, the amendment attracted speeches of unreserved support from Lord Lane, former Lord Chief Justice of England, and Lord Lowry, former Lord Chief Justice of Northern Ireland. When the vote came 142 peers voted Content and 126 Not Content.[131] After analysing the vote, Ackner said that no fewer than seventeen 'judges of distinction' had voted against the Government in the division on 26 June, and not one in their favour.[132]

Judicial dissatisfaction on this scale may have alarmed the draftsman, for on Third Reading the Government tabled amendments of its own. They gave effect to the intention of the amendment carried against it the previous week, but recast the provision for appeal by persons convicted of murder against the judicial recommendation so as to eliminate certain technical deficiencies. When moving the new amendments, the Minister of State explained that they had been tabled because the Government took the view that the Bill should not leave the House in a technically unsound condition. She made it clear, ominously, that the tabling of the amendments had been undertaken without prejudice to whatever view the House of Commons might take of the matter. The Government's reaction would be put before the Commons by the Home Secretary when the Bill was returned there for further consideration.[133]

To complete the discomfiture of ministers, another voice of unrivalled authority was raised in support of the amendment from its own side. Lord Hailsham, Lord Chancellor for nearly twelve

[131] *Parl. Debates*, HL, 565 (5th ser.), cols. 554–6.
[132] *Parl. Debates*, HL, 565, col. 969, 3 July 1995.   [133] Ibid., col. 943.

years,[134] had spent as much of his long and remarkable career in Conservative politics as in the practice of law. He had been unable to attend the House during the Report Stage, but had read the debate since. He was left with intense sympathy for Baroness Blatch who had been given 'an absolutely unrelenting brief by the Home Office with no room for manoeuvre at all and without any technical knowledge of her own to bring to her support if she wished to relent in any way'.[135] Speaking as a politician, Hailsham said it was 'absolutely lamentable' that the Government should find itself in opposition to what was virtually a united judiciary. He believed that the Government ought to have given way, and still ought to give way, on the substantive issue. It was 'extreme folly' to disregard professional opinion to this extent. He did not think that he had ever known such unanimity amongst the Law Lords.[136]

Two weeks later, when the Commons considered the Lords amendments on 17 July, the right to appeal against the judicial recommendation was the sole contested issue, more than fifty detailed amendments made in the Lords having been agreed without a division. The debate was a short one in which the Home Secretary, the Opposition front-bench spokesman for Home Affairs, Jack Straw, and the Liberal Democrat spokesman, Alan Beith, were the only speakers. In moving that the Commons disagree with the redrafted clause added by the Government in the Lords on Third Reading, Howard repeated the same reasoning, in places word for word, which had been rejected by the Lords. He said that in deference to those who had spoken in favour of the new clause, he had considered their arguments with great care. However, he remained of the view that the proposed right of appeal was not only unnecessary but would introduce anomalies of its own into the tariff-setting procedure.[137] He could not see the sense or logic in having a right of appeal against a recommendation that was the first stage of a multi-stage process.[138]

Both Straw and Beith gave greater weight to the views of the Lord Chief Justice. Taylor, they pointed out, was at the centre of the process and evidently did not share the Home Secretary's belief

---

[134] Lord Hailsham served two terms as Lord Chancellor, from 20 June 1970 to 5 Mar. 1974 and from 5 May 1979 to 13 June 1987. The total of eleven years and nine months made him the longest serving Lord Chancellor in the twentieth century.

[135] *Parl. Debates*, HL, 565, col. 954.　　　　　　　　　　[136] Ibid., cols. 955.

[137] *Parl. Debates*, HC, 263, *op. cit.*, col. 1353, 17 July 1995.

[138] Ibid., col. 1361.

that the current arrangements were working well. Other than that, little reference was made to the dangers of the rift developing between the executive and the judiciary against which Hailsham had warned. In a vote on strict party lines, with the Whips active to ensure that the Government's unyielding stance was supported, the Commons disagreed with the new clause by 254 to 225 votes.[139] The Lords did not insist on their amendment, and the Criminal Appeal Act 1995 received the Royal Assent on 19 July.

Only months later, in December 1995, with its membership less influenced by party loyalties and better informed about the way in which an appeals procedure would fit in with the wider considerations which were the subject of its inquiry into the mandatory life sentence for murder, the House of Commons Home Affairs Committee came to the opposite conclusion. Noting that at present there was no clear provision for an appeals procedure against the trial judge's recommendation, although a prisoner might make representations to the Home Secretary before the tariff was set, the Committee concluded that there should be a right of appeal against the judicial recommendation on the tariff in mandatory life-sentence cases in the same way as there was against the 'relevant part' of a discretionary life sentence. Their report continued:

We believe that a right of appeal would not just act in the interests of the offender, but could also be in the public interest. If sentencing for murder were to be at the discretion of the judiciary then, as with sentencing for other serious crimes, either side would have rights of appeal; if the sentence were to be mandatory, then whether the responsibility for setting the tariff were to rest with the judiciary or with the Home Secretary, we believe that the judge should declare his tariff or his recommendation as to tariff in open court, and that both the defence and the Attorney-General (acting on referral from the prosecution) should have a right of appeal.[140]

X

Serious as it was, the controversy over the merits of an appeal against the judicial recommendation diverted attention away from

[139] *Parl. Debates*, HC, 263, *op. cit.*, cols. 1362–5.
[140] House Commons, Session 1995–96, Home Affairs Committee, First Report, *Murder: The Mandatory Life Sentence* (HC 111), HMSO, London, 1995, paras. 91–3, p. xxxii–iii.

the main reason why the legislation had been introduced, namely to strengthen the process of criminal justice by providing greater safeguards against the possibility of further miscarriages of justice on the scale which had led to the establishment of the Royal Commission. Throughout the time that the Bill was before Parliament, its central purpose tended to get submerged in debate on points of detail where there was greater scope for adversarial cut and thrust. The scrutiny it received was certainly not perfunctory, but there was an eclectic quality which distinguishes parliamentary proceedings from the thorough and systematic approach of a Royal Commission. No more than cursory attention was given, for example, to the paramount importance of adequate funding if the new statutory body was to fulfil the proactive investigative role on which the Royal Commission had set such store.

Nor was there any sustained display of parliamentary interest in a feature which many of the critics believed had contributed so significantly to the long delay in rectifying the wrongful convictions of the Birmingham Six and the Guildford Four. The conventional adherence by the Home Office to the requirement for fresh evidence before the Home Secretary would be justified in exercising his power to refer a case to the Court of Appeal was replaced by new criteria. In the future, when considering whether to refer a case to the Court of Appeal, the Criminal Cases Review Commission would be guided by a statutory provision. A broader test had been devised which was intended to encompass the variety of circumstances where it appeared that there might be grounds for doubting the safety of a conviction or the validity of a sentence in law.

The effect of Section 13(1) of the Criminal Appeal Act 1995 is that the Commission may refer a conviction if there exists any argument or evidence, not already raised in court proceedings, which gives rise to a real possibility that the conviction, verdict, or finding would not be upheld were the reference to be made. Under Section 13(2) the criteria do not preclude the Commission from making a reference if there are exceptional circumstances which justify making it. Although the inclusion of the word 'argument' broadens the grounds for reference unquantifiably, and may in itself lead to much argument in the courts, the Home Office was keen to see that the constitutional proprieties were respected and preserved by ensuring that neither the argument nor the evidence would be adequate to support a reference if they had been considered previously by the courts.

On those aspects of the legislation which did engage their interest the two Houses showed a fair degree of complementarity. Whereas in the Commons the principal issues pursued were the independence of investigations if carried out only by police officers and the risk of the new Commission being overwhelmed by appeals relating to sentences rather than convictions, in the Lords the dominating issue was the unsuccessful attempt to attach a right of appeal to the judicial recommendation on the tariff in mandatory life sentence cases. All in all, by the customary standards of law-making at Westminster, the Criminal Appeal Act was an orderly reform. It was facilitated from the start by the willingness of some broad-minded ministers who had held the office of Home Secretary to relinquish the thankless task of investigating cases of alleged wrongful conviction and referring them where appropriate to the Court of Appeal. The first Royal Commission for more than a decade acquitted itself creditably by reporting within a tight two-year timetable and producing generally acceptable proposals on almost all of the main issues.

Next came a period of deliberation within Whitehall, resulting in the publication of a discussion paper on the general principles of reform, the grounds for further appeal when all normal remedies were exhausted, and the establishment and powers of an independent Criminal Cases Review Commission. After a pause for consultation, a Bill was drafted and the preparatory work put in hand by the civil servants. Having languished for a time on the reserve list for the Government's legislative programme, it found a place at the eleventh hour due to the unexpected withdrawal of a larger Bill with a higher political priority. The parliamentary scrutiny was not skimped or rushed, although in the Commons the ability of the Government business managers to secure a majority at each stage for what was looked on by most MPs as a technical bill was never in doubt.

As opinion towards criminal policies hardened, on both sides of the Commons chamber, there was some truth in Mullin's jibe that the Bill was one of the few pieces of Government legislation on which the Opposition seemed to be keener than the Government. In the Lords too the Government got its way in the end, although leaving behind misgivings, not confined to the higher judiciary, that expediency and appeal to populist sentiment sometimes counted for more than the demands of justice or the lessons of practical experience in the minds of the ministers then in charge at the Home Office.

11

Compensation for Victims: A Disorderly Reform

If the inauguration of a new system of criminal appeals was an example of an orderly reform, as measured by the conventional standards of Westminster legislation, the same could not be said of the maladroit way in which policy changes were introduced in providing compensation from public funds for the victims of violent crime. The wry civil service aphorism 'once something begins to go wrong, it goes on going wrong' could have been coined to fit the erratic sequence of events which preceded the passage of the Criminal Injuries Compensation Act 1995.

Financial compensation as a form of restitution has had a place in court proceedings since 1907,[1] but is effective only if the offender has the means to compensate the victim for the injury, loss, or damage caused by his criminal act. Each year large numbers of court orders are made in the Magistrates' courts and the Crown Court requiring offenders to compensate their victims. In 1994 a total of 90,000 defendants convicted of criminal offences in the Magistrates' courts in England and Wales were ordered to pay compensation. In the Crown Court, 6,400 defendants convicted of the more serious indictable offences were made subject to similar orders. Twenty-three per cent of all offenders sentenced for crimes of violence against the person in the Crown Court were ordered to pay compensation to their victims, and 59 per cent of those sentenced for the same category of offence in the Magistrates' courts. In that year

---

[1] The Probation of Offenders Act 1907 gave the courts power to order the offender to pay damages for injury or compensation for loss of stolen goods or money in cases where they discharged an offender on recognizance or on probation. Radzinowicz and Hood, Vol. 5, *A History of English. Criminal Law and its Administration from 1750*, say that magistrates were loath to make much use of it. *Op. cit.*, p. 655.

the average amount of compensation payable for violent offences was £153 in the Magistrates' courts and £926 in the Crown Court.[2] Compensation orders have precedence over fines or costs and can be imposed with no other penalty.

In some cases orders can be extended to include the proceeds of the sale of forfeited property. All too often, however, the means of the offender are so limited that the amounts are pitifully small, and time is allowed to pay sums of a few pounds a week over several months. As a result, court-ordered compensation can raise victims' expectations, only to dash them with irregular payments keeping alive the distress caused by the crime, not infrequently terminating with the reconviction of a persistent offender. The effectiveness of the system of collection also varies. A still greater weakness in looking to the offender to compensate the victim is the regrettable fact that no more than a minority of all offences recorded by the police result in the culprit being identified and brought before the courts. In 1994 the percentage of notifiable offences[3] cleared up was 26 per cent. As the gravity of the crime increases, so does the incidence of police involvement. Thus while overall violent crime increased in 1994 by 6 per cent to a total of 311,700 offences, the clear-up rate improved marginally from 65 to 66 per cent.[4]

The policy of reinforcing court-ordered compensation with payments made from public funds, to the victims of crimes of violence and those who were injured in attempting to apprehend the offenders or to prevent crime, was introduced with all-party support in 1964. In launching the scheme, the Government of the day stated that while it could not accept liability for injuries caused to people

---

[2] Home Office, *Criminal Statistics England and Wales 1994* (Cm. 3010), HMSO, London, 1995, p. 178.

[3] Notifiable offences recorded by the police cover the more serious offences, including most indictable offences or those which are triable either way (i.e. in the Magistrates' courts or the Crown Court).

[4] The clear-up rate is the ratio of offences cleared up in a year to offences recorded in the year. An offence is said to be cleared up where a person has been charged, summonsed, or cautioned, or where the offence is admitted and could be taken into consideration with other offences by the court. In some cases no further action is taken, for example where a person is already serving a custodial sentence for another offence, or the offender is under the age of criminal responsibility, or the victim is unable to give evidence. *Criminal Statistics England and Wales 1994, op. cit.*, p. 220. The percentage of total violent crime cleared up remained close to two-thirds throughout the decade 1984–94, with only small variations above and below the figure of 65 per cent in 1984 and 66 per cent in 1994, ibid., pp. 17 and 45.

by the acts of others, it believed the public felt a sense of responsibility for and sympathy with the innocent victims. It was right to give practical expression to this feeling by the provision of compensation on behalf of the community.[5] Compensation payments would be made *ex gratia* (i.e. in the exercise of executive discretion) from money provided through a grant in aid, and not as a statutory right. The amounts would be assessed by a Compensation Board[6] on the basis of common law damages for comparable personal injuries. Awards would be in the form of a lump sum rather than a periodical pension, and in general would cover pain and suffering, loss of amenity, and prospective future earnings. Compensation would be payable only where there had been an appreciable degree of injury directly attributable to a criminal offence involving the use of force. Theft or damage to property, by far the largest categories of offence, were excluded. The national scheme, which started on 1 August 1964, applied in Scotland as well as in England and Wales, but not in Northern Ireland where there were separate arrangements.

The British scheme was the first of its kind in Europe, being preceded by a state scheme for compensation to victims of crimes of violence introduced in New Zealand in 1963. The idea took root and spread rapidly. By 1978 nineteen jurisdictions in English-speaking countries alone had introduced a variety of compensation schemes for criminal injuries, depending on the policy approach, political stimulus, or administrative method adopted. By 1983, thirty-three states in America, and all but one of the Canadian provinces, had victim compensation statutes in place. In Europe by the mid-1980s, schemes were in operation in Austria, Denmark, France, the Federal Republic of Germany, the Republic of Ireland, the Netherlands, and in Scandinavia, Norway and Sweden.[7]

It is hard to identify the pressures leading to the near simultaneous shift in emphasis in so many different systems of criminal

---

[5] Home Office and Scottish Home and Health Department, *Compensation for Victims of Crimes of Violence* (Cmnd. 2323), HMSO, London, 1964, para. 8, p. 4.

[6] The 1964 White Paper, ibid., named the Board, clumsily if accurately, the Victims of Crimes of Violence Compensation Board. In the amended scheme, announced by the Home Secretary in the House of Commons in June 1964, the title was changed to the Criminal Injuries Compensation Board. A person of wide legal experience was to be appointed as chairman, initially with five other legally qualified members. *Parl. Debates*, HC, 697 (5th ser.), cols. WA 89–94, 24 June 1964.

[7] M. Wright, 'State compensation for criminal injuries: a short comparative survey', *Justice of the Peace*, 1 Aug. 1987, p. 489.

justice. In modern times the interests of the victim have been subordinated to those of the centralized state.[8] Yet when the state failed to protect the individual, the victim often was left without redress or compensation of any kind. Rising levels of crime, particularly violent crime and the fear and sympathy it engendered, must have been a factor, although not the only one. The portrayal of crime by the mass media, with a vividness made possible by the new electronic media, had the effect of focusing public attention on the personal harm or injury suffered by the victim at the expense of the abstract idea of crime as an offence against society as a whole. These factors coincided with other less specific considerations, such as the increased wealth of national societies in the developed world leading to an expansion of welfare payments to many people experiencing disability or disadvantage.[9] Such influences may have impinged on the consciences of elected representatives, stirring in the minds of the more calculating an instinct that, if caught at the right moment, a potential wave can be channelled to political advantage. In Britain at least there is no evidence to suggest that victims themselves were agitating for greater recognition and recompense. Victims were an unacknowledged group of individuals, not a self-aware community. There was no identifiable victims' movement; no formal organization, nor associations claiming victims as their clients.[10]

Political persuasion, low-key but persistent, was maintained in the 1950s through the activities of penal reformers, with Margery Fry in the forefront. Recognizing that the ideals of restitution by offenders towards their victims were impracticable in a system where so few offenders were detected and charged, and so many of those who were brought to justice were impecunious, she argued that the Government should take on the role of the offender at second hand and compensate the victim.[11] When finally adopted by central government, having been urged in the early 1960s by study

[8] See Chapter 2, 'The Victim', in *Responses to Crime*, 1987, pp. 27–61.

[9] See J. Haldane and A. E. Harvey, 'The Philosophy of Compensation', in *Compensating the Victim of Crime*, Report of an Independent Working Party, Victim Support, London, 1993, pp. 57–65.

[10] This account of the early origins of criminal injuries compensation in Britain draws on Paul Rock's masterful study of the Home Office and the rise of Victim Support: *Helping Victims of Crime*, Clarendon Press, Oxford, 1990, p. 59 *et seq.* Paul Rock is Professor of Sociology at the London School of Economics.

[11] Ibid.

groups on the political left and right (on criminal policies closer together then than later), with their memberships ranging from Lord Longford to a promising young Conservative lawyer and Parliamentary candidate named Geoffrey Howe,[12] the mainspring for the establishment of a publicly financed system of criminal compensation was to be found in the work of a small group of people who might be described as professional reformers. In Paul Rock's felicitous phrase, compensation was the outsider's gift, not the insider's demand.[13]

It was not the result of any mass campaign waged by victims themselves: they were not banded together, and they did not form a corporate group. Little was known about their needs, hopes, or character; there was no consultation about what they might want. There was never much evidence that victims were urgently seeking change of the kind proffered or that substantial monetary compensation was what they actually sought.[14]

In summary, then, the inauguration of a system of state-financed compensation for personal injuries resulting from crimes of violence was an authentic example of a consensus measure which was decided on what were seen at the time as its intrinsic merits. It owed little or nothing to the rampant populism that was to become the dynamo for governmental initiatives in the arena of criminal justice in the closing years of the twentieth century.

II

In its first full year of operation, 1965–6, the Criminal Injuries Compensation Board received 2,452 applications and made 1,164 awards. The cost of compensation was £403,000, the equivalent of £4.03 million at 1993–4 prices. The cost of administration added a further £60,000. A decade later, in 1975–6, the number of applications had risen to 16,690, with 11,500 awards being made. In that year the number of cases resolved was 13,599, with a very similar total of 13,940 applications outstanding. Ten years after that, in

[12] Solicitor-General 1970–2; Minister for Trade and Consumer Affairs 1972–4. Chancellor of the Exchequer 1979–83; Secretary of State for Foreign and Commonwealth Affairs 1983–9; Lord President of the Council and Leader of the House of Commons 1989–90. Created a life peer as Lord Howe of Aberavon in 1992.

[13] *Helping Victims of Crime*, pp. 52–3.   [14] Ibid., p. 87.

1985–6, the applications had more than doubled to 39,697, with awards rising to 22,534. By then, however, a large and apparently ineradicable gap had opened between the number of cases resolved each year and the number of applications which were still outstanding at the year end on 31 March. The totals for 1985–6 were 29,965 cases resolved, compared with 51,490 applications outstanding. The gap was widening each year and in 1987–8, the session in which Parliament made the discretionary scheme statutory, 29,153 cases were resolved (slightly less than two years earlier), while the backlog of outstanding applications had risen to 78,087. The cost also had escalated steeply, far outstripping the rate of inflation. At actual prices, the cost of compensation in that year was £52.043 million. An additional £6.759 million in administration costs brought the total costs of £58.80 million, the equivalent of £82.68 million at 1993–4 prices.[15]

From the late 1970s onwards it was Home Office policy to legitimate the payment of compensation to victims of crime, which had become such a substantial item of the Department's annual expenditure, by placing it on a statutory basis. The Treasury and Public Accounts Committee both attached importance to legislation for reasons of parliamentary and financial propriety. The policy was also consistent with the findings of the Royal Commission on Civil Liability and Compensation for Personal Injury which had recommended in 1978 that the criminal injuries compensation scheme for Great Britain should be put on to a statutory basis; that it should continue to be based on tort damages; and that consideration should be given to applying to the criminal injuries compensation scheme the Royal Commission's proposals for changes in the assessment of tort damages.[16]

Despite these endorsements, doubts were germinating in the minds of some Home Office officials about whether it would be possible or prudent to continue with the open-ended commitment which was inherent in the current scheme. The next step was an inter-departmental working party set up in March 1984 under Home Office chairmanship. The membership comprised represen-

---

[15] An historical record, from which these statistics have been extracted, was published as Annex A to the White Paper presented to Parliament in December 1993 by the Secretary of State for the Home Department and the Secretary of State for Scotland. *Compensating Victims of Violent Crime: Changes to the Criminal Injuries Compensation Scheme* (Cm. 2434), HMSO, London, 1993, p. 8.

[16] *Report*, Vol. I (Cmnd. 7054–I), HMSO, London, 1978, paras. 1591–2, 1595.

tatives of the Scottish Home and Health Department, the Northern Ireland Office, the Treasury, the Lord Chancellor's Department, and the Criminal Injuries Compensation Board. At first, the working party was inclined to favour a move towards a system of fixed awards, based on a tariff graduated to reflect the gravity of the injuries suffered. Such a change would be a way of checking the uncontrolled flow of financial resources required to meet the ever-rising cost in real terms of the claims assessed under the common law damages scheme, at the same time avoiding the cumbersome process of individual assessment which had caused lengthy delays. To the orderly civil service mind, advantage was also seen in replacing the value judgments of two dozen or so individual Board members with a more explicit published scheme founded on certain defined principles.

David Mellor, at the time a junior Home Office Minister,[17] and a barrister by profession, was strongly opposed to the idea of a tariff-based scheme. He anticipated that there would be trouble if the level of awards under a tariff scheme were lower than those which had become the expected scale of financial recompense for those who had suffered personal harm from criminal injuries. The Home Secretary, Douglas Hurd, was uncommitted and did not feel that the arguments for making a change were sufficiently compelling. When the final version of the report of the inter-departmental working party was agreed in late 1986, it accepted that compensation should continue to be paid to the victims of criminal violence on the basis of civil damages, subject to certain well recognized exceptions, and that the scheme should be placed on a statutory basis. The working party concluded that compensation should be restricted to the victims of violent crime and their dependants. Personal injuries caused by the commission of any criminal acts other than crimes of violence should not qualify, nor should damage to property. One of the most important aspects of a statutory scheme was that compensation would no longer be awarded by executive discretion. Anyone who satisfied the conditions would have a legal and enforceable right to compensation.

[17] Parliamentary Under-Secretary of State: Dept. of Energy 1981–3; Home Office 1983–6. Minister of State: Home Office 1986–7; Foreign and Commonwealth Office 1987–8; Dept. of Health 1988–9; Home Office 1989–90. Minister for the Arts 1990. Chief Secretary to the Treasury 1990–2. Secretary of State for National Heritage 1992.

There were sixty-eight recommendations in all, most of which were accepted by the Government. The Home Secretary confirmed his intention to put criminal injuries compensation on to a statutory basis, and that extra public funds would be made available in future years to enable applications to be dealt with more expeditiously.[18] The opportunity came in the criminal justice legislation introduced in 1986. A General Election was held in June 1987 before this part of the Bill had completed its passage through Parliament, with the result that it was not enacted until another Criminal Justice Act was passed in the following year.[19]

In retrospect, the incorporation into statute of the hitherto discretionary scheme was the first mistake in a chain of errors that was to reach a climax seven years later. The interconnected problems of the unwillingness of the Treasury to provide the funds necessary to implement the new statutory provision, and the long administrative delays being encountered by the Criminal Injuries Compensation Board (CICB), meant that it was impracticable for the Home Secretary to make the Commencement Order necessary to bring Part VII of the Act into effect at the same time as the bulk of the other provisions. With a backlog estimated to reach 100,000 by 1990, the Home Affairs Select Committee of the House of Commons added its voice to that of the CICB in pressing for urgent action to increase the number of staff and speed up computerization.[20]

In the later stages of the controversy, when the Government faced a legal challenge in the courts, it was keen to point out that in 1989 it was the CICB which had requested the Home Office to postpone bringing into force the provisions of the legislation on the

---

[18] *Parl. Debates*, HC, 103 (6th ser.), col. WA 539, 6 Nov. 1986. The report of the working party was published the same day: Home Office and Scottish Home and Health Department, *Criminal Injuries Compensation: A statutory scheme*, HMSO, London, 1986.

[19] Part VII of the Criminal Justice Act 1988, comprising ten sections, Sections 108–17, and two schedules, Schedules 6 and 7, provided for the setting up of a statutory body to administer a scheme for the payment of compensation as of right for criminal injuries.

[20] House of Commons, Session 1989–90, Home Affairs Committee, Second Report, *Compensating Victims Quickly: The Administration of the Criminal Injuries Compensation Board* (HC 92), HMSO, London, 1990. Not all delays were due to staff shortages or systems. According to the nature of the case, it was often necessary to make enquiries of the police, hospitals, doctors, employers, or other sources with knowledge about the applicant's circumstances, either to determine eligibility under the scheme or to quantify the loss sustained. Criminal Injuries Compensation Board, *Twenty-Second Report* (Cm. 42), HMSO, London, 1986, p. 1.

grounds that to do so 'would disrupt work and add to arrears'.[21] The chairman, Lord Carlisle of Bucklow, asked the then Home Secretary for 'a reasonable period of stability or quietude' to get on and see what the Board could do.[22] In a statement on 8 December 1989 the Home Secretary accepted the Board's request, at the same time announcing changes, including discretion to delegate some decision-making to staff and revised provisions for oral hearings, which would come into effect as part of a revised scheme on 1 February 1990. The immediate priority for senior staff was to concentrate on reducing the backlog, rather than on drafting the rules necessary for the introduction of a statutory scheme. The House of Commons Home Affairs Committee reported itself satisfied that the statutory scheme should not be brought into force in the foreseeable future.[23]

Despite the best efforts of the Board, which had grown to over forty part-time members supported by 380 civil servants in London and Glasgow, the task proved overwhelming. In the year 1991–2, 61,400 applications were made (an increase of 21 per cent on the previous year), and 60,113 cases were resolved, with 81,190 applications outstanding. 39,249 awards were made at a cost of £143.66 million. Operating expenses of £13.10 million accounted for 8.4 per cent of the total expenditure.[24] Ministers acknowledged the Board's determination to reduce delays and improve procedures, and set up a management review carried out by a team of officials from the Home Office and Treasury and a firm of management consultants. Even with the increases in administrative resources, hard fought for and reluctantly granted, the backlog of unresolved cases, which had reached about 96,000 in December 1989,[25] remained stuck at an unacceptably high level. The delegation of certain categories of decision to staff helped to reduce the amount of time taken in dealing with applications, but the problem of obtaining reports more speedily from police, medical, and other sources appeared to be insurmountable. In the more complicated cases delays of a year or more in the final settlement of claims were not unusual.[26]

---

[21] *Parl. Debates*, HC, 163 (6th ser.), col. WA 411, 8 Dec. 1989.

[22] HC 92, *op. cit.*, Q 99, p. 15.   [23] Ibid., para. 39, p. xv.

[24] *Compensating Victims of Violent Crime: Changes in the Criminal Injuries Compensation Scheme* (Cm. 2434), *op. cit.*, p. 8.

[25] *Parl. Debates*, HC, 163, col. WA 410, 8 Dec. 1989.

[26] In 1992–3, 57 per cent of cases were wholly resolved within one year of application, compared with 48 per cent in the previous year. About 15 per cent of cases

Surveying this bleak outlook, the conclusion reached by the Home Secretary, Kenneth Clarke, was that the system of individual assessment of applications on the basis of common law damages was no longer sustainable. It was not only costly, but also incapable of delivering the standard of service which claimants were entitled to expect, namely a service by which awards were made moderately quickly, and in an understandable and predictable manner. The time had come for change.

In a written answer to a pre-arranged question in the House of Commons on 23 November 1992, Clarke gave notice of the Government's intention to replace the still discretionary Criminal Injuries Compensation Scheme with a simplified procedure based on a tariff structure. In his view, it offered the 'best prospect of providing quicker payments to claimants through a means that is fair, straightforward and understandable'.[27] Savings in cost were not mentioned; instead, the statement referred to an additional £180 million which would be made available to meet compensation claims, over and above the current provision of £530 million, during the next three years. Further work was needed, the Home Secretary said, to develop the practical aspects of the new arrangements. It was anticipated that the work would be completed by the first half of 1993, when a White Paper would be published setting out the details. The tariff scheme was planned to come into operation early in 1994.

From this moment on, Government policy was that the link between financial compensation for the victims of violent crime and common law damages would be severed. In the future, injuries of comparable seriousness were to be grouped or banded together in a tariff of awards, with each band attracting a single lump-sum payment. The Home Secretary's statement was made without any prior consultation, even with the CICB's chairman.[28] Carlisle, who had sat in Margaret Thatcher's first Cabinet and was a former ministerial colleague, was asked to go and see the Home Secretary at short notice, and was told that the decision would be announced to

took longer than eighteen months before applicants had received and accepted an offer of compensation. Criminal Injuries Compensation Board, *Twenty-Ninth Report* (Cm. 2421), HMSO, London, p. 1. The annual report of the Board was presented to Parliament in March 1993, but was not published until 9 March 1994.

[27] *Parl. Debates*, HC, 214 (6th ser.), WA cols. 461–2, 23 Nov. 1992.

[28] Lord Carlisle had succeeded Sir Michael Ogden QC as Chairman of the Criminal Injuries Compensation Board in 1989.

Parliament the following day. He was dumbfounded, not simply by the discourtesy, but by the implications of the switch in policy. A personal letter to Clarke, written immediately after his interview and now reproduced with the writer's permission, showed the depth of his feelings.

Rt Hon Kenneth Clarke MP
Home Secretary
50 Queen Anne's Gate
London
SW1H 9AT   20 November 1992

When I saw you yesterday you specifically requested that I should not disclose the contents of our discussion to any of my colleagues on the Board until after you had made a statement to Parliament.

I feel, therefore, that I must express in writing to you my concern at the effect of what is intended and in particular to express my surprise and very great concern that the Home Office should decide to alter the very basis of the Scheme without any prior consultation with the Board as to the practicality of what is proposed, and with apparently little serious thought having been given to its consequences.

Your desire to achieve a Scheme which deals more expeditiously with applications, which achieves as great a degree of consistency as is possible, and which has regard to your concern at the increasing cost of the Scheme, is one which I am sure is shared by all Members of the Board.

However, to sever the link with Common Law Damages and to go instead to a wholly tariff based system, administered bureaucratically which rather than compensating the individual for his actual loss will instead pay a particular sum for a particular type of injury, is to my mind a retrograde step, which will undermine the great merit of the Scheme, without achieving the objectives which you have set.

I believe that it will, for the reasons we discussed, be far more expensive in terms of the overall cost; will not achieve great savings in time, in dealing with individual applications, and will be difficult to justify and defend.

The Common Law Basis of the current Scheme had been repeatedly stressed by Ministers of this and previous Governments, as the great strength of the Scheme.

Since you were kind enough to express your recognition of the enormous strides that have been achieved by the Board over recent years in accelerating its procedures, I am at a loss to understand what benefit will now accrue from what you propose.

The cost of the Scheme will as at present remain open-ended, in that it will still be subject to the volume of crime and the number of applications.

I repeat my view that further steps could be taken within the present framework of the Scheme as enacted by Parliament in 1988, which would achieve greater efficiency at the least possible administrative cost.

As I said, should you choose to discuss the matter further before making any statement I and my colleagues remain ready to discuss ways in which these objectives might be achieved.

Since the timetable which we discussed for the transitional arrangements is likely to be considerably longer than my term as Chairman of the Board, you will appreciate that I am in no way motivated by self-interest in expressing the views that I do.

The heart of the objections, then and later, was that while a flat-rate tariff might be quicker and less expensive to administer than the complex and time-consuming system of individual assessment (and there was no agreement on this point), it would be unable to take account of the different effect of similar injuries on different people according to their individual circumstances. Nor would it allow for loss of earnings or future earning capacity. Compensation would cease to reflect a particular victim's losses; payments would be related instead to the category of injury without regard to the age, sex, or personal circumstances of the victim. The tariff award structure would be based on the median level of awards made by the CICB for the same injuries. Under the new regime some victims would receive more than before, and some less. Those who would lose out most heavily would be those whose injuries were the most serious and permanent in their effect.

III

The crux of the problem facing the Home Office post 1988 is illustrated in Table 15. The out-turn figures over the five years 1988–93 show a consistent pattern of increase under all headings. It was the expenditure line which was the cause of the most acute concern. In 1992–3 the cost of compensation reached £152.2 million, estimated to rise to £170 million in 1993–4, and £193 million in 1994–5. The larger numbers of applicants, and the efforts (only partially successful) to reduce the backlog meant that heavy administration costs had been incurred in addition; increasing over the same three years from £14.2 million to £17.4 million to £19 million. These statistics were published in March 1994 as the Government's expenditure plans for 1994–95 to 1996–97 for the Home Office and the

TABLE 15. *Criminal Injuries Compensation: Out-turn and Plans, 1988–97*

	1988–89 out-turn	1989–90 out-turn	1990–91 out-turn	1991–92 out-turn	1992–93 out-turn	1993–94 estimated out-turn	1994–95 plans	1995–96 plans	1996–97 plans
Number of applications	43,385	53,655	50,820	61,400	65,977	71,250	77,000	83,100	89,800
Number of cases resolved	38,830	38,620	53,384	60,113	58,688	64,000	72,000	77,000	87,000
Number of final awards	27,752	27,926	35,190	39,249	36,638	39,700	46,800	53,700	57,200
Applications outstanding[a]	82,642	87,780	81,828	81,190	86,951	94,200	99,200	105,300	108,000
Manpower (average in post in year)	312	332	368	380	387	410	460	480	490
Expenditure on compensation[b] (£ million)[c]	69.4 (88.6)	72.8 (86.9)	109.3 (120.7)	143.7 (149.2)	152.2 (152.5)	170.0 (164.6)	193 (180)	204 (183)	151 (132)
Expenditure on administration[b] (£ million)[c]	7.5 (9.6)	9.1 (10.9)	10.3 (11.4)	13.1 (13.6)	14.2 (14.2)	17.4 (16.9)	19 (18)	19 (17)	19 (17)
Administration cost per case resolved[b] (£)	193	235	193	218	243	271	265	245	217
Applications resolved per staff member	124	116	145	158	152	156	157	160	178

[a] At 31 March.
[b] Includes contribution from Scottish Home and Health Department.
[c] Figures shown in brackets indicate expenditure in real terms at 1992–3 prices using the GDP deflator.

Source: Home Office.

Charity Commission[29] which accompanied the Public Expenditure Statistical Supplement to the Financial Statement and Budget Report for the same period.[30] Evidence sworn on behalf of the Home Office when the decision to introduce the tariff based scheme was challenged in the courts disclosed that if no change had been made the annual cost of the old scheme was estimated to rise to about £550 million by the year 2000–01. Under the tariff scheme the annual cost of compensation by that date was estimated to be reduced to the order of £225 million.[31]

Head 1 of the Home Office vote in the supply estimates laid before Parliament for the year ending March 1995 related to criminal injuries compensation, among other items. In his recital of the facts, when giving judgment in the Court of Appeal on the application for judicial review, the Master of the Rolls, Sir Thomas Bingham, said:

A note referred to the old non-statutory scheme under which compensation was assessed on the basis of common law damages and to the plan to introduce a new scheme based on a tariff for injury awards to take effect on 1 April 1994. It was stated that the new scheme would apply to all applications received on or after the date of introduction.

Further reference was made to the Criminal Injuries Compensation Authority which would administer the new tariff scheme. The Appropriation Act 1994 received the royal assent on 21 July 1994. The sum granted by the Act and appropriated to the Home Office under head 1 was the sum contained in the March estimates.[32]

This nugget of budgetary information provides the clue to the severe restraints on the Home Secretary's freedom of action. Put simply: there was no Parliamentary authority for the expenditure that would be needed to fund a continuation of the common law damages scheme for new applications.

The opposition of the CICB to any severance of the link with common law damages was heartfelt, and perhaps to be expected from a Board composed entirely of lawyers who were experienced personal injury practitioners. They were accustomed to a painstak-

---

[29] Cm. 2508. The expenditure figures included a contribution from the Scottish Home and Health Department.

[30] Cm. 2519.

[31] *R.* v. *Secretary of State for the Home Department, ex parte Fire Brigades Union and Others,* [1995] 2 AC 513 at 518.

[32] Ibid., at 518–19. Bingham succeeded Lord Taylor as Lord Chief Justice in May 1996.

ing case-by-case approach, calculating payments in line with the amounts which would have been awarded by the courts to the injured party in a civil action following familiar principles developed to compensate victims of tort. It is a mistake to think, as some did, that the opposition of the lawyers, then and later, arose purely from professional self-interest. A more generous explanation can be found in the different ways of looking at the issue. For lawyers, it is the instant case that matters; the situation of the individual, whether seeking redress in the courts or claiming compensation for criminal injuries from the CICB. Against the insistence on individual assessment was the argument that greater consistency and clarity would be achieved by the adoption of published criteria based on principles of equity and proportionality which would be applied to all victims. The application of published scales was also likely to be a great deal quicker than individual assessment.

The latter approach was developed by an independent working party convened by the National Council of Victim Support in May 1992, six months before Clarke's statement. Concurrently, therefore, while Home Office officials were preparing the functional details of a new tariff-based scheme, the Victim Support working party, under the chairmanship of David Faulkner, formerly the Deputy Under Secretary responsible for the Criminal Departments at the Home Office,[33] was surveying the same territory, but from a broader viewpoint. Its substantial report examined carefully the purpose of compensation; the principles upon which payments should be made by the state, the offender, or other sources; and the proper scope of a state compensation scheme.[34]

The context of the working party's conclusions and recommendations went beyond the payment of compensation, relating financial recompense to the recognition and support which the state, and society as a whole, gives to the victims of crime and the provisions made for victims of other forms of personal tragedy and misfortune. It proposed a system of scale payments to be applied by a new compensation agency, instead of referring cases for individual assessment by legally qualified Board members. Such a system

---

[33] Before his retirement, Faulkner had been the senior civil servant responsible for the preparation of the Criminal Justice Act 1991; see *Responses to Crime* (Vol. 2), pp. 211–54. Since 1992 he has been a Fellow of St. John's College, Oxford, and Senior Research Associate at the Oxford Centre for Criminological Research.

[34] *Compensating the Victim of Crime*, Victim Support, 1993.

would be tariff-based, but there were a number of important conditions to be satisfied if a tariff scheme was to be adopted. These included the conditions that scales should be set at acceptable levels, and regularly reviewed and updated; that there should be an effective system of appeals; that there should be a new social security benefit (described as a criminal injuries benefit) to compensate victims for loss of earning capacity; and that the lower limit of £1,000 should be removed. Further recommendations covered psychological rather than physical injuries; the vexed subject of the exclusions relating to the character of the applicant, as indicated by a person's previous convictions or unlawful conduct; and the importance of compensation payments being excluded from the calculation of assets in determining eligibility for income support.[35]

A week after the publication of the report of the Victim Support working party on 7 December 1993, the Government published its delayed White Paper on *Compensating Victims of Violent Crime*.[36] It was a far briefer document, containing only seven pages of text before setting out a detailed tariff of payments for a long list of physical injuries. Shock or nervous shock was defined to include a number of psychological symptoms. Disability included impaired work or school performance, significant adverse effects on social relationships, and sexual dysfunction.[37] The Government had decided that compensation should no longer be assessed on the basis of common law damages. Instead, injuries of comparable severity would be grouped or banded together in a tariff of awards. Each band would attract a single lump-sum payment. There would be twenty-five tariff levels, with awards ranging from £1,000 to £250,000. Tariff levels would be based on the CICB's past award levels, and it had been estimated that the average claimant would be no worse off than under the current scheme. No separate payments would be made for loss of earnings or medical expenses. The rules of eligibility, including the minimum threshold for awards of £1,000, and the exclusion on grounds of the applicant's character or conduct, would remain largely as before.[38] The new scheme would come into force on 1 April 1994 and cases lodged on or after that date would be dealt with under the tariff scheme. It was expected to take around two years to clear cases lodged under the

---

[35] Ibid., pp. 34–6.   [36] Cm. 2434; *op cit.*   [37] Ibid., p. 13.
[38] Ibid., pp. 4–5.

current rules. During this period the old and the new schemes would run in parallel.[39]

The differences of principle between the Government and the main 'user' organization, Victim Support, were not as great as between the Government and the CICB, wedded as it was to the principle of common law damages. Ministers should have been aware that Victim Support is primarily a service organization.[40] Through its 376 local schemes it assists large numbers of victims each year to make claims for criminal injuries compensation.[41] With more sensitive handling, Victim Support might have been drawn into a constructive dialogue to try and get round the awkward corners. It was, after all, the stated objective of the Government to provide a better, as well as a less costly, service to victims. In other Government initiatives, for example the Citizens' Charter, the views of the user were considered to be paramount. Yet there was no consultation, either before Clarke's initial statement or during in the thirteen-month period it took to work out the tariff scheme.

In an attempt to bridge the gap, Victim Support, jointly with the Mannheim Centre at the London School of Economics, held a one-day conference at the School on 23 February 1994 to provide a forum for discussion on the White Paper and its own working party's report. The aim was to avoid ritual exchanges on the merits or demerits of the status quo *versus* the tariff, and to suggest practical improvements that might be made to the Government scheme before it was implemented. In particular, Victim Support spokesmen and others present wanted to press for a postponement of the implementation date of 1 April 1994. There were several outstanding points which needed to be considered and talked through, with a reasonable prospect of reaching consensus on some if not all

---

[39] Ibid., p. 7.

[40] Victim Support, the abridged name for the National Association of Victims Support Schemes, is a large charitable organization providing help for the victims of crime. In 1994–5 16,219 volunteers and 811 paid staff offered emotional support and practical assistance to the victims of 1,028,067 crimes. Most of these victims had been referred by the police soon after the crime was reported, but some will have contacted local Victim Support schemes directly. Personal contact is achieved with about one-third of all referrals. In addition, Victim Support's witness service in 54 Crown Court centres assisted 58,593 people attending court for trials. Victim Support, *Annual Report 1995*, pp. 14–16.

[41] Victim Support assisted 11,631 claimants for compensation in 1994–5. *Annual Report 1995*, p. 15.

of them if adequate time were allowed for discussion and representations. In addition, it was important to avoid confusion which would cause distress to victims and lead to uncertainty in the minds of those who would be advising them.

The Home Secretary and Tony Blair, then Opposition spokesman on Home Affairs, were invited to attend, together with representatives from the CICB, the Bar Council, the Law Society for England and Wales and the Law Society of Scotland, the Association of Personal Injury Lawyers, the police, the Trades Union Congress (TUC), and some trade unions whose members were at risk of injury as a result of criminal actions. Tony Blair, albeit on an easier wicket, accepted immediately, attended, spoke about Opposition policies towards victims and proposals for improving the White Paper proposals, and responded courteously to questions raised in discussion. Michael Howard declined, although it was agreed that the Home Office officials concerned with the administration of criminal injuries compensation should attend. However, it is not the job of civil servants to justify government policies; that is the task of ministers. After some negotiation, David Maclean, the Minister of State, was deputed as the emissary. In a short but confrontational speech, the Minister said that blameless victims of crimes of violence should receive a generous award for their injuries quickly, and with as little fuss and inconvenience to them as possible. The criminal injuries compensation scheme was an important part of the commitment to ensure that the needs of victims were properly recognized and that they were treated with consideration and respect. The scheme was among the most generous in the world, paying out more than all European schemes put together, and only slightly less than was paid for the whole of the United States.[42]

This defensive assertion, then and on the many occasions when it was to be repeated in Parliament, was the sole reference to the heavy cost of the current scheme, and the projections for the future. It was left unsaid that in the year commencing 1 April 1994 the Home Office vote only provided enough funds for new applications under the tariff scheme. The unavailability of any further finance is the most likely explanation for ministers' apparent decision to brazen it out. Whereas Victim Support had demonstrated that there

---

[42] Home Office, *Press Release*, 40/94, 23 Feb. 1994.

were respectable arguments in favour of changing to a tariff scheme, the lack of frankness in admitting (and justifying) the most compelling reason for the change in policy was to cause the Government acute embarrassment. The impatience displayed by ministers, and their reluctance to consult or listen, left the ground parched and combustible when the spark was struck.

IV

One of the speakers at the LSE conference was Owen Tudor, Assistant General Secretary of the TUC with responsibility for Equality and Social Policy. Encouraged by some solicitors specializing in compensation work, the TUC had joined the Association of Personal Injury Lawyers in 1993 in forming a pressure group called the Victims' Campaign for Compensation Rights (VCCR). The title was in fact a misnomer, since it was not an organization formed by or directly representative of victims. Unlike Victim Support, the VCCR was a single-issue campaigning body. In the early stages its activities were mainly directed towards publicizing the deleterious effect that the Government's intended tariff scheme would have on large claims for serious injuries, which in some cases would lead to markedly smaller awards being made. According to its General Secretary, the TUC was concerned to protect the interests of union members who were criminally injured during the course of their work. Criminal assaults at work were on the increase. Bank staff were caught up in armed raids, nurses were assaulted by patients, teachers attacked by pupils, and fire-fighters had to cope with the results of arson. Unions dealt with 40–50 per cent of all criminal injuries cases.[43]

Although the VCCR had kept in touch with Victim Support, by the Autumn of 1993 it became clear that the two organizations had different agendas. Apart from the tariff question, Victim Support argued, as it always had done, against both a lower limit and the reduction or refusal of awards because of previous convictions for unrelated offences. It had also opposed the practice of counting compensation as capital for social security means-testing purposes. These matters were of little interest to the VCCR, which was

[43] J. Monks, *The Times*, 11 Apr. 1995.

dedicated to saving the *status quo ante*. Victim Support was critical of the Government's proposed tariff without an allowance for loss of earnings, and on this item at least there was an identity of interest. But there was no co-ordinated campaign. Victim Support concentrated on publicizing its own working group's report, and setting up the conference the following February as a possible stepping stone to the consultation which had been so notably absent.

The decision to apply for judicial review in the courts was taken by the VCCR, co-ordinated by Andrew Dismore, a personal injury specialist with a London firm of solicitors,[44] and backed by the TUC. Although it had been reported earlier that the Law Society of England and Wales was considering initiating proceedings against ministers,[45] in the event it was ten unions or staff associations[46] which joined the TUC in making an application to the High Court on 22 March for judicial review of the Home Secretary's decisions. Leave was granted, and although Counsel for the Home Secretary said that the application for leave was misconceived, he did not oppose it on the grounds that there was an arguable issue of public interest.[47] The unions' application was heard in the Queen's Bench Divisional Court on 23 May 1994, notwithstanding a jurisdictional challenge that on the evidence only four of the ten applicants had a right to bring proceedings. Counsel for the unions argued that in refusing to implement the statutory scheme, first launched in 1964 under common law, the Home Secretary had flouted the will of Parliament. As enacted, the statute expressed the will of Parliament, and Parliament was unlikely to have authorized a member of the Government to postpone its operation indefinitely.

The Court disagreed. Some sections of the Act came into force on the date it received the Royal Assent, 29 July 1988, and others two months later. Under Section 171(1) the remaining provisions were to come into force 'on such day as the Secretary of State may by order made by statutory instrument appoint and different days may be appointed . . . for different provisions or different purposes of the same provision'. Although in certain cases the word 'may'

---

[44] Robin Thompson and Partners.

[45] [1994] *Law Society Gazette*, 16 Feb. 1994.

[46] The Fire Brigades Union, National Association of Schoolmasters and Union of Women Teachers, Unison, GMB, Prison Officers' Association, Royal College of Nursing, Transport and General Workers' Union, ASLEF, Civil and Public Services Association, and NatWest Staff Association.

[47] *The Times*, 23 Mar. 1994.

had been interpreted as imposing a duty, this was not one of them. No obligation was expressed or implied. Precedents were available to the draftsman to impose an obligation as to commencement if this was desired. He had not done so. The power to activate was permissive, leaving the Home Secretary with a discretion, but no obligation, to bring the relevant provisions into force. In his judgment, Staughton LJ said that once the conclusion had been reached that the Home Secretary was not obliged to bring the statutory provisions into force, he could not see anything irrational or improper in his deciding not to do so, or in bringing in another scheme under the common law. The application was dismissed and leave granted to appeal to the Court of Appeal.[48]

Before following the *Fire Brigades Union* case through the Court of Appeal to the House of Lords, it is worth making a detour to scrutinize more closely than was done in the courts the current parliamentary practice on Acts not brought into force. The non-implementation of legislation is an important, if little noticed, byway from the junction where legislative power branches off into executive action. It is far more common than is usually realized for statutory provisions to remain unimplemented for lengthy periods of time. A provisional list prepared by the Statutory Publications Office at the Houses of Parliament showed that a total of 168 statutes were either not in force, or not fully in force, at 31 December 1994.[49] Of these, 105 had been enacted before 1 January 1990, forty-five before 1 January 1980, and ten before 1 January 1970. Some provisions shown as not in force, or not fully in force, were only arguably so, while others were virtual technicalities because they related to provisions which were spent, or of no more than vestigial effect.[50] In contrast, some entire Acts had not been brought into effect, dating back nearly seventy years to the Easter Act 1928. More recent examples of unimplemented Acts of Parliament were the Children Act 1973, Motor Cycle Noise Act

---

[48] *R.* v. *Secretary of State for the Home Department, ex parte Fire Brigades Union and Others*, [1994] PIQR p. 320 at 327. Personal Injuries and Quantum Reports (PIQR) are published by Sweet and Maxwell.

[49] *Primary Legislation partly or wholly prospective as at end of 31 December 1994*. I am indebted to J. M. Davies, Clerk Assistant, House of Lords, for this hitherto unpublished information.

[50] Ibid.; Introductory note.

1987, Antarctic Minerals Act 1989, Smoke Detectors Act 1991, two Acts passed in 1993,[51] and four in 1994.[52]

Acts, or parts of Acts, may remain unimplemented for a variety of reasons, including a change of Government, shortage of financial or manpower resources, changes in policy, or lack of agreement with bodies required to be consulted. Complex legislation may take time to implement, and Parliament has in general been content to leave it to the minister concerned to decide whether the administrative basis for implementing a new policy is in place, or whether there are other considerations to be taken into account. In some instances second thoughts may induce a change in policy. A good example is the Football Spectators Act 1989 which required a membership scheme to be established for football clubs so as to control crowd behaviour. Policy changed when it was realized that such a scheme might cause more problems than it would solve.

However common the practice, it is not only constitutional purists who may be uneasy about allowing the intentions of Parliament, as expressed in primary legislation, to be postponed so readily by the executive. Commencement orders which enable a minister to appoint a date or dates for the coming into force of one or more provisions of an Act are almost never subject to parliamentary control.[53] There is no obligation for a minister to make a commencement order at all, or to give any explanation to Parliament of the reasons for non-implementation. In Australia, where the non-proclamation (as it is known) of Commonwealth legislation had become a controversial issue, with vital sections of Acts never being brought into force because of ministerial or bureaucratic opposition,[54] a remedy has been devised. Since 1988 the Senate has required yearly reports on provisions that have not been brought into force, with explanations of why that is the posi-

[51] Osteopaths Act 1993 and Road Traffic (Driving Instruction by Disabled Persons) Act 1993.

[52] Antarctic Act 1994, State Hospitals (Scotland) Act 1994, Chiropractors Act 1994 (except Section 42 and Schedule 2), and Social Security (Incapacity for Work) Act 1994.

[53] House of Lords, Session 1993–4, Select Committee on the Scrutiny of Delegated Powers, *Review of the Committee's Work* (HL 90), HMSO, London, 1994, para. 11, p. 2.

[54] See A. Lynch and D. Creed, 'Management and Mousetraps: The non-proclamation of legislation', *The Parliamentarian*, July 1994, pp. 194–9. Anne Lynch is Deputy Clerk of the Senate; David Creed is Secretary to the Senate Standing Committee on Regulations and Ordinances, Commonwealth of Australia.

tion and of what is to be done (e.g. enforcement or repeal).[55] Some Australian Acts now provide that if provisions are not brought into force within a specified time, they lapse automatically unless the period of time is extended by Parliament.[56] Regular notification by the executive to the legislature is a practical way of keeping under review statutory provisions which have not been implemented. Although its adoption would not reverse the erosion of Parliamentary supremacy at Westminster, it would at least be a step in the right direction.

V

From this excursus it will be seen that not only was there nothing unlawful about the Home Secretary's failure to bring into operation the scheme of compensation for criminal injuries approved by Parliament in 1988, provided that he had good grounds for postponement and kept the possibility of implementation under review, but that ministers had acted within the current conventions. There was, however, a second and stronger limb to the argument of unconstitutionality which had not been tested in the judgment of the Divisional Court. This was the decision of the Government to introduce by executive discretion a new and radically different scheme while the 1988 scheme, approved by Parliament but unimplemented and unrepealed, was still on the statute book. It was on that issue that Sir Thomas Bingham MR found against the Home Secretary. Even after the 1988 Act had been passed, he said, the Secretary of State would not have been open to legal challenge had he continued the old non-statutory scheme without bringing the new statutory provisions into force, so long as the reasons for postponement fell within the wide discretion accorded to him.[57] If he wished to change the basis of compensation he could have invited Parliament to repeal the statutory provisions. Since there had been Criminal Justice Acts in 1991 and 1993, and the Criminal Justice

---

[55] Michael Ryle, formerly Clerk of Committees in the House of Commons and Secretary of the Hansard Society's Commission on the Legislative Process 1991–3, provided the author with information about the Australian experience.

[56] Lynch and Creed, *op. cit.*, p. 199.

[57] *R.* v. *Secretary of State for the Home Department, ex parte Fire Brigades Union and Others*, [1995] 2 AC 513 at 522.

and Public Order Act in 1994, there had been no lack of opportunity.

Enactment of a tariff scheme in substitution of the 1988 provisions, Bingham said, was one course open to the Home Secretary; or if the 1988 scheme was simply repealed he could have used his prerogative powers to introduce the tariff scheme. What he could not lawfully do, however, 'so long as the 1988 provisions stood unrepealed as an enduring statement of Parliament's will, was to exercise prerogative powers to introduce a scheme radically different from what Parliament had approved'.[58] Accordingly, he would declare that by implementing the tariff scheme the Home Secretary had acted unlawfully and abused his prerogative or common law powers. Hobhouse LJ dissented, saying that it was not possible for the applicants to make out their case that there was something unlawful about what the minister had done in introducing the tariff scheme.[59] Morritt LJ then joined the Master of the Rolls in allowing the appeal and granting a declaration, substantially for the same reasons.[60]

The division of opinion continued in the speeches of the Law Lords when an appeal by the Home Secretary against the judgment of the Court of Appeal, and a cross-appeal by the Fire Brigades Union and Others, were decided by the Appellate Committee on 5 April 1995. In dismissing both the appeal and the cross-appeal, Lord Browne-Wilkinson, in an opinion agreed by Lords Lloyd and Nicholls, stated that it would be most undesirable for the courts to intervene in the legislative process by requiring an Act of Parliament to be brought into effect. In doing so, the courts would be treading dangerously close to the area over which Parliament enjoyed exclusive jurisdiction, namely the making of legislation. In the absence of a clear statutory duty, the court should hesitate long before holding that such a provision as Section 171(1) of the Criminal Justice Act 1988 imposed a legally enforceable duty on the Secretary of State. It did not follow, however, that because the Secretary of State was not under any duty to bring the Section into effect, he had an absolute and unfettered discretion whether or not to do so. So to hold would lead to the conclusion that both Houses of Parliament had passed the Bill through all its stages, and the Act

---

[58] *R. v. Secretary of State for the Home Department, ex parte Fire Brigades Union and Others*, [1995] 2 AC 513 at 522–3.
[59] Ibid., at 534.　　　　　　　　　　　　　　　[60] Ibid., at 538–9.

received the Royal Assent, merely to confer an enabling power on
the executive to decide at will whether or not to make the
Parliamentary provisions a part of the law. Such a conclusion was
not only constitutionally dangerous, but flew in the face of common sense.

In Browne-Wilkinson's opinion, the tariff scheme was both
inconsistent with the statutory scheme contained in the 1988 Act,
and intended to be permanent. Its introduction made it impossible,
or at least more expensive, to reintroduce the old discretionary
scheme or the statutory enactment of it in the 1988 Act. If the
power in Section 171(1) was conferred on the Home Secretary with
a view to bringing the provisions into force, he could not himself
procure events to take place and rely on the occurrence of those
events as the grounds for not bringing them into force. By introducing the tariff scheme the Home Secretary had debarred himself
from exercising the statutory power for the purposes and on the
basis which Parliament intended. For these reasons, in Browne-
Wilkinson's judgment, the Home Secretary's decision to introduce
the tariff scheme, at a time when the statutory provisions and his
power under Section 171(1) were on the statute book, was unlawful and an abuse of power.[61]

The relationship between the courts and the executive also dominated the speech of Lord Mustill, with whose reasoning and conclusion to allow the appeal and dismiss the cross-appeal Lord Keith
of Kinkel agreed. After an historical review, matched in thoroughness only by Bingham's judgment in the Court of Appeal, Mustill
pointed out that although the issues arising on the appeal were of
great constitutional importance, they were limited in range. There
were only two questions of law which called for decision. First, did
Section 171(1) impose a legally enforceable duty on the Secretary
of State to bring into force all the provisions of the Act, including
Part VII on criminal injuries compensation, and secondly, was
either the winding up of the existing scheme or the inauguration of
the new scheme, or both, a breach of a duty created by Section
171(1), or an abuse of the prerogative power? In answering the first
question he joined with the other Law Lords in concluding that the
1988 Act did not compel the Secretary of State to bring its provisions into force as soon as practicable, and that the continuing

[61] Ibid., at 550–1, 552–4.

omission to implement the statutory scheme did not amount to any breach of duty arising from Section 171(1). On the second question, Mustill dissented from the majority in his opinion that so long as the Home Secretary and his successors in office performed in good faith the duty to keep the implementation of Part VII under review, there was no ground for the court to interfere.[62]

Few judges have thought longer and harder than Mustill, or expressed themselves better, about the limits of judicial review and the distinctions between the respective roles of government, Parliament, and the courts. Although in this case he was in the minority, Mustill's concluding observations are worth reproducing in full and pondering upon:

It is a feature of the peculiarly British conception of the separation of powers that Parliament, the executive and the courts each have their distinct and largely exclusive domain. Parliament has a legally unchallengeable right to make whatever laws it thinks right. The executive carries on the administration of the country in accordance with the powers conferred on it by law. The courts interpret the laws, and see that they are obeyed. This requires the courts on occasion to step into the territory which belongs to the executive, to verify not only that the powers asserted accord with the substantive law created by Parliament but also that the manner in which they are exercised conforms with the standards of fairness which Parliament must have intended. Concurrently with this judicial function Parliament has its own special means of ensuring that the executive, in the exercise of delegated functions, performs in a way which Parliament finds appropriate. Ideally, it is these latter methods which should be used to check executive errors and excesses; for it is the task of Parliament and the executive in tandem, not of the courts, to govern the country. In recent years, however, the employment in practice of these specifically Parliamentary remedies has on occasion been perceived as falling short, and sometimes well short, of what was needed to bring the performance of the executive into line with the law, and with the minimum standards of fairness implicit in every Parliamentary delegation of a decision-making function. To avoid a vacuum in which the citizen would be left without protection against a misuse of executive powers the courts have had no option but to occupy the dead ground in a manner, and in areas of public life, which could not have been foreseen 30 years ago. For myself, I am quite satisfied that this unprecedented judicial role has been greatly to the public benefit. Nevertheless, it has its risks, of which the courts are well

---

[62] *R. v. Secretary of State for the Home Department, ex parte Fire Brigades Union and Others*, [1995] 2 AC 513 at 560–7.

aware. As the judges themselves constantly remark, it is not they who are appointed to administer the country. Absent a written constitution much sensitivity is required of the parliamentarian, administrator and judge if the delicate balance of the unwritten rules evolved (I believe successfully) in recent years is not to be disturbed, and all the recent advances undone. I do not for a moment suggest that the judges of the Court of Appeal in the present case overlooked this need. The judgments show clearly that they did not. Nevertheless some of the arguments addressed would have the court push to the very boundaries of the distinction between court and Parliament established in, and recognised ever since, the Bill of Rights 1688. 300 years have passed since then, and the political and social landscape has changed beyond recognition. But the boundaries remain; they are of crucial significance to our private and public lives; and the courts should I believe make sure that they are not overstepped.[63]

VI

Replying to Opposition criticism in the House of Commons, Michael Howard stressed that it was the method of introduction, and not the merits, of the tariff scheme which had been found to be unlawful. He was not slow to point out that of the ten judges who had considered the matter during the protracted legal proceedings, five held in his favour and the other five against.[64] It was, he argued with some justification, a grey area of the law in which it was perfectly possible not only for reasonable Secretaries of State but for judges, of the High Court and above, to come to different conclusions.[65]

In the twelve months since the replacement of the non-statutory common law damages scheme by the first tariff scheme on 1 April 1994, CICB Board members had no responsibility for processing

---

[63] Ibid., at 567–8.

[64] Both judges in the Divisional Court (Staughton LJ and Buckley J) rejected submissions that the Home Secretary had acted unlawfully and refused the declarations sought. The Court of Appeal, Bingham MR and Morritt LJ with Hobhouse LJ dissenting, concluded by a majority that the applicants were entitled to succeed on the second but not the first issue before the court, and declared that by implementing the tariff scheme the Home Secretary had acted unlawfully and abused his prerogative. The House of Lords, by a majority of three Lords of Appeal (Browne-Wilkinson, Lloyd, and Nicholls) to two (Keith and Mustill), dismissed the appeal by the Secretary of State from the majority decision of the Court of Appeal, and the cross-appeal by the respondents.

[65] *Parl. Debates*, HC, 260 (6th ser.), col. 738, 23 May 1995.

new applications. The tariff scheme was essentially an administrative one in which decisions were made by staff under the arrangements contained in the White Paper published in December 1993. During this period the CICB continued to process applications made before 1 April 1994 and to hear appeals. Only a few days before the changeover, when leave had been granted by Owen J to the unions to apply for judicial review on 22 March, an assurance had been given on behalf of the Home Secretary that no individual claimant would be prejudiced, and no final award would be made to any claimant, pending the matter being resolved by the courts. On receiving this assurance, the applicants did not press for interim relief by way of an injunction to stay the implementation of the tariff scheme until the legal proceedings had been completed.

Almost exactly a year later, as soon as the Home Office learned of the judgment in the House of Lords, it stopped the payment of awards under the tariff system. To honour the assurance that individual claimants would not be prejudiced, the Criminal Injuries Compensation Authority (in effect the administrative staff of the CICB) embarked on a review of about 72,000 applications which had been made under the tariff scheme in the twelve months from 1 April 1994 to 5 April 1995. Of these only about 16,000 had been decided, some of which were subject to appeal. It was estimated that additional expenditure amounting to approximately £85 million was likely to be incurred to meet the extra costs of bringing up the tariff awards to the higher levels of compensation which would have been payable under the common law damages scheme, as revised in 1990.

The CICB, whose corporate life had been drawing to an end, was revived in order to deal with new cases coming in from 5 April 1995 and all outstanding applications for a hearing. The temporary expedient would continue until such time as the Government could introduce and pass legislation through Parliament to repeal Sections 108 to 117 of the Criminal Justice Act 1988, and enact a new criminal injuries compensation scheme based on tariff principles. Apart from the heavy administrative costs arising out of the double change, the impact on another performance indicator, that of delay, was equally adverse. The number of cases outstanding at 31 March 1995, shortly before the decision of the House of Lords, was just below a historic high of 110,000. Home Office projections were that the Board would resolve some 78,000 cases under the reinstated common law damages scheme in 1995–6, leaving the backlog of uncleared cases at just under 110,000.[66] This compared with the forecast of 105,300 applications outstanding in 1995–6 which had been published in the Home Office *Annual Report 1994*.[67]

In the same way as the Criminal Appeal Bill earlier in the session, the Criminal Injuries Compensation Bill was the beneficiary of an unusually light Parliamentary session. Thus the Government's business managers were able to insert a short, although controversial, measure into the legislative programme as late as May 1995. The Bill, which had its Second Reading in the Commons on 23 May, completed all its stages and was sent to the Lords on 29 June, three weeks before the start of the Summer Recess. Despite being a single-issue bill, on introduction amounting to only twelve clauses and one schedule, it was strenuously contested and consumed a total of over twenty-four hours of Parliamentary time in the House of Commons. The adversarial stance taken by Howard and Maclean, and the tactic of the Opposition to exploit to the full the Home Secretary's embarrassment at the judicial rebuff, obscured the real improvements made from the original tariff scheme to the revised tariff scheme which was now proposed. In the unforeseen interval between the two, the Government had been able to take account both of the experience gained from the twelve-month operation of the first tariff scheme, and the representations made by Victim Support, the VCCR, the CICB, and others about the likely impact that an unamended tariff approach would have on victims who had suffered serious injuries, or on households where a fatality had been caused by an act of criminal violence.

As a result of the special interest and parliamentary pressures, the Home Office agreed to make several important changes. The first was that the tariff should be enhanced to provide payment for loss of earnings and special care for those most seriously affected by their injuries. In the new scheme, incapacitation after twenty-eight weeks from the date of the injury would bring an entitlement to a separate payment for loss of earnings, whether employed or self-employed. As had been the practice under the common law scheme, the payment would be subject to a cap of one-and-a-half

---

[66] *Parl. Debates*, HL, 566 (5th ser.), cols. WA 106–7, 23 Oct. 1995.
[67] Cm. 2508, *op. cit.*, Table 9 (ii), p. 53.

times the national average industrial wage. The qualifying period of twenty-eight weeks was aligned to the period for which statutory sick pay was payable. In cases of incapacity for more than twenty-eight weeks, there would be eligibility for payment for special care to cover actual costs from the date of injury, and future costs reasonably incurred. This provision was intended to cover the same type of item which was compensated under the common law damages scheme, including the cost of private medical treatment if in all the circumstances both the treatment and the cost were reasonable. Payment could cover the costs of home mobility equipment and fittings, special wheelchairs, and fees for care in a nursing home.

The next category for which improved provision was made, an especially poignant one, was for the family of a victim who had lost his or her life. In fatal cases, reasonable funeral expenses would continue to be reimbursed and a fixed payment made. Under the previous tariff scheme, a fatal award of £10,000 was shared between all qualifying claimants, of which there could be several. The new arrangements allowed for each qualifying claimant to receive an award of £5,000, unless there was only one qualifying claimant who would receive the £10,000 award. In addition, there would be a payment for loss of dependency and loss of mother's support. Payment for dependency again would be capped at one and a half times the national average industrial wage.

Under the new tariff scheme, the upper limit for any award would be raised to £500,000, double that payable under the first tariff scheme. The final new feature was a provision to enable payments to be made by way of structured settlements. This meant that for higher-value awards the victim could opt for payment for life, or other specified period. The payments would be index-linked and tax-free.[68]

These enhancements, although falling short of meeting the full range of criticisms of the tariff scheme by the relevant interests, represented a significant shift by the Government on some of the main issues, i.e. loss of earnings, medical care costs, structured settlements, and bereavement awards. In the view of Victim Support, substantial shortcomings remained, including the criteria for exclusion from eligibility, and especially the minimum award of £1,000

---

[68] *Parl. Debates*, HC 260, *op. cit.*, cols. 734–6.

below which no injury would be compensated, the definitions of criminal injury and accidental injury, and the reduction in the time-limit for making an award from three years to two.[69] When Howard announced the changes at the start of his speech moving the Second Reading on the Bill in the Commons he was listened to attentively, but thereafter he was constantly interrupted in a noisy and fractious House. Jack Straw, who had succeeded Tony Blair as Opposition Front Bench Spokesman on Home Affairs the previous year, spoke next. He moved a reasoned amendment, declining to give the Bill a Second Reading because it was based on cutting the amount of cash available to compensate victims and failed to place them at the centre of the criminal justice system.[70] After a debate lasting five hours, the Commons divided in a vote on the Labour amendment which was lost by 229 to 274 votes.[71]

The Standing Committee considering the Bill had eight sittings between 8 June and 27 June, amounting to a total of 16 hours and 36 minutes (see Table 16).[72] Maclean led for the government and Alun Michael for the Labour Opposition. Alan Beith, Deputy Leader of the Liberal Democrats, was also a member of the Committee. Table 17 shows that out of a total of five new clauses and sixty-one amendments, only six amendments, all tabled by the Government, were made and included in the Bill. In three cases, clear undertakings were given in reply to Opposition amendments, and so the long hours were not spent entirely in vain. However, the iron grip of party discipline in the Commons, as effective off the floor as in votes of the whole House, impairs the quality of scrutiny brought to bear on Government bills. Some will have been hastily drafted, the Criminal Injuries Compensation Bill falling into this category, and a series of votes on strict party lines is not the best way of remedying drafting deficiencies, nor of testing how far the Government has thought through all of the practical effects once the legislation is implemented.

An attempt to subject the details of the enhanced tariff scheme

---

[69] Victim Support prepared a detailed response to the Draft Criminal Injuries (Tariff-based) Compensation Scheme after it had been published in Aug. 1995.

[70] *Parl. Debates*, HC 260, *op. cit.* The wording of the reasoned amendment is printed at col. 741.

[71] Ibid., cols. 807–11.

[72] The author acknowledges his thanks to Paul Evans, a Deputy Principal Clerk in the Public Bill Office at the House of Commons, for compiling the statistical information in Tables 16 and 17.

TABLE 16. *Criminal Justice Compensation Bill 1994–5: House of Commons Standing Committee, hours of sitting*

	Morning hrs/mins	Evening hrs/mins
8 June 1995	2.30	—
13 June 1995	2.30	2.13
15 June 1995	2.30	2.19
20 June 1995	2.01	—
22 June 1995	1.58	—
27 June 1995	1.55	—
Total Time:	16 hours 36 minutes	

Source: Public Bill Office, House of Commons.

to Parliamentary control having been rejected, the only small change made in Standing Committee was to clarify the right of the adjudicators forming an appeals panel under the provisions of the Bill to exercise an advisory role. This would enable the panel, composed of persons experienced in criminal injuries compensation work, to tender advice to the Secretary of State. Maclean indicated that a panel of about fifty adjudicators (including some former CICB members) would be needed to deal with the likely number of appeals. He accepted that it should be one of the functions of the panel to give advice on any matters relating to the working of the scheme as a whole, and not just on the appeals procedure. Nor would the panel be confined to responding to points put to it by the Government. It would be able to initiate advice whenever it thought fit. Although Opposition amendments on this advisory function were tabled and debated, both in Standing Committee and on Report, they were not pressed to a division. Home Office ministers gave, and repeated, an undertaking that an express provision would be included on the face of the Bill making it clear that the panel of adjudicators should be able to offer advice on all matters relating to the scheme.[73]

It was not much to show for sixteen and a half hours spent in Committee. The really important changes between the first and

[73] Section 5(6) of the Criminal Injuries Compensation Act 1995 states that 'The Scheme shall include provision as to the giving of advice by adjudicators to the Secretary of State'.

TABLE 17. *Criminal Injuries Compensation Bill 1994–5: new clauses and amendments in the House of Commons*

	(a) No. tabled		(b) No. made		of (b) Government		of (b) Opposition		of (b) Other Members	
	New Clauses	Amend-ments	New Clauses	Amend-ments	New Clauses	Amend-ments	New Clauses	Amend-ments	New Clauses	Amend-ments
Standing Committee	5	61	0	6	—	6	0	0	0	0
Report stage	3	4	0	0	—	—	—	—	—	—

14 Amendments were withdrawn. In the case of 3 of these withdrawals, a clear undertaking was given.
Source: Public Bill Office, House of Commons.

second tariff schemes were contained not in the legislative framework of the Act, but in the detailed content of the scheme. The crucial negotiations leading to the enhanced provisions took place at the pre-legislative stages, rather than in Parliament. When the Bill returned from Standing Committee to the floor of the House for Report Stage and Third Reading on 29 June, there were three further divisions. On one of these, a new clause proposed by the Opposition to ensure that the administration of the scheme fell within the jurisdiction of the Parliamentary Commissioner for Administration (the Ombudsman), there was no difference of principle between the two sides. The Government was worried, though, about the resource implications if there were large numbers of complaints from disappointed claimants for compensation. Although rejected in the Commons, the Government brought forward its own new clause conceding the point at a later stage in the Lords.[74]

The final vote resulted in the defeat of another reasoned amendment tabled by the Opposition on Third Reading and, unusually, selected for debate. The numbers voting, 260 on the Government side and 202 on the Opposition,[75] belied the fact that the House had been very thinly attended throughout the afternoon. No Government back-bencher spoke during nearly three hours of debate; indeed Straw complained that for much of the time not a single Conservative back-bench MP had been present in the Chamber. For good measure, he added that the Liberal Democrat benches also had been vacant for almost the whole of the debate.[76]

VII

In contrast to the Commons, the Lords had taken a keen interest in the principles of compensation, and the most appropriate type of system, from the moment the Government published its White Paper in December 1993.[77] The opening skirmish in what was to be an epic war of words was a debate initiated by Lord Ackner a

---

[74] Section 10 of the Criminal Injuries Compensation Act 1995 inserted a new subsection into the Parliamentary Commissioner Act 1967 stating that the administrative functions exercisable by an administrator of the Criminal Injuries Compensation Scheme should be taken to be administrative functions of a government department to which the 1967 Act applied.

[75] *Parl. Debates*, HC, 262 (6th ser.), cols. 1134–5, 29 June 1995.

[76] Ibid., col. 1129.   [77] Cm. 2434, *op. cit.*

month before the tariff scheme was due to be brought into effect on 1 April 1994. For the next twenty months the controversy over how victims should be compensated for injuries suffered as a consequence of the criminal violence of others, and the proper reach of ministerial power, afforded a vivid and unusual instance of the interplay between the legislative, deliberative, and judicial roles of the House of Lords.

The debate on 2 March fuelled the discontent aroused by the Government's peremptorily announced decision to alter the basis for compensating victims of crime, at the same time adding a new dimension. Ackner's opening speech was blunt and condemnatory. In asserting that the new scheme would provide a better service for victims, he accused the Government of hypocrisy. It was a cost-cutting exercise. The proposed scheme was 'grossly unfair', since those who suffered the more serious injuries and the more substantial losses would receive 'but a fraction' of the compensation currently provided. Some striking examples were cited. A psychiatric nursing sister whose arm had been so badly injured that she had been assessed as unfit for any work had been awarded a total of over £126,000 by the CICB. Under the new scheme she would receive £5,000. A police officer, whose back was seriously injured, had received a total of £121,000 under the old scheme, made up of loss of earnings over seven years and an award for items of special damage. Under the new scheme he would receive £7,500. Finally, and most damagingly, Ackner argued that the Government's proposed action was an abuse of power.[78]

Sixteen speakers followed in a debate that lasted until after midnight. They included four Law Lords, one of whom, Lord Nolan,[79] chose the occasion for his maiden speech, and a well respected Scottish judge.[80] Carlisle and Colnbrook[81] were former Conservative

[78] *Parl. Debates*, HL, 552 (5th ser.), col. 1072, 2 Mar. 1994.

[79] QC 1968; Recorder of the Crown Court 1975–82. Judge of the High Court of Justice, Queen's Bench Division 1982–91; Lord Justice of Appeal 1991–3; Lord of Appeal in Ordinary 1994–. Chairman, Committee on Standards in Public Life 1994–.

[80] Lord Morton of Shuna, a Senator of the College of Justice in Scotland from 1988 until his death in 1995.

[81] Sir Humphrey Atkins MP was created a life peer taking the title of Lord Colnbrook in 1987. Deputy Chief Whip and Government Chief Whip in the House of Commons 1970–4; Opposition Chief Whip 1974–9. Secretary of State for Northern Ireland 1979–81; Lord Privy Seal (at the Foreign Office) 1981–2. Resigned with Lord Carrington over the invasion of the Falklands in 1982.

Cabinet ministers, and Alexander of Weedon, Chairman of JUS-
TICE, also spoke from the Conservative benches. On the Opposition side, the Shadow Lord Chancellor, Irvine of Lairg, opened
from the front bench supported, amongst others, by Longford and
Baroness Dean, a former Union General Secretary.[82] With the sole
exception of the unfortunate minister designated to reply, Lord
Fraser of Carmyllie,[83] every speaker irrespective of party affiliation
was strongly critical of both the detail of the tariff scheme and the
Government's handling of the change. Time and again instances
were given of the magnitude of the discrepancies that would result
between the amount of compensation awarded under the new
scheme compared with the old; time and again speakers hammered
home the point that such fundamental changes were being made
arbitrarily by ministers, with neither Parliament nor the interested
parties, including a directly relevant non-departmental public body
in the shape of the CICB, being consulted in advance. Such a
debate could not have happened in the Commons, and it acted as
a trigger for the next development.

The new dimension was the weight of authority provided for the
proposition that in substituting the tariff scheme by executive discretion while the previous common law damages scheme as was still
on the statute book, ministers had disregarded the express will of
Parliament, and might have acted unlawfully. Only the courts could
decide the issue of legality, but the prospect of a successful application for judicial review strengthened the hands of the activists in
the Association of Personal Injuries Lawyers and the VCCR.
Before the Lords debate there had been some discussion about
mounting a challenge in the courts, but no decisions had been
reached. After it, there was no delay in securing the practical
assistance necessary from the TUC and a number of trade unions
and staff associations in the public and private sectors whose members were likely to be affected by the change. Consequently, ten
days before the introduction of the tariff scheme on 1 April,

[82] Brenda Dean (Baroness Dean of Thornton-le-Fylde) was General-Secretary of
SOGAT '82 1985–91, having been President of that Union 1983–5. Co-Chairman,
Women's National Commission 1985–7; Member, General Council of the TUC,
1985–92. Created a life peer in 1993.

[83] Peter Fraser, MP for South Angus 1979–83 and Angus East, 1983–7, was
Solicitor-General for Scotland 1982–9. He was created a life peer as Lord Fraser of
Carmyllie in 1989, and was Lord Advocate of Scotland 1989–92. Minister of State:
Scottish Office 1992–5; Department of Trade and Industry 1995–.

Counsel for the unions appeared in front of a single judge and obtained leave to apply to the Divisional Court of the High Court for a judicial review of the Home Secretary's decision.

Victim Support considered a report on the Lords debate at a meeting of its National Council on 15 March. Conscious that as a charity it could not properly contribute to the costs of legal action, it decided to maintain its policy of calling for a postponement to allow sufficient time for consultation and further deliberation before the new scheme was introduced. The stance was to take a sympathetic interest, but no direct part, in the court proceedings, meanwhile keeping the lines open with Home Office officials and being ready to come forward when the moment was ripe with proposals for improvements on the key points. By now it was becoming clear that there would have to be some provision for loss of earnings and for reduction in earning capacity in the future. There was scope too for sounding out the ground on numerous other proposals which had been so carefully explored by its own working party. In the event, under the skilful guidance of its director, Helen Reeves, and the then chairman, Mary Tuck, who was very experienced in the ways of Whitehall,[84] Victim Support's approach was largely vindicated by events.

The next opportunity for the Lords to return to the compensation issue, this time in its legislative rather than deliberative role, was when the Criminal Justice and Public Order Bill came before the House in the Summer of 1994. An amendment proposed by Ackner to bring the dormant sections of the Criminal Justice Act 1988 into effect six months after the Criminal Justice and Public Order Act 1994 received the Royal Assent was carried against the Government by a comfortable majority. Its subsequent rejection by the Commons, and the later proceedings in the Lords, were described in Chapter 4. At that stage the Divisional Court had heard and dismissed the application for judicial review, finding that there had been nothing irrational or improper in the Home Secretary's decision not to bring the 1988 provision into force, or to replace it with another scheme under the common law. Pending the hearing of an appeal by the Court of Appeal, the judgment in the Divisional Court altered the terminology, but not the substance, of the censure to which the Government was becoming accustomed

---

[84] Before her retirement in 1990 Mary Tuck had been Head of the Research and Planning Unit at the Home Office for six years.

in the Lords. The charges of gross unfairness to victims were reiterated, the main difference being that instead of alleging unlawfulness on the part of the Home Secretary, Ackner and his supporters now spoke dismissively of the 'technical legality of the Minister's action' and 'a serious affront' to Parliamentary democracy.[85]

In the following Session, the Lords addressed itself to the Bill which the Government had been compelled to introduce in order to regularize the situation after the Appellate Committee had agreed with the Court of Appeal that the Home Secretary's action in implementing the tariff scheme at a time when the very different statutory provisions of the 1988 Act were still on the statute book was indeed unlawful and an abuse of his prerogative power. As we have seen, the Criminal Injuries Compensation Bill had passed through the House of Commons with no more than minimal amendment. In the Lords, where the Government could not rely so heavily on the discipline of the party whip, and needed to persuade enough of the very large group of cross-benchers of the merits of their proposals,[86] the task was more formidable.

Baroness Blatch, the hard-worked Home Office Minister of State who had taken the Criminal Appeal Bill through the House earlier in the Session, was again in charge. Her speech in moving the Second Reading on 19 July was matter-of-fact, explaining that the Bill provided statutory backing for the payment of compensation to victims of violent crime on the basis of an enhanced tariff scheme. The previous tariff scheme which had run from 1 April 1994 to 5 April 1995 had been withdrawn immediately when the House in its judicial capacity had ruled that the method of introduction had been unlawful, and the former scheme reinstated. As Howard had done in the Commons, she emphasized that the legal judgment related solely to the method of the tariff scheme's introduction, and was not concerned with the merits of the scheme itself,[87] although that was a question which had not been before the courts. Her statement failed to satisfy at least one exasperated cross-bencher, a retired Law Officer and Law Lord[88] who inter-

---

[85] *Parl. Debates*, HL, 555 (5th ser.), col. 1832, 16 June 1994.

[86] At 31 July 1995 there were 289 cross-bench peers in the House of Lords.

[87] *Parl. Debates*, HL, 566 (5th ser.), col. 293, 19 July 1995.

[88] Lord Simon of Glaisdale had been Solicitor General 1959–62, while sitting in the House of Commons as Conservative MP for Middlesborough West, 1951–62. He was President of the Probate, Divorce and Admiralty Division of the High Court of Justice 1962–71, and a Lord of Appeal in Ordinary 1971–7.

vened at the end of her speech to ask why she had no words of con-
trition on behalf of the Home Secretary for having acted illegally;
for having done so in the knowledge that there was a fifty-fifty
chance that he was acting illegally; and for the fact that he was in
any case acting unconstitutionally by producing his own scheme in
place of that enacted by Parliament which was still on the statute
book awaiting his bringing it into force?[89]

Other speakers on the Government benches, including myself,
were inclined to be more generous, complimenting the Home
Secretary on the prompt and uncomplaining way in which he had
accepted the majority decision of the House of Lords. The measure
being presented to Parliament was a Bill to rectify an error of judgment and to make lawful an administrative action which had been
found by the highest courts to be unlawful.[90] With some exceptions,
once the Second Reading was out of the way, the mood of the
House was to look forward and not back.

The Committee Stage, as is normal in the Lords, took place on
the floor of the House on two successive days, 16 and 17 October
1995. The Report Stage followed on 31 October, with the Bill
receiving a Third Reading, after further debate, on 5 November.
The amount of time spent on the Bill shown in Table 18,[91] just
under fourteen hours, does not include the duration of the Second
Reading debate (3 hours, 32 minutes). Even so, the total of 17
hours, 20 minutes fell short of the Commons total of over twenty-
four hours. The value of the Lords as a revising chamber is better
illustrated in Table 19, showing that in total over 100 new clauses
or amendments were tabled, fourteen of which were incorporated
in the final Act, more than double the Commons total of six. It is
unwise, however, to read too much into these figures, particularly
since most of the small number of amendments of substance which
were enacted and attributed to the Government owed their origin
to the efforts of the Opposition parties, or to MPs or peers on the
Government side of each House.

The author writes with first-hand experience of one such, for at
the start of the first day in Committee on 16 October 1995 I moved
a series of amendments intended to draw attention to some comments made by the Select Committee on the Scrutiny of Delegated

---

[89] *Parl. Debates*, HL, 566, *op. cit.*, col. 297.   [90] Ibid., col. 317.
[91] Thanks are due to Edward Wells in the Public Bill Office at the House of Lords
for compiling the statistics in Tables 18 and 19.

TABLE 18. *Criminal Injuries Compensation Bill 1994–5*: House of Lords, hours of sitting

Stage	Date	Hours/minutes
Committee Stage	16 October 1995	4.21
	17 October 1995	3.50
Report Stage	31 October 1005	4.46
Third Reading	5 November 1995	1.01
Total Time:	13 hours 58 minutes	

Source: Public Bill Office, House of Lords.

Powers. Its report,[92] ordered to be printed on 21 July, the day the House went into Recess, had not been available at the time of the Second Reading debate. The main points raised by the Scrutiny Committee were that the power to establish a scheme for compensation was a delegated legislative power (para. 6); that important elements of the legislation and its administration were included in the scheme rather than in the body of the Bill (para. 7); that the Bill was unusual in not making the document embodying the delegated legislation a statutory instrument; and that the exercise of the majority of the powers would not be subject to parliamentary control (para. 9).[93] Coming from an all-party Select Committee whose remit was to report whether the provisions of any bill inappropriately delegated legislative power, this was an unmistakable warning signal. As Lord Renton observed, there had been a growth in recent years of ministerial documents which were non-legislative but which purported to have legislative effect. The examples he cited were codes of practice, guidance offered under statute, departmental directives, and, as in the case before the House, schemes. If such documents were merely administrative, or explanatory of legislation which had been approved by Parliament, that was well and good. If, on the other hand, they purported to have a legislative effect of which Parliament had not approved, then there was a need for vigilance.[94]

[92] House of Lords, Session 1994–5, 14th Report, Select Committee on the Scrutiny of Delegated Powers, *Criminal Injuries Compensation Bill and other bills* (HL 95), HMSO, London, 1995.
[93] *Parl. Debates*, HL, 566, *op. cit.*, col. 584.
[94] Ibid., col. 585.

TABLE 19. *Criminal Injuries Compensation Bill 1994–5: new clauses and amendments in the House of Lords*

	(a) No. tabled		(b) No. made		By whom tabled Government		By whom tabled Opposition		By whom tabled Other Members	
	New Clauses	Amend-ments	New Clauses	Amend-ments	New Clauses	Amend-ments	New Clauses	Amend-ments	New Clauses	Amend-ments
Committee	17	55	1	11	1	11	15	31	1	13
Report Stage	6	21	—	—	—	—	6	19	—	2
Third Stage	—	6	—	2	—	2	—	4	—	—
Total	23	82	1	13	1	13	21	54	1	15

Source: Public Bill Office, House of Lords.

After consulting the chairman of the Delegated Powers Scrutiny Committee, Lord Alexander of Weedon, and obtaining some expert advice on the drafting, I tabled amendments making the scheme itself, and not simply the contents of the proposed tariff and alterations to it, subject to parliamentary control. Additional amendments covered other points in the Scrutiny Committee's report, some of which had already been met by the circulation of a draft of the proposed rules and procedures of the new scheme to the interested parties during the Recess. These included members of both Houses of Parliament who had taken part in the earlier debates, the Law Society, the Bar Council, the Association of Personal Injury Lawyers, Victim Support, the TUC, the police representative organizations, and the equivalent bodies in Scotland. Useful comments had been received on the draft proposals, some of which would be included in the final version of the scheme.[95]

The main feature, that of parliamentary control over delegated legislation, was conceded by the Government shortly before the first day the Bill was in Committee. Amendments in the name of Baroness Blatch, similar in effect to my own, were tabled which would require the Secretary of State to lay a draft of the scheme before Parliament, and not to implement it unless the draft had been approved by a resolution of each House. This meant that the entire scheme would be subject to prior parliamentary approval by the affirmative resolution procedure. Later changes would require parliamentary approval either by the affirmative or the negative resolution procedure, depending whether or not they affected key elements of the scheme. After a short debate, in which general satisfaction was expressed, I withdrew my amendments in favour of those tabled by the Government. When the Lords amendments were considered by the Commons, Maclean explained that the degree of parliamentary control had altered significantly. Specific approval would be required for every aspect of the new arrangements before 'we can kick off'.[96] Thus the first, and most important, amendment to the Bill in the Lords was achieved by consensus in both Houses. It was a characteristic which hitherto had been conspicuously absent in the parliamentary proceedings on the revised system for compensating victims of crime.

---

[95] See Baroness Blatch, ibid., cols. 588–9.
[96] *Parl. Debates*, HC, 265 (6th ser.), col. 744, 7 Nov. 1995.

The Criminal Injuries Compensation Act 1995 received the Royal Assent on 8 November, in the last moments before Parliament was prorogued at the end of the 1994–5 session. The timetable had been very tight, but both Houses had co-operated in getting the Bill through just in time to meet the date of 1 April 1996 which had been set for the introduction of the new statutory scheme. On that date, the interim arrangements, i.e. the reinstated common law damages scheme, was due to cease. Unlike the ill-fated Part VII of the Criminal Justice Act 1988 (which was repealed), the provisions of the 1995 Act came into force once it received the Royal Assent. Before the new arrangements could be implemented each House of Parliament had to approve the enhanced tariff scheme. This was duly done in the Commons on 6 December and in the Lords on 11 December. In a short debate on a motion that the draft scheme laid before Parliament on 16 November be approved, Baroness Blatch and the Opposition front-bench spokesmen each had their final say.[97] The only other speaker was Lord Carlisle, still chairman of the CICB, who had been closer to the frustrating and deeply unsatisfactory sequence of events than any other member of either House.

In his final Parliamentary comment on a quintessentially disorderly reform, Carlisle put his finger accurately on a factor that is often overlooked in studies of law-making. He remarked in particular on the extent to which the atmosphere in the House had changed since Lord Ackner had first raised the issue after the publication of the White Paper, and when the Government had been defeated during the passage of the Criminal Justice and Public Order Act in 1994. He continued:

The reason that the atmosphere has changed is that the scheme has greatly changed. I, for one, welcome those changes—although, sadly, the Government still stick to an inflexible tariff. One does not have to repeat again all the arguments against such a scheme, but at least the present scheme gets rid of what to my mind were the totally unacceptable features of the Government's original proposals. If those proposals had gone through, all the savings that are intended to be made would have been made at the cost of those most badly injured in any assault. By refusing to pay for loss of earnings and earnings capacity, as the Government had intended, all of those savings would have been borne by the worst injured.

I believe that those trades unions which chose to challenge that scheme by judicial review have had their actions thoroughly exonerated. The

[97] *Parl. Debates*, HL, 567 (5th ser.), cols. 1102–13, 11 Dec. 1995.

changes that have come about as a result of the defeat of that original scheme which was ruled unlawful by the Judicial Committee of this House are to the great advantage of future victims. However, it is sad that that had to be achieved in that way. If only the Home Office had been willing at an earlier stage to consult, to listen, to reflect and to amend its own proposals, taking account of the criticisms that were being made, I believe that it would have been possible to achieve a system which would have been acceptable to all parties, which would have achieved the Government's aims and which would, I suspect, have saved a great deal more than the present scheme will save.[98]

VIII

It is now time to draw together the strands of the last three Chapters, and then to end. This Chapter has brought out the extent to which the executive discretion of ministers is curtailed, both by the courts and by Parliament. Judicial review is more of an effective constraint than parliamentary accountability, but it has spread so fast and reached waters so deep that the waves are getting higher and the weather rougher. Although ministers customarily accept findings by the courts that their actions have been unlawful, and alter their policies accordingly, they tend to do so grudgingly and there are growing signs of friction. As Lord Mustill argued so cogently in his observations at the conclusion of his dissenting judgment in the *Fire Brigades Union* case,[99] Parliament, the executive, and the courts each have their distinct, and largely exclusive, domain. The boundaries between them are not static, and in recent years the courts have occupied some of the dead ground to ensure that the individual is not left without protection against misuse of executive power. However, the boundaries remain and should not be overstepped. These cautionary remarks were prompted by the greater degree of activism in judicial review which had seen an increase from 491 applications to the High Court for leave to challenge administrative decisions by public authorities in 1980 to 3,604 in 1995.[100] Only a minority were successful, but that was enough to create an antagonism between judges and ministers.

[98] *Parl. Debates*, HL, 567, *op. cit.*, cols. 1106–7.
[99] [1995] 2 AC 513 at 567–8.
[100] Letter from Michael Huebner, Chief Executive of the Court Service, 21 Mar. 1996.

The narrative of Chapter 10 described the voluntary surrender of ministerial discretion brought about by the inability of the established system of criminal appeals to remedy some of the most notorious instances of miscarriage of justice in English penal history. Since Home Office ministers agreed at an early stage to relinquish the responsibility for decisions to re-open cases of alleged wrongful conviction when the normal appeal procedures had been exhausted, it was possible to proceed in an orderly and methodical way in devising an alternative system. In contrast, the gradual erosion of ministerial control over life sentence prisoners, the subject of Chapter 9, was a story of reluctant retreat on the part of ministers. In February 1996, the European Court of Human Rights made a further encroachment into disputed territory in ruling that young persons convicted of murder should have access to a court-like body to decide on their continued detention after the expiry of the fixed minimum period.[101] As a result, one more category of prisoners sentenced to indefinite detention will be transferred from the arbitrary procedures applicable to mandatory life sentence prisoners to the quasi-judicial procedures governing release decisions on discretionary life sentence prisoners. Indeterminate sentences without subsequent judicial control are unknown elsewhere in Europe for juveniles, and children sentenced in England and Wales for murder serve longer periods in custody than elsewhere.[102]

The fact that the latest fetter on executive discretion stemmed from a European institution brought out the worst in that strain of public opinion which is antagonistic to all things European. The point at issue, however, was one of general application, and quite separate from issues of national sovereignty. At the heart of the relationship between the liberty of the subject and the power of the state lies the principle that it is for an independent judiciary, and not for politicians dependent on popular support, to decide on the degree of punishment which a crime deserves.

[101] European Court of Human Rights, *Hussain* v. *United Kingdom* (55/1994/502/584), Judgment, Strasbourg, 21 Feb. 1996. Subject to editorial revision before reproduction in final form in the *Reports of Judgments and Decisions* for 1996 and the EHRR series.

[102] 84 per cent of the 217 prisoners in custody at 17 Feb. 1995 convicted of murder and sentenced under Section 53 (1) of the Children and Young Persons Act 1933 will spend a minimum of ten years in custody before their release can be considered, and 20 per cent will spend over twenty years. *Children and Homicide*, JUSTICE, London, 1996, p. 29. This report, of a working party convened by JUSTICE, reviews the appropriate treatment for children who commit, or are accused of, homicide.

Index

NOTE: All references are to England and Wales unless otherwise stated.